GLOBALIZATION

GLOBALIZATION

Encyclopedia of Trade, Labor, and Politics

Volume 2

Ashish K. Vaidya, Editor

A B C ⬙ C L I O

Santa Barbara, California • Denver, Colorado • Oxford, England

Library of Congress Cataloging-in-Publication Data is available from the Library of Congress.

ISBN: 1-57607-826-4
E-ISBN: 1-57607-827-2

09 08 07 06   10 9 8 7 6 5 4 3 2 1

This book is also available on the World Wide Web as an e-
book. Visit http://www.abc-clio.com for details.

ABC-CLIO, Inc.
130 Cremona Drive, P.O. Box 1911
Santa Barbara, California 93116-1911

This book is printed on acid-free paper.
Manufactured in the United States of America

Contents

GLOBALIZATION
Encyclopedia of Trade, Labor, and Politics

Volume 1

Volume 2

PART THREE

International Blocs and Organizations

Andean Community

The Andean Community (Communidad Andina, CAN), also known as the Andean Pact (Pacto Andino) or the Andean Group (Grupo Andino), is a customs union and subregional organization endowed with international legal status and with political and social dimensions. Its members are Bolivia, Colombia, Ecuador, Peru, and Venezuela, which together form the geographic region surrounding the Andes Mountains in South America. The five member countries occupy a total area of approximately 4.7 million square kilometers stretching from the Atlantic to the Pacific oceans and linked by the mineral-rich Andes Mountains, with a combined population of 105 million people and a gross domestic product (GDP) of over $290 billion.

Intra-Andean exports reached $5.68 billion in 2001. The organization was formed in 1969 with the signing of the Andean Subregional Integration Agreement in Cartagena, Colombia (subsequently known as the Cartagena Agreement). Venezuela joined in 1974. Chile was an original member but withdrew in 1976. Peru partially withdrew in 1992, opting out of the common external tariff (CET) but not the other institutions. Panama applied for membership in 1995 and presently has observer status. The main goals of the Cartagena Agreement are to promote the formation of a common market, accelerate the growth of member countries, and promote job creation. The agreement also seeks to reduce the external vulnerability of the members and improve their joint position within the global economy.

To achieve these goals, the Andean Group, as it was then called, initially sought to implement the import-substitution model of development. Since 1989, the Andean Community has adopted open-market policies and sought growth through international trade. Today the Andean Community is one of the most advanced integration processes in the developing world, based on a customs union, elaborate institutional structures, a unique intellectual property regime, some common rules regarding services, and other economic, political, and social cooperation schemes. Still, intraregional total trade flows remain low in the Andean Community compared, for example, to the Central American Common Market (CACM).

A Fast Start

Throughout the 1970s, the Andean Group was based on free trade systems that aimed to form a local market for liberalized trade in goods and services among the member countries, free from competition from outside nations. The instruments of Andean integration as set out in the Cartagena Agreement were: (1) a liberalization program, designed to generate restricted competition within the area; (2) a common external tariff, to protect the enlarged market against imports from the rest of the world; (3) sectoral industrial development programs, to induce new advanced import-substitution activities; (4) a common policy toward direct investment and common developmental finance programs; (5) harmonization of economic and social policies and of national legislation, where relevant; (6) programs designed to accelerate the development of the agricultural sector; (7) physical integration through transportation enhancement; and (8) preferential treatment for Bolivia and Ecuador.

The 1970s are regarded as the Golden Age of the Andean Community. For example, between 1974 and 1979, total intra-Andean trade increased by 154 percent, from $439 million to more than $1.1 billion, and intra-Andean nonfuel exports increased by 307 percent, from $230 million to $937 million. In addition to trade growth, a number of key decisions were adopted to help achieve the goals of the Cartagena Agreement. Within five years the pact's statute book included details of the minimum common external tariff; internal tariff dismantling programs; industrial development programs for petrochemicals and metal engineering; a common set of rules on foreign investment and industrial property; a convention on double taxation; rules on competitive practices such as dumping; a statute for Andean multinational companies; guidelines on harmonization of industrial policy; an agreement on international road transport rules, including standards on weights and measurements for road haulage vehicles; a priority road network and an industrial development program for the motor industry; and a number of special provisions for Bolivia and Ecuador. However, this period coincided with favorable external factors (such as the Venezuelan and Ecuadoran oil booms and the Colombian coffee boom), which generated rapid income growth in most Andean nations. When global conditions turned, so did regional integration.

Stalled Integration and Reacceleration

Intra-Andean trade experienced a prolonged crisis in the 1980s as a result of the commodity and debt crises that afflicted all Andean nations. By the early 1980s, the Andean Group had become virtually dormant as a result of unilateral efforts by its members to participate in the emerging global economy. The common external tariff was never approved; liberalization for competitive goods was systematically postponed; and industrial development programs were designed only for a few sectors and proved cumbersome and operationally deficient, particularly as a result of the political criteria used to allocate new activities.

As economic crises began to subside, the Andean countries again turned to regional trade. By the mid-1980s, Andean Community members were concluding bilateral trade agreements in an attempt to restart intraregional trade, but in direct contravention of Cartagena Agreement rules. Eight bilateral agreements were signed covering 809 items. The greatest number were between Colombia and Ecuador.

By the late 1980s, market reforms and economic integration took place in all the Andean countries. The members began a new proposal to tear down trade barriers, strengthen the Andean free trade zone, and prepare it for integration into agreements with other trade communities in North and South America. The import-substitution program was abandoned in favor of market opening. The members approved changes in the agreement, enabling foreign investors to develop and expand on intra-Andean trade, and agreed to abolish export subsidies and tariffs on goods produced in member countries.

The December 1989 summit of the Andean Community presidents in the Galapagos Islands in Ecuador was the crucial turning point. In this meeting, the member states decided, in what is called the Galapagos Declaration, that the most restrictive provisions, such as managed trade, should be rapidly phased out; that a free trade zone would be in place by December 1993 (1995 for Bolivia and Ecuador), with a small list of exceptions; and that a customs union would be established by December 1997 (1999 for Bolivia and Ecuador). After 1989, the Andean Group received renewed political stimulus but was rapidly detached from its original import-substitution elements. Emphasis was placed on intraregional trade liberalization; the elimination of restrictive provisions regarding foreign direct investment and intellectual property rights; and the design of complementary tools to trade liberalization, such as regional unfair trade legislation and free transportation in the area. The November 1990 presidential summit in La Paz, Bolivia, sped up the commitments with a decision to consolidate the free trade zone by December 1991 for all members and to have the customs union in place by December 1993 (1995 for Bolivia and Ecuador).

The effort has proved fruitful. Intra-Andean trade over the decade of 1991–2001 was marked by heavy average growth. The volume of trade may be deceiving, both as it rises and falls, since it is critically affected by the price of oil. For example, total Andean exports in 2001 declined by 9.7 percent, but exports of nontraditional products increased by 1.2 percent; intra-Andean exports also rose by 9.8 percent overall. In the same year, intra-Andean fuel exports declined by 42.5 percent, but intra-Andean non-fuel exports increased by 21.5 percent.

Moreover, significant progress was made in terms of land, marine, and air transportation; regulations were issued based on decisions concerning international transportation of passengers and cargo; progress was made in the regulation of multimodal transportation operators; and guidelines were set for the interpretation of Open Skies policies on a subregional level and with respect to international carriers. An Andean decision about liberalization of trade in services was also elaborated in order to increase commercial links and promote technological development.

In April 1992, Peru's president, Alberto Fujimori, declared a self–coup d'état. This political event led Venezuela to suspend diplomatic relations with the Peruvian government, creating a conflictive political environment within the community. In response, Peru suspended its trade liberalization obligations with all Andean countries and opted to partially withdraw from its treaty obligations, requesting that other countries allow it to participate as a conditional member of the free trade zone. In June, this unilateral decision was replaced by a common agreement to allow Peru to stay temporarily out of the Andean Community. In an atmosphere of flexibility characteristic of the Andean Group, Peru was granted a temporary waiver of compliance in exchange for a promise to negotiate bilateral trade agreements with each of the other four Andean Group members.

The bilateral agreements were to compensate the other members for Peru's decision to maintain its own tariff structure. Peru established a free trade area with Bolivia and provisional agreements with Colombia, Ecuador, and Venezuela. It has yet to fully rejoin the Andean Group and has been permitted to keep its own tariff system while expanding its trade with the region through bilateral agreements. Other issues remain. Ecuador, for example, has not yet abandoned its traditional pattern of demanding preferential treatment within the Andean Community. In addition, the ratio of intraregional trade to total trade, known as the integration coefficient, is still relatively low (below 10 percent as of 2002, the latest data available).

The Common External Tariff

Implementation of the common external tariff has proved elusive since the Andean Community was formed in 1969. Several declarations throughout the community's history have committed the members to a CET, were breached, and later restated. For example, the Galapagos Declaration of December 1989 designed a series of mechanisms for the restart of the integration scheme, among them the creation of a common external tariff, the harmonization of economic policies, and the signing of bilateral agreements that strengthen trade between the countries of the region. In 1991, the Act of Barahona was signed, establishing an outline for the creation of a regional free trade zone that specified that Andean members implement a common external tariff. In 1992, four of the member countries, excluding Peru, agreed to adopt a common external tariff and a customs union, and the Andean Free Trade Area was formed. In 1995, the common external tariff and customs union went into effect. Different tariff levels were set at 0 percent, 5 percent, 10 percent, 15 percent, and 20 percent.

Ecuador exempted 400 products from the CET, whereas Colombia and Venezuela exempted 270. Bolivia kept its tariff structure, with rates of 5 percent and 10 percent. In the Santa Cruz Declaration of January 2002, the Andean presidents stipulated that "Bolivia, Colombia, Ecuador, Peru and Venezuela will apply a common external tariff by December 31, 2003 at the latest." On April 14, 2003, the Andean countries reached final agreement on the CET. The primary goal of the common external tariff is to keep tariffs low on raw materials, inputs, and capital goods needed for industrialization, while setting higher duties on finished goods. Despite the difficulties in adopting the common external tariff, its establishment and that of the customs union has increased intra–Andean Community trade. And even with setbacks, the common external tariff scheme brought the average tariff level down to 13.6 percent in 1998 from 33 percent in 1989. Nevertheless, the goal of becoming a fully integrated customs union remains only partially accomplished.

Effects of Integration

From 1970 to 2001, total intracommunity exports increased more than fifty-fold, from $111 million to $5.63 billion. Intracommunity manufacturing exports increased by ninety-four times, from $54 million to more than $5 billion. Intracommunity airline flights increased from 128 a week to 496 a week, and accrued intracommunity investment expanded seventy-four-fold, from $15 million to more than $1.1 billion. Total Andean Community debt also in-creased dramatically, with total external debt expanding from $8 billion to $116 billion in the same period.

The effects of regional market liberalization took effect immediately. From 1970 to 1979, Andean trade multiplied tenfold, growing at an annual rate of 29 percent. As a percent of total Andean trade, intraregional trade grew from 4 percent in 1970–1974 to 5.7 percent in 1980–1982. In the 1980s, intraregional trade experienced a prolonged crisis as a result of the commodity and debt crises that afflicted all members. Intraregional trade fell to 3.8 percent at its lowest point in this decade. Members used devaluation and trade restrictions in an attempt to correct trade imbalances, in violation of the Cartagena Agreement. Intraregional trade reached a low point in 1986 at less than half the level of the early 1980s. By the end of the decade, the group was close to collapsing. In an attempt to avoid disintegration, flexibility was allowed, including the postponement of treaty obligations and managed trade.

Following the rebirth of the community with the Galapagos Declaration, intraregional trade boomed again. Between 1989 and 1993, intraregional trade tripled, rising from less than $1 billion to more than $2.8 billion, with an annual growth rate of 34.5 percent, and accounted for 8 percent of total Andean trade by 1992. In 1990–1996, intraregional trade continued to grow at an average annual rate of 20 percent, totaling 11.9 percent of total Andean trade by the end of this period. By 1998, intraregional exports reached $5.3 billion, from $111 million in 1970. Colombia and Venezuela account for most of the trade volume. Colombia is Venezuela's largest market for nonpetroleum exports.

Although the aggregate figures may be small, qualitatively they are significant, especially when certain structural factors are taken into account. All Andean Community member states are primarily commodity exporters with relatively similar factor endowments and rich mineral wealth. Primary exports account for as much as 80 percent of the Andean Community's exports worldwide in such commodities as oil, metals, coffee, bananas, and shrimp. Transport costs within the region are very high and in general more expensive than shipping to industrialized countries such as the United States. In qualitative terms, however, intra-Andean trade is very important because of its high concentration of nontraditional or manufactured exports and intra-industry trade. Manufacturing exports account for 63 percent of intra-Andean trade (equivalent figures for both Mercosur and CACM are about 60 percent). The largest increases occurred in chemicals, textiles, and natural resource–intensive manufactures.

From Andean Group to Andean Community

The Andean Community has important political and social dimensions and institutions on which the member countries have increasingly focused their energies. An extensive institutional structure characterizes the Andean Community today, making it unique among integration schemes in the developing world, with many similarities to the European Union. A series of successive declarations and amendments to the Cartagena Agreement led to the present elaborate institutional structure.

In 1987, the member states of the Andean Group decided to give the treaty a new direction. They signed the Quito Protocol, an amending instrument through which the member states sought new horizons for the subregional integration process, including further strengthening of economic and commercial relations. Also, they reiterated the autonomous nature of the Andean integration process and reaffirmed the institutional structure established by the treaty.

In mid-1995, the member states sought to modernize and reinforce the then Andean Pact and convert it into the Andean Community, to be governed by similar structures to those instituted by the European Union. They agreed to restore the administrative structure, to improve the agility and efficiency of the decision-making process, and to broaden the scale of regional integration to include political as well as economic affairs. The Protocol of Trujillo, signed in March 1996, codified and integrated the Cartagena Agreement and its respective modifying instruments—the Additional Instrument for the accession of Venezuela (1973); the Protocol of Lima (1976); the Protocol of Arequipa (1978); the Protocol of Quito (1987); and the Protocol of Trujillo—creating the Andean Community and establishing the Andean Integration System, with its series of bodies and institutions.

The Andean Community announced its commitment to establish a common market by 2005 enabling the free circulation of goods, services, capital, and people. To this effect, in June 2001 national identification documents were recognized as the sole requirement for intra-Andean tourist travel. Goods have circulated freely since 1993. Free circulation of capital, people, and services are still being addressed.

Institutions of the Andean Community

The Trujillo Protocol in 1996 added nine bodies to the existing institutions to make up the new framework of the Andean Community, called the Andean Integration System (Sistema Integracion Andina, SAI). The institutions of the SAI are as follows:

- Presidential Council
- Council of Foreign Ministers
- Andean Community Commission
- Andean Parliament (1979)
- Court of Justice of the Andean Community (1979)
- General Secretariat
- Consultative Council on Business, Labor and Cultural Affairs
- Andean Development Corporation (Corporacion Andina de Fomento, CAF) (1968)

- Latin American Reserve Fund (1978)
- Andean Promotion Fund
- Simon Bolivar University
- Simon Rodriguez Group (Convenio Simon Rodriguez) (1973)
- Directorate of the Andean Integration System
- Andean Subregional Association of State Telecommunications Companies (Asociacion de Empresas Estatales de Telecommunicaciones del Acuerdo Andino, Aseta) (1974)
- Andean Satellite Telecommunications Organization (Organizacion Andina de Telecommunicaiones por Satelite, OATS) (1988)

The Presidential Council, composed of the presidents of the member states, is the supreme body of the Andean Community, providing political leadership. It defines the integration process of the region, provides instruction and recommendations to the other institutions, and evaluates the development and results of the integration process. The Council of Foreign Ministers is the second highest institution in the Andean Integration System. It is the executive body in charge of the implementation of the integration process and of foreign relations. Together the Presidential Council and the Council of Foreign Ministers preside over the entire Andean Integration System, allowing presidents the direct responsibility for designing policy and ordering its implementation.

The Andean Council of Foreign Ministers shares legislative authority with the Andean Community Commission. The commission is made up of a representative from each of the governments of the Andean Community member countries. Each government provides a regular representative and one alternate. The commission's president, the representative of the country that also holds the council presidency, serves a term of one year. The commission formulates, implements, and evaluates the policies of Andean subregional integration relating to commerce and investment, adopts measures for fulfilling the objectives of the Cartagena Agreement, coordinates the joint position of the member countries in international forums and negotiating sessions, and represents the Andean Community in areas of its domain. Each country exercises one vote in approving decisions. Initially, the commission adopted decisions by a two-thirds vote by the member countries. Under the rules of the Trujillo Protocol, an absolute majority is necessary to adopt decisions, a change that has facilitated approval of community proposals. Certain issues require a qualified majority, or no negative vote.

The General Secretariat is a permanent executive body with its seat in Lima. The secretary general of the Andean Community is a single individual elected by consensus in an extended meeting by the Andean Council of Foreign Ministers. The secretary general administers the Andean subregional integration process, oversees the fulfillment of community commitments, maintains permanent links with member countries and the executive bodies of other regional cooperation organizations, and enforces the decisions of the extended meetings of the Andean Council of Foreign Ministers and of the Andean Community Commission.

The Court of Justice of the Andean Community, headquartered in Quito, Ecuador, reviews the legality of community decisions to ensure uniform application in the territories of the member states, acts as arbiter and resolves disputes on the part of the members and between institutions of the Andean Community, and oversees labor disputes. It has five magistrates, with two alternates per magistrate, who are nationals of the member countries.

The Andean Parliament, located in Bogotá, Colombia, represents the people of the Andean Community. Currently, the Andean Parliament is made up of representatives of the National Congresses. The Parliament is constituted by representatives elected by a universal, direct vote for five-year terms. It lacks real legislative authority but participates in the promotion of the integration process by drafting regulations, by making suggestions to the bodies of the System Project of Rules of Common Interest, by promoting the legislative harmony of member countries, and by promoting cooperative relations and coordination with the parliaments of member countries and of third countries.

The Andean Community formally applied for and was granted observer status in the United Nations General Assembly. In 2002–2003, it participated in a single voice in the negotiations for a Free Trade Area of the Americas.

Anastasia Xenias

See Also Economic Integration; Common Market of the South (MERCOSUR); Latin American Free Trade Association (LAFTA)

References

Andean Community, "Key Andean Community Indicators," http://www.communidadandina.org.
Bywater, Marion. 1990. *Andean Integration: A New Lease on Life?* Special report no. 2018. London: The Economist Intelligence Unit.
Comunidad Andina. 1999. *How to Do Business in the Andean Community: Trade and Investment Guide.* Peru: Andean Community General Secretariat.
Josling, Timothy Edward. 1997. *Agricultural Trade Policies in the Andean Group: Issues and Options.* World Bank Technical Paper 364. Washington, DC: World Bank.
Morawetz, David. 1974. *The Andean Group: A Case Study in Economic Integration among Developing Countries.* Cambridge: MIT Press.
Puyana de Palacios, Alicia. 1982. *Economic Integration among Unequal Partners: The Case of the Andean Group.* New York: Pergamon.

Asia Pacific Economic Cooperation (APEC)

The Asia Pacific Economic Cooperation (APEC) forum was formally established in 1989. Though its emergence coincided with the end of the Cold War, its origins can be traced to the broad economic and geopolitical changes of the late 1960s and 1970s. By the 1970s, the United States had been overtaken by Japan as East Asia's most significant source of foreign aid and investment. The growing regional economic significance of Japan and the relative economic decline and politico-military reorientation of the United States (in the context of the rapprochement between the United States and the People's Republic of China in 1972 and the U.S. withdrawal from, and eventual defeat in, the Vietnam War between 1973 and 1975) increasingly coincided with efforts on the part of Japanese officials and economists to encourage regional economic integration and the creation of some form of Asia-Pacific organization.

The formal promulgation of an Asia-Pacific policy by the Japanese Foreign Ministry in late 1966 is often regarded as the start of Tokyo's effort to create a regional trade organization. This led to persistent but unsuccessful efforts by the Japanese economist Kiyoshi Kojima and Japan to promote a Pacific Free Trade Area (PAFTA) that would encompass the United States, Japan, New Zealand, Canada, and Australia, as a counterweight to the European Economic Community. Although the PAFTA idea received limited support, it eased the way for the establishment in April 1967 of the Pacific Basin Economic Council (PBEC). The PBEC is composed of nationally based business organizations.

Meanwhile, the first Pacific Trade and Development (PAFTAD) conference was held in 1968, primarily providing a forum for economists. The continued lack of interest in a formal trade organization in the region led Kojima to introduce a less ambitious proposal centered on the idea of an Organization for Pacific Trade and Development (OPTAD), which would be modeled on the Organisation for Economic Co-operation and Development (OECD). This proposal also languished until the late 1970s, when it was revived in a report for the U.S. Senate Committee on Foreign Relations written by prominent U.S. economist Hugh Patrick and Australian economist Peter Drysdale. It was proposed that this version of OPTAD would encompass all the non-Communist nation-states in the region, including some Latin American countries.

As with previous initiatives, very few governments in the region were actually interested in making a commitment; however, the proposal did lead to the establishment of the Pacific Economic Cooperation Conference (PECC), which sought to provide a forum for academics, business representatives, and government officials. The PECC, which later became the Pacific Economic Cooperation Council, had its first meeting in Canberra in late 1980 and included representatives from the United States, Japan, Canada, Australia, New Zealand, Korea, Malaysia, Thailand, Indonesia, Singapore, and the Philippines. During the 1980s, the governments of China, Taiwan, and Brunei and the members of the South Pacific Forum also began sending delegates to the

PECC. Hong Kong, then Mexico, Chile, and Peru, joined the PECC in 1991–1992, and a number of other Latin American countries, along with the USSR (Russia after 1991), gained observer status in the early 1990s. The PECC brought together academics, business leaders, and government officials, but a key characteristic of its operation was the unofficial role played by governments.

The failure to establish a governmental organization focused on regional economic issues between the 1960s and the 1980s, and the timing of the establishment of APEC at the beginning of the 1990s, underscore the close relationship between geopolitical and security considerations, on the one hand, and economics and trade, on the other. The Cold War had clearly inhibited any form of expansive regionalism in East Asia and the Asia Pacific: From the outset, governments in the region were wary of an economic organization that might have security implications and thus limit its membership to capitalist economies, whereas the United States was opposed to an organization in which the USSR and its allies might have a forum for the discussion of security questions. However, with the end of the Cold War, APEC could be set up as a major institutional forum for the articulation and accommodation of a revised and reconfigured version of various long-standing geopolitical and geo-economic visions for the Asia-Pacific region. (In fact, the term "Asia Pacific" itself only began to enjoy widespread currency in the 1990s.) In the early post–Cold War era, influential liberal narratives on economic development and international relations increasingly represented the Asia Pacific as destined to become an ever more integrated region of prosperous free-trading nation-states.

At the same time, governments and economic elites in Northeast and Southeast Asia were concerned that the post–Cold War international political economy was shifting toward economic blocs centered on Western Europe (through the EU) and North America (through the North American Free Trade Agreement, or NAFTA), and they viewed some form of regional economic grouping, although not necessarily the form that APEC took at its establishment, as an important counterweight to wider post–Cold War political and economic trends. For example, APEC, as it was constituted in 1989, was challenged by Prime Minister Mahathir Mohamad of Malaysia, who proposed the establishment of a trading bloc, initially called the East Asian Economic Group (EAEG), which would exclude the United States, Australia, and New Zealand as well as all other "non-Asian" nation-states. In this context, Mahathir refused to attend APEC's first heads-of-government meeting in Seattle in 1993. However, by the time of the annual summit in November 1998, which was held in Kuala Lumpur, he was the presiding host, and his East Asian Economic Group, in the form of the East Asian Economic Caucus, had been incorporated into APEC.

Apart from concerns about the possible formation of economic blocs in the post–Cold War era and the need to respond in kind, elites in Asia were also unsure about Washington's attitude toward both APEC and security issues in the region after the Cold War. At the outset, Washington was preoccupied with the situation in Europe, but in a 1991 visit to East Asia, George H. W. Bush's secretary of state, James Baker, reaffirmed a U.S. commitment to the region, emphasizing the continued importance of Washington's bilateral security arrangements. These arrangements maintained, in a somewhat revised fashion, the basic, and primarily bilateral, politico-military alliance structure of the Cold War in the region. This did not necessarily mean that the United States actively opposed regional and multilateral economic (or even security) initiatives; however, it needs to be emphasized that it was the Australian government that took the lead, with the particularly active involvement of the Japanese government (rather than the U.S. government), in the establishment of APEC.

With its establishment APEC was portrayed by many of its supporters as an example of "open regionalism," in contrast to the preferential trading practices that characterize the EU and NAFTA. The Eminent Persons Group (EPG), which laid down much of the early organizational framework for APEC, made it clear that APEC was not intended to be like the European Union, which involved the relinquishment of national sovereignty in the context of both deepening economic integration and formal political institutionalization. By contrast it emphasized that APEC would be a much looser organization of "like minded economies" seeking to remove "barriers to economic exchange among members in the interest of all." C. Fred Bergsten (former chair of the EPG and director of the Washington-based Institute for International Economics) also emphasized that the organization should not only play a central role in regional trade liberalization, but also act as a "force for world-wide liberalization" (Bergsten 1994).

Nevertheless, the focus at the first major meeting in Seattle in late 1993 (and at the second major meeting in Bogor, Indonesia, in November 1994) was squarely on trade liberalization within APEC. On the final day of the Bogor meeting, the leaders from the eighteen member countries agreed in principle to the virtual elimination of tariff barriers and obstacles to capital flows within the APEC region by the year 2020 (2010 for developed nations and 2020 for developing nations). This meshed with an increasingly influential strand of economic and political thinking grounded in the idea that economic transformation and integration of the region was connected to a new East-West synthesis. The public articulation of synthetic cultural (as well economic and political) visions of the region's future by prominent politicians and intellectuals facilitated consensus building aimed at easing tensions in and around APEC.

An important example of the East-West synthesis was the 1995 book, *Asia Pacific Fusion: Japan's Role in APEC,* by Yoichi Funabashi, the former chief diplomatic correspondent for *Asahi Shimbun.* Funabashi's book was, in part,

a reply to Samuel Huntington's famous 1993 warning of the potential for a "clash of civilizations" in the Asia Pacific and elsewhere. Funabashi, who has close links to the Institute for International Economics in Washington and had served as head of *Asahi Shimbun*'s Washington, DC, bureau, argued that "the Asia-Pacific experiment to bring the greatest civilizations of the world into one dynamic sphere of confluence will lead to a new era of prosperity into the next century." He emphasized that "the economic and cultural dynamics in the Asia-Pacific, suggest that in at least this region, economic interdependence and cross-fertilization among civilizations can perhaps transcend the barriers of race and ideology." He concluded that "the growing fusion of the Asia Pacific is offering Japan" and other countries in the region "more room to harness elements of both East and West" (Funabashi 1995, 10–11).

This view was certainly at least superficially apparent at the annual APEC summit in Osaka, Japan, in November 1995. This meeting produced what was called an "Action Agenda." Meanwhile, the organization's rejection of binding trade agreements was celebrated by participants, such as Fidel Ramos (then president of the Philippines), as evidence of the "Asian Way" at work. The Asian Way in this instance amounted to verbal assurances by all member governments that they would make every effort to meet the economic liberalization goals of APEC. Thus, regardless of the alleged antipathy between East and West, which was a focus of considerable debate in the early 1990s, APEC emerged as a major site of elite integration in the Asia Pacific, and this was facilitated by the domestication of influential East Asian visions of progress to the narratives on globalization via an emphasis on a synthesis between East and West.

Despite the efforts at elite consensus building and the emerging East-West synthesis, the end of the Cold War and the continued spread of economic liberalism contributed to considerable tension in the Asia Pacific. For example, in the post–Cold War era, relations between the

U.S. and Japanese governments, an important axis of the APEC process, continued to be beset by friction on a range of economic issues, especially those related to trading practices. In fact, the growing economic significance of the region generally, and of China in particular, combined with growing concern in North America about the latter's increasing politico-military power, also contributed to uncertainty regarding the post–Cold War character of the region. At the same time, the consensual character of agreements made at APEC meetings pointed to the organization's weak institutionalization. Although the annual meeting in the Philippines in November 1996 proceeded much as earlier meetings, the organization's diverse membership faced a serious challenge with the onset of the Asian financial crisis in July 1997. As problems mounted, APEC's inability to make formal and binding decisions became a source of frustration for many.

By the time of the annual meeting in Vancouver in November 1997, the Asian financial crisis was a serious problem. In fact, in the view of some observers, by the time of the Vancouver summit, APEC had become virtually irrelevant. In particular, the prominent role that the International Monetary Fund (IMF) began to play in the management of the Asian financial crisis provided the United States (which was seen to have been ambivalent about APEC from the outset) with the opportunity to encourage economic liberalization and deregulation in the region far more effectively than it could under the auspices of APEC. In the second half of 1997, the IMF embarked on major efforts to restore financial stability to the region via loan packages to the governments of Thailand, Indonesia, and South Korea. The loans were conditional on the implementation of a range of austerity measures and liberal economic reforms.

The IMF's intervention directly challenged the nascent multilateral and consensual approach to regional economic issues embodied by APEC. In fact, the overall approach taken by the IMF challenged East Asian ideas about how

the region had achieved its economic success: From the point of view of the IMF, the crisis flowed from the inefficiencies and distortions that were characteristic of the various state-centered approaches to capitalist development that prevailed in East Asia (what became known pejoratively as "crony capitalism"). Not surprisingly, Prime Minister Mahathir in particular was quick to dispute IMF explanations for the crisis, at the same time as his government also rejected IMF advice and interference. Mahathir and a number of other politicians and commentators placed the blame for the region's problems at the door of foreign currency speculators. In some instances, they even argued that foreign currency traders had deliberately acted to undermine the economies of East Asia. For example, Mahathir singled out the well-known fund manager George Soros and charged him with masterminding a deliberate attempt to sabotage the economic dynamism of Malaysia and the other countries of the region.

Of course, Mahathir's opposition to the IMF's handling of the financial crisis was grounded in his earlier opposition to APEC and his promotion of an East Asian Economic Group, which, as already noted, had been partially accommodated in APEC as the East Asian Economic Caucus. Although Mahathir's initiative in the early 1990s had flowed from concerns about the membership and orientation of APEC, as well as the rise of NAFTA and the EU, it was also an attempt to curb the growing flow of Chinese-Malaysian capital to China by linking China more tightly into a regional economic cooperation network. By the late 1990s, the EAEC enjoyed considerable independence within the framework of APEC and was made up of the governments of the Association of Southeast Asian Nations (ASEAN) plus Japan, South Korea, and China (ASEAN+3). This lineup apparently reflected the perception in ASEAN that Japan and South Korea were the driving economic forces in the region. Indeed, both were the source of major investment flows, while China was the main destination for overseas Chinese capital moving out of ASEAN. The exclusion of Hong Kong and Taiwan from this list also catered to Beijing's sensitivities. At the same time, Mahathir's vision at least remained focused on Japan as the leading economic power in the region, and a major economic force internationally. Although the economic malaise that has gripped Japan since the beginning of the 1990s, and the continued salience of the Cold-War-era U.S.-Japan relationship, has meant that the Japanese government and Japanese corporations have not played as significant a role in the region in the post–Cold War era as many had anticipated, Mahathir has continued to emphasize the need for the Japanese government to act as the "voice of Asia" at meetings of the G-7 and elsewhere.

Certainly, given the obvious inability of APEC to address the Asian financial crisis, there were early efforts by Tokyo to play a more significant role. At the annual IMF–World Bank meeting in Hong Kong in mid-1997, the Japanese government floated the idea of an Asian Monetary Fund (AMF), proposing that upward of $100 billion be set aside and that an institutional infrastructure to administer it be created in order to be prepared for any future crises of the kind then destabilizing Southeast Asia. A key characteristic of the AMF proposal was the absence of the conditions attached to the IMF's loan packages. The approach envisioned by proponents of the AMF was one that worked to maintain the restrictions on foreign ownership, of financial institutions in particular, and that sustained the economic practices that East Asian elites associated with rapid capitalist development. Representatives from the United States, Europe, and the IMF voiced strong opposition to an Asian Monetary Fund, while officials from Hong Kong, Malaysia, and Thailand expressed considerable enthusiasm. Meanwhile, other East Asian leaders made clear their frustration with the IMF's approach to the crisis.

The idea of an Asian Monetary Fund was formally discussed and rejected at the November 1997 APEC Finance Minister's meeting. Prior to the annual APEC meeting in 1998, the idea of an Asian Monetary Fund was again raised; however, no effort to implement such a scheme materialized. Given its size and organizational frailty, APEC has, since the Asian crisis (and in the wake of 9/11 and the launch of the war on terrorism), served primarily as an opportunity for the region's leaders to get together to hold a range of bilateral meetings on specific issues often completely unrelated to regional economics and trade, while publicly reaffirming their long-term commitment to the nonbinding economic goals of the organization.

Mark Berger

See Also Economic Integration; Association of Southeast Asian Nations (ASEAN); International Monetary Fund (IMF)

References

Berger, Mark T. 1999. "APEC and Its Enemies: The Failure of the New Regionalism in the Asia-Pacific." *Third World Quarterly: Journal of Emerging Areas* 20, no. 5.
———. 2004. *The Battle for Asia: From Decolonization to Globalization.* London: RoutledgeCurzon.
———. 2004. "The US-China-Japan Triangle and the Geo-Political Economy of Regionalism in the Asia-Pacific." In Dominic Kelly and Wyn Grant, eds., *The Politics of International Trade: Actors, Issues, Processes.* Basingstoke: Palgrave Macmillan.
Berger, Mark T., and Mark Beeson. 2004. "APEC, ASEAN and American Power: The Limits of the New Regionalism in the Asia-Pacific." In Morten Bøås, Marianne H. Marchand, and Timothy M. Shaw, eds., *The Political Economy of Regions and Regionalisms.* Basingstoke: Palgrave Macmillan.
Bergsten, C. Fred. 1994. "APEC and the World Economy: A Force for Worldwide Liberalisation." *Foreign Affairs* 73, no. 3.
Camilleri, Joseph A. 2000. *States, Markets and Civil Society in Asia Pacific: The Political Economy of the Asia-Pacific Region.* Vol. 1. Cheltenham: Edward Elgar.
Funabashi, Yoichi. 1995. *Asia Pacific Fusion: Japan's Role in APEC.* Washington, DC: Institute for International Economics.
Higgott, Richard. 2000. "Regionalism in the Asia-Pacific: Two Steps Forward, One Step Back?" In Richard Stubbs and Geoffrey R. D. Underhill, eds., *Political*

Economy and the Changing Global Order. New York: Oxford University Press.

Korhonen, Pekka. 1998. *Japan and Asia Pacific Integration: Pacific Romances, 1968–1996.* London: Routledge.

Ravenhill, John. 2001. *APEC and the Construction of Pacific Rim Regionalism.* Cambridge: Cambridge University Press.

Takashi, Terada. 1998. "The Origins of Japan's APEC Policy: Foreign Minister Takeo Miki's Asia-Pacific Policy and Current Implications." *Pacific Review* 11, no. 3.

Association of Southeast Asian Nations (ASEAN)

The governments of Thailand, Singapore, the Philippines, Malaysia, and Indonesia formally established the Association of Southeast Asian Nations (ASEAN) on August 8, 1967. Brunei joined in January 1984, and the end of the Cold War saw the entry of Vietnam (July 1995), Burma (July 1997), Laos (July 1997), and Cambodia (April 1999). Although East Timor gained independence from Indonesia in 2001 and initially sought early entry into ASEAN, it has met opposition on this score from the government of Burma; its entry to ASEAN has not only been postponed, apparently indefinitely, but as of mid-2003 it was still being refused entry to the much larger, twenty-three-member ASEAN Regional Forum (ARF).

ASEAN was originally established in the context of the deepening of the Cold War in Southeast Asia. By the mid-1960s, even though they differed with regard to the level of support they wanted to provide for escalating U.S. involvement in the Vietnam War, anti-Communist governments in the region had a shared concern about local Communist-led insurgencies in their respective nations. The founding members of ASEAN were also interested in establishing a mechanism for the resolution or avoidance of disputes such as the complicated military and diplomatic struggle that had flowed from the setting of Malaysia's borders to include Sarawak and Sabah in the early 1960s.

The failure of the South-East Asia Treaty Organization (SEATO), set up in February 1955, also contributed to the emergence of ASEAN. The formation of SEATO followed the French withdrawal from Indochina and the parallel consolidation of the Democratic Republic of Vietnam (North Vietnam) under Ho Chi Minh and of the Republic of Vietnam (South Vietnam) under Ngo Dinh Diem. The United States sponsored the establishment of SEATO, and most of its members (the United States, Australia, New Zealand, Britain, France, Pakistan, Thailand, and the Philippines) were not even in Southeast Asia. From the outset it was envisioned as more of a military alliance for the defense of South Vietnam than a regional security organization. Even at the height of the Vietnam War, SEATO never assumed an active military role. At the same time, although the establishment of ASEAN was a response to the apparent weakness of SEATO and various postcolonial and Cold War security concerns, the members of ASEAN also placed considerable emphasis on economic collaboration.

ASEAN represented one of the earliest, and now represents by far the most long-lived, efforts to establish a regional intergovernmental organization in Southeast Asia. In fact, although Southeast Asia is now widely understood as that part of Asia that lies east of India and south of China (and contains Burma, Thailand, Malaysia, Singapore, Indonesia, Brunei, the Philippines, Cambodia, Laos, Vietnam, and most recently East Timor), the routinized treatment of Southeast Asia as a political, economic, or geographical unit only dates to the era of decolonization and the early Cold War. Although the term has been traced to the nineteenth century, and was used by some policymakers, colonial officials, and journalists by the 1930s, it took on greater significance during World

War II, when the theater of war under the direction of Lord Mountbatten was formally identified as the "South-East Asia Command" between 1943 and 1946. At the same time, the area covered by the South-East Asia Command did not coincide with contemporary Southeast Asia insofar as it never included the Philippines or all of French Indochina. After the war, meanwhile, the French government sought to promote a Southeast Asia Union centered on a reconfigured French Indochina (Vietnam, Laos, and Cambodia). This was challenged by the Southeast Asian League, which was set up in 1947 by the Laotian Prince, Souphanouvong (the "Red Prince"), who became its first general secretary. Neither of these organizations survived for long, but by the time of the establishment of SEATO in 1955, and then ASEAN a little more than a decade later, the idea of Southeast Asia as a discrete region was firmly established.

Apart from SEATO, which was formally disbanded in June 1977, ASEAN also had a more immediate predecessor in the form of the Association of Southeast Asia (ASA). Thailand, Malaya (later Malaysia), and the Philippines set up the ASA on July 31, 1961. It was hoped it would serve as an alternative to the already faltering SEATO; however, the ASA was undermined within a year or two by the outbreak of a dispute between Malaya and the Philippines over Sabah, in northern Borneo. The ASA was further weakened when Manila took the side of Jakarta in the escalating territorial conflict (the "Konfrontasi") that pitted the Indonesian government against the Malayan and British governments, and their allies, over the inclusion of Sarawak and Sabah (and briefly Brunei) in the planned postcolonial polity of Malaysia (which was also expected to include Singapore).

With the eventual resolution of the Konfrontasi and the consolidation of Malaysia to include Sarawak and Sabah, but not Singapore and Brunei, the ASA was briefly resuscitated in 1966, but was dissolved in 1967 in favor of the newly created, and more broadly based, ASEAN. The Association of Southeast Asian Nations, which was briefly known as the South East Asia Association for Regional Cooperation (SEAARC), formally emerged under the auspices of the ASEAN Declaration promulgated in Bangkok on August 8, 1967, by the governments of Indonesia, Malaysia, the Philippines, Singapore, and Thailand. Immediately prior to the establishment of ASEAN, the idea of regional governmental cooperation in Southeast Asia was receiving both private and public support from U.S. policymakers, academics, and the print media.

ASEAN's main goals, as already suggested, were presented as economic and social cooperation; however, a key implicit objective was political cooperation, and the founding document also reflected an intention to influence regional political and military affairs. These latter concerns were reflected in the declaration in November 1971 of Southeast Asia as a Zone of Peace, Freedom and Neutrality (ZOPFAN). However, despite gestures such as ZOPFAN, ASEAN did very little for almost ten years after its initial establishment in 1967. And even when the organization eventually had its first summit meeting in February 1976, it was clear that ASEAN still did not have anything resembling a unified strategic outlook. During Vietnam's occupation of Kampuchea (Cambodia) from December 1978 to the end of 1989, however, ASEAN was united in its opposition to Vietnam's violation of Cambodian sovereignty.

The end of the Cold War led eventually to Vietnam, Laos, and Cambodia becoming members of ASEAN. Burma (Myanmar) also became a member in this period, and by the end of the 1990s ASEAN included all of the nation-states in Southeast Asia. Starting in January 1992, ASEAN also entered into a security dialogue with governments outside of Southeast Asia. The specific instrument for this process was the Post-Ministerial Conference (PMC), a meeting between the foreign ministers of the United States, Russia, and China, along with other East Asian governments, on the one hand, and the foreign ministers from the ASEAN governments, on the other. This meeting led to the establishment of the ASEAN Regional Forum in July 1993, which held its first formal meeting in Bangkok in July 1994. These years also saw the promulgation of a formal commitment to an ASEAN Free Trade Area (AFTA). Meanwhile, ASEAN played a key role in the formation of the Asia-Europe Meeting (ASEM), which met in Bangkok for the first time in March 1996.

ASEAN was the focus of considerable international controversy at the time of the entry of Burma (Myanmar) and Cambodia into the organization. The acceptance of Burma into ASEAN in July 1997, and the failure of the organization's members to criticize the Rangoon-based military government's terrible human rights record, attracted the opprobrium of governments outside the region. It also highlighted the organization's continued blanket commitment to respecting the sovereignty of other members and the principle of noninterference into their affairs. The question of the human rights record of the military government of Myanmar has not gone away. It surfaced again at the June 2003 meeting of ASEAN in Phnom Penh. There is particular international concern, and concern within ASEAN, expressed most forcefully by the Malaysian government, about the fact that the government in Rangoon is slated to assume the rotating secretary-generalship of ASEAN in 2006.

Meanwhile, ASEAN members did defer the entry of Cambodia into the organization when Hun Sen led a coup in Phnom Penh shortly before its scheduled induction in July 1997. Cambodia's membership was subsequently ratified in April 1999 against the backdrop of growing problems with the formation and maintenance of consensus in the organization as it expanded in size. The Asian financial crisis (1997–1998) and disagreements over how to handle it (Thailand and Indonesia accepted the financial assistance and reform package proffered by the International Monetary Fund [IMF], while Malaysia rejected IMF support and advice) also contributed to disarray and ineffectiveness in ASEAN at the end of the 1990s.

As the issue of Myanmar's entry makes clear, ASEAN has always emphasized its commitment to consensus and respect for the sovereignty of member governments. Although ASEAN watches the European Union with interest, it has no apparent commitment to political integration. However, there has been some attempt to move toward what Rodolfo C. Severino, a former secretary-general of ASEAN (2000–2002), described as a "more rules-based association." Speaking in Kuala Lumpur in 2001, Severino, a former undersecretary for foreign affairs in the Philippines, argued that "regional agreements may need national legislation to carry them out" and that a move in this direction "would help strengthen the national legal systems of the member-states as well as the rule of law in the region as a whole" (Severino 2001). The main activity of ASEAN remains an annual meeting between the foreign ministers of the member governments, preceded by a meeting of senior officials. The daily operations of the ASEAN secretariat are managed by a standing committee that is based in the capital city of whichever member government is scheduled to provide the venue for the next annual meeting.

Meanwhile, the emergence of ASEAN+3 (ASEAN and China, Japan, and South Korea) in the late 1990s is probably the most important ASEAN-related development in the region. This trend has meant that ASEAN (or more precisely ASEAN+3) is seen as more significant than the Asia Pacific Economic Cooperation (APEC) forum. For many commentators, the Asian financial crisis breathed new life into the specifically East Asian efforts to develop a regional political and economic organization that is far less inclusive than the apparently moribund APEC. In this situation ASEAN has the potential to play an important role. The events of 1997–1998 demonstrated that East Asia continued to be vulnerable to external economic trends. For governments and business elites in the region, the crisis highlighted the need for an effective regional organization that could manage economic instability.

This is the context in which ASEAN, and especially ASEAN+3, emerged as potential frameworks for the explicitly pan-Asian organization that had been promoted for many years by the long-serving prime minister of Malaysia, Mahathir Mohamad (1981–2003). Mahathir is seen as having been vindicated in his use of capital controls (contrary to the IMF's approach to Thailand, Indonesia, and South Korea), insofar as he steered the Malaysian economy through the economic crisis of the late 1990s far better than the IMF-backed governments of Thailand and Indonesia did. The war on terrorism also initially enhanced Mahathir's ability to control political opposition in Malaysia, and his wider support for the struggle against Islamic fundamentalists in the region and beyond also improved his relationship with the United States. However, his harsh criticisms of the U.S.-led war on Iraq in early 2003 had the reverse effect. Furthermore, although he may use less strident language, compared to his earlier calls for an exclusive East Asian regional organization, Mahathir continued up to the end of his term as prime minister of Malaysia in October 2003 (and beyond) to promote an exclusive form of regional cooperation that would challenge the U.S.-led globalization project. For example, writing in a World Economic Forum publication the year before he stepped down as prime minister, he emphasized that "with the global economy in trouble, Asian countries should intensify their regional cooperation in trade and finance, including such initiatives as an East Asian Economic Grouping and a regional monetary fund" (Mahathir 2002, 10).

Regardless of the continued salience of Pan-Asian economic regionalism, it remains unclear whether ASEAN+3 will emerge at the center of an independent regional political and economic organization of the type that Mahathir has been promoting since the beginning of the 1990s. Certainly there are a number of broad reasons why the nation-states of ASEAN might move toward ever-tighter integration with the main nation-states of Northeast Asia.

Although proponents of regional integration often point to an ostensibly common history and cultural background, more important factors facilitating regional integration probably relate to a continued commitment to state-guided development, or the "developmental state," along with certain similarities in the organization of economic activities. This is strengthened by the important role of overseas Chinese businesses in the region and increasingly strong regional investment flows and trading relationships. There is considerable debate about how important some of these trends and ostensibly shared characteristics are in terms of facilitating regional economic and even political integration, but when they are linked to the resentment about the unilateral way in which the United States and the IMF handled the Asian financial crisis, and the often unilateral approach that the administration of President George W. Bush is taking to diplomacy and military affairs, as well as trade and finance, there is clearly the potential for increased regional mobilization and even regional institution-building by governments and elites in Asia.

It is also clear that, unlike APEC, the regionalism associated directly and indirectly with ASEAN+3 is focused far more on money and finance than it is on trade. Both China and Japan have significant monetary reserves, and they are both viewed as potential anchors for any wider effort to develop an effective regional monetary mechanism. At the same time, the main obstacle to greater regional integration, led by Japan and/or China, apparently has little to do with any bilateral disagreements between the two major regional players. Nor does it even appear to be related directly to Tokyo's long-standing willingness to defer to Washington. The main reason that the governments of Japan and China apparently remain willing to leave the overall management of regional monetary relations to the IMF is that Tokyo and Beijing are both reluctant to make open-ended financial or monetary commitments to other governments in the region.

This situation apparently flows from the limits that the wider global political economy imposes on even the largest national economies today. The growing power of financial capital, in particular, has been at the forefront of the construction of an international economic order that is characterized by a growing disjuncture between the production of goods and services and an increasingly deregulated financial system. At this point even the largest and most powerful economies in the region are limited by the ability of the global financial markets to shape global economic policy. It is also worth noting that China's rapid economic development and concomitant politico-military rise is viewed in many quarters as a challenge to ASEAN. At the same time, Japan continues to exert a powerful influence over Southeast Asia, an influence that has a contradictory rather than a straightforward unifying effect on the region. Meanwhile, the resurgence of bilateral trade negotiations in the region and beyond over the past few years highlights the decline of APEC, the continued frailty of the WTO, and the important countervailing tendencies that will thwart any straightforward movement toward stronger regional economic and political integration centered on the East Asian region generally or ASEAN specifically.

Mark Berger

See Also Economic Integration; Asia Pacific Economic Cooperation (APEC); South Asian Association for Regional Cooperation (SAARC)

References

Acharya, Amitav. 2000. *The Quest for Identity: International Relations of Southeast Asia.* Singapore: Oxford University Press.

———. 2001. *Constructing a Security Community in Southeast Asia: ASEAN and the Problem of Regional Order.* London: Routledge.

Berger, Mark T. 2004. *The Battle for Asia: From Decolonization to Globalization.* London: RoutledgeCurzon.

Emmerson, Donald. 1984. "Southeast Asia—What's in a Name?" *Journal of Southeast Asian Studies* 15. no. 1, 1–21.

Higgott, Richard. 2000. "Regionalism in the Asia-Pacific: Two Steps Forward, One Step Back?" In Richard Stubbs and Geoffrey R. D. Underhill, eds., *Political Economy and the Changing Global Order.* New York: Oxford University Press.

Johnston, Alastair Iain. 2003. "Socialization in International Institutions: The ASEAN Way and International Relations Theory." In G. John Ikenberry and Michael Mastanduno, eds., *International Relations Theory and the Asia-Pacific.* New York: Columbia University Press.

Mahathir bin Mohamad. 2002. "Globalization: Challenges and Impact on Asia." In Frank-Jürgen Richter and Pamela C. M. Mar, eds., *Recreating Asia: Visions for a New Century.* Singapore: John Wiley and Sons.

McMahon, Robert J. 1999. *The Limits of Empire: The United States and Southeast Asia since World War II.* New York: Columbia University Press.

Narine, Shaun. 2002. *Explaining ASEAN: Regionalism in Southeast Asia.* Boulder: Lynne Rienner.

Severino, Rodolfo C. 2001. "The ASEAN Way and the Rule of Law." Speech delivered September 3, Kuala Lumpur. In *International Law Conference on ASEAN Legal Systems and Regional Integration.* Sponsored by the Asia-Europe Institute and the Faculty of Law, University of Malaya, Kuala Lumpur, http://www.asean.or.id/newdata/asean_way.htm.

Stubbs, Richard. 2002. "ASEAN Plus Three: Emerging East Asian Regionalism?" *Asian Survey* 42, no. 3, 440–455.

Australia New Zealand Closer Economic Relations Trade Agreement (ANZCERTA)

The Australia New Zealand Closer Economic Relations (CER) Trade Agreement, sometimes called ANZCERTA, came into effect on January 1, 1983. It is usually known by its short title, Closer Economic Relations, or its abbreviation, CER. A free trade agreement (FTA) as provided for in Article 24 of the General Agreement on Tariffs and Trade (GATT), it is comprehensive and nondiscriminatory. It reports to the GATT Secretariat.

CER in a Nutshell

The CER Agreement contains provisions for the following:

- Free trade in goods. Since 1990 there have been no tariffs or quantitative restrictions on trade in goods, and goods traded between the parties are not subsidized.
- Free trade in services. New Zealand and Australian service providers can access each other's markets with only minor restrictions in air services, coastal shipping, broadcasting, third-party insurance, and postal services.
- Mutual recognition of goods and occupations. A good (with five exceptions) that can legally be sold in one country can also be sold in the other, and a person

who is registered to practice an occupation in one country (save medical practitioners) is entitled to practice an equivalent occupation in the other.
- Free labor market. A long history of arrangements, collectively known as the Trans-Tasman Travel Arrangement, allow Australians and New Zealanders to visit, reside, and work in either country without restriction. These arrangements have been supplemented by a Social Security Agreement, the Reciprocal Health Agreement, and the Child Support Agreement.
- Government Procurement. Progressive agreements provide for a single trans-Tasman government procurement market.
- Investment. Most investments from one party no longer require approval by the government of the other.
- Taxation. Double taxation is eliminated, and company taxes and imputation policies are being harmonized.
- Customs, quarantine, and biosecurity measures. These have been harmonized and no longer constitute barriers.

The evolution of CER displays five notable features. First, CER did not evolve as a consequence of natural complementarity but rather was the outcome of negotiations and decisions by Australian and New Zealand political leaders, who were obliged to cope with European protectionism. Second, CER was innovative inasmuch as its negotiators started with a notional assumption of total free trade and then accommodated sensitive issues with a negative list approach and other devices, such as deferral arrangements, memoranda of understanding, and intra-industry pacts. Third, CER was evolutionary inasmuch as it started with goods in 1983, progressed to services in 1987, then tackled other constraints on trade and investment in a series of pragmatic steps extending to the present. Fourth, CER gradually broke new ground with agreements to recognize professional and educational credentials and food and safety standards in both countries and to eliminate other "beyond-the-border" constraints on trade. Competition laws have made antidumping and countervailing regulations unnecessary. Fifth, CER is uniquely efficient, inasmuch as it operates without a secretariat or a dispute resolution body, but rather is managed by existing political and administrative bodies and private-sector enterprises.

Recent Developments

During the 1990s, business laws were further harmonized by New Zealand legislation including the Reciprocal Enforcement of Judgments Amendment Act, the Securities Act, the Consumer Guarantees Act, and the Financial Reporting Act, each with its Australian counterpart, and by accession, alongside Australia, to the Patent Co-operation Treaty and the Convention on the Settlement of Investment Disputes. By 1993, agreements were reached to harmonize rules of origin, industry assistance, and technical barriers to trade. Judges were exchanged among civil courts dealing with CER-related torts, and a body of "CER law" began to accumulate.

CER had reached a high plateau by the mid-1990s; that is, all major issues had been dealt with, and progress gave way to consolidation.

The two governments focused on how to harmonize company laws, tax policies, and other regulations affecting trade. Subsequent meetings by prime ministers and administrators dealt with problems arising in the broader trans-Tasman relationship, such as disputes over access for New Zealand apples affected by Fire Blight, regulation of national airlines, administration of immigration and refugee policies, and welfare eligibility of resident noncitizens. Noneconomic issues engaging the leaders included New Zealand's lag in defense capability and its exclusion from military relations with the United States, which contrasted with Australia's close military relationship with the United States and contribution to the war against Iraq. These issues played a role in coordination of counterterrorism approaches.

Neither government is contemplating moving to a customs union, monetary union, or other merger of the two economies or political systems. The policy is not about duplication or merger, but rather harmonization. That is, the governments and leading associations of each country will continue to formulate their own laws, policies, procedures, and practices, but these will deliberately be made compatible with those of the other, even as they continue to differ in title, idiom, and detail. The precedents they have set and the experience they have gained have facilitated subsequent FTA negotiations with Singapore and other members of the Association of Southeast Asian Nations (ASEAN), Chile, and the United States.

Assessment of CER

In 2003, Australia and New Zealand leaders celebrated twenty years of harmonious operation of CER. Trade and economic relations between the two economies at that time were still enjoying vigorous and sustained growth. In the 1990s, trans-Tasman trade increased by an annual average of 9 percent, which exceeded the average growth of Australia's international trade of 8.5 percent and the annual growth in New Zealand's international trade of 6.3 percent. As a proportion of total trade, New Zealand's merchandise trade with Australia grew from an average of 13.9 percent to 21 percent in the period 1985–2000; Australia's proportion of trade with New Zealand grew from 4.1 percent to 7.1 percent in the same interval. New Zealand did especially well; its merchandise exports to Australia rose steadily, from NZ$1,037 million in 1983 to NZ$6,217 million in 2002, and the trade ratio improved from two-to-one in Australia's favor to virtual parity during the first decade of CER. Australia became New Zealand's best trading partner, New Zealand became Australia's third best trading partner, and each strengthened its position as the other's best customer for manufactured goods.

Furthermore, trans-Tasman investment grew from NZ$2 billion to NZ$32 billion during the period 1983 to 2000. Intra-industry trade, intercorporate alliances, trade in services, and movement of tourists and migrants also registered increases in the 1980s and 1990s over corresponding figures for the 1970s, increases attributed directly or indirectly to CER. CER is paralleled by a Closer Defence Relationship (CDR), close and frequent political and administrative sector consultations, and a joint institution, the Australia New Zealand Food Authority. Under negotiation is a binational therapeutics goods regulatory agency. Also, citizens of each country may reside and work in the other, creating a single labor market.

Historical Background and Motivation

For a century and a half, the trade relationship between Australia and New Zealand remained harmonious and mutually advantageous, but not deep or close. The two countries' leaders had discussed closer economic cooperation sporadically since the 1880s, signed trade agreements in 1922 and 1933 extending British preferential tariff rates to each other, and negotiated a Trade Understanding to grant special import licenses in 1956. But as recently as 1960, only 4 percent of New Zealand exports went to Australia, and a similar proportion of Australia's exports went to New Zealand. Throughout much of the twentieth century, the two countries looked in opposite directions, New Zealand trading through Panama, Australia through Suez.

Their mutual aloofness was shaken by faraway events. In 1961, Britain declared its intent to seek membership in the European Economic Community (EEC). This jeopardized New Zealand's and Australia's privileged access to the British market. At the same time, world prices for bulk agricultural commodities were declining as other countries became self-sufficient and began supplying world markets. New Zealand's and Australia's export growth slowed, and by the later 1960s, as the two countries continued borrowing and importing, and to support their high standards of living, their balance of payments fell deeper into deficit. Their export industries, which were dependent on the British market, mainly for agricultural and light industrial products, had to either find new outlets or enlarge traditional ones.

Faced with these prospects, the governments of New Zealand and Australia began to take an interest in each other's markets. The attractions were several. They included proximity and familiarity; cultural, legal, and monetary similarity; an unrestricted labor pool; and substantial cross-Tasman direct investment linkages in, for example, manufacturing, banking, finance, and insurance. New Zealand traders were attracted by the potential of the Australian market to absorb dairy products facing exclusion from the British market. Conversely, New Zealand had become the largest market for Australian light manufactures and was seen also as a proving ground and a stepping stone to markets farther afield, a view soon to be adopted by New Zealand toward Australia as well.

CER's Predecessor, 1965–1978

Converging interests stimulated the political leaders to spearhead a five-year negotiating effort beginning in 1960. The specific objective was to liberalize bilateral trade in forest products, but selected manufactures were also included for consideration. The result of the subsequent negotiations and compromises was the New Zealand Australia Free Trade Agreement of 1965, popularly known as NAFTA. The heart of NAFTA was a list of products that would be traded freely, without tariffs or quotas, between the partners. This list was to be expanded at semiannual meetings by representatives of the two governments.

Despite the hopes of the negotiators, NAFTA soon bogged down, increasingly becoming an institution of managed trade. Industry lobbies used their veto power to delay additions to the free trade list. Although the number of items enjoying free trade had risen from approximately 1,000 at the inception of the agreement in 1965 to 1,760 by 1974, this still represented only 37 percent of the items on the New Zealand Customs Tariff list. Many of the additions were of little trade value or were not competitive. The inordinate amount of time and effort spent by negotiators yielded small gains, particularly for Australia. For example, New Zealand was particularly prone to using import licenses and quotas to protect motor vehicles and parts and steel products, items Australia was particularly keen to export to New Zealand.

CER Negotiations, 1978–1983

By 1978, the trade ministers of the two governments were well aware that NAFTA was no longer good enough. Furthermore, the failure of the GATT Tokyo Round to reduce the subsidization of European and American agriculture exports stimulated a defensive reaction in New Zealand and Australia, on the one hand, and on the other a determination to set up a re-

formed and liberalized market regime to exemplify what GATT should be. These impulses converged on the conclusion that NAFTA had to be drastically reformed or superseded altogether by a new trans-Tasman trade regime. New Zealand political leaders were inclined to reform NAFTA, but Australian leaders conceived bolder innovations.

The result was a joint statement by prime ministers in 1978 pledging to liberalize trans-Tasman trade. Joint committees were set to work to explore options. Trade and industry ministers met to review progress and to encourage the newly formed Australia–New Zealand Business Council to bring business leaders into the initiative. In New Zealand, indefatigable speeches to business groups by Minister of Customs Hugh Templeton created a favorable climate of opinion that dissolved latent protectionist impulses. Industry leaders initially were cautious, particularly toward any weakening of import licensing or diminution of export incentives, but over time modern, export-oriented firms, such as Fisher and Paykel and Feltex, and the Dairy Board, declared themselves in favor of liberalization. Older and more protected sectors and enterprises took longer to convince.

The prime ministers in March 1980 adopted five principles to guide their negotiation on a "closer economic relationship," marking the initiation of this portentous label. These principles were:

- the freest possible movement of goods;
- an outward-looking approach to trade;
- favorable treatment of each other's citizens;
- consideration of each other's interests; and
- frequent consultation.

The essence of their approach was simple but profound: Liberalization was to be effected by making *all* goods duty free (some immediately, some after five years) except those on a deferred list, which was to be kept "as short as possible." This turned NAFTA's free-trade-list approach on its head by putting the burden of proof on any exception to the overarching principle of duty-free access.

Five Difficult Issues and Their Resolution

During the ensuing negotiations, five issue-clusters preoccupied the negotiators. They are summarized, with indications of how they were resolved, as follows.

1. *Tariff Reduction.* Tariff schedules differed considerably, so the two parties decided to reduce tariffs in three phases to protect vulnerable industries. First, all tariffs were to be reduced immediately to a maximum of 25 percent. Second, tariffs were then to be reduced by five percentage points per year so that most tradables would be duty free in five years. Third, products to be protected were to be put on a deferral list for further negotiations.

2. *The Deferral List.* Each side was tempted to defer tariff cuts as long as possible. The New Zealand negotiators assembled a lengthy list of sensitive products, one that initially included automobile and steel products, wines, agricultural chemicals, teas, wool grease and woolen yarn products, pineapples, aerated waters, and prepared vegetables. The Australians submitted a shorter list in which dairy products, horticultural products, textiles, plastics, and household appliances (whiteware products) predominated. Australia then called for the deferral period to end in 1992. New Zealand held out for an indefinite period for its sensitive industries but compromised in 1995. Thus, interim protection by deferral lists smoothed the way to a CER agreement but did not become entrenched.

3. *Subsidies and Monopolies.* The New Zealand side was worried about subsidies, rebates, or price supports of Australian wheat, wine, tobacco, sugar, and canned fruit, whereas the Australian side was concerned about New Zealand statutory monopoly marketing of dairy products (the Dairy Board), wheat (the Wheat Board), tropical fruits and grapes (Fruit Distributors), vegetables, and berry fruit. Eventually each party surrendered subsidies and monopolies as applied to trade with the other. The New Zealand government revoked the Wheat Board's monopoly in 1987 and deregulated the wheat market.

4. *Government Purchasing.* New Zealand wanted to be included in the "buy Australia" policies of the federal and state governments. The Australian federal government speedily adjusted federal preferences so as not to discriminate against New Zealand suppliers, but it was powerless to change state government purchasing policies. Despite persistent representations by New Zealand, this issue was not resolved until 1989.

5. *Intermediate Goods.* "Buy Australia" policies and higher tariffs encouraged Australian manufacturers to use materials and components ("intermediate goods") from Australian suppliers whose prices tended to be higher than world market prices. New Zealand manufacturers, by contrast, purchased intermediate goods from world markets at the cheapest available prices, so the final products tended to be less expensive than the Australian equivalent and had potential to capture larger market shares if traded freely. Australian negotiators urged New Zealand to allow a compensation for this structural advantage and used this rationale to defer tariff freeing of several sensitive products.

Intra-Industry Agreements

At the same time, many industries began to play a creative role in the negotiations. In late 1981 and early 1982, the carpet, wine, dairy, and steel industry associations met with their trans-Tasman counterparts to draft industry agreements. These were essentially intra-industry orderly marketing arrangements brokered by and later underwritten by the governments. The carpet agreement set up a ten-year phase-in schedule for Australian synthetic-carpet access to the New Zealand market, thereby allowing the New Zealand carpet industry time to adjust and compensating it by allowing immediate free access for wool carpet to the Australian market. The wine agreement of February 11, 1982, negotiated by the Wine Institute of New Zealand and the Australian Wine and Brandy Corporation, eased New Zealand's adjustment by delaying the commencement of the tariff reduction schedule until 1986.

The dairy industry agreement of April 13, 1982, was worked out by a Joint Dairy Industry Consultative Committee representing the New Zealand Dairy Board, the Australian Dairy Corporation, the Australian Dairy Farmers Federation, and the Australian Dairy Products Federation. The committee pledged to consult in order to avoid undermining the returns or price structures of the industries, to avoid dumping or unfair trading practices, and to cooperate in international markets. New Zealand was to restrain its exports of cheddar to a pace no faster than total market growth in Australia and to avoid exporting milk or cream except in the event of a shortfall in Australia. An official memorandum of understanding pledged that dairy trade was to be "liberalized progressively under the CER in such a way as not to result in unfair competition between industries or disruption to industries of either country."

Steel was dealt with in an attachment noting that trade in deferred iron and steel products would be made compatible with CER "as soon as practicable." These intra-industry arrangements, although less visible than the government-to-government negotiations, proved essential to making CER work.

A "Heads of Agreement" was signed on December 14, 1982, and CER was brought into operation on the first day of 1983.

The 1988 CER Review

The 1984 general election in New Zealand brought a Labour government to power. The new finance minister, Roger Douglas, initiated a radical economic reform program characterized by sweeping deregulation, privatization, and the liberalization of imports of goods, capital, and entrepreneurial expertise. These policies were subsequently applied to the next review of CER, in 1988, and New Zealand negotiators were instructed to achieve full free trade in goods as soon as possible, to eliminate nontariff and qualitative barriers and "beyond-the-border" trade distortions, and to extend free trade practices to new areas such as services.

Following the 1978–1982 precedent, the negotiators started with a goal of complete liberalization, then acknowledged those issues that proved sensitive to either side, then set about isolating and minimizing them. To keep the negotiations moving closer to the liberal idea, they employed nonreciprocal concessions, which differ from tradeoffs because they are not synchronized, one-for-one deals, but concessions made by each side at varying times. The concessions made by each side are summarized in Table 1.

Consolidation of CER in the 1990s

In 1989, the two governments freed all services trade not on the exemption list. New Zealand subsequently freed trade in domestic air services, postal services, radio and television broadcasting, short-wave and satellite broadcasting, and stevedoring, and Australia freed banking, postal services, and construction, engineering, and general consultancy. New Zealand finally gained equal treatment in bidding for contracts let by state governments. Australia abolished export incentives and bounties applying to trans-Tasman trade, and in turn New Zealand abolished import monopolies on apples, pears, and bananas. By 1990, full free and unsubsidized trade in goods was achieved, five years ahead of schedule.

In the early 1990s, the two governments began to dismantle the "second-generation" bar-

Table 1: Concessions by New Zealand and Australia in the 1988 CER Review Negotiation

New Zealand agreed to:
- Removal of import monopolies
- Exceptions for Australia from the services liberalization protocol
- An exemption for Australia from its Export Market Development Tax Incentive from July 1, 1990, and phaseout of its nonperformance export incentives
- A Record of Understanding that the New Zealand Dairy Board would treat sales in Australia the same as sales in the New Zealand domestic market
- Removal of its demand for a disputes settlement mechanism
- Conclusion of the 1988 review with a collection of declarations, protocols, and memoranda reflecting the diversity of the two sides rather than a consolidated document reflecting the linkage that New Zealand sought at the outset

Australia agreed to:
- Removal of antidumping provisions in the CER agreement, and application of domestic competition laws to complaints regarding unfair competition
- Removal of two export subsidy programs for goods exported to New Zealand, and further discussion of motor vehicles
- Removal of bounties paid directly for exports to New Zealand by July 1, 1990
- Long-term disciplines and consultations for industry assistance policies
- Plans to conclude a services protocol
- Promotion of the New Zealand bid to gain nondiscriminatory access to procurement by state governments

Notes: New Zealand failed to achieve agreements on issues involving investment and a number of services sectors. The Australian exclusion list remained longer than New Zealand's and included key sectors, such as banking and insurance, as well as air services and consultancy. Useful memoranda of understanding were signed, however, on technical barriers to trade, quarantine, customs, and business laws.

riers to free trade that had proved politically intractable during the first two rounds of 1978–1982 and 1988. They abolished antidumping measures; signed a draft Agreement on Standards, Accreditation, and Quality to make the certifications, credentials, and quality standards of each country acceptable to the other; and set in motion negotiations to harmonize business laws.

The governments agreed in 1991 to set up a Joint Accreditation System to raise their quality management systems to international standards and provide for mutual recognition of each other's certifications of them. In 1992, the governments signed a memorandum of understanding to make progress toward a single trans-Tasman aviation market; this foreshadowed the freeing of trade in aviation services, a major sector still on the exemption list, by 1994. Prime ministers Robert Hawke and Geof-frey Palmer pledged to work for free trade in services by 1995.

Stephen Hoadley

See Also Economic Integration; North American Free Trade Agreement (NAFTA); General Agreement on Tariffs and Trade (GATT)

References

Catley, Bob, ed. 2002. *NZ-Australia Relations: Moving Together or Drifting Apart?* Wellington: Dark Horse.

Closer Economic Relations. 1997. Canberra: Department of Foreign Affairs and Trade.

Edwards, Stephen, and Sir Frank Holmes. 1994. *CER: Economic Trends and Linkages.* Wellington: National Bank of New Zealand and Institute of Policy Studies.

Hoadley, Stephen. 1995. *New Zealand and Australia.* Wellington: New Zealand Institute of International Affairs.

Holmes, Frank. 1996. *The Trans-Tasman Relationship.* Wellington: Institute of Policy Studies.

Impact of the CER Trade Agreement. 1995. Canberra: Bureau of Industry Economics Report 95/17, September.

Lloyd Peter J. 1987. "Australia–New Zealand Trade Relations: NAFTA to CER." In Keith Sinclair, ed., *Tasman Relations: New Zealand and Australia, 1788–1988.* Auckland: Auckland University Press.

New Zealand Australia Closer Economic Relations Trade Agreement (with Exchange of Letters). 1983.

Wellington: New Zealand Treaty Series 1983, no. 1, Ministry of Foreign Affairs, Government Printer, http://www.dfat.gov.au/geo/new_zealand/anz_cer/an zcerta1.pdf (cited March 30, 2003).

New Zealand Ministry of Foreign Affairs and Trade. "CER Background" and "Positive Points," http://www.mft. govt.nz/foreign/regions/australia/ausdefault.html (cited March 30, 2003).

Caribbean Community (CARICOM)

The Caribbean Community, or CARICOM, is the primary instrument of Caribbean regional integration. Its mission is "to provide dynamic leadership and service, in partnership with Community institutions and Groups, toward the attainment of a viable, internationally competitive and sustainable Community, with improved quality of life for all" (CARICOM, http://www.caricom.org). CARICOM was established as the Caribbean Community and Common Market on August 1, 1973, by the Treaty of Chaguaramas, which was signed by the prime ministers of Barbados, Guyana, Jamaica, and Trinidad and Tobago. In February 2002, it was modified as the Revised Treaty of Chaguaramas Establishing the Caribbean Community Including the CARICOM Single Market and Economy (the Revised Treaty), and CARICOM was reformulated as the Caribbean Community, incorporating a single market, or CSME (CARICOM Single Market and Economy). CARICOM's secretariat is located in Georgetown, Guyana, and its secretary-general is Edwin Carrington. It encompasses a secondary instrument of subregional integration, the Organization of Eastern Caribbean States (OECS), which is recognized as an Associate Institute within the Treaty of Chaguaramas (Blake 2001, 482).

CARICOM was originally composed of Anglophone Caribbean countries. The membership subsequently expanded to include other countries of the region. CARICOM's fifteen member countries are Antigua and Barbuda, the Bahamas (a member of the community but not the common market), Barbados, Belize, Dominica, Grenada, Guyana, Haiti, Jamaica, Montserrat, St. Kitts and Nevis, St. Lucia, St. Vincent and the Grenadines, Suriname, and Trinidad and Tobago. Antigua and Barbuda, Belize, Dominica, Grenada, Montserrat, St. Kitts and Nevis, St. Lucia, and St. Vincent and the Grenadines are designated as less developed countries (LDCs). Barbados, Guyana, Suriname, Jamaica, and Trinidad and Tobago are designated as most developed countries (MDCs). Associate members include Anguilla, Bermuda, British Virgin Islands, Cayman Islands, and Turks and Caicos Islands. CARICOM observers include Aruba, Colombia, Dominican Republic, Mexico, Netherlands Antilles, Puerto Rico, and Venezuela. Several CARICOM members belong to the OECS. OECS member states include Anguilla, Antigua and Barbuda, British Virgin Islands, Dominica, Grenada, Montserrat, St. Kitts and Nevis, St. Lucia, and St. Vincent and the Grenadines.

CARICOM evolved out of a fifteen-year movement for regional integration in the Caribbean and followed two previous attempts at regional economic integration: the British West Indies Federation, and the Caribbean Free Trade Association (CARIFTA). The British West Indies Federation was an attempt at pre-independence unification. It was created in 1958 under the direction of the British government and included ten British colonial islands. Although envisaged as both a political and customs union, the federation had more of a political orientation. It disbanded in 1962, in part because of the withdrawal of two of its largest member countries, Jamaica and Trinidad and

Tobago, which gained their independence from Britain in 1962. However, the leaders of both countries continued to support the movement for integration. After the federation dissolved, Caribbean leaders continued to meet outside of a formal alliance to foster regional cooperation and collaboration.

Rules of the Revised Treaty

The Revised Treaty is a comprehensive document that incorporates provisions governing institutional arrangements; establishment, services, capital, and movement of community nationals; sectoral development; trade policy; transport policy; disadvantaged countries, regions, and sectors; competition policy and consumer protection; and dispute settlement. The treaty makes concessions in certain cases for the LDCs. With regard to trade policy, the Revised Treaty in Chapter Five establishes a common external tariff (CET) for extraregional imports and compels free intraregional trade on the bases of nondiscrimination and most-favored-nation treatment for goods that satisfy the community's Rules of Origin criteria; prohibits import duties, export duties, quantitative restrictions, and internal taxes and other fiscal charges on intraregional imports; defines allowable and prohibited subsidies; and permits member states to take action against dumped imports if these imports cause injury or pose a threat to a domestic industry (Organization of American States, http://www.sice.oas.org).

With regard to the movement of labor and capital, the Revised Treaty in Chapter Three defers the treatment of monopolies to member states, allowing them to decide whether the public interest necessitates restriction of the right of establishment in any industry or sector; requires member states to eliminate discriminatory restrictions on banking, insurance, and other financial services; forbids the introduction of new restrictions on the movement of capital and requires the facilitation of free capital flows; requires coordination of

member-state foreign-exchange policies to facilitate the movement of capital between them and third states; and provides for the free movement of labor within the community (ibid.).

With regard to sectoral policy, the Revised Treaty in Chapter Four delineates a Community Industrial Policy emphasizing the goal of "market-led, internationally competitive and sustainable production of goods and services for the promotion of the region's economic and social development"; specifies the sectors of interest, namely micro and small enterprises, services, tourism, and agriculture; outlines the priorities for each sector; and establishes a Community Investment Policy that addresses macroeconomic policy convergence, fiscal policy harmonization, monetary convergence, monetary union/single currency, a harmonized system of investment incentives, stable industrial relations, appropriate financial institutions and arrangements, supportive legal and social infrastructure, and modernization of the role of public authorities (ibid.).

Structure and Mission of CARICOM

CARICOM aims to improve the region's standards of living and work; stimulate full employment of labor and other factors of production; foster sustained economic development and convergence; expand trade and economic relations with external states; enhance levels of international competitiveness; organize for increased production and productivity; and enhance member states' economic leverage and effectiveness in dealing with external entities (CARICOM, http://www.caricom.org). The institutions of CARICOM are intergovernmental, with no supranational decisionmaking capacity such as that found in the European Community (Axline 1978, 956). CARICOM itself has no supranational body. Its primary organs are the Conference of Heads of Government (the conference) and the Community Council of Ministers (the council). The conference—

the highest organ—provides policy direction for the community, concludes treaties on behalf of the community, and negotiates relationships between the community and external entities (ibid.). The Bureau of the Conference, a subsidiary body, acts on behalf of the conference between meetings. The Council administers the community's financial obligations and coordinates its economic integration, functional cooperation, and external relations.

Four ministers councils support the conference and council. They are the Council for Trade and Economic Development, the Council for Foreign and Community Relations, the Council for Human and Social Development, and the Council for Finance and Planning. Bodies of the community include the Legal Affairs Committee, the Budget Committee, and the Committee of Central Bank Governors. CARICOM has several institutions implementing its programmatic work, including the Caribbean Disaster Emergency Response Agency, the Caribbean Meteorological Institute, the Caribbean Food Corporation, the Caribbean Environment Health Institute, the Caribbean Agriculture Research and Development Institute, the Caribbean Regional Center for the Education and Training of Animal Health and Veterinary Public Health Assistants, the Assembly of Caribbean Community Parliamentarians, the Caribbean Center for Development Administration, and the Caribbean Food and Nutrition Institute. Associate institutions of the community include the Caribbean Development Bank, the University of Guyana, the University of the West Indies, the Caribbean Law Institute/Caribbean Law Institute Center, and the Secretariat of the Organization of Eastern Caribbean States.

History of CARICOM

The prime minister of Trinidad and Tobago convened the first Conference of Heads of Government in July 1963, which was attended by the prime ministers of Barbados, British Guiana, Jamaica, and Trinidad and Tobago. Several conferences followed, and in December 1965 the leaders of Antigua, Barbados, and British Guiana signed an agreement to create the Caribbean Free Trade Association. The fourth Conference of Heads of Government ratified this agreement and formally established CARIFTA with the concurrence that a common market would be achieved over the course of several stages. The CARIFTA agreement was actualized on May 1, 1968. Membership comprised the original ten members of the federation, plus Guyana. Belize joined in 1971.

CARIFTA was essentially a free trade zone; it was neither a customs union nor a common market and therefore allowed for the least degree of integration. It lessened controls on intraregional trade but did not establish uniform requirements for external trade or establish a common market for productive factors such as labor and capital. The CARIFTA arrangement also did not include any mechanisms to limit the impact of free intraregional trade on the smallest, most vulnerable economies. Its structural weaknesses notwithstanding, CARIFTA achieved a degree of success. In 1968, it accomplished its first integration measures by lowering tariffs and quantitative restrictions in the region. During the following decade, CARIFTA stimulated intraregional trade, which increased substantially. In addition, CARIFTA stimulated interest within the region in transforming the Caribbean from a free trade area to a customs union. Eventually, it was replaced by CARICOM, which deepened the integration process.

At the seventh Conference of Heads of Government in October 1972, Caribbean leaders elected to reformulate CARIFTA into a regional community encompassing a common market. At the subsequent conference, held in Georgetown, Guyana, in April 1973, the leaders of eleven CARIFTA member countries signed the Georgetown Accord, which laid the groundwork for the Caribbean Community and Common Market. CARICOM was established by the

Treaty of Chaguaramas four months later. Although the treaty was signed initially only by the four countries of the region that were independent at that time, within a year Antigua and Barbuda, Belize, Dominica, Grenada, Montserrat, St. Kitts and Nevis, St. Lucia, and St. Vincent had signed.

CARICOM underwent several changes after the eighth Conference of Heads of Government in 1987. The conference elected to establish the CSME to replace the common market, which had proven ineffective. The conference also proposed the introduction of a parliamentary opposition institution to enhance the community's decisionmaking process. The Assembly of Caribbean Community Parliamentarians was formally established shortly after the tenth Conference of Heads of Government. Another significant development occurred at this juncture in CARICOM's history as well: The community adopted the Grand Anse Declaration and Work Program for the Advancement of the Integration Movement in 1989 at the tenth Conference of Heads of Government. The declaration outlines an agenda of enhanced integration to be implemented over the four-year period from 1989 to 1993. The overall objective was to make CARICOM a common market in practice as well as in name, something that had eluded the organization in the sixteen years since it was founded (Erisman 1992, 136).

Member states committed to the following obligations in the declaration: implementation of a comprehensive CET by January 1991, a uniform standard for handling Rules of Origin trade questions, and a Harmonized Scheme of Fiscal Incentives; revitalization of the Caribbean Multilateral Clearing Facility to handle currency exchanges and payments and extend credit; elimination of all barriers to intraregional commerce by July 1991; and institutionalization of air-sea transport cooperation (ibid., 136). Caribbean leaders created the West Indian Commission to monitor the community's progress and ensure that member states met their obligations. The commission, comprising seventeen Caribbean experts, was

tasked with preparation of a comprehensive report inclusive of recommendations for moving the region forward during the twenty-first century to be presented at the following conference. This report, entitled *Time for Action: Report of the West Indian Commission,* was published in 1992. The community revisited the Grand Anse Declaration in 1999 at the Seventh Special Session of the conference in Chaguaramas and assessed the progress that had been achieved in implementing its agenda. That same year, the nineteenth Conference of Heads of Government established a Caribbean Supreme Court called the Caribbean Court of Justice (CCJ) to officiate disputes concerning the interpretation and application of the Treaty of Chaguaramas and serve as the final appellate court for all member states (Blake 2001, 490). The Consensus of Chaguaramas summarizes the conclusions reached at the Seventh Special Session and serves as a blueprint of the community's plans for executing the CSME and CCJ in the twenty-first century.

Preparation for the CSME is an integral part of CARICOM's agenda. The CSME was negotiated in nine protocols amending the Treaty of Chaguaramas and its provision for the common market. The final two protocols were signed in 2000, paving the way for the realization of the CSME. In 2000, a quasi-cabinet was formed, and the leader of each member state was assigned a portfolio of responsibility pertaining to the creation of the CSME. Jamaica, for example, is tasked with external negotiations, the Bahamas with tourism, and Guyana with agriculture, agricultural diversification, and food security. The CSME aims to open access to the region's productive resources to all regional producers of goods and services; facilitate the location of businesses wherever investors deem most viable; and enhance the policy environment across the region (ibid., 483–484). To achieve these aims, new institutional arrangements such as COFAP, COTED, and a Committee of Governors of Central Banks were created to ensure that the national economies converge to form a single economy.

Realization of the CSME is crucial to CARICOM's success and the region's future in light of each member country's small size and economic vulnerability in a rapidly globalizing international political economy. Unfortunately, implementation of the policy measures has not matched the urgency of the negotiations creating them (ibid., 485). Critics allege that the CSME is no different from the preexisting common market because it is premised on the maintenance of frontiers, within which it will ostensibly liberalize access markets (Brewster 2003). According to these critics, the CSME, and CARICOM itself, is stymied by member states' apparent inability to cede the requisite degree of political and economic sovereignty to CARICOM.

CARICOM's Agenda

CARICOM states practice free trade with each other and "outreach" trade with external countries. For many years, CARICOM pursued regional development via widening, or expansion. However, its leadership found that widening alone was not sufficient for maximizing development; CARICOM had to deepen the integration process via economic cooperation, foreign policy coordination, and functional cooperation. These are CARICOM's three pillars of regional integration. Economic cooperation implies a common market based on the principles of free trade, a common external tariff, commitment to the removal of nontariff barriers to trade, harmonized fiscal incentives, and free intraregional capital mobility. Functional cooperation targets issues such as health, education, labor, finance, agriculture, industry, communications, transport, energy, mining and natural resources, science and technology, the law, information, and women's affairs. Foreign policy coordination involves the negotiation of political and economic affairs with extra-regional countries and organizations.

CARICOM has advanced significantly in all three dimensions. With regard to economic in-

tegration, it established a common external tariff and is moving toward becoming a single-market economy. For functional cooperation, it created several mechanisms for advancing regional human and social development, including the Caribbean Examination Council to standardize exam requirements across the region. Regarding foreign policy coordination, CARICOM established the Regional Negotiating Machinery (RNM) in 1997 to negotiate for all member states as one voice or bloc in international trade negotiations such as those conducted by the World Trade Organization (WTO), those related to the Free Trade Area of the Americas (FTAA), and negotiations between the European Union and the African, Caribbean and Pacific States (ACP). CARICOM, empowered by the Charter of Civil Society, has also played an instrumental role in fostering democratic stability in the region, particularly in Guyana, Haiti, and St. Kitts and Nevis.

Despite these accomplishments, CARICOM realized that the challenges of globalization required further widening along with deepening. Various global developments are restructuring the international relations of CARICOM states (Lewis 2002, 190). One such development is the globalization of production and finance, which has compelled countries to eliminate national barriers to the movement of goods, services, capital, and finance (Bernal 1994, 182). Another is the erosion of trade preferences under the WTO and its emphasis on trade liberalization. The EU first extended trade preferences to its former colonies in the ACP group under the Lomé Agreement to help them transition into the world economy as sovereign entities. The preferences were challenged in 1996, when the United States filed a claim at the WTO alleging that the EU discriminated against more efficient banana producers of other regions, namely Central and South America, the base of operations for U.S.-domiciled fruit multinational corporations such as Dole and Chiquita. This compelled the EU to reformulate Lomé with an eye toward phasing it out completely within a short period. The Lomé Agreement, renamed the Cotonou Agreement after Cotonou, Benin, where the agreement was renegotiated in 2000, extended preferences to 2006, when they are slated for complete elimination. In 2003, a tripartite coalition of Brazil, Australia, and Thailand filed a claim at the WTO alleging the same complaint with regard to Lomé/Cotonou's EU-ACP sugar regime.

Trade pundits predict that sugar, bananas, and other traditional Caribbean exports will fail without preferences because they simply cannot compete with more efficient, lower cost producers. Given the predominantly agricultural orientation of CARICOM economies, this would have severe implications for member states. Another global trend that has restructured CARICOM's international relations is the intensification and increasing regionalization of international economic relations (Blake 2001, 491; Lewis 2002, 189). The creation of trade groupings such as the WTO, the North American Free Trade Agreement (NAFTA), and the pending FTAA has particular relevance to CARICOM, challenging it to devise strategies for coping in a hemisphere dominated by regional economic blocs and the eventuality of a free trade area extending from Canada to Argentina.

In 1994, CARICOM merged with other Latin American/Caribbean Basin states to form the Association of Caribbean States (ACS), a regional zone of cooperation. CARICOM was also instrumental in the creation of the Caribbean Forum of African, Caribbean and Pacific States (CARIFORUM). The community has linked with regional integration groupings in other parts of the world, such as the Southern African Development Community (SADC). In 2001, it concluded its first free trade agreement, the CARICOM–Dominican Republic Free Trade Agreement. The community has trade agreements with three other countries, Venezuela, Colombia, and Cuba. CARICOM is active at the Organization of American States (OAS), the United Nations, and the Summit of the Americas, a hemispheric grouping of states formed to foster cooperation in trade. It has also taken steps to safeguard its regional natural and human resource capital. In 1999, the region's leaders mobilized to reject the Caribbean Sea as transit for nuclear waste materials. In the aftermath of the September 11, 2001, terrorist attacks on the United States, the community mobilized to create a strategy to buffer the tourism sector—the region's most lucrative income earner—from extreme vulnerability to external shocks.

Structure and Performance of CARICOM Economies

CARICOM states are predominantly primary-commodity export economies. They are small, open economies that are highly trade-dependent. Agriculture, tourism, and mineral extraction are the region's leading economic sectors. All member states rely on agriculture, especially the sugar and banana industries, for employment and foreign exchange earnings. Although tourism is significant for the whole region, some states have been more proficient at developing a marketable product than others—for example, the all-inclusive destination package was pioneered in Jamaica. Some CARCIOM states possess large stores of mineral resources that are in high demand globally. Trinidad has oil and Jamaica has bauxite/alumina. CARICOM countries have prioritized economic diversification and technological innovation via the incorporation and utilization of information and communication technologies (ICT). However, twenty to thirty years after independence, the economies remain natural-resource based, and manufacturing still constitutes a relatively small percentage of regional gross domestic product (GDP). CARICOM does not have a regional currency. With the exception of the OECS states, which utilize the Eastern Caribbean dollar, CARICOM countries maintain their own national currencies.

Most CARICOM states have large debt-to-GDP ratios owing to extended periods of borrowing from private banks and international

Table 1: Data on Pertinent Economic Sectors

ANTIGUA AND BARBUDA
Gross Domestic Product by Industry at Factor Cost in Constant 1990 Prices
Percentage Distribution

Industry	1999	2000	2001
Total	100.0	100.0	100.0
Agriculture	3.5	3.5	3.5
Mining & Quarrying	1.9	1.9	1.9
Manufacturing	2.5	2.5	2.5
Electricity & Water	3.6	3.9	4.1
Construction	13.0	13.5	13.8
Wholesale & Retail Trade	9.5	9.7	9.8
Hotels & Restaurants	13.3	12.8	11.8
Transport	11.3	11.6	11.3
Communications	11.3	10.2	10.6
Banks & Insurance	10.9	10.8	10.8
Real Estate & Housing	7.2	7.3	7.4
Government Services	16.1	16.1	16.2
Other Services	6.5	6.6	6.6
Less: Imputed Service Charges	10.5	10.3	10.3

Source: Caricom Secretariat

THE BAHAMAS
Gross Domestic Product by Industry at Factor Cost in Constant 1990 Prices
Percentage Distribution

Industry	1993	1994	1995
Total	100.0	100.0	100.0
Agriculture & Fishing	3.4	3.3	3.2
Mining & Manufacturing	4.0	4.0	4.0
Electricity & Water	3.1	3.2	3.2
Construction	3.8	3.4	2.7
Wholesale & Retail Trade	12.7	13.6	14.9
Hotels & Restaurants	11.3	11.5	11.6
T/Port, Storage & Comm.	8.9	8.8	9.1
Financial Intermediation	3.6	3.7	4.0
Real Estate, Rent & Business	12.1	11.5	11.0
Public Admin. & Defense	7.3	7.4	7.3
Education	4.2	3.8	4.3
Health	2.9	3.0	3.1
Other Com., Soc. & Pers. Serv.	6.2	6.0	6.1
Dummy Financial Corporation (Fisim)	-2.5	-2.3	-2.4
Net Indirect Taxes	13.9	13.4	14.4
Statistical Discrepancy	5.2	5.7	3.6

Source: Caricom Secretariat

BARBADOS
Gross Domestic Product by Industry at Factor Cost in Constant 1990 Prices
Percentage Distribution

Industry	1999	2000	2001
Total	100.0	100.0	100.0
Agriculture	6.1	6.2	6.0
Mining & Quarrying	1.0	0.9	0.8
Manufacturing	9.3	9.0	8.5
Electricity, Gas & Water	4.0	3.8	4.1
Construction	7.4	7.3	7.2
Wholesale & Retail Trade	19.9	20.1	19.8
Tourism	14.8	15.5	15.0
Transport, Storage & Comm.	8.3	8.2	8.6
Business & General Services	16.8	16.8	17.3
Government Services	12.5	12.2	12.7

Source: Caricom Secretariat

BELIZE
Gross Domestic Product by Industry at Factor Cost in Constant 1990 Prices
Percentage Distribution

Industry	1999	2000	2001
Total	100.0	100.0	100.0
Agriculture	15.4	14.6	14.3
Forestry & Logging	1.7	1.0	1.2
Fishing	5.4	5.5	7.2
Mining	0.7	0.8	0.7
Manufacturing	15.4	16.6	16.2
Electricity & Water	1.6	1.6	1.6
Construction	6.0	6.2	6.5
Trade, Hotels & Restaurants	18.3	20.5	19.5
Transport & Communications	14.5	13.5	13.5
Finance & Insurance	4.7	5.1	5.0
Real Estate & Bus. Services	5.9	5.4	5.3
Public Administration	6.8	6.4	6.4
Community & Other Services	6.7	6.2	6.1
Less: Imputed Services Charges	3.3	3.5	3.4

Source: Caricom Secretariat

DOMINICA

Gross Domestic Product by Industry at Factor Cost in Constant 1990 Prices
Percentage Distribution

Industry	1999	2000	2001
Total	100.0	100.0	100.0
Agriculture	18.4	18.1	16.8
Mining & Quarrying	0.8	0.8	0.8
Manufacturing	6.5	7.0	6.2
Electricity & Water	4.3	4.3	4.7
Construction	7.7	7.8	7.8
W/Sale & Retail Trade	12.7	12.9	13.1
Hotels & Restaurants	2.5	2.3	2.4
Transport	10.0	9.7	9.5
Communications	12.3	11.7	11.3
Banks & Insurance	12.9	12.9	13.8
Real Estate & Housing	3.4	3.5	3.7
Government Services	17.4	18.1	19.8
Other Services	1.3	1.3	1.4
Less: Imputed Service Charges	10.3	10.4	11.3

Source: Caricom Secretariat

GRENADA

Gross Domestic Product by Industry at Factor Cost in Constant 1990 Prices
Percentage Distribution

Industry	1999	2000	2001
Total	100.0	100.0	100.0
Agriculture	8.9	8.2	8.2
Mining & Quarrying	0.5	0.6	1.0
Manufacturing	8.2	8.7	8.4
Electricity & Water	5.0	5.3	5.8
Construction	8.4	9.2	8.1
W/Sale & Retail Trade	11.5	11.2	11.3
Hotels & Restaurants	7.8	7.5	7.4
Transport	14.5	13.5	13.7
Communications	12.5	14.2	13.0
Banks & Insurance	9.8	10.1	11.1
Real Estate & Housing	4.2	4.0	4.2
Government Services	14.1	12.9	13.9
Other Services	2.7	2.9	3.2
Less: Imputed Service Charges	8.2	8.4	9.3

Source: Caricom Secretariat

GUYANA

Gross Domestic Product by Industry at Factor Cost in Constant 1990 Prices
Percentage Distribution

Industry	1999	2000	2001
Total	100.0	100.0	100.0
Agric., Forestry & Fishing	36.4	33.1	33.6
Mining & Quarrying	10.9	11.7	11.9
Manuf. & Processing[1]	6.5	5.8	5.6
Construction & Engin.	7.8	8.4	8.4
Distribution	7.4	7.9	7.8
Transport & Communication	8.3	9.0	9.2
Rental of Dwellings	1.6	1.7	1.7
Financial Services	5.5	5.8	5.4
Government	12.1	12.9	12.6
Other Services	3.5	3.7	3.7

[1] Includes Electricity and Gas
Source: Caricom Secretariat

JAMAICA

Gross Domestic Product by Industry in Constant 1990 Producers' Prices
Percentage Distribution

Industry	1999	2000	2001
Total	100.0	100.0	100.0
Agric., Forestry & Fishing	8.0	7.0	7.3
Mining & Quarrying	9.1	8.9	9.1
Manufacturing	15.7	15.7	15.5
Electricity & Water	5.2	5.4	5.3
Construct. & Installation	7.5	7.4	7.5
Distributive Trade	20.4	20.5	20.2
T/Port, Comm. & Storage	15.4	16.5	17.3
Finance & Insur. Services	13.4	14.8	14.6
Real Estate & Bus. Services	9.0	9.0	8.9
Producers of Gov't Services	6.3	6.3	6.2
Miscellaneous Services	11.2	11.7	11.3
H/Hold & Private NPIs	0.5	0.4	0.4
Less: Imputed Service Charges	21.6	23.6	23.6

Source: Caricom Secretariat

MONTSERRAT

Gross Domestic Product by Industry at Factor Cost in Constant 1990 Prices

Percentage Distribution

Industry	1999	2000	2001
Total	100.0	100.0	100.0
Agriculture	1.2	1.8	1.5
Mining & Quarrying	0.1	0.1	0.1
Manufacturing	0.9	0.9	0.9
Electricity & Water	2.3	2.4	2.7
Construction	27.8	18.4	17.6
Wholesale & Retail Trade	5.8	5.0	4.8
Hotels & Restaurants	1.2	1.2	1.6
Transport	7.0	6.8	7.2
Communications	8.6	11.8	8.6
Banks & Insurance	6.5	11.1	11.7
Real Estate & Housing	7.5	8.2	8.8
Government Services	30.7	31.4	33.5
Other Services	6.2	7.3	7.9
Less: Imputed Service Charges	5.6	6.5	7.0

Source: Caricom Secretariat

SAINT LUCIA

Gross Domestic Product by Industry at Factor Cost in Constant 1990 Prices

Percentage Distribution

Industry	1999	2000	2001
Total	100.0	100.0	100.0
Agriculture	7.2	7.4	5.9
Mining & Quarrying	0.6	0.7	0.5
Manufacturing	6.2	6.0	6.1
Electricity & Water	4.3	4.6	5.1
Construction	9.4	9.0	9.0
Wholesale & Retail Trade	13.5	12.6	11.3
Hotels & Restaurants	13.1	13.4	12.7
Transport	11.1	10.9	10.9
Communications	8.8	9.3	11.0
Banks & Insurance	10.4	10.7	11.6
Real Estate & Housing	7.0	7.2	7.8
Government Services	12.1	12.2	13.1
Other Services	4.8	5.0	4.9
Less: Imputed Service Charges	8.6	9.0	9.7

Last Updated in March 2003

Source: Caricom Secretariat

ST. KITTS AND NEVIS
Gross Domestic Product by Industry at Factor Cost in Constant 1990 Prices
Percentage Distribution

Industry	1999	2000	2001
Total	100.0	100.0	100.0
Agriculture	5.2	4.5	5.0
Mining & Quarrying	0.4	0.6	0.4
Manufacturing	11.8	12.4	11.1
Electricity & Water	1.8	1.9	1.9
Construction	15.4	18.8	19.2
Wholesale & Retail Trade	15.0	13.8	13.8
Hotels & Restaurants	6.0	4.3	4.4
Transport	7.6	7.8	7.9
Communications	10.3	9.9	10.1
Banks & Insurance	12.2	12.9	12.5
Real Estate & Housing	2.7	2.7	2.7
Government Services	15.7	15.3	15.4
Other Services	4.1	4.0	4.1
Less: Imputed Service Charges	8.1	8.8	8.5

Source: Caricom Secretariat

ST. VINCENT AND THE GRENADINES
Gross Domestic Product by Industry at Factor Cost in Constant 1990 Prices
Percentage Distribution

Industry	1999	2000	2001
Total	100.0	100.0	100.0
Agriculture	11.5	12.1	11.2
Mining & Quarrying	0.3	0.3	0.3
Manufacturing	6.9	6.2	6.1
Electricity & Water	5.9	6.2	6.9
Construction	10.4	8.9	9.5
W/Sale & Retail Trade	16.6	17.7	18.3
Hotels & Restaurants	2.4	2.5	2.4
Transport	13.6	13.6	13.7
Communications	10.3	11.1	9.7
Banks & Insurance	9.3	9.8	10.2
Real Estate & Housing	2.6	2.6	2.7
Government Services	16.0	15.4	15.8
Other Services	1.6	1.7	1.8
Less: Imputed Service Charges	7.7	8.1	8.5

Source: Caricom Secretariat

SURINAME

Gross Domestic Product by Industry at Factor Cost in Constant 1990 Prices
Percentage Distribution

Industry	1997	1998	1999
Total	100.0	100.0	100.0
Agriculture	8.0	6.9	6.6
Mining & Quarrying	13.2	22.7	24.6
Manufacturing	8.4	8.6	7.8
Gas, Water & Electricity	9.3	10.0	10.0
Construction	2.1	2.6	2.7
Trade, Restaurants & Hotels	26.3	19.4	18.2
T/Port, Storage & Commun.	7.1	5.7	5.1
Finan. & Bus. Services	12.3	9.9	10.1
Public Administration	14.7	14.4	15.2
Pers., Soc. & Other Comm. Serv.	2.1	2.2	1.0
Less: Imputed Service Charges	3.6	2.4	1.3

TRINIDAD AND TOBAGO

Gross Domestic Product by Industry in Constant 1990 Market Prices
Percentage Distribution

Industry	1998	1999	2000
Total	100.0	100.0	100.0
Agriculture, Fishing & Forestry	2.4	2.7	2.5
Mining & Quarrying	14.4	13.7	12.5
Manufacture	15.5	17.7	19.4
Electricity & Water	1.6	1.5	1.6
Construction	11.5	11.6	11.4
Distribution Services	13.7	13.9	14.3
Hotels, G/ Houses & Restaurants	1.9	1.9	1.9
T/Port, Storage & Commun.	11.8	11.6	11.0
Fin., Ins., Real Est. & Bus. Services	9.3	8.9	8.6
General Government	13.3	12.3	12.2
Educ. Cult. & Comm. Services	4.6	4.4	4.2
Personal Services	2.8	2.7	2.6
Less: Imputed Service Charge	2.9	2.9	2.2

Source: Caricom Secretariat

Table 2: FDI Inflows to the Caribbean Community (US$million)

Country	1990	1991	1992	1993	1994	1995	1996	1997	1998	1999
The Bahamas		n.a.	7	27	23	107	88	210	147	145
Barbados	(17)	7	19	4	13	12	13	15	16	15
Belize	11	15	19	8	15	21	17	12	18	3
Guyana	17	13	170	46	107	74	92	52	47	48
Jamaica	8	133	178	42	130	147	1874	203	369	520
OECS*	138	166	1127	36	161	186	113	182	232	257
Suriname**	182	—	—	—	—	—	7	12	10	5
Trinidad and Tobago	109	169	1379	78	516	299	320	1,000	732	633
CARICOM	448	503	495	699	965	846	834	1,686	1,571	1,626

* All (Antigua and Barbuda, Dominica, Grenada, St Kitts and Nevis, St Lucia, St Vincent and the Grenadines) except Montserrat.
** Included only from year of accession to CARICOM.
Source: Caribbean Trade and Investment Report, 2000.

financial organizations such as the World Bank and International Monetary Fund (IMF). The high debt-service ratios, their concentration on a few primary commodity exports, the vagaries of international commodity markets, the high incidence of agricultural protectionism in world trade, and the susceptibility of tourism to exogenous shocks all make CARICOM economies extremely vulnerable. In 1998, the region had a combined GDP of $24 billion, income per capita of $3,900, and a ratio of imports and exports to GDP of more than 100 percent (Stotsky et al. 2000, 22). Interestingly, GDP and per capita growth rates have been more dramatic for the smaller LDCs than for the larger MDCs. The region's trade and capital flows are concentrated on the United States, and most of its exports are marketed to the United States, EU countries, and Canada under preferential trade arrangements—the Caribbean Basin Initiative (CBI), Lomé/Cotonou, and the Caribbean-Canadian Agreement, (CARIBCAN), respectively (Bernal 1994, 175).

Foreign direct investment inflows to the region increased threefold from 1990 to 1999 (CARICOM 2000). These flows continue to target the region's primary commodity sectors—namely mining, energy, and agriculture—but are increasingly targeting tourism and labor-intensive manufacturing. The report also indicates that for the period 1990–1998, intrare-gional imports accounted for 8 to 10 percent of the region's total imports, whereas intraregional exports accounted for 12 to 23 percent of total exports. From 1990–1998, the region's total exports increased by 4 percent, whereas total imports increased by 55 percent. This difference reflects CARICOM's trade imbalance with external countries.

The regional market is more significant to some CARICOM countries than others. The OECS countries, for instance, export far more to CARICOM than do other countries. Trinidad and Tobago constitute another leading exporter (of petroleum, primarily) to the community. The three leading importers of CARICOM goods are Barbados, Jamaica, and Trinidad and Tobago, with 40, 21, and 14 percent, respectively. Implementation of the CET has facilitated the community's intra- and extra-regional trade. By 2000, more than half of the member states had implemented the final reductions of the CET (Stotsky et al. 2000, 24).

Major Issues Facing the Caribbean

CARICOM member countries are small, open microstates that have had a collective history of colonialism and underdevelopment. A majority of the states are islands. Sustainable development in small states like these is impeded by

Table 3: CARICOM Statistical Profile, 2000–2003 Averages (unless otherwise noted)

Country	Area	Population	Unemployment	GDP ($US, PPP)	GDP per Capita ($US, PPP)	GDP composition by sector	Exports ($US)	Imports ($US)	Exchange rate ($US)	External Debt Outstanding ($US)	Investment Income ($US, 1999)
Antigua & Barbuda	443 sq km	67,897	11%	$750 million	$11,000	Agriculture: 3.9% Industry: 19.2% Services: 76.9%	$40 million	$357 million	ECD2.7/US1, fixed rate since 1976	$231 million (1999)	$41.2 million
Bahamas	13,940 sq km	297,477	6.9%	$5.2 billion	$17,000	Agriculture: 3% Industry: 7% Services: 90% (1999)	$560.7 million	$1.86 billion	BSD/US1	$371.6 million	$616.8 million
Barbados	431 sq km	277,264	10%	$4 billion	$14,500	Agriculture: 6% Industry: 16% Services: 78%	$227 million	$987 million	BBD2/US1	$692 million	$104.4 million
Belize	22,966 sq km	266,440	9.1%	$1.28 billion	$4,900	Agriculture: 18% Industry: 24% Services: 58%	$290 million	$430 million	BZD2/US1	$475 million	$616.8 million
Dominica	754 sq km	69,655	23%	$380 million	$5,400	Agriculture: 18% Industry: 24% Services: 58%	$50 million	$135 million	ECD2.7/US1, fixed rate since 1976	$161.5 million	$42.9 million
Grenada	344 sq km	89,258	12.5%	$440 million	$5,000	Agriculture: 7.7% Industry: 23.9% Services: 68.4%	$78 million	$270 million	ECD2.7/US1, fixed rate since 1976	$196 million	$38.4 million
Guyana	214,970 sq km	702,100	9.1%	$2.7 billion	$4,000	Agriculture: 35% Industry: 21% Services: 44%	$500 million	$575 million	GYD187.3/US1	$1.2 billion	N/A
Haiti	27,750 sq km	7,527,817	More than two-thirds of labor force do not have formal jobs	$12 billion	$1,700	Agriculture: 30% Industry: 20% Services: 50%	$298 million	$1.14 billion	Gourde29.3/US1	$1.2 billion (1999)	N/A

continues

Table 3: CARICOM Statistical Profile, 2000–2003 Averages (unless otherwise noted) *continued*

Country	Area	Population	Unemployment	GDP ($US, PPP)	GDP per Capita ($US, PPP)	GDP composition by sector	Exports ($US)	Imports ($US)	Exchange rate ($US)	External Debt Outstanding ($US)	Investment Income ($US, 1999)
Jamaica	10,991 sq km	2,695,867	15.4%	$10 billion	$3,900	Agriculture: 6% Industry: 31% Services: 63%	$1.4 billion	$3.1 billion	JA48.4/US1	$5.3 billion	$168.1 million
Montserrat	102 sq km	8,995	6% (1998)	$29 million	$3,400	Agriculture: 5.4% Industry: 13.6% Services: 81% (1996)	$700,000	$17 million	ECD2.7/US1, fixed rate since 1976	$8.9 million (1997)	$-5.9 million
St. Kitts & Nevis	261 sq km	38,763	4.5% (1997)	$339 million	$8,800	Agriculture: 3.5% Industry: 25.8% Services: 70.7%	$47 million	$152 million	ECD2.7/US1, fixed rate since 1976	$171 million	$82.0 million
St. Lucia	616 sq km	162,157	16.5% (1997)	$866 million	$5,400	Agriculture: 7% Industry: 20% Services: 73%	$68.3 million	$319.4 million	ECD2.7/US1, fixed rate since 1976	$214 million	$68.4 million
St. Vincent and the Grenadines	389 sq km	116,812	22% (1997)	$339 million	$2,900	Agriculture: 10% Industry: 26% Services: 64%	$53.7 million	$185.6 million	ECD2.7/US1, fixed rate since 1976	$167.2 million	$45.1 million
Suriname	163,270 sq km	435,449	17%	$1.5 billion	$3,500	Agriculture: 13% Industry: 22% Services: 65%	$445 million	$300 million	2,346.8 Gilder/US1	$321 million	N/A
Trinidad and Tobago	5,128 sq km	1,104,209	10.8%	$11.1 billion	$9,500	Agriculture: 1.6% Industry: 43.2% Services: 55.2%	$4.2 billion	$3.8 billion	6.2TTD/US1	$2.8 billion	N/A

Sources: CIA *World Factbook* and CARICOM Secretariat Statics website.

Table 4: CARICOM Sociopolitical Profile, 2000–2003 Averages (unless otherwise noted)

Country	Natural resources	Environmental issues	Life expectancy at birth (years)	HIV/AIDS adult prevalence rate	Literacy*	Government type	Capital
Antigua & Barbuda	N/A	Water management; deforestation	71.31	N/A	89%	Constitutional monarchy	Saint John's
Bahamas	Salt, aragonite, timber	Coral reef decay; solid waste disposal	65.71	3.5%	95.6%	Constitutional parliamentary democracy	Nassau
Barbados	Petroleum, natural gas	Pollution of coastal waters from effluents and waste disposal; soil erosion; contamination of aquifers due to illegal solid waste disposal	71.84	1.2%	97.4%	Parliamentary democracy	Bridgetown
Belize	Timber	Deforestation; water pollution from sewage, industrial effluents, agricultural runoff; solid and sewage waste disposal	67.36	2%	94.1%	Parliamentary democracy	Belmopan
Dominica	Timber	N/A	74.12	N/A	94%	Parliamentary democracy; Republic within the Commonwealth	Roseau
Grenada	Timber	N/A	64.52	N/A	98%	Constitutional monarchy with Westminster-style parliament	Saint George's
Guyana	Bauxite, gold, diamonds, hardwood timber	Water pollution from sewage and agricultural and industrial chemicals; deforestation	63.09	2.7%	98.8%	Republic within the Commonwealth	Georgetown
Haiti	Bauxite, copper, calcium carbonate, gold, marble	Deforestation; soil erosion; inadequate supplies of potable water	51.61	6.1%	52.9%	Elected government	Port-au-Prince
Jamaica	Bauxite, gypsum, limestone	Deforestation; coastal water pollution from waste disposal and effluents; damage to coral reefs; air pollution from vehicle emissions	75.85	1.2%	87.9%	Constitutional parliamentary democracy	Kingston
Montserrat	N/A	Land erosion on slopes cleared for cultivation	78.36	N/A	97%	Overseas territory of the United Kingdom	Plymouth (abandoned in 1997 due to volcanic activity; interim government buildings constructed at Brades Estates in the northwest area of Montserrat)

continues

Table 4: CARICOM Sociopolitical Profile, 2000–2003 Averages (unless otherwise noted) *continued*

Country	Natural resources	Environmental issues	Life expectancy at birth (years)	HIV/AIDS adult prevalence rate	Literacy*	Government type	Capital
St. Kitts & Nevis	N/A	N/A	71.57	N/A	97%	Constitutional monarchy with Westminster-style parliament	Basseterre
St. Lucia	Forests, minerals (pumice), geothermal potential	Deforestation; soil erosion	73.08	N/A	67%	Westminster-style parliamentary democracy	Castries
St. Vincent and the Grenadines	N/A	Coastal water pollution from effluents and waste disposal	73.08	N/A	96%	Parliamentary democracy	Kingstown
Suriname	Timber, bauxite, gold, nickel, copper, platinum, iron ore	Deforestation as timber is cut for export; pollution of inland waterways due to mining	69.23	1.2%	93%	Constitutional democracy	Paramaribo
Trinidad and Tobago	Petroleum, natural gas, asphalt	Water pollution from agricultural chemicals and effluents; oil pollution of beaches; deforestation; soil erosion	69.59	2.5%	98.6%	Parliamentary democracy	Port-of-Spain

*Age 15 and over has attended school and/or can read or write.
Source: CIA World Factbook.

their capacity limitations in key areas such as product and factor markets, public- and private-sector administrative and institutional structures, and negotiating power and leverage vis-à-vis external countries and organizations (Blake 2001, 481). Regional cooperation provides a means of ameliorating size-related capacity constraints to development and is thus an integral part of Caribbean development strategy (ibid.). Because individual member states are highly susceptible to external influence, CARICOM has been called an example of externally vulnerable integration (Bernal 1994, 171). Nevertheless, the degree of functional cooperation and foreign policy coordination is fairly strong. CARICOM has been less successful with regard to economic integration. This more expansive integration effort is constrained to a large degree by the small size, limited resources, and external orientation of CARICOM's member states as well as the similarity of their economies and productive structures.

CARICOM's ability to contribute to development in the region is limited by the constraints of member-state underdevelopment, dependence, and their tendency to pursue nationalistic, not regional, solutions to pressing economic problems (Axline1978, 969). These forces have fostered disincentives for full-fledged integration. Critics assert that because national interest is so predominant and entrenched, CARICOM has never been serious about economic or political integration (Payne and Sutton 2001, 174). CARICOM is alleged to be an exercise in regionalization, not integration; it is a regionalized economy and polity in which the preservation of the institution of the nation-state is paramount (ibid.). Personality politics, elite politics, and interest-group lobbying are said to encumber effective policymaking at the regional level and implementation at the national level. Put simply, national governments are pursuing domestic politics infused with an elite perspective within a regional framework (ibid.).

To attain any semblance of collective self-reliance, CARICOM members must transcend their present regime of nominal multilateral cooperation and incorporate a higher degree of politico-economic integration (Erisman 1992, 138). Actualization of the CSME and effective implementation at the national level of rational decisions made at the regional level are imperative in this regard. CARICOM must also address several policy imperatives to foster sustained development in member states. It must encourage production and export diversification, export market penetration, improved productivity, and enhanced competitiveness.

Michelle Benjamin Calhoun

See Also Economic Integration

References

Axline, Andrew. 1978. "Integration and Development in the Commonwealth Caribbean: The Politics of Regional Negotiations." *International Organization* 32, no. 4: 953–973.

———. 1979. *Caribbean Integration: The Politics of Regionalism.* London: Frances Pinter.

Beckford, George, ed. 1984. *Caribbean Economy: Dependency and Backwardness.* Mona, Jamaica: Institute of Social and Economic Research.

Benn, Denis, and Kenneth Hall. 2001. *The Caribbean Community: Beyond Survival.* Kingston: Jamaica: Ian Randle.

Bernal, Richard L. 1994. "CARICOM: Externally Vulnerable Regional Economic Integration." In Roberto Bouzas and Jaime Ros, eds., *Economic Integration in the Western Hemisphere.* Notre Dame: University of Notre Dame Press.

Blake, Byron. 2001. "Experiences and Opportunities for Capacity Sharing through Regional Co-operation and Integration: The Case of the Caribbean Community." In David Pertez et al., eds., *Small States in the Global Economy,* London: Commonwealth Secretariat.

Brewster, Havelock. 2003. *The Caribbean Single Market and Economy: Is It Realistic without Commitment to Political Unity?* Georgetown: Guyana: CARICOM Secretariat.

Brewster, H., and C. Y. Thomas. 1967. *The Dynamics of West Indian Economic Integration.* Mona, Jamaica: Institute of Social and Economic Research.

Caribbean Community. 2000. *Caribbean Trade and Investment Report 2000,* http://www.caricom.org.

Caribbean Community Secretariat. 1981. *The Caribbean Community in the 1980s: Report by a Group of Caribbean Experts.* Georgetown, Guyana: CARICOM Secretariat.

———. 1988. *Caribbean Development to the Year 2000: Challenges, Prospects and Policies.* Georgetown: Guyana: CARICOM Secretariat.

Demas, William G. 1965. *The Economics of Small Countries with Special Reference to the Caribbean.* Montreal: McGill University Press.

Erisman, H. Michael. 1992. *Pursuing Postdependency Politics: South-South Relations in the Caribbean.* Boulder: Lynne Rienner.

Girvan, Norman, and O. Jefferson. 1971. *Readings in the Political Economy of the Caribbean.* Trinidad: New World Group.

Hall, Kenneth O. 2003. *Re-Inventing CARICOM: The Road to a New Integration.* Kingston: Jamaica: Ian Randle.

Inter-American Development Bank. 1984. *Ten Years of CARICOM: Papers Presented at a Seminar on Economic Integration in the Caribbean.* Washington, DC: IDB.

Lewis, G. K. 1968. *The Growth of the Modern West Indies.* London: Macgibbon and Kee.

Lewis, Patsy. 2002. *Surviving Small Size: Regional Integration in Caribbean Ministates.* Kingston: Jamaica: University of the West Indies Press.

Organization of American States, http://www.sice.oas.org.

Payne, Anthony. 1980. *The Politics of the Caribbean Community, 1961–79: Regional Integration among New States.* New York: St. Martin's.

Payne, Anthony, and Paul Sutton. 2001. *Charting Caribbean Development.* Miami: University Press of Florida.

Stotsky, Janet, et al. 2000. "Trade Liberalization in the Caribbean." *Finance and Development* (June): 22–25.

West Indian Commission. 1994. *Time for Action: The Report of the West Indian Commission.* Largo, MD: International Development Options.

The Central American Common Market (CACM)

The Central American Common Market (CACM) is a free trade organization formed in 1960 by Guatemala, Honduras, Nicaragua, and El Salvador; Costa Rica joined two years later. The organization came into being with the General Treaty of Central American Economic Integration (Tratado General de Integración Económica Centroamericana), signed in Managua, Nicaragua, on December 13, 1960. It entered into force on June 4, 1961, for Guatemala, El Salvador, and Nicaragua; on April 27, 1962, for Honduras (with reservation); and on September 23, 1963, for Costa Rica. Panama has remained outside the regional scheme because of its special status based on the Panama Canal, but has maintained limited free trade treaties with each CACM country.

According to the treaty, CACM was created "for the purpose of reaffirming [the] intention to unify the economies of the four countries and jointly to promote the development of Central America in order to improve the living conditions of their peoples" (para.1, sec. 1). It was one of four regional economic integration organizations created during the Latin American export boom of the 1960s. The CACM and the three other Latin American trading blocs, the Latin American Free Trade Association, the Caribbean Free Trade Association (CARIFTA), and the Andean Community, were similar in their initial endorsement of regional integration behind temporary protectionist barriers as a way to continue an economic policy of import-substitution industrialization that was popular among developing countries in the region at that time.

The CACM was considered the most successful integration attempt by developing countries. By the mid-1960s, the group had made advances toward economic integration, and by 1970 trade between member nations had risen more than tenfold over 1960 levels. In 1967, at the conference of American presidents at Punta del Este, Uruguay, it was decided that the CACM, together with the Latin American Free Trade Association, would be the basis for a comprehensive Latin American common market. During this period, imports doubled, and a common tariff was established for 98 percent of the trade with nonmember countries. However, the CACM's effectiveness waned following Honduras's withdrawal in the wake of the 1969 Soccer War with El Salvador. The CACM stagnated throughout the 1970s and virtually collapsed during the prolonged Central American political and debt crises of the 1980s, revitalizing only after its overhaul and the partial inclusion of Panama in the early 1990s. By the early 1990s, little progress toward a Latin American common market had been made.

Past Attempts at Regional Cooperation

The CACM was preceded by other regional attempts at economic and political union. The earliest of these was the Central American Federation, or Central American Union, a political confederation (1825–1838) comprising the republics of Central America—Costa Rica, Guatemala, Honduras, Nicaragua, and El Salvador. United under a common governor in

Spanish colonial times, these countries gained independence in 1821 and were briefly annexed to the Mexican empire formed by Agustín de Iturbide. The nations joined in a loose federation in 1825, with Manuel José Arce (1825–1829) as the first president of the group. He was succeeded by Francisco Morazán (1830–1838). Political and personal rivalries between liberals and conservatives, poor communication, and the fear of the hegemony of one state over another led to dissolution of the congress in 1838 and the defeat (1839) of Morazán's forces by Rafael Carrera. In 1842, Morazán made an abortive attempt to reestablish the federation from Costa Rica. Later efforts by Nicaragua, Honduras, and El Salvador failed, and the attempts at regional union of Justo Rufino Barrios (1885) and José Santos Zelaya (1895) only increased existing enmities. The United States proposed a union at the Central American conference of 1922–1923 that was not favorably received. Integration attempts emerged again in 1951 with the formation of the Organization of Central American States (Organización de Estados Centroamericanos, or ODECA).

The post–World War II movement toward Central American economic integration began with a wave of bilateral free trade treaties signed among Guatemala, Honduras, El Salvador, Nicaragua, and Costa Rica between 1950 and 1956. By the end of this period of bilateral negotiations, each country had become party to at least one of the treaties, which involved free trade in a limited range of products. Although primarily a political entity, ODECA represented a significant step toward the creation of other regional multilateral organizations. Toward the end of the decade, with the assistance of the United Nations Economic Commission for Latin America and the Caribbean (ECLAC), concrete plans for regional economic integration emerged. In 1951, ECLAC delegates decided to proceed with formal integration discussions, and in 1952 they formed the Central American Economic Cooperation Commission, composed of the ministers of econ-

omy and other relevant officials from the participating governments, to engage in fact-finding under the auspices of the United Nations. The CACM treaties emerged shortly thereafter.

Treaties and Institutions of the CACM

The CACM boasts a complex and detailed legal framework. In 1958–1959, three important integration agreements were signed: the Multilateral Treaty on Free Trade and Central American Economic Integration (Tratado Multilateral de Libre Comercio e Integración Económica Centroamericana), the Integration Industries Convention (Régimen de Industrias de Integración, or RII), and the Central American Tariff Equalization Convention (Convenio Centroamericano sobre Equiparación de Gravámenes a la Importación). The Multilateral Treaty on Free Trade and Central American Economic Integration provided for intraregional free trade in 239 groups of Central American products and a ten-year phase-in of intraregional free trade in all Central American goods. The Central American Tariff Equalization Convention was a complementary agreement to the multilateral treaty, establishing a common external tariff (CET) on 270 products, including all those listed under the treaty, and proposing a harmonization of tariffs on an additional 200 products within five years. The convention would thereby provide the common barrier to extraregional imports under which Central American producers would conduct a liberalized trade.

The RII was the most controversial program and would be the most difficult to implement. As originally conceived, it was to direct the flow of capital investment into the region by granting special incentives and privileges to firms given "integration industries" status. In order to prevent costly duplication of capital investment, firms whose products had small consumer markets in the region would be given a virtual monopoly within the CACM. The Central American countries were supposed to distribute integration industry plants among themselves in an equitable and efficient manner. The integration regime envisioned by these agreements never fully entered into force, however, but was instead superseded by the General Treaty of Central American Economic Integration of 1960, which became the basis for the CACM. The general treaty went into effect for Guatemala, El Salvador, and Nicaragua in June 1961 and for Honduras and Costa Rica in April and July 1962, respectively.

In addition to the RII, the general treaty established a permanent secretariat (Secretaría Permanente del Tratado General de Integración Económica Centroamericana, SIECA) and a development bank (Banco Centroamericano de Integración Económica, BCIE). A Central American Clearing House (Cámara Centroamericana de Compensación de Monedas) was established in 1963 to promote the use of local currencies in the settlement of short-term trade deficits between pairs of CACM member states, and a Central American Monetary Council (Consejo Monetario Centroamericano) was set up in 1964 to promote monetary union.

U.S. Influence in Regional Integration

There was a strong U.S. interest in the CACM's success from its inception. The United States provided financial and technical contributions to the integration process, and presidents John F. Kennedy and Lyndon B. Johnson became personally involved. The general treaty represented a compromise between the ECLAC-inspired approach and the policy preferences of the United States. The latter proposed several significant changes to the ECLAC integration scheme, the main difference being the establishment from the outset of intraregional free trade as the norm, rather than as the exception as provided for in the multilateral treaty. Under the U.S. plan, all products would be subject to intraregional free trade unless ex-

empted. The United States was also opposed to the idea of granting monopoly status to integration industries within the region. In exchange for adoption of its plan, the United States promised to provide funding for the various institutions of the CACM and to increase its economic aid to Central America.

In February 1960, Guatemala, El Salvador, and Honduras accepted the U.S.-sponsored integration scheme and signed the Tripartite Treaty (Tratado Tripartito) in Esquipulas, Guatemala, establishing intraregional free trade as the norm and excluding an RII mechanism. The Tripartite Treaty evoked strong objections from ECLAC, which saw its guiding role in Central American integration undermined by U.S. involvement in the process. In response to protests from ECLAC and the government of Nicaragua, the United States and the parties to the Tripartite Treaty agreed to negotiate a compromise integration treaty to supersede all prior free trade agreements. The General Treaty of Central American Economic Integration was signed in Managua, Nicaragua, by four of the five republics (Costa Rica delayed signing by two years) on December 13, 1960, with ECLAC conceding on the free trade issue and the United States conceding on the inclusion of the RII.

U.S. interest in the region continues today. Negotiations to create a U.S.–Central American Free Trade Agreement (US-CAFTA) were launched in San Jose, Costa Rica, in January 2003. The talks involved the five CACM members and the United States. The United States is CACM's biggest market, the source of several billion dollars' worth of migrant remittances annually, and provides the de facto or de jure currency of the region. El Salvador adopted the U.S. dollar as the official currency in 2002, and Guatemala allows a legal parallel circulation of dollars along with the national currency, the quetzal. Throughout Central America, U.S. dollars are commonly used for commercial loans and bank accounts as well as informal transactions.

CACM's Impact on the Regional Economy

During the 1960s and 1970s, the CACM had a significant positive impact on trade flows, economic growth, and industrial development in Central America. Intraregional exports as a percentage of total exports grew dramatically—from 7.5 percent in 1960 to 26.9 percent in 1970—before declining to 23.4 percent in 1975 and to 14.7 percent in 1985 (SIECA). The total value of trade within the region grew from US$33 million in 1960 to US$1.1 billion in 1980, but dropped to US$421 million in 1986. By 1967, 95 percent of all goods traded within the region had attained duty-free status, and 90 percent of traded goods were covered by the CET. The goods exempted from intraregional free trade were mainly traditional agricultural exports destined for global markets.

Most of the new intraregional trade was in consumer goods, a large share of which consisted of processed foods. By 1970, food processing was the single most prominent industrial activity within the CACM, accounting for approximately half of gross industrial output. The preference for consumer goods production was built into the CACM tariff structure, which imposed a high CET on extraregional consumer goods but did not impede the import of intermediate or capital goods.

In addition to the protection afforded to consumer goods by the CET on consumer imports, CACM member states also promoted investment in industry by introducing generous tax incentives and exemptions for new and existing industrial firms. To help promote balanced development, the four original CACM member states signed the Convention of Fiscal Incentives for Industrial Development (Convenio Centroamericano de Incentivos Fiscales al Desarollo Industrial) in 1962 to equalize grants of tax incentives to industrial firms. The convention allowed Honduras and Nicaragua to offer temporarily broader tax breaks to industrial firms than the other two more industrialized republics. Honduras became the main beneficiary of this differentiated treatment, gaining in 1969 an extension of its preferential taxation status.

Another important incentive to industrial development within the CACM was the implementation of regional infrastructure development projects. Several infrastructure development organizations were established during the 1960s to improve intraregional transport and communications: the Regional Telecommunications Commission (Comisión Técnica de las Telecomunicaciones de Centroamérica, or COMTELCA), the Central American Corporation of Air Navigation Services (Corporación Centroamericana de Servicios de Navegación Aérea, or Cocesna), the Central American Maritime Commission (Comisión Centroamericana de Transporte Marítimo, or Cocatram), and the Central American Railways Commission (Comisión Centroamericana de Ferrocarriles, or Cocafer). These organizations were financed mainly by the Regional Office for Central America and Panama (ROCAP) of the U.S. Agency for International Development (AID) as part of the Alliance for Progress initiative. AID/ROCAP also financed a Regional Highway Program to improve highway routes considered vital to intraregional trade.

Total net economic benefits of integration were estimated at 3 or 4 percentage points of regional GDP in 1972. Expressed as a single present discounted value for all future years, the decision to integrate was worth an estimated $3 billion by 1972. Economic integration created an estimated 150,000 jobs, or 14 percent of the increase in total employment from 1958 to 1972.

Regional Integration Setbacks

By the late 1960s, issues of unequal distribution of the benefits of integration began to arise among the members. The poorest member, Honduras, especially, but also Nicaragua and Costa Rica, felt that the CACM free trade arrangements favored the countries with the largest industrial base—Guatemala and El Salvador—and did not offer enough opportunities for industrialization. Instead, they believed, patterns of raw materials production for finished goods imports were repeating, reinforcing themselves on a regional scale and creating trade deficits among the members.

Increasing tensions throughout the summer of 1969 erupted into hostilities on July 14, when Salvadoran air and land units made an incursion into Honduran territory. The ensuing four-day war claimed 2,000 lives and led to the forced repatriation of about 150,000 Salvadorans. The war is often referred to as the Soccer War, or "Futbol War," because the violence broke out in both countries during the 1969 soccer championship qualifying rounds for the 1970 World Soccer Cup. The deeper causes of the conflict, however, had to do with population migration and subsequent territorial claims by El Salvador on Honduras.

Diplomatic and commercial relations between El Salvador and Honduras were suspended for a decade thereafter, as was air transport between the two countries. Honduras withdrew from the CACM in December 1970 after it failed to persuade the other member states to enact further reforms in its favor. Honduras subsequently conducted trade with CACM countries on a bilateral basis until 1986. Honduras's withdrawal from the CACM, although not significant in terms of lost trade volume, represented a symbolic collapse of the organization as a vehicle for promoting coordinated regional growth.

Despite Honduras's withdrawal from the CACM and its suspension of commercial relations with El Salvador, Central American intraregional trade rose steadily throughout the 1970s, exceeding US$1 billion by 1980, before dropping to half that level in the mid-1980s. Most efforts to coordinate industrial and macroeconomic policies had been abandoned, however, well before the general treaty expired in 1982.

The fiscal problem that had plagued Central America in the 1960s carried over to the 1970s, when it was aggravated by a series of external shocks: the acceleration of world inflation and higher dollar prices for imports; the first oil crisis of 1973, which caused a quadrupling of dollar prices of oil; natural disasters in Nicaragua (1972 earthquake), Honduras (Hurricane Fifi in 1974), and Guatemala (1976 earthquake); major declines in several world commodity prices; and the second oil shock of 1979. The 1980s ushered in the Third World debt crisis, beginning with the Mexican default on sovereign loans in 1982. Real wages fell, debt grew, inflation rose (except in Honduras), and the trade balance deteriorated for each CACM. In 1982 alone, GDP fell in all five CACM republics for the first time since 1932. Also in the 1980s, the CACM was rocked by brutal civil wars in Nicaragua and El Salvador.

Resumption of Progress

A reactivation of Central American economic integration was made possible with the signing of the Central American Peace Agreement (Esquipulas II) in August 1987. Esquipulas II laid the political groundwork for concerted action to renew the integration system following restoration of peace and democracy in the region. Formal action to restart the integration process was taken at the eighth summit of Central American presidents, held in Antigua, Guatemala, in June 1990. The participants at the Antigua summit approved the Economic Action Plan for Central America (Plan de Acción Económico de Centroamérica, or Paeca), which foresaw a new conceptual and legal basis for a Central American economic community.

Further progress toward integration was made at the tenth Central American presidential summit, held in San Salvador, El Salvador, in July 1991, when the five original participants agreed to include Panama in certain aspects of the new economic community. The eleventh summit, held in Tegucigalpa, Honduras, modified several CACM institutions and incorporated them into the System of Central American Integration (Sistema de Integración Centroamericana, SICA), an umbrella organization encompassing both political and economic integration efforts. Honduras fully rejoined the integration process in February 1992 upon the signing of the Transitional Multilateral Free Trade Agreement with the other Central American republics.

Central American integration was given a further boost with the signing of the North American Free Trade Agreement (NAFTA) by Canada, Mexico, and the United States. In August 1992, a Framework Free Trade Agreement was signed by the five Central American republics and Mexico, establishing procedures for the formation of a free trade area that entered into force in December 1996. Inclusion of Central America in a free trade area with Colombia and Venezuela was also foreseen in the Caracas Commitment adopted at a regional summit in February 1993. The signing of the Central American Free Trade treaty, along with the Dominican Republic (CAFTA-DR), be-tween the members of CACM and the United States in August 2005, promises further integration in the region.

Anastasia Xenias

See Also Economic Integration; North American Free Trade Agreement (NAFTA)

References

Balassa, Bela. 1971. "Regional Integration and Trade Liberalization in Latin America." *Journal of Common Market Studies* 10, no. 1 (September).

Bulmer-Thomas, Victor. 1987. *The Political Economy of Central America since 1920.* New York: Cambridge University Press.

Cline, William R., and Enrique Delgado, eds. 1978. *Economic Integration in Central America.* Washington, DC: Brookings Institution.

Ivin, George, and Stuart Holland, eds. 1989. *Central America: The Future of Integration.* Boulder: Westview.

Secretaría Permanente del Tratado General de Integración Económica Centroamericana. *Cuadernos de la SIECA: Estadísticas Analíticas del Comercio Intracentroamericano.* SIECA.

———. *Series Estadísticas Seleccionadas de Centroamérica.* SIECA.

Common Market of the South (Mercosur)

The Mercado Comùn del Sur, or Common Market of the South (Mercosur), is a customs union (that is, a free trade area with a common external tariff, or CET) among the countries of Argentina, Brazil, Paraguay, and Uruguay. It originated in 1991 with the Treaty of Asunción, which established a free trade area and outlined a transition schedule to a common market. In 1994, the Protocol of Ouro Preto gave Mercosur customs union status by introducing a common external tariff on a large number of products. The protocol also renewed the commitment among member states to a transition process, which is expected to lead to the establishment of a common market in 2006. In 1996, Chile and Bolivia joined the free trade area (but not the customs union) as "associate countries." Mercosur is entirely governed by intergovernmental structures, without any autonomous central institution.

Historical Overview

The effort to bring about economic integration in Latin America can be traced back to the Latin American Free Trade Association (LAFTA, or ALALC in Spanish), created in 1960 with the objective of achieving a free trade zone through a gradual reduction of tariffs over a period of twenty years. Difficulties in enforcing the reductions led to LAFTA's collapse in 1980. That same year, the Treaty of Montevideo established the Latin American Integration Association (LAIA, or ALADI in Spanish), signed by Argentina, Bolivia, Brazil, Chile, Colombia, Ecuador, Mexico, Paraguay, Peru, Uruguay, and Venezuela as an alternative to LAFTA. LAIA established a preferential trade zone among its members and a legal framework for the formulation of bilateral and multilateral trade agreements. It has a more flexible structure than LAFTA because it does not have to abide by a schedule for tariff reductions. Mercosur was created under the legal framework of LAIA.

The idea of a bilateral agreement between Argentina and Brazil started in November 1985 with the Iguazu Declaration, in which these countries expressed their desire to establish political and economic cooperation. Both countries had regained their democracies after enduring years of military dictatorships, and they saw in their cooperation a way to stabilize their economies. In July 1986, in the Argentine-Brazilian Integration Act, Argentina and Brazil defined the basis of future negotiations toward the promotion of a common economic area. A set of twenty-four protocols reducing tariffs in specific sectors soon followed. In November 1988, the Integration, Cooperation and Development Treaty established a ten-year transition period toward the creation of the common economic area. The treaty called for cooperation in two areas: commerce, through the elimination of tariff and nontariff barriers to trade, and trade policy, through gradual harmonization.

Argentina and Brazil stated the basis of their economic integration and cooperation in several agreements and acts that followed the Integration, Cooperation and Development Treaty. The Act of Buenos Aires established January 1995 as a starting date for the common market and set up a Bilateral Common Group responsible for determining the measures that would be needed to achieve this goal. In December 1990, the countries signed the Accord of Economic Complementation (LAIA's Accord of Economic Complementation #14). During 1991, Uruguay and Paraguay decided to join the agreement at a slower pace of integration, and in December of that year the four countries signed the Treaty of Asunción.

The Treaty of Asunción, with only twenty-four articles, contains the basic set of rules defining and governing Mercosur. As a frame treaty, it only sets the legal basis under which Mercosur is to be governed; as negotiations advance, new rules are put in place to complement and modify the original agreement. Besides creating a free trade area, it set January 1995 as the target date for establishing a customs union and introduced a set of instruments to help with the transition process. The treaty set a preliminary organizational structure, with a Common Market Council and a Common Market Group to administer Mercosur during the transition. It did not provide for the creation of central institutions with supranational powers. All decisions would be made by consensus of the member states. Since Mercosur was created within the framework of LAIA, it is open to all LAIA signatories. Several protocols were later added to the Treaty of Asunción to address institutional and operational issues. The Protocol of Brasilia (1991) established a system of dispute settlement among member states. It was later complemented by the Protocol of Olivos (2002).

The Ouro Preto Protocol of 1994 brought Mercosur a step closer to achieving a common market. It established a customs union as a transition arrangement, set up a common external tariff, and defined a schedule of gradual CET convergence. The customs union is imperfect, however, because the CET applies to only 85 percent of the products traded among the countries. A set of "sensitive" items and country-specific lists of products are exempt from the CET, including capital goods, telecommunication products, and computers. Difficulties encountered in reaching agreement on common policies also excluded the automobile, sugar, and textile sectors from the CETs. Following the Ouro Preto protocol, negotiations for deeper integration called for new legal measures related to methods of fair competition, antidumping, and safeguard rules. Yet little progress was made on most of these issues, especially on those related to domestic subsidies to industries and public enterprises.

By the end of the 1990s, economic problems in the two major countries of Mercosur, along with the devaluation of Brazil's currency, led to numerous trade disputes between Argentina and Brazil, threatening Mercosur's future. To reestablish confidence in Mercosur, in June 2000 its member countries signed the Relaunch of Mercosur agreement. The objective of this program was to strengthen the customs union while recognizing the central role of convergence and macroeconomic coordination in advancing the integration process. To this end, the Relaunch agreement provided a working schedule for negotiating a set of targets for economic convergence. In spirit, it is similar to the Treaty of Maastricht that launched the European Union and the euro zone in 1992. It established priority for negotiations on several topics, including market access; customs; incentives to investment; production and exports, including the free trade zones; common external tariffs; fair competition; resolution of controversies; and external relations. Some progress has been made in the harmonization of statistics, that is, in the presence of a core set of statistics in all member states. In order to ease the convergence process, elimination of national exceptions to the common external tariff was postponed until 2006.

In April 2001, in the face of deep economic crisis in Argentina, Mercosur authorized the country to abandon the common external tariff until the end of 2002. In particular, Argentina temporarily abolished the tariffs on imports of capital goods from third parties and imposed a unilateral tariff on consumption goods of 35 percent (Mercosur sets both at 14 percent).

Organization of Mercosur

The ultimate purpose of Mercosur is to expand the national markets of the member states in order to accelerate their economic, scientific, and technological development. This purpose is to be achieved through the optimal use of available resources, the preservation of the environment, the coordination of macroeconomic policies, the improvement of communications, and complementation of all sectors of the economy. More specific objectives include "the free movement of goods, services, and factors of production; the establishment of a common external tariff and a common trade policy; the coordination of macroeconomic and sectoral policies; and harmonization of the legal systems" (Treaty of Asunción).

The organizational structure of Mercosur was established in the Ouro Preto Protocol. Mercosur has six decisionmaking bodies that operate at the presidential, ministerial, and technical levels. None of these bodies has supranational powers.

The highest body of Mercosur is the Council of the Common Market (CCM). The council is responsible for the political leadership of the organization and for ensuring the achievement of the common market. It is composed of the foreign affairs and economic ministers of the member states. The presidency of the CCM rotates among members, in alphabetical order, for terms of six months. The council meets at least twice a year with the participation of the presidents of the member states. Its main duties are to rule on proposals submitted by the Common Market Group and to negotiate with other countries or entities on behalf of Mercosur. The CCM also appoints directors of Mercosur's Administrative Secretariat. The council rules are issued in the form of decisions to be implemented by the member countries.

The executive body of Mercosur is the Common Market Group (CMG). The CMG is composed of four members and four alternates for each country, appointed by their governments, and is coordinated by the ministries of foreign affairs. Its main duty is to enforce decisions of the CCM and monitor compliance. In addition, the CMG proposes draft decisions to the CCM and organizes and prepares reports for the council. The CMG supervises Mercosur's Administrative Secretariat by approving its budget and supervising its activities. The CMG also approves procedural rules for the Trade Commission and the Economic-Social Consultative Forum. Its decisions take the form of resolutions.

Both the CCM and the CMG were created by the Treaty of Asunción to preside over Mercosur through the transition period to the common market. Both groups were ratified in the Ouro Preto Protocol. The protocol completed the institutional organization of Mercosur by adding four more entities to Mercosur: the Mercosur Trade Commission, the Joint Parliamentary Commission, the Socioeconomic Consultative Forum, and the Administrative Secretariat.

The Mercosur Trade Commission (MTC) is responsible for assisting the Common Market Group and for monitoring the application of the common trade policy instruments related to the operation of the customs union. It consists of four members and four alternates per country, meets at least once a month, and it is coordinated by the ministries of foreign affairs. The MTC submits proposals to the CMG regarding the development of common trade policy instruments, and it makes decisions pertaining to the application of the common external tariff. It also proposes new trade and customs regulations and revises tariff rates on specific products, and it is responsible for setting up and supervising Mercosur's technical committees. Finally, the MTC receives complaints from its associated national sections related to dispute settlement.

The Joint Parliamentary Commission (JPC) brings together representatives from the national parliaments of each country. Each representative is approved by his country's parliament. The commission's role is to ensure that each country applies CCM decisions and CMG resolutions at the national level. To this end, the JPC assists countries with the harmonization of legislation and submits recommendations to the CCM and the CMG.

The private enterprises and social groups of Mercosur are represented in the Socioeconomic Consultative Forum. Composed of an equal number of representatives from each country, the forum makes recommendations to the CMG.

Mercosur's Administrative Secretariat provides operational support to the other institutional organs. Headquartered in Montevideo, Uruguay, it holds the official archives of Mercosur, publishes and disseminates the decisions and resolutions adopted by the legislative and executive bodies, and organizes the meetings of the CCM, the CMG, and the MTC. The director of the Administrative Secretariat is chosen by the CMG and appointed for a two-year term, which may not be renewed.

Rules Governing Mercosur

The rules that determine the functioning of Mercosur are stated in the Treaty of Asunción and the protocols that amended and complemented the treaty. The treaty itself established a trade liberalization program to be followed by the member countries during the transition period to the common market. The program called for a reduction in tariffs on goods originating in member countries from an average level of 47 percent in June 1991 to 0 percent in January 1995. The elimination of the tariffs was to occur gradually, at a rate of 7 percent per semester. The liberalization program authorized country-specific lists of goods to be exempted from the tariff reductions. The number

of goods in the lists was also to be reduced gradually throughout the transition period. After December 1994, the tariffs on these products were to be eliminated linearly and automatically over a period of four years, at a rate of 25 percent a year. Paraguay and Uruguay would have a one-year moratorium before having to begin the process.

Further integration was achieved through the introduction of a common external tariff in the Ouro Preto Protocol. The CET required the application of a uniform treatment to imports from third parties, starting in 1995 for Argentina and Brazil, and 1996 for Uruguay and Paraguay. The CET covered approximately 85 percent of traded products, with tariffs ranging from 0 percent to 20 percent, and an average of 11 percent. Exceptions were allowed in the form of country-specific lists of goods and sensitive items (including 900 capital goods and 200 telecommunication and computer items) and sectors (automobile and sugar). In the exempt sectors, countries apply a national regime of tariffs that cannot favor imports from outside Mercosur countries over imports from members of Mercosur. Brazil's exception list, with 29 products, concentrates primarily on chemical and petrochemical goods, milk, and raw textile materials. Argentina's (221 products) focuses on chemicals and steel, paper, and footwear. The lists for Paraguay and Uruguay (427 and 950 goods, respectively) contain mainly agricultural products. Under an agreement reached in the year 2000, a country can change up to 50 of the products included in its country-specific list of exempt items every 90 days, provided that it does not increase the total number of items on the list. The tariffs on the products that appear on the country-specific lists are subject to adjustments that will converge to the common tariff by no later than 2006.

The main sectors receiving special treatment under Mercosur are the automobile and sugar industries. The treaty kept in place the national tariff regimes in automobile trade that existed prior to the creation of Mercosur; after several rounds and bilateral agreements, a Common Regime for the Automobile Sector was signed in October 2001. The objective of the common regime is to lay the groundwork for the achievement of free trade in automobiles and their parts in the Mercosur area and to create the basis for an integrated and competitive regional industry. The restrictions on trade in automotive products are to be faded out by 2006. The regime imposes a common external tariff of 35 percent; establishes rules on the import of vehicles and their parts as well as on environmental protection and safety standards; and puts into place a transition mechanism from the national regime to the common regime, including harmonization of the national protection systems. The sugar sector is also excluded from the common external tariff and the zero internal tariff. National tariff regimes on the import of sugar from inside or outside Mercosur are applied, and tariffs applied to imports from other Mercosur countries cannot exceed the tariffs applied to third parties.

Although there are no specific rules regarding the textile sector in intra-Mercosur transactions, textile imports from nonmember countries are exempt from the common external tariff until 2006. A Technical Textile Committee has been created to study the need for a common trade policy on textiles. The results of the study and committee recommendations are to be presented to the Mercosur Trade Commission by June 2006. Mercosur's accords are bound by the resolutions on textiles adopted by the World Trade Organization (WTO).

Rules governing the investment sector are established in the Colonia Protocol for the Promotion and Protection of the Reciprocal Investments in Mercosur, signed in 1994. Under the Colonia Protocol, the member countries agree to promote each other's investments and to give home-country treatment to all investments originating in a member country. The protocol allows for countries to have temporary

exceptions in some sectors. Argentina has exceptions in areas such as airlines, nuclear plants, insurance, and fisheries; Brazil in telecommunications, insurance, construction, and financial intermediation; Paraguay in airlines, electricity, water, phone companies, and oil; and Uruguay in oil, electricity, telecommunications, and mines.

Given that the Treaty of Asunción offers preferential treatment to goods originating in member countries, the treaty enumerates a set of criteria for determining a product's country of origin. These "rules of origin" are stated in Annex II of the treaty. There are three main criteria that are used to determine whether a product is considered to have originated in a Mercosur country: (1) The good's production process uses exclusively materials originating from the Mercosur area; (2) Mercosur accounts for more than 60 percent of the value added to the product (this rules out products that are only assembled or packaged in a Mercosur country); (3) the good is produced with foreign parts but is transformed in a Mercosur country to the extent that its category under the Mercosur Customs Product Classification changes. Goods originating in a Mercosur country are identified by a certification of origin that is attached to their export documentation.

The treaty also establishes specific rules on internal free trade zones (that is, areas within a country that operate under special tariff and tax regimes). Mercosur countries have the right to establish free trade zones, but products originating in such zones are subject to the common external tariff. The member countries agreed that the special customs areas of Tierra de Fuego and Manaos would be preserved until 2013.

Two measures in the treaty are designed to protect domestic industries against unfair competition from other member countries: a set of safeguard clauses and a dispute-settlement procedure. Countries may levy safeguard measures on products from other member countries that benefit from the Mercosur agreement and that represent a danger for their domestic industries, particularly if imports of the product increase sharply in a short period of time. The Common Market Group, upon request of the affected country, holds consultations on whether measures should be taken and on the nature of these measures. Safeguard clauses have been extended until 2006.

Disputes between member states are subject to dispute-settlement procedures laid down in the Brasilia Protocol and modified in the Olivos Protocol. Countries are encouraged to solve their disputes through direct negotiations, and they are required to inform the CMG of the state of the negotiations through the Administrative Secretariat. If the dispute is not resolved in fifteen days, it is taken to the CMG. Over a period of thirty days, the CMG reviews the petition and formulates a recommendation. If the countries do not agree with the recommendation, they can request the intervention of an arbitration committee. The committee is composed of three arbitrators selected from a previously specified list (one from each country involved in the dispute and a third selected at random). The arbitration committee makes a decision based on majority vote in sixty to ninety days. Countries may appeal the committee decision to a Permanent Committee of Revisions within fifteen days of the ruling. The appeal is limited to the legal interpretations on which the ruling was based.

The Treaty of Asunción is essentially an economic treaty and does not mention explicitly social issues, except to state that economic development should occur within a framework of "social justice" in order to improve the standards of living of the population. Nevertheless, the member countries have agreed to collaborate in the areas of employment, education, and the environment. With respect to employment, one of Mercosur's objectives is the achievement of free movement of labor once the status of common market is reached. A Working Group on Employment was designed to study labor-market integration. The harmonization of labor policies among member countries is a difficult issue, given their differ-

ent degrees of economic development and labor regulations. In 1992, a Plan for the Sector of Education was approved by the members of Mercosur. Several working groups were created to study cooperation in areas such as higher education, especially in technology-related fields and information systems. The main agreement related to education is the Protocol of Integration in Education and the Recognition of Studies, Degrees and Certificates, signed in August 1994 in Buenos Aires. Under this agreement, university degrees obtained in one Mercosur country may be recognized in any other country of Mercosur. Regarding environmental issues, Mercosur established a working group to set objectives on environmental policy. The main recommendations of the group relate to the harmonization of environmental policies, sustainable development in the use of renewable natural resources, reduction of pollutants in production processes, and the creation of common environmental criteria.

External Relations of the Members

The Protocol of Ouro Preto gave Mercosur the status of a legal entity under international law. As such, it can negotiate as a bloc with entities of other countries and with international bodies. Mercosur has initiated bilateral agreements with various blocs as well as with individual countries.

Chile and Bolivia have signed agreements to be associate members of Mercosur, with the option of fully joining the common market. Chile signed a trade agreement with Mercosur in June 1996 in Portero de Funes, Argentina, under the legal framework of ALADI. The agreement calls for cooperation and integration in the economic, scientific, and technological arenas as well as the promotion of bilateral investments in order to achieve a free trade area in ten years. A trade liberalization program was established, with gradual and automatic reductions in tariffs. Chile has not joined the customs union, since it is already a more open country than the Mercosur bloc: Chile's unique tariff on imports of 11 percent is lower than the common external tariff applied by Mercosur. In December 1995, Mercosur and Bolivia signed the Agreement of Economic Complementation in Punta del Este, Uruguay, with the objective of preparing for an agreement to establish a free trade area in ten years. The agreement was ratified in February 1997 under the ALADI legal framework. The purpose of the agreement was to intensify economic and trade relations between the parties, to harmonize legislation, to promote and protect investment, and to establish common projects in transportation and communications.

Since its creation, Mercosur has enjoyed good relations with the European Union. In 1992, Mercosur and the European Union signed the Agreement for Interregional Cooperation between the EU and Mercosur with the objective of developing a project of cooperation in technical issues related to the establishment of a common market. Negotiations progressed from technical assistance to commercial matters, and in Madrid in December 1995, both blocs signed the Economic and Trade Cooperation Agreement with the objective of strengthening relations and preparing the way to create an interregional association. The agreement covers political and institutional relations, trade and cooperation on integration issues, and other fields of mutual interest. The EU exports capital goods, automobiles, and other advanced technological products to Mercosur, and imports mainly agricultural products and foodstuffs from Mercosur. Indeed, agricultural products account for half of the Mercosur-EU trade. A large share of Mercosur's exports to the EU are duty free. Furthermore, the EU has an interest in the Mercosur area, with high levels of foreign direct investment, especially in Argentina.

Mercosur has established relations as well with other blocs in North and South America. Relations with the United States started with the Rose Garden Treaty, also known as "4+1,"

signed in June 1991 in the framework of the Initiative for the Americas. The agreement states the intentions of both parties to advance to freer trade and to promote and facilitate reciprocal investments. Mercosur and the United States also express in the agreement their willingness to negotiate on liberalization policies and on the protection of intellectual property rights. The agreement established the Consultative Council on Commerce and Investments to oversee progress in the negotiations. More recently, Mercosur has initiated external relations with Canada. Mercosur and Canada signed an Act of Understanding in June 1998 in Buenos Aires, Argentina, with the objective of deepening their relationship in terms of investment and trade. A Consulting Group of Cooperation on Commerce and Investment was created to set up a plan of action to consider the main areas of interest of each group. Mercosur has also initiated bilateral relations with Mexico.

Since 1998, Mercosur has promoted relations with other trade blocs in Latin America. In April 1998, Mercosur established "frame agreements" with the Andean Community and the Central American Common Market (CACM). The frame agreement with the Andean Community has the objective of creating a free trade area between the regions in order to promote economic development. Both blocs agreed on a schedule for further meetings to specify the terms of the agreement. The Frame Agreement of Trade and Investment signed with the CACM aims at stronger relations through trade, investment, and technological transfer in order to promote and protect investment.

Mercosur's efforts to establish relations have reached other areas of the globe as well. In December 2000, at Florianopolis, Brazil, Mercosur and South Africa signed a frame agreement with the objective of strengthening their relationship, promoting trade, and laying the groundwork for the creation of a free trade area. A negotiating committee was set up to establish a working schedule for the negotiations.Mercosur is currently negotiating bilateral trade agreements with Japan and Venezuela, and it plans to negotiate as a bloc in the creation of the Free Trade Area of the Americas (FTAA), expected to begin by December 2005.

Mercosur in Numbers

Mercosur is the fourth largest economic bloc in the world, with a gross domestic product (GDP) in 1999 of $11.5 billion. The average GDP per capita in the bloc for 1999 was about $5,000 (one-fifth that of the United States). Mercosur includes four countries that are diverse in terms of their size and level of development. The biggest country in Mercosur is Brazil, with an area of 8,551,965 square kilometers (5,302,218 square miles) and a population of 174.4 million people. Brazil's GDP per capita in 1999 was $4,524. Brazil is rich in natural resources and has well-developed manufacturing and service sectors that produce 29 percent and 62 percent of GDP, respectively. Its main industries include textiles, footwear, machinery and equipment, and automobiles. The second country in terms of size is Argentina, with an area of 2,776,890 square kilometers (172,671 square miles) and a population of 37.4 million people. GDP per capita in Argentina for 1999 was $7,709. Argentina is also rich in natural resources and has very fertile land. Its main industries include food processing, chemicals, and automobiles, and its main exports are agricultural products, fuels, and automobiles. The industrial sector represents about 32 percent of GDP and the service sector 62 percent.

Paraguay's area is 406,750 square kilometers (252,185 square miles) and the country has a population of 5.7 million people. With a GDP per capita in 1999 of $1,505, Paraguay is the poorest country in Mercosur. Its economy is characterized by a large agricultural sector that mainly operates at a subsistence level (the agricultural sector produces only 28 percent of

GDP but employs 45 percent of the population). The informal sector, which includes all economic activities that are not officially regulated and which operates outside the market system, is also very important in Paraguay. Paraguay's main imports are machinery and equipment, and it exports electricity and agricultural products. Uruguay, with an area of 176,220 square kilometers (109,256 square miles) and a population of 3.36 million people, is the smallest country in the region. Its GDP per capita in 1999 was $6,102. Uruguay has a highly efficient agricultural sector, which accounts for about 10 percent of GDP. The country's main exports are primary goods and manufactures derived from primary goods. Its imports include metal products and machinery and equipment.

Mercosur's performance as a trading bloc is described by its trade flows. The geographic distribution of Mercosur exports in 2002 reveals the importance of trade within the bloc: Mercosur countries received 24 percent of Mercosur exports. European Union countries received 23 percent, East Asia 15 percent, and the United States 14 percent. The main sources of Mercosur imports are the EU, with 26 percent, and the United States, with 22 percent. The main sectors exported by Mercosur are food and beverages (representing 39 percent of total exports), manufacturing goods not based on natural resources (37 percent), and manufactured products based on mining and other natural resources (20 percent). Mercosur's foreign direct investment goes mainly to the automotive sector (36 percent), followed by commerce and construction (12 percent) and chemistry and pharmaceuticals (11 percent).

Mercosur was a great success in its early stages. Intra-Mercosur trade went from 9 percent in 1990, prior to the Treaty of Asunción, to 25 percent in 1997. But during 1999, Mercosur seemed to be in trouble, with intra-Mercosur trade reduced to 20 percent. A devaluation of Brazil's currency in 1999 reduced Argentina's competitiveness in the Brazilian market by about 40 percent, threatening a tariff war between Argentina and Brazil. Furthermore, incentives to strike bilateral deals with other countries undermined the customs union. Because the organization does not have a centralized enforcement institution, it is hard to enforce the customs union. Brazil has so far blocked attempts to create a permanent dispute-settlement tribunal that could enforce the rules agreed upon in the Mercosur framework. Negotiations are still in progress to set up this type of organization. Mercosur is currently pursuing free trade agreements with the EU, India, and China.

Claustre Bajona

See Also Economic Integration; Andean Community; Latin American Free Trade Association (LAFTA)

References

"Another Blow to Mercosur." 2001. *The Economist,* March 29.

Central Intelligence Agency. 2001. *The World Factbook 2001,* http://www.odci.gov/cia/publications/factbook.

Coffey, Peter. 1988. *Latin America–MERCOSUR.* Boston: Kluwer Academic Publishers.

Embassy of Uruguay, Washington, DC. *MERCOSUR,* http://embassy.org/uruguay/econ/mercosur.

Foreign Trade Information System. *Trade Agreements,* http://www.sice.oas.org/TRADEE.ASP#MERCOSUR/MERCOSUL.

Inter-American Development Bank, Department of Integration and Regional Programs, http://www.iadb.org/intal/tratados/mercosur.htm.

International Development Research Center. *MERCOSUR,* http://www.idrc.ca/lacro/investigacion/mercosur2.html#Trade and Investment Statistical Information.

Mercosur.org, http://www.mercosur.org.

Mercosur.org. *Boletín de Indicadores Macroeconómicos del Mercosur,* http://www.mercosur.org.uy/espanol/sinf/varios/INDICEMAC.HTM#I_Sector_Real.

Mercosur.com. Business Information Community, http://www.mercosur.com.

Roett, Riordan. 1999. *MERCOSUR: Regional Integration, World Markets.* Boulder: Lynne Rienner.

Common Market for Eastern and Southern Africa (COMESA)

The Common Market for Eastern and Southern Africa (COMESA) was established in 1993 to replace a Preferential Trade Area (PTA) set up in December 1981. The original PTA agreement included eight countries and covered a range of measures to promote a greater degree of free trade among members and cooperation in industry, transport, and communication. COMESA, now with twenty member states, deals with a comprehensive slate of trade and economic issues and policies in the region. The member states are Angola, Burundi, Comoros, Democratic Republic of the Congo, Djibouti, Egypt, Eritrea, Ethiopia, Kenya, Madagascar, Malawi, Mauritius, Namibia, Rwanda, Seychelles, Sudan, Swaziland, Uganda, Zambia, and Zimbabwe.

History of African Integration

Even before the independence of African states, many African intellectuals called for an African League. Conferences held for that purpose began in 1900 with the London Conference, followed by the Paris Conference in 1919, the Brussels Conference in 1921, and the New York Conference in 1927. The Manchester Conference in 1945 marked a turning point in African calls for unity because of the fact that it was well attended and the conference was instrumental in pushing for a unified Africa. As African nations began to gain their independence, African leaders came to believe that integration would enable states that were still occupied to gain their independence and provide the best means for independent states to maintain their newly gained freedom.

The first formal initiative for African integration was presented by Komi Nokoroma on March 6, 1957, who called for an African Conference on the issue. This conference was held April 15–24, 1958, with representatives from all of the African independent states in attendance, including Libya, Sudan, Tunisia, Morocco, Ethiopia, Liberia, Ghana, and Egypt. Other initiatives that aimed at African integration included the Mali Federation in 1959 and the Currency Union of Western Africa in 1962.

The African states have formed four organizations for regional integration since that time. The first was the Economic Community for Western African States, formed with fifteen member states in 1975. The second was the Southern African Development Coordination Conference (SADCC), established in 1980 by the states of southern Africa. In 1993, the SADCC was replaced by the Southern African Development Community (SADC), which constitutes the third regional organization. The fourth organization, the Maghareb Union, was established in 1984 to pursue economic integration among its member states in northern Africa: Morocco, Mauritania, Algeria, Tunisia, and Libya. Nevertheless, ideological debates presented obstacles to reaching specific objectives for economic integration.

In 1991, the African states signed the Declaration of the Economic African Community. This declaration aimed at a number of objectives, mainly economic integration and currency union, to take place in six stages over thirty-four years. Several agencies and organizations were established to implement the declaration's articles and objectives. These included a Ministerial Council, an African Parliament, a Social Economic Committee, a General Secretariat, and a Justice Court. The member states faced obstacles, however, in achieving the wide range of activities that the declaration set forth. COMESA represented an attempt by the member states to bridge the gap between the declaration's ambitious articles and objectives and the real situation of the African states.

In November 1993, PTA countries signed a treaty transforming PTA into COMESA. COMESA started with the ten member states that ratified the treaty: Burundi, Ethiopia, Kenya, Madagascar, Malawi, Mauritius, Rwanda, Somalia, Tanzania, and Zambia. At an inaugural summit held in Lilongwe, the capital city of Malawi, in December 1994, two additional countries, Angola and Congo, joined COMESA. The last eight member states joined in 2000 and as of 2003, there were twenty member states.

In February 2000, COMESA held a conference in Cairo, Egypt. A new confidence in the common market's future was apparent. With the eight new member states, the COMESA area stretched from the Mediterranean in northern Africa to Madagascar in the Indian Ocean. The organization was preparing to implement its free trade area by October 31, 2000. At the same time it faced formidable problems, however. Much of the region remained desperately poor and underdeveloped, and a number of member states—Mozambique, Malawi, and Tanzania, for example—suffered from a high rate of illiteracy.

Objectives of COMESA

The Treaty of COMESA mentioned numerous sectors and activities. Fulfillment of the entire COMESA mandate is regarded as a long-term objective. In the effort to become more effective as an institution, COMESA has defined its strategic focus within its mandate, over the next three to five years, as being promotion of regional integration through trade development and investment. An important objective in the pursuit of this strategy is to enable member states to make the adjustments necessary to become part of the global economy within the framework of the World Trade Organization (WTO) regulations and other international agreements.

COMESA encourages cooperation in the development of natural and human resources for the good of all member states and their peoples. It is hoped that it will become a large economic and trading unit capable of overcoming some of the barriers faced by individual member states. Leaders hoped to remove all internal trade tariffs by the year 2000 in order to implement a free trade area; to facilitate the removal of structural and institutional weaknesses in member states to enable them to attain collective and sustained development; to facilitate trade liberalization and customs cooperation, including the introduction of a unified computerized customs network across the region; to improve the administration of transportation and communications to ease the movement of goods, services, and people across national borders in COMESA countries; to create an enabling environment and legal framework that would encourage the growth of the private sector; to establish a secure investment environment; to adopt common sets of standards on economic issues and achieve the harmonization of macroeconomic and monetary policies throughout the region, free movement of capital and investment, a payments union based on the COMESA Clearing House, and a monetary union with a common currency; and to adopt common visa arrangements, including the right of establishment, leading eventually to the free movement of bona fide persons.

COMESA Institutions

COMESA is made up of eight institutions: (1) the Authority of Heads of State Government, the supreme policy organ of COMESA, responsible for the executive functions of the common market and the achievement of its aims and objectives; (2) the Council of Ministers, which determines COMESA programs and activities and monitors and reviews financial and administrative management of the organization; (3) the Committee of Governments of the Central Bank, which manages the COMESA Clearing House and ensures implementation of the monetary and financial cooperation programs; (4) the Intergovernmental Committee, composed of permanent secretaries from the member states; (5) technical committees, responsible for various economic sectors and for administrative and budgetary matters; (6) the Secretariat, headed by a secretary general, which provides technical support and advisory services to the member states in the implementation of the treaty; (7) the Consultative Committee of the Business Community and other Interest Groups, to provide a link and facilitate dialogue between the business community and other interest groups and organs of the common market; and (8) a Court of Justice, which ensures the proper interpretation and application of the provisions of the treaty and adjudicates disputes that arise among the member states regarding these interpretations and applications. The Court of Justice was established by the COMESA Treaty and became fully operational in 1998.

In addition, a number of institutions have been established for promoting subregional cooperation and development, including the COMESA Trade and Development Bank, located in Nairobi, Kenya; the COMESA Clearing House, in Harare, Zimbabwe; the COMESA Trade Association of Commercial Banks, also in Harare; the COMESA Leather Institute, located in Ethiopia; the COMESA Re-Insurance Company, in Nairobi, which provides reinsurance within the region; the COMESA Metallurgical Industries Association; the Eastern and Southern African Business Association; the Federation of National Association of Women in Business in COMESA; and the Pharmaceutical Manufacturers of Eastern and Southern Africa. Finally, other bodies exist to promote cross-border initiatives, form common industrial policies, and pursue a monetary harmonization program.

Achievements of COMESA

COMESA has made good progress in several areas, including the following: (1) elimination of nontariff barriers (the classic nontariff barriers, such as quantitative restrictions, licensing, import permits, and restrictive foreign exchange controls, have been largely eliminated); removal of tariff barriers (as of April 1, 1999, two countries had achieved a 90 percent tariff reduction, eight countries had reached an 80 percent tariff reduction, one country had surpassed a 70 percent reduction, and three countries had met a 60 percent reduction); the adoption of a single COMESA Customs Document (COMESA-CD) to replace the previous multiplicity of documents (up to thirty-two in some countries) covering clearance of customs warehousing, reexport, and transit purposes; incorporation of efficient customs management systems to facilitate data and revenue collection and establish the basis for a harmonized tariff, including the Automated System of Customs Data, installed in twelve countries, and Eurotrace, in nineteen; simplification of rules of origin, with more scope for import content, by the adoption of a 35 percent local value-added criterion (these rules are undergoing further changes to take developments at the WTO into account, as a result of a study financed by the U.S. Agency for International Development); implementation of a Customs Bond Guarantee Scheme to facilitate transit traffic and reduce the cost of financing transit goods; and establishment of a Trade Information Network, which now has some forty-seven computerized focal points set up in twenty member states to provide information on export and import opportunities available in COMESA countries, including trade flow analyses, company registers, comparative COMESA tariffs, nontariff barriers, and macroeconomic profiles of member states. In addition, COMESA has set up its own Web site (http://www.comesa.int) to provide information to business interests from within and outside of the COMESA region.

COMESA Member States

The total area of the twenty COMESA member states is 12.88 million square kilometers (7,985,600 square miles), and the total population of these states reached 385 million in the year 1999. COMESA's membership exhibits great political, geographical, and linguistic diversity as well as differences in natural resources and industrial strengths. These differences maximize the benefits to be gained by COMESA countries through economic integration and cultural and social exchanges.

Angola is located in southern Africa with 1,246,700 square kilometers (481,353 square miles) of total area and 10,145,267 in population. Its main natural resources are petroleum, diamonds, iron ore, and phosphates. The official language is Portuguese, although some people speak Bantu and other African languages, and the country is governed by a transitional government, nominally a multiparty democracy with a strong presidential system.

Burundi, located in central Africa with 27,830 square kilometers (10,745 square miles) of total area and 6,054,714 in population, contains nickel, uranium, and rare earth oxides. The main industries are light consumer goods. The official languages are Kirundi and French, and the government is a republic.

Comoros is located in southern Africa with 2,170 square kilometers (838 square miles) and 578,400 in population. The country's main industries are textiles, food processing, and chemicals. The official language is Arabic, and some people speak French. Comoros is a republic.

Democratic Republic of the Congo, located in central Africa, has 2,345,410 square kilometers (905,568 square miles) of total area and 51,964,999 in population. Its main natural resources are cobalt, copper, and cadmium. The main industries are mining, mineral processing, and consumer products, and the official languages are French and Lingala.

Djibouti, in eastern Africa, has 22,000 square kilometers (8,494 square miles) of total area and 451,442 in population. Its main natural resource is its geothermal areas. Industries are limited to a few small-scale enterprises. The official language is Arabic, though many people speak French. Djibouti is a republic.

Egypt, located at northern Africa, covers 1,001,450 square kilometers (386,662 square miles) and has a population of 68,359,979. Egypt's main natural resources are petroleum and natural gas. Its predominant industries are textiles, food processing, tourism, and chemicals. The official language is Arabic. Egypt is a republic.

Eritrea, located in eastern Africa, with 117,600 square kilometers (45,406 square miles) of total area and 4,135,933 in population, contains gold, potash, and zinc. The main industries are food processing, beverages, and clothing and textiles. The official language is Afar, with a minority speaking Amharic. Eritrea has a transitional government.

Ethiopia, located in eastern Africa, covers 1,104,303 square kilometers (426,372 square miles) and has a population of 64,117,452. Its main natural resources are gold, platinum, and copper. The official language is Amharic, though some people speak Gallinya or Tigrinya. Ethiopia is a federal republic.

Kenya, in eastern Africa, has 582,650 square kilometers (224,962 square miles) of total area and 30,399,770 people. Kenya's main natural resources are gold, limestone, and soda ash. Its industries are plastics, furniture, batteries, and textiles. The main languages are English and Swahili. Kenya is a republic.

Madagascar, located off the coast of southeastern Africa with 587,040 square kilometers (226,657 square miles) of total area and 15,506,472 in population, contains graphite, chromites, and coal. The official language is Malagasy, and some people speak French. Madagascar is a republic.

Malawi, in southeastern Africa, covers a total area of 118,480 square kilometers (45,745 square miles) and has a population of 10,385,849. Malawi's main natural resources are limestone and arable land. Its main industries are tobacco, tea, and sugar. The official languages are Chichewa and English. Malawi is a multiparty democracy.

Mauritius, an island east of Madagascar off the southeastern coast of Africa, with 1,860 square kilometers (790 square miles) of total area and 1,179,368 in population, offers arable land and good locations for fishing. The main industries are food processing and textiles. The official language is Creole, but some people speak English. Mauritius is a republic.

Namibia, in southern Africa with 824,292 square kilometers (318,260 square miles) of total area and 1,771,327 in population, contains diamonds and copper. The top industries are meat packing, fish processing, and dairy products. Some people speak English, but African languages are also common. Namibia is a republic.

Rwanda, in central Africa with 26,338 square kilometers (10,169 square miles) of total area and 7,229,129 in population, has natural resources of gold and cassiterite. Its main industries are cement, agricultural products, and small-scale beverages. The official language is Kinyarwanda; French and English are also official languages. Rwanda is a republic.

The Seychelles are a chain of islands located off the east coast of Africa north of Madagascar with 455 square kilometers (176 square miles) of total area and 79,326 in population. The main natural resources are fish, copra, and trees, and the main industries are fishing, tourism, and processing of coconuts and vanilla. The official languages are English and French. The country is a republic.

Sudan, located in northern Africa with 2,505,810 square kilometers (967,499 square miles) of total area and 35,079,814 in population, offers petroleum and natural gas. Its main industries include textiles, food processing, and chemicals. The official language is Arabic, but Nubian and English are also spoken. The government is a transitional one.

Swaziland, in southeastern Africa, covers 41,290 square kilometers (6,704 square miles) and has a population of 7,262,372. Swaziland's main natural resources are hydropower potential and timber. The main industries are machinery, chemicals, watches, textiles, and precision instruments. The official language is French, though some people speak German and Italian. Swaziland's political system is a monarchy.

Uganda, located in eastern Africa with 236,040 square kilometers (91,136 square miles) of total area and 23,317,560 in population, contains copper and cobalt. The official language is English, and some people speak Luganda. Uganda is a republic.

Zambia, located in southern Africa with 752,614 square kilometers (290,586 square miles) of total area and 9,582,418 in population, offers copper, cobalt, and zinc. The main industries are copper mining and processing and also construction. The official language is English, though some people speak Bemba and other African languages. It is a republic.

Zimbabwe, in southern Africa, covers 390,580 square kilometers (150,830 square miles) and has a population of 11,342,521. Its main natural resources are coal and chromium ore, and its top industries are mining, steel, and wood products. The official language is English; some people speak Shona and other African languages. Zimbabwe is a republic.

Nilly Kamal El-Amir

See Also Economic Integration; East African Community (EAC); Economic Community of Central African States (CEEAC); Southern African Development Community (SADC); Franc Zone

References

Abdel-Rahman, Hamdy. 2001. "Africa and US Policy: From Isolation to Partnership." *International Politics Journal,* no. 144 (April): 192–204.

Ali, Khaled. 2001. "New Regionalism in Africa." *International Politics Journal,* no. 144 (April): 185–191.

Arnold, Guy. 2001. *A Guide to African Political and Economic Development.* London: Fitzrog Dearborn.

Auda, Abdel-Malek. 2002. "The Issues of Arab-African Relations." *International Politics Journal,* no. 148 (April): 30–34.

Bibers, Samia. 2001. "Sert's Summit and the Declaration of the African Union." *International Politics Journal,* no. 144 (April): 205–209.

Selim, Mohammad. 2002. *The Development of International Politics in the Nineteenth and Twentieth Centuries.* Cairo: Dar Al-Fajir Al-Jadid.

Shalabi, Ibrahim. 1993. *International Organization.* Beirut: Dar El-Gamaa.

Commonwealth of Independent States (CIS)

On December 8, 1991, near Minsk, Belarus, the Commonwealth of Independent States (CIS) was agreed upon by the leaders of Russia, Ukraine, and Belarus. On December 13, the Central Asian Republics of Kazakhstan, Kyrgyzstan, Tajikistan, Turkmenistan, and Uzbekistan expressed their desire to be a part of the new organization in a joint statement. By December 21, the Commonwealth grew to eleven member countries: Armenia, Azerbaijan, Belarus, Kazakhstan, Kyrgyzstan, Moldova, Russia, Tajikistan, Turkmenistan, Ukraine, and Uzbekistan. Two years later, Uzbekistan's parliament approved the agreement and Georgia joined as well. By this time, all of the former republics of the Soviet Union except for the Western-supported Baltic states of Estonia, Latvia, and Lithuania had become part of the CIS.

As the USSR began to crumble, the Commonwealth of Independent States agreement represented an effort to preserve economic, military, and foreign ties between the former republics of the USSR. Attempting to stay away from the tsarist and Soviet past, St. Petersburg and Moscow were not chosen as the capital of the new Commonwealth. Instead, the leadership chose the Belorussian city of Minsk.

The Fall of the Soviet Union

After many months of uncertainty, the Commonwealth agreement represented a voluntary cohesion and a possibility for mutually beneficial cooperation for the former Soviet republics. The events leading up to the agreement began with the selection of Mikhail Gorbachev as the leader of the Soviet Communist Party and the USSR in 1985.

Gorbachev, a fifty-four-year-old agricultural specialist from southern Stavropol, was frustrated with the slow pace of change and reform within the USSR. Beginning in 1986, he moved in a new reform-oriented direction labeled as "radical" by Communist hard-liners. He advocated *glasnost* (openness) in the media and culture and *perestroika* (restructuring) in the government and economy, hoping to spark reform while maintaining the Communist Party's domination of power and the socialistic features of the Soviet system.

Gorbachev's policies led to the legalization of entrepreneurship and cooperative small businesses, but the public sector remained overwhelmingly dominant and resisted attempts at reform. This lack of change in the public sector resulted in reform that was far from comprehensive and very disruptive. Consequently, there was a further slowdown in economic growth, and shortages of goods led to frequent panics and protests. Gorbachev's new policies resulted in worsened economic turmoil, building up to a contraction of the USSR's gross national product (GNP) in 1990.

The perestroika policies enabled a wide range of government reform to take place, and there was a push for competitive elections with multiple-candidate ballots throughout the early months of 1987. At a national conference of the Communist Party, Gorbachev's plan for government restructuring was approved, promoting the freedoms of expression, assembly, and organization. Soon after, the constitution of the USSR was amended to replace the Supreme Soviet legislative body with the Congress of People's Deputies, a new legislative body with 2,250 members. In the spring of 1989, elections were held across the USSR, and though the majority of the seats were occupied by Communist Party members, many dissidents were able to obtain seats as well.

As a result of his reforms, Gorbachev alienated himself from both sides of the political spectrum. Communist Party hard-liners and conservatives believed that he was a traitor to the Party. The liberals, led by Boris Yeltsin, a former member of the Politburo whom Gorbachev had passed over for leadership, attacked his actions for not instituting even more drastic reform. By 1990, opposition to Gorbachev had arisen in every republic within the USSR. Reacting to criticism, the Soviet Parliament and the Communist Party allowed non-Communist parties to participate in each republic's elections. In a surprising turn of events, Yeltsin's Democratic Russia Party won a narrow advantage in the Russian republic's parliamentary elections in March 1990. The success of the Democratic Russia movement continued, and on June 12, 1991, Yeltsin was elected to the presidency of Russia, winning over a field of five candidates.

The other Soviet republics began to benefit from the uncertainty in Gorbachev's administration and were now able to stand up to Moscow. The USSR no longer had the will or the power to prevent political transformations within its republics. Communist governments throughout the Soviet sphere of influence began to fall. The tearing down of the Berlin Wall was one of the most dramatic examples of this new reality. Across the USSR, different republics' legislatures, including Russia's legislature, passed resolutions asserting their sovereignty. Lithuania and Georgia were extreme cases; their legislatures asserted complete independence from the USSR.

For over a year, Gorbachev dwelled on whether to use oppressive or conciliatory measures to deal with the republics. In the spring of 1991, he selected the course of reconciliation and offered to renegotiate the original Union Treaty of 1922 that had created the USSR. In August 1991, a new draft Union Treaty had been agreed upon, and seven republics were prepared to sign the agreement on August 20, 1991. However, the signing never happened owing to a Communist hard-liner coup attempt on August 19, 1991, while Gorbachev was vacationing in the Crimea. The coup failed, the military withdrew its tanks from Moscow, and Gorbachev was completely discredited by the situation. Boris Yeltsin, who had rallied pro-democracy supporters in front of the Russian Parliament, was viewed as a hero of change. These events led to the resignation of Gorbachev as the general secretary of the Communist Party of the Soviet Union on August 24, 1991. By November 1991, Yeltsin had dissolved the Communist Party within Russia.

Between August 20 and 31, Estonia, Latvia, Ukraine, Belarus, Moldova, Kyrgyzstan, Uzbekistan, and Azerbaijan joined Lithuania and Georgia in declaring their independence from the USSR. By October, Tajikistan, Armenia, and Turkmenistan had also separated from the USSR, officially leaving only Russia and Kazakhstan in the union.

A few months later, in December, the Commonwealth of Independent States agreement was signed. On December 26, 1991, the powerless Soviet parliament passed its final resolution officially ending the Soviet Union. The purposes, functions, and structure of the new organization are outlined within the Charter of the CIS.

The Goals and Functions of the CIS

The CIS Charter outlines a wide range of purposes and principles in its first section and articles. It emphasizes the independence and equality of each member state of the CIS. It embraces cooperation between the independent states, specifically in economic, political, environmental, humanitarian, and cultural areas. The charter also emphasizes the need for action on certain issues, calling for reductions in the military, the elimination of nuclear bombs and other weapons of mass destruction, and the promotion of human rights. All future agreements made under the auspices of the CIS must conform to these principles.

The main functions of the organization outlined in the charter are collective defense; conflict prevention and resolution; economic, social, and legal cooperation; and finance. The collective defense function protects international security, helps to achieve disarmament goals, and promotes cooperation and coordination among states. To attain this type of military relationship, the charter calls on member states to enact methods of consultation and plans for mutual defense in accordance with Article 51 of the United Nations Charter.

The conflict prevention and the peaceful resolution of dispute function of the CIS require all member states to undertake every possible diplomatic means for the resolution of a dispute. Member states must not act in a way that damages another state and must move toward peaceful coexistence. If two states wish to do so, they may submit their dispute to arbitration by the CIS Council of Heads of States, a committee made up of the leaders of each member state. Also, at any time the Council of Heads of States has the authority to recommend a solution to any given dispute among member states that threatens the organization.

Economic, social, and legal cooperation is stressed in the charter as one of the main goals of the CIS. The charter calls for the eventual establishment of a free trade area, incorporating all member states, based upon a common market economy. Socially, the development of joint programs is crucial to the integration of the CIS. The sharing of transportation and communications expertise and technology, as well as energy resources assistance, are listed in the charter in order to achieve higher levels of interdependence and cooperation. Legally, it highlights the need for the respect of intellectual property and respect for common environmental standards. Also, member states are directed to eliminate legal contradictions that exist from one member state to another, specifically relating to various government regulations.

The last major function applies to financing the organization. The CIS's expenditures are distributed among the participating members under the authority of the Council of Heads of States. The council is also responsible for replying to questions concerning the financial and administrative activities of the CIS. Also, member states are expected to individually pay the expenditures of their representatives and their assistants while attending to their duties at the CIS.

The Organs of the CIS

The aforementioned Council of Heads of States is just one body within the CIS. There are many other structures, or committees, which are charged with fulfilling the purposes and functions set forth by the charter. Scheduled to meet twice a year, the Council of Heads of States is the supreme authority within the CIS and is able to address principal issues. The Council of Heads of Governments, scheduled to meet four times a year, is the coordinating body directly below the Council of Heads of States in the line of authority. This council primarily deals with the promotion of cooperation on economic and social matters. On both councils, member states are represented equally and actions are decided by general consent. The councils have the authority to establish other permanent or temporary bodies to address CIS issues. Joint sessions of the two bodies may be conducted, and the councils reside permanently in the city of Minsk.

The Inter-Parliamentary Assembly is another body set forth under the CIS Charter that is made up of delegations from each member state. This assembly, established in March 1995, is a consultative body that deals with cooperation issues and develops proposals to better achieve the goals of the CIS to bring before the councils of higher authority.

The Economic Court is a judicial body beneath the two top councils. Its main purpose is to ensure the attainment of previous economic commitments under the CIS framework. It deals with interstate economic issues and is given the power to interpret the economic provisions of CIS agreements.

The Council of Foreign Ministers works to ensure cooperation between CIS member states on foreign policies of mutual interest. This council acts primarily on orders from the Council of Heads of States and the Council of Heads of Governments.

The Council of Defense Ministers is responsible for coordinating CIS member states' military policies. To attain this goal, it prepares and holds meetings often to organize the activities of interstate military observers. Also, the council has the authority to plan for the creation of collective forces for peacekeeping operations. There is a Council of Collective Security as well, created under the Agreement on Collective Security of May 15, 1992, that works with the Council of Defense Ministers to deal with security issues. Along with this council, a Council of Commanders-in-Chief of Frontier Troops, a subsidiary body of the Council of Heads of States, is responsible for the coordination of troops guarding the frontiers of the CIS and its member states.

In the area of economic policy, the Economic Council is the main executive body. This council works to implement the economic decisions of the Council of Heads of States and the Council of Heads of Governments. Its primary goal is to work toward the creation of a CIS free trade zone, as well as to work on minor issues of economic cooperation. This council is made up of the deputy heads of government from each member state.

The primary administrative body of the CIS is the Executive Committee. It organizes the meetings and activities of all the major bodies of the CIS and also pursues an economic platform. Along with the Economic Council, the Executive Committee works toward the creation of a CIS free trade zone.

The major body within the CIS framework that deals with financial issues is the Interstate Bank. It organizes and implements interstate settlements between member states' central bank agencies, primarily on trade and currency issues.

The last major body of the CIS is the Interstate Statistical Committee, which was established by a decision of the Council of Heads of Governments in December 1991. It assists the statistical organizations from member states, promoting the use of similar statistical techniques throughout the Commonwealth. It also promotes information exchange among states and other international organizations and maintains a common CIS statistical database on the social and economic situations within the CIS and its member states.

The CIS since Its Establishment

Since Russian President Boris Yeltsin, Chairman Stanislav Shushkevich of Belarus, and Ukrainian President Leonid Kravchuk created the CIS on December 8, 1991, many CIS meetings and agreements have advanced the CIS along its path toward obtaining its goal of increased cooperation in many fields. Soon after the CIS's creation and following two foundational meetings, the Council of Heads of States and the Council of Heads of Governments met on February 14, 1992, to deal with the dismantling of the former USSR's military. They came to an agreement about the impermissibility of the use of force and the basic structure of CIS strategic forces. By the time of the next meeting, which took place in Kiev on March 20, 1992, the Council of Heads of States completed the formation of the CIS defense forces, the CIS United Armed Forces (UAF). Then, in a meeting at Tashkent, Uzbekistan, on May 15, 1992, the Treaty on Collective Security was signed, providing the basic collective defense program and arms reduction plan for the CIS.

By October 9, 1992, the CIS was prepared to make commitments toward economic coordination. At a summit in Bishkek, Kyrgyzstan, a joint meeting of the Council of Heads of States and the Council of Heads of Governments was held, and the issues of a single monetary system, economic coordination policies, and the free movement of citizens of CIS member states were discussed. Then, at a later meeting in Minsk, Belarus, on April 16, 1993, the issues of a single free market and the protection of human rights were debated, primarily driven by Boris Yeltsin of Russia and Nursultan Nazarbayev of Kazakhstan. At a two-day summit in Moscow on May 14 and 15, 1993, the Council of Heads of States established the Economic Union, pending approval from individual member states. The Economic Union was based upon the free movement of goods, services, labor, and capital. It also coordinated tax policies, customs, and other fiscal programs. The council delegates hoped that the Economic Union would lead to the establishment of favorable conditions for economic growth. By April 15, 1994, all CIS states agreed to the eventual creation of the free trade zone, but it was not immediately established.

Meanwhile, CIS peacekeeping operations were under way in areas of Georgia and Tajikistan. Between 1996 and 1997, the primary councils focused on the creation of newer subsidiary bodies to deal with the goals of the CIS Charter more effectively. By April 29, 1998, efforts were still in progress to improve CIS procedures. New protocols were agreed upon, and leaders pushed for increased military cooperation.

On January 25, 2000, at a summit in Moscow, Boris Yeltsin's successor, Russian President Vladimir Putin, was elected as chairman of the Council of Heads of States. His priorities were to counter international terrorism and reduce organized crime. At a two-day summit on June 20 and 21, 2000, joint efforts were agreed upon to combat extremism within the CIS, and an Anti-Terrorism Center was created. The CIS also embraced Russia's recent approval of the Nuclear Test Ban Treaty.

At a joint meeting of the councils in Minsk, Belarus, on November 30, 2000, the Anti-Terrorism Center was given its full list of responsibilities: to struggle against extremism, to establish and maintain a database of terrorists and terrorist organizations, and to facilitate combined operations by CIS member states.

Some months later, at a meeting in Minsk on May 31, 2001, the Council of Heads of Governments made steady progress on many issues, including health care, information exchange, education, the economy, and technical cooperation. Numerous important documents were signed, including one on the creation of a Coordinating Council on taxation issues made up of the tax agency directors of individual member states.

By late November 2001, preparations were under way to celebrate the tenth anniversary of the CIS. At the Jubilee Summit on November 29 and 30, 2001, meetings were held by the Council of Foreign Ministers and the Council of Heads of Governments. Sixteen major issues were discussed by the foreign ministers, and the heads of governments debated over twenty major issues. The outcome of the meetings included an action plan by the foreign ministers to increase the efficiency of the coordination of foreign political activities, and the heads of governments adopted a decision on the plans for the sixtieth anniversary of the Great Patriotic War (World War II) memorial programs and made significant progress on educational cooperation agendas. Also, there was a CIS declaration at the summit strongly in favor of antiterrorist action in Afghanistan by the United States and its allies.

At the next major meeting, on October 7, 2002, in Chisinau, Moldova, the Council of Heads of Governments, chaired by Kazakhstan's prime minister, Imangaliy Tasmagambetov, discussed an extensive agenda of twenty-five issues. Substantial agreements were made concerning energy cooperation, such as shared power supply and increased energy production effectiveness. Another agreement, detailing measures to improve interstate television and radio, was passed as well.

On the same date, a meeting of the Council of Heads of States also occurred. The council awarded Russian President Vladamir Putin an Honorary Badge of the CIS for his work to strengthen and develop the organization. There were further discussions concerning the establishment of the CIS free trade zone, and a special session of the council was proposed to deal solely with economic issues. Consequently, the Economic Council was given specific instructions to prepare for the summit. Also at the meeting, Armenia requested CIS observers for its elections in March 2003, and the request was granted.

Conclusion

Although the CIS has progressed substantially over the past decade, many problems remain. Each CIS member state is different from the others in areas such as literacy, higher education, human rights, natural resources, access to shipping, multiculturalism, and infrastructure. Some CIS states excel in a few of these areas, but none of the countries stand out in every area. Also, there are a few problems that all CIS countries face, including widespread corruption and nepotism, limited acceptance of the market economy, lack of capital, and ethnic discrimination. In spite of these problems, the CIS continues to work toward economic and social progress and prosperity into the twenty-first century.

Arthur Holst

See Also Economic Integration; Emerging Markets and Transition Economies

References

Bucknell University. "Russian History," http://www.departments.bucknell.edu/russian/history.html (cited May 2, 2003).

Charter of the Commonwealth of Independent States. "English—Unofficial Translation," http://therussiasite.org/legal/laws/CIScharter.html (cited May 1, 2003).

Commonwealth of Independent States, www.cis.minsk.by (cited May 1, 2003).

Eisenhower Institute. "Russia and the Commonwealth of Independent States," www.eisenhowerinstitute.org (cited May 2, 2003).

Global Corruption Report. 2003. "The Commonwealth of Independent States," www.globalcorruptionreport.org.

Interstate Statistical Committee of the Commonwealth of Independent States, http://www.cisstat.com (cited May 1, 2003).

Multinational Electronic Services Corp. "Commonwealth of Independent States Economic and Market Trends," http://www.mes-corp.com/W4_7f.htm (cited May 5, 2003).

"Official Russian Document," http://www.cis.minsk.by/russian/cis_doc2.htm (cited May 1, 2003).

Olcott, Martha Brill, Anders Aslund, and Sherman W. Garnett. 2000. *Getting It Wrong: Regional Cooperation and the Commonwealth of Independent States.* Washington, DC: Brookings Institution.

Radio Liberty, Inc. "CIS: Debt Another Tie Binding Commonwealth of Independent States to Russia," www.rferl.org (cited May 1, 2003).

Shoemaker, M. Wesley. 2001. *Russia and the Commonwealth of Independent States 2001.* Washington, DC: Stryker Post.

Smolansky, Bettie M., and Oles M. Smolansky, eds. 2001. *The Lost Equilibrium: International Relations in the Post-Soviet Era.* Bethlehem, PA: Lehigh University Press.

Stroev, E. S., Leonid Solomonovich Bliakhman, and Mikhail I. Krotov. 1999. *Russia and Eurasia at the Crossroads: Experience and Problems of Economic Reforms in the Commonwealth of Independent States.* New York: Springer Verlag.

Webber, Mark, and Richard Sakwa. 1999. "The Commonwealth of Independent States, 1991–1998: Stagnation and Survival." *Europe-Asia Studies* (May).

Council of Arab Economic Unity (CAEU)

On June 3, 1957, the Economic and Social Council of the Arab League established the Council of Arab Economic Unity (CAEU), also known as the Economic Unity Council. Decision Number 85, which was promoted by Jordan, Kuwait, Morocco, Syria, and the United Arab Republic, implemented the Arab Economic Unity Agreement, which had evolved from a decision made by the Political Committee of the Arab League in 1956. The motion to create the Council for Arab Economic Unity was ultimately approved by a majority vote of the Economic and Social Council. The CAEU Charter states that the organization's goals are to promote freedom of movement of people and capital within the Arab world; to enhance the freedom to exchange domestic and global commodities and products among member nations; to encourage freedom of residence, work, employment, and the practice of economic activity; to support freedom of transit and the use of common transportation measures at Arab seaports and airports; and to promote the rights of ownership and inheritance within the region.

In practice, the council has worked to promote greater economic cooperation among Arab countries and to bring an end to the intense competition among them that in the past tended to weaken the economies of the various Arab states. Because of enormous profits from oil resources, there has been increased emphasis on inter-Arab unity and development since the early 1970s, when Arab nations realized for the first time that oil gave the Arab world an influential voice in global politics.

The CAEU was a direct descendent of the Economic Council of the Arab League, which had begun as the Arab Joint Defence and Economic Cooperation Council in 1950. The Economic Council had originally been designated as the economic arm of its parent organization, the Arab League. The initial charter of the Economic Council had limited membership to members of the Arab League; an amendment that passed on June 2, 1960, extended Economic Council membership to nonmember states as well as to member states. The architects of the Economic Council believed that development was the key to advancing Arab interests and intended to focus resources on achieving this goal. Once the Council for Arab Economic Unity was developed, however, the Economic Council became virtually redundant, and political maneuvering within the Economic Council has seriously weakened the influence of this organization.

By May 30, 1964, CAEU was operating out of its headquarters in Cairo, Egypt. Over the next several decades, it continued to promote Arab self-reliance, creating a large number of companies and trade federations that were designed to foster Arab cooperation across the economic spectrum. Membership in the council is limited to members who have joined the Arab League, the parent organization of CAEU. The original CAEU Charter was signed by eleven countries—Egypt, Iraq, Jordan, Kuwait, Libya, Mauritania, Somalia, Sudan, Syria, United Arab Emirates (UAE), and Yemen—and the Palestine Liberation Organization.

In June 1973, CAEU met in Cairo and set up

a five-year plan aimed at furthering cooperation with other inter-Arab agencies and with global organizations such as the United Nations and the World Bank, both of which had already been instrumental in furthering the goals of Arab countries. The council's eventual goal was to develop an integrated Middle East Economic Community by 1981. In addition to pursuing its stated goals, the Council for Arab Economic Unity often serves as a liaison among regional organizations that deal with promoting greater economic cooperation in the Arab world.

Within the council, a vast disparity among levels of development among the member states has continued to exist, leading to constant internal friction. From the beginning, CAEU was weakened by the fact that only fourteen of the twenty existing Arab states opted for membership during the first decade and a half of the organization's existence. Financial problems also beset CAEU from its inception. At least 80 percent of the council's annual budget has traditionally been provided by four of its members, and the remaining members have frequently neglected to remit membership dues. As a result, the council has at times been unable to pay its staff for years at a time.

Despite the council's efforts, inter-Arab disputes have persisted throughout the history of the organization. For example, in 1962, when the Gamal Abdel-Nasser administration turned Egypt toward socialism, other Arab nations reacted by drawing away from the heavily industrialized nation. Tensions were further exacerbated when Egypt signed a peace agreement with Israel. Arab unity was subsequently threatened by the Iraqi invasion of Kuwait in 1991, which served as the impetus for the Gulf War in which the United States and its allies succeeded in forcing Iraq out of Kuwait. Arab unity is also weakened by economic factors: Although the population of the Arab world, 380 million, constitutes a major share of the global population, trading among Arab nations amounts to less than 10 percent of total world trade. Additionally, more than $800 million in

Arab funds remains deposited in foreign banks.

Trade Unions and Joint Stock Companies

In the 1970s, CAEU began to bring a number of trade organizations under its authority in order to strengthen the economic unity of the Arab world. These organizations, which maintain branches in a number of Arab cities, included the Arab Steel Union, headquartered in Algiers; the Arab Textile Industries Union, based in Damascus; the Arab Union for Chemical Fertilizers, with offices in Cairo; and several unions headquartered in Baghdad, including the Arab Union for Engineering Industries, the Arab Union for Fish Producers, the Arab Union for Food Industries, and the Arab Union for Paper Industries.

Other unions included the Arab Sugar Union, with headquarters in Khartoum; the Arab Union for Land Transport, based in Amman; the Arab Union for Leather Industries (temporarily frozen); the Arab Union for Maritime Forwarders; and the Arab Railways Union, the Arab Union for Seaports, and the Arab Union for Cement and Building Material, headquartered in Baghdad. The impact of these unions has been enormous for both Arab and neighboring nations. For instance, the Arab Union for Cement and Building Material conducts training courses in non-Arab African countries. Additionally, this union has worked diligently to promote knowledge of the environment, holding conferences in which both Arab nations and international firms participate.

Over the next two decades, CAEU created the Arab Cooperative Union, which joined existing unions together under the auspices of the council. Other additions to CAEU unions included the Arab Union for Producers of Medicines and Medical Accessories and the Union of Arab Organisations of Tourism, both headquartered in Amman; the Arab General Union for Insurance, the Union of Arab Investors, and the Union of Arab Contractors, all based in Cairo; the General Union of Arab Peasants and Agricultural Cooperatives, headquartered in Tripoli; the Arab Union of Hotels and Tourism, in Beirut; and the Arab Union for the Manufacturing of Tyres and Rubber Products, with offices in Alexandria. In 2000, CAEU added the Federation of Arab Businessmen's Council and the Councils of Plastic Production and Chemical Industries to the existing unions that operate under its authority.

The council has also created four joint stock companies that coordinate Arab economic activity: the Arab Mining Company and the Arab Pharmaceutical Company, both based in Amman; the Arab Company for Livestock Development, headquartered in Damascus; and the Arab Company for Industrial Investment, in Baghdad.

The Arab League

The League of Arab States, popularly known as the Arab League, was created in 1945 in the closing days of World War II. The league, open to all independent Arab states, was designed to strengthen security ties in the region by encouraging policies and activities among members that advance the well-being of the Arab world as a whole. From the outset, the Arab League planned to create spin-off agencies that would meet the specialized needs of its members. Despite the Arab League's emphasis on Arab unity, member states sometimes come into conflict with one another. In such cases, the league serves as mediator.

The original charter of the League of Arab States was signed on March 2, 1945, by Egypt, Iraq, Lebanon, Saudi Arabia, Syria, Trans-Jordan, and Yemen. The powers of the Arab League are lodged in an executive council composed of representatives from each member state, with each state having one vote. Activities of the league are divided among six committees, each designed to deal with specific Arab issues: economic and financial matters, com-

munications, cultural relations, nationality and passports, social affairs, and health problems. Some of the founders of the Arab League cherished an underlying but never-realized hope that all Arab states might someday join together under a single Arab government.

In addition to supporting the Council for Arab Economic Unity, the Arab League, under the guidance of the Economic Council, established the Arab Fund for Economic and Social Development (AFESD), which began operations in February 1972 with an initial capital outlay of 100 million Kuwaiti dinars, divided into 10,000 shares. The purpose of the AFESD was to fund Arab development projects that were seen as promoting Arab unity and development, particularly those that involved joint-Arab activities.

By December 1975, the Arab Fund, working in conjunction with the United Nations Conference on Trade and Development and the Council for Arab Economic Unity, set up a program to identify projects that would benefit from receiving AFESD contributions. The plan called for the Arab Fund, the United Nations, and individual Arab governments to make initial contributions of $9,396,000, $6,268,000, and $3,500,000, respectively. The project was modeled after an earlier joint project developed by the Economic Commission for Western Asia (ECWA) and the United Nations Industrial Development Organization (UNIDO) that evolved from a joint meeting in Beirut in November 1974. The Arab Fund/United Nations project, which worked in conjunction with the Council for Arab Economic Unity and other Arab organizations, was particularly aimed at advancing technical knowledge and cooperation in the Arab world.

By the beginning of the twenty-first century, the Arab League was composed of twenty-two member states, including all the countries of North Africa, most Middle Eastern states, and Djibouti and Somalia. The member states included Algeria, Bahrain, Comoros, Djibouti, Egypt, Iraq, Jordan, Kuwait, Lebanon, Libya, Mauritania, Morocco, Oman, Palestine,

Qatar, Saudi Arabia, Somalia, the Sudan, Syria, Tunisia, United Arab Emirates, and Yemen. In addition to the Economic and Social Council, the Council for Arab Economic Unity, and the Arab Fund, the Arab League has also created a number of other agencies in response to particular needs that have developed within the Arab world, including the Arab Labor Organisation (ALO), the Industrial Development Centre for the Arab States (IDCAS), and the Arab Monetary Fund (AMF).

The new century brought major problems to the Arab League. In addition to dealing with Arab/Israeli tensions, global terrorism signaled an unprecedented interference in Arab affairs. When Taliban-supported terrorists attacked the World Trade Center in New York City and the Pentagon in Washington, DC, on September 11, 2001, the United States retaliated by attacking Afghanistan in November and followed this up with an attack on Iraq that was aimed at annihilating Saddam Hussein, who was accused of having ties with terrorist groups and harboring weapons of mass destruction. In March 2003, the United Arab Emirates asked Saddam Hussein to go into hiding. When other members disagreed, bitter divisions occurred within the Arab League. Further tensions developed when the United States–appointed Iraqi Governing Council asked to be granted membership in the Arab League. However, when the league granted membership to the Iraqi provisional government, only Libya boycotted the league.

Arab Common Market

In August 1964, the Council for Arab Economic Unity formed the Arab Common Market, modeled in large part on the European Common Market. Initially, Egypt, Iraq, Jordan, Kuwait, Syria, and the United Arab Republic signed the charter. These six countries were subsequently joined by Algeria, Morocco, the Sudan, Tunisia, and Yemen. Even though Kuwait was the first country to sign the agreement, the country

never became an official member of the Arab Common Market, and Lebanon, Saudi Arabia, and Libya also refused to join. The Arab Common Market began official operations on January 1, 1965. Each member was given an equal vote, establishing a simple majority to approve most resolutions. Major decisions, however, require a two-thirds majority vote. Executive authority continues to be lodged in the Council for Arab Economic Unity. Separate committees were established to deal with particular functions such as administration, technology, and data collection and analysis.

The charter stated that although the headquarters of the Arab Common Market would remain in Cairo where the Council for Arab Economic Unity was headquartered, meetings could be held in any Arab city. Each member state was expected to contribute to the overall budget of the Arab Common Market. The charter established that the presidency would rotate among the member states each year. Over the next several years, Libya, Mauritania, the Sudan, and Palestine became members of the Arab Common Market, and North Yemen was allowed to take part as an observer.

The goals of the Arab Common Market, set up to be implemented over a six-year period, were to simplify customs activities under a single authority; to codify tariff legislation; to establish consistent import and export procedures among member states; to revise and unify transportation and transit laws; to oversee trade and payment agreements between foreign governments and Arab states; to coordinate agricultural, industrial, real estate, and monetary activities; to coordinate labor laws among member states; and to initiate social security legislation. Initial goals placed annual reduction of agricultural tariffs at 20 percent and those on manufactured goods at 10 percent.

Implementing the dictates of the Arab Common Market involved liberalizing domestic and foreign trade in both agricultural and industrial products. Member states were allowed to exempt certain goods and services from the new trade liberalization policies. Initially, the member countries benefited from the tariff liberalization and bilateral agreements with other states within the Arab Common Market; however, it soon became apparent that liberalizing trade among the member nations provided greater benefits to the more developed nations within the Arab Common Market, creating discord among less developed nations. Some members, such as Jordan, also claimed that they were hurt financially from losing customs duties. Both Syria and the Sudan insisted that a mandated lack of competition with the Egyptian industrial sector could cause a rise in domestic unemployment.

Additional problems developed within the Arab Common Market because Kuwait refused to ratify the charter, and Jordan, Syria, Iraq, and Egypt chose to restrict the number of domestic products that were covered by Arab Common Market policies. Further problems developed as individual member states began to reinstate customs, tariffs, taxes, and fees that worked against a common Arab economy. The general consensus is that the Arab Common Market has made little progress toward accomplishing its goal of furthering Arab regional development. This failure to successfully create a completely functional Arab Common Market brought the CAEU close to total collapse in the early 1980s.

Arab Economic Cooperation

From the 1940s until the 1960s, Arab politicians and economists focused their attention on building Arab trade among members of the Arab League and paying off the foreign debts of member nations. Unfortunately, the architects of various schemes that were proposed lacked the ability to deal with the unique problems involved in fostering Arab economic cooperation. For reasons unique to each Arab nation, proponents of Arab economic unity were forced to fight an uphill battle and were ultimately unable to check the inherent inter-Arab

competition that continued to thrive. Although member nations gave lip service to economic unity, various Arab countries continued to block efforts toward liberalizing trade and promoting cooperation. Additionally, a number of projects that might have helped to realize the goals of the Council for Arab Economic Unity never received the support they needed to get past the various committees that considered them.

CAEU works closely with other Arab organizations, such as the Gulf Cooperation Council (GCC), which was created in 1981 when Bahrain, Kuwait, Oman, Qatar, Saudi Arabia, and the United Arab Emirates joined together to deal with the economic, political, and military sectors within the Gulf region with an overall goal of promoting Arab unity and prosperity.

Arab scholar Khalil Ibrahim Al-Kanaani believes that the greatest obstacle to Arab integration has been backwardness or underdevelopment and dependency on foreign governments. He maintains that all Arab countries that are still considered underdeveloped have been consistently "exploited by others" (Al-Kanaani 2002). This dependency on foreign nations, in his view, has led to a continued weakness in Arab economic relationships, a vast disparity in the industrialized and nonindustrialized Arab economies, enormous gaps in the expansion of Arab industrial economies, and a detrimental foreign interference in Arab public policy.

The Twenty-First Century

By the beginning of the twenty-first century, there again seemed to be some doubt as to whether the Council for Arab Economic Unity would survive. The council had been seriously weakened by the tensions generated during the Gulf War of the early 1990s. After Iraq invaded Kuwait, the latter responded by withdrawing from the council. When the United Arab Emirates left the council in 1999, CAEU was left with no representation among the Gulf states.

The loss of the economic support of these two oil-producing nations substantially contributed to CAEU's economic breakdown.

Critics claim that the Council for Arab Economic Unity has never reached its full potential, and some detractors insist that the whole history of the organization has been marked by failure. The lack of capital has been an obstacle to the realization of CAEU goals since its inception. The fact that since the early 1990s CAEU has been hindered economically by the failure of some Arab states to pay dues has added to the organization's financial woes. A number of problems have arisen because some CAEU members are not completely loyal to the goals of the council, and competition among member states has continued to hamper efforts to reach the goal of Arab economic unity. Since membership is voluntary, CAEU lacks the authority to punish violations of the council's rules or to prevent member states from signing agreements with nonmember countries that serve to defeat the stated purposes of the council. Nevertheless, the Council for Arab Economic Unity is known for its perseverance. In 2002, it developed a plan to expand the economies of fifteen Arab states through investment in thousands of Arab entrepreneurs within the Arab world.

Elizabeth Purdy

See Also Economic Integration; Gulf Cooperation Council (GCC); League of Arab States (LAS)

References

Al-Kanaani, Khalil Ibrahim. 2002. "The Integration Attempts in the Fourth World: The Case of the Arab World," January, http://www.druid.dk/conferences/winter2002/gallery/al-kanaani.pdf (cited December 1, 2003).

Casadio, Gian Paolo. 1976. *The Economic Challenge of the Arabs.* Westmead, UK: Saxon House.

Demir, Sooman. 1979. *Arab Development Funds in the Middle East.* New York: Pergamon.

El-Agraa, Ali M. 1997. *Economic Integration Worldwide.* London: Macmillan.

Flowers, E. C., Jr. 1961. "The Arab League in Perspective." Pp. 1–29 in *The Citadel Monograph Series.* Charleston, SC: Citadel.

"Issues Facing the Arab Common Market," http://www.arabicnews.com (cited December 1, 2003).

McDonald, Robert W. 1965. *The League of Arab States: A Study in the Dynamics of Regional Organization.* Princeton, NJ: Princeton University Press.

Sayigh, Yusif A. 1978. *The Determinants of Arab Economic Development.* New York: St. Martin's.

———. 1991. *Elusive Development: From Dependence to Self-Reliance in the Arab Region.* London and New York: Routledge.

East African Community (EAC)

The East African Community (EAC) is a regional bloc in East Africa consisting of Kenya, Uganda, and Tanzania. The current "new" EAC was established in 2001 at a ceremony held in Arusha, Tanzania, reviving an earlier effort of regional integration in East Africa that had been abandoned in 1977. The EAC Treaty foresees an ever closer economic and ultimately policy union of its member states, a group that is not confined entirely to the founding members—currently, Burundi and Rwanda enjoy observer status in the EAC, and both countries have applied for accession to the community. The accession of Rwanda is planned for 2006.

A further treaty signed in March 2004 set up a customs union and entered into force on January 1, 2005. The EAC operates on the basis of five-year development strategies that spell out the policy guidelines, priority programs, and implementation schedules of the organization. The first EAC Development Strategy, in 1997–2000, was implemented during the formation of the revitalized EAC and before the EAC Treaty was signed. The second phase took place in 2000–2005. Both plans emphasized economic cooperation and development with a strong focus on the social dimension. The role of the private sector and civil society is considered as central to the regional integration and development of an internationally competitive single market and investment area in East Africa.

In 2004, the East African Community covered a region of 1.8 million square kilometers (about 695,000 square miles), with a combined population of some 80 million people and a combined gross domestic product (GDP) of US$33 billion. The region includes vast natural resources, and the three member states, Kenya, Tanzania, and Uganda, are relatively prosperous compared to their neighbors, which include the Democratic Republic of the Congo, Ethiopia, Sudan, and Somalia.

Rules of the Treaty Establishing the EAC and EAC CU

The treaty establishing the EAC was signed by heads of state of the partner states on November 30, 1999, in Arusha, Tanzania, and entered into force on July 7, 2000; the formal launch of the EAC followed on January 15, 2001. The treaty is organized along twenty-nine chapters that lay out the principles and objectives of the community; establish its organs; and specify priority areas of cooperation, calling for ever closer integration in the form of a customs union, to be followed by a common market and monetary union. The ultimate objective is to establish a political federation of East African States.

Negotiations for the customs union protocol had begun shortly after implementation of the EAC and were finally concluded in March 2004 with the signature of the EAC Customs Union Protocol by the heads of state and government. After ratification by the three member states, the EAC Customs Union (CU) entered into force on January 1, 2005. Its main underpinnings are a common EAC Customs Management Act and a common external tariff applied to all imports into the customs union. The common external tariff has three tariff bands—0, 10, and 25 percent—that apply to all imports except for a list of ten sensitive products that carry additional protection. Intraregional tariff liberalization will be achieved after a five-year transition period during which Uganda and Tanzania will gradually phase out tariffs on a selected list of Kenyan imports. Imports from Uganda and Tanzania already enter duty free into all partner states.

The EAC Treaty and CU Protocol name only Kenya, Tanzania, and Uganda as members of the community and customs union but provide for the possibility of granting membership, association, or observer status to other countries upon agreement by the original member states.

Structure and Objectives of the EAC

Structure
The community's main organs are the Summit of Heads of State and Government, the Council of Ministers, the Coordinating Committee, Sectoral Committees, the East African Court of Justice, the East African Legislative Assembly, and the Secretariat.

- The summit, comprising heads of state and government of partner states, gives general direction toward the realization of the objectives of the community and customs union. It meets at least once a year to consider the annual progress report and may hold extra meetings as necessary.
- The Council of Ministers, the main decisionmaking institution, is made up of ministers from the partner states responsible for regional cooperation. Among its functions, the council promotes, monitors, and keeps under review the implementation of the programs of the community and ensures the proper functioning of the regional organization.

- The Coordinating Committee consists of permanent secretaries and reports to the Council of Ministers; it is responsible for regional cooperation and coordinates the activities of the Sectoral Committees.
- The Sectoral Committees conceptualize programs, set priorities in the various sectors, and monitor implementation of the programs; the Council of Ministers establishes the committees on the recommendation of the respective Coordinating Committee.
- The East African Court of Justice has jurisdiction over the interpretation and application of the EAC Treaty.
- The East African Legislative Assembly consists of twenty-seven elected members, nine from each partner state plus the three ministers responsible for regional cooperation, the secretary general, and the counsel to the community; it provides a democratic forum for debate and has a watchdog function.
- The Secretariat is the executive organ of the community. It is based in Arusha, headed by the secretary general, and ensures that regulations and directives adopted by the Council of Ministers are properly implemented.

The EAC also includes a number of autonomous institutions that have been established upon the initiative of the Council of Ministers. Currently, the EAC's autonomous institutions are:

- The Lake Victoria Development Program,
- the East African Development Bank,
- the Lake Victoria Fisheries Organisation, and
- the Inter-University Council for East Africa.

Objectives
The EAC aims to improve and strengthen cooperation on the basis of the historical ties and understanding between the peoples of East Africa—that is, of Kenya, Tanzania, Uganda,

and any other East African state that may accede to the community and customs union. The community focuses on cooperation in trade liberalization and development, investment and industry, harmonization of standards, monetary and financial cooperation, infrastructure and services, human resources, science and technology, agriculture and food security, environment, natural resources management, tourism and wildlife management, and health, social, and cultural activities.

The EAC Treaty emphasizes that regional integration be people centered, market driven, and aimed at the provision of an adequate enabling environment. The vision is to create an "export oriented economy in which there shall be free movement of goods, persons, labor, services, capital, information and technology" guided by "the principle of subsidiarity with emphasis on multilevel participation and the involvement of a wide range of stakeholders in the process of integration."

To achieve its vision and goals, the EAC has made a commitment to:

- promote sustainable growth and equitable development of partner states, which includes promoting rational utilization of the region's natural resources and protection of the environment;
- strengthen and consolidate long-standing political, economic, social, cultural, and traditional ties by partner states and between the peoples of the region, thereby promoting a people-centered, mutual development;
- enhance and strengthen participation of the private sector and civil society;
- promote mainstreaming of gender in all EAC programs and enhancement of the role of women in development;
- promote good governance, including adherence to the principles of democratic rule of law, accountability, transparency, social justice, and equal opportunities and gender equality; and
- promote peace and stability within the

region and good neighborliness among the partner states.

History of the East African Community

The East African Community is the oldest regional arrangement in sub-Saharan Africa, dating back to 1917, when Kenya and Uganda set up the first African Customs Union. These nations were later joined by Tanganyika in 1927 to form the East African Customs Union under British colonial rule. Subsequent agreements gave birth to the East African High Commission (1948–1961), the East African Common Services Organization (1961–1967), and the East African Community (1967–1977)—now often referred to as the "first EAC." Disputes among the three East African countries regarding the unequal distribution of benefits stemming from the customs union, coupled with ideological differences among their leaders, resulted in the dissolution of the first EAC in 1977.

On November 30, 1993, regional cooperation efforts were resumed with the signature of the Agreement for the Establishment of the Permanent Tripartite Commission for East African Co-operation. In 1997, negotiations started for the upgrading of the Tripartite Commission, leading to the signature of the Treaty for the Establishment of the East African Community in Arusha on November 30, 1999. The treaty entered into force on July 7, 2000, but the EAC was launched formally on January 15, 2001.

The EAC's Agenda

Since its relaunch, the overall performance of the revitalized EAC has been fairly satisfactory, even remarkable in some respects. Among its main achievements, the EAC has established an institutional architecture; achieved convertibility of East African currencies; enhanced coordination in macro and budgetary policies; reduced internal tariffs; set up a common external tariff and an EAC Customs Union; and revived regional cooperation in a number of important fields (Lake Victoria, natural resources, immigration, and the like).

The implementation of the various phases of regional integration since the entry into force of the "new" EAC has been translated into action in multiyear strategies. The first EAC Development Strategy, launched in 1997, covered a period of four years, 1997–2000. It focused on setting up the institutional and legal architecture of the East African integration process. The strategy in place for 2001–2005 emphasizes two main areas: (1) achieving a customs union and a common market, which should set the foundations for a strong and internationally competitive single market and an investment area in the region; and (2) enhancing the supply capacity in the region, with a focus on agriculture, industry, tourism, and natural resources—in particular, management of Lake Victoria. As a result, the three member states have concluded ten protocols and agreements since 1997; however, only two of them (the Protocol on Standardization, Quality Assurance, Metrology and Testing, and the Protocol on the Establishment of the East African Community Customs Union) have been ratified and entered into force.

So far, EAC integration progress has relied primarily on intergovernmental cooperation, based on consensus and assigning a very limited role to supranational organizations, particularly the EAC Secretariat. However, with the entry into force of the EAC Customs Union, the role of the Secretariat needs to be strengthened so that it can effectively monitor and follow up on the implementation of the CU Protocol and the new Common Customs Management Bill. In this regard, a new Customs and Trade Directorate has been created that will be staffed by up to twelve people.

Structure and Performance of the EAC and EAC Economies

In 2004, the three EAC member states, Kenya, Tanzania, and Uganda, had a collective GDP of US$33.2 billion. Kenya is the largest of the three economies, with a GDP of US$15.1 billion and a population of 31.3 million; it is also the richest, with US$390 per capita gross national income (GNI—Atlas method). Tanzania's GDP is US$10.6 billion, its population 35.2 million, and its GNI per capita US$290. Uganda's GDP is US$7.5 billion, its population 24.3 million, and its GNI per capita US$240 (IMF 2004c; The World Bank has a database available online: http://www.worldbank.org/data/countrydata/countrydata.html .)

The differences in GDP and per capita GNI among the EAC economies have been declining in the past decade. Several reasons lie behind this trend toward regional economic convergence. Uganda and Tanzania have experienced relatively high rates of GDP growth in the past ten years, averaging 6.5 percent and 4.8 percent, respectively (IMF, 2004c). Major advances in macroeconomic stabilization and structural reforms, as well as the impact of higher foreign direct investment, have driven economic growth in both countries. For instance, inflation has fallen steeply, from two-digit rates in the 1970s and 1980s to stable average rates of around 5 percent in 1994–2004. In stark contrast, Kenya's economic performance has been disappointing for the past three decades. The GDP rate of growth has been on a sustained declining trend over this period. The annual rate of real GDP growth fell from 7.5 percent in the 1970s to only 1.9 percent in the 1990s. Although significantly lower than in the 1980s, inflation is still closer to two-digit rates, and foreign direct investment remains at very low levels. This sluggish performance is primarily the reflection of pervasive governance problems and the slow pace of structural reforms (see IMF 2003, 2004a, 2004b).

International trade plays a crucial role for the three EAC economies. Kenya is the most open of the three countries, with a trade in goods ratio to GDP of 44.5 percent; Uganda is second with 36.7 percent, and Tanzania is the last with 27.1 percent (World Bank 2004). The European Union is the main trading partner of

Table 1: Change in the Structure of the EAC's Economies

(% of GDP)	Kenya			Tanzania			Uganda		
	1984	1994	2004	1984	1994	2004	1984	1994	2004
Agriculture	30	28	13	n.a.	42	41	50	46	29
Industry	16	15	16	n.a.	14	15	10	13	19
Manufacturing	10	9	11	n.a.	7	7	6	6	8
Services	41	42	52	n.a.	37	35	31	34	43

Source: World Bank's staff calculations based on National Authorities data.

EAC countries, absorbing around 30 percent of its total exports in 2003. EAC imports are more diversified: Around a quarter come from the EU, about 20 percent from Asia, and about 20 percent from the Middle East. Trade between EAC members has grown significantly over the past decade. Between 1991 and 2003, the share of exports to the region increased sixfold, reaching 19 percent in 2003. The share of regionally sourced imports increased sevenfold over the same period, accounting for about 8 percent in 2003. Intraregional trade is dominated by exports from Kenya to Uganda.

Foreign direct investment (FDI) directed to the EAC countries has increased significantly over the past decade, from only US$72 million in 1994 to a historical record of US$517 million in 2004. Tanzania is the frontrunner in attracting FDI, with three-fifths of the total investment in the region; Uganda is second, with one-third, and Kenya is the laggard, with only 12 percent (IMF 2004a, b).

Poverty remains an important concern for the EAC countries, despite the recent positive economic performances of Uganda and Tanzania. As a result of three decades of extremely weak economic growth, poverty incidence in Kenya is currently over 50 percent. After a steady decline in poverty during the 1990s, income poverty has recently worsened in Uganda, rising up to 38 percent of the population in 2003 from 34 percent in 2000. Tanzania's sharply improved growth performance has had, in contrast, a notable impact on poverty, which has declined consistently over the past decade. However, despite these signifi-

cant improvements, the percentage of the population below the national poverty line was still around 35 percent.

Data on Pertinent Economic Sectors

There are major differences in levels of economic development between the EAC countries. Kenya remains the most industrialized of the three economies, with a manufacturing sector that accounts for 11 percent of its GDP. Although Uganda's industry has expanded significantly over the past ten years, from 13 percent of the GDP in 1994 to 19 percent in 2004, manufacturing remains small in comparison with Kenya's.

The importance of agriculture varies significantly across the three EAC economies. The rural sector remains the largest in Tanzania, with 41 percent of the GDP, whereas Uganda and Kenya have exhibited a sharp decrease over the past decade. The share of agriculture in the GDP declined by more than half in Kenya and by 37 percent in Uganda. Services have shown a vigorous growth in Uganda and Kenya but have declined slightly in Tanzania in this period.

Manufacturing has been the most dynamic economic sector in Uganda and Tanzania, with average rates of growth of 11.6 percent and 5 percent, respectively, in 1993–2003. Services and government consumption, in contrast, have been the main drivers of economic growth in Kenya, with 5.5 percent and 2 percent, respectively.

Table 2: Structure of the Economy

	Kenya	*Tanzania*	*Uganda*
Average annual growth 1993–2003			
Agriculture	1.6	3.7	3.9
Industry	1.4	6.5	11
Manufacturing	1.4	5	11.6
Services	2	4.4	7.6
Private consumption	1.7	5.4	6.2
General government consumption	5.5	-0.4	6.5
Imports of goods and services	7.2	4.8	10.7

Source: World Bank's "At-a-Glance Tables" 2004

Table 3: EAC Statistical Profile

	Kenya	*Tanzania*	*Uganda*
Poverty and Social			
2003			
Population, mid-year (millions)	32.2	36	25.5
GNI per capita (Atlas method, US$)	400	290	250
GNI (Atlas method, US$)	12.8	10.6	6.2
Most recent estimate			
Poverty (% of population below national poverty line)	55	35	38
Urban population (% of total population)	36	36	12
Life expectancy at birth (years)	45	47	42
Infant mortality (per 1,000 live births)	77	85	88
Child Malnutrition (% of children under 5)	20	44	38
Access to an improved water source (% of population)	57	56	55
Illiteracy (% of population age 15+)	15	21	69
Gross primary enrollment (% of school population)	96	105	127
Key Economic Ratios and Long-term Trends			
2003			
GDP (US$ billions)	14.3	10.1	6.3
Gross domestic investment/GDP	12.9	18.6	20.7
Exports of goods and services/GDP	24.9	18.3	12.3
Gross Domestic Savings/GDP	8.2	9.5	6.6
Gross National Savings/GDP	12.8	9.3	7.1
Total debt/GDP	47.2	74	62.5
Total Debt service/exports	15.8	5.2	11
Present value of debt/GDP	31.2	19.2	30.8
Present value of debt/exports	123.4	109.4	269.2

Source: World Bank's "At-a-Glance Tables"

Major Issues Facing the EAC

In spite of the important achievements made during the first few years since the revival of the East African Community in 1997, progress in regional integration has slowed down in recent years. One of the reasons for this slowdown is that regional issues have not always been a priority for national bureaucracies, and the regional authorities lacked the means to further the agenda faster. One example is that, out of the ten protocols and agreements signed since 1997, eight are still not ratified: the Agreement for the Avoidance of Double Taxation and the Prevention of Fiscal Evasion; the Protocol on Decision-Making by the EAC Council; the Protocol on Combating Drug Trafficking in the East African Region; the Tripartite Agreement on Road Transport; the Tripartite Agreement on Inland Waterway Transport; the Protocol on the Establishment of the Inter-University Council for East Africa; the Search and Rescue Agreement; and the Protocol for the Sustainable Development of Lake Victoria Basin.

To address this problem, in August 2004 the EAC members established a Committee on Fast Tracking Regional Integration to examine ways and means to deepen and accelerate the process of integration. By October, the committee had adopted a timetable that recommended: (1) the formation of the EAC Common Market, the achievement of free movement of EAC citizens and persons, and the establishment of an EAC identity card by 2007; (2) the formation of an EAC monetary union by 2010; (3) the approval of an EAC Constitution and election of an EAC president by 2012; and (4) the establishment of an EAC Federation by 2015.

The committee also highlighted the need to restructure and strengthen the EAC Secretariat as a matter of urgency if the organization was to fulfill its mandate. A new system of direct financing for EAC institutions was proposed by which member states would remit either 1 percent of their customs revenue or 0.0025 (one-quarter of 1 percent) of their external imports directly to the EAC.

At this stage, it is clear that the long-term success of the community will also involve finding mechanisms to better redistribute the benefits deriving from the integration process. It is important to remember that at the root of the breakup of the community in 1977 there was a disagreement over the sharing of costs and benefits from regional integration. These issues are currently reemerging, with Uganda and Tanzania raising concerns that Kenyan producers will gain from duty-free access to their markets while the Tanzanian and Ugandan governments will lose tariff revenues. In the long run, unless the benefits of regional integration are perceived as being fairly distributed, the whole process may again be derailed.

Furthermore, moving toward deeper integration will require a solution to conflicts caused by the overlapping membership of EAC countries in other regional integration agreements. Currently, Kenya and Uganda belong to the Common Market for Eastern and Southern Africa (COMESA), and Tanzania is a member of the Southern African Development Community (SADC). Both COMESA and SADC have signed free trade agreements and are negotiating the formation of customs unions. Since countries cannot participate in more than one customs union, EAC members will have to make some critical decisions to avoid risking the benefits of further regional integration in East Africa.

Finally, in the long run, if the community is to reap the full benefits of integration it will need to fully embrace the idea of open regionalism, gradually liberalizing its markets to improve economic competitiveness and ensure a better insertion into the global economy. This process should be reinforced by an acceleration of the "deep integration" agenda toward the establishment of a real common market and by stepping up regional cooperation in other areas, such as regional transport networks, standards harmonization, energy and telecommunications, and the like.

Christiane Kraus, Lucio Castro,
and Manuel de la Rocha

See Also Economic Integration; Common Market for Eastern and Southern Africa (COMESA); East African Community (EAC); Economic Community of Central African States (CEEAC); Southern African Development Community (SADC); Franc Zone

References

Castro, Lucio, Christiane Kraus, and Manuel de la Rocha. 2004. *Regional Trade Integration in East Africa: Trade and Revenue Impacts of the Planned East Africa Community Customs Union.* World Bank Africa Region Working Paper Series No. 72. August. Washington, DC: World Bank.

East African Community. 1999. *Treaty for the Establishment of the East African Community.* Arusha, Tanzania: EAC.

———. 2000. *EAC Development Strategy 2001–05.* Arusha, Tanzania: EAC.

East African Community Secretariat, http://www.eac.int. ———. 2004. *Report of the Committee on Fast Tracking Regional Integration to Examine Ways and Means to Deepen and Accelerate the Process of Integration.* November. Arusha, Tanzania: EAC.

Hope, D., V. Bhowon, and F. Ruhindi. 2003. *East African Community—Study to Develop a Legal, Institutional and Administrative Structure for the Customs Union.* Pretoria: Imani Development.

Imani Development. 2003. *A Review of the East African Community Development Strategy, 2001–2005.* Final Report. June. Pretoria: Imani Development.

International Monetary Fund. 2003. *Kenya: 2003 Article IV Consultation—Staff Report; Staff Supplement; Public Information Notice on the Executive Board Discussion; and Statement by the Executive Director for Kenya.* Country Report No. 03/199, July 9. Washington, DC: IMF.

———. 2004a. *Tanzania: 2004 Article IV Consultation and Second Review under the Three-Year Arrangement under the Poverty Reduction and Growth Facility—Staff Report; Staff Statement; and Public Information Notice and Press Release on the Executive Board Discussion.* Country Report No. 04/285, September 7. Washington, DC: IMF.

———. 2004b. *Uganda: Third Review under the Three-Year Arrangement under the Poverty Reduction and Growth Facility and Request for Waiver of Performance Criteria—Staff Report; Press Release on the Executive Board Discussion; and Statement by the Executive Director for Uganda.* Country Report No. 04/289, September 9. Washington, DC: IMF.

———. 2004c. World Economic Outlook Database. September. http://www.imf.org/external/pubs/ft/weo/2004/02/data/index.htm.

N'geno, Nehemiah K. 2002. *The Status of Regional Trade Liberalization in East Africa.* Unpublished manuscript. Washington, DC: World Bank.

World Bank. 2004. World Development Indicators 2004. Washington, DC: World Bank. http://www.worldbank.org/data/countrydata/countrydata.html.

Economic and Social Council (ECOSOC)

The United Nations Economic and Social Council (ECOSOC) was established at the inception of the UN in 1945 under the UN Charter. It comprises fifty-four members elected by the UN General Assembly for three-year terms based on the principle of geographical representation.

ECOSOC's goals and objectives are deeply rooted in the primary reason for the UN's existence. The Preamble to the UN Charter states, "We the peoples of the United Nations are determined to save succeeding generations from the scourge of war, which twice in our lifetime has brought untold sorrow to mankind, and to reaffirm faith in fundamental human rights, in the dignity and worth of the human person, in the equal rights of men and women and of nations large and small." ECOSOC thus is charged with initiating studies and reports concerning international economic, social, educational, cultural, and health matters. Specifically, it coordinates the work of fourteen specialized and regional commissions as well as several UN agencies. These duties correspond to the main stated aims of the United Nations: the maintenance of international peace and security; the improvement of relations between nations; the promotion of social progress; and the advancement of living standards and human rights.

Structure and Functions of ECOSOC

There are six chief organs of the UN established under the UN Charter. These are the General Assembly, the Security Council, the International Court of Justice, the Trusteeship Council, the Secretariat, and the Economic and Social Council. The establishment of ECOSOC under the founding UN Charter was a significant addition to the organizational framework inherited from the League of Nations. Its creation reflected a new preoccupation among the Allied nations of World War II about the potential for unmet economic and social needs to become a source for future conflict. ECOSOC thus contributed to the UN's overarching goal of preventing war through the promotion of the economic and social development of member nations.

The sections of the charter establishing ECOSOC as a principal organ of the United Nations include Article 7 and Chapters IX and X. ECOSOC is principally responsible for the economic and social activities of the United Nations and its specialized agencies. It operates under the authority of the General Assembly.

The rules governing ECOSOC membership allocate fourteen representatives to African states, eleven to Asian states, six to Eastern European states, ten to Latin American and Caribbean states, and thirteen to Western European and other states.

Article 62 of the Charter empowers ECOSOC to "make or initiate studies and reports with respect to international economic, social, cultural, educational, health, and related matters" and to make recommendations regarding these issues to the General Assembly, member nations, and specialized agencies. In addition to reports and recommendations,

ECOSOC may prepare draft conventions for submission to the General Assembly.

On economic and social issues, which include the environment and development, the United Nations operates under certain constraints. Its founders were unwilling to allow the United Nations to carry out economic and social activities in a country without the nation's consent. They thus specified that "nothing contained in the present Charter shall authorize the United Nations to intervene in matters which are essentially within the domestic jurisdiction of any state or shall require the Members to submit such matters to [dispute] settlement under the present Charter (http://www.un.org/esa/coordination/ecosoc/b wi2003/BWIInfoNote.pdf).

The General Assembly and ECOSOC have established well over fifty programs and subsidiary organs, many of which critically affect development and environment issues. ECOSOC coordinates the activities of this system, but, like the General Assembly, it can only recommend actions to the agencies and to member governments, not dictate policy or programs. ECOSOC also receives regular reports from these programs and organs and examines their administrative budgets (http://www.un.org/ esa/coordination/ecosoc/about.htm).

ECOSOC coordinates the activities of the International Labour Organization (ILO); the Food and Agriculture Organization (FAO); the World Health Organization (WHO); the United Nations Educational, Scientific and Cultural Organization (UNESCO); and the World Intellectual Property Organization (WIPO). It also oversees nine functional commissions, including the Commission on Human Rights, the Commission on Narcotic Drugs, and the Commission on the Status of Women; and five regional economic commissions, including commissions for Africa, Europe, Latin America and the Caribbean, Asia and the Pacific, and Western Asia. It also receives reports from eleven UN funds and programs, including the United Nations Children's Fund (UNICEF), the United

Nations Development Programme (UNDP), and the United Nations Environment Programme (UNEP) and issues policy recommendations to the UN system and to member states. Thus, ECOSOC is responsible for promoting higher standards of living, full employment, and economic and social progress; identifying solutions to international economic, social, and health problems; facilitating international cultural and educational cooperation; and encouraging universal respect for human rights and fundamental freedoms (http://www. un.org/esa/coordination/desc.htm).

Indeed, ECOSOC's purview extends to over 70 percent of the human and financial resources of the entire UN system (http://www. un.org/esa/coordination/ecosoc/about.htm). In its quest for long-term development and welfare establishment, ECOSOC works closely with academics, representatives from large business sectors, and more than 2,100 registered nongovernmental organizations (NGOs). In this way, ECOSOC differs from the other UN bodies that mostly involve member governments only.

Each year the council holds a four-week session in July, alternating between New York and Geneva, that is attended by national ministers, chiefs of international agencies, and other high-ranking officials. The focus of these annual sessions are themes of global significance. The theme of the 2003 session, for example, was "promoting an integrated approach to rural development in developing countries for poverty eradication and sustainable development." The 2005 meetings held in New York made further progress towards ECOSOC's commitment to meeting the goals of the UN Development Agenda. At this annual session, the council usually adopts a declaration providing policy guidance and recommendations for action.

The subsidiary bodies, commissions, and committees of ECOSOC carry out their work year round. Apart from the substantive session convened annually in July, supplementary formal meetings as well as informal panels on topical issues are held throughout the year.

ECOSOC and Nongovernmental Organizations

The Committee on Non-Governmental Organizations, a standing committee of ECOSOC, was established by Council Resolution 3(II) on June 21, 1946. Its membership consists of representatives from nineteen countries, including five from African states, four from Asian states, two from Eastern European states, four from Latin American and Caribbean states, and four from Western European and other states.

The committee's mandate is set out in Council Resolution 1996/31. The main tasks of the committee are to consider applications for consultative status and requests for reclassification submitted by NGOs; consider quadrennial reports submitted by NGOs; implement the provisions of Council Resolution 1996/31 and monitor the consultative relationship; and deal with other issues at ECOSOC's request (http://www.peacewomen.org/un/ngoadvocacy/ngostatus.html).

ECOSOC offers consultative status to NGOs working on issues discussed as part of ECOSOC's brief, such as the rights of women. ECOSOC's website describes NGOs in consultative status as "technical experts, advisers and consultants to governments and Secretariat." All NGOs with consultative status can attend all UN conferences and meetings and designate UN representatives.

Requests for consultative status are handled by the Non-Governmental Organizations Section of the Department of Economic and Social Affairs (DESA) of the United Nations in New York. Organizations applying for consultative status fill out a questionnaire, which is then forwarded to the Committee on Non-Governmental Organizations. This committee makes its recommendations to ECOSOC, which makes the final decision.

Depending on the scope of their work, NGOs can have three different types of consultative status with ECOSOC:

- General status is for NGOs who work on most of ECOSOC's issues. These NGOs can propose agenda items to ECOSOC and speak in front of ECOSOC and its subsidiary bodies, and can circulate statements at ECOSOC and subsidiary body meetings. Organizations such as the Muslim World League, Rotary International, and the International Planned Parenthood Association all have General Status.
- Special status is for NGOs who work on a few areas of ECOSOC's mandate. They can speak at ECOSOC's subsidiary bodies and circulate short statements both at ECOSOC and subsidiary body meetings. The All-India Women's Conference, the African Women Jurists' Association, the Hong Kong Federation of Women's Centres, Amnesty International, and the Women's International League for Peace and Freedom are all examples of NGOs in Special Consultative Status.
- Roster status is for NGOs whose work has limited relation to ECOSOC, and whose work is normally more technical than an NGO with another status. While being in consultative status, they cannot speak or circulate statements at meetings. The Confederation of German Forest Owners Associations, the International Association of Hydrogeologists, the International Confederation of Midwives, and the Latin American Plastics Institute all have Roster Status (http://www.peacewomen.org/un/ngoadvocacy/ngostatus.html).

Policy Leadership

ECOSOC has taken a lead role in key policy areas in recent years. In 1999, it issued a "Manifesto on Poverty" that in many respects anticipated the formulation of the Millennium Development Goals that were approved at the UN Millennium Summit in New York. The council's Ministerial Declaration in 2000 proposed specific actions to address the digital divide, leading directly to the formation in 2001 of the Information and Communication Technologies (ICT) Task Force. In 2002, ECOSOC's consideration of African development resulted in the first formal international endorsement of the New Partnership for Africa's Development (NEPAD).

Since 1998, ECOSOC has held a special high-level meeting with the Bretton Woods institutions immediately following the spring meetings of the World Bank and the International Monetary Fund (IMF). These meetings originated with UN reform measures adopted at the fiftieth session of the General Assembly, specifically Assembly Resolution 50/227, and are meant to facilitate a free-flowing dialogue among ministers of finance returning from the Washington meetings, on the one hand, and ministers of development cooperation and ministers and high-level officials of foreign affairs, on the other. Civil society and private-sector representatives have also participated in these meetings.

The 1998 meeting was held against the backdrop of the Asian financial crisis, and ministers discussed how to maintain the focus on long-term development amidst economic and financial upheavals. The next meeting, in 1999, addressed the functioning of international financial markets and stability in financing for development in the broader context of issues related to promoting recovery, ensuring cross-sectoral coherence, and mobilizing the cooperation of all actors in the development process. In 2000, the meeting discussed the theme of strengthening international financial arrangements and eradicating poverty, whereas in 2001 the meeting addressed two themes: (1) development financing, in particular poverty eradication, official development assistance, and debt; and (2) a development-friendly international financial system with public and private responsibility in the prevention of financial crises.

The title of the 2002 meeting was "Dialogue on the Outcome of the International Conference on Financing for Development and of the Meetings of the Development Committee and International Monetary and Financial Committee." This meeting, held just one month after the International Conference on Financing for Development, which adopted, in March 2002, the Monterrey Consensus, was the first opportunity to lay down the foundation for "staying engaged" as called for in the consensus. The 2003 meetings focused on social development, while the 2004 meetings emphasized human rights.

These ECOSOC meetings have been considered important for deepening the dialogue between the United Nations and the Bretton Woods institutions and for strengthening their partnership for achieving the development goals agreed upon at the global conferences of the 1990s. In the Millennium Declaration, heads of state and government declared their resolve to further strengthen ECOSOC, building on its recent achievements, to help it fulfill the role ascribed to it in the UN Charter. The Assembly subsequently encouraged the deepening of the dialogue between the council and the Bretton Woods institutions in the special high-level meetings (http://www.un.org/esa/coordination/ecosoc/bwi2003/BWIInfoNote.pdf).

Strengthening ECOSOC for the Twenty-first Century

Several studies have been carried out reviewing the United Nations system, its successes and shortcomings, and the changes and reforms that might allow it to function in a more systematic and effective manner. The end of the Cold War led to expectations of a UN renaissance. This, however, has not happened. Instead, the end of the Cold War saw the exacerbation of political, ethnic, economic, and social tensions. New information and communications technologies have fostered the dissemination of inspiring concepts of civil, political, economic, and social human rights across the world but at the same time have created a much greater awareness of the disparities between rich and poor.

Adequate policies to address global poverty and deprivation are lacking. Global population is increasing, and unemployment is growing rapidly. Food security, health concerns, and environmental degradation have become pressing issues of concern. The result has been that the UN system is operating in a world of much greater complexity and is in greater demand than ever before. It is often stretched to the limits of its capacity (http://www.ncrb.unac.org/unreform/selected/Childers-Urquhart.html; see also Childers and Urquhart 1994). Bridging the divide between rich and poor nations has been one of the cornerstones of the UN's social and economic policy. But the "economic and social advancement of all peoples" is farther away today than before, as can be witnessed from the inequities of the North-South divide.

Although the UN Charter vested responsibility for coordinating "the activities of specialized agencies" with ECOSOC, it has been pointed out that over time, the membership of ECOSOC has become too large to be effective. This has led to a certain degree of failure in its attempts to play its designated role of coordinator among the various organizations of the UN system. Moreover, the council has too many items on its agenda to be able to do full justice to all of them, especially now that it meets for only one session each year. Failure to allow sufficient time to carry out its business has held back the proper implementation of ECOSOC's reforms.

Some remedies have been suggested. For instance, in theory there have been suggestions of "a revived ECOSOC, empowered by Member States to coordinate the UN's economic and social policies across a broad front, with a smaller membership and regular operating procedures working throughout the year to supervise the progress made toward sustainable develop-ment" ("A Report of the Independent Working Group on the Future of the United Nations"). In practice, however, this may never happen.

The Independent Working Group on the Future of the United Nations reported correctly that economic and social activities must go hand in hand, and that what is required for this is an integrated, comprehensive approach. While preserving this overall coherence and purpose, however, the UN must have a structure that will permit effective and focused deliberation. To achieve this, the group suggested that "the functions of the ECOSOC be taken over by *two* UN bodies that will fulfill the Charter's original purposes, but with a very different structure, authority, mandate and membership," recommending "a new Economic and a new Social Council," each with a specific portfolio of responsibilities. Together, the working group said, "they would then constitute the Global Alliance for Sustainable Development" (ibid.; see also "Maintaining Peace through the United Nations in the Twenty-first Century").

The Independent Working Group report further suggested that the Economic Council could focus on "coordinating monetary, financial and trade policies at the global level, as well as addressing the economic aspects of sustainable development including job creation, poverty alleviation and protection of the environment, responsibility for which it would share with the Social Council." The Social Council, in turn, would be responsible for "supervision and integration of all UN agencies, and international institutions, programs and offices involved with all social issues, including social development, humanitarian questions, human rights and restoration of states under stress" (ibid.). Since the work of the councils would be interrelated by nature, they could work closely together, and also with the Security Council when the occasion required it. Other UN agencies, such as the UNDP, UNICEF, and the United Nations Population Fund, would report to these two new councils.

The working group, and many others, believe that the reformulation of ECOSOC into two councils, jointly functioning as the Global Alliance, would help to counter the criticisms that have been leveled against ECOSOC because it would reflect the profound transformations that have taken place in the world since the founding of the United Nations.

Conclusion

It is evident that ECOSOC, under the larger umbrella of the United Nations, plays an enormous role, with many difficult and diverse tasks at hand. Unfortunately, many of the achievements and major tasks of the UN are currently overshadowed by its image as an organization that is failing to meet the challenges of a new security situation, particularly in international disputes. Understandably, many believe that there are areas where the UN is in need of improvement and reform, and that ECOSOC is one of these. One must bear in mind, however, that the UN can only achieve what its member states allow it to. The United Nations will face many fresh challenges in the new millennium. It can meet these challenges through greater cooperation among nations, greater awareness of the world's population, and the continued work of concerned people around the globe.

Shoma Munshi

See Also United Nations Conference on Trade and Development (UNCTAD); Sustainable Development

References

Blackwell, David. "A review of *Renewing the United Nations System* by Erskine Childers and Brian Urquhart." Dag Hammarskjold Foundation, Uppsala, Sweden, 1994. 213 pp. David Blackwell, World Federalists of Canada, June 1995. http://www.ncrb. unac.org/unreform/selected/Childers-Urquhart.html.

Childers, Erskine, and Brian Urquhart. 1994. *Renewing the United Nations System.* Uppasala, Sweden: Dag Hammarskjold Foundation.

Maintaining Peace through the United Nations in the Twenty-First Century, http://www.ony.unu.edu/ seminars/MaintingPeace15June.html.

Ford Foundation. "The United Nations in its Second Half Century: A Report of the Independent Working Group on the Future of the United Nations." http:// www.library.yale.edu/un/UN_Report.txt. Also available from Office of Communications, Ford Foundation, 320 East 43rd Street, New York, New York 10017.

"A Report of the Independent Working Group on the Future of the United Nations," available online at http://www.library.yale.edu/un/un 1 e3d2.htm.

http://www.munuc.org/del/2003pdf/EcoSoc%20 Committee%20History.pdf. This is the web site for the Model United Nations of the University of Chicago.

http://www.peacewomen.org/un/ngoadvocacy/ ngostatus.html.

http://www.un.org/esa.

http://www.un.org/esa/coordination/desc.htm.

http://www.un.org/esa/coordination/ecosoc/about.htm.

http://www.un.org/esa/coordination/ecosoc/bwi2003/ BWIInfoNote.pdf.

The Economic Community of Central African States (ECCAS)/ *Communaute Economique des Etats d'Afrique Centrale (CEEAC)*

It has long been recognized that regional integration is an important key to socio-economic development, especially where the markets of individual countries may not be large enough to facilitate effective trade. Thus it is not surprising that each of the world's major continental or sub-continental regions has at least one major regional integration arrangement. Primary examples include the Association of South East Asian Nations (ASEAN), the Latin American Integration Association (LAIA), and the European Economic Community (EEC). Africa is no exception. Indeed Africa has a long history of regional cooperation and integration initiatives dating back to colonial times when the British established the East African Community, and the French, the *Union Douaniere de l'Afrique de l'Ouest*. Realizing the benefits of regional integration, some African countries, soon after independence, established alliances such as the Ghana-Guinea-Mali alliance to facilitate co-operation among them. However, it was not until the UN Economic and Social Council (ECOSOC) adopted its Resolution 671 (XXV) on April 29, 1958, to establish the United Nation Economic Commission for Africa (UNECA) that the foundation was laid for the evolution and growth of regional integration in Africa (Adedeji 2002). Currently there are 14 regional economic communities in Africa, which includes the Southern African Development Community (SADC); the Economic Community of West African States (ECOWAS); the Common Market for Eastern and Southern Africa (COMESA); and the Economic Community of Central African States (ECCAS), which is the subject matter of this article.

The Economic Community of Central African States (ECCAS) / *Communaute Economique des Etats d'Afrique Centrale (CEEAC)* is a regional bloc made of the 11 countries in Central Africa. The member countries include Angola, Burundi, Cameroon, Central African Republic, Chad, Congo, Democratic Republic of Congo, Equatorial Guinea, Gabon, Rwanda, Sao Tome, and Principe. The current headquarters of the ECCAS is based in Gabon.

Brief History and Present Status

The decision to establish a Central Africa–wide economic community was hatched at the summit of the Central African Customs and Economic Union (UDEAC) held in December

1981. However, the community was not established until October 18, 1983, when the UDEAC members and the members of the Economic Community of the Great Lakes States (CEPGL) (Burundi, Rwanda, and then Zaire) as well as Sao Tome and Principe, came together to form the organization. Angola retained an observer status until 1999, when it became a full member (Cosme and Fiacre 2001).

ECCAS began operations in 1985. However, after operating for about seven years, it fell into inactivity from 1992 until 1998, a situation that resulted primarily from the non-payment of membership fees by the member states. At the Second Extra-Ordinary Summit of ECCAS held in Libreville on February 6, 1998, ECCAS was re-launched under the chairmanship of President Pierre Buyoya of Burundi. The Heads of State/Government present at the summit committed themselves to the resurrection of the organization. Since then, the community has been quite active on a number of fronts.

In January 1999, a mini-summit of ECCAS leaders held in Gabon deliberated on the problems facing the community. They agreed on the creation of a third Deputy Secretary-General Post, specifically designated for Angola. Angola formally joined the community during this summit. In 1999, ECCAS made formal contact with the African Economic Community (AEC) and signed the Protocol on Relations between the AEC and the RECs, thus re-establishing the community's role as one of the designated pillars of the AEC. The AEC again confirmed the importance of ECCAS as the major economic community in Central Africa at the third preparatory meeting of its Economic and Social Council (ECOSOC) in June 1999.

The Tenth Ordinary Session of Heads of State and Government took place in Malabo, Equatorial Guinea, in June 2002. This summit decided, among other things, to adopt a protocol on the establishment of a Network of Parliamentarians of Central Africa (REPAC), and to adopt the standing orders of the Council for Peace and Security in Central Africa (COPAX), including the Defense and Security Commission (CDC), Multinational Force of Central

Africa (FOMAC), and the Early Warning Mechanism of Central Africa (MARAC). Rwanda was also officially welcomed upon its return as a full member of ECCAS (http://www.iss.co.za/AF/RegOrg/unity_to_union/eccasprof.htm).

The Eleventh Ordinary Session of Heads of State and Government in Brazzaville during January 2004 welcomed the fact that the Protocol Relating to the Establishment of a Mutual Security Pact in Central Africa (COPAX) had received the required number of ratifications to enter into force. The summit also adopted a declaration on the implementation of NEPAD in Central Africa as well as a declaration on gender equality.

The Twelfth Session was held in Brazzaville, the Republic of Congo, on June 8, 2005. The session challenged member countries to resolve their differences and work together to face the common challenges facing the community. Among other things, the members focused on transport and communication problems, which have stifled any meaningful integration. A key agreement was the request to donor agencies to help fund the Sangmelima-Djoum-Sanké-Ouesso road, which would link the Republic of Congo and Cameroon.

ECCAS has been designated a pillar of the African Economic Community (AEC) alongside the Economic Community of West African States (ECOWAS), Common Market for Eastern and Southern African (COMESA), Southern African Development Community (SADC), and Arab Maghreb Union (AMU).

Primary Aims and Objectives

Like other regional integration arrangements, ECCAS intends to eliminate customs duties and any other charges having an equivalent effect levied on imports and exports between member states. To facilitate further cooperation among member states it seeks to abolish quantitative restrictions and other trade barriers. Similarly, progressive abolition of obstacles to the free movement of persons, goods, services, and capital and to the right of establishment between member states is outlined. A comprehensive trade policy vis-à-vis third states necessitates the establishment and maintenance of an external common customs tariff. The ECCAS aims to promote rapid development in States that are landlocked, semi-landlocked, island or part-island and/or belong to the category of the least advanced countries. To achieve this goal it seeks to establish a Co-operation and Development Fund and harmonization of national policies in order to promote community activities, particularly in industry, transport and communications, energy, agriculture, natural resources, trade, currency and finance, human resources, tourism, education, culture and science, and technology. Achieving collective self-reliance, raising the standard of living of its peoples, increasing and maintaining economic stability, fostering close and peaceful relations between member states, and contributing to the progress and development of the member states remain prime objectives of this bloc.

Structure of ECCAS

To achieve its objectives, ECCAS is governed by several institutions such as the Conference of Heads of State and Government; the Council of Ministers; the Court of Justice; the General Secretariat; the Consultative Commission; and finally any specialized technical committee or organ set up or provided for by the establishing treaty.

The Conference of Heads of State and Government is the supreme organ of the organization and responsible for implementing the goals of the community. Among other things, it defines the general policy and major guidelines of the community and directs and harmonizes the socio-economic policies of member states. It has been granted the right to take any action under this treaty for achieving the aims of the community and to establish its rules of procedure and approve the rules of procedure of the Council of Ministers. It approves the organization chart of the General Secretariat of the

community. It is vested with the power to appoint the Secretary-General, the Deputy-Secretaries-General, the Financial Controller and the Accountant; and to delegate to the Council of Ministers, if it wishes, the authority to take decisions and issue directives on matters within its competence; and to refer a matter to the Court of Justice when it confirms by a two-thirds majority vote that a member state has not met one or more of its obligations arising from the treaty, from a decision or a directive of the conference or from a regulation of the Council of Ministers.

The conference meets once a year in regular session, although special sessions may be convened by its chairperson or at the request of a member state, provided such a request is supported by two thirds of the conference members. The office of chairperson is held every year by one of the Heads of State in the French alphabetical order of the member states specified in the treaty.

The conference is assisted by the Council of Ministers in the performance of its duties. The council, which meets twice a year, is made up of ministers responsible for economic development matters, or of any other minister appointed for the purpose by each member state. It makes recommendations to the conference on any action aimed at achieving the aims of the community in the context of the general policy and major guidelines defined and adopted by the conference; guides the activities of the other subordinate institutions of the community; submits the draft budget of the community to the conference and proposes to the conference the annual contribution of each member state; prepares its rules of procedure and submits them to the conference for approval; and exercise any powers granted to it under the treaty and any powers that may be delegated to it by the conference.

Relevant Treaties/Protocols/Accords

ECCAS or its members have been signatories to several treaties and accords since its inception.

These include (1) Protocol on Relations between the African Economic Community and Regional Economic Communities; (2)treaty establishing the African Economic Community; (3)the trilateral agreement on peace and military cooperation between Angola, the Congo and the Democratic Republic of the Congo; (4) the bilateral agreement on military cooperation between Cameroon and Chad; (5) border agreements between Gabon, Equatorial Guinea, and São Tomé and Principe; Equatorial Guinea and Cameroon; and Cameroon, Chad, and the Central African Republic; and (6) creation of the Council for Peace and Security in Central Africa (COPAX) in February 1999 to promote, maintain, and consolidate peace and security in Central Africa.

First, most of these treaties aim at fixing accurate sea and land borders between the member states, an important step in bringing peace and stability to the region considering the fact that border disputes have been one of the major causes of conflicts in the region. Second, the member states hope that through these agreements, they can jointly control and defend their borders and curb armed incursions, thereby making life safer for their nationals who live along the borders.

The creation of COPAX, a forum for political dialogue that meets in the event of a serious threat to peace and security in one or several countries, is a good way of dealing conflicts. The signing of a pact of non-aggression in 1996 by the heads to restore confidence between the various heads of state of the sub-region will go a long way to prevent conflicts. Another important dimension to the treaties is the linkage to the African Economic Community. This is in fact the long range objective of all the regional integration arrangements in Africa.

The ECCAS' Agenda

According to Article 6 of the ECCAS treaty, the community was to be established progressively over a period of twelve years, subdivided into three four-year stages:

Stage 1: Establishment of stability of the fiscal and customs regime existing at the date of entry into force of the treaty, and the carrying out of studies to determine the timetable for the progressive removal of tariff and non-tariff barriers to intra-community trade; and setting a timetable for increases or decreases in the customs tariffs of member states with a view to the adoption of a common external tariff.

Stage 2: Creation of a free trade area, once application of the timetable for the progressive elimination of tariff and non-tariff barriers to intra-Community trade is achieved.

Stage 3: Establishment of the customs union with the adoption of a common external tariff.

Laudable as the agenda is, most of it is yet to be implemented more than two decades after the community was established.

An Overview of the Economic Performance of ECCAS

An assessment of all the 14 regional arrangements in Africa by ECA staff indicates that EC-CAS is one of the least integrated. Trade among member states is still insignificant. In 1999, exports to and imports from member countries accounted for only 1.3 percent and 2.6 percent of total trade, respectively. Such results are not satisfactory when compared to 12.1 percent and 11.3 percent, respectively, for ECOWAS.

Overall, the community's economic growth has been mixed. Recent statistics from the Central African States Development Bank (BDEAC) indicate that economic growth in the sub-region dropped 7.7 percent in 2004 to 6.3 percent in 2005. Inflation rates in the sub-region, however, were estimated at 2 percent over the same period.

ECCAS has been making efforts to build its capacity. In May 2004, ECCAS signed a grant arrangement of $2 million with the African Capacity Building Foundation (ACBF) to build and strengthen the institutional capacity of the community.

Major Issues Facing ECCAS

Despite the re-organization and the apparent activities going on in the community, lack of unity among member states still remains a stumbling block to the organization's operation. For instance, the recent War in the Democratic Republic of Congo saw Rwanda and Angola supporting opposing sides.

The current most important issues with regard to ECCAS are conflict resolution, promotion of peace and stability, good governance, and economic reconstruction and development. The region has experienced, and continues to experience, more strife than all the other regions put together. The constant conflicts have undermined development efforts and made it difficult for the region to come down to real peacemaking as the conflicts have been spilling across the borders and some states have had to get involved in the conflicts of their neighbors. These issues, among others, prevented ECCAS from achieving its primary objective of establishing a common market area by the year 2000.

Integration has also been hampered by lack of efficient transportation systems in the region. Twenty years after formal integration was launched, none of the capital cities of the region are linked by good highway or railway systems between member states. Efforts at establishing a regional airline, Air CEMAC, have not been fruitful. This is a major hindrance to the movement of people and goods within and across the borders of member states.

Another key challenge is peace and stability. There is no gainsaying that socio-economic development cannot take place in an atmosphere of chaos and political instability. While Africa as a whole has faced wars, social upheavals, and conflicts, the ECCAS area has experienced more instability than any of the other regions. Until peace and political stability are secured

in the area, socio-economic development will continue to elude the region.

ECCAS in Numbers

Angola

The country of Angola encompasses an area of 481,354 square miles (1,246,700 square kilometers). Its population is 13.3 million with a GDP of $11.6 billion (1999). The labor force is 5 million (1997 est.), with approximately 85 percent employed in agriculture and 15 percent in the industry and service sectors combined. The GDP per capita of Angola is $1,038. Angola has the following natural resources: petroleum, diamonds, iron ore, phosphates, copper, feldspar, gold, bauxite, and uranium. Major industries include petroleum; diamonds, iron ore, phosphates, feldspar, bauxite, uranium, and gold; cement; basic metal products; fish processing; food processing; brewing; tobacco products; sugar; and textiles. With respect to agriculture, Angola produces bananas, sugar cane, coffee, sisal, corn, cotton, manioc (tapioca), tobacco, vegetables, plantains; livestock; forest products; fish. Its main exports are crude oil, diamonds, refined petroleum products, gas, coffee, sisal, fish and fish products, timber, and cotton. Angola's main export trading partners include the United States (with a 63 percent share of total exports), France, Chile, and China. Its primary imports are machinery and electrical equipment, vehicles and spare parts, medicines, food, textiles, and military goods. Angola's main import partners include Portugal, the United States, South Africa, France, Brazil, and Spain.

Burundi

The country of Burundi encompasses an area of 10,745 square miles (17,299 square kilometers). Its population is 6.2 million with a GDP of $4.2 billion (1999). The labor force of 1.9 million is mainly employed in agriculture (93 percent share of total workforce), with the remaining employed in the following sectors: government, industry and commerce, and services. The GDP per capita of Burundi is $730. Burundi has the following natural resources: uranium, rare earth oxides, peat, cobalt, and copper. Major industries include: light consumer goods such as blankets, shoes, and soap; assembly of imported components; public works construction; and food processing. With respect to agriculture, Burundi produces coffee, cotton, tea, corn, sorghum, sweet potatoes, bananas, manioc (tapioca); beef, milk, and hides. Its main exports are coffee, tea, sugar, cotton, and hides. Burundi's main export partners are Switzerland, Benelux, Germany, and the United Kingdom. Its main imports are capital goods, petroleum products, and foodstuffs, while its main import partners are Japan, Kenya, Germany, Zambia, and France.

Cameroon

The country of Cameroon encompasses an area of 183,567 square miles (475,440 square kilometers). Its population is 16.1 million with a GDP of $31.5 billion (1999). The labor force is mainly employed in agriculture (70 percent share of labor force) and in the industry and service sector (13 percent share), and the remaining employed in other sectors. The GDP per capita of Cameroon is $2,038 (1999). Cameroon has the following natural resources: petroleum, bauxite, iron ore, and timber. Major industries include petroleum production and refining, food processing, light consumer goods, textiles, and lumber. With respect to agriculture, Cameroon produces coffee, cocoa, cotton, rubber, bananas, oilseed, grains, root starches, livestock, and timber. Its main exports are crude oil and petroleum products, lumber, cocoa beans, aluminum, coffee, and cotton. Its main export partners are Italy (25 percent share of exports), Spain (20 percent), France (16 percent), and the Netherlands (7 percent). Its primary imports are machines and electrical equipment, transport equipment, fuel, and food. Cameroon's main import partners are France (25 percent share), the United States (8 percent), Nigeria (8 percent), and Germany (6 percent).

Central African Republic

The Central African Republic (CAR) encompasses an area of 240,535 square miles. Its population is 3.7 million with a GDP of $5.8 billion (1999). The GDP per capita of the Central African Republic is $1,684. It has the following natural resources: diamonds, uranium, timber, gold, and oil. Major industries include diamond mining, sawmills, breweries, textiles, footwear, and the assembly of bicycles and motorcycles. With respect to agriculture, the CAR produces cotton, coffee, tobacco, manioc (tapioca), yams, millet, corn, and bananas. Its main exports are diamonds, timber, cotton, coffee, and tobacco, and its main export partners are Benelux (36 percent share of exports), Côte d'Ivoire (5 percent), Spain (4 percent), Egypt (3 percent), and France. The CAR's main imports include food, textiles, petroleum products, machinery, electrical equipment, motor vehicles, chemicals, pharmaceuticals, consumer goods, and industrial products. Its main import partners are France (30 percent share of total imports), Côte d'Ivoire (18 percent), Cameroon (11 percent), and Germany (4 percent).

Chad

The country of Chad encompasses an area of 495,755 square miles. Its population is 9.5 million with a GDP of $7.6 billion (1999). The labor force is mainly employed in agriculture (85 percent), with only 15 percent in the industry and service sectors combined. The GDP per capita is $1,006. Chad has the following natural resources: uranium, kaolin, and fish. Major industries include cotton textiles, meat packing, beer brewing, natron (sodium carbonate), soap, cigarettes, and construction materials. With respect to agriculture, Chad produces cotton, sorghum, millet, peanuts, rice, potatoes, and manioc (tapioca). Its main export partners are Portugal (30 percent) and Germany (14 percent), as well as France, South Africa, Costa Rica, and Thailand. Its main import partners include France (41 percent), Nigeria (10 percent), Cameroon (7 percent), and India (6 percent).

Democratic Republic of Congo

The Democratic Republic of Congo (DRC) encompasses an area of 905,446 square miles (1,457,768 square kilometers). Its population is 53.6 million with a GDP of $35.7 billion (1999). The labor force is primarily employed in agriculture (65 percent share), with 16 percent in industry and 19 percent in the service sector. The GDP per capita of the DRC is $707 (1999). The DRC has the following natural resources: cobalt, copper, cadmium, petroleum, gem diamonds, gold, silver, zinc, manganese, tin, uranium, radium, bauxite, iron ore, coal, and timber. With respect to agriculture, the DRC produces coffee, sugar, palm oil, rubber, tea, quinine, cassava (tapioca), palm oil, bananas, root crops, corn, and fruits. Its main exports are diamonds, copper, coffee, cobalt, and crude oil and its main export partners are Benelux (52 percent share of total exports), the United States (14 percent), South Africa (9 percent), and Finland (4 percent). Its primary imports are foodstuffs, mining and other machinery, transport equipment, and fuels, and the DRC's main import partners are South Africa (25 percent), Benelux (14 percent), Nigeria (7 percent), and Kenya (5 percent).

Republic of Congo

The Republic of Congo encompasses an area of 132,046 square miles (342,000 square kilometers). Its population is 3.8 million with a GDP of $4.15 billion (1999). The GDP per capita of Congo is $1,530. Congo has the following natural resources: petroleum, timber, potash, lead, zinc, uranium, copper, phosphates, and natural gas. Major industries include petroleum extraction, cement kilning, brewing, sugar milling, palm oil, soap, and cigarette making. With respect to agriculture, Congo produces cassava (tapioca), sugar, rice, corn, peanuts, vegetables, coffee, and cocoa. Its main exports are petroleum, lumber, plywood, sugar, cocoa, coffee, and diamonds, while its primary imports are petroleum products, capital equipment, construction materials, and foodstuffs. Congo's main trading partners are the United States, Benelux, Germany, Italy, Taiwan, China, France, Belgium, and the United Kingdom.

Equatorial Guinea

The country of Equatorial Guinea encompasses an area of 10,830 square miles (28,051 square kilometers). Its population is 0.5 million with a GDP of $960 million (1999). The GDP per capita of Equatorial Guinea is $2000. Equatorial Guinea has the following natural resources: oil, petroleum, timber, small unexploited deposits of gold, manganese, and uranium. Major industries include petroleum, fishing, sawmilling, and natural gas. With respect to agriculture, it produces coffee, cocoa, rice, yams, cassava (tapioca), bananas, palm oil, and nuts. Its main exports are petroleum, timber, and cocoa, while its export partners are the United States (62 percent), Spain (17 percent), China (9 percent), Japan (3 percent), and France (3 percent). Its primary imports are petroleum and manufactured goods and equipment, and its main import partners include the United States (35 percent), France (15 percent), Cameroon (10 percent), Spain (10 percent), and the United Kingdom (6 percent).

Gabon

The country of Gabon encompasses an area of 103,346 square miles (267,667 square kilometers). Its population is 1.4 million with a GDP of $7.9 billion (1999). The labor force is about 600,000 with the sectoral shares being agriculture (60 percent), services and government (25 percent), and industry and commerce (15 percent). The GDP per capita of Gabon is $6,444. Gabon has the following natural resources: petroleum, manganese, uranium, gold, timber, and iron ore. Major industries include food and beverage, textile, lumber and plywood, cement, petroleum extraction and refining, and chemicals. With respect to agriculture, Gabon produces cocoa, coffee, sugar, palm oil, and rubber. Its main exports are crude oil (75 percent), timber, manganese, and uranium, while its main export partners are the United States (68 percent), China (9 percent), France (8 percent), and Japan (3 percent). Its primary imports are machinery and equipment, foodstuffs, chemicals, petroleum products, and construction materials with France (39 percent), the United States (6 percent), the Netherlands (5 percent), and Cameroon (5 percent), being its main import partners.

Rwanda

The country of Rwanda encompasses an area of 10,169 square miles (26,338 square kilometers). Its population is 8.4 million with a GDP of $5.9 billion (1999). The labor force is 3.6 million (1997 estimate) with 90 percent employed in agriculture. The GDP per capita of Rwanda is $720. Rwanda has the following natural resources: gold, cassiterite (tin ore), wolframite (tungsten ore), and methane. Major industries include cement, small-scale beverages, soap, furniture, shoes, plastic goods, and textiles. With respect to agriculture, Rwanda produces coffee, tea, pyrethrum (insecticide made from chrysanthemums), bananas, beans, sorghum, and potatoes. Its main export is cocoa (90 percent) while its primary export partners include Kenya, Spain, Pakistan, Belgium, Germany, and Brazil. Rwanda imports foodstuffs, machinery and equipment, steel, petroleum products, cement, and construction material, mainly from France, Benelux, the United States, Tanzania, and Kenya.

Sao Tome and Principe

The country of Sao Tome and Principe encompasses an area of 386 square miles (1,001 square kilometers). Its population is 200,000 with a GDP of $169 million (1999). The labor force is mainly employed in agriculture. The GDP per capita of Sao Tome and Principe is $1,100. Major industries include textiles, soap, beer, and fish processing. With respect to agriculture, Sao Tome and Principe produces cocoa, coconuts, palm kernels, copra, cinnamon, pepper, coffee, bananas, and papayas. Its main

export is cocoa (90 percent) mainly to the Netherlands (51 percent), Portugal (6 percent), and Germany (6 percent), while its primary imports are machinery and electrical equipment, food products, and petroleum products from Portugal (26 percent), France (18 percent), Japan, Belgium, and Angola.

Kwadwo Konadu-Agyemang

See Also Economic Integration; Common Market for Eastern and Southern Africa (COMESA); East African Community (EAC); Economic Community of Central African States (CEEAC); Southern African Development Community (SADC); Franc Zone

References

Adedeji, Adebayo. 2002. *History and Prospects for Regional Integration in Africa.* Paper presented at the Third Meeting of the African Development Forum Addis Ababa, 5 March 2.

African Development Bank. 2001. *Selected Statistics on African Countries 2001.* Abidjan: ADB. Central Intelligence Agency. *The World Factbook.* Washington, DC: CIA.

Cosme, H. E., and Y. Fiacre. 2001. "The Economic Community of Central African States and Human Security." In Goucha, M., and Cilliers, J., eds. *Peace, Human Security and Conflict Prevention in Africa.* Proceedings of the UNESCO-ISS Expert Meeting held in Pretoria, South Africa. July 23–24.

Population Reference Bureau (PRB). 2004. *Population Data Sheet.* Washington, DC: Population Reference Bureau.

UNICEF 2000 *Statistical Data.* http://www.unicef.org/statis/ (accessed January 20, 2002).

United Nations Economic Commission for Africa. 2000.

United Nations Development Program. 2001. *Human Development Report.* New York: Oxford University Press.

World Bank. 2004. *World Development Report.* New York: Oxford University Press.

http://www.polisci.com/almanac/organs/intorg/20054.htm.

http://www.iss.co.za/AF/RegOrg/unity_to_union/pdfs/eccas/ECCASoverview.pdf.

http://www.iss.co.za/AF/RegOrg/unity_to_union/eccasprof.htm.

http://www.polisci.com/almanac/organs/intorg/20054.htm.

Economic Organization of West African States (ECOWAS)

Historical Background

The treaty of Lagos, establishing the Economic Commission of West African States (ECOWAS), was signed in May 1975 by 15 states, with the objective of promoting economic and political co-operation and integration, leading to the establishment of an economic union in West Africa.

Many African countries had gained independence by the 1960s. At that time the Organization of African Unity (OAU) and the United Nations Economic Commission emphasized to independent African leaders the necessity for economic integration for African countries. In a bid to respond positively to this demand these leaders made assiduous efforts to achieve that goal. Unfortunately their efforts did not yield the desired result. "Most countries which had just become independent were not willing to surrender their sovereignty to such an organization. Furthermore, these African countries had strong ties with their former colonial Masters, which they considered more important than integration in Africa" (Venn 2000, 171). Equally the leaders of these countries had divergent political and economic ideological beliefs and, thus, lacked sincere confidence in one another.

Despite the lack of commitment of some African leaders to set up an economic organization, Uganda, Kenya, and Tanzania formed the East African Community in 1967 with the aim of creating a common market and good trade relationships among themselves. Unfortunately this community collapsed in 1977. Subsequently in October 1973 the West African countries Sierra Leone and Liberia formed the Mano River Union (MRU). Guinea, a neighboring country, joined in 1980. The formation of this union was intended to be an experiment in interstate cooperation with the ultimate objective of creating an economic integration among the three countries. It was assumed that this would be a lesson for member countries of the OAU in order to establish an African Economic Community.

Despite the aforementioned problems, Nigeria and Togo were instrumental in establishing an economic community in West Africa. Therefore, the treaty setting up the Economic Community of West African States was signed in Lagos on the May 28, 1975. Fifteen countries were the original signatories. Cape Verde registered in 1977, which increased the membership to sixteen at which time the treaty of ECOWAS commenced full operation. The ECOWAS headquarters is located in Lagos and at the time of establishment the total combined population of the countries was about 125 million.

After the formal establishment of ECOWAS, the leaders realized the necessity to intensify their undertakings to include more treaties: a treaty was drafted in 1991–1992 to increase political co-operation and economic integration. This revision was signed in July 1993. The revised treaty aims at the provision of a com-

Map of ECOWAS Members

mon market and a single currency, while politically it is determined to establish a West African parliament, an economic and social council, and an ECOWAS court of justice to replace the existing Tribunal and enforce community decisions. The treaty also formally assigns the community with the responsibility of preventing and settling regional conflicts. A protocol of nonaggression was signed at the third Conference of the Heads of State and Government. In 1990 a Standing Mediation Committee was formed to mediate disputes between member states. ECOWAS is also intended to maintain and enhance economic stability, foster relations among member states, and contribute to the progress and development of African-continent trade, cooperation, and self-reliance.

Member Nations

ECOWAS is comprised of member nations that can be categorized into three groups, based on their colonialization history: Anglophone, Francophone, and Lusophone. The Gambia, Sierra Leone, Liberia, Ghana, and Nigeria comprise the Anglophone group. Mau-

ritania, Mali, Senegal, Guinea, Cote d'Ivoire (Ivory Coast), Burkina Faso, Togo, Benin, and Niger are members of the Francophone group, whereas Guinea-Bissau and Cape Verde make up the Lusophone group.

The Gambia

The Gambia became independent from Britain on February 18, 1965. It formed a short-lived federation of Senegambia with Senegal between 1982 and 1989. In 1991 the two nations signed a friendship and cooperation treaty. A military coup in 1994 overthrew The Gambia's president and banned political activity, but in 1996 a constitution was created and a presidential election successfully occurred, followed by parliamentary balloting in 1997. This completed a nominal return to civilian rule. The capital city is Banjul.

The Gambia lies between the north part of the Atlantic Ocean and Senegal. The climate is tropical with a hot, rainy season from June to November and a cooler, dry season from November to May. The Gambia has an area of 11,300 square kilometers and has a population of 1,501,050. African-language speakers comprise 99 percent (Mandinka 42 percent, Fula 18 percent, Wolof 16 percent, Jola 10 percent, and Serahuli 9 percent) and others 4 percent. The official languages are English, Mandinka, Wolof, Fula, and other vernaculars. The literacy rate is 40.1 percent.

The Gambia is a republic under multiparty democratic rule divided into five administrative regions: Central River, Lower River, Bank, Upper River, Western.

The Gambia has a limited agricultural base without important mineral or natural resources. For their livelihood 75 percent of the population depends on crops and livestock. Small scale manufacturing activity depends on processing of peanuts, fish, and hides. Re-export trade constitutes major segment of economic activity, as does tourism. The main exports are peanut products, fish, cotton, lint, palm kernel, and re-exports of goods. The GDP derives from 33 percent agriculture, 13 percent industry, and 54 percent service oriented. The currency is the Dalasi (GMD).

Sierra Leone

In 1462 a Portuguese Explorer called Pedro da Cintra discovered Sierra Leone. Initially he called the country "Sierra Lyoa" in Portuguese, which means Lion Mountain, due to the topographical configuration and climatic conditions experienced by the explorers.

Sierra Leone was used as a slave trade outpost for many years until Granville Sharpe, the English philanthropist, abolished the slave trade. Part of the legacy of the slave trade can still be seen in the United States among the Gullah, who still retain many cultural traits from their origins in Sierra Leone.

Sierra Leone served as the seat of government for other British colonies along the West Africa Coast. The first college for higher education was called Fourah Bay College, which was established in 1827. This enabled the country to become known for its early achievements in medicine, law, and education, giving it the rep-

utation as the "Athens of West Africa." Sierra Leone became independent on April 27, 1961, from Britain.

Sierra Leone's recent history has been marred by a rebel war, which began in 1991 and lasted until July 7, 1999, when a peace agreement was signed between the government and the Revolutionary United Front (R.U.F) the group that waged war for eleven years.

The country lies north of the Atlantic Ocean, between Guinea and Liberia. The capital city, Freetown, provides natural anchorage and berthing facilities for ships at the Queen Elizabeth II Quay, the third largest natural harbor in the world. The climate is tropical with a hot, humid summer rainy season from May to December, and a winter dry season from December to April. Sierra Leone has an area of 71,740 square kilometers and a population of 5,732,681. English is the official language but the people speak Krio as the lingua franca. The literacy rate is 18 percent. Sixty percent of the population is Muslim, 10 percent is Christian, and indigenous beliefs comprise 30 percent.

Sierra Leone's government is a constitutional democracy made up of four administrative regions: the North, East, South, and the Western Area, which includes Freetown, the capital city. It is a very poor country with tremendous inequality in income distribution but does have substantial mineral, agricultural and fishing resources. The economy and social infrastructure are not well developed and serious social disorders continue to hamper economic development owing to the civil war. Plans continue to reopen the rutile and bauxite mines that were shut down during the war. Diamond mining is the major source of hard currency. The economy depends upon the maintenance of domestic peace and continued receipt of substantial aid from abroad, which is essential to offset the severe trade imbalance and supplement government revenues. Sixty-eight percent of the population is below the poverty line. Exports are diamonds, rutile, bauxite, coffee, cocoa, and fish. The GDP is comprised of 49 percent agriculture, 31 percent industry, and 21 percent service. The official currency is leones (le).

Liberia

Portuguese explorers established contacts with Liberia as early as 1461 and named the area the Grain Coast because of the abundance of grains of malegueta pepper. In 1663 the British established trading posts on the Grain Coast, but the Dutch destroyed these posts a year later. There were no further reports of European settlements on the Grain Coast until the arrival of the freed slaves in the early 1800s.

Freed slaves from the United States founded Liberia, which means "land of the free," in 1820. Called Americo-Liberians, they first arrived in Liberia and established a settlement in Christopolis, now named Monrovia after U.S. President James Monroe on February 26, 1820. These 86 immigrants formed the nucleus of the settler population of what became known as the Republic of Liberia, with its capital city being Monrovia.

Thousands of freed slaves from America soon arrived during the proceeding years, leading to the formation of more settlements culminating in a declaration of independence on July 26, 1847, from the United States. The Republic of Liberia adopted America styles of life and established thriving trade links with other West African countries.

Liberia borders the Atlantic Ocean, between Cote d'Ivoire and Sierra Leone. Its climate is tropical with a hot, humid dry winter full of hot days and cool to cold nights. Summers are wet and cloudy with frequent heavy showers. It has an area of 111,370 square kilometers and has a population of 3,317,176 made up of 95 percent indigenous tribes (including Kpell, Bassa, Gio, Kru, Grebo, Mano, Krahn, Gola, Gbandi, Loma, Kissi, Vai, Dei, Bella, Mandingo, and Mende), 2.5 percent Americo-liberians (descendants of immigrants from the United States who had been slaves), and 2.5 percent Congo people (descendants from immigrants

from the Caribbean who were slaves). English is the official language, but there are also 20 ethnic group languages, of which a few can be written and used in correspondence. The literacy rate is 15 percent. Twenty percent of the population are Muslim, 40 percent are Christian, and 40 percent maintain indigenous beliefs.

Liberia is a republic. It is endowed with rich water, mineral resources, and forests and climate favorable to agriculture. It is a producer and exporter of basic products—primarily raw timber and rubber. Civil war and misgovernment have destroyed much of the economy, especially the infrastructure in and around Monrovia. Many businessmen have fled the country, taking capital and expertise with them. The restoration of the infrastructure and the raising of income in this ravaged economy depend on the settlement of the civil war, the implementation of sound macro- and micro-economic policies, including the investment of foreign investments and generous support from donor countries. Exports are rubber, iron, timber, diamonds, coffee, and cocoa. The GDP is composed of 74 percent agriculture, 7 percent industry, and 19 percent service. The currency is Liberian dollars (LRD).

Ghana

Ghana initially was formed from the merger of the British colony of the Gold Coast and Togoland trust territory. On March 6, 1957, Ghana became the first country in Africa to gain its independence. Its capital city is called Accra. A series of coups resulted in the suspension of the constitution in 1981 and the banning of political parties. A new constitution, restoring multiparty politics, was approved in 1992. Lieutenant Jerry Rawlings, head of state since 1981, won the presidential elections in 1992 and 1996 but was constitutionally prevented from running for the third term in 2000. John Kufour, who defeated the former Vice President Atta Mills in a free and fair election, thus succeeded the president. Ghana has a constitutional democracy.

Ghana borders the Gulf of Guinea, between Cote d'Ivoire and Togo. It is smaller in size than Oregon and has ten administrative regions: Ashanti, Brog-Ahafo, Central, Eastern, Upper, Greater Accra, Northern, Western, and Volta. The climate is tropical, that is, warm and comparatively dry along the southeast coast, hot and humid in southwest, and hot and dry in the North. Ghana's total population numbers 20,467,747, which is broken down into 98.5 percent Black African, 44 percent Akan, 3 percent Gurma, 1 percent Yoruba, 16 percent Moshi-Dogomba, 13 percent Ewe, and 8 percent Ga. The official language is English. Sixteen percent of the population is Muslim, 63 percent Christian, and 21 percent maintain indigenous beliefs.

Well endowed with natural resources, Ghana has roughly twice the per capita output of the poorer counties in West Africa. However, Ghana remains heavily dependent on international and foreign financial and technical assistance. The domestic economy still revolves around subsistence agriculture, which accounts for 36 percent of the Gross Domestic Product (GDP) and employs 60 percent of the work force. Export products include gold, cocoa, timber, tuna, bauxite, aluminum, manganese, ore, and diamonds. Import products include capital equipment, petroleum, and foodstuff.

Nigeria

Nigeria became independent on October 1, 1960. The capital city is Abuja since December 12, 1991, when the capital was formerly transferred from Lagos. It divides administratively into 36 parts and one territory.

Nigeria borders the Gulf of Guinea, between Bennin and Cameroon. The climate varies from equatorial in the south, to tropical in the center, and arid in the north. Nigeria has an area of 923,768 square kilometers and has a population of 133,881,703. As Africa's most populous country, Nigeria has more than 250 ethnic groups. The most politically influential are the Hausa and Fulani (29 percent), Yoruba (21 percent), Ibo/Igbo (18 percent), Ijaw (10 percent), Kanuri (4 percent), Ibibio (3.5 percent), and Tiv (2.5 percent). The official languages are English, Hausa, Yoruba, Ibo, and Fulani, and the literacy rate is 68 percent. Fifty percent are Muslims, 40 percent are Christians, and 10 percent maintain indigenous beliefs.

The oil-rich Nigerian economy, long hobbled by political instability, corruption and poor macroeconomic management is undergoing substantial reform under the new civilian government. Former military rulers failed to diversify the economy away from over dependence on the capital-intensive oil sector. Exports are petroleum and petroleum products (95 percent), cocoa, and rubber. The currency is the naira (NGN).

Mauritania

Independent from France as of November 28, 1960, Mauritania annexed the southern third of the former Spanish Sahara (now called Western Sahara) in 1976, but relinquished it after three years of raiding by the Polisario Guerrillas Front seeking independence for the territory. It is a one party state and also continues to experience ethnic tensions between its black minority population and the dominant Maur (Arab-Berber) populace.

Mauritania borders the north Atlantic Ocean, between Senegal and Western Sahara. The climate is desert, constantly hot, dry, and dusty. It is 1,030,700 square kilometers in size and has a population of 2,912,584, made up of 40 percent racially mixed Maur and Black ethnicity, 30 percent Maur, and 30 percent Black. One hundred percent of the population is Muslim. The official languages are Hassaniya Arabic, Pulsar, Soninke, Wolof, and French and the literacy rate is 41.7 percent.

The country is a republic divided into 12 regions and 1 capital district: Adrar, Assaba, Brakna, Dalkhlet-Nouadhibou, Golgol, Guidi-maka, Hodh Ech, Chargui, Tagant, Inchiri, Nouakchott, Tiris Zemmour, and Trarza,

Half of the population depends on agriculture and livestock for livelihood, though many of the nomads and subsistence farmers were forced into the cities by recurrent droughts in the 1970s and 1980s. Mauritania has extensive deposits of iron ore, which accounts for nearly 40 percent of total exports. Decline in the world demand for ore, however, has led to cutbacks in production. Mauritania's coastal waters are among the richest fishing areas in the world, but overexploration by foreigners threatens the key source of revenue. The first deep water port opened near Nouakchott in 1986. In 2001 exploratory oil wells in the tracts 80 kilometers offshore indicated potential extraction at current oil prices. Exports are iron ore, fish and fish products, and gold. The GDP is made up of 25 percent agriculture, 29 percent industry and 46 percent service. The national currency is the ouguiya (MRD).

Mali

The Sudanese Republic and Senegal became independent of France in 1960 as the Mali Federation. When Senegal withdrew after only a few months, what formerly made up the Sudanese Republic was renamed Mali, with a new capital city of Bamako. Dictatorship ended in 1991 with a transitional government, and in the 1992 general elections Alpha Konare came to power.

Mali is situated southwest of Algeria and is 1.24 million square kilometers. The climate is subtropical to arid; hot and dry from February to June; rainy, humid, and mild from June to November; and cool and dry November to February. It has a population of 11,626,219 that is comprised of 50 percent Mande (Bambara, Malinke, Soninke), 17 percent Peul, 12 percent Voltaic, 6 percent Songhai, 10 percent Tuareg and Moor, and 5 percent others. Ninety percent

of the population is Muslim, 11 percent is Christian, and 9 percent maintain indigenous beliefs. The official language is French, Bambara (80 percent) and numerous African languages, and the literacy rate is 46.6 percent.

Mali is a republic. It is among the poorest countries in the world, with 65 percent of its land area desert or semi desert and with a highly unequal distribution of income. Economic activity is largely confined to the riverine area irrigated by the Niger. Ten percent of the population is nomadic and 80 percent of the work force is engaged in farming and fishing. Mali is dependent on foreign aid and vulnerable to fluctuations in world prices for cotton and gold. Exports are cotton, gold, and livestock. The GDP is made up of 45 percent agriculture, 17 percent industry, and 38 percent service. The national currency is the Communaute Financiere Africaine franc (XOF).

Senegal

Senegal became independent from France on April 4, 1960, when it joined with The Gambia to form the nominal confederation of Senegambia in 1982. However, the envisaged integrity of the two nations was never carried out and the union dissolved in 1989. The country Senegal then remained on its own and chose Dakar as its capital city. Since 1982, despite peace talks, a southern separatist group sporadically clashes with the government forces. There is a long history of international peacekeeping participation in Senegal.

Senegal lies along the southern Atlantic Ocean, between Guinea-Bissau and Mali and is 196,190 square kilometers in area. The climate is tropical with a hot, humid, rainy season from May to November with strong southeast winds and a dry season from December to April dominated by hot, harmattan wind. It has a population of 10,580,307 comprised of 94 percent Muslims, 5 percent Christians (Roman Catholic), and 1 percent retain indigenous beliefs. The official languages are French (official),

Wolof, Polaar, Jola, and Mandinka, and the literacy rate is 40.2 percent.

A republic under multi-party democratic rule, it is divided into ten administrative regions: Dakar, Diourbel, Fatick, Kaolack, Koida, Louga, Saint Louis, Tambacounda, Thies, and Ziguinchor, plus another area called Matam.

In January 1994, Senegal undertook an ambitious economic reform program with the support of the international donor community. This reform began with a 50 percent devaluation of Senegal's currency, the CFA franc that was linked at a fixed rate to the French franc. Government price controls and subsidies have been steadily dismantled. After seeing its economy contract by 2.1 percent in 1993, Senegal made an important turnaround, with real growth in GDP averaging 5 percent annually from 1995 to 2002. Annual inflation was pushed down to less than 1 percent, but rose to an estimated 3.3 percent in 2001 and 3.0 percent in 2002. 1993 Investment rose steadily from 13.8 percent of GDP to 16.5 percent in 1997. As a member of the West African Economic and Monetary Union (WAEMU), Senegal is working toward greater regional integrity with a unified tariff. Exports are fish, groundnuts (peanuts), petroleum products, cotton, and phosphate. The GDP is made up of 18 percent agriculture, 27 percent industry and 55 percent service. The national currency is the Communaute Financiere Africaine franc (XOF).

Guinea

Independent from France since October 2, 1958, Guinea only had her first democratic elections in 1993 when General Lansana Conte, head of the military government, was elected president of the civilian government. He was reelected in 1998.

Guinea is bounded by the northern part of the Atlantic Ocean, and it lies between Guinea-Bissau and Sierra Leone. From June to November the climate is a hot and humid, monsoon-type of rainy season with southwesterly winds, and from December dry season with northeasterly harmattan winds. It is 245,857 square kilometers in area and has a population of 9,030,220 of which 40 percent are Peuhl, 30 percent are Malinke, 20 percent are Sousou, and 10 percent are smaller ethnic groups. Eighty-five percent of the population is Muslim, 8 percent is Christian, and 7 percent maintain indigenous beliefs. The official language is French.

The country is a republic divided into 33 prefectures and one special zone: Beyla, Boffa, Boke, Conakry, Coyah, Labe, Fria, Faranah, Dabola, Dalaba, Dabola, Dinguiraye, Dubreka, Yomou, Tougue, Macenta, Lola, lelouma, Kissidougou, Koubia, Kindia, Telimele, Pita, Siguiri, Kankan, Kerouare, Gueckedou, Mali, Mandina, Nzerekore, Kouroussa, Gaoual and Forecariah.

Guinea possesses mineral, hydropower and agricultural resources, yet remains an underdeveloped nation. It boasts over 30 percent of the world's bauxite reserves and is the second-largest bauxite producer in the world. In 1999 the mining sector accounted for 75 percent of exports. Exports are bauxite, aluminum, gold, diamonds, coffee, fish, and imports are primarily petroleum products, metals, transport equipment, textiles, and foodstuff. The GDP is made up of 25 percent agriculture, 37 percent industry, and 38 percent service. The currency is the Guinean franc (GNF).

Cote d'Ivoire

Cote D'ivoire's has maintained a close relationship with France since it achieved independence. The development of cocoa production for export and foreign investment made Cote d'Ivoire one of the most prosperous of the tropical African states, but did not protect it from political turmoil. In December 1999, the first military coup in the history of the country overthrew the government of President Henri Konan Bedie. Junta leader Robert Guei held elections in 2000, but excluded prominent opposition leader Alassane Ouattara by blatantly rigging the polling results and declaring himself winner. Popular protest forced Guei to step aside and brought runner-up Laurent Gbagbo to power. Gbagbo spent two years consolidating his weak mandate but was unable to appease his opponents, who launched a failed coup attempt in September 2002. Rebel forces claimed the north half of the country and in January granted minority positions in a unity government. There are several thousand French and West African troops in Cote d'Ivoire to maintain peace and the peace accord.

Cote d'Ivoire borders the North Atlantic Ocean between Ghana and Liberia.There are only three seasons: warm and dry from November to March, hot and dry from March to May, and hot and wet from June to October. The climate is tropical along the coast and semiarid in the far north. It has an area of 322,460 square kilometers and has a population of 16,962,491 divided into 42.1 percent are Akan, 17.6 percent Voltaiques or Gur, 17.6 percent Northern Mandesx, 11 percent Krous, 10 percent Southern Mandes, and 7.8 percent of other origins (130,000 Lebanese and 20,000 French).

In 1960 Cote d'Ivoire established a Republic multi-party presidential regime, divided into 58 departments. The capital city is Yamoussoukro, but since 1983, Abijan remains the commercial and administrative center. The United States and other countries have their embassies in Abijan. It is among the world's largest cocoa, coffee, bean, and palm oil producing countries. Consequently the economy is highly sensitive to fluctuations in international prices for these products and to weather conditions. Despite the government's attempts to diversify, the economy is still largely dependent on agriculture and related activities, which engage roughly 68 percent of the population. After several years of lagging performance, the Ivorian economy began a comeback in 1994. Exports are coffee, cocoa, beans, bananas, palm kernel, corn, sweet potatoes, sugar, cotton, rubber, and timber. The national currency is the Communaute Financiere Africaine franc (XOF).

Togo

French Togoland became Togo and independent on April 27, 1960. In 1967, General Gnassingbe Eyadema was installed as military ruler. He was Africa's longest-serving head of state. Despite the façade of multi-party elections instituted in the 1990s, the government continues to be dominated by President Eyadema, whose rally of the Togolese People Party (RPT) has maintained power almost continually since 1967. Dictatorship formally ended in 1991 with transitional government, and the 1992 general election brought Alpha Konare to power.

French Togo sits between Bennin and Ghana. The capital city is Lome. It is 56,785 square kilometers in area and has a population of 5,429,299. There are 37 ethnic groups but the most important are the Ewe, Mina, and Kabre, who make up 99 percent of the population. Europeans and Syrian-Lebanese comprise less than 1 percent. Twenty percent of the people are Muslim, 29 percent are Christians, and 51 percent maintain indigenous beliefs. The official language is French.

This sub-Saharan economy is heavily dependent on both commercial and subsistence agriculture, which provides employment for 65 percent of the population. Cocoa and coffee generate 40 percent of export earnings and cotton is the most important cash crop. Togo is the world's fourth largest producer of phosphate, but 2002 production fell to 22 percent due to power shortages and cost of developing new deposits. The GDP is 42 percent agriculture, 21 percent industry, and 37 percent service.

Niger

Although Niger gained its independence from France 33 years ago, it was not until 1993 that there were free and fair elections. A 1995 Peace accord ended a five-year Tuareg insurgence in the north. Coups in 1996 and 1999 were followed by the creation of a national reconciliation council that effected a transition to civilian rule by December 1999. The capital city is Niamey.

Niger is southeast of Algeria and is 1.267 million square kilometers in area. The climate is that of a desert: mostly hot, dry, dusty, tropical in the extreme south. It has a population of 11,058,590 that is made up of 56 percent Hausa, 22 percent Djerma, 8.5 percent Fula, 8 percent Tuareg, 4.3 percent beriberi (Kanouri), 1.2 percent Arab, Toubou and Gourmantche, and about 1,200 foreign expatriates. Eighty percent of the population is Muslim and the remainder are Christians and indigenous believers. The official languages are French, Hausa, and Djerma. Niger is a republic divided into seven administrative departments, Agadez, Diffa, Dosso, Maradi, Niamey, and Tillaberi and the capital district of Zinder.

As a poor, landlocked nation, Niger's economy centers on subsistence agriculture, animal husbandry, and re-export trade, and increasingly on depleted uranium mining because of declining world demand. Exports are uranium ore, livestock, cowpeas, and onions, and imports are foodstuff, machinery, vehicles and parts, petroleum, and cereals. The GDP is 39 percent agriculture, 17 percent industry, and 44 percent service. The national currency is the Communaute Financiere Africaine franc (XOF).

Bennin

Dahomey achieved independence from France in 1960. The name changed to Bennin in 1975. From 1974 to 1989, the country was socialist; free elections were reestablished in 1991.

Bennin borders Bennin, between Nigeria and Togo and is 12,620 square kilometers in area. The climate is tropical, and hot humid in the south while semiarid in the north. It has a population of 7,041,490 that is declining because of the devastation of HIV/AIDS. Twenty percent of the people are Muslim, 30 percent are Christian, and 50 percent maintain indigenous beliefs. The official languages are French,

Fon, and Yoruba (south), and various tribal dialects (6 in the North). The literacy rate is 40 percent.

In December 1989 the multiparty democratic rule dropped Marxism and Leninism and in February 1990 adopted democratic reforms. On April 4, 1991, Bennin officially made the transition to a multiparty system. It is divided into 12 provinces: Atakora, Alibori, Atlantique, Borgou, Collines, Couffo, Donga, Littoral, Mono, Oueme, Plateau, and Zou.

Bennin's economy remains underdeveloped and dependent on subsistence agriculture, cotton products, and regional trade. Exports are cotton, crude oil, palm products, and cocoa; and imports are foodstuffs, capital goods, and petroleum. The GDP growth rate is 5.04 percent. The national currency is the Communaute Financiere Africaine franc (XOF).

Burkina Faso

Burkina Faso, formerly known as Upper Volta, became independent from France on August 5, 1960. Government instability in 1970s and 1980s was followed by multi-party elections in the early 1990s. Several hundred thousand farm workers migrate south every year to Cote d'Ivoire and Ghana. It is 274,200 square kilometers in area and has a population of 13,228,460. North of Ghana, its capital city is Ouagadougou. The nationality of the people is Burkinabe. The climate is tropical with a warm, dry winter and a hot, wet summer. The Mossi comprise over 40 percent of the population, followed by Gurusi, Senufo, Lobi, Bobo, Mande and Fulani. Fifty percent of the people are Muslim, 10 percent are Christian, and 40 percent maintain indigenous beliefs. French and native African languages belonging to the Sudanic family are spoken by 90 percent of the population. The literacy rate is 26.6 percent.

Burkina Faso is a parliamentary republic divided into 30 administrative regions. It is one of the poorest countries in Africa. Landlocked, it has few natural resources, a fragile soil, and a highly unequal distribution of income. About 90 percent of the population is engaged in agriculture (mainly subsistence), which is vulnerable to variations in rainfall. Industry remains dominated by unprofitable government-controlled co-optations. Following the African franc currency devaluation in January 1994, the government updated its development program in conjunction with international agencies, and exports and economic growth have increased. Maintenance of macroeconomic progress depends on continued low inflation, reduction in the trade deficit, and reforms designed to encourage private investment. International crisis in Cote d'Ivoire continues to hurt trade and industrial prospects and deepens the need for international assistance.

Guinea-Bissau

Guinea-Bissau became unilaterally declared independence on September 24, 1973, but was not recognized by Portugal until September 10, 1974.

In 1994, 20 years after independence from Portugal, the first multi-party legislature and presidential elections were held. A bloody civil war in 1998 created hundreds of thousands of displaced persons. A military junta ousted the government in 1999. The interim government turned over power in February 2000 when the opposition, Kumba Yala, took office following two rounds of transparent elections. Transition back to democracy is complicated due to a crippled economy devastated during the war.

Guinea-Bissau lies between Guinea and Senegal. The climate is tropical with a generally hot and humid monsoon-type rainy season from June to November and a dry season from December to May. It has a population of 1,360,827, of which 45 percent is Muslim, 5 percent is Christian, and 50 percent maintain indigenous beliefs. The official language is Portuguese, but Crioulo is widely spoken.

It is a republic divided into nine regions: Bafata, Biombo, Bissau, Bolema (or Bolama, Bi-

jagos), Cacheu, Gabu, Oio, Quinara, and Tombali. The capital city is Bissau.

Guinea-Bissau is one of the poorest countries in the world. Bissau depends mainly on farming and fishing. Intermittent fighting between Senegalese-backed government troops and a military junta have destroyed the government infrastructure and seriously damaged the economy. Exports are fish, cashew, palm kernel, and peanut. Although it has potential for gold, phosphate, bauxite, and oil mining, the exploration cost is more than the country presently can afford.

Cape Verde

These inhabited islands were discovered and colonized by the Portuguese in the fifteenth century and subsequently became trading centers for African slaves. They later became an important coal restocking and supply stop for whaling and transatlantic shipping. Most Cape Verdeans have both African and Portuguese ancestors. Cape Verde achieved independence from Portugal on July 5, 1975.

A group of islands in the North Atlantic Ocean, west of Senegal, Cape Verde is 4,033 square kilometers in area. The population of 412,137 of which 71 percent are Creole (Mulato), 28 percent are African, and 1 percent are European. The country is mostly Roman Catholic infused with indigenous beliefs, and Protestant (mostly Church of Nazarene). The official languages are Portuguese, Crioulo (a blend of Portuguese and West African words) and the literacy rate is 76.6 percent. The climate is temperate with warm, dry summers and meager and very erratic precipitation.

Cape Verde is a republic whose economy suffers from a poor natural revenue base including serious water shortages exacerbated by cycles of long-term droughts. The economy is service-oriented, with commercial, transportation, tourism and public services activity accounting for 72 percent of the GDP. Although nearly 70 percent of the population lives in the rural areas, the share of agriculture in GDP in 2001 was only 11 percent, of which fishing accounts for 1.5 percent. Eighty-two percent of the country's food is imported. Fishing potential (mostly lobster and tuna) is still not fully exploited, thus the economy is financed by foreign aid and remittance from immigrants.

Goals and Objectives of ECOWAS

ECOWAS was developed to accomplish the following objectives: (1) Abolish custom duties levied on trade among member states. (2) Eliminate quantitative and administrative restrictions on trade among member states, and moreover to establish a common tariff for non-member countries and eliminate tariffs and other trade obstructions, and to establish a common external tariff among member countries. (3) Eliminate obstacles restricting people's free movement, services, and capital among member states. In 1979 a protocol for free circulation of the region's citizens and rights of residence and establishment of commercial enterprises was signed. (4) Harmonize agricultural policies and promotes of common projects in member states, in the field of marketing, research and agro-industrial enterprises. "An Agricultural Development Strategy was adopted in 1982, aiming at sub-regional self-sufficiency by the year 2000. The strategy included plans for selecting seeds and cattle species, and called for solidarity among member states during international commodity negotiations. Seven seed selection and multiplication centers and eight livestock-breeding centers were designated in 1984" (http://www.focusintl.com/whos0004.htm). It establishes a common policy in joint development of transportation communications, energy, and other infra-structural facilities. A work program for energy development, involving a regional analysis of energy issues and plans for increasing efficiency and finding an alternative source, was planned in 1981. The creation of an Energy Resources Development Fund was ap-

proved in 1982. (6) Harmonize economic, industrial, and monetary policies and eliminate disparities in income levels of member states. (7) Establish a fund for co-operation, compensation, and development. (8) Prevent and settle regional disputes. (9) Undertake the responsibility to protect, preserve, and enhance the natural environment of the region and co-operate in the event of natural disasters. Article 29 of the ECOWAS Treaty justifies this point. (10) Urge member states to harmonize and co-ordinate their policies and programs in the field of natural resources. Article 31 of ECOWAS Treaty substantiates this fact.

Structure of ECOWAS

The Authority is the highest institution of the community. Composed of heads of states and government or their accredited representatives, it meets once a year. It essentially directs and controls the performance of the executive functions of the community. All of its decisions are binding on all the community's institutions. The Office of the Chairman of ECOWAS is based on an annual rotation among members of the Authority.

The Council of Ministers is made up of two representatives of each member state. The council meets twice a year, although there is provision for extra-ordinary meetings. The office of the Chairman of the Council of Ministers also rotates annually. It is responsible for reviewing the functioning and development of the community. The council makes recommendations to the Authority on the efficient functioning of the community and gives directions to all subordinate community institutions.

The Executive Secretariat is headed by the Executive Secretary, who is the principal executive officer of the community. The Authority, on the recommendation of the Council of Ministers, appoints the Executive Secretary and two Deputy-Executive Secretaries. The Executive Secretary is elected for a four-year term, which can be renewed once. The position is responsible for the daily administration of the Community. Past Executive Secretaries of ECOWAS include: Aboubakar D. Quattara, 1977–1984, from Ivory Coast; Momodu Munu, 1985–1989 from Sierra Leone. The current Secretary General is Dr. Muhammad Ibn Chambers, Nigerian by nationality.

The Tribunal is responsible for the maintenance of law and justice as enshrined in the Treaty of ECOWAS. It is called upon to settle all disputes of ECOWAS. *The Technical and Specialized Commissions* have been created to focus efforts on particular venues. These are the the Trade, Customs, Immigrations, Monetary and Payments Commission; the Industry, Agriculture and Natural Resources Commission; the Transport, Telecommunications and Energy Commission, and the Social and Cultural Affairs Commission. Each member state provides one representative to the commissions, who periodically submit reports and recommendations through the Executive Secretary to the Council of Ministers.

Advantages of ECOWAS

Establishment of ECOWAS has created a larger market for the sale of goods among member countries. Invariably this has led to the appreciation of the economies, incremenal increase in marketing levels, and large-scale production in some member countries. The treaty provides for the free movement of persons, services and capital, which has enhanced members' ability to benefit from skills and expertise of advanced member counties. Membership in ECOWAS is reducing the high incidence of smuggling, which has historically caused serious loss of revenue for the country into which the goods have been smuggled.

Harmonization of prices of goods among member states has put member countries in an advantageous and effective bargaining position with regard to their products and thus afforded them better terms of trade negotiation with the outside world. Setting up an economic commu-

nity of this nature gives ECOWAS countries the likelihood of increasing foreign investment in many business areas.

Problems of ECOWAS

There is inequality in terms of population, geographical size, and resource endowment among ECOWAS countries. In this regard there is a fear by other members that Nigeria, with vast size, large population, and resources could dominate the community.

Presently the levels of trade are low, therefore political leaders need to increase trade among member countries if ECOWAS is to succeed as an economic union.

Prospect of trade among member countries is still poor as there is a huge currency barrier. "The multiplicity of currencies among members is a serious drawback. Presently most West African States settle their accounts in foreign currencies such as the US dollar, pound sterling and CFA franc"(Venn 2000, 175). It could be advantageous to remove these currency barriers.

Lack of direct communication lines among ECOWAS countries is a hindrance to the community. This is negating co-operation and integration among West African countries. The road, rail, and telecommunications systems were built to serve individual countries instead of linking them.

As most of the member countries were colonies of France and Britain, there is still a prevailing problem of common ideological orientation and common language. Also within the ECOWAS are rival groupings, such as the French-speaking West African Economic Community (CEAO).

Free movement of citizens of member states of the community is creating problems of migration of labor from states experiencing economic hardship into the more affluent states. Nigeria asked over a million citizens of ECOWAS without proper documents to leave the country or face legal action.

Since the formation of ECOWAS, leaders of member countries intended to prioritize environmental issues, but success is yet to be attained. "Even though ECOWAS has laudable policies in favor of the environment, not much has been done to mobilize resources to tackle problems confronting member states in their quest for sustainable development. A number of countries have embarked on a course of structural adjustment and trade liberalization and with programs on serious environmental and socio-economic problems" (http://www.focusintl.com/whos0004.htm). It appears much effort is required to successfully achieve the objectives of this treaty.

Saffa-woya Rogers

See Also Economic Integration; Common Market for Eastern and Southern Africa (COMESA); East African Community (EAC); Southern African Development Community (SADC; Franc Zone

References

Deng, M., Francis and William I. Zartman. 1991. *Conflict Resolution in Africa.* Washington, DC: The Brookings Institution.

Diamond, Larry, J. Linz, and Seymour Martin Lipset. 1995. *Politics in Developing Countries: Comparing Experiences with Democracy.* Boulder: Lynne Rienner Publishers.

Francis, David. 2003. *Uniting Africa: Building Regional Security Systems.* Boulder: Lynne Rienner.

Huntington, Samuel P. 1968. *Political Order in Changing Societies.* New Haven: Yale University Press.

Richard, Paul. 1996. *Fighting for the Rain Forest: War, Youth and Resources in Sierra Leone.* Wageningen, Holland: University of Wageningen.

Stewart, Ian. *Freetown Ambush, A Reporter's Year in Africa.* Albany (Aukland): Pengiun Books Ltd.

Venn, Oladipo H. B. 2000. *Essentials of Government for Ordinary Level Examinations.* (Second Ed.) London: Evans Brothers Limited.

European Economic Area (EEA)

The European Economic Area (EEA) is the result of a cooperative economic agreement reached in 1991 between the European Community (forerunner of the European Union) and the seven member countries of the European Free Trade Association (EFTA). The EEA treaty was signed by the foreign ministers of the member states in May 1992 and came into effect on January 1, 1994. Treaty provisions allow the free movement of goods, persons, services, and capital among EEA countries. Lichtenstein, Switzerland, Norway, and Iceland are able to trade with the member states of the European Union without restriction and without having to pay tariffs at their borders. These countries therefore enjoy access to the single European market while not assuming the full responsibilities of a European Union membership.

Genesis of EFTA and EEA

The idea of a free trade agreement in Europe goes back to the early 1950s and the European Economic Community (EEC). After World War II, several European countries sought closer political, economic, and social ties to achieve higher economic growth on a continent that was largely destroyed by the war itself. In 1951, the leaders of six governments and states, namely Belgium, France, Italy, Luxembourg, the Netherlands, and West Germany, signed the Treaty of Paris with the aim of ensuring a lasting peace and security in Europe, especially to reconcile France and West Germany. The Treaty

of Paris established the European Coal and Steel Community (ECSC). This treaty became the cornerstone of European integration and economic liberalization and ultimately led to the creation of the European Union with the Maastricht Treaty in 1993. The ECSC created a free trade area among the signing members in areas such as coal, steel, scrap, and iron. It also established several institutions to better manage coordination of the new community. Among these institutions was an administrative authority, a Council of Ministers to act as a legislative body, an Assembly to formulate common policy, and a Court of Justice to solve disputes and interpret the treaty.

In 1957, the six signing countries of the ECSC created the European Economic Community (EEC). From then on, a common market shaped the political landscape, abolishing economic borders among the member states. The EEC also held the door open to other countries wishing to join the community. Furthermore, it abolished trade barriers such as tariffs and inspections to guarantee the free movement of goods, labor, services, and capital within the community. This liberal ideology prevails today in the European Economic Area. Moreover, the community developed its own external trade and agricultural policy. The signing of the EEC made it mandatory for member states to revise domestic legislation in order to abolish internal tariffs and adopt the new supranational provisions of the treaty. In 1968, the member states were required to replace policies that discriminated against goods, services, and people to promote domestic industries with policies giving foreign investors equal rights to domestic ones.

Most important, the EEC created four institutions that have remained in place: (1) the European Commission, the administrative body of the community (and now the European Union); (2) the Council of Ministers, the legislative organ; (3) an Assembly, an early form of the European Parliament; and (4) the European Court, the judicial entity. The commission created for the EEC and the one for the ECSC were merged into a single commission by the Treaty of Brussels in 1965. Ever since, the commission has consisted of a permanent civil service staff governed by commissioners, who are appointed by the member states for a five-year term.

The treaties fostered the process of European integration and created far-reaching competencies for the member states, but thus far they had left out those European countries that had not yet joined the EEC. Although the United Kingdom, Denmark, Ireland, Greece, Portugal, Austria, and Spain belonged to Europe geographically, and historically had close economic relationships with the rest of Europe, their economies were not fully integrated into the single European market because they had not signed the treaties. This created an enormous economic disadvantage for those countries because they still had to pay tariffs and customs at the borders of EEC countries. In order to eliminate this economic hardship, EFTA was created on May 3, 1960, among both EEC member states and states that had resisted joining the EEC for domestic political reasons. The Stockholm Convention, adopted on January 4, 1960, granted EFTA countries the same economic rights as the EEC member states, allowing free movement of goods, services, people, and capital and creating the largest single market in Europe, with only one customs union.

In the 1970s and 1980s, the EEC, which had become the European Community (EC) in 1967, enlarged to include new members. The United Kingdom, Denmark, and Ireland joined in 1973, Greece in 1981, and Portugal and Spain in 1986. The EC was transformed into the European Union by the Maastricht Treaty in 1993, and on January 1, 1995, Sweden, Austria, and Finland joined, leaving only Iceland, Switzerland, Liechtenstein, and Norway outside the group of Western European nations that had become EU member states. However, these countries continued their membership in EFTA. Norway has held two national referendums, one in 1972 and the second in 1994, about its application for membership in the EU, and on both occasions the voters rejected the Norwegian government's attempt to join.

The European Economic Area replaced EFTA in 1994. Norway, Liechtenstein, and Iceland, in particular, initiated the consultations leading to the agreement. EEA member states today include Austria, Belgium, Denmark, Finland, France, Germany, Greece, Iceland, Ireland, Italy, Liechtenstein, Luxembourg, the Netherlands, Norway, Portugal, Spain, Sweden, and the United Kingdom, to make up the largest free trade zone in Europe. Besides the privileges based on freedom of movement, membership gives Norway, Liechtenstein, Switzerland, and Iceland the right to consult with the European Commission during policy and legislation formation processes. In other words, they enjoy consultative status on commission matters in Brussels, but not the right to vote on policy decisions, which is an exclusive right held only by EU member states.

Social policy, consumer protection, environmental regulations, business law, and statistics are policy areas affected by the EEA. In these fields, Norway, Iceland, and Liechtenstein must adopt the rules and regulations of the European Union. The EEA agreement's primary function is to ensure equal conditions for competition among European businesses, people, and goods. The European Union's "Acquis Communautaire," which lists the rules and regulations for business cartels, state monopolies, and state aid (subsidies) for specific businesses, markets, or regional blocks, leans on the articles of the EEA dealing with competition laws.

Free Movement Policies

The freedom-of-movement principles embodied in the EEA treaty are fundamental to the success of the single European market. They cover freedom of movement in four areas: goods, services, capital, and people.

Goods

One of the major requirements for the free flow of goods is the elimination of customs duties and other qualitative restrictions at the border. Free movement of goods has its roots in the European Coal and Steel Community; however, the EEA agreement extended the principle to harmonize legislation related to technical regulations and to remove technical barriers to trade. The EEA agreement also identifies the principle of mutual recognition of standards and testing.

Services

The EEA agreement guarantees the free flow of services for businesses, eliminating the requirement of nationality to offer business services in any EEA state. Also, businesses can offer services across borders without restrictions and without the fear of repercussions or punishment by the state. These services include financial services, information and technology services, audiovisual services, and postal services.

Capital

The free flow of capital is one of the foremost requirements to ensure the completely free flow of goods and services. It includes free capital transfers across EEA borders, cross-border investments, and transborder loans. The provisions of the EEA agreement not only ensure exchange controls but also require nondiscrimination against foreign investors in domestic legislation pertaining to capital movement. In other words, in any EEA member country, investors from other EEA nationalities possess the same rights as domestic investors. Only under exceptional circumstances, such as domestic currency devaluations, can the free flow of capital be restricted.

People

The EEA agreement adopted similar provisions to the Schengen Agreement in 1985, which also ensures the free movement of people. The free movement of people has thus become one of the fundamental rights of the people of Western Europe. Citizens of EEA member countries may live, work, study, and establish businesses anywhere within the borders of the region.

EEA Institutions

The decisionmaking process within the EEA is characterized by what may be called a "two-pillar system." EEA/EFTA countries—Norway, Iceland, Switzerland, and Liechtenstein—did not transfer legislative competencies to an EEA organ; in other words, the EEA institutions do not accept direct decisions by the European Commission or even the European Court of Justice. In order to fill this gap, the EEA agreement set up specific EEA/EFTA bodies matching their counterparts in the European Community. They include an EEA Court, a Surveillance Authority, and a Standing Committee.

Joint EEA Bodies

EEA Council. The EEA Council's primary responsibility is to support the policy formation process and to lead the implementation and development of the EEA agreement. Its counterpart on the EU side would be the European Council, which meets to discuss and develop EU policies. The foreign ministers of the EEA/EFTA countries meet twice a year for consultation. The meeting is supplemented by the European commissioner for external relations, the high representative for the European Union's common foreign and security policy, and the current and forthcoming presidents of the EU. The composition of the council already insinuates that the consultations in the council go beyond traditional economic policies and include a political dialogue about general external policies, including security policies. The presidency of the council rotates between the EU side and the EFTA side every term. The council also deals with recommendations and resolutions of the EEA Joint Parliamentary Committee and the EEA Consultative Committee.

EEA Joint Parliamentary Committee. The Joint Parliamentary Committee debates and discusses a wide range of issues and policies. It seeks to contribute to a better understanding among EU and EFTA states in fields defined by the EEA agreement through increased dialogue and consultations. The European Parliament as well as the parliaments of the EEA/EFTA countries send parliamentarians to this committee, which meets twice a year. The chairmanship of the committee rotates each year between the European Parliament side and the EFTA side.

It is the task of the parliamentarians to scrutinize and monitor the legislation of the European Community that touches upon the fields negotiated in the EEA agreement. The parliamentarians enjoy the right to ask the EEA Council (in writing or orally) about policies or policy intentions. Once the Joint Parliamentary Committee has finalized its discussions and reached a conclusion on an issue, it publishes its views and recommendations in the form of a written report or resolution. Between 1998 and 2002, the committee published more than twenty-two resolutions.

EEA Consultative Committee. The Consultative Committee is largely a voice for workers, employers, and other nongovernmental organizations of the EEA member countries and meets once a year. It is composed of members of the European Economic and Social Committee (EESC) and EEA representatives from the EFTA Consultative Committee and provides a forum in which social partners have a chance to meet and discuss policies. The EESC is a nonpolitical body that gives representatives of Europe's socio-occupational interest groups and others a formal platform to express their points of view on EU issues. Its opinions are forwarded to the larger institutions, including the EEA Council, the Commission, and the European Parliament. It thus has a key role to play in the European Union's decisionmaking process. Article 96 of the EEA agreement asks this committee to evaluate the economic and social aspects of the EEA and to provide guidance and recommendations to other EEA bodies.

EEA Joint Committee. The EEA Joint Committee is responsible for the daily management of the EEA agreement and serves as the primary decisionmaker in the EEA. In this committee, representatives from the European Union as well as the EEA/EFTA countries jointly develop policies regarding the EEA treaty. This forum of political exchange is not just consultative in character; it may incorporate European Community legislation into the EEA agreement. Because of its importance, the committee meets once a month on the ambassador level of the EEA/EFTA countries, with representatives of the European Commission and the European Union member states. Four subcommittees assist the EEA Joint Committee in making informed decisions. Each subcommittee deals with an aspect of the freedom of movement. The subcommittees are supported by outside consultants such as academics and think-tank representatives.

However, constitutionally the EEA/EFTA countries are not allowed to adopt legislation of the EC into their national legislation. Therefore, whenever the original EEA agreement needs to be changed, a separate annex to the original agreement has to be drafted. This process is seen as an essential step to ensuring the homogeneity of the EEA.

EEA and EFTA Bodies
EFTA Standing Committee. The EFTA Standing Committee provides a forum in which all EEA/EFTA states may consult with each other on a regular basis. Here EEA/EFTA countries can freely discuss important economic and political issues and reach a common agreement

prior to meeting with their counterparts from the European Union in the EEA Council. Therefore, only representatives from Iceland, Liechtenstein, and Norway are members of the committee. The chairmanship of the Standing Committee rotates among these three countries. However, representatives from Switzerland and the EFTA Surveillance Authority enjoy observer status.

The EFTA Standing Committee is subdivided into four committees that assist the general committee in the decisionmaking process. Each subcommittee focuses on one area of the freedom of movement principles. In addition, a legal and institutional subcommittee assists the Standing Committee in constitutional questions.

EFTA Surveillance Authority

The EFTA Surveillance Authority is responsible for overseeing uniform implementation of the EEA agreement. It ensures that the rules and procedures outlined in the EEA agreement are not breached or interpreted differently by different entitites and monitors implementation of EEA regulations in national legislation. In the two-pillar system, the EFTA Surveillance Authority is the controlling authority for EEA/EFTA states that are not EU members, and the European Commission is the central authority for EU states. The EFTA Surveillance Authority possesses control and investigative mechanisms similar to those of the European Commission.

EFTA Court

The EFTA Court operates in parallel to the European Court of Justice, handling matters that affect the EEA/EFTA states. Therefore, it has jurisdiction only in EEA/EFTA states, mostly in matters dealing with infringement actions. Its main responsibility is to settle disputes between two or more EEA/EFTA states.

EEA Enlargement

The European Union enlarged on May 1, 2004, to comprise twenty-five member states. The enlargement process has a direct impact on the EEA agreement, which states in Article 128 that countries that apply for EU membership should also apply for EEA membership. Therefore, the EEA countries negotiated EEA applications for Cyprus, the Czech Republic, Estonia, Hungary, Latvia, Lithuania, Malta, Poland, Slovenia, and the Slovak Republic in 2003. These states became members of the EEA on May 1, 2004, creating an internal market of more than 450 million people. However, the legislation that provides for EEA enlargement still awaits ratification by all twenty-eight member states.

Benjamin Zyla

See Also Economic Integration; European Union

References

Bossuat, Gerard. 1997. "European Economic Areas since 1914: Old Realities and European Unity." *European Review* 5, no. 3: 323–329.

Gestöhl, Sieglinde. 1994. "EFTA and the European Economic Area, or the Politics of Frustration." *Cooperation and Conflict* 29, no. 4: 333–336.

Hitris, Theo. 1994. *European Community Economics.* 3d ed. New York: Harvester Wheatsheaf.

Laursen, Finn. 1991. "EFTA Countries as Actors in European Integration: The Emergence of the European Economic Area (EEA)." *International Review of Administrative Science* 57: 543–555.

Smith, Alasdair, and Helen Wallace. 1993. "The European Union: Towards a Policy for Europe." *International Affairs* 70, no. 3 (July): 429–444.

Swann, Dennis. 2000. *The Economics of Europe: From Common Market to European Union.* London: Penguin.

"Treaty Establishing the European Community." 1957. *American Journal of International Law* 51, no. 4 (October): 865–954.

European Union

The European Economic Community, later restyled the European Union, was one of many attempts to reduce tensions in a Europe recovering from World War II. It has developed into a loose confederation of 25 member states bound together through common trade, social, and economic policies. The European Union came into being on November 1, 1993, as a result of the 1992 Treaty on European Union (Maastricht Treaty). It has at its heart a three-pillar structure to support the project of European cooperation. The three policy areas covered by this structure were primarily existing areas of European interest subdivided to provide a compromise solution to treaty issues rather than to create new powers.

The first pillar covers policy responsibility for agriculture, economic and monetary union, immigration and asylum, and internal markets. The second pillar deals with common foreign and security policy (CFSP) and international cooperation and policies to preserve the peace and the security of the European Union. The third pillar covers Justice and Home Affairs (JHA), with responsibility for cross-border crime, police cooperation, and criminal law. The new treaty also set out a timetable for economic and monetary union and for the introduction of a single currency, the euro.

Historical Overview

The idea of European unity, born in the aftermath of World War II, was based on the desire to preserve peace, promote free trade, and guarantee the free movement of people within Europe. The concept of a European community evolved from the early days of the European Coal and Steel Community in 1952. The European Economic Community (EEC), established in 1957 by the Treaty of Rome, brought together six European countries (France, West Germany, Belgium, the Netherlands, Luxembourg, and Italy) in an attempt to abolish customs duties and trade barriers among the member states and in the process create a common market for goods and services. It was renamed the European Community in 1967. The original six members were joined in 1973 by Britain, Denmark, and Ireland, with further enlargement in 1981 when Greece joined, followed by Spain and Portugal in 1986.

In 1993, as the result of the Treaty on European Union, the European Community was reborn as the European Union. Austria, Finland, and Sweden joined in 1995, and in 2004. The admittance of the Eastern European countries culminated a lengthy process involving a study of the applicants' politics, culture, economic development, human rights records, and so on. The 1993 European Council in Copenhagen opened the door of EU membership to Central and Eastern European countries and set out clear requirements for attaining it, including the stability of institutions guaranteeing democracy, the rule of law, human rights and respect for and protection of minorities, the existence of a functioning market economy, and the capacity to cope with competitive pressures and market forces within the union. The ability to take on the obligations of membership, including adherence to the aims of political, economic, and monetary union, is also a qualifying factor. In addition, the EU itself must have the ability to absorb proposed new members without endangering the momentum of European integration.

EU Institutions

The EU consists of four main institutions: the European Commission, the European Parliament, the European Court of Justice, and the Council of Ministers.

The European Commission

The European Commission is the administrative and executive body of the EU and is headed by twenty commissioners who serve for a period of five years. There is one commissioner from each of the smaller member states and two from each larger one. They are nominated by the respective national governments and approved by the European Parliament. The commissioners have a duty to act in the interests of the EU and independently of their national governments. Only by showing such impartiality can they effectively mediate points of conflict between member states when they arise. The purpose of the commission is to further the goals of the EU and to implement policy and legislation. It fulfills three distinct roles: initiating proposals for legislation, acting as the guardian of the treaties, and serving as the manager and executor of EU policies and international trade relationships. Its draft proposals for legislation are subject to approval by the Council of Ministers and the European Parliament. The commission is based in Brussels, Belgium, with a staff of 16,000.

The commission is the initiator of the legislative process; indeed, EU law cannot be made without a proposal from the commission. In preparing its proposals, the commission must take account of its main objectives: to consult with pressure groups, trade unions, industry, and individual governments; to identify the European interest—that is, to ensure that a proposal reflects what is best for Europe as a whole rather than what is best for any individual member state; and to respect the principle of "subsidiarity" by taking action only when it is decided that a matter can be dealt with more effectively at the EU level than at the national level.

The commission acts in a watchdog capacity to ensure that individual states do not breach their treaty obligations. It has the power to initiate legal proceedings against member states in the Court of Justice; it can also take action against individuals and corporations that break EU treaty law.

As manager and executor, the commission oversees the EU's annual budget and enforces the treaty's competition rules. It regulates acquisitions and mergers and can take action to prevent third countries from dumping surplus goods on the community market.

The European Parliament

Members of the European Parliament (MEPs) are democratically elected to five-year terms. There are 626 MEPs representing the 370 million people of the fifteen member states. The parliament employs 3,850 people and is primarily based in Brussels; the headquarters of the parliament's civil service is based in Luxembourg, but for one week every month it decamps to Strasbourg, France. The most important powers of the parliament can be divided into three distinct categories: supervision of the executive function, legislative duties, and power over the budget. Among other things, MEPs approve the European budget, question European commissioners, approve international agreements, and approve the appointment of the European Commission.

The importance of the role fulfilled by parliament in supervising the executive function is highlighted every five years when it appoints the president and members of the commission. The parliament conducts political supervision of EU policies through comprehensive questioning of the representatives of the commission and the Council of Ministers, who jointly share the executive power of the EU.

Under the original Treaty of Rome, the parliament was given a purely consultative role in legislative matters. However, subsequent treaties have amended and strengthened its powers to the degree that it can now amend and adopt legislation; in the process, it has assumed a power-sharing role with the Council of Ministers. There are several ways in which this power-sharing role has been put into place. First, the consultation procedure regarding legislative proposals requires the parliament to issue opinions on commission proposals before they can be adopted by the council. Second, the parliament is allowed to amend proposals in the interest of improving them. Proposed legislation is given two readings in the European Parliament in order to provide ample opportunity for review and amendment. Decisionmaking power is shared equally by the parliament and the Council of Ministers through a procedure that aims to secure consensus on the texts so that they can be endorsed by both the council and the parliament. Finally, international agreements, such as those outlining the tasks and powers of the European Central Bank, or the accession of new member states, must obtain parliamentary assent.

The EU's annual budget is approved by the European Parliament. Initial budgetary proposals are submitted by the commission but are subject to modification and amendment by the parliament. The parliament, in cooperation with the Council of Ministers, is responsible for determining expenditures on environmental projects, education, regional funds, and social programs. The parliament does not have any budgetary powers over costs arising from international agreements or agricultural spending, however. The parliament's Committee on Budgetary Control continuously monitors expenditures in an effort to ensure that money is spent toward the agreed purposes.

Much of the parliament's work is done by its twenty special committees, which scrutinize the activities of other EU institutions and oversee proposals for new EU laws. The topics covered by special committees include citizens' freedoms and rights; justice and home affairs; employment and social affairs; fisheries; regional policy; transport and tourism; women's rights and equal opportunities; foreign affairs; human rights; and common security and defense policy. European citizens have the right to petition the parliament on matters that fall within the EU's area of responsibility. The parliament works in eleven official languages and employs more than 1,000 translators.

European Court of Justice

The European Court of Justice is based in Luxembourg and adjudicates all legal issues and disputes involving EU law. Its decisions fall into two main categories. Preliminary rulings are rulings of interpretation of law and are held in the language of the national court that referred the case in the first instance. The court's other rulings are in response to various kinds of direct actions initiated by institutions against other institutions; in these, the language of the case is chosen by the applicant. The court is composed of fifteen judges and nine advocates general appointed by common accord from the member states for renewable periods of six years. The court sits in chambers of three or five judges, or in plenary session if requested and if the case merits such action.

Council of Ministers

The Council of Ministers, made up of ministers from the member states, approves EU legislation and policy, establishes political objectives, coordinates national policies to ensure that they are in line with EU policies, and resolves differences between the council itself and other institutions. The presidency of the council rotates every six months among member states, with one term from January until June, and another from July until December. The country holding the presidency hosts a meeting of the heads of state, known as the European Council, every six months. In recent years these meetings have become the scene of violent, large-scale environmental demonstrations.

The Council of Ministers has its headquarters in Brussels, where most of its work is done, though council meetings take place in Strasbourg three times a year. Some matters are decided by unanimous decisions, but the vast majority are decided by qualified majority voting. There are a number of policies related to the first pillar (agriculture, transportation, environment, and energy) that are decided in council by qualified voting with member states carrying different weights. France, Germany, the United Kingdom, and Italy carry ten votes each; Spain carries eight votes; Portugal, the Netherlands, Belgium, and Greece five votes each; Austria and Sweden four votes each; Denmark, Finland, and Ireland three votes each; and Luxembourg two votes, for a total of eighty-seven votes. At least sixty-two votes must be cast in favor when a commission proposal is involved, and in other cases, although sixty-two votes are still required, these must be cast by at least ten member countries. Those policy areas from pillar one that require unanimity include taxation, industry, and culture. Unanimity is the rule in the other two pillars, CFSP and JHA. EU law adopted by the council may take one of several forms: regulations, which are directly applied without the need for national measures to implement them; directives, which bind member states to the objectives to be achieved while leaving the national authorities some leeway in implementing them; decisions, which are binding in all their aspects upon those to whom they are addressed; and recommendations and opinions, which are not binding.

Common Agricultural Policy

Established in 1962, the Common Agricultural Policy (CAP) was intended to increase agricultural production, provide a fair standard of living for those working within the agricultural community, stabilize markets, guarantee supplies to the consumer, and ensure product availability at a reasonable price. The CAP is based on three interdependent principles: (1) the initial concept of a single market with common market rules, which was followed in 1968 by the unification of prices, marking the completion of a single agricultural market; (2) the requirement for member states to show preference to products grown within the community, which results in the imposition of import duties on foreign goods, making them too expensive to compete in the European marketplace (in tandem with this, EU export subsidies allow community products to compete on the world market); and (3) financial subsidies to farmers, which are administered through a central pool to ensure that no individual member country is able to utilize the subsidies to unfairly prop up its own national agricultural community.

The CAP allows a wide range of products to be brought into member states, providing a high degree of choice for the consumer. It sets common quality standards for fruit and vegetables throughout the European Union, permits cross-border trade in which traders need not be present when buying goods, and guarantees consistent quality. This standardization of products, along with regulations governing the labeling of products, means a high level of protection for the European consumer.

The downside is that European prices are kept artificially high to compensate producers. Prices are usually set at the level of the member state where production is dearest, resulting in an artificially large gap between European prices and the prices on the world market. Farmers are guaranteed a minimum price for their products, and if there is a surplus, the community undertakes to stockpile that surplus for sale on the world market at a later date, even if that means selling at a price below that paid by community citizens. As a result, the community often subsidizes the sale of goods on the world market at a loss rather than enjoying a reduced price in Europe, which, it is felt, might threaten the fixed price system. The stockpiling of surplus agricultural goods has brought about the "beef mountain," "butter mountain," "wine lake," and so on. The policy of guaranteeing a price and a market for goods has led to overproduction, with some farmers being paid not to grow crops and to leave large sections of land fallow, while some large corporate farmers are able to earn sums in excess of a million euros from community subsidies. With the enlarged membership that took place in 2004, especially of Eastern European agricultural countries, the European Union is in the early consultative stages of restructuring the CAP.

Common Fisheries Policy

The Common Fisheries Policy (CFP) is intended to ensure a sustainable fishing industry within the union. This is to be achieved by limiting the number of each species caught by vessels in community waters, using a licensing system and quotas set each year by the Council of Ministers, based on scientific advice on the state of existing fish stocks. These quotas, or total allowable catches (TACs), are divided among the member states according to historic fishing patterns, with the individual members assuming responsibility for ensuring that the quotas are respected and stocks are not overfished. The CFP has had mixed results, prompting widespread protest from within the fishing community. There is continuing conflict among member states, as CFP rules allow vessels from one member state to obtain a license to fish in the territorial waters of another member state, thereby reducing the fish stocks available for home vessels.

The Spanish and Portuguese, in particular, have been heavily criticized for fishing in UK waters, using large vessels and large nets that threaten to destroy future breeding stock. Within EU waters, fishing is now totally banned in some areas in an attempt to regenerate stock. There are also limits to the length of time a fishing vessel can spend at sea within any one year; rules about the type of fishing gear that can be used, including net size; and minimum sizes for each species of fish. The decommissioning of fishing vessels, which in effect reduces the size of national fleets, is one method of conservation encouraged by the EU, but the results have been varied, as owners who choose to accept large payments to scrap older vessels sell their licenses for sums as high as half a million euros, allowing large modern vessels, usually with corporate owners, to operate on several fishing licenses, thus obtaining almost unlimited access to fishing stocks.

Monetary Union

On January 1, 1999, the euro replaced the national currencies of eleven member states: Austria, Belgium, Finland, France, Germany, Ireland, Italy, Luxembourg, the Netherlands, Portugal, and Spain. Greece joined this group on January 1, 2001. Not all member states chose to adopt the euro as their currency. The exceptions were the United Kingdom, and Sweden, which chose not to join the euro group. On January 1, 2002, euro banknotes and coins were introduced, and national currencies were phased out as existing coins and notes were withdrawn from circulation.

There were many reasons for the monetary union. It was thought that a common currency would ensure that a reunified Germany would remain tied to the ideal of European integration within an expanding EU, that it would ensure economic efficiency within the EU and improve the standard of living, and that it would help to develop a greater sense of European identity—the major stumbling block to total European federalization. It was hoped that the introduction of a single currency would increase the trading of goods and services between the participating countries and strengthen the single market, and that travelers would benefit from the introduction of the euro because they would no longer need to worry about currency exchange. However, the decision of the EU to produce euro notes with twelve regional designs caused confusion. Some European shopkeepers initially refused to accept notes issued in other member countries (especially in Greece, Italy, and Spain). This problem has since been resolved, but it serves to demonstrate that at the grassroots level Europeans are still not operating as a single European state.

The adoption of the euro as a single currency has made the EU a major international monetary power. More important, countries that have adopted the euro no longer have an independent monetary policy. Individual governments no longer have control over interest-rate levels. These and all other decisions affecting EU monetary policy are now set by the European Central Bank (ECB) from its headquarters in Frankfurt. The ECB was established on June 1, 1998, and has as its main objective price stability in the euro area, which it achieves in part by influencing the interest rate. Those countries joining the EU in the future must adopt the euro eventually but have to wait at least two years from the time of joining the EU before they can apply to join the European monetary union. They must also meet a number of economic criteria if they wish to join at a later date, including low interest rates, sound public finances, stable exchange rates, and low inflation.

Common Foreign and Security Policy

Common foreign and security policy (CFSP) is contained within the second pillar of the EU. Although member states are expected to act in cooperation and through consensus to formulate common foreign and security policy goals, they are not required to adhere to a single foreign policy. While enshrining the single market and European integration, the Treaty of Rome did not endow the EEC with any external pow-ers except to conclude international trade agreements. European foreign policy derives directly from the national foreign policies of the member states and, since it is achieved primarily by consensus, need not necessarily be followed by all. An example of this principle may be seen in the mixed reaction within the EU over the U.S.-led invasion of Iraq in 2003. There was a common EU policy condemning the Iraqi regime and supporting United Nations intervention, and, when action was taken, the bulk of European states were supportive. However, France and Germany were vehemently opposed to any military action and called for the withdrawal of coalition forces. In other words, there is no single, unified EU foreign policy; rather, individual member states still have the ability to fall back on national interests.

The EU has become a major player on the world political stage, although at times this has been hindered by conflicting messages from the individual member states. The political divide over the invasion of Iraq in 2003 demonstrated the deficiencies of a system lacking political uniformity. In an effort to present a cohesive single voice on world issues, proposals were put forward in June 2003 to create an elected European president and foreign secretary. Sanctions on Iraq, involvement in Eastern Europe, and the almost unanimous European reaction to the terrorist attacks of September 11 have shown that Europe can act as a single force when required to do so.

Defense Policy

There has been little advance in creating a unified European defense policy despite some attempts to do so. In the aftermath of the Cold War, cuts in national defense budgets limited any advance in this direction, with a continued reliance on the North Atlantic Treaty Organization (NATO) as the dominant stabilizing military force in Europe. The crises in Kosovo and

Bosnia showed that Europe was unable to produce either a coherent policing policy or the means to enforce any form of peacekeeping policy. Britain and France are both members of the UN Security Council and both nuclear powers, which would give any common European defense policy credibility on the world stage.

The problem has been with the coordination of ground forces. Various attempts have been made over the years to create a single European military force, but although the member states are quite prepared to coordinate their efforts to achieve a unified economic policy, they have not been prepared to relinquish independent control of their armed forces. A unified military must have a unified central command answerable to the European Commission and not to the individual member states. This realignment has been the stumbling block. With a combined strength of more than 2 million troops and 6,000 combat aircraft, even before the membership of the EU increased in 2004 the potential was there for the EU to assume the role of a superpower, a counterbalance to U.S. dominance. This potential increased when the new members were admitted and the military potential of Poland, Hungary, and the Czech Republic was added to the EU.

There is no common EU defense policy, and in fact there has never been a common view of European defense. Several member countries, including Britain, Portugal, and Holland, view the continuing security relationship with the United States as of prime importance; others, such as Germany, France, Spain, and Italy, advocate an independent Europe operating free of U.S. intervention or assistance. While the Cold War dominated world politics, the Atlanticist policy was followed, and NATO was the European defense arm of choice. Since the collapse of the former Soviet Union and the removal of the threat to Europe, policy has been changing, and the Europeanist point of view has been gaining ground. There is a grow-

ing desire within the EU to move from Cold War dependence on the United States to a new partnership of equals. In tandem with this, several individual member states maintain loyalty and special interest in their former colonies and reflect this in their national defense policies.

The Western European Union (WEU) was revived in the 1990s as a means to creating a centralized military presence in Europe. Originally created as the Western Union by the 1948 Brussels Treaty and consisting of Britain, France, Belgium, the Netherlands, and Luxembourg, the Western Union became the Western European Union in 1954 when Italy and West Germany joined. The WEU was always in the shadow of NATO, and the organization lay dormant until it was revived to stimulate European military cooperation. In 1992, following a meeting of WEU foreign and defense ministers at Petersburg, near Bonn, the responsibilities of the revived WEU were clearly outlined. Military units from the member states could be deployed under the authority of the WEU for a variety of peacekeeping and humanitarian tasks. These forces are known collectively as the Forces Answerable to the WEU (FAWEU) and include troops from Britain, Holland, France, Italy, Spain, and Portugal. The force has operated in Serbia and Montenegro to monitor the UN embargo and has helped train the Croatian and Albanian police forces.

However, as might have been expected, the fragmented security policy of the EU has caused problems for the FAWEU. In an attempt to move toward a European Army, Germany and France took the step of creating the Eurocorps in 1992. The 60,000-strong Eurocorps has been operational since 1995, and Germany and France have been joined by Belgium, Spain, and Luxembourg. It was originally conceived with three main aims: to lead to a credible European Army that would provide the backbone of the CFSP, to give the EU an independent military arm, and to supply a military alternative for the EU in the event that the

United States decided to withdraw from its commitment to defend Europe.

Justice and Home Affairs

The third pillar of the EU covers the field of justice and home affairs, bringing together the justice departments of the fifteen member states to increase dialog, mutual assistance, and joint effort and cooperation among their police, customs, and immigration departments. Cooperation in civil matters deals with divorce, child custody, and bankruptcy where these matters overlap into two or more member states. Criminal matters covered include illicit trafficking in drugs, arms, toxic waste, and nuclear materials. Europol, the European police office based in The Hague in the Netherlands, was created to combat all forms of international crime. It is intended to play a major part in furthering cooperation among individual police forces in the fight against terrorism, drugs, and organized crime. It became fully operational in July 1999.

Welfare and Social Policy

The social policy of the European Union dictates that EU bodies serve mainly in a regulatory capacity. Social welfare programs are thus still administered and delivered at the national level, as are programs in education, housing, and health care. This is in keeping with the EU's policy of becoming involved only when it is deemed that such action would be more effective than action at the level of the individual member state. European social policy has evolved as a by-product of European integration and was not included in the Treaty of Rome, as the original six signatories had broadly similar social systems. Over the ensuing years, national welfare systems have expanded enormously, both in the provision and the extent of services, and continual expansion has created greater diversity of social policy

within the EU. The idea that a common social welfare policy can be created from such diversity has become increasingly impractical as well as undesirable. However, in a Europe that is achieving ever greater economic and political integration, there is still a call for greater coordination and compatibility across systems. The new role of social policy is to enable the process of economic integration to take place. For example, in health care, a practical result of social coordination is that surgical patients can be transferred from one member state to another—say, from Britain to France—to reduce the time patients have to wait for treatment.

Faced with the prospect of ten additional member countries in 2004, issues such as jobs, schools, health care, and quality of life began to form a key part of the European debate. It is inconceivable that a centralized European welfare state would take over the financing and delivery of health care systems, education, housing, or environmental protection from individual member-state governments. Welfare provision will continue to be the responsibility of national and subnational bodies, but greater integration of policy could become part of the developing political process. The task facing EU social policy makers is enormous. An integrated European social policy will be achieved not by enforcing a single unified standard but by linking together the many diverse systems and standards that already exist within the expanding EU.

Global Relations

With the introduction of a common currency and the creation of a Central European Bank, the EU has come of age as a global power. It was already the world's largest trading bloc before the expansion to twenty-five member countries in 2004, and with the expansion it became a dominating force in world trade. It is the biggest industrialized marketplace, with, at present, a population of 375 million, just over 6 percent of the world's population, accounting for 28 percent of global gross domestic product (GDP). Owing in part to the accessibility of the single market, the EU has become increasingly important to those multinationals that hitherto concentrated on the North American market. Moreover, the EU is home to some of the world's largest companies. The common economic and trade policies are at present major factors in the economic power of the EU. Once a common policy has been reached by the member states through the Council of Ministers, the European Commission undertakes trade agreements and negotiates on behalf of the EU as a whole, thereby operating from a position of strength and presenting a single European voice.

The United States and Europe

The EU is the largest market for U.S. goods, with 20 percent of U.S. exports destined for member states. At the same time, the United States is also the largest external market for EU goods, receiving over 24 percent of EU exports. The two largest economies in the world, the European Union and the United States together account for about half of the entire world economy, with a combined global trade amounting to 40 percent of world trade. Although there are similarities in their foreign policy, there is a continuing divide between the European Union and the United States, with the differences of opinion increasing and becoming more substantive in recent years.

This gap has been caused in part by the emergence of the EU as a powerful political voice on the world stage and the corresponding reduction in U.S. influence, especially in Central and Eastern Europe. There have been major trade and policy disputes, including one over the Cuban Liberty and Democracy Act, which was introduced by the United States in 1996 as a result of the downing of two civilian aircraft by the Cuban military. The act made provision for foreign companies investing in Cuba to be sued in U.S. courts. The reaction of the EU was to threaten sanctions against U.S. companies and individuals. The dispute was resolved in May 1998 when the United States agreed to lift the sanctions on European companies. This was followed in 1999 by the end of the so-called "Banana War" when the EU conceded to U.S. demands to open up its internal market to bananas produced in Latin America by U.S. companies. Until then, preference had been given to bananas produced in former colonies of European states. In 2001, President George W. Bush signaled his intention to renege on the U.S. commitment to the Kyoto Protocol agreement of 1997, which was aimed at the reduction of global levels of carbon dioxide emissions. The relationship between the European Union and the United States is rocky at best, with both parties following protectionist economic principles. Although the United States has good relationships with a number of individual member states, it has been unable to come to terms with the concept of a common market and European integration.

The Future

The focus of the European Union has changed in recent years, especially with the expansion of its membership to include former Soviet bloc countries in 2004. The direction of EU policy is changing from one emphasizing Atlantic cooperation to one that takes account of wider European expansion, and in the process the EU is becoming a dominant power in Eastern Europe. The EU signed trade and cooperation agreements with almost all Eastern European states even before their membership became a reality, and investment loans and food aid were made readily available. The inclusion of Eastern European states within the EU, and EU involvement in Central and Eastern Europe, have served to focus EU interest and foreign policy in that direction. The union is no longer led by a small group of Western European countries, and no longer dominated by the relationships among France, Germany, and Britain.

The enlargement of the EU should bring significant benefits to existing member states as well as to new ones. The addition of new, rapidly growing economies and a rise in population of over 100 million are expected to stimulate employment and economic growth. European integration is being extended through widened cultural diversity. Social policy will be extended eventually to those sections of European society most in need of assistance. With the addition of the poorer East European states, the short-term burden of economic stability will fall on the established members, especially since some of the new members depend heavily on inefficient agrarian economies. The EU gross domestic product increased by only about 4 percent with the addition of the ten new members. But with the underlying EU principle of freedom of movement, the crisis will come with the westward migration of cheap Eastern European labor and those seeking an instant improvement in social and working conditions. The existing health and social services structure will struggle to cope with the influx. The recent failure to ratify the European Constitution is a major setback to the efforts of the EU to move towards greater political and social unification.

Derek Young

See Also Economic Integration; European Economic Area (EEA); North American Free Trade Agreement (NAFTA); Organisation for Economic Co-operation and Development (OECD)

References

Anderson, P., and K. Eliassen. 2001. *Making Policy in Europe.* 2d ed. London: Sage.

Barnes, I., and P. M. Barnes. 1995. *The Enlarged European Union.* London: Longman.

Blomberg, E., and A. Stubb. 2003. *The European Union: How Does It Work?* Oxford: Oxford University Press.

Budd, S. A. 1992. *The European Community—A Guide to the Maze.* London: Kogan Page.

Corbett, R., F. Jacobs, and M. Shackleton. 2000. *The European Parliament.* 4th ed. London: Cartermill.

Dehousse, R. 1998. *The European Court of Justice.* London: Macmillan.

George, V., and P. Taylor-Gooby, eds. 1996. *European Welfare Policy—Squaring the Welfare Circle.* London: Macmillan.

Kagan, R. 2003. *Paradise and Power—America and Europe in the New World Order.* London: Atlantic.

Kleinman, M. A. 2002. *European Welfare State?* Houndmills: Palgrave.

McCormick, J. 2001. *Environmental Policy in the European Union.* Houndmills: Palgrave.

———. 2002. *Understanding the European Union.* Houndmills: Palgrave.

Newman, M. 1997. *Democracy, Sovereignty and the European Union.* London: Hurst.

Nicoll, W., and T. C. Salmon. 1994. *Understanding the New European Community.* Hemel Hempstead: Harvester Wheatsheaf.

Peterson, J., and M. Shackleton. 2002. *The Institutions of the European Union.* Oxford: Oxford University Press.

Shanks, M. 1977. *European Social Policy, Today and Tomorrow.* Oxford: Pergamon.

Shore, C. 2000. *Building Europe—The Cultural Politics of European Integration.* London: Routledge.

Siedentop, L. 2000. *Democracy in Europe.* London: Penguin.

Franc Zone

At present the Franc Zone consists of France; its overseas departments, territories, and territorial communities, including Mayotte, Saint Pierre et Miquelon, Monaco, and the Comoros; and the countries of two African monetary unions. Membership in the Franc Zone has not remained constant over the years of its existence. Initially, the zone consisted of France and its colonies. In the nineteenth century, it consisted of France, the Sarre, Monaco, and French colonies around the world. As the former colonies achieved independence, on different dates over several years, some chose to leave the zone. In 1954, the three states of the former French Indochina, Cambodia, Laos, and Vietnam, left the zone after four years of participation. The Maghreb countries soon joined them in exiting the zone, with Tunisia and Morocco leaving shortly after independence in 1958 and 1959, respectively. Algeria left in 1963.

The Franc Zone persisted in Africa. With the independence of African countries in the 1960s, only Guinea, under Sekou Toure, and Mali, under Modibo Keita, opted to create their own currencies and abandon participation in the West African Monetary Union (Union Monétaire Ouest-Africaine, UMOA) that united the other countries of the former French West Africa. Mauritania left the UMOA in 1972, but Mali eventually returned in 1984. Guinea-Bissau joined in 1997. In Central Africa, no country left the zone, and Equatorial Guinea joined in 1985.

In Africa, the Franc Zone is divided into two distinct groupings. The West African countries are members of the West African Economic and Monetary Union (WAEMU, or Union Economique et Monétaire de l'Afrique), whereas the Central African countries are members of the Central African Economic and Monetary Community (Communauté Economique et Monétaire de l'Afrique, CEMAC). WAEMU members include Benin, Burkina Faso, Côte d'Ivoire, Guinea-Bissau, Mali, Niger, Senegal, and Togo. Members of CEMAC include Cameroon, Central African Republic, Chad, Congo Brazzaville, Equatorial Guinea, and Gabon. The monetary system, which operates via two central banks, the Central Bank of West African States (Banque Centrale de l'Afrique de l'Ouest, BCEAO) for WAEMU and the Bank of Central African States (Banque des Etats de l'Afrique Centrale, BEAC) for CEMAC, has no equivalent elsewhere.

The CFA franc is used by more than 80 million people in West and Central Africa. The currency was created by France for use in its African colonies as early as 1939, but it only became widely implemented on December 26, 1945, the date when France ratified the Bretton Woods Agreement and made its first declaration of parity to the International Monetary Fund (IMF). At the time of its institution, CFA stood for Franc des Colonies Françaises d'Afrique (Franc of the French Colonies of Africa). In 1958, it came to stand for Franc de la Communauté Financière d'Afrique (Franc of the African Financial Community). Today the acronym stands for Communauté Financière Africaine in the WAEMU and for Cooperation Financière en Afrique Central in the CEMAC.

The Franc Zone supports an agenda of currency cooperation between France's Ministry of the Treasury and the fourteen African member states. It was developed to facilitate the transfer of funds; the conversion of currency at a fixed rate; and the centralization of all monetary reserves of the African countries in the French Treasury. Proponents argue that this provides members with three primary advantages: an increased degree of currency stability, which encourages decreased rates of inflation; a direct channel for foreign trade; and increased interdependence among African member countries.

Under the arrangement, African state members of the Franc Zone surrendered the management of their foreign exchange reserves to the French Treasury in exchange for convertibility of the CFA franc. A single currency was maintained, but trade barriers were erected between countries and the single market of colonial times was dismantled. Thus, the CFA money supply was primarily based on the volume of trade between France and its African partners.

For half a century, the zone was characterized by stable rules of function that were subject only to limited adjustments. Three primary features marked the monetary and exchange rate regime for CFA francs. The currencies, which were issued by the two multinational central banks in Africa, maintained a fixed and adjustable rate defined first in French francs and more recently in euros. Their convertibility was guaranteed by France through an operational account opened by the French Treasury in the name of the African central banks of the zone.

The African countries of the Franc Zone agreed to deposit 65 percent of their foreign exchange reserves in this operational account within the French Treasury in exchange for France's guarantee of the CFA franc's convertibility. They also granted France a veto over the monetary policy of the Franc Zone's monetary policy whenever this special account was overdrawn. Critics suggest that this relationship has had dire consequences for African Franc Zone members over the past half-century.

The Franc Zone benefited France by providing a broad market for its products, a regular supply of inexpensive raw materials, political influence, a strategic military presence in Africa, and allies in international arenas. In addition, a great share of local savings was transferred to France. Critics contend, however, that in return African countries have been hampered by weak trade performance, tight money, high interest rates, large-scale capital flight, and massive debt repayments that prevent investment in health, education, housing, food production, training, and industry.

Over the course of its existence, the Franc Zone has transformed from a protective zone in the 1950s, practicing strict exchange control for the French franc along with import quotas for countries outside of the zone, to an instrument in opening African countries to foreign trade. From independence to the mid-1980s, the Franc Zone members showed positive economic results encouraged by rising prices for raw materials and the results of a weak French franc. The Franc Zone showed satisfactory real gross domestic product (GDP) growth in the immediate postindependence period by comparison with other sub-Saharan countries.

With the move to floating international exchange rates in 1973, and the resulting instability of exchange rates for major world currencies, the Franc Zone provided African member countries with a relatively stable exchange rate in relation to their primary trading partners. This partly explains why the economies of African countries of the Franc Zone were relatively more open than other African economies in the 1960s and 1970s. Between 1975 and 1985, average annual real GDP growth in the CFA Franc Zone rose to 4.6 percent.

Throughout the 1980s, African Franc Zone countries were subjected to structural adjustment programs, under the IMF and World Bank, directed toward addressing deficits in balance of payments and public finances. Between 1985 and 1993, the Franc Zone experienced a period of deep crisis, sparked by the decline in raw materials prices beginning in 1976, and extended by France's strong franc policy begun in 1985. Traditional exports, especially cacao, coffee, cotton, and oil, fell into deficit, and revenue from export taxes dwindled. At the same time, the appreciation of the French franc led to price increases on imports. Currency reserves for African members decreased regularly until France intervened as a lender of last resort.

Between 1986 and 1993, budget deficits moved from an average of 5 percent of GDP to 7.4 percent of GDP. Governments responded by pursuing internal adjustments, such as wage restraints, tax increases, and price guarantees for farmers, rather than external adjustments such as altering the CFA franc/French franc exchange rate. Beginning in 1988, capital flight became a major and ongoing problem. Anticipation of devaluation, in 1993, amplified this particular situation.

Prior to January 1994, adjustments were achieved primarily through budgetary policies rather than devaluation, an often difficult process given that with a monetary union such policies required the agreement of all member governments. Successive devaluations of the French franc and the appreciation of the dollar in the early years of the 1980s assisted the implementation of this strategy. In the second half of the decade, the situation of the African Franc Zone countries deteriorated considerably.

In preparation for participation in the European monetary union, the French government tied the franc to the German mark. This led to an appreciation of the CFA franc against the dollar and against several European currencies. At the same time, the terms of exchange for African Franc Zone members suffered a dramatic deterioration resulting from the decline of international market prices for their primary export products. This occurred at a time when industrial products from Franc Zone countries in Africa were competing with products from neighboring countries that had experienced massive devaluations of their cur-

rencies. This encouraged a reversal of the growth seen in previous decades as exports in the zone failed to keep up with those of other African countries.

Unwilling to finance public deficits in the zone, France requested intervention by the IMF and the World Bank, which demanded a devaluation of the CFA franc as a precondition for the granting of any aid. In January 1994, the CFA franc experienced a devaluation of 50 percent, and the Comoran franc was devalued by 33 percent. The rate of exchange had remained fixed for forty-eight years.

It has been noted that, though currency devaluation is a common phenomenon in much of Africa, this move was specifically intended to send African leaders a message that France was adopting a new and potentially more disciplinary and stringent stance toward economic management. France threatened to slash the aid to any country that did not adopt the devaluation. At the time of devaluation, only Côte d'Ivoire had been able to prepare any studies dealing with the possible economic effects of devaluation. The IMF, along with the World Bank and especially the U.S. State Department, had long been pressing both France and the African Franc Zone states to devalue the currency. The devaluations of the CFA franc were primarily payments-improving, unlike devaluations in Anglophone Africa, which were trade-liberalizing. Devaluation has typically been used, owing to inflationary consequences, to change the real value of debt and wage contracts, especially to reduce real wages in those sectors where nominal wages were not decreasing.

The devaluation of the CFA franc was only accepted by African heads of state under the joint pressures of the IMF and the French government. This led some African member governments to question France's commitment to the Franc Zone and caused some doubt about the future of the zone. Indeed, the devaluation of the CFA franc had a devastating effect on the economies of the African countries. It resulted in deteriorating economic conditions leading to rising unemployment and skyrocketing prices. The devaluation also provided an opportunity for foreign investors to benefit from a widespread privatization of state assets. Under the auspices of the IMF and the World Bank, lucrative sectors, including energy, water supplies, telecommunications, and banks, were privatized at very low prices to Western companies.

At the time of devaluation, the Franc Zone countries in Africa decided to develop the two monetary unions into economic and monetary unions. These economic unions included three main planks: the gradual implementation of a common market; multilateral monitoring of public finance, accompanied by harmonized tax policies; and the institution of regional policies. Recently countries of western Africa have expressed intentions to develop a broad monetary union integrating the countries of the Economic Community for West African States (ECOWAS) and the members of WAEMU.

At the beginning of 2002, the Franc Zone was faced with a major change as the French franc was replaced by the euro. The CFA franc became pegged to the new European currency. The exchange rate against the euro was automatically determined under this substitution. Because the exchange rate between the euro and the French franc, one euro for 6.55957 francs, was fixed by the Council of the European Union on December 31, 1998, and because the CFA franc was exchanged at the rate of 100 CFA francs for one French franc, the fixed rate of the CFA franc became one euro for 655.957 CFA francs.

At the time of adoption of the Maastricht Treaty in 1993, the French government asserted that the monetary arrangements of the Franc Zone could not be affected because the French Treasury, rather than the Banque de France, guarantees the convertibility of the CFA franc. This was in keeping with Article 109, paragraph 5, of the treaty, which affirms that member states of the European Union retain the right to conclude international agreements where they do not contravene the economic and monetary agreements of the EU.

France's relations with the Franc Zone countries was not dealt with in the Maastricht Treaty, but the treaty did provide for the possibility of monetary and foreign exchange arrangements with third countries through Article 109 (3). On July 1, 1998, members of the Monetary Committee of the EU presented a recommendation allowing France to maintain the main features of its agreement with the Franc Zone. The reasoning for this recommendation was that the guarantee of convertibility of the CFA franc against the French franc was based on a budgetary commitment from the French Treasury without involvement from the Banque de France. The French Treasury would guarantee an unlimited convertibility of the CFA franc into euros without monetary implications for the Banque de France or the European Central Bank. Furthermore, the impact of the guarantee of convertibility of the CFA to the euro on monetary conditions in the euro area was judged to be limited, considering the relative sizes of the euro area and the Franc Zone.

While the CFA franc was pegged to the French franc, most investment in the zone was French. It is now expected that with the currency pegged to the euro, more investment will come from other European countries. In 1996, trade with the EU accounted for 51 percent of the total external trade of CFA Franc Zone countries. France's share stood at 25 percent. IMF estimates suggest that a 1 percent increase in euro area GDP impels an increase of the CFA franc countries' exports of 0.6 percent and an increase in GDP of 0.2 percent.

The maintenance of price stability in the euro area is expected to allow the Franc Zone to sustain relatively low inflation with positive impacts on the real exchange rate and on external competitiveness. In the longer term, proponents expect that the Franc Zone countries, because they mainly export primary commodities priced in U.S. dollars, will benefit from an expanded use of the euro in quoting prices on commodity markets. It is also expected that in the long term capital movements between the Franc Zone and the euro area, not only France, will experience ongoing trade liberalization. This would be coupled with ongoing trade liberalization within the Franc Zone. Critics, however, suggest that this will be impelled through neoliberal macroeconomic policies and through the restructuring of domestic financial systems in ways that will not benefit local populations in the African member countries.

This transformation also made the admission of new countries into the Franc Zone more complex, since it required any potential candidate for entry to negotiate not only with France and the union to which it sought admission but also with the other states of the EU. Indeed, any change in the scope of the agreement, including the admission of new members, or in the character of the agreement, such as in the guarantee of convertibility of the African franc at a fixed rate, would require a decision of the Council of the European Union. France was given the responsibility of informing other EU members about the ongoing functioning of the zone.

Critics contend that the guarantee of the operational account both under the French franc and the euro has implied monetary and budgetary discipline that has negatively impacted the populations of Franc Zone countries. Proponents argue that the convertibility of currencies and the stability of exchange rates are essential to the development of external trade for African countries that do not otherwise have easy access to prospective markets. This is seen to be all the more promising with access to the European markets for industrial products. Proponents also argue that the guarantee of convertibility at a fixed rate provided by the operational account also buffers African Franc Zone countries, with primarily raw material exports, against violent external shocks that would impel a dramatic depreciation in exchange rates. Assumptions about positive growth and price effects are predicated on improved access of Franc Zone countries to European financial markets.

Political instability, matched with increasingly unfavorable terms of trade, the recent rise

in the euro, and the ongoing threat of massive capital flight, have called into question the future of the Franc Zone. Overall, and crucially, the zone remains marked by increasingly impoverished populations and unfavorable trends in GDP. Lack of diversification in external trade, difficulties financing productive investment, and the amount of external debt remain crucial matters facing the zone. Trade has not encouraged growth in the zone, as it has consisted primarily of exports of unprocessed raw materials, subject to volatile prices, and imports of manufactured goods and services. The highly valued CFA franc has discouraged exports while encouraging imports of foodstuffs and manufactured goods. Rural areas and agriculture have not benefited from development programs, and major contributions to GDP from industry have come almost exclusively from oil.

Europe has taken in approximately 35 percent of the zone's exports while providing 45 percent of its imports. Trade within the zone has been consistently weak, representing less than 10 percent of total formal trade. The reliance on foreign markets is reflected in the banking system, which offers little toward addressing the development needs of local economies. The primary business of the banks remains the financing of the needs of international trade rather than investment.

The African countries of the zone suffer crushing debt burdens, which greatly limit budget policies and states' financing of growth. On average, the external public debt represents approximately 100 percent of GDP for African member countries, with the figure for Congo Brazzaville at approximately 200 percent of GDP and for Guinea-Bissau at more than 400 percent. The West African countries, including Côte d'Ivoire and the deeply impoverished Sahel countries of Mali, Burkina Faso, and Senegal, depend on exports of cotton and gold, as well as some light industrial production in Côte d'Ivoire. These countries have followed IMF programs of structural adjustment and have suffered years of economic pain.

The Central African countries are in a different position. Gabon, a major oil producer with a population of just over 1 million people, suffers from debt and budgetary problems exacerbated by dependence on petroleum. Cameroon accounts for half of the economic weight of the Central African part of the zone but has suffered an extended period of economic decline. Congo Brazzaville, an oil-dependent nation, has been the world's most indebted country per citizen and has suffered decades of civil war. Chad has few economic links with its neighbors in the monetary union. Terms of trade for the Central African countries plummeted by more than 20 percent with the collapse of oil prices in 1998.

There have been signs of an increasing gap between the economic developments of West and Central Africa. In the West African region in 1998, growth occurred at a rate of 5.1 percent, whereas Central African countries recorded growth of 4.3 percent. Both figures were lower than those for the previous year. Since 1999, the WAEMU has suffered a difficult period, in part because of the political and economic crises in Côte d'Ivoire. Successive coups in the country, which accounts for 40 percent of the zone's GDP, along with a decline in export prices for agricultural commodities and increases in the price of oil, have combined to reduce growth in the WAEMU. Conversely, the CEMAC, which includes oil-producing countries such as Cameroon, Chad, Congo Brazzaville, Equatorial Guinea, and Gabon, has experienced economic improvement due to the increase in oil prices. GDP growth in the WAEMU dipped to 0.8 percent in 2000, while the CEMAC saw growth reach 3.5 percent.

These large discrepancies lead some commentators to suggest that the two halves of the zone may not be able to remain together. Some have suggested that the fixed value of the currency is removed from reality and that either a split in the zone or another large devaluation will occur. Reliance on exports of primarily unprocessed raw materials, low levels of savings for financing the economy, and the possibility of increases in the value of the euro suggest ongoing obstacles to growth. The prospects of slow growth for the African members of the zone suggest to some that changes may occur in the agreements governing the zone. Recommendations have included allowing greater flexibility in the exchange rate, decoupling the two main groups in the zone, or undertaking both of these approaches at the same time.

Critics note that the policies of constraint in the name of price stability have been harsh for these extremely poor countries, which have experienced decades of depressed demand. The policies have meant that African Franc Zone countries have experienced a combination of factors fueling speculation and capital flight, including currency convertibility, growing interest rates, and low inflation. Others argue that the entire arrangement is a neocolonial anachronism. This is a sentiment that is beginning to find an audience in France.

Jeffrey Shantz

See Also Economic Integration; Common Market for Eastern and Southern Africa (COMESA); East African Community (EAC); East African Community (EAC); Economic Community of Central African States (CEEAC); Southern African Development Community (SADC)

References

Konate, Adama. 2001. "Challenges Facing the CFA Franc." *Conjoncture.* October, pages 2–12.

Mbaye, Sanou. 2004. "France Killing French Africa." *Taipei Times,* http://www.taipeitimes.com/News/edit/archives/2004/01/29/2003096656.

General Agreement on Tariffs and Trade (GATT)

The General Agreement on Tariffs and Trade (GATT) was the outcome of an international conference held in Geneva in 1947 with twenty-three countries as signatories (see Table 1). Established as part of the preparatory negotiations for an International Trade Organization (ITO) that would stipulate rules for freer and less discriminatory trade, it was intended to be merely a temporary treaty to serve until the ITO was implemented. But signatory countries, notably the United States, never ratified the ITO; thus, by default, the GATT became the basis on which successive rounds of negotiations were conducted (see Table 2). Hence, the GATT was not formally an international organization, but an intergovernmental treaty. Consequently, instead of member states, it had contracting parties. With no formal institutional structure and very little publicity, the GATT persisted in making a revolutionary demand upon the nation-state—to perpetually relinquish its sovereign right to raise tariff rates. The endurance of an international regime on such a basis, for so long, was without precedent (see Table 3).

The GATT was conceived as one leg of a tripod that was to manage postwar international economic relations. The International Monetary Fund (IMF) was assigned to repair the disintegration that had befallen the international monetary system prior to the war; the International Bank of Reconstruction and Development (IBRD, or World Bank) was to offer long-term capital assistance; and the GATT was intended to reverse the protectionist and discriminatory trade practices that had become widespread during the prewar years of the Great Depression.

The Great Depression and New Perspectives

During the Great Depression of the 1930s, tariff levels soared, reflecting the sentiment of economic nationalism after World War I. Countries expressed economic nationalism during the interwar period through protectionism, exchange controls, and competitive devaluation of national currencies. In the United States, Congress passed the Hawley-Smoot Tariff Act of 1930, establishing the highest tariff rates in the nation's history. By 1932, the average tariff rates on dutiable imports had reached almost 60 percent. Coupled with the economic depression of the time, the high trade barriers caused U.S. imports to decline sharply. Merchandise imports fell from $4.3 billion in 1929 to $1.3 billion in 1932. Also, exports fell as U.S. trading partners mounted retaliatory tariffs. Even the British, who had been the champions of free trade, passed an import duties act in 1932 that increased tariffs on goods imported from countries outside the British Commonwealth. In fact, more than sixty countries raised tariffs within two years.

The devastating experience of the early 1930s awakened many countries to the economic realization that trade is mutually beneficial. In the developed world, it was widely believed that the most important lesson of the 1930s was that peace, prosperity, and free trade

Table 1: GATT Participants, 2005

Country	Date	Country	Date
Angola	April 8, 1994	Macau	January 11, 1991
Antigua and Barbuda	March 30, 1987	Madagascar	September 30, 1963
Australia	January 1, 1948	Malawi	August 28, 1964
Austria	October 19, 1951	Malaysia	October 24, 1957
Bahrain	December 13, 1993	Maldives	April 19, 1983
Bangladesh	December 16, 1972	Mali	January 11, 1993
Barbados	February 15, 1967	Malta	November 17, 1964
Belgium	January 1, 1948	Mauritania	September 30, 1963
Belize	October 7, 1983	Mauritius	September 2, 1970
Benin	September 12, 1963	Mexico	August 24, 1986
Bolivia	September 8, 1990	Morocco	June 17, 1987
Botswana	August 28, 1987	Mozambique	July 27, 1992
Brazil	July 30, 1948	Myanmar (Burma)	July 29, 1948
Brunei Darussalam	December 9, 1993	Namibia	September 15, 1992
Burkina Faso	May 3, 1963	Netherlands	January 1, 1948
Burundi	March 13, 1965	New Zealand	July 30, 1948
Cameroon	May 3, 1963	Nicaragua	May 28, 1950
Canada	January 1, 1948	Niger	December 31, 1963
Central African Rep.	May 3, 1963	Nigeria	November 18, 1960
Chad	July 12, 1963	Norway	July 10, 1948
Chile	March 16, 1949	Pakistan	July 30, 1948
Colombia	October 3, 1981	Papua New Guinea	December 16, 1979
Congo, Rep. of	May 3, 1963	Paraguay	January 6, 1994
Costa Rica	November 24, 1990	Peru	October 7, 1951
Côte d'Ivoire	December 31, 1963	Philippines	December 27, 1979
Cuba	January 1, 1948	Poland	October 18, 1967
Cyprus	July 15, 1963	Portugal	May 6, 1962
Czech Republic	April 15, 1993	Qatar	April 7, 1994
Denmark	May 18, 1950	Romania	November 14, 1971
Djibouti	December 16, 1994	Rwanda	January 1, 1966
Dominica	April 20, 1993	Senegal	September 1963
Dominican Republic	May 19, 1950	Sierra Leone	May 19, 1961
Egypt	May 9, 1970	Singapore	August 20, 1973
El Salvador	May 22, 1991	Slovak Republic	April 15, 1993
Fiji	November 16, 1993	Slovenia	October 30, 1994
Finland	May 25, 1950	Solomon Islands	December 28, 1994
France	January 1, 1948	South Africa	June 13, 1948
Gabon	May 3, 1963	Spain	August 29, 1963
Gambia	February 22, 1965	Sri Lanka	July 29, 1948
Germany	October 1, 1951	St. Kitts & Nevis	March 24, 1994
Ghana	October 17, 1957	St. Lucia	April 13, 1993
Greece	March 1, 1950	St. Vincent & the Grenadines	May 18, 1993
Grenada	February 9, 1994	Suriname	March 22, 1978
Guatemala	October 10, 1991	Swaziland	February 8, 1993
Guinea	December 8, 1994	Sweden	April 30, 1950
Guinea Bissau	March 17, 1994	Switzerland	August 1, 1966
Guyana	July 5, 1996	Tanzania	December 9, 1961
Haiti	January 1, 1950	Thailand	November 20, 1982
Honduras	April 10, 1994	Togo	March 20, 1964
Hong Kong	April 23, 1986	Trinidad & Tobago	October 23, 1962
Hungary	September 9, 1973	Tunisia	August 29, 1990
Iceland	April 21, 1968	Turkey	October 17, 1951
India	July 8, 1948	Uganda	October 23, 1962
Indonesia	February 24, 1950	United Arab Emirates	March 8, 1994
Israel	July 5, 1962	United Kingdom	January 1, 1948
Italy	May 30, 1950	United States	January 1, 1948
Jamaica	December 31, 1963	Uruguay	December 6, 1953
Japan	September 10, 1955	Venezuela	August 31, 1990
Kenya	February 5, 1964	Yugoslavia	August 25, 1966
Korea, Rep. of	April 14, 1967	Zaire	September 11, 1971
Kuwait	May 3, 1963	Zambia	February 10, 1982
Lesotho	January 8, 1988	Zimbabwe	July 11, 1948
Liechtenstein	March 29, 1994		
Luxembourg	May 19, 1950		

Source: World Trade Organization, 2004.

Table 2: GATT Trade Rounds, 1947–1995

Name of Round	Period & Number of Parties	Subject and Modalities	Outcome
Geneva	1947 23 countries	Tariffs; item-by-item offer-request negotiations.	Concessions on 45, 000 tariff lines
Annecy	1949 29 countries	Tariffs; item-by-item offer-request negotiations.	5,000 tariff concessions; 9 accessions
Torquay	1950–1951 32 countries	Tariffs; item-by-item offer-request negotiations.	3,700 tariff concessions; 4 accessions
Geneva	1955–1956 33 countries	Tariffs; item-by-item offer-request negotiations.	Modest reductions
Dillon	1960–1961 39 countries	Tariffs; item-by-item offer-request negotiations, motivated in part by need to rebalance concessions following creation of the EEC.	4,400 concessions exchanged; EEC proposal for a 20 percent linear cut in manufactures tariffs rejected
Kennedy	1963–1967 74 countries	Tariffs; formula approach (linear cut), and item-by-item talks. Nontariff measures: antidumping, customs valuation.	Average tariffs reduced by one-third to 6 percent for OECD manufactures imports; voluntary codes of conduct agreed for all nontariff issues except safeguards
Tokyo	1973–1979 99 countries	Tariffs; formula approach with exceptions. Nontariff measures: antidumping, customs valuation, subsidies and countervailing duties, import licensing, product standards, safeguards, special and differential treatment of developing countries.	Average tariffs again reduced by one-third on average; agriculture and textiles and clothing subjected to rules; creation of WTO; new agreements on services, and TRIPs; majority of Tokyo Round codes extended to all WTO members
Uruguay	1986–1994 103 countries in 1986, but 117 as of end of 1993	Tariffs; formula approach and item-by-item negotiations. Nontariff measures: all Tokyo issues, plus services, intellectual property, preshipment inspection, rules of origin, trade-related investment measures, dispute settlement, transparency, and surveillance of trade policies.	

Source: Bernard M. Hoekman and Michel M. Kostecki, eds., *The Political Economy of the World Trading System* (Oxford: Oxford University Press, 2001), p. 101.

Table 3: From GATT to WTO: A Chronology

Date	Events
1947	The GATT is drawn up to record the results of tariff negotiations among twenty-three countries. The agreement enters into force on January 1.
1948	GATT provisionally enters into force. Delegations from fifty-six countries meet in Havana, Cuba, to consider the final draft of the ITO; fifty-three countries sign the so-called Havana Charter establishing an ITO in March.
1949	Annecy Round of tariff negotiations.
1950	China withdraws from the GATT. The U.S. administration abandons efforts to seek congressional ratification of the ITO.
1951	Torquay Round of tariff negotiations. The intersessional committee is established to organize voting by airmail ballot on issues concerning use of trade measures to safeguard the balance of payments. Germany (Federal Republic) accedes to the GATT.
1955	A review secession modifies numerous provisions of the GATT. A move to transform the GATT into a formal international organization fails. The United States is granted a waiver from GATT disciplines for certain agriculture policies. Japan accedes to the GATT.
1956	Fourth Round of MTNs is held in Geneva.
1957	Creation of European Economic Community.
1960	A council of representatives is created to manage day-to-day activities. The Dillon Round is started (concluded in 1961).
1961	The Short-Term Arrangement permitting quota restrictions on exports of cotton textiles is agreed upon as an exception to the GATT rules.
1962	The Short-Term Arrangement becomes the Long-Term Agreement on cotton textiles. It is renegotiated in 1967 and extended for three years in 1970, then replaced by the Multi-Fiber Agreement (MFA) in 1974.
1964	The Kennedy Round begins (concluded in 1967).The United Nations Conference on Trade and Development (UNCTAD) is created to press for trade measures to benefit developing countries.
1965	Part IV (on Trade and Development) is added to the GATT, establishing new guidelines for trade policies of—and toward—developing countries. A Committee on Trade and Development is created to monitor implementation.
1967	Poland becomes the first centrally planned country to accede to the GATT.
1973	The Tokyo Round is initiated (concluded in 1979).
1974	The Agreement Regarding International Trade in Textiles, better known as the Multi-Fiber Agreement (MFA), enters into force, restricting export growth to 6 percent per year. It is negotiated in 1977 and 1982 and extended in 1986, 1991, and 1992.
1982	A GATT ministerial meeting—the first in almost a decade—fails to agree on an agenda for a new round. A GATT work program is formulated with a view to establishing an agenda for a new MTN.
1986	The Uruguay Round begins (concluded in 1994).
1988	A GATT ministerial meeting to review progress in the Uruguay Round is held in Montreal in December. The mid-term review is completed only in April 1989.
1990	Canada formally introduces a proposal to create a Multilateral Trade Organization that would cover the GATT, the GATS, and other multilateral instruments agreed upon in the Uruguay Round. A ministerial meeting is Brussels fails to conclude the Uruguay Round.
1993	In June, the U.S. Congress grants fast-track authority to the U.S. administration—under which it cannot propose amendments to the outcome of negotiations—setting a December 15 deadline for talks to be concluded. The Uruguay Round is concluded on December 15 in Geneva.
1994	In Marrakech, on April 15, ministers sign the Final Act establishing the World Trade Organization (WTO) and embodying the results of the Uruguay Round.
1995	The WTO enters into force on January 1.

Source: Bernard M. Hoekman and Michel M. Kostecki, eds., *The Political Economy of the World Trading System* (Oxford: Oxford University Press, 2001), pp. 39–41.

were inextricably linked. The GATT's guiding principles reflected the prevailing liberal consensus on free trade as a generator of world prosperity and as conducive to stable peace. As early as 1934, America took steps in the direction of free trade with the Reciprocal Trade Agreements Act. Secretary of State Cordell Hull offered to reduce American tariffs in exchange for equivalent concessions from its trading partners. Any such reduction would be extended to other countries enjoying most-favored-nation (MFN) treatment by virtue of preexisting trade treaties. With the United States moving into a position of leadership and the declining role of Great Britain, the global trading order changed shape. Whereas Britain had sustained a policy of unilateral free imports regardless of its trade deficit, the United States would seek contractual and reciprocal freeing of trade.

The GATT borrowed two elements from the model laid out by U.S. tariff bargaining, reciprocity and MFN treatment. In the preamble, the contracting parties to the GATT agreed to enter into reciprocal and mutually advantageous arrangements directed toward the substantial reduction of tariffs and other barriers to trade and to the elimination of discriminatory treatment. These two basic principles— MFN treatment and reciprocity of concessions—were further specified in Article I and Article XXVIII (see Table 4).

Postwar Planning and the GATT

Soon after the entry of the United States into World War II, talks were started between the United States, the rising power, and Britain, the declining power, on trade and monetary collaboration to be conducted after the war. In the backdrop was the Keynesian revolution, which had led to an acceptance at the national level of two related ideas: that market forces were not automatically self-regulating, and that certain forms of government intervention were therefore required from time to time. Concurrently,

it was also conceded at the international level that government management was necessary; disagreement was confined to the extent of such intervention, not whether it was called for. It was widely accepted by both sides that the collapse of the 1930s was largely due to the lack of international consultative mechanisms, which had left economic affairs at the mercy of unregulated market forces.

The postdepression era paved the way for fundamental changes in the international trade and monetary system. In this context, the aim of the Bretton Woods Agreements was to reestablish by international agreement a reasonable reproduction of the gold-standard system, that is, the conditions for an international system that would secure the combination of currency convertibility, capital mobility, and free trade. Three major institutions—the IMF, the World Bank, and the ITO—were planned to achieve this objective. They were also to be given powers of multilateral surveillance to ensure that rules were not capriciously breached. It was thought that with multilateral surveillance, a reenactment of the collapse of the 1930s could be averted.

The first two institutions were created as a result of the conference held at Bretton Woods, New Hampshire, in 1944. There, the signatories undertook to maintain the interconvertibility of their currencies and to refrain from competitive devaluations and from bilateral currency arrangements that would discriminate among trading partners in current transactions. The appropriate financial arrangements were thus laid out for multilateral trade and free exchange to develop. Commercial policy, however, was not directly involved, and negotiations on this particular issue went much more slowly. There were two reasons for this: differences in the British and American views, and internal differences within each government. In the United States, the more ardent free-traders in the Department of State, inspired by Cordell Hull's global vision, confronted sectoral interests in the Department of Agriculture as well as in Congress.

Table 4: Major GATT Articles

Article	Summary
I	General MFN requirement.
II	Tariff schedule (binding).
III	National treatment.
V	Freedom of transit goods.
VI	Allows antidumping and countervailing duties. Superseded by the GATT 1994 Agreement on Antidumping and the Agreement on Subsidies and Countervailing Measures.
VII	Requires the valuation of goods for customs purposes be based on actual values.Superseded by the GATT 1994 agreement on the implementation of Article VII.
VIII	Requires that fees connected with import and export formalities be cost based.
IX	Reaffirms MFN for labeling requirements and calls for cooperation to prevent abuse of trade names.
X	Obligation to publish trade laws and regulations; complemented by the WTO's Trade Policy Review Mechanism and numerous notification requirements in specific WTO agreements.
XI	Requires the general elimination of quantitative restrictions.
XII	Permits trade restrictions if necessary to safeguard the balance of payments.
XIII	Requires quotas to be administered in a nondiscriminatory manner.
XVI	Establishes the GATT 1947 rules on subsidies.
XVII	Requires that state trading enterprises follow MFN.
XVIII	Allows developing countries to restrict trade to promote infant industries and to protect the balance of payments.
XIX	Allows for emergency action to restrict imports of particular products if these cause serious injury to the domestic industry.
XX	General expectations provision—allows trade restrictions if necessary to attain noneconomic objectives (health and safety).
XXI	Allows trade to be restricted if necessary for national security reasons.
XXII	Requires consultations between parties involved in trade disputes.
XXIII	GATT's main dispute-settlement provision, dealing with violation or nonviolation complaints.
XXIV	Sets out the conditions under which the formation of free trade areas or customs unions is permitted.
XXVIII	Allows for renegotiation of tariff concessions.
XXVIII	Calls for periodic MTNs to reduce tariffs.
XXXIII	Allows for accession.
Part IV	Calls for more favorable and differential treatment of developing countries.

Source: Bernard M. Hoekman and Michel M. Kostecki, eds., *The Political Economy of the World Trading System* (Oxford: Oxford University Press, 2001), pp. 146–147.

Negotiations for the International Trade Organization began in 1946. Successive conferences took place from 1946 to 1948 in London, New York, Geneva, and Havana. The final version of the ITO Charter was drawn up in Havana in March 1948, but it never came into effect. The initial proposal for the ITO was largely conceived by Department of State officials; however, anticipating a strong rebuff, President Harry S. Truman never submitted it to Congress for ratification. In fact, only two countries, Australia and Liberia, ever ratified it.

In 1947, President Truman was determined to use his congressional power to negotiate under the Reciprocal Trade Agreements Act, which had been renewed in 1945 for a period of three years. This law authorized the president to reduce import duties by up to 50 percent in return for equivalent concessions by other countries. The administration proposed to negotiate such trade agreements simultaneously and to embody them in one multilateral treaty. The General Agreement on Tariffs and Trade was drawn up as the general framework of rights and obligations for the twenty-two countries—of which nine were less developed countries (LDCs)—participating in tariff negotiations sponsored by the United States. The GATT came into being before the Havana Conference but in accordance with the draft ITO Charter that was being discussed. It was originally envisaged as the first of a number of agreements that were to be negotiated under the auspices of the ITO. When it became clear that the Havana Charter would not be ratified by the United States, the General Agreement became, by default, the underpinning of an international institution.

Thus, the GATT is not technically an organization of which countries become members, but a treaty with contracting parties. Nevertheless, it has assumed the commercial policy role that was planned for the ITO, without incorporating the wider provisions of the Havana Charter on restrictive business practices, commodity agreements, economic development, and full employment policies. It mainly deals, instead, with the reduction of tariffs on trade in manufactures.

Fundamental Principles of the GATT

Although the text of the GATT is highly technical, consisting of thirty-eight articles covering everything from MFN treatment in tariff concessions to details about quotas, subsidies, and other trade policies, its broad outlines are simple enough. In essence, the GATT contains three fundamental principles regulating trade policy.

The first principle is that trade should be concluded on the basis of nondiscrimination. Accordingly, contracting parties are bound by the most-favored-nations clause in the application of import and export duties and changes in their administration. In addition, the use of import quotas is permitted under the rules, but these are to be administered on a nondiscriminatory basis. Any departure from these fundamental rules is hedged with conditions and safeguards. Thus, countries may protect themselves against unfair competition—for example, dumping and export subsidization—by implementing measures limited to imports from the countries employing the unfair methods, but the conditions under which such measures can be taken are strictly limited and defined. When countries are compelled to restrict the volume of imports in order to safeguard foreign exchange reserves, the strict application of the rules of nondiscrimination might lead to a greater degree of discrimination than the financial situation in fact requires. Here again—but within narrow limitations and subject to international consultation—the rule of nondiscrimination is relaxed. However, the MFN clause is also qualified so as to permit contracting parties to enter into genuine customs unions and free trade areas, the purpose of which is to facilitate trade between the constituent territories and not to raise barriers, and a series of criteria is laid down designed to ensure that arrangements are "trade creating" and not "trade diverting."

The second major principle is that protection should be afforded to domestic industries exclusively through customs tariffs and not through other commercial measures. Thus the use of import quotas as a means of protection is explicitly condemned. The use of import quotas for other purposes—notably to safeguard the balance of payments—is governed by a formidable series of criteria and conditions, coupled with procedures for consultations. There are also numerous provisions designed to prevent the use of administrative techniques as a means of protection additional to the tariff, as well as provisions designed to prevent the use of subsidies as a means of obtaining unfair advantages in export markets or as a means of hampering imports.

The third principle is inherent throughout the GATT. The sum total of detail rules, which are built around the basic framework, constitutes a code that is voluntarily accepted by GATT contracting parties to govern their trading relationships. The importance of this code can be measured by the fact that it is accepted and applied by forty-two countries whose foreign trade accounts for some 85 percent of the total volume of world trade. Among the twenty-three founding parties of the GATT, nine were LDCs. GATT participants are drawn from all parts of the world, and have interests as diverse as their geographical locations, but most of them are united in the conviction of the beneficial effects of expanding world trade on an orderly basis.

GATT's Operational Structure

When discussing the basic principles and mechanisms of the GATT, it is important to consider that it operates on two interrelated levels. On the first level, the GATT brings together a body of principles. It is an international, contractual agreement by which each signatory commits itself to treat all other signatories according to the MFN standard. On the second level, the GATT is a forum where countries negotiate tariff reductions according to the legal framework provided by the agreement. GATT countries are not required to abolish the tariff automatically; rather, tariffs are the negotiable item. Countries make specific agreements to reduce particular tariffs in exchange for a reciprocal reduction from a trading partner. In the absence of such an agreement, a contracting party is not obliged to make a reduction.

The key component of the General Agreement is the MFN clause, which imposes on the contracting parties the obligation to grant each other equality of treatment. The MFN clause was specifically designed to outlaw preferential arrangements, and as a corollary, to prevent the struggle to obtain and secure such arrangements. The widespread use of discriminatory trade and currency arrangements was believed to have contributed to the political tension of the prewar era, and consequently, to war. The GATT expressed the belief that a liberal trading system would convert competition aimed at controlling territories into competition for price. If every country undertook to apply the same tariff to all its foreign suppliers, competition for markets would be open but confined to prices; it would therefore contribute to economic efficiency rather than leading to economic warfare. Many of the proponents of the GATT and intellectuals of the postwar economic order believed that there was a link between free trade and the possibility of international peace.

Besides regulating competition in the international market, the GATT also aimed to regulate the methods and mechanisms by which a country could protect its domestic producers from international competition. In theory, countries were supposed to have no other form of protection but tariffs. Being the sole legal device, tariffs are also, in principle, the sole negotiable item in the GATT. Protection through nontariff measures (NTMs), such as import quotas, was to be banned. No provision was therefore made for negotiations to reduce NTMs. Furthermore, a new class of provisions was added in 1964 to incorporate some of the innovations that LDCs had lobbied for. These provisions were brought together under Part IV. The core provision of this part was that LDCs would no longer be required to offer reciprocity in tariff negotiations.

In contrast to the IMF and the World Bank, which operate under a system of weighted voting, in the GATT each country is entitled to only one vote. Voting rules vary according to the subject under discussion. An amendment to Part I (containing the obligation to grant MFN treatment) and to Articles XIX (safeguard action in imports) and XXX (amendments) can only be passed if it is unanimously agreed upon. Amendments to other parts become effective once they have been accepted by a two-thirds majority, but are only effective among those who have agreed to them. This highlights the contractual rather than mandatory nature of the GATT. Equally, a two-thirds majority is required to grant a waiver to a government wanting to take measures that are incompatible with its obligation—for example, an import surcharge. All other decisions are taken by a majority of votes cast (Article XXV).

The accession of a new GATT country requires a two-thirds majority vote. No one country can exercise the power of veto. Majority rule was preferred over unanimity to obviate a situation in which the accession of a country might be impeded by a GATT country with little interest in the proposed country's market or by one competing with it. However, GATT signatories that have not assented to the accession of a particular country are not obliged to apply the provisions of the agreement vis-à-vis the new participant (Article XXXV). In other words, countries are not forced to grant equal treatment to all participating countries, although this is the desired end result.

The GATT's core function is to arrange periodical conferences, or "rounds," at which the participants bargain for mutual concessions. In the early stages, there were no provisions for secretariat services; the secretariat was provided by the Interim Commission of the ITO,

which was made available to the GATT by the United Nations in 1952. A Committee for Agenda and International Business was formed in 1951 to exercise surveillance functions, and a Council of Representatives, with broader decisionmaking powers, replaced this committee in 1960. The Council of Representatives holds regular sessions concerned with the granting of waivers, the application of the GATT rules, the accession of new signatories, and general trade policy issues.

Altogether, these provisions aimed to establish as open and liberal a system as possible that would allow trade to increase global efficiency. The GATT aimed to codify this system, which was thought to be more realistic than absolute free trade. The founding GATT countries considered absolute free trade the first best policy but acknowledged that it would not be politically feasible to enforce it at all times or regardless of domestic employment levels. The GATT was regarded as a pragmatic compromise, a "second best" solution, by which domestic interests were offered some protection from the international market, but foreign suppliers would be allowed to compete for a share of the domestic market. With the creation of an appropriate institution, there would, moreover, be a framework for collective discipline. With such collective rules, it was hoped that the international trading system would strengthen in order to avoid strains similar to those of the 1930s, which had resulted in a scramble for self-protection.

The GATT adopted the traditional MFN principle of nondiscrimination with two innovations. The first innovation was that negotiations for tariff reductions in GATT take place simultaneously. The second was that these reductions are safeguarded against future rises. Whereas Article I ensures that tariff concessions are to be extended to all contracting parties, Article II provides future stability to these concessions. The agreed rates are "bound" and put together in "schedules" for each country. Once bound, the rates can only be raised following renegotiation with the country holding the "initial negotiating rights" (Article XXVIII), that is, the country that has bargained and "paid" for the concession in the first place, as well as with those that might have become principle supplying countries since that time. Concessions thereby become the collective right of the contracting parties, regardless of which country has negotiated them. A contracting party that wishes to raise the bound tariff must be prepared to offer compensation or risk retaliation (Article XIX).

Given that legally bound tariffs are an integral part of the General Agreement, a new GATT country automatically benefits from the cumulative effect of all concessions negotiated prior to its arrival. The new country is therefore expected to pay an "entry fee" on accession, and it must enter into tariff negotiations with established contracting parties before becoming a full participant. The general thrust of activities in the GATT is to maintain a balance of concessions.

To ensure that all foreign suppliers would stand on equal footing in their competition for a part of the domestic market, the General Agreement only accepted the tariff as a legitimate device for safeguarding the domestic market. There was yet a second reason for the legitimacy of the tariff as opposed to quantitative restrictions. In the minds of those who had done most to initiate and push forward the GATT project, a strong dislike of quantitative regulation, as something inconsistent with, and inimical to, a self-adjusting price system, played a prominent part in the GATT formulation. The quantitative restrictions on trade were prohibited on the grounds that they allow discrimination among foreign exporters and, by predetermining the volume of trade, alter the "correct" price relations. In principle, they could only be applied in strictly limited, carefully defined circumstances.

A further provision designed to ensure nondiscrimination stipulated that once foreign goods passed the frontier, they would be ensured equal rights of competition with domestic goods. They were to be given "national treat-ment" (as defined in Article III), that is, they would not be subject to measures of a discriminatory nature, such as higher taxes, vis-à-vis those goods produced domestically.

The major trading countries were successful in putting these provisions into practice. Trade liberalization among them was accomplished through removal of quantitative restrictions, as convertibility of their currencies was restored, and through a series of multilateral trade negotiations under the GATT. The GATT has sponsored seven rounds of negotiations, following the pace set by U.S. trade legislation. In other words, the GATT is largely an international counterpart of U.S. tariff policy. Various rounds of negotiations have concentrated primarily on tariff reduction, but gradually, broader issues concerning the problems of LDCs and nontariff measures have come to the fore. During the Tokyo Round, for example, a whole series of codes on nontariff measures was negotiated and concluded, apart from the tariff reductions, and the improvement of some elements of the General Agreement in favor of LDCs was also discussed.

Overview of Negotiation Rounds

GATT principles have guided the trade policies of the major industrial countries since the late 1940s. By the early 1990s, eight rounds of negotiations on tariff reductions and other multilateral trade issues had been held. These rounds had achieved remarkable success in lowering trade barriers, and particularly in reducing tariffs. The rounds are named after the places at which they were launched or the people who were influential in launching them, though, with the exception of the early sets of negotiations, held in Annecy, France, and Torquay, United Kingdom, the actual negotiations occurred in Geneva, where the GATT Secretariat is based.

The following rounds have been concluded: the first Geneva Round (1947), the Annecy Round (1949), the Torquay Round (1950–

1951), the second Geneva Round (1955–1956), the Dillon Round (1960–1961), the Kennedy Round (1963–1967), the Tokyo Round (1973–1979), and the Uruguay Round (1986–1994) (see Table 2). The first five rounds dealt almost exclusively with tariffs. The first round in Geneva achieved substantial multilateral tariff reductions through some 123 bilateral agreements that were extended on a most-favored-nation basis to all participants. The total of 45,000 tariff concessions represented about half of world trade. Tariff reductions in each of the four bargaining rounds held during the following fifteen years were relatively minor. The Annecy Round, the second Geneva Round, and the Dillon Round each resulted in modest tariff reductions. The Torquay Round accomplished a 25 percent tariff reduction in relation to the 1948 level. Starting with the Kennedy Round, attention began to shift toward nontariff trade restrictions and to the problem of trade in agricultural products. The Kennedy Round achieved remarkable multilateral trade negotiations. Inspired by the Trade Expansion Act of 1962 under the John F. Kennedy administration, this round of bargaining resulted in average tariff reductions of 35 percent for industrial products. In addition, it included much broader country coverage, as countries such as Japan and West Germany acceded to the GATT.

The Kennedy Round dealt exclusively with the nontariff measures that were already covered by the GATT, but the Tokyo Round addressed policies that were not subject to GATT disciplines—for example, product standards and government procurement. Also, the Tokyo Round concluded with major countries agreeing to cut average tariffs by 35 percent for industrial products. The tariff reductions amounted to more than $155 billion in 1977. An important feature of the Tokyo Round was a first-time agreement to limit the growth of nontariff barriers. The negotiations produced codes covering several nontariff trade barriers that included subsidies and countervailing duty code, government procurement code, technical standards code, customs valuation code, and import licensing code. A failure of the Tokyo Round, however, was the inability of participating countries to agree on safeguards code. Safeguards are temporary measures, such as higher duties, quotas, and voluntary export restraints, used to protect industries threatened by imports. Agreement on a safeguards code is vital for free trade because governments are often pressured by protectionist interest groups to impose such temporary measures.

The trend set by the Tokyo Round continued in the Uruguay Round, which included trade in services, intellectual property, and rules of origin. This round of negotiations aimed to eliminate trade barriers and domestic subsidies in agriculture, remove barriers to trade in services, establish patents and copyright agreements, and eliminate restrictions on international investments. The Uruguay Round led to further liberalization of international trade, including not only tariff reductions but also the elimination of tariffs for certain product groups, the reintegration of agriculture trade and textiles and clothing into the trading system, and the expansion of GATT disciplines. The GATT 1994 embodies a series of agreements on specific issues—many of them renegotiations of Tokyo Round codes. Criteria for a new GATT allowed contracting parties to bypass the need to formally amend the GATT 1947 and at the same time to ensure that the results of the round were a single undertaking that applied to all. In 1995, the World Trade Organization (WTO) was established to oversee the function of the GATT, the General Agreement on Trade in Services (GATS), and the Agreement on Trade-Related Aspects of Intellectual Property Rights (TRIPS).

Jitendra Uttam

See Also Antidumping and Countervailing Duties; Nontariff Barriers; Protectionism; Tariffs; Technical Barriers to Trade; World Trade Organization (WTO); Copyrights and Intellectual Property

References

Bagwell, Kyle, and Robert Staiger. 1999. "An Economic Theory of GATT." *American Economic Review* 89: 215–48.

Camps, Miriam, and William Diebold, Jr. 1986. *The New Multilateralism.* New York: Council on Foreign Relations.

Curzon, Gerard. 1965. *Multilateral Trade Diplomacy.* London: Michael Joseph.

Hoekman, Bernard M., and Michel M. Kostecki, eds. 2001. *The Political Economy of the World Trading System.* Oxford: Oxford University Press.

Jackson, John H. 1990. *Restructuring the GATT System.* London: Pinter.

Long, Oliver. 1987. *Law and Its Limitations in the GATT Multilateral Trade System.* London: Graham and Tortman; Boston: Nijhoff.

Low, P. 1993. *Trading Free: The GATT and the US Trade Policy.* New York: Twentieth Century Fund.

Roessler, Frieder. 1985. "The Scope, Limits and the Function of the GATT Legal System." *World Economy* 8: 287–298.

Schott, Jeffrey J., ed. 1990. *Completing the Uruguay Round: A Results-Oriented Approach to the GATT Trade Negotiations.* Washington, DC: Institute for International Economics.

Winham, Gilbert. 1990. "GATT and the International Trade Regime." *International Journal* 15: 786–822.

Group of 8 (G8)

The Group of Eight (G8) is an informal gathering of world leaders who meet each summer, usually in June or July, to discuss and deliberate on matters of mutual interest and of global ramification. The member countries are Canada, France, Germany, Italy, Japan, Russia, the United Kingdom, and the United States. The European Union is also represented, by the leader of the country holding presidency of the European Council and the president of the European Commission in a given year.

Historical Overview

In 1975, at the invitation of French President Giscard d'Estaing, leaders of Italy, West Germany, Japan, the United Kingdom, and the United States had an informal gathering at the Château of Rambouillet, near France. The leaders discussed major world issues of the time, particularly the 1973 Arab-Israeli conflict and the ensuing oil crisis that had ravaged several world economies. Canada joined this exclusive group as the seventh member at the 1976 summit held in Puerto Rico. Russia began to participate in 1991, though not as a full member, and only after the main summit was concluded. It was allowed to participate fully at the 1998 Birmingham Summit after a consensus was reached among the G7 nations to admit it to the group.

G8 leaders currently do not plan to expand the number of countries formally accepted to the group; however, in recent years, tangible efforts have been made to invite other countries and institutions to participate on a limited basis to advance particular initiatives, especially the developing and least developed countries of Asia and Africa. For example, the Kananaskis G8 Summit of 2002 invited the leaders of five African countries to participate in developing a new initiative known as the New Partnership for Africa's Development (NEPAD). Unlike the United Nations and other international forums, the G8 Summit has no official language policy, as the summit meetings are basically consultative in nature. The heads of state and government who attend the meetings speak in their own native languages, with simultaneous translation into English and French for the worldwide audience.

The chair of the G8 rotates among the member countries. Recent summits have been chaired by France (2003), the United States (2004), and the United Kingdom (2005); upcoming summits will be chaired by Russia (2006), Germany (2007), Japan (2008), Italy (2009), and Canada (2010). The country holding the chair proposes the summit location, sets the agenda, and takes care of logistics and related matters. The chair is the host for the summit and acts as the chief spokesperson for the G8 for the year (January through December). Meetings of the foreign ministers and finance ministers of the eight countries are also held each year preceding the G8 summit meetings.

Table 1:   Group of Eight Country Statistics

Country	Area	Population	GDP	GDP per Capita	Exports	Imports
Canada	9,984,670 sq km (3,854,083 sq mi)	32,207,113	$934.1 billion	$29,300	Chemicals, plastics, fertilizers, wood pulp, timber, crude petroleum, natural gas, aluminum	Machinery and equipment, crude oil, chemicals, electricity, durable consumer goods
France	547,030 sq km (211,154 sq mi)	60,180,529	$1.558 trillion	$26,000	Machinery and transportation equipment, aircraft, plastics, chemicals, iron and steel, beverages	Machinery and equipment, vehicles, crude oil, aircraft, chemicals
Germany	357,021 sq km (137,810 sq mi)	82,398,326	$2.16 trillion	$26,200	Machinery, vehicles, chemicals, food stuffs, textiles	Machinery, vehicles, chemicals, textiles, metals
Italy	301,230 sq km (116,275 sq mi)	57,998,353	$1.455 trillion	$25,100	Engineering products, textiles and clothing, motor vehicles, production machinery, chemicals, food, beverages	Chemicals, transport equipment, energy products, textiles and clothing, food, beverages, and tobacco
Japan	377,835 sq km (145,844 sq mi)	127,214,499	$3.651 trillion	$28,700	Motor vehicles, semiconductors, office machines, chemicals	Machinery and equipment, fuels, foodstuffs, chemicals, textiles, raw materials
Russia	17,075,200 sq km (6,591,027 sq mi)	144,526,278	$1.409 trillion	$9,700	Petroleum and petroleum products, natural gas, wood and wood products, metals, chemicals	Machinery and equipment, consumer goods, medicines, meat, sugar, semi-finished metal products
United Kingdom	244,820 sq km (94,501 sq mi)	60,094,648	$1.528 trillion	$25,500	Manufactured goods, fuels, chemicals, food, beverages, tobacco	Manufactured goods, machinery, fuels, food stuffs
United States	9,629,091 sq km (3,716,829 sq mi)	290,342,554	$10.45 trillion	$36,300	Capital goods, automobiles, industrial supplies and raw materials, consumer goods, agricultural products	Crude oil and refined petroleum products, machinery, automobiles, consumer goods, industrial raw materials

Note: Population figures are 2003 estimates. Gross domestic product (GDP) and GDP per capita are 2002 estimates.

G8 Initiatives

The 2003 G8 Summit:
Weapons of Mass Destruction

At the 2003 G8 Summit held in Evian, France, a G8 declaration recognized the increased proliferation of weapons of mass destruction (WMD) and other dangers posing a real threat to global peace and security. The G8 member countries resolved to tackle the WMD issue individually and collectively, working both among themselves and with other partners, including the United Nations and its specialized agencies. The declaration stressed the role of international treaty regimes, such as Nuclear Nonproliferation Treaty (NPT), the Comprehensive Test Ban Treaty (CTBT), and the Vienna-based International Atomic Energy Agency (IAEA), and highlighted the need for concerted efforts to prohibit the use of chemical weapons.

In light of the events of September 11, 2001, the G8 nations endorsed a set of principles to prevent the spread of WMDs and other materials of mass destruction to terrorists and those who harbor them. In the regional sphere, the G8 nations expressed grave concern about North Korea's enrichment of processed uranium, its plutonium production, and its failure to comply with IAEA safeguards, urging North Korea to desist from threatening its neighbors, particularly Japan and South Korea. A similar request was made to Iran, asking it to sign and implement IAEA protocols without delay or conditions and to fully comply with its obligations under the NPT.

International Terrorism

In light of increasing recent incidents of international terrorism the world over, the G8 nations have reassessed counterterrorism methods and conducted capacity-building assistance measures. With this mission in place after the 2003 summit, they have focused on three main areas of counterterrorism activity: (1) measures denying terrorists any safe haven or sanctuary anywhere and ensuring that they

are brought to justice quickly; (2) measures denying terrorists the means to commit terrorist acts (for example, preventing the financing of terrorism); and (3) measures bolstering domestic security and creating fail-proof mechanisms for crisis and disaster management. The G8 nations lent support to the United Nations Security Council's Counter-Terrorism Committee (CTC), including providing assistance in drafting and enforcing customs and border-control legislation, assistance in drafting and enforcing immigration laws pertaining to interstate travel and in streamlining procedures related to asylum/refugee status, and assistance in developing procedures for counterterrorism law enforcement. It was hoped by the G8 countries that these measures would curb acts of terrorism, stem illicit drug trafficking and other forms of organized crime, and assist countries in drafting counterterrorism legislation.

Through its Counter-Terrorism Action Group (CTAG), established in 2003, the G8 is committed to creating the necessary political will to fight terrorism around the globe and to coordinating capacity-building with other nations. In this context, the G8 nations have decided to provide funding, expertise, and training facilities for this purpose and to prioritize needs and expand counterterrorism capacities.

Public Health Issues

In the new millennium, global health crises have reached epidemic proportions. G8 nations, in partnership with developing countries, the private sector, nongovernmental organizations (NGOs), and other multilateral organizations, are determined to develop a proactive approach.

It was decided at the 2003 Evian Summit to fight diseases such as HIV/AIDS, tuberculosis, and malaria by initiating actions in such areas as institution building, human resource development, public-private partnerships, medical research, and promotion of public health at the microcommunity level. A Global Fund was also proposed to develop strategies for mobilizing all available resources in order to secure sustainable, long-term financing for management of health-care goals. For fighting diseases mostly affecting developing countries, including those on the African continent, G8 nations agreed to encourage research for developing effective, affordable, and safe drugs and vaccines and other forms of treatment and care for these diseases. In this context, G8 nations welcomed the long-term commitment of pharmaceutical companies in providing essential medicines, particularly those relating to HIV/AIDS, tuberculosis, and malaria, at affordable and discounted prices. In a renewed commitment to eradicate polio, the G8 decided to provide additional funding of US$500 million at the Kananaskis Summit of 2002. Severe Acute Respiratory Syndrome (SARS) received attention from G8 nations at Evian, where it was decided to develop global collaboration in containing the disease through disease surveillance; laboratory, diagnostic, and research efforts at various levels; and prevention, care, and treatment, working in close coordination with the World Health Organization (WHO) and other major health groups.

Water Policy

G8 nations are committed to developing an action plan on water because of its importance to public health and human security. In this context, emphasis was laid on promoting good governance and capacity-building to pursue a viable water policy and financial resources for the water and sanitation sector. In line with the World Summit on Sustainable Development (WSSD), convened by the UN, G8 nations gave high priority to ameliorating water and sanitation problems in developing nations. They expressed readiness in helping to mobilize domestic resources for water-infrastructure financing through the development and strengthening of capital markets and through encouraging financial institutions to consider such proposals liberally. Local water management systems in rural areas, sewage facilities in urban areas, and safe drinking water for all were given highest priorities. These matters

were to be dealt with in part through a concerted effort geared toward empowerment of local communities and action groups. Apart from supporting water-monitoring capacity in partner countries, G8 nations also voiced support for enhanced collaboration in water-cycle research and other related efforts. G8 nations also encouraged coordination between the United Nations and the World Bank for streamlining the water sector.

Sustainable Development

G8 nations have recognized the need to support sustainable development around the world. At the 2003 summit, it was stressed that this could be achieved through cooperative efforts among various countries. These efforts, leaders agreed, should focus on cutting pollution, reducing greenhouse emissions, and finding other ways to address the onerous prospect of global climate change from an objective viewpoint. The discussion focused on three areas: (1) seeking cleaner, more sustainable, more efficient use of energy; (2) encouraging coordination of global observation strategies as they pertain to climate change and global warming; and (3) pursuing agricultural sustainability and productivity and the conservation of biodiversity resources. In accordance with the WSSD resolution, G8 nations also voiced support for promoting energy efficiency in the use of all types of resources and encouraged the diffusion of advanced, energy-efficient methods of pollution reduction as well as measures dealing with public procurement and the provision of economic incentives and information. It was also decided by G8 nations to develop a workable strategy to promote rapid innovation and marketing of clean technologies by working in unison with the Milan Conference of the Parties of the United Nations Framework Convention on Climate Change, the International Energy Agency, the UN Economic Convention for Europe, the Expert Group on Technology Transfer, and other entities.

G8 nations are committed to accelerating the development of fuel-cell and hydrogen-related technologies (in transportation and power generation), working in close collaboration with industry to remove impediments to making fuel-cell-based vehicles at competitive prices; to developing internationally usable codes and standards in appropriate existing energy-related organizations; and to working toward cleaner, more efficient fossil fuel technologies. To achieve these objectives, it was decided at the Evian Summit to create a Global Environment Fund that could help finance energy-efficient, renewable, cleaner fossil fuel technologies and sustainable use of energy.

In the areas of agriculture and biodiversity, at the 2003 summit, the G8 nations agreed to support the International Treaty of Plant Genetic Resources for Food and Agriculture by conducting negotiations over an agreement for facilitating access to plant genetic resources for agricultural research. In this context, G8 nations are determined to contribute significantly to the Consultative Group for International Agricultural Research (CGIAR), the Global Forum for Agricultural Research (GFAR), and other North-South and South-South partnerships, with priority assigned to helping the rural poor of Asia and Africa. The expectation, from the G8 perspective, is that by promoting sustainable agricultural technologies and practices, famine can be prevented and productivity and nutrition enhanced. Recognizing the urgent need to tackle problems of food security, coupled with the need to address other structural problems, such as chronic poverty, the alarming rate of HIV/AIDS cases, poor governance, and economic mismanagement, the G8 nations at Evian 2003 created the G8 Africa Action Plan in support of the New Partnership for Africa's Development.

Since the 2002 Kananaskis Summit, G8 nations have provided US$3.3 billion in emergency assistance to mitigate Africa's pressing needs, including US$1.7 billion for sub-Saharan Africa. Another US$3.2 billion has been committed for long-term agricultural and food security assistance. Working in close collaboration with various governments in Africa as well as with UN relief agencies, nongovernmental organizations, and other entities that are part of the international community, G8 nations have instituted plans for improving the efficiency and timeliness of aid committed to Africa. For longer term initiatives to address food security problems in Africa, G8 nations have focused on core areas, such as rural and agricultural development, as well as ways to deal with poverty and national development, adopting a strategic approach that relies less on official development assistance and more on increasing trade opportunities for developing countries. By creating new, innovative agricultural policies at the national and regional levels, G8 nations hope to develop a climate of productive investment in agricultural infrastructure that will promote food crops and encourage improved agricultural technologies across the African continent.

Other Issues
At the Evian 2003 Summit, it was decided to develop models for promoting efficiency and transparency in the day-to-day governance of the developing countries of Asia and Africa through the use of new information technologies. In view of the impact and benefit of the computer on the information superhighway in the new millennium, emphasis was laid on promoting information and communications technologies to a wider global audience. At the 2000 Okinawa Summit, the potential of these technologies for enabling global economies, including those of developing countries, to expand, for enhancing public welfare in all sectors, and for promoting social bonds among people of different cultures was emphasized. In keeping with the process of globalization, and in the hope of bridging the digital divide, G8 nations decided to create a Digital Opportunities Task Force, in collaboration with the Global Digital Divide Initiative of the World Economic Forum and the Global Business Dialogue on Electronic Commerce. To maximize the benefits of IT and ensure that the new technologies are spread to one and all, including those with

marginal or no resources, G8 nations created the Okinawa Charter on the Global Information Society, which aims to bring the computer revolution to the developing world on an equitable and affordable basis. At the same time, G8 nations, aware of the limitations and rapid pace of IT and its potential negative impacts on global society, asked the task force to weigh carefully all the pros and cons of IT.

On the debt issue, G8 nations at Evian 2003 reaffirmed their commitment to the Heavily Indebted Poor Countries (HIPCs) Initiative that was launched at the 1999 Cologne Summit. At the 2002 Kananaskis Summit, the member countries pledged to pay up to US$1 billion to support this project and expressed satisfaction that twenty-six of the world's poorest countries were benefiting from debt relief. It was also decided to accelerate the HIPC process by asking the International Monetary Fund (IMF) and the World Bank to identify the specific needs in each of these poor countries and to make recommendations as to the areas that should take priority. In keeping with the commitment made during the Kananaskis Summit, the G8 nations pledged US$850 million to an HIPC Trust Fund and have asked official and commercial creditors to participate in this initiative. However, concern was expressed over the fact that a number of HIPC countries were being affected by military conflicts that prevented full implementation of debt relief and poverty reduction measures. Some countries, such as Benin, Bolivia, Burkina Faso, Honduras, Mauritania, Mozambique, Senegal, Tanzania, and Uganda, were recognized for their efforts in implementing the HIPC Initiative by assisting the poor and continuing to work toward economic reforms, whereas other countries were encouraged to work steadily to devise more effective methods of financial resource management and new, innovative poverty reduction strategies.

Cultural diversity is recognized by G8 nations as a source of social and economic dynamism that has the real potential of enriching

human life in the twenty-first century. In this regard, the role of the United Nations Educational, Scientific and Cultural Organization (UNESCO) in celebrating diversity through creative expression was welcomed by the G8 nations. At the 2000 Okinawa Summit, the leaders stressed the need for increasing interaction and dialogue among peoples, groups, and individuals to bring greater understanding among various cultures of the world. Preservation and promotion of cultural heritage were also given high priority, as they help to enhance cultural diversity and to foster creative cultural interaction. Along these same lines, G8 nations pledged to support projects dedicated to protecting and preserving art and archeological objects in developing countries, as well as UNESCO's projects on Masterpieces of the Oral and Intangible Heritage of Humanity. For nurturing interest, understanding, and respect for diverse cultures, the G8 nations supported an initiative for a new kind of educational curriculum that fosters understanding among different cultures and encourages educational institutions to promote exchanges of students, teachers, researchers, and scholars so as to derive maximum benefit from the richness of culturally diverse peoples.

Toward a twenty-first century of deeper peace of mind, issues such as crime and drugs have been given due emphasis by the G8 countries. In this respect, G8 nations at the 2000 Okinawa Summit supported the United Nations Convention Against Transnational Organized Crime and related protocols on firearms, smuggling of migrants, and trafficking in persons, as well as the establishment of an effective legal framework against transnational organized crime (TOC). High-tech crimes, such as cyber crimes, now have the potential to seriously threaten security and confidence in the global information order, and hence meaningful dialogue with computer-related industries was mounted by G8 nations in the Okinawa Charter on Global Information Society in 2000. On drug trafficking and abuse, the G8 nations supported the recommendation of the 1998 UN Special Session on containing the world drug problem as well as other regional initiatives to reduce both the supply and demand of drugs, with the ultimate aim of ending narcotics production and trafficking. G8 nations have also shown a commitment to combating the illicit diversion of precursor chemicals for the production of illegal drugs and to addressing the growing new threat from amphetamines and other synthetic drugs that could have a very devastating impact on the world's youth. Financial crimes, including money-laundering across and within national boundaries, were also perceived as a serious threat, especially to economic stability, and hence G8 nations, working in concert with other countries, instituted an action plan to put a dent in this menace. Enhanced investigation, prosecution of crime, and judicial cooperation were recommended to various groups for bringing about maximum punitive impact.

On regional issues, G8 nations at the 2003 Evian Summit voiced support for peace in Iraq and reconstruction of the war-torn country. It was hoped that Iraq would soon emerge as a fully sovereign, stable, and democratic country at peace with its neighbors. Similar support was also extended by the G8 nations to President Hamid Karzai's government in Afghanistan.

On the Israel/Palestine issue, at the 2003 summit the G8 expressed a hope that the Roadmap to Peace would bring about viable improvements in the Middle East, with Israel and a new state of Palestine existing side by side in peace and harmony with one another.

On North Korea, at the 2003 summit the G8 nations supported multilateral efforts by the countries of Asia to reduce tensions. At Evian 2003, the G8 opted to seek a comprehensive solution to the crisis over North Korean nuclear proliferation and other humanitarian issues, such as the abduction of Japanese nationals by North Korea, through dialogue and peaceful means.

2004 G8 SUMMIT

The 2004 G8 summit took place in Sea Island, Georgia, USA, June 8-10, 2004. A foundation had been laid at the Evian 2003 summit, during which the G8 leaders had recognized the dangers emanating from the proliferation of weapons of mass destruction and international terrorism as the pre-eminent threat to international peace and security. At the 2004 summit, G8 countries adopted an Action Plan on Nonproliferation to reinforce the global nonproliferation regime. This Action Plan enhanced and expanded ongoing efforts, such as the Proliferation Security Initiative (PSI), which included all G8 members, and the G8 Global Partnership Against the Spread of Weapons and Materials of Mass Destruction. The Action Plan addressed transfers of enrichment and reprocessing equipment and technologies, and took tangible steps to strengthen Vienna-based International Atomic Energy Agency (IAEA) and to counter bioterrorism.

The challenges faced by Africa were discussed in-depth at the Sea Island summit. These included vital issues of enormous significance to Africa such as armed conflict, HIV/AIDS, famine, and poverty. The G8 leaders made a commitment (a) to launch a G8 Action Plan on Expanding Global Capability for Peace Support Operations; (b) to initiate a G8 Action Plan on Applying the Power of Entrepreneurship to the Eradication of Poverty; (c) to endorse and establish a Global HIV Vaccine Enterprise to accelerate HIV vaccine development; (d) to take all necessary steps to eradicate polio by 2005; (e) to launch a new initiative on Ending the Cycle of Famine in the Horn of Africa, Raising Agricultural Productivity, and Promoting Rural Development in Food Insecure Countries; (f) to reaffirm commitment to fully implement and finance the Heavily Indebted Poor Countries (HIPC) initiative; and (g) to continue the pace of sustainable development by endorsing the Reduce, Reuse, and Recycle ("3 R's") Initiative.

On regional issues such as North Korea, the G8 leaders addressed the DPRK nuclear issue by supporting the Six-Party Talks as well as efforts made by all concerned parties to achieve a comprehensive solution by diplomatic means. They also discussed other security and humanitarian issues, such as the abductions of Japanese nationals.

2005 G8 SUMMIT

The 2005 G8 summit took place in Gleneagles, England, July 6-8, 2005.

The G8 leaders reaffirmed that the proliferation of weapons of mass destruction and their delivery systems, together with international terrorism, remain the scourge in today's world. As at the previous 2004 Sea Islands summit, the leaders reaffirmed their commitments and called on all states to uphold in full international norms on non-proliferation and to meet their arms control and disarmament obligations. Emphasis was laid on meeting proliferation challenges decisively, through both national and multilateral efforts. In this respect, the G8 leaders expressed particular concern about the threat of proliferation in North Korea and Iran.

On Africa, the G8 leaders agreed (a) to provide extra resources for Africa's peacekeeping forces so that they could deter, prevent and resolve conflicts in Africa more effectively; (b) to give enhanced support for greater democracy, effective governance and transparency, and to help fight corruption; (c) to boost investment in quality health and education, and to take concrete action in combating HIV/AIDS, malaria, TB, and other killer diseases; and (d) to stimulate growth, to improve proper investment climate and to make trade work for Africa, including by helping to build Africa's capacity to trade and working to mobilize the extra investment in infrastructure that is needed for a pro-business environment. The G8 leaders also agreed to double aid for Africa by 2010. It was also agreed that the World Bank should

have a leading role in supporting the partnership between the G8, other donors, and Africa, helping to ensure that additional assistance was effectively co-ordinated and utilized. It was also agreed at the Gleneagles summit that all of the debts owed by eligible heavily indebted poor countries to the International Monetary Fund and the African Development Fund should be cancelled.

On regional issues, G8 leaders reconfirmed their commitment to the Partnership for Progress and a Common Future with the Region of the Broader Middle East and North Africa, based on genuine co-operation between the G8 and the governments, businesses, and civil society of the region.

The G8 leaders also reviewed the international relief operations of the tsunami disaster of December 26, 2004, that ravaged a vast number of countries along the Indian Ocean. The leaders underlined their support for UN work on post-tsunami humanitarian aid and reconstruction, as well as confirming their long-term commitment to reduce the risk from future disasters and to encourage reform of human security.

Mohammed Badrul Alam

See Also Global Economic Growth; Organisation for Economic Co-operation and Development (OECD); Conflict, Cooperation, and Security; Human Rights

References

Group of Eight. 2000. Okinawa Summit 2000, " Summit Documents," http://www.g8.fr/evian/english/navigation/g8_documents/archives_from_previous_summits/okinawa_summit_._2000.html (cited July 23, 2000).

————. 2002. Kananaskis Summit 2002, "Summit Documents," http://www.g8.fr/evian/english/navigation/g8_documents/archives_from_previous_summits/kananaskis_summit_._2002.html (cited June 27, 2002).

————. 2003. Evian Summit 2003, "Summit Documents," http://www.g8.fr/evian/english/home.html (cited June 3, 2003).

————. 2004. Sea Island, Summit 2004. "Summit Documents," http://www.g8seaisland.com/en/index.cfm.

———. 2005. Gleneagles Summit 2005. "Summit Documents," http://www.g8.gov.uk.

Landes, David S. 1999. *The Wealth and Poverty of Nations: Why Some Are So Rich and Some Are So Poor.* New York: W. W. Norton.

Osnos, Peter, and William Shawcross, eds. 2003. *Allies: The U.S, Britain, and Europe in the Aftermath of the Iraq War.* Boulder: Perseus.

Porter, Michael E. 1998. *Competitive Advantage of Nations.* New York: Free Press.

Rogers, Adam. 1993. *The Earth Summit: A Planetary Reckoning.* Los Angeles: Global View.

Smith, Adam. 2003. *The Wealth of Nations.* New York: Bantam Classics.

Stiglitz, Joseph E. 2003. *Globalization and Its Discontents.* New York: W. W. Norton.

Gulf Cooperation Council (GCC)

The Gulf Cooperation Council (GCC) is an international organization composed of six states in the Persian Gulf region: Saudi Arabia, the United Arab Emirates (UAE), Qatar, Bahrain, Oman, and Kuwait. It exists to try to provide a more multilateral approach to international relations, trading, and economics. The organization was created in 1981, partly in response to the Islamic Revolution in Iran and the Iran-Iraq War, which in different ways highlighted security issues in the Gulf region and demonstrated the weakness of individual voices and the need for increased cooperation. The headquarters of the GCC are in Riyadh, Saudi Arabia.

The states of the Gulf region share a common geography and climate. They are hot and dry and possess few natural resources apart from the oil available to some. The GCC is dominated in terms of size, population, and overall income by Saudi Arabia, which has some 84 percent of the total land area of nearly 2.7 million square kilometers (1,042,476 square miles), 79 percent of the total population of 27.9 million people, and 55 percent of the total regional gross national product of $340,971 million. Further, Saudi Arabia is accorded considerable prestige by virtue of its being the birthplace of the Islamic religion. Its ruler is considered the protector of the Holy Places, and all Muslims of sufficient means are required to conduct a pilgrimage (the Hajj) to Mecca in the kingdom at some stage.

Of the other members, Qatar and Bahrain are small island states with little other than oil and international banking to support themselves, while Kuwait is still recovering from the Iraqi invasion of 1990–1991. Oman lacks oil and is therefore the poorest of the states. Only the UAE has sufficient population, wealth, and status to offer much balance to Saudi Arabia in the organization. The UAE's federal governmental structure offers a vision of future governance in an integrated region, but it could only be made to work if Saudi Arabia devolved into smaller political units, which would be anathema to the ruling royal family.

Although the GCC leadership likes to stress the homogeneous cultural and ethnic background of the region, this emphasis disguises some important differences among and within states, and these are intensified somewhat by the presence of large numbers of migrant workers in the region (many of whom remain resident for a number of years), who are often excluded from benefits of GCC policy decisions. The strong Islamic nature of the states involved has led to similarities in legal systems, but the degree to which those strictures are applied to non-Muslims varies. One common factor is the nondemocratic nature of the states; although democratization is slowly proceeding in, for example, Bahrain, free speech and open political debate are often still discouraged in the region either by decree or by custom. The lack of democratic influences is connected with other factors, such as the lack of recognition of organized labor movements, which means that the GCC states individually and collectively are unable to join groups such as the International Labour Organization (ILO); this, in turn, means that GCC states have fewer opportunities to participate in multilateral international discussions.

Relations among the member states and between member states and their near neighbors are not always harmonious. A particularly contentious issue is that of border demarcation, especially with reference to the various small islands in the Gulf. Disputes over territory are rendered more important by the possible presence of oil and the potential wealth that it represents. Border disputes often result from the imposition of artificial boundaries by colonial powers such as Britain, whose controlling influence was not removed from the region until the 1970s. The history of the region as one of small communities open to the outside world and engaging with it through trade and cultural exchange, combined with the harshness of the climate and the small size of its populations, has meant that spatial boundaries came to be considered as less important than mutual ties and obligations between and among rulers and their families and connections.

Creation of the GCC

The Iranian Revolution of 1979, in which a hereditary, pro-Western ruler, the Shah of Iran, was replaced by a theocratic Islamic state under the spiritual and political leadership of Ayatollah Khomeini, demonstrated an actual threat to the monarchs of the Gulf region. The outbreak of the Iran-Iraq War, in which Western powers mostly supported the secularist aggressor Saddam Hussein against the Islamic victim Iran, also illustrated instability in regional security. This conflict was complicated by a variety of cross-border ethnic and ideological conflicts of interest that led to Iranian reprisals on Kuwaitis, for example, who were considered to be too helpful in providing materiel to the Iraqi military. Creating a regional forum and organization in such a context meant providing an arena in which solidarity could be demonstrated and expressed. Meanwhile, aspects of economic and technical coop-

eration could be expected to promote even higher standards of living sufficient to take peoples' minds off violent struggle.

The GCC Charter

The charter establishing the GCC is composed of twenty-two articles that outline the organization's basic purpose, constitution, and methods of operation. The introductory rubric supplies the philosophical basis for the GCC by describing member states as:

Being fully aware of the ties of special relations, common characteristics and similar systems founded on the creed of Islam which bind them; and

Desiring to effect coordination, cooperation and integration between them in all fields; and,

Having the conviction that coordination, cooperation, and integration between them serve the sublime objectives of the Arab Nation; and,

In pursuit of the goal of strengthening cooperation and reinforcement of the links between them; and

In an endeavour to complement efforts already begun in all essential areas that concern their peoples and realize their hopes for a better future on the path to unity of their States; and

In conformity with the Charter of the League of Arab States which calls for the realization of closer relations and stronger bonds; and

In order to channel their efforts to reinforce and serve Arab and Islamic causes. (Gulf Coooperation Council Charter 1981)

In other words, the organization exists both to achieve economic objectives, such as reducing transaction costs and boosting investment, and as a means by which cultural, technological, and environment protection links can be enhanced. However, perhaps more important is the emphasis placed upon the notion of an Arab nation that is Islamic in character. It is clear that these concerns are at least in part a response to the dangerus international events outlined above and help provide a common purpose for Arab states. Subsequent consistent agitation on behalf of the Palestinian people, however much it may be informed by genuine feeling and belief, has served the same purpose of uniting people against a common enemy so as to deter questioning of domestic rulers. Nevertheless, the rise to importance of fundamentalist Islam has highlighted the tensions implicit in the establishment of an international organization embracing the tenets of Western forms of globalization and integration of markets and also maintaining a distinctive Arab Islamic character.

The GCC Charter further states "that the basic objectives are to effect coordination, integration and inter-connection between Member States in all fields, strengthening ties between their peoples, formulating similar regulations in various fields such as economy, finance, trade, customs, tourism, legislation, [and] administration, as well as fostering scientific and technical progress in industry, mining, agriculture, water and animal resources, establishing scientific research centres, setting up joint ventures, and encouraging co-operation of the private sector." This is a very wide-ranging charter that would require considerable detailed multilateral discussions among well-informed experts in a wide range of fields. Consequently, not all areas of the charter have been fully explored. The nondemocratic nature of most of the GCC states has meant that policy decisions may be taken very quickly but may therefore lack some popular and institutional support.

Structure and Objectives

The lead body of the GCC is the Supreme Council, which is composed of the heads of the member states and which meets annually (or more often for extraordinary sessions). This body determines substantive policy matters by unanimous vote or procedural issues by a simple majority of the six members (with four states representing a quorum). The presidency rotates among the heads of the states in an order determined by the position of each state's name in the Arabic alphabet.

The Supreme Council is supported by a number of administrative bodies, including the Consultative Commission, the Commission for the Settlement of Disputes, the Ministerial Council, and the Secretariat-General, which is composed of a number of bodies devoted to political and economic affairs, patents, delegation to the EU, and other matters.

An official communiqué describing the 83rd Ministerial Council Session, held in Jeddah, Saudi Arabia, on June 8, 2003, indicates which areas are receiving the most attention (GCC, Ministerial Council 2002). Economic aspects include proposals for a customs and monetary union, improvements and innovations in science and technology, research and the environment, and military cooperation issues. Meanwhile, political aspects are restricted to little more than platitudes about the dangers posed by any state threatening the status quo. Like the founders of the Association of Southeast Asian Nations (ASEAN), GCC member states know that their organization could not survive criticism—or even rigorous scrutiny —of each others' regimes.

Economic Issues

The basis of economic agreement between the GCC states has been the Unified Economic Agreement between the Countries of the Gulf Cooperation Council, established in November 1981. This was replaced twenty years later by the Economic Agreement among the GCC States (GCC, Supreme Council, 2001). The Unified Economic Agreement required the member states to exercise nondiscriminatory treatment to all other members in areas such as trade exchanges, movements of capital and individuals, financial and monetary cooperation, and transportation and communications. These provisions relate to national subjects of member states and not the temporary migrant labor force that is such an important component of each member state. This helps to reinforce the privileged position of national subject–owned businesses and resources in the member state area. The Unified Economic Agreement set a basis for low tariffs and openness in trade relations that are usually considered advantageous for developing countries. However, economic matters are still frequently subservient to dogmatic political issues, and while this continues to be the case there is less opportunity for trade diplomacy (Wilson 1998).

One problem that the GCC faces in multilateral trade negotiations stems from the refusal of Saudi Arabia to deal with firms that also do business with Israel, which it does not recognize. This policy contravenes World Trade Organization (WTO) regulations, which require nondiscriminatory treatment, and means that GCC states must negotiate on a bilateral rather than a multilateral or organizational basis. This considerably weakens the positions of the smaller GCC states, in particular. A second problem, one that has been influential in previous attempts to organize cross-border Arab or Muslim trade blocs, is that trade patterns differ from cultural or religious boundaries. Moreover, the disparities in levels of development between member countries mean that flows of goods or capital tend to be unidirectional rather than bi-directional.

A meaningful Gulf-related trade system would need to include both Iran and Iraq, while special provisions would also need to be made for India. If that occurred, then complementarities of natural resource allocations would enable more complete flows to occur. The six members of the GCC currently have little opportunity to provide sustainable agricultural produce because of their geographical conditions, and the lack of labor means that manufacturing will always be on a small scale. Iran and Iraq, however, could (if international events did not interfere) provide agriculture, and India could provide labor; each of these three countries would also be suitable recipients of GCC outward capital investment.

More recent negotiations have focused on the possibility of a Gulf monetary union with a single currency. A summit meeting at the end of 2001 led to an announcement that such a union would be established on January 1, 2010. The union is expected to provide benefits to those states able to continue providing stable macroeconomic conditions, and to reduce transaction costs between states in an era in which diversification away from hydrocarbon production will be increasingly necessary. Nevertheless, considerable work remains to be done to ensure that the necessary financial infrastructures are in place throughout the region (Fasano and Iqbal 2002). This will be a demanding task, as the majority of the economy remains in the state sector, and governments are more likely to talk about the benefits of free trade for the organization than to try to achieve it (Smith 1998).

There is an increasing need for economic cooperation among GCC states to focus on diversification from oil-based industries to others in which they can develop some form of competitive advantage with existing labor markets. These industries must also be sustainable environmentally within a harsh climate. Moreover, GCC states need to identify best practices in managing the substantial overseas holdings that oil revenues have enabled some them to accumulate, especially to shield them from possible adverse future economic shocks. Future competitiveness in the oil and gas extraction industries will depend on enhanced capabilities in marketing and organization as much as technical skills (Al Sa'-doun 2000).

Political Issues

The institutional weakness of the GCC is apparent in the communiqué issued at the conclusion of the 84th session of the Ministerial Council on September 3, 2002, which began: "The Ministerial Council condemned the ill-intentioned campaign by some Western media to which the Kingdom of Saudi Arabia was subjected, and which was designed to give an unbalanced and unfair image of the Kingdom's international relations and of its handling of the events" (GCC, Ministerial Council 2002).

This defensive tone suggests, at the very least, that piqued feelings have colored discussions in GCC meetings. The charges that may in fact have been made by "some Western media" are simply brushed aside; it is difficult to imagine a member state other than Saudi Arabia requiring a Ministerial Council communiqué to begin in such a way. This form of engagement with the outside world has the danger of making the GCC and its rulers appear out of touch and even irrelevant. In an international political environment in which it appears that the norms of international cooperation and engagement are about to be renegotiated, organizations are under greater pressure than ever to produce a clear and coherent message of their purpose and resolve.

The GCC and the First Gulf War

The invasion of Kuwait by Iraq followed from the bloodthirsty stalemate of the Iran-Iraq War and was also provoked by the desire of the regime of Saddam Hussein of Iraq for more oil. Historically, Kuwait was considered by some to be a part of Iraq and, prior to the invasion, some Kuwaitis at least had offered ambivalent signals about their support for Iraq. Kuwait had supplied Iraq with materials during the Iran-Iraq War and had suffered attack by Iran in retaliation. Arab countries generally deplored the act of aggression by Iraq, not least because it was by no means certain that further invasions

might not be attempted in the Gulf region. Consequently, Saudi Arabia took a leadership role in supporting the U.S.-led military action to free Kuwait and, significantly, permitted U.S. troops to be stationed in the kingdom. Although U.S. forces have made use of other bases in the Gulf region without major incident, the presence in Saudi Arabia was immediately controversial, since that country is considered to be the home of Muslim holy places in which no nonbeliever should be permitted. This was cited by Osama bin Laden in partial explanation for his role in subsequent terrorist attacks on the United States.

The first Gulf war revealed the GCC to occupy a difficult and somewhat contradictory role in the international political environment: Although it would wish to propagate public policies demonstrating Islamic principles, it was forced for the sake of security to ally with Western powers considered by some to be improper partners. The leaders of member states have had to juggle the desire to provide freedom of religious expression with the threat of dissidence generally and some internal and external calls for greater democratization. At the same time, internal problems remain, as difficulties in border demarcation provide numerous grounds for bilateral disputes, and the possible presence of oil related to those disputes makes them all the more intense (Alnajjar 2000).

The GCC, Terrorism, and the Second Gulf War

The greater focus on the GCC region as a potential source of terrorism has highlighted problems in financial infrastructure and governance because of the dangers of money laundering and the sponsorship of terrorism. The second Gulf war has proved far more divisive of public opinion in the GCC region than the first and is likely to increase internal pressure for states to declare themselves at odds with the policies of the United States. One outcome has been the relocation of U.S. military forces from Saudi Arabia to Qatar; the latter is a country with a much smaller population that in recent times has been easier to control.

One of the unexpected outcomes of globalization has been to enable people to come together and create communities with various common features and characteristics. This is mediated through information and communications technology as well as greater ease in moving people and items around the world. These communities are not always benign in nature, and governments and organizations, the GCC not least among them, will need to provide more transparency to minimize the risk that they are in some way conspiring with such groups. GCC member states fully appreciate the damage and dangers of terrorism, in part because it threatens their own continuance. They will need to compromise their own traditional secrecy to communicate this understanding.

The need to respond to calls for democratization, to create a coherent foreign policy platform, and to integrate more states into the GCC are all likely to be defining features of a future GCC.

Future Prospects

A post–Saddam Hussein Iraq is a potential entrant to the GCC, as is Yemen. It is possible for integration in the GCC to become both wider (spatially) and deeper (functionally) (Asoomi 2003). The GCC would face enhanced difficulties under such circumstances in maintaining its focus as a genuinely regional force while looking for greater opportunities through broader and more meaningful membership in

the same way that the European Union is doing. This will prove a significant challenge, especially as it appears that the United States is currently bent on forcing change in the region at a much greater pace than the region itself would otherwise be likely to pursue.

John Walsh

See Also Economic Integration; Council of Arab Economic Unity (CAEU); League of Arab States (LAS)

References

Al Sa'doun, Abdul Wahab. 2000. "GCC Petrochemical Industry Must Unite to Compete." *Oil and Gas Journal* 98, no. 46 (November 13): 52–58.

Alnajjar, Ghanim. 2000. "The GCC and Iraq." *Middle East Policy* 7, no. 4 (October): 92–99.

Asoomi, Mohammed. 2003. "GCC, Iraq Can Play a Significant Role." *Gulf News,* May 9, http://www.gulfnews.com/Articles/Opinion.asp?ArticleID=86965.

Co-operation Council for the Arab States of the Gulf. 1981. The Co-operation Council Charter, http://www.gcc-sg.org/CHARTER.html.

Fasano, Ugo, and Zubair Iqbal. 2002. "Common Currency." *Finance and Development* 39, no. 4 (December): 42–45.

Gulf Cooperation Council, http://www.gcc.sg.org.

Gulf Cooperation Council, Ministerial Council. 2002. "Press Communiqué Issued by the Ministerial Council of the Gulf Cooperation Council at Its Eighty-Third Session Held in Jeddah" (June), http://www.gcc-sg.org/session83.html.

Gulf Cooperation Council, Supreme Council. 2001. "Final Communiqué Adopted by the Supreme Council of the Gulf Cooperation Council at Its Twenty-Second Session" (Muscat, Oman, December 30–31), http://www.gcc-sg.org/session22.html.

Smith, Dexter Jerome. 1998. "Non-Oil Industry in the GCC." *Middle East* no. 278 (May): 41–43.

Wilson, Rodney. 1998. "The Changing Composition and Direction of GCC Trade." *The Emirates Occasional Papers.* Abu Dhabi: Emirates Centre for Strategic Studies and Research.

International Bank for Reconstruction and Development (IBRD)

The International Bank for Reconstruction and Development (IBRD), popularly known as the World Bank, was a product of the waning days of World War II as forward-thinking individuals realized that unprecedented measures were needed to rebuild countries around the world that had been devastated by the war. Although the first loans were directed toward this purpose, the IBRD soon evolved into the foremost provider of low-interest and no-interest loans with liberal repayment plans to developing countries that were unable to obtain loans through regular channels, particularly poor countries in Asia, Africa, and Latin America. IBRD loans have been granted for a variety of needs that encompass the construction of electric power plants, roads, railways, ports, and natural gas pipelines as well as the advancement of telecommunications, agriculture, industry, water supplies, education, health, and debt relief. Because the bank maintains an AAA credit rating, it has little trouble generating funds to provide loans to developing countries.

In order to remain relevant, the IBRD has constantly reinvented itself through internal restructuring and the creation of new agencies and initiatives designed to meet the specific needs of the developing world. One way that the IBRD has done this is by furnishing technical and research assistance as well as financial assistance to developing countries. Although loans are generally made in U.S. dollars, the IBRD now pays local contractors, suppliers, and workers in their own currencies in an effort to further stimulate local economies.

The expanded organization, known as the World Bank Group, is made up of the International Bank for Reconstruction and Development, the International Development Association (IDA), the International Finance Corporation (IFC), the Multilateral Investment Guarantee Agency (MIGA), and the International Centre of Settlement for Investment Disputes (ICSID). The focus of the World Bank Group has shifted toward concentrating on the eradication of poverty by cutting the vast disparities in the high-income and low-income countries of the world. As a continued part of its efforts to remain more responsive to member nations, the IBRD maintains offices in Washington, DC, in the United Nations building and in the financial center in New York City, and in Paris, France. Additionally, the IBRD has offices in a number of host counties.

The United States has been the largest shareholder in the International Bank for Reconstruction and Development since the inception of the organization and was the motivating force behind it. The IBRD was particularly the brainchild of Harry Dexter White, who served as an adviser to U.S. Secretary of the Treasury Henry Morgenthau, and the internationally known British economist John Maynard Keynes. Although the bank has no official language, English is the official working language. Spanish and French translators are available at IBRD meetings, and reports are often published in several languages.

Although much criticism has been leveled at the IBRD throughout its history, no other organization has come close to achieving such far-reaching goals in the areas of eradicating poverty and promoting development in the poorest countries of the world. The success of the IBRD is best documented through the fact that since its inception the organization has lent approximately $1 trillion to countries around the world. During 2002 alone, the IBRD lent approximately $11.2 billion to support ninety-nine operations in thirty-seven separate countries. The bank has also committed itself to the Millennium Development Goals that were announced at a September 2000 United Nations summit. The Millennium Goals aim to promote school enrollment, decrease child mortality, improve maternal health, eradicate disease, and provide access to clean water for developing nations.

Membership and Subscriptions

The International Bank for Reconstruction and Development currently has 189 member nations, constituting most of the nations of the world. Any country that chooses can apply for membership in the IBRD. Thirty nations signed the Articles of Agreement at the inception of the IBRD in December 1945; ten others joined in 1946, and more in the years that followed. Poland joined in January 1946 but withdrew from the IBRD in March 1950. Czechoslovakia's membership has been permanently suspended according to stipulations of the Articles of Agreement, which state that membership can be withdrawn whenever a member fails to live up to its obligations to the bank. After a one-year grace period, suspension is put into effect through a majority vote of the Board of Governors.

Each member country is required to pay a subscription to join the IBRD. Two percent of all subscriptions must be paid in gold or in U.S.

dollars, and this entire amount is always available to the bank for lending. An additional 18 percent of each country's subscription may be paid in its own currency and is available for bank lending only upon approval by that country. The final 80 percent of each subscription is earmarked as a backup in case the IBRD needs to call on it to meet its financial obligations. In this way, the International Bank for Reconstruction and Development has been able to make loans to high-risk countries at low or no interest. The bulk of the funding for IBRD activities is provided by the forty richest countries. Periodically, bank funds are replenished by member countries and by other industrialized countries, such as Switzerland and New Zealand, that donate money to help developing countries. For example, in 2002, replenishment funds amounted to close to $9 billion. These funds were further supplemented by $6.6 billion generated from various bank activities.

Voting Rights and Governance

Once a country becomes a member of the International Bank for Reconstruction and Development, the country automatically receives 250 votes. Member nations can buy additional votes by purchasing shares at $100,000 each. IBRD decisions are generally decided by majority vote; therefore, those countries with large shares of stocks find it easy to influence decisionmaking. The United States is the major shareholder, holding almost a quarter of the voting power.

The Board of Governors of the IBRD is technically at the top of the governing hierarchy of the bank. It meets annually in September, at the same time that the governors of the International Monetary Fund (IMF) meet. In practice, most of the power of the IBRD is lodged in the hands of the five executive directors, a group appointed by the largest stockholders (the United States, Great Britain, France, China, and India), and the eleven directors elected from the remaining member nations. Each director is required to maintain close ties with an alternate director who can make decisions when necessary. In a meeting held at IBRD headquarters, executive directors are elected for two-year terms. The power of the executive directors stems from the fact that each one represents the interests of the members in his or her voting bloc and may promote or block legislation that protects or harms the interests of his or her constituents.

The administrative body of the IBRD is made up of a president, vice presidents, officers, and staff members. The president is elected by the executive directors for a five-year term that is renewable only once. The staff members are appointed by the president to oversee particular functions of the bank. Major IBRD departments include Operations Evaluation, Institutional Integrity, and Internal Auditing. The administration of the bank is charged with carrying on the day-to-day activities. The president votes only in the case of a tie, even though he is charged with responsibility for establishing the agenda of the bank.

IBRD Loans

Once a nation becomes a member of the World Bank Group, the country is eligible to apply for a loan. Loans may be made to member governments, political subdivisions of member governments, and business, agricultural, or industrial organizations within each country. The Articles of Agreement of the IBRD mandate that any bank loan not made to a governmental entity must be guaranteed by the member government, a central bank, or some other legitimate agency within the project country. IBRD loans are generated from a number of sources, including member countries, bank missions, bank officials, resident representatives of the bank, resident missions, and United Nations agencies. Other provisions of the bank's charter require bank officials to make sure that IBRD-funded loans are used only for those purposes

stated in the terms of the loan and that the loans could not be obtained from traditional commercial sources. The charter prohibits the IBRD from insisting that the project country spend loan funds in the countries or territories of other member nations.

Once a particular project has been suggested, IBRD officials appraise the project and analyze the loan according to established procedures. Specifically, World Bank loans are evaluated according to:

1. *Economic factors,* including domestic demands for goods and services and the availability of local resources.
2. *Technical factors,* centering on project details such as the scale, layout, design, and location of the project in addition to the process by which the project will be carried out, the availability of equipment, and a schedule of costs and timing for the project.
3. *Institutional factors,* chiefly concerning the availability and skills of local management and the possible presence of external project influences.
4. *Procurement and commercial factors,* dealing with the availability of project materials and the processes by which these goods will be bought and sold.
5. *Financial factors,* including an overall evaluation of the costs of the project.

Historical Overview

During the first three weeks of July 1944, forty-four nations and a number of observers and technicians came together at the United Nations Monetary and Financial Conference at the Mount Washington Hotel in Bretton Woods, New Hampshire, to draw up the Articles of Agreement for the International Bank for Reconstruction and Development (and the International Monetary Fund as a separate institution). The 730 delegates drew up an unprecedented plan for redefining global monetary transactions and scheduled IBRD operations to go into effect on June 25, 1946.

During the first week of March 1946, the Board of Governors met for the first time in Savannah, Georgia, and the positions of Executive Directors, representing the member nations, were established. By the fall of 1946, Eugene Meyer, the first IBRD president, announced that the bank had approved its first loan applications to Chile, Czechoslovakia, Denmark, France, Luxembourg, and Poland. By August 1952, former Allied enemies West Germany and Japan had also become members of the bank.

On May 9, 1946, the bank awarded its first loan, $250 million to the Crédit National of France. The following month, the bank's first fact-finding mission was dispatched to Poland, and three years later the bank initiated its first economic survey in Colombia. On July 15, 1949, the bank offered $250 million on the U.S. bond market. The first Asian loan was granted to India in August 1949, with $34 million earmarked for railway development. During the following year, the bank allotted its first Middle Eastern loan, with $128 million directed toward constructing a flood control system in Iraq.

By 1950, the IBRD had approved approximately $350 million in loans to developing nations but had actually disbursed less than one-third of those funds. During the following three years, it made loans that would be equivalent to $1.8 billion by twenty-first-century standards. By the end of fiscal year 1958, the IBRD had actually distributed around $700 million to developing nations, with approximately $200 million of those funds directed to India and Pakistan.

During the first couple of decades of its existence, the IBRD was focused on the reconstruction of nations still recovering from World War II and on promoting increased attention to international investment and trade. In practice, this meant that the bank raised money by borrowing through bond markets and from central banks of high-income nations as well as through subscriptions from member countries. In turn, the bank lent money, provided advice on various development issues, and coordinated financial investment from private sources.

Bank Presidents

Eugene Meyer, the first president of the IBRD, resigned in December 1946 after only six months in office. Most of his time in office had been spent in administrative duties such as setting up offices, recruiting personnel, and generating funds for the bank's operations. According to the Articles of Agreement, the operational power of the bank was lodged in the executive directors, who were chosen by member nations. However, when John J. McCloy was invited to become the second president of the World Bank, he refused to accept the position unless executive power was given to the president. This designation was made, McCloy took office on March 17, 1947, and all future presidents of the bank retained the extended power.

In July 1949, Eugene Black became the third president of the IBRD. It was during Black's presidency that the emphasis of the bank's activities shifted from administration and reconstruction to development. The bank began financing the construction of electric power plants, ports, roads, and railways. In October 1952, the IBRD announced a major restructuring, and Area Departments and a Technological Operations Department were added to the bank's existing structure. Under Black's leadership, the Economic Development Institute (EDI) was established on March 11, 1955, and began operating in January of the following year.

In January 1963, George D. Woods became the fourth president of the IBRD. Woods was considered to be one of the most innovative of the bank's presidents. It was Woods who insisted on using local currency to pay the ongoing expenses of projects as a means of stimulating local economies. The first loans made to advance education were also made under Woods, and he relaxed the bank's position on making loans to state-owned industries and development finance companies. Woods directed major bank resources toward agriculture for the first time in its history. The result was that a number of loans were made to wealthy farmers with the idea that the poorest people would benefit from increased jobs and production.

On April 1, 1966, Robert McNamara began what became one of the most influential IBRD presidencies. The fact that McNamara brought his experience as U.S. secretary of defense to the position enhanced the bank's reputation. During his term, he also enhanced his own reputation. McNamara effectively redirected the bank's activities, making it more a development agency committed to alleviating worldwide poverty than a rigid financial institution. Under his administration, the bank increased its lending capabilities from around $1 billion to over $12 billion per year. In an often-quoted speech in Nairobi in 1973, McNamara first identified the concept of "absolute poverty," which he defined as "a condition of deprivation that falls below any rational definition of human decency." From that point onward, the entire direction of aid to developing countries was changed.

In July 1981, Alden W. Clausen became the sixth president of the World Bank Group, initiating a reorganization plan that involved the bank's analysis, research, and policy activities. Subsequent changes included the creation of new positions, including vice presidents for economics and research, operations policy, and energy and industry. Clausen's administration was somewhat hampered by the worldwide economic crisis of the 1980s.

In July 1986, Barber Conable became the seventh president of the World Bank Group. Over the next year, Conable launched a major reorganization of the bank, separating all func-

tions into operations, finance, administration, and policy, planning, and research, with a senior vice president in charge of each department. In December 1987, under Conable's guidance, the bank launched the Special Program of Assistance (SPA), which focused on debt relief in sub-Saharan Africa, and the Social Dimensions of Adjustment (SDA), a joint program with the African Development Bank and the United Nations Development Programme (UNDP). In March 1990, the World Bank established the Global Environment Facility (GEF), a pilot program to provide grants for various investment and technical projects, in conjunction with the UNDP and the United Nations Environment Programme.

Toward the end of Conable's presidency, an international controversy developed over the bank's financing of the India Narmada River Sardar Sarorar dam. In response, Conable appointed an independent commission to investigate the bank's role in the scandal. The commission reported that both the World Bank and India were guilty of "gross delinquency" that had resulted in the displacement of more than 200,000 of India's poorest farmers.

Investigations into the World Bank's activities continued after September 1991, when Lewis T. Preston was named the eighth president of the World Bank Group. What became known as the Wapenhans Report, named after World Bank Vice President Willi Wapenhans, who directed the study, identified a "culture of loan approval" deeply entrenched throughout the management of the bank that was detrimental to the quality of bank operations and to the overall reputation of the World Bank Group. The Wapenhans Report stated that more than one-third of all projects thus far financed by the bank had been failures.

On June 1, 1995, James D. Wolfensohn was named the ninth president of the World Bank Group. Concerned about the bank's reputation in the wake of the Wapenhans Report, Wolfensohn hired a consulting firm to suggest ways that the bank could be restructured to become more efficient, responsive, and effective. This reorganization created a number of technical networks that made the bank staff more productive. Initially, these networks included sections on Human Development; Poverty Reduction and Economic Management; Private Sector Development and Infrastructure; and Environment, Rural and Social Development. A fifth network, Core Services, was added later. The reorganization also called for downsizing the regional departments located in various member countries and replacing them with fifty-five to sixty country managers, who were given administrative and operational responsibilities. Wolfensohn has been credited with directing the bank toward more humanistic goals.

World Bank Group Institutions

The World Bank Group consists of five institutions, with each institution playing a distinct role in support of the mission to fight poverty and improve living standards for people in the developing world. The term "World Bank Group" encompasses all five institutions. The term "World Bank" refers specifically to two of the five, IBRD and IDA.

International Finance Corporation (IFC)
To its chagrin, the World Bank realized in the early 1950s that some developing nations were refusing to borrow from the bank because of its insistence on involving national governments through loan guarantees. The fact that the governments of some host countries were unresponsive to local needs, while others were corrupt, often resulted in undesired governmental interference in IBRD projects. The bank responded by creating the International Finance Corporation, which did not require government guarantees of bank loans. On July 20, 1956, the Articles of Agreement for the IFC went into effect. Any IBRD member was eligible to become a member of IFC. Each member country purchases shares in IFC, and voting is based on the number of shares held, just as it is

with the IBRD. Similarly, the board of directors of the IFC has conceded a good deal of power to the executive directors. Even though the IFC acts independently of IBRD, the president of the World Bank Group serves as the president of the IFC. A few months after it began operation, the IFC announced that its first investment would be to the firm Siemens do Brasil to expand manufacturing.

The IFC was created specifically to work with the private sector in developing countries to alleviate poverty and speed up development. The seventy-five member countries of IFC have generally directed projects toward promoting private-sector development, aiding the financial mobilization of private companies, and providing technical advice and assistance to governments and businesses.

International Development Association (IDA)
At the insistence of the United States and out of a new understanding of the part that poverty plays in preventing progress in developing nations, in 1960 the IBRD created the International Development Association to provide a means of making concessionary loans to the poorest member-nations unable to meet the standards for bank loans. For a number of years, the poorest developing countries had been asking the IBRD to liberalize loan policies so that they could qualify for loans for essential projects. Membership in the IDA is open to any country. Initial subscriptions amounted to $912.7 million; on May 12, 1961, IDA extended its first credit to Honduras. During the first few years of its existence, the IDA distributed around $1 billion a year to developing nations. During this period, the United States began to play a lesser role in World Bank activities, and the reputation of the bank rose in response.

By 1970, the IDA could claim 107 members. The countries were divided into two categories: Part I Countries, which are considered high-income and developed, and Part II Countries, which are poorer and less well developed. The rules governing subscription in the two categories are designed to be most responsive to the needs of poorer countries. IDA loans are interest-free and are payable over a fifty-year period, with a grace period of ten years before any payments are due at all. Over the following ten years, Part II Countries repay the loans at a 1 percent rate. For the remaining thirty years of the loans, payments are made at 3 percent. The only cost above the actual loan is a payment of three-fourths of 1 percent for administrative costs.

The entire subscription for Part I Countries is made available to IDA. However, only one-tenth of Part II Countries' subscription funds are available for lending. The other nine-tenths is composed of the individual country's own currency and is available to the IDA only upon approval by that country. The IDA is therefore able to call upon four methods of funding: member subscriptions; replenishments from Part I Countries and nonmember contributors such as Switzerland and New Zealand; transfers from the IBRD; and its own generated income.

The success of the IDA is best illustrated by the amount distributed annually to low-income countries—for example, $8.1 billion to sixty-two countries in 2002. Most of the funds were directed toward poverty-reduction efforts, the development of social services, environmental protection measures, and economic growth. Established IDA policy places strong emphasis on providing loans to enhance economic growth, supporting the social sectors, improving governance, protecting the environment, helping countries to recover from conflict, and promoting trade and regional integration.

International Centre of Settlement for Investment Disputes (ICSID)

On October 14, 1966, the International Centre of Settlement for Investment Disputes was established under the Convention on the Settlement of Investment Disputes between States and Nationals and Other States. The specific function of the ICSID is to deal with disagreements that arise between investors and the various host countries. Before the creation of the ICSID, the president of the World Bank Group and various bank employees dealt with disputes on a case-by-case basis, resulting in such a burden that bank officials were unable to devote proper attention to other matters. The ICSID is governed by an Administrative Council, which is chaired by the president of the World Bank Group, and a secretary general. It meets only when the IBRD and the IMF hold their regular annual meeting. Members of the ICSID are also members of the IBRD.

Cases are referred to the ICSID on a purely voluntary basis. Once both parties in a dispute agree to accept the ICSID decision, neither can unilaterally withdraw from the agreement. All states that contract with the IBRD are required to accept and enforce all ICSID decisions, which may be based either on conciliation or on arbitration. The ICSID maintains close ties with other arbitrating authorities, including the Permanent Court of Arbitration, the Regional Arbitration Centres of the Asian-African Legal Consultative Committee, the Australian Centre for International Commercial Arbitration, the Australian Commercial Disputes Centres, the Singapore International Arbitration Centre, and the Gulf Cooperation Council Commercial Arbitration Centre.

Multilateral Investment Guarantee Agency (MIGA)

In April 1988, the fifty-seven member Multilateral Investment Guarantee Agency became an essential component of the World Bank Group. MIGA's chief purpose is to work with the private sector to facilitate financing for development projects by guaranteeing loans that could not otherwise be obtained. MIGA operates under four guiding principles:

1. It must keep its focus on its clients.
2. It serves the interest of investors, lenders, and host countries by supporting private enterprise and promoting foreign investment.

3. It is required to work with other insurers, government agencies, and relevant international organizations to promote its goals.

4. It must constantly strive to better the lives of people in emerging economies by working with host countries to promote their individual goals.

In practice, MIGA supports an improved infrastructure that includes construction and improvements to roads, power plants, hospitals, schools, and access to clean water. Since its inception, MIGA has guaranteed more than 500 loans to seventy-eight developing countries, with total coverage exceeding $10 billion.

New Paradigm

As part of the bank's new paradigm that focuses on making the organization more responsive and accountable, bank-financed projects now call for individual countries to take active roles in alleviating poverty and furthering development. Since 1999, the bank has worked with the International Monetary Fund to create Comprehensive Development Frameworks (CDFs). Under the leadership of President James D. Wolfensohn, the IBRD established four goals for these CDFs:

1. All projects must focus on achieving long-term, holistic development.
2. All projects are results directed.
3. The host countries own all projects.
4. All projects are considered partnerships between the IBRD and host countries.

Agriculture

A major part of the new paradigm for the International Bank for Reconstruction and Development is a shift in its position on agriculture. Between 1949 and 1984, the bank pursued what was known as a policy of "benign neglect" toward agriculture because it lacked an understanding of the importance of the agricultural sector in the economies of the developing nations. During the 1960s, approximately 6 percent of the bank's total loans were directed toward agriculture; over the next fifteen years, that percentage more than quadrupled.

By 1984, the IBRD had committed more than $30 billion to agricultural development. As part of this new emphasis on agriculture, the bank began to invest in tractors, irrigation structures, and other means of improving productivity on farms, particularly in Latin America and sub-Saharan Africa. During the 1980s, loans to India and Mexico, the two major borrowers from the World Bank, surpassed $500 million. On May 1, 1971, the Consultative Group on International Agricultural Research (CGIA) was established, and in May 1985 the Special Facility for Sub-Saharan Africa began operations.

Disease Control

In addition to contributing to agriculture, the International Bank for Reconstruction and Development has begun to realize the importance of eradicating disease in member countries. For instance, it worked with the Soros Foundation and almost 200 other organizations in 1997 on a project aimed at eradicating tuberculosis in Russian prisons after the Soros team identified a strain of tuberculosis that was resistant to traditional drug treatment and had the potential to generate a major outbreak of tuberculosis in the Soviet Union. The plan to circumvent this outbreak, known as the Global Plan to Stop TB, was announced at World Bank headquarters in October 2001. The proposal called for appropriations of $9.3 billion for the program, with $4.8 billion coming from affected and donor countries.

After health experts announced that approximately 14,000 people around the world were being infected by the HIV virus each day, the IBRD pledged a major portion of its resources toward eradicating HIV/AIDS. The bank cosponsors UNAIDS, the international umbrella group that works toward eliminating this highly infectious disease. The IBRD also created the Multi-Country HIV/AIDS Program (MAP) in partnership with African and Caribbean governments to provide resources to civil and community organizations committed to fighting the HIV/AIDS epidemic. By the beginning of the twenty-first century, the bank had directed over $1.6 billion toward fighting HIV/AIDS, with half of that amount being spent in sub-Saharan Africa. A large part of the funding is directed toward educating the public about HIV/AIDS, especially in that region, and guaranteeing bank funding to any country with an effective HIV/AIDS strategy.

Debt Relief

Through the Heavily Indebted Poor Countries program, the IBRD has become heavily involved in providing debt relief to developing countries. Through HIPC, twenty-six countries have received funding that allows them to save more than $40 billion in debt payments. This enables these countries to allocate more money toward improving the lives of local citizens with enhanced housing, education, health, and welfare programs. Examples of improved social benefits include an initiative to increase elementary school enrollment in Rwanda, improved access to maternal and child health care in Honduras, and sex education programs for groups that are considered at high risk for HIV/AIDS in Cameroon.

Education

In its new persona, the bank has become an active player in improving access to education in developing countries, including the use of distance learning to make knowledge more accessible. Since education became a major focus, the bank has awarded around $33 billion in loans and credits to 83 countries to be used for 157 educational projects. In Bangladesh, for example, bank funds have been used to promote the education of girls who were previously denied access to education. In India, the bank has funded the India District Primary Education Program aimed at increasing the female literacy rate. In Latin America, the bank has been instrumental in helping Brazil, El Salvador, and Trinidad and Tobago to set up assessment programs that target educational areas that need improvement.

Corruption

The International Bank for Reconstruction and Development has frequently been accused of financing corruption in developing countries by continuing to lend money to governments that are well known for their corrupt practices. Jeffrey Winters, for instance, claimed that "since its founding, the World Bank has participated mostly passively in the corruption of roughly $100,000,000,000 of its loan funds intended for development" (Winters 2002, 101).

Most critics point to the Indonesian loans as the epitome of IBRD-financed corruption, suggesting that the bank could somewhat redeem its tarnished reputation by granting the current Indonesian government debt relief from loans that were obtained by the notoriously corrupt Suharto administration, which was defeated by a democratically elected government in 1999. Over a period of several years, investigators learned that bank funds had been systematically stolen by the corrupt government, leaving the taxpayers of Indonesia responsible for the government-guaranteed loans that were never used in development projects.

The democratically elected government of Indonesia announced plans to pursue the matter before the International Court of Justice in order to seek debt relief. Indonesian officials charged the bank with lending approximately $30 billion to the corrupt Suharto regime. Some independent sources contend that the World Bank was aware of deep corruption in the Indonesian government as early as 1968 but that it nevertheless continued to extend loans to the corrupt regime.

For several years after the Indonesian scandal broke, the bank cut funding to Indonesia from about $1 billion a year to around $400 million per year. However, in December 2003, the bank announced a new funding plan for Indonesia, even though documentation for continued government corruption was readily available. Evidence of corruption included the siphoning of 30 percent of a $76 million urban development fund paid to government officials in Sulawesi and a kickback scam in Garut wherein local officials were demanding that schools remit payments to them before they could be considered as eligible for bank funds.

Bank officials announced that new funding was dependent on the Indonesian government creating an anticorruption commission and improving government procurement methods. The IBRD planned to begin loan allotments at $580 million a year and increase them by up to $850 million a year by 2007. If, however, the Indonesian government initiates total compliance with bank terms, that amount could reach $1.2 billion a year by 2007. The World Bank defended its actions by arguing that despite the country's rich natural resources, too many people in Indonesia were suffering from poverty to deprive them of much-needed assistance.

In an effort to cut down on corruption in host countries, in 1996 the International Bank for Reconstruction and Development began a concentrated effort to promote anticorruption programs. The bank has initiated stricter oversight of projects in host countries. Furthermore, in approximately 100 developing countries, the bank has engaged in such diverse anticorruption activities as training judges and teaching journalists investigative reporting skills.

The Role of the United States

Throughout the history of the International Bank for Reconstruction and Development, the bank has been criticized for being too heavily influenced by the United States. Although this dependence on American funding was necessary in the years after World War II, when the United States was the only major world power that had not been ravaged by the war, contin-

ued dependence generated a good deal of resentment. The bank has been known to sacrifice both human and natural resources in host countries in order to promote progress in developing counties. In response to this tendency, the U.S. Congress instructed the American executive director to vote against using bank funds in any country that consistently violates human rights. Subsequent proposed amendments to the original International Financial Institutions Act of 1977 have attempted to prohibit assistance to countries that work against the interests of the United States.

At the beginning of the twenty-first century, without offering additional funding from the United States, President George W. Bush began to push the bank toward a system of grants rather than loans, arguing that since grants would not have to be paid back, recipient countries would be less burdened. The problem with this approach is that the bank's charter has limited the availability of bank funds for grants. For example, grant funding for the International Development Association is only $100 million.

In November 1999, the U.S. Congress established the Meltzer Committee and charged it with generating recommendations on the role of the United States in the future of the World Bank. The Meltzer Committee issued a report in March 2000 that accused the bank of being too heavily bureaucratic, insisting that many of the bank's functions could be taken over by the private sector. Furthermore, the committee recommended that countries with per capita incomes of more than $4,000 be made ineligible for bank loans and that limits be placed on those countries with incomes of $2,500 or more. Essentially, the International Bank for Reconstruction and Development as it exists would be disbanded under the Meltzer Committee plan by merging the International Development Agency and the IFC and dissolving the MIGA entirely. Critics claim that such a plan would benefit highly industrialized nations such as the United States at the expense of still developing countries.

Criticisms of the World Bank

From its inception, the International Bank for Reconstruction and Development has been the target of heavy criticism. Critics on the Left have accused the bank of being an "imperialist institution for imposing one view of the development process," whereas detractors on the Right insist that the bank is a "hangover from the interventionist early post-war era" (Gilbert and Vines 2000, 10–11). Whatever one feels about the World Bank, the bottom line is that the organization has served a purpose that no other organization or country has been willing or able to fill.

In her 1982 critique of the World Bank, Cheryl Payer identified ten functions that the World Bank has historically filled:

The Bank has served to accelerate the flow of funds from wealthier nations and the private sector to developing nations.

The Bank has provided a means of directing funds for investment, transportation, and communications to previously remote locations.

The Bank has promoted the activities of multinational corporations, including the mining sector.

The Bank has functioned as a channel for improving the legal principles that govern foreign investment in developing nations.

The Bank has improved production of foreign exports within developing countries.

The Bank has protected its own legitimacy by denying loans to any country that has a history of repudiating international debts or nationalizing foreign property.

The Bank has opposed minimum wage laws, trade union activity, and other measures of improving national income of developing nations.

The Bank has purchased project materials through international competitive bidding, resulting in favoritism of large multinational companies.

The Bank has continually expressed opposition to protection for locally owned businesses and industry.

The Bank has favored project goals that deny control of basic resources of land, water, and forests to local residents. (Payer 1982, 19)

Even by the bank's own standards, its projects have not always been successful. For example, in a study published in 2001, the World Bank admitted that out of ten projects undertaken in Africa, only two were absolute successes. The bank identified two other African projects as failures; the other six were deemed to be only partially successful.

The harshest critics of the International Bank for Reconstruction and Development contend that from the beginning the reconstruction goals of the bank were too lofty to be achieved because other programs and institutions, such as the Marshall Plan implemented by President Harry S. Truman, were better suited to reconstructing war-ravaged countries. Other critics suggest that whatever original purpose the bank might have served has long become obsolete, maintaining that it has not responded quickly enough or extensively enough to the changing needs of globalization.

Critics have also charged that members of the IBRD career staff have been prone to fall into mindsets that often work against efficiency and responsiveness. George Soros, for example, has suggested that IBRD's staff should be limited to five-year terms of employment, renewable only once, and that continued employment should be based entirely on the quality of performance rather than the amount of loans disbursed (Soros 2002). A number of critics have suggested that the bank needs to revise its charter in order to bring an end to the influence that certain governments exercise within the bank's governing structure. They claim that voting power sometimes allows self-interested governments to push through loans that promote their own interests or to block those loans that have the potential to create opposition to their interests.

Elizabeth Purdy

See Also Global Economic Growth; Inequality; International Financial Markets; Financial Services; International Monetary Fund (IMF); Foreign Aid

References

Acheson, A. L. K., Martin F. J. Prachowny (Editor), J. F. Chant (Editor). 1972. *Bretton Woods Revisited: Evaluations of the International Monetary Fund and the International Bank for Reconstruction and Development.* Toronto: University of Toronto Press.

Caufield, Catherine. 1996. *Masters of Illusion: The World Bank and the Poverty of Nations.* New York: Henry Holt.

Devarajan, Shantayanan, Shanta Devarajan, David Dollar, and Torgny Holmgren. 2001. *Aid and Reform in Africa: Lessons from Ten Case Studies.* Washington, DC: World Bank.

Gilbert, Christopher L., and David Vines. 2000. *The World Bank: Structure and Policies.* New York: Cambridge University Press.

International Bank for Reconstruction and Development. 1954. *The International Bank for Reconstruction and Development, 1946–1953.* Baltimore: Johns Hopkins University Press.

Jaycox, Edward. 1988. "What Can Be Done in Africa? The World Bank Response." Pp. 19–52 in Stephen K. Commins, ed. *Africa's Development Challenges and the World Bank: Hard Questions, Costly Choices.* Boulder: Lynne Rienner.

McLellan, Elisabeth P., ed. 2003. *The World Bank: Overview and Current Issues.* New York: Nova Science.

Mikesell, Raymond F. 1972. "The Emergence of the World Bank as a Development Institution." Pp. 70–84 in A. L. K. Acheson, et al., *Bretton Woods Revisited: Evaluations of the International Monetary Fund and the International Bank for Reconstruction and Development.* Toronto: University of Toronto Press.

Payer, Cheryl. 1982. *The World Bank: A Critical Analysis.* New York: Monthly Review Press.

Perlez, Jane. 2003. "World Bank Again Giving Large Loans to Indonesia" *New York Times Online,* December 2.

"Report on Implementation of Recommendations Made by the International Financial Institutions Advisory Commission." 2002. October, http://www.treas.gov/ press/releases/reports/meltzerreport.pdf (cited December 1, 2003).

Rich, Bruce. 2002. "The World Bank under James Wolfensohn." Pp. 26–53 in Jonathan R. Pincus and Jeffrey A. Winters, *Reinventing the World Bank.* Ithaca, NY: Cornell University Press.

Salda, Anne C. M. 1995. *World Bank.* New Brunswick, NJ: Transaction.

Soros, George. 2002. *George Soros on Globalization.* New York: PublicAffairs.

Winters, Jeffrey. 2002. "Criminal Debt." Pp. 101–130 in Jonathan R. Pincus and Jeffrey A. Winters, *Reinventing the World Bank.* Ithaca, NY: Cornell University Press.

World Bank. 1970. *One Hundred Questions and Answers.* Washington, DC: World Bank.

———. 1971. *World Bank and IDA: Questions and Answers.* Washington, DC: World Bank.

———. 2003. "What Is the World Bank?" http:// www. worldbank.org (cited December 1, 2003).

Yudelman, Montague. 1985. *The World Bank and Agricultural Development: An Insider's View.* New York: World Resources Institute.

International Labour Organization (ILO)

The International Labour Organization (ILO), established as an autonomous institution in 1919 by the Treaty of Versailles, became, in 1946, the first specialized agency associated with the United Nations. It brings together representatives of workers, employers, and governments with the goal of improving worldwide working conditions by formulating benchmark international labor standards, encouraging countries to adopt these standards, and shining a spotlight on those that violate the most basic norms. Advocates see it as "the conscience of the world"—an important voice for achieving harmony between workers and employers and helping to improve workers' lives. Critics, however, view it as an ineffectual debating society that has had little impact on labor issues.

Origins of the ILO

The ILO traces its origin to the European movement to adopt international protective labor legislation in the first half of the 1800s. Among the leaders were Scottish industrialist Robert Owen, who proposed international labor standards at the 1818 Congress of Aix-la-Chapelle, and Alsatian Daniel Legrand, who tirelessly lobbied government leaders throughout Western Europe to adopt child-labor restrictions, limitations on night work, Sunday rest provisions, and other labor laws. Much of the support for these laws came from socialists, academic social scientists, and religious groups—especially after Pope Leo XIII's encyclical *Rerum Novarum* (1891) justified and

encouraged the adoption of labor standards. A meeting of social reformers led to the establishment of the International Association for Labor Legislation (IALL) and a permanent International Labour Office in 1900. In 1906, the IALL arranged a diplomatic conference, which approved the first two labor "conventions"— one prohibiting night work for women, and the other prohibiting the use of white phosphorus in matches—both of which were widely enacted in Western Europe.

At the end of World War I, the establishment of a more powerful international labor commission was considered urgent by many of the victorious allies, who saw the passage of protective labor legislation as "insurance" against the threat of communism. The Versailles Peace Conference appointed a Labor Commission of fifteen members from the United States, Britain, France, Italy, Japan, Belgium, Cuba, Czechoslovakia, and Poland. Chaired by Samuel Gompers, president of the American Federation of Labor (AFL), the commission agreed to create the International Labour Organization, which they envisioned as a unique body with a "tripartite" structure. Each nation would have four voting delegates—two representing their government, one representing workers, the other representing employers.

However, the new organization was given little power. Although the ILO Constitution (which was adopted April 16, 1919, becoming part XIII of the Treaty of Versailles) warned that "the failure of any nation to adopt humane conditions of labour is an obstacle in the way of other nations which desire to improve the conditions in their countries," the ILO was only granted the power to adopt conventions on specific labor issues (by a two-thirds vote)—it could not enforce them. ILO members promised to submit conventions before their national lawmaking bodies and to report on their status and enforcement. In addition, they officially bound themselves under international law to abide by any convention they ratified. Despite these provisions, however, the ILO could do little to induce nations to adopt these conventions or to enforce them in nations that did ratify them.

The ILO between World War I and World War II

Thirty-nine countries sent delegations to the ILO's first conference, held in Washington, DC, in October 1919, which selected the organization's leadership and adopted conventions on maximum hours of work, unemployment, maternity protections, night work for women, and child labor. However, divisions between rich and poor countries were evident, and a month later, the U.S. Senate voted against membership by the United States. U.S. business advocates, and many labor advocates as well, were skeptical of the ILO because of the socialist ideas of many of its leaders, including its first president, Frenchman Albert Thomas. Although the United States eventually joined in 1934, the ILO was primarily a European concern during its first two decades. Its headquarters were in Geneva, and most of its funding and staff were European—with much of its personnel coming from its predecessor, the International Labour Office.

Despite its initial prestige, the ILO immediately had trouble convincing nations to ratify conventions that legally raised their labor standards. International competitors refused to go first, fearing that ratifications would raise labor costs and give their rivals an advantage. Some proponents of labor legislation in the United States hoped that they could circumvent court

rulings against these laws by having the Congress ratify ILO conventions, which would then have the status of treaty obligations. However, the United States ratified only a handful of ILO conventions, most dealing with maritime issues, and none very important. Thus, the ILO had little success in achieving its most fundamental mission of raising legal labor standards via coordinated international action, and critics dismissed it as an impotent debating society.

Soon the organization was wracked by another persistent problem. In 1923, the credentials of the Italian workers delegate, who was appointed by the fascist labor union, were challenged on the grounds that he did not represent a workers organization in accordance with ILO rules, but instead a mixed organization of employers and workers. He was nevertheless seated. However, Italy clearly did not recognize freedom of association among its workers, and the ILO struggled in vain to adequately define this condition.

In 1930, the ILO adopted an important convention, No. 29, requiring the suppression of forced and compulsory labor in all forms (with exceptions for military services and emergencies). This became the most widely ratified convention in its history. During the 1930s, the organization turned its attention to offering solutions to the economic slump, especially work sharing and shorter hours, but it became virtually impossible for it to push for higher labor standards. In addition, it began to offer "technical assistance" to less developed nations. The first of these missions, in 1930, assisted Greece in establishing a government-run social insurance system. The following year, China sought help in organizing factory inspections, whereas Egypt invited the ILO to advise it on the best methods of setting up a labor department.

The outbreak of World War II devastated the ILO, cutting its funding and prompting its remaining staff to move from Geneva to Montreal. Its major task during the war years was to plan for the peace, in the realization that it would be unlikely to play an important role in the postwar reconstruction unless it captured the limelight. Despite its leaders' best efforts and a renewed focus on the ILO as "revolution insurance," the ILO failed again in its aim of becoming a major postwar player. Some would argue that it never really had a chance—what nation could cede power and sovereignty to this divided organization in which national governments received only half the votes? In addition, the ILO was seen by some as an embarrassing reminder of the failed League of Nations. As the postwar international landscape emerged, the United Nations and its agencies (such as the United Nations Relief and Rehabilitation Administration) took upon themselves tasks that the ILO had hoped to undertake. Analysts argue that both the United States and the Soviet Union sought to downplay the ILO's role because neither had adequate power or influence in the organization.

The Declaration of Philadelphia

As these events unfolded, the ILO held its twenty-sixth annual conference from April 20 to May 12, 1944, in Philadelphia, where it issued a declaration expanding its tasks and restating the fundamental principles of the organization: "that a) labor is not a commodity, b) freedom of expression and of association are essential to sustained progress, c) poverty anywhere constitutes a danger to prosperity everywhere, and d) the war against want requires to be carried on with unrelenting vigour within each nation, and by continuous and concerted international effort in which the representatives of workers and employers, enjoying equal status with those of governments, join with them in free discussion and democratic decision with a view of the promotion of the common welfare."

The declaration then asserted that "all human beings, irrespective of race, creed or sex, have the right to pursue both their material well-being and their spiritual development in conditions of freedom and dignity, of economic security and equal opportunity" and recognized "the solemn obligation" of the ILO

to further programs around the world aiming to achieve full employment and increased living standards; job satisfaction; training and mobility of labor; fair sharing of the fruits of progress and a minimum living wage to all; recognition of the right to collective bargaining; the extension of social security measures providing basic income and comprehensive medical care to all; adequate protection of life and health among workers in all occupations; child welfare and maternity protection; adequate nutrition, housing, and facilities for recreation and culture; and equality of educational and vocational opportunity. Finally, the declaration pledged cooperation with other international bodies in accomplishing these goals. The declaration implicitly envisioned expanded and activist governmental programs, and it clearly repositioned the ILO's agenda beyond its initial negative task of banning abusive work conditions.

ILO leaders knew that this declaration was a vague expression of hope and a consciously crafted assertion of the agency's potential. However, the powers meeting in San Francisco to establish the United Nations gave virtually no attention to the ILO, and despite its acceptance in December 1946 as the first international agency to officially associate with the UN, the ILO was unable to achieve the power, influence, and funding of other postwar organizations, such as the World Bank or the International Monetary Fund. Likewise, despite its continued hopes to coordinate international labor standards, it was never able to achieve the cooperation of the General Agreement on Tariffs and Trade (GATT), which did achieve substantial progress in coordinating a movement toward reduced international trade barriers.

The ILO during the Cold War

Like many other international agencies, the ILO was torn by the tensions of the Cold War. It continued in its traditional mission of encouraging countries to enact more stringent labor legislation, expanded its technocratic missions to less developed countries, and increased its efforts to collect and interpret data on labor conditions around the world. For such efforts, the ILO was award the Nobel Peace Prize on its fiftieth anniversary in 1969.

Although its membership, budget, and staff grew, however, debates became even more divisive and the viability of its tripartite structure was called into question. The United States and other nations complained that newly independent developing countries and Communist one-party states used ILO meetings as a stage to attack developed countries. They protested that these nations' worker and employer representatives were government mouthpieces lacking the independent voice envisioned in the organization's charter, and that they failed to respect the organization's pivotal goal of freedom of association. The conflict escalated after the Soviet Union's decision to join the ILO in 1954 and culminated in the mid-1970s, when a Russian was nearly elected chair of the ILO's Governing Body. The Arab-Israeli conflict further politicized the organization.

At the urging of AFL President George Meany, the United States, whose dues amounted to one-quarter of the ILO's budget, announced its withdrawal (effective two years later) from the organization in 1975, citing its "appallingly selective concern" for human rights. In response, ILO leaders moved to refocus the organization toward its stated goals and pressed the issue of freedom of association more strongly—for example, condemning Soviet treatment of labor dissidents. The United States rejoined the ILO in 1980, with the Ronald Reagan administration seeing it as one more weapon in the battle against Soviet ideology. True to its new direction, in 1984 the ILO Conference accepted a report from a special commission of inquiry concluding that Poland had violated ILO conventions regarding union and workers rights in suppressing the Solidarity labor movement.

Throughout these decades, U.S. business leaders were skeptical of the ILO. In 1952, for example, American employer representative Charles McCormick criticized the organization as "hostile to the American free competitive enterprise" system. Employer representatives complained that the ILO's Convention No. 87 on Freedom of Association (adopted in 1948) and Convention No. 98 on the Right to Organized and Collective Bargaining (1949) were so broad that they would give undue power to organized labor, and that they clashed with provisions of the Taft-Hartley Act of 1947. They decried the socialism implicit in ILO conventions, including those on the need for universal health insurance. Employer representative William McGrath was openly hostile to the ILO and worked to adopt the Bricker Amendment, which would have instituted constitutional protections against adopting laws via ratification of ILO conventions.

Additional ILO activities during this period included the establishment of the International Institute for Labour Studies in Geneva in 1960, an educational research institute bringing together international experts on social and labor policy. In 1965, the ILO opened the International Training Center in Turin, Italy. It provides training programs for directors in charge of technical and vocational institutions, managers in private and public enterprises, trade union leaders, and technicians, primarily from developing countries. Some 90,000 people have received training there since its establishment. The ILO's technical and development assistance programs were also expanded. ILO experts have traveled around the globe providing technical advice on the improvement of systems of labor statistics, methods of labor inspection, arrangements for employment services, systems of pensions, unemployment benefits, and the like.

The ILO in Recent Years

In the past two decades, the ILO has become more harmonious and has refocused its attention on raising the lowest of labor standards around the world. During the 1990s, concerns about the effects of "globalization" brought a renewed attention to international labor standards and the role of the ILO. The ILO has shared these concerns, worrying aloud about the penchant of governments and employers to dilute work standards in order to compete with cheaper labor in other parts of the world.

In accordance with this rising concern, the ILO approved in 1998 a Declaration on Fundamental Principles and Rights at Work. The declaration advocates freedom of association and the effective recognition of the right to collective bargaining; the elimination of all forms of forced or compulsory labor; the effective abolition of child labor; and the elimination of discrimination in respect to employment and occupation. Perhaps the strongest push came in the area of child labor. Convention No. 182, on the Worst Forms of Child Labor, called for immediate and effective measures to secure the prohibition and elimination of forms of child labor such as slavery, forced recruitment in armed conflict, prostitution and pornography, and work likely to harm the health, safety, or morals of children. In less than three years, 132 countries ratified this convention—the fastest ratification rate ever. In attacking child labor, the ILO took a coordinated approach with other organizations as part of the International Programme on the Elimination of Child Labour (IPEC). The ILO's media-savvy campaign included publication of *Global Report 2002: A Future without Child Labour,* a World Day against Child Labour (June 12, 2003), and even a collaboration with FIFA (the Federation Internationale de Football Association) bringing child labor to the attention of soccer fans through the "Red Card to Child Labor" campaign. Similarly, the ILO launched a coordinated international publicity campaign in 2003—the Global Campaign on Social Security and Coverage for All—to encourage countries to extend social security to more of their citizens.

In 1999, for the first time in its history, the ILO imposed penalties on a member state—

Burma (Myanmar)—for allowing forced labor. These penalties, though largely symbolic, are part of a larger international campaign of moral suasion and trade sanctions. Along these lines, nations have begun turning to the ILO to help administer labor standards tied to trade agreements. For example, the United States paid the ILO to monitor conditions in the Cambodian garment industry when it expanded Cambodia's import quota in 1999.

Despite these developments, the ILO's standing continues to be weak in the United States, which has ratified only 14 of the ILO's 184 conventions. This compares with 105 ratifications by Spain, 97 by France, and 65 by Britain. However, ratifications don't always mean much in practice—Iraq under Saddam Hussein had ratified 59 conventions, and Cuba has ratified 73.

Current Status and Structure of the ILO

The ILO maintains its original tripartite structure. The International Labour Conference is its supreme deliberative organ and meets annually to adopt international labor conventions and recommendations. The Governing Body (elected by the conference for a three-year term) is the executive council and meets three or four times a year to implement policies and programs and supervise the work of the International Labour Office (which serves as the ILO's secretariat, operational headquarters, research center, and publishing house). The Governing Body has the same tripartite (government-worker-employer) structure, with fifty-six regular members. Of the twenty-eight representing government, ten are appointed by the members of "chief industrial importance" (presently Brazil, China, France, Germany, India, Italy, Japan, Russia, the United Kingdom, and the United States).

The International Labour Office is headed by a director-general and employs 1,900 officials, representing more than 110 nationalities, at its Geneva headquarters and in forty field offices around the world. Regional offices are located in Abidjan, Lima, Beirut, and Bangkok. The director-general of the ILO (since 1999) is Juan Somavia of Chile. His predecessors have been Albert Thomas of France (1919–1932), Harold Butler of the United Kingdom (1932–1938), John Winant of the United States (1939–1941), Edward Phelan of Ireland (1941–1948), David Morse of the United States (1948–1970), Wilfred Jenks of the United Kingdom (1970–1973), Francis Blanchard of France (1973–1989), and Michel Hansenne of Belgium (1989–1999).

The director-general's global reports, prepared in a four-year cycle, cover freedom of association, forced labor, child labor, and discrimination. These reports are credited with the decision in 2001 to allow the formation of worker committees in Saudi Arabia and unions in Bahrain. Other widely distributed publications include *World of Work* (a quarterly magazine in fifteen languages aimed at a popular audience), the scholarly *International Labour Review,* the *Bulletin of Labour Statistics,* and *Key Indicators of the Labour Market.* In addition, the ILO continues to publish hundreds of specialized studies with titles such as *Safety and Health in the Use of Chemicals at Work: A Training Manual* (1993), *Sending Workers Abroad: A Manual for Low- and Middle-Income Countries* (1997), *Localizing Global Production: Know-How Transfer in International Manufacturing* (1997), *HIV/AIDS and Employment* (1998), *Employment Revival in Europe Labour: Market Success in Austria, Denmark, Ireland and the Netherlands* (2000), *Social Security Pensions: Development and Reform* (2000), *Current International Recommendations on Labour Statistics* (2000), *Action against Sexual Harassment at Work in Asia and the Pacific* (2001), and *Combating Child Labour: A Handbook for Labour Inspectors* (2002).

ILO conventions are attended by roughly 2,000 delegates from 176 member states each year and have again attracted the attention of world leaders. The 2003 conference, for example, was addressed by King Abdullah II of Jordan; President Thabo Mbeki of South Africa, who used the forum to push for global income redistribution; and Brazilian President Lula da Silva, who criticized rich countries for their agricultural subsidies.

The ILO's total income in its 2000–2001 budget was $467 million, with the top contributors being the United States (22 percent), Japan (19 percent), Germany (10 percent), France (6 percent), and Britain (5.5 percent).

Proponents argue that the need for the ILO has never been greater and point to its recent activities as evidence for its potential. However, even strong advocates of international labor standards question the organization's effectiveness. Kimberly Ann Elliott and Richard B. Freeman, for example, concluded that "most reasonably informed people have little idea what the letters I-L-O stand for"; they were not optimistic about the ability of this "90-pound weakling of UN agencies" and "toothless tiger" to raise and enforce labor standards. The ILO's power is seemingly still limited to shining a spotlight on the world's worst labor conditions and hoping that this leads to change.

Robert Whaples

See Also Labor Markets and Wage Effects; Labor Rights and Standards

References

Alcock, Antony. 1971. *History of the International Labor Organization.* New York: Octagon.

Elliott, Kimberly Ann, and Richard B. Freeman. 2003. *Can Labor Standards Improve under Globalization?* Washington, DC: Institute for International Economics.

Galenson, Walter. 1981. *The International Labor Organization: An American View.* Madison: University of Wisconsin Press.

International Labour Organization, www.ilo.org.

Lorenz, Edward C. 2001. *Defining Global Justice: The History of U.S. International Labor Standards Policy.* Notre Dame, IN: University of Notre Dame Press.

International Monetary Fund (IMF)

The International Monetary Fund (IMF) is an independent international organization established by the Bretton Woods Agreements of 1944. It is responsible for ensuring the stability of the international monetary and financial system and has had an important impact on the world economy and its member countries. To meet its objectives, the IMF performs three main functions—surveillance, technical assistance, and financing. Originally, surveillance entailed ensuring that exchange rates stayed relatively fixed. Now it requires only that national exchange rate policies be consistent with the smooth functioning of the international monetary system (that is, that there are no beggar-thy-neighbor policies). The IMF also serves as the lender of last resort, lending large sums to countries in balance of payments difficulty. The IMF can perform regulatory functions up to a point in enforcing the Articles of Agreement by making its loans conditional on specified changes in the economic behavior of the borrowing country. This practice is known as "conditionality" and has drawn much criticism from around the world.

Objectives and Functions of the IMF

Although the IMF has sometimes been called a central bank for central bankers, its role is much more limited than this description implies. The formal objectives of the IMF are stated in Article I of its Articles of Agreement. These are:

1. to promote international monetary co-operation through a permanent institution which provides for consultation and collaboration on international monetary problems;
2. to facilitate the expansion and balanced growth of international trade, and to contribute thereby to the promotion and maintenance of high levels of employment, real income and the development of the productive resources of all members;
3. to promote exchange stability, to maintain orderly exchange arrangements among members, and to avoid competitive exchange depreciation;
4. to assist in the establishment of a multilateral system of payments in respect of current transactions between members and in the elimination of foreign exchange restrictions which hamper the growth of world trade;
5. to give confidence to members by making the general resources of the Fund temporarily available to them under adequate safeguards, thus providing them with the opportunity to correct maladjustment in their balance of payments without resorting to measures destructive of national or international prosperity;
6. to shorten the duration and lessen the degree of disequilibrium in the international balances of payments of members.

The purpose of the IMF was to establish a new world order based on an open exchange and trading system that would operate under international scrutiny and control. Following the competitive devaluations and exchange rate instability of the Great Depression, exchange rates were recognized as matters of international importance. The IMF created an international code of conduct to be observed by all members, and in turn, it would make funding available to smooth the balance of payments difficulties of members. Members would subscribe to and have available to them a pool of currencies that they could draw upon in times of external payments difficulties. Initially the Fund was to promote and enforce an international system of fixed exchange rates established in terms of the U.S. dollar (which was in turn set to gold). Apart from a cumulative initial change of 10 percent, par values could be changed only on a proposal by the member and subject to a finding by the Fund that the member's balance of payments was in fundamental disequilibrium.

Significant changes in the international monetary system have also led to changes in the IMF. One of the most significant changes was the move to floating exchange rates following the U.S. decision to close the gold window and de-link the dollar-gold exchange standard on August 15, 1974. The Second Amendment to the Articles of Agreement was drafted and agreed upon under the Jamaica Agreement of January 1976 and came into effect on April 1, 1978. By resolving issues that led to the second amendment, the Jamaica Agreement ended the negotiations for a reformed international monetary system. The second amendment then spelled out the main themes of a reformed international monetary order. Some of the main points were:

1. Each member could adopt the exchange regime of its choice; however, members were "to seek to promote stability by fostering orderly underlying economic and financial conditions" and to avoid manipulating the exchange rate to gain unfair advantage.

2. A system of par values (that is, global fixed exchange rates, as in Bretton Woods) could be introduced again if 85 percent of the total voting power of the membership agreed, but it would not be based on gold.

3. The role of gold would be permanently reduced through the elimination of gold as a common denominator of the monetary system, obligatory gold payments to the IMF, and the requirement that the IMF hold 50 percent of its reserves in gold.

4. The special drawing right was bolstered to become the principal reserve asset of the international monetary system.

The IMF remains a powerful international institution with an important role in maintaining a stable international economic order.

Governance, Membership, and Quotas

The IMF, like the World Bank, has a representative form of government. The senior decision-making body of the Fund is the Board of Governors. Day-to-day management of the IMF is in the hands of the managing director, who reports to the twenty-four-member Executive Board. The executive directors meet several times a week and represent all of the member states of the IMF. The largest creditors to the Fund are permitted to appoint one executive director each. Presently these are the United States, the United Kingdom, Germany, France, and Japan (the five nations originally assigned the largest amount of privilege and responsibility according to the IMF quota system, each of which has appointed an executive director since 1946), as well as Saudi Arabia, China, Russia, and Switzerland, which have been elected by their respective member state groups. The managing director is ultimately responsible to the Board of Governors, which meets once a year. The votes of member states are weighted according to a formula embodied in the IMF quota system, which is designed to reflect both the importance of each country in the world economy and the importance of world trade for each economy.

The IMF Board of Governors meets jointly with the Board of Governors of the World Bank Group each year. Following an inaugural meeting held in Savannah, Georgia, in March 1946, the first official joint annual meeting of the two boards was held in Washington, DC, in September 1946. These annual meetings have taken place in September each year since. The second meeting was held in London in 1947. The third (1948), fourth (1949), fifth (1950), and sixth (1951) meetings were held in Washington, DC. The seventh (1952) was held in Mexico City. Thereafter, it became conventional to hold two consecutive annual meetings in Washington and every third meeting in another member country. For example, meetings have been held in Istanbul, Tokyo, Toronto, Belgrade, Berlin, Manila, Nairobi, and Rio de Janeiro.

Membership in the IMF is now almost universal, but this was not always the case. Representatives from forty-five countries attended the International Monetary Conference at Bretton Woods, New Hampshire, in July 1944. The IMF came into existence when twenty-nine of those countries ratified the agreement and sent representatives to the formal signing ceremony on December 27, 1945. Fifteen of the remaining sixteen countries ratified the agreement in subsequent years, with New Zealand (1961) and Liberia (1962) ratifying last. Germany and Japan both joined in 1952. The one exception to the rule was the Soviet Union, which did not ratify the Bretton Woods Agreement. The USSR was an active member at the 1944 conference and had been allocated a quota of $1.2 billion, the third largest behind the United States and the United Kingdom. Although the USSR did not become an IMF member, the fifteen sovereign countries created after the Communist

collapse that were part of the former Soviet Union all became members in the period June 1992 to April 1993.

Three founding members withdrew from the Fund: Poland in 1950, alleging that the Fund had failed to fulfill the expectations of its founders; Czechoslovakia in 1955, in a dispute as to whether it was required to provide data to the Fund; and Cuba in 1964, following protracted negotiations on overdue payments to the Fund. Poland and Czechoslovakia rejoined in 1986 and 1990, respectively. China's request for the ouster of the Chinese National Government in Taiwan was rejected in 1950 but accepted thirty years later. Switzerland became a member in 1992 following a long association as a nonmember. The quotas of Yugoslavia and Czechoslovakia were reassigned to the component states that accepted membership following the breakup of those nations.

The Board of Governors is the only authority in the Fund that can approve membership applications, and it does this by a simple majority vote. There are three criteria for membership: The applicant must be a country, it must be in control of its external relations, and it must be willing to perform the obligations of membership contained in the Articles of Agreement. Geographic or economic size, population, the existence of a national currency or central bank, and type of political regime have no bearing on membership. Denial of membership to the Fund automatically entails denial of membership in the World Bank and thus cuts off development finance to the country.

Member countries must deposit their currencies in the IMF in an amount defined by a quota system that also defines each member nation's voting rights, its maximum access to financing, and its share of Special Drawing Right (SDR) allocations. A member's quota is expressed in SDRs and is equal to the subscription the member must pay in full to the Fund before the membership becomes effective. Up to 25 percent must be paid in reserve assets (SDRs or hard currencies); the remainder is paid in the member's own currency. Each member has 250 basic votes plus one additional vote for each SDR 100,000 of quota. The size of a quota is determined by economic factors that reflect a member's relative position in the world economy, such as trade flows, reserves, and national income. Quotas are reviewed at least once every five years and reassigned as necessary. Initially, only the United States, France, the United Kingdom, Japan, and West Germany had enough voting rights based on quota to appoint a member to the Executive Board. Over time, specific countries were allocated higher quota responsibility and thus additional voting rights. In 1992, Switzerland, Saudi Arabia, China, and Russia each had enough votes to appoint a member to the Executive Board. Major policy decisions taken by the Board of Governors require a high majority vote—85 percent of all quota-based votes; certain other decisions require a 70 percent majority vote, but most decisions require only a simple majority.

IMF Programs and Activities

Surveillance

In its surveillance capacity, the IMF monitors the economic and financial policies of member states and provides consultation and regular dialogue about the national and international consequences of those policies. It also may offer economic and financial policy advice. Regular consultations between the Fund and each member country (developing and industrial) have been required under Article IV since passage of the Second Amendment of the Articles of Agreement in 1978 (prior to 1978 they were voluntary). These consultations may be held annually or once every two years. Since 1987, a "bicyclic" approach has been adopted where a full consultation takes place every two years and a simplified, interim consultation in the intervening year. During these consultations, IMF economists visit the member country to collect data and hold discussions with government and central bank officials, and often pri-

vate-sector representatives, members of parliament, and leaders of civil society and labor unions. The consultations provide the data the Fund needs to exercise surveillance. The Fund analyzes a member nation's economic development and policies; examines its fiscal, monetary, and balance of payments accounts; and assesses how policies influence its exchange rates and external accounts. Discussions with member countries, staff reports on their economies, and the adjustment programs that are supported by the Fund are all confidential, with no limitations on the period of confidentiality.

The IMF also continuously reviews global economic developments in what is known as "multilateral surveillance." In its biannual *World Economic Outlook* (WEO), IMF staff analysts discuss prospects for the world economy and provide in-depth studies of specific issues and challenges. The IMF also publishes a biannual *Global Financial Stability Report* (GFSR), which provides assessments of the stability of global financial markets and identifies potential systemic weaknesses that could lead to crises.

One area of surveillance is monitoring of exchange rates. The Fund is charged under the Articles of Agreement with exercising "firm surveillance over the exchange rate policies of its members" to help assure orderly exchange arrangements and promote a stable exchange rate system. It has approved three principles to guide members in their conduct of exchange rate policy: (1) to refrain from manipulating the exchange rate or the international monetary system in order to gain an unfair advantage or prevent balance of payments adjustment (beggar-thy-neighbor policies); (2) to intervene in the exchange markets, if necessary, to counter disorderly conditions; and (3) to take the interests of other members into account in developing intervention policies, including the interests of countries in whose currencies they are planning to intervene.

In 1978, the Second Amendment to the Articles of Agreement produced several changes. One of the most significant was the expansion of the Fund's surveillance function to include, de facto, all the monetary and financial policies of its members. Because countries could now elect the exchange regime of their choice and would not have to gain Fund approval to change parity, in other words, the Fund surveillance function was expanded to a broader but less specific arena of operation. In order for "firm surveillance" of the system to now be effective, the Fund needed to apply its monitoring and consultation activities not only to exchange rates but also to other national economic and financial policies, whether the country being monitored used the Fund's resources or not. Exchange rate, monetary, and fiscal policies remain at the center of IMF surveillance on issues ranging from the choice of exchange rate regime to ensuring consistency between the exchange rate regime and the stance of fiscal and monetary policy.

Structural policies were added to the IMF's surveillance agenda in the 1980s as economic growth slowed in many industrial countries in the wake of the second oil price shock. The debt crisis in the developing world and the fall of communism further underlined the need for structural change in many countries. Financial-sector issues were added to IMF surveillance in the 1990s following a series of banking crises in both industrial and developing countries. In 1999, the IMF and the World Bank decided to create a joint Financial Sector Assessment Program (FSAP) specifically designed to assess the strengths and weaknesses of countries' financial sectors. Other issues of concern are institutional issues, such as central bank independence, financial-sector regulation, corporate governance, and policy transparency and accountability. Assessment of risks and vulnerabilities has expanded from the traditional focus on the current account and external debt to include risks from large and volatile capital flows.

Training and Technical Assistance
The objective of IMF technical assistance, as described in Article I of the IMF's Articles of Agreement, is "to contribute to the development of the productive resources of member countries by enhancing the effectiveness of economic policy and financial management." The IMF Institute was established in 1964 to provide training in economic management to officials of the Fund's member countries and to help members design and implement effective economic policies. Since then, it has trained more than 13,000 officials at its headquarters in Washington, DC, and about 8,000 officials overseas from almost all of the member countries. The IMF provides technical assistance in its areas of expertise, including fiscal policy, monetary policy, and macroeconomic and financial statistics, mostly free of charge.

About three-quarters of IMF technical assistance goes to low- and lower-middle-income countries. Most of the institute's overseas training is conducted in regional training centers in Austria, Brazil, China, Côte d'Ivoire, Singapore, and the United Arab Emirates, and occasionally in large member countries and in countries with special circumstances. Courses at headquarters are offered in four languages— Arabic, English, French, and Spanish. In the regional training centers, courses are offered in English and in the primary language of the region. In January 2000, the institute launched its first distance learning program, with a course on financial programming and policy.

Financing
The resources of the Fund consist of gold, SDRs, currencies of members' paid in quota subscriptions, undistributed net income (interest payments) derived from the use of those resources, and borrowed funds from member governments, central banks, or the Bank for International Settlements. The value of those resources is in SDR, the Fund's unit of account. From these resources the IMF administers its financing facilities. The Fund does not provide development finance. Development finance is long-term financing directed to a specific project or sector of the economy. This is the function of the World Bank. The Fund provides

short-term to medium-term balance of payments financing in support of macroeconomic adjustment programs.

The Fund's financing is available at slightly below market rates and is generally repayable in terms of three to five years or slightly longer, but never more than ten years. Technically, IMF financing operations are purchases and repurchases of member currencies, not loans. When a member draws on the Fund's resources, it *purchases needed currencies* by exchanging its own currency. In repayments to the Fund, a member *repurchases its own currency* from the Fund with a designated currency usable in international payments (for example, U.S. dollars). The Fund pays interest on that portion of a member's currency holdings that it uses to meet the drawings of other members.

The Fund aims to be self-financing. The objective is to cover expenses from revenue, mainly from interest payments arising from loans and credits. The basic rate of interest applied to the use of the Fund's ordinary resources (distinct from borrowed resources, where the rate covers the cost to the IMF of borrowing the funds plus a small margin for the Fund) is set at the beginning of each financial year based on the estimated income and expenses of the Fund in the year ahead. The Fund also charges a uniform service charge of 0.5 percent on amounts purchased from the ordinary resources of the Fund beyond the reserve tranche (purchases from the reserve tranche, formerly called the "gold tranche," do not have a charge). The Fund has usually had a surplus income over expenditures.

The balance of payments adjustment is at the center of the use of IMF financial resources. Members may draw on amounts they have deposited with the IMF—based on their quota, in either their own currency or the currency of other countries, as needed—only when they have a balance of payments problem. Each member may draw up to 150 percent of its quota in one year and no more than 450 percent of its quota in total outstanding debt. For extensive drawings, a member country

must work out a balance of payments adjustment program acceptable to the IMF. In time of crisis, quota limits may be waived by a vote of the Executive Board. The IMF may thus aid a troubled country up to its total available resources.

The IMF's resources were primarily used by industrial countries in the first twenty years after World War II. From 1966 to 1977, industrial and less developed countries made about equal use of Fund resources. Beginning in 1978, IMF total credits and loans to developing countries accelerated remarkably, rising from approximately SDR 6 billion in 1977 to a peak of nearly SDR 40 billion in 1984, before beginning to decline in 1985. In the same period, credits and loans to industrial countries dwindled from approximately SDR 6 billion in 1977 to approximately SDR 1 billion in 1986.

In the 1950s, IMF financing went almost entirely to industrial countries in need of postwar assistance. In the 1960s and until the first oil crisis of 1973, IMF financing to industrial and developing countries was roughly equivalent, at approximately SDR 1 billion to each in any given year. IMF financing to industrial and developing nations jumped equally following the first oil crisis, but after 1978 the face of IMF financing dramatically turned to developing countries, causing a definitive change in the Fund. The last year that a major industrial country made use of the Fund's resources was 1976, when eight industrial countries drew a total of SDR 2.6 billion. From 1976 to 1984, several small industrial countries made limited use of the Fund's resources, but since 1984 no industrial country has done so and all of the Fund's activity has been with less developed countries, who have continuously made increasing use of Fund resources.

In the 1980s, Fund policy with respect to delinquent debtors also began to shift. As more and more countries began running into debt servicing difficulties and began to default in their obligations to the IMF, the Fund was beginning to feel the effect of the debt crisis on its own operations. If a member fails to fulfill any of its obligations under the Articles of Agreement, the Fund has the right to declare that member ineligible to use the Fund's general resources, and from 1985, the Fund began to do so in an unprecedented number of cases. The Fund may also issue a declaration of noncooperation or suspend a member's voting rights and representation in the Fund. If a member is judged not to be cooperating with the Fund, not paying off its debt, or even freezing its arrears, a series of further steps can eventually lead to the compulsory withdrawal of the member from the Fund. By April 1992, overdue obligations had risen from $1.2 billion in 1987 to a peak of $3.5 billion, and eight members were declared ineligible. No member has been forced to withdraw from the Fund, however.

The General Agreement to Borrow (GAB) was created in October 1962 when the Fund arranged to borrow, in certain circumstances, specified amounts of currencies from eleven industrialized countries, including ten members of the Fund (Belgium, Canada, France, Germany, Italy, Japan, the Netherlands, Sweden, the United Kingdom, and the United States) plus Switzerland, which was not a member at the time. The ten member countries of the GAB originated the Group of Ten, which was to become prominent in international monetary affairs in later years. The GAB provided the Fund with up to $6 billion in lenders' currencies to help finance purchases by GAB participants in the event of a financial crisis. GAB countries recognized that, owing to their financial size, in the event of a crisis for any one of them the Fund might not have the resources available to provide drawings of the magnitude that may be required. Between 1964 and 1970, the GAB was activated six times, to help finance four large drawings of the United Kingdom and two by France. In the 1970s, it was activated three times to help finance drawings by the United Kingdom (1977), Italy (1977), and the United States (1978). In 1982, among other reforms, arrangements were agreed with Saudi Arabia to associate that country on a bilateral basis with the GAB.

The first oil crisis of 1973 gave rise to balance of payments difficulties of unprecedented magnitude for most oil-importing countries. Drawings from normal credit tranches would have been inadequate. Financing, rather than adjustment, was the main objective. In 1974 and 1975, as a result of the sharp rise in oil prices in 1973, the Fund established a special oil-financing program to help members meet the increased import costs of petroleum and related petroleum products. The program involved recycling so-called petrodollars, that is, borrowing from those IMF members that had a balance of payments surplus (seventeen lenders, mainly the oil-exporting countries) and lending to oil-importing countries that were in deficit. Conditionality on the use of the oil facilities was minimal, and repayment terms were generous (repayments were to begin after four years and be completed within seven years). A total of fifty-five member countries drew SDR 6.9 billion under the program. A special Oil Facility Subsidy Account was created to reduce the cost of oil facility funds by half for the eighteen members most seriously affected by the oil crisis as determined by the secretary general of the United Nations.

In 1986, the Fund established the Structural Adjustment Facility to provide financial resources on highly concessional terms to support medium-term (three years) macroeconomic and adjustment programs in low-income countries facing protracted balance of payments problems. Within this program, annual policy programs are formulated by the member country and supported by financing from the Fund in annual disbursements. Interest rates on structural adjustment loans are set at 0.5 percent a year, and repayments are made in five to ten years. Other financing facilities include the Supplementary Financing Facility, the Supplementary Financing Facility Subsidy Account, and the Systemic Transformation Facility (established in 1993 and designed to assist former planned economies in transition). In 1963 and 1989, the Compensatory and Contingency Financing Facility was introduced to extend the Fund's financing to members in balance of payments difficulties because of (1) temporary export shortfalls; (2) adverse external contingencies; (3) excess cost of cereal imports; and (4) excess cost of oil imports (temporarily). This program allows members to draw on the Fund to offset export shortfalls caused by factors largely beyond their control (such as crop failures or natural disasters). It may also cover workers' remittances and international buffer stocks.

The IMF is also actively working to reduce poverty in countries around the globe, both independently and in collaboration with the World Bank and other organizations. The IMF provides financial support through its concessional lending facility—the Poverty Reduction and Growth Facility (PRGF)—and through debt relief under the Heavily Indebted Poor Countries (HIPC) Initiative. In most low-income countries, this support is underpinned by Poverty Reduction Strategy Papers (PRSP). These papers are prepared by country authorities—in consultation with civil society and external development partners—to describe a comprehensive economic, structural, and social policy framework that is being implemented to promote growth and reduce poverty in the country. Since 1962, the IMF has also provided emergency assistance to member countries afflicted by natural disasters—such as floods, earthquakes, hurricanes, or droughts. IMF financing can help to offset resulting shortfalls in export earnings and/or increased imports for recovery and reconstruction and help countries to avoid a serious depletion of their external reserves.

The resources of a Trust Fund created in 1976 were to be used exclusively for the purpose of providing loans to poorer developing countries, subject to very light conditionality, with concessional interest rates of 0.5 percent and a maturity of ten years. The Trust Fund made its final disbursement in gold in 1981. Its business was converted into the Special Disbursement Account, the structural adjustment facility, in 1986, and the enhanced structural adjustment facility in 1987, with additional funds from loans and grants contributed by aid agencies of member countries. Lack of fulfillment of the agreed-upon program of restructuring in the first year required additional corrective measures with benchmarks in the subsequent years of the program. Reforms implemented under the enhanced structural adjustment facility were particularly far-reaching with regard to both macroeconomic policy measures and structural reforms, but allowed up to 255 percent of quota. Commitments under three-year programs ended in 1992 when the entire resources of the trust were committed (SDR 6 billion).

Special Drawing Rights (SDRs). The SDR system was the first international reserve asset arrangement to be created by international law. It came into existence through the First Amendment to the Articles of Agreement. SDRs are purely book entries maintained by the IMF and do not have any traditional reserve backings such as gold or hard currency reserves. They are used by members in settling accounts within the IMF, by some other international organizations (such as development banks), and in some private arrangements. SDR deposits in the IMF carry a market-weighted interest rate but are not traded in international capital markets (except for a brief period in 1980–1981). The principal characteristics of the special drawing right are:

1. It was voluntary but universal, open to all Fund members, and specified that allocations or cancellations would be made in proportion to each participating member's quota and remain stable for a period of five years.
2. It would be created on the books of the Fund backed by an international agreement (the Fund's Articles of Agreement).
3. It would be available for use through the Fund on a voluntary basis by mutual agreement of both transacting parties, by national monetary authorities, and by

a limited number of official holders, but was not for use in private markets.

4. Its value was initially determined in terms of gold, then (after 1978) by a basket of currencies.

Allocations of SDRs are made by the Fund to those members who agree to participate in the SDR Department. The first basic period of SDR allocation was for three years (1970–1972), with a total of SDR 9.3 billion allocated. The second basic period was 1973–1977, during which no SDRs were allocated. The third period was 1978–1981, when SDR 12.1 billion were allocated. On April 30, 1992, a total of SDR 21.4 billion were in circulation, of which SDR 20.8 billion were held by participants and SDR 0.7 billion were held by the IMF. To enhance the attractiveness of the SDR, the Executive Board decided in 1980 to reduce the basket from sixteen to five currencies (U.S. dollar, German mark, French franc, British pound sterling, and Japanese yen) and to raise the interest rate on SDR deposits to market rates. The largest weight in the basket belongs to the U.S. dollar (40 percent). Despite such measures, however, the role of the SDR in the international monetary system has been limited. At present it is only a minor supplement to international reserves, amounting to less than 3 percent of world reserves. Nor is it used extensively except in transactions with the IMF itself.

Conditionality

Before a member state can use the Fund's financial resources, it must represent that it has a need to make the purchase "because of its balance of payments or its reserve position or developments in its reserves." Three conditions—the requirement of a balance of payments need, temporary use, and adequate safeguards—distinguish the IMF's lending operations from those of the World Bank. When a country borrows from the IMF, its government makes commitments on economic and financial policies—a requirement known as "conditionality." Conditionality is the link between the approval or continuation of the Fund's financing and the implementation of specified elements of economic policy by the country receiving this financing. It provides assurance to the IMF that its loan will be used to resolve the borrower's economic difficulties and that the country will be able to repay promptly, so that the funds become available to other members in need.

The policies to be adopted are designed not just to resolve the immediate balance of payments problem but also to lay the basis for sustainable economic growth by achieving broader economic stability—for example, by containing inflation or reducing public debt. Policies may also address structural impediments to healthy growth, for instance price and trade liberalization, measures to strengthen financial systems, or improvements in governance. Together, such policies constitute a member country's "policy program," which is described in a letter of intent, which may or may not have a memorandum of economic and financial policies attached to it, that accompanies the country's request for IMF financing. The specific objectives of a program and the types of policies adopted depend on a country's circumstances.

Most IMF loans feature "phased disbursements." This allows the IMF to verify that a country is continuing to adhere to its commitments before disbursing successive installments. Program monitoring relies on several tools:

- *Performance criteria* are specific conditions that have to be met for the agreed amount of credit to be disbursed. There are two types: quantitative and structural.
- *Quantitative performance criteria* typically involve macroeconomic policy variables such as international reserves, monetary and credit aggregates, fiscal balances, or external borrowing. For ex-

ample, a program might include a minimum level of net international reserves, a maximum level of central bank net domestic assets, or a maximum level of government borrowing.

- *Structural performance criteria* vary widely across programs but could, for example, include specific measures to restructure key sectors such as energy, to reform social security systems, or to improve financial sector operations.
- *Indicative targets* may be set when there is substantial uncertainty about economic trends beyond the first months of the program. As uncertainty is reduced, these targets will normally be established as performance criteria, with appropriate modifications as necessary.
- *Structural benchmarks,* though less critical for meeting the program's objectives, may help the Board assess a country's progress on structural reforms. Failure to achieve them would not necessarily interrupt Fund financing, however.
- *Program reviews* serve as an opportunity for a broad-based assessment by the Executive Board of progress within the program and provide a forum in which to discuss policies and introduce changes that may have become necessary in light of new developments.

Although the use of IMF resources has involved some element of conditionality since the 1950s, formal guidelines were not developed until 1968, and the scope of conditionality has expanded particularly since the early 1980s. Up to the early 1980s, IMF conditionality focused primarily on macroeconomic policies. Subsequently, however, the complexity and scope of the structural performance criteria attached to IMF credit increased significantly. This broadening and deepening of conditionality reflected both an increased emphasis on the need for supply-side measures to strengthen the fundamentals underlying economic growth and the IMF's growing in-

volvement in low-income and transition countries, where structural problems were particularly severe. In the process, tensions arose between the desire to cover aspects of policy central to program objectives and the importance of minimizing intrusion into national decisionmaking processes. Against this background, the 1979 Guidelines on Conditionality underscored the principle of parsimony and the need to limit performance criteria to the minimum number needed to evaluate policy implementation. They also stressed that the Fund should pay due regard to a country's social and political objectives, economic priorities, and circumstances.

Since 1979, a major expansion of conditionality has taken place, particularly in the structural area. Although structural measures were rarely an element in Fund-supported programs until the 1980s, by the 1990s almost all programs included some element of structural conditionality. The expansion of structural conditionality was also reflected in increasing numbers of performance criteria, structural benchmarks, and prior actions. These changes were the result of several factors. First, the Fund placed increasing emphasis on economic growth as a policy objective, with the recognition that raising growth on a sustainable basis requires strengthening the supply side through structural reforms. Second, the Fund became increasingly involved with groups of countries in which structural reforms were viewed as a particularly important part of an overall policy package, such as low-income countries and transition economies. Third, there was an increasing awareness that the monetary and fiscal policy objectives often depend critically on structural conditions—including the removal of extensive market distortions and the establishment of institutional underpinnings for effective policymaking in a market economy.

Members' drawing privileges on their reserves at the Fund are divided into tranches (or portions), each amounting to 25 percent of the total member's quota. The first 25 percent tranche can be drawn at any time without challenge (this was originally called the "gold tranche," as this portion of the quota was paid in gold). The second tranche requires moderate conditionality. The third and fourth tranches (the upper tranches) require substantial justification and agreement by the Fund on a sound corrective program. Use of the upper tranches is done through a standby arrangement that normally has repayment terms of one year (although members often renew this), quarterly phasing of drawings, and performance criteria to aid in program assessment.

History of the IMF

1944: Bretton Woods

From July 1 to 22, 1944, the International Monetary and Financial Conference was held in Bretton Woods, New Hampshire, with representatives from forty-four countries. At this conference the Articles of Agreement of the IMF and World Bank were drafted. On December 27, 1945, the IMF's Articles of Agreement entered into force, with twenty-nine governments, collectively representing 80 percent of the IMF's originally agreed-upon financial quotas, signing the agreement. From March 8 to 18, 1946, the inaugural meeting of the IMF Board of Governors was held in Savannah, Georgia. Here it was decided that the IMF's headquarters would be in Washington, DC. In addition, the by-laws were adopted and the first executive directors were elected. Camille Gutt of Belgium became the first managing director of the IMF on May 6, 1946.

The Bretton Woods par value system was a fixed exchange rate system based on gold. Changes could be made in the value of the currency only with the concurrence of the Fund. Otherwise, exchange rate movements were to be confined to a margin of 1 percent on either side of the declared parity. The concept of "fundamental disequilibrium" was central to the working of the system. A member was not allowed to propose a change in the par value of its currency without the need to correct a "fun-

damental disequilibrium." The term was not explicitly defined, and the Fund reviewed proposals on a case-by-case basis, allowing for significant flexibility in interpretation. The breakdown of the Bretton Woods par value system in 1971 led to a generalized system of floating exchange rates by 1973. A fundamental disagreement rapidly emerged (and still exists) among countries as to whether currencies should float freely (mainly the U.S. view) or the exchange rate should be influenced by central bank intervention (mainly the European view).

Despite ideological differences, two notable examples of international monetary cooperation and planning among the industrial countries occurred among the Group of Seven industrialized countries (Canada, France, Germany, Italy, Japan, the United Kingdom, and the United States) in 1985 and 1987: the Plaza Accord and the Louvre Accord, respectively. In the Plaza Accord, the Group of Seven agreed to cooperate in reducing the value of the dollar. At the Louvre Accord, they agreed to cooperate to foster stability around current currency levels at the time. Both accords involved significant central bank intervention and coordination in foreign exchange markets and monetary policy.

1947–1966: Building an Institution

On September 27, 1947, the first joint annual meeting of the Board of Governors of the IMF and the World Bank Board of Governors opened in Washington, DC. On December 18, 1946, initial par values of exchange rates to the U.S. dollar were agreed for most members. On March 1, 1947, the IMF began financial operations. France was the first member country to draw financial resources from the Fund when it received $25 million on May 8, 1947. On February 13, 1952, the Fund codified its policies on the use of its resources, establishing the tranche policies. The Fund also developed a general framework for the use of its financial resources in "standby arrangements." The Fund's first standby arrangement was with Belgium on June 19, 1952, which was followed by arrangements with France and the United Kingdom in 1956. Also in 1952 the Fund began to have annual consultations with members maintaining exchange restrictions, as directed by Article XIV. Exchange restrictions were in place until December 29, 1959, when fourteen Western European countries made their currencies externally convertible for current transactions. This was the first major step toward an open multilateral trading system. In 1961, nine more West European countries joined convertibility, resulting in all major currencies being convertible.

In 1959, the first increase in Fund quotas became effective, raising total quotas from $9.2 billion to $14 billion. In 1962, the General Agreements to Borrow went into effect. Under these agreements, the ten largest industrial members, plus Switzerland, agreed to lend the IMF the equivalent of $6 billion immediately if called for to prevent a disruption of the international payments system. The arrangements inspired the formation of the Group of Ten. In 1963, the compensatory financing facility was established to allow members with temporary shortfalls in their export earnings to draw on the Fund's resources. Oil facilities, the buffer stock financing facility, the emergency assistance facility, and the structural adjustment facility were established later.

On September 27, 1963, in his opening address to the annual meeting, Managing Director Pierre-Paul Schweitzer of France announced the IMF's intention to become involved in international liquidity of the monetary system. This was a contradiction of the Group of Ten's efforts to make international liquidity a matter of concern only to the industrial nations and to limit any scheme for reserve creation to those countries. Six months later, on March 3, 1964, the IMF proposed the creation of a new reserve asset through the IMF. This proposal produced the Special Drawing Right (SDR) scheme three years later. In 1966, a second increase to IMF quotas was approved at 25 percent for each member, with special additional increases for sixteen members. The second wave of quota increases brought total available financing by the Fund to $21 billion.

1967–1979: Turbulent Times

In the late 1960s and for most of the next decade, the Fund oversaw the end of the international monetary order set up at Bretton Woods, attempted to reduce the effects of severe exchange rate crises, and saw a vastly increased membership as a result of the decolonization movement. Together, these events produced a substantial increase in the use of Fund resources as well as new policies governing their use. They also led to the First Amendment to the Articles of Agreement, to the SDR, and to new responsibilities and activities in technical assistance and training. In 1974, recognizing that the era of fixed exchange rates was over, the IMF produced its "Guidelines for the Management of Floating Exchange Rates."

The growing liquidity problems in the international monetary system were becoming evident in the mid-1960s. In an attempt to address the issue and alleviate pressures in the system, the Fund sought the creation of a new reserve asset, and it was agreed that the executive directors of the Fund, representing all Fund members, would hold a series of meetings with deputies of the Group of Ten to discuss reserve creation schemes. The initial meetings, which took place in Washington, DC, from November 28 to 30, 1966, brought representatives of less developed countries face to face with their counterparts from the industrial countries for the first time in discussing problems of international liquidity, bringing the IMF a step closer to the creation of a universal reserve scheme. A second meeting took place from January 25 to 26, 1967, in London, where delegates began to seriously consider a plan based on SDRs. The executive directors and deputies of the Group of Ten met two more times in 1967, from April 25 to 26 and from June 19 to 21. On August 26, the Group of Ten met in London and agreed on voting majorities and reconstitution provisions for an SDR facility.

In 1968, a two-tiered market for gold was established as a result of a decision by the central banks from seven industrial nations to buy and sell gold at the official price of $35 an ounce only in transactions with monetary authorities. Private transactions in gold were left to be determined by market forces. This marked the beginning of the end of the par value system of exchange rates based on gold. From June 4 through June 19, 1968, heavy use was made of the Fund's financial resources when France drew $645 million and the United Kingdom drew $1.4 billion under a standby arrangement approved in November 1967 under what many viewed as favorable terms. On September 20, 1968, executive directors representing the developing countries successfully pressed for the adoption of guidelines that would ensure uniform and equitable treatment for all members in the use of the Fund's financial resources.

On June 20, 1969, a new standby arrangement was approved for the United Kingdom for $1 billion. A few weeks later, on August 10, France devalued the franc by 11 percent and drew on a new standby arrangement for $985 million a month later. In the face of persistent balance of payments surpluses, in September the Federal Republic of Germany allowed the deutsche mark to float, but a month later it ended the float and revalued the currency by 8.39 percent. The Special Drawing Right Account was established that same year, setting the stage for a distribution of SDRs in 1970–1972. On October 2, 1969, the IMF Board of Governors approved the allocation of SDR 9.3 million to 104 participants over a period of three years beginning January 1, 1970. The United States was the largest participant, receiving an allocation of SDR 867 million. Botswana was the smallest, receiving SDR 504,000.

In 1970, a third general increase in quotas was approved, raising total quotas by 36 percent to $28.9 billion. On November 25 of that year, the International Tin Agreement became the first commodity agreement for which use

of the buffer stock financing facility was authorized. From May 9 to 11, 1971, in the face of heavy capital movements, the Federal Republic of Germany and the Netherlands allowed their currencies to float. Austria revalued its currency, and Belgium and Luxembourg enlarged their free trade market for capital transactions. On July 16, 1971, the first purchases under the buffer stock financing facility were made by Bolivia and Indonesia.

On August 15, 1971, the United States announced that it would no longer freely buy and sell gold for the settlement of international transactions, thus suspending the convertibility of the dollar held by official institutions. The announcement in effect ended the Bretton Woods system. For the next four months, global exchange rates were in total disarray, with Fund members introducing various exchange rate arrangements, including free-floating rates. There was an attempt to maintain a fixed rate system for another eighteen months under the Smithsonian Agreement. On December 17–18, 1971, the Group of Ten concluded the Smithsonian Agreement, providing for the realignment of the major currencies and an increase in the official price of gold from $35 to $38 an ounce. It was the first time that exchange rates had been negotiated at an international conference. As part of the Smithsonian Agreement, the IMF formally established a temporary regime of central rates and wider margins set at 2.25 percent on either side of an established central rate, thereby providing for an overall margin of 4.5 percent.

On March 20, 1972, the IMF Board of Governors authorized the Fund to express its accounts in terms of the SDR instead of U.S. dollars. On April 24, the exchange rate mechanism of the European Monetary System went into effect for six currencies, limiting margins to 2.25 percent, half the margin established under the Fund's temporary regime of central rates—the so-called "snake-in-the-tunnel." On June 23, the United Kingdom floated the pound sterling. This was the first break in the pattern of rates established by the Smithsonian Agreement. Switzerland floated the Swiss franc on January 23, 1973, and on March 19 of that year, the European Community countries introduced a joint float for their currencies against the U.S. dollar. This marked the beginning of generalized floating and the end of the attempt to maintain an international system of fixed exchange rates.

Between July 1972 and June 1974, several meetings were held by the Committee of Twenty (or the Committee of the Board of Governors on Reform of the International Monetary System and Related Issues) to reform the international monetary system. The Committee of Twenty produced an Outline of Reform but was not successful in implementing full-scale reform. In 1973, the first oil crisis hit as the six members of the Organization of Petroleum Exporting Countries (OPEC) increased prices for crude oil dramatically. The disruption to the world economy made any agreement on international monetary reform difficult. However, the committee agreed on a number of important points, such as an oil facility and medium-term assistance to developing countries. On August 22, 1974, the first use was made of the IMF's oil facility, and on September 13, 1974, an extended facility was established to give medium-term financing assistance to developing countries with terms of up to ten years in order to address structural changes in their economies (such as an oil price rise). In 1975, the United Kingdom drew SDR 1 billion under the oil facility, and in 1977 the IMF approved a two-year standby arrangement for the United Kingdom for SDR 3.36 billion—the largest amount ever approved.

To address developmental and structural issues within the developing world, IMF members agreed in 1975 to sell one-sixth of the IMF's gold (or 25 million ounces) for the benefit of developing members through the establishment of a Trust Fund. It also agreed to return one-sixth of the Fund's gold to all members, sold at the official price of SDR 35 an ounce, in proportion to their quotas. This process was completed in stages by 1980. In 1977,

the first Trust Fund loans were made to twelve member nations. The Trust Fund was later folded into the structural adjustment facility and other programs.

1980–1990: New Direction

The 1980s showed a marked turn in the IMF toward financing the needs of less developed countries. In 1981, the Executive Board introduced a policy of "enlarged access." Under the new policy, the Fund could approve standby or extended arrangements for up to 150 percent of a member's new quota each year, for a period of three years, with a cumulative limit of 600 percent of quota. To make this enlarged access operative, the Executive Board authorized the managing director to borrow from the Saudi Arabian Monetary Agency. The Fund concluded an agreement for up to SDR 12 billion over a six-year period. At the same time, the compensatory financing facility was amended to cover financing to members that encountered balance of payments difficulties caused by an excessive rise in the cost of cereal imports that were largely beyond the control of the member. The amendment was expected to be of particular benefit to low-income countries.

On December 23, 1982, the Fund approved a three-year extended arrangement for Mexico of SDR 3.6 billion to support a medium-term adjustment program. The Group of Ten agreed to a major enlargement of the General Agreements to Borrow, from SDR 6.4 billion to SDR 17 billion, in January 1983, with additional lenders and revisions in its terms to allow all members to draw on the Fund. The same month, the Fund approved a standby arrangement and compensatory financing for Argentina totaling SDR 2 billion, and another SDR 1.7 billion in December 1984. The Fund approved an extended arrangement for Brazil for SDR 5 billion in February 1983. The same month, an increase in quotas was recommended to enlarge total Fund quotas from SDR 61 billion to SDR 90 billion. In May 1984, the Fund entered into a borrowing arrangement with Saudi Arabia for a maximum of SDR 1.5

billion. It also concluded four new short-term borrowing agreements that year totaling SDR 6 billion with the Saudi Arabian Monetary Agency, the Bank for International Settlements, Japan, and the National Bank of Belgium.

1991–2001: Increasing Criticism

In 1990, the managing director of the IMF, for the first time, outlined a timetable for dealing with members having overdue obligations to the Fund. This timetable included compulsory withdrawal from the Fund up to two years after the emergence of arrears. The Executive Board then adopted the "rights" approach to overdue obligations. A member in arrears to the Fund would be able to earn rights conditioned on a satisfactory performance under an adjustment program monitored by the Fund. This process would lead to a disbursement by the Fund once the member's overdue obligations had been cleared and upon approval of a successor arrangement by the Fund. In 1992, a Third Amendment to the Articles of Agreement provided for the removal of voting rights of "ineli-gible members," and the Fund terminated the "enlarged access" policy in effect since 1981 under which the Fund supplemented its quota resources with borrowed funds. Through various quota increases, Fund resources had now grown to SDR 145 billion ($200 billion).

Anastasia Xenias

See Also Balance of Payments and Capital Flows; Currency Crisis and Contagion; Exchange Rate Movements; Inequality; International Financial Markets; International Indebtedness; Asia Pacific Economic Cooperation (APEC); International Bank for Reconstruction and Development (IBRD)

References

Cooper, Richard. 1975. "Prolegomena to the Choice of an International Monetary System." *International Organization* 29, no. 1: 63–97.

———. 1987. *The International Monetary System: Essays in World Economics.* Cambridge: MIT Press.

Humphreys, Norman K. 1993. *Historical Dictionary of the International Monetary Fund.* Metuchen, NJ: Scarecrow.

Latin American Free Trade Association (LAFTA)

Organizing the Americas into a regional free trade area has a long history. The vision of regional integration across all of Latin America can be traced back to Simon Bolivar and the nineteenth century. In more modern times, two waves of integration have encompassed the region as a whole. The first culminated in the mid–twentieth century with the creation of the Latin American Free Trade Area (LAFTA); the second began in the 1990s with the initiative to create a Free Trade Area of the Americas that would encompass Latin America, the United States, and Canada.

The Era of Regional Integration

Economic integration became popular in Latin America in the 1950s and 1960s, spearheaded by the United Nations Economic Commission for Latin America and the Caribbean (ECLAC), then under the leadership of Secretary General Raul Prebisch. Prebisch was a staunch advocate of regional economic integration and import-substitution industrialization as a method of economic development. With the encouragement of ECLAC, a number of regional initiatives took shape in Latin America during this period encompassing small groups of countries (the Central American Common Market, the Andean Group, and Mercosur). These regional groupings survived and to varying degrees flourished into the twenty-first century. There was also an attempt at a free trade area that would encompass all of Latin America that preceded and in some cases gave rise to the smaller regional groupings. In 1960, the Latin American Free Trade Association was created by Argentina, Brazil, Chile, Mexico, Paraguay, Peru, and Uruguay with the Treaty of Montevideo. This group was later joined by Bolivia, Colombia, Ecuador, and Venezuela. A highly ambitious program, LAFTA covered 90 percent of the entire area, population, and gross national product (GNP) of Latin America.

From April 12 to 14, 1967, the Organization of American States (OAS) sponsored a meeting of the heads of state of Latin American countries and the United States at Punta del Este, Uruguay. At that meeting, the heads of state of the Western Hemisphere approved the Declaration of the Presidents of America (or the "Punta del Este Declaration"), an agreement that committed the countries of Latin America, supported by the United States, to proceed in launching a region-wide Latin American Common Market (LACM). The LACM was to be created beginning in 1970 and be "substantially in operation a period of no more than fifteen years." The goal was to turn all of Latin America into a single economy no later than 1985. The declaration received full approval from all OAS members (all countries of Latin America except Cuba plus the United States). According to the Punta del Este Declaration, the LACM would be "based on the complete development and progressive convergence of the Latin American Free Trade Association and of the Central American Common Market taking into account the interests of the Latin American countries not yet affiliated with these systems. . . . We will join in efforts to increase substantially Latin American foreign trade earnings."

In August 1967, at the annual meeting of LAFTA's Council of Ministers in Asunción, the first major attempt at implementation of the LACM, negotiations stalled. Problems encountered were attributable to the large differences in economic development of the member countries and the related conflicts of interest that ensued. The economies of Latin America varied widely in terms of industrialization, market size, transportation and communication infrastructure, and standard of living. The major concern was that economic integration might actually intensify, rather than resolve, existing inequalities. The seventh annual conference of LAFTA later in 1967 encountered similar negotiating difficulties on the inclusion of wheat and petroleum (which accounted for over 25 percent of intra-LAFTA trade).

LAFTA cut tariffs on about 7,500 items in its first two years, but after that initial burst of enthusiasm, negotiations became more difficult, and LAFTA's goal of eventual free trade became increasingly unrealistic. The main reason for the slowdown in tariff reductions was a lack of commitment to integration largely due to disparate levels of industrial development. Momentum for action on recommendations for tariff concessions slowed, and the number of concessions actually approved from among those recommended began to steadily decrease. Agricultural and metal products, which accounted for 70 percent of intra-LAFTA trade, proved the most difficult to provide concessions for, whereas manufactures (primarily chemicals, equipment, and machinery), accounting for only 20 percent of intra-LAFTA trade, provided over half of all concessions. Despite stated intentions to attain the opposite results, there were indications that LAFTA was promoting uneven development. Accumulating data showed that trade advantage was moving in favor of the more developed countries at the expense of the less developed ones.

There were also structural impediments to integration. The Punta del Este Declaration affirmed the need to "lay the physical foundations for a Latin American economic integration through multinational projects in transportation, telecommunications and power, and border regions." However, transportation and communications facilities were generally inadequate to promote regional integration and trade. Physical obstacles rooted in geography, such as vast distances, mountainous terrain, and dense jungles, entailed large financial investments overwhelming for most countries. Financial challenges such as access to capital, settlement of accounts, inflation, and currency instability added to problems in advancing integration. Moreover, Latin American countries traditionally relied heavily on customs receipts for government revenue. Reducing tariff barriers under regional integration had the effect of depriving governments of less developed countries of important sources of income that could otherwise be used for development projects.

Some financial assistance for regional integration was provided by the Inter-American Development Bank (IDB). The IDB was formed in 1959 at the initiative of Latin American countries to be the region's primary multicultural resource for channeling financial and technical resources to individual countries as well as the region. Colloquially, the IDB was referred to as the "Bank for Integration." The IDB sought to alleviate some of the structural impediments that were obstacles to integration, and it continues to support economic and social development and regional integration in Latin America and the Caribbean through loans to public institutions and private projects. IDB financing is typically in infrastructure and capital markets development, although a wide variety of projects have been funded. Headquartered in Washington, DC, it is owned by twenty-six borrowing member countries in Latin America and the Caribbean and twenty creditor industrialized countries. In 1965, the IDB added the Institute for Latin American Integration to its operations to carry out research, training, and advisory activities, and in 1966 it added the Pre-investment Fund for Latin American Integration to arrange and finance feasibility studies related to multinational integration projects. The IDB's many funded projects could not sufficiently address the problems of divergent development and structural impediments to regional economic integration, although the situation has significantly improved over the forty-five years of its operations.

New Efforts at Pan-American Free Trade

The initiative for a Free Trade Area of the Americas began in the 1990s. On June 27, 1990, U.S. President George H. W. Bush spoke in favor of a free trade zone for North and South America. In December 1994, President Bill Clinton hosted the Miami Initiative for the American hemispheric free trade conference of all thirty-four states in the Americas except Cuba. At the same time, a new, smaller regional trade area was negotiated. The debate on the free trade area of the United States, Canada, and Mexico was concluded in 1993, and the North American Free Trade Agreement (NAFTA) was established on January 1, 1994. In 1996, the second hemispheric meeting of the trade ministers of the Americas added further momentum to the Free Trade Area of the Americas (FTAA) movement. Four ministerial meetings took place during this preparatory phase: the first was in June 1995 in Denver; the second in March 1996 in Cartagena, Colombia; the third in May 1997 in Belo Horizonte, Brazil; and the fourth in March 1998 in San Jose, Costa Rica. Formal negotiations were launched at the Second Summit of the Americas in Santiago, Chile, in April 1998. Annual ministerial meetings followed in Toronto in 1999 and Buenos Aires in 2000.

The Third Summit of the Americas took place in Quebec, Canada, in April 2001. At this meeting, the heads of state and government endorsed the decision of the ministers to prepare a first draft of an FTAA agreement in all four official languages (English, Spanish, Portuguese, and French) to be available to the public on the Internet. This task was completed on July 3, 2001 (see http://www.ftaa-alca.org). FTAA negotiations saw several meetings from 2001 to 2003. However, difficulties in reconciling the positions, mainly of the United States and Brazil, the cochairs and two main partners in the effort, resulted in stalled pan-American efforts and renewed interest by the United States in smaller agreements, such as the Central American Free Trade Area (CAFTA).

The differences that stalled the talks were similar to concerns of past efforts, which divided more developed and less developed nations in the Americas. Some countries, led by Brazil, wanted to exclude areas such as copyright and patent protection, investment, and government procurement. The United States wanted to exclude agricultural subsidies. The broader concern was that the FTAA not produce large benefits to the most developed states (especially the United States) to the detriment of the less developed ones. Though efforts to create an FTAA have slowed, the long history of attempts at a pan-American free trade area indicate that the initiative is likely to resurface in the future.

Anastasia Xenias

See Also Economic Integration; Andean Community; Common Market of the South (Mercosur); North American Free Trade Agreement (NAFTA)

References

Bouzas, Roberto, and Jaime Ros. 1994. *Economic Integration in the Western Hemisphere.* Notre Dame, IN: University of Notre Dame Press.

Dell, Sidney. 1966. *A Latin American Common Market?* New York: Oxford University Press.

Dorn, James A., and Roberto Salinas-León, eds. 1996. *Money and Markets in the Americas: New Challenges for Hemispheric Integration.* Studies on the Economic Future of the Western Hemisphere. Vancouver: Fraser Institute.

Hilton, Ronald, ed. 1969. *The Movement toward Latin American Unity.* New York: Praeger.

Prebisch, Raul. 1959. "The Role of Commercial Policies in Underdeveloped Countries." *American Economic Review,* papers and proceedings, May.

United Nations. 1963. *Toward a Dynamic Development Policy for Latin America.* New York: United Nations.

United Nations Conference on Trade and Development. 1964. "I: Final Act and Report." New York: United Nations.

Urquidi, Victor. 1962. *Free Trade and Economic Integration in Latin America.* Berkeley: University of California Press.

Wionczek, Miguel S. 1965. *Latin American Free Trade Association.* New York: Carnegie Endowment for International Peace.

League of Arab States (LAS)

The League of Arab States (LAS), known informally as the Arab League, was established in 1945 and is considered the first initiative for regional organization in the twentieth century. The United Nations Charter was signed on June 26, 1945, whereas the LAS Charter was signed on March 22, 1945. The Organisation for European Economic Co-operation (OEEC), the forerunner to the Organisation for Economic Co-operation and Development (OECD), was launched in 1948.

The countries making up the LAS had a total population of 270 million in 1999 and covered an area of about 14 million square kilometers (5.4 million square miles). The strength of the league lies in the geographical and economic position of its member states. The LAS aims to bring the Arab nations into an independent unit that can have a significant influence in world affairs. From the seven founding countries, it has grown to include twenty-two member states.

Historical Overview

Arab thinkers have supported the idea of Arab unity since the eighteenth century. The concept gained popularity especially during the period from 1839 to 1897, when it was promoted by Mohammad Abdo and Gamal El-Din Al-Afghany. The desire for Arab unity intensified and grew over the years that followed. Political and economic barriers, particularly arising from colonialism, however, prevented these hopes from becoming reality. World War I–era efforts were frustrated by the Treaty of Sevres in 1920, which divided the Arab region into twenty-five separate entities, mostly under British and French domination. The idea of Arab unity was given new impetus by Britain, however, during World War II.

The first real steps toward Arab unity and the establishment of the League of Arab States took place in 1944 as many Arab countries were gaining their independence. Seven countries attended the Alexandria Conference in September to lay the groundwork for the LAS: Egypt, Iraq, Lebanon, Saudi Arabia, Syria, Transjordan (now Jordan), and Yemen, the organization's founding members.

In July of the same year, a preparatory committee had been charged with the task of arranging a General Arab Conference. The results of the conference confirmed the dynastic and nationalistic rivalries impeding unification or federation of the Arab states and testified as well to the growing influence of Egypt in the region. The Alexandria Protocol issued at the close of the conference made vague allusions to the possibility of eventual Arab unity but basically envisaged a loose grouping of states that would restrict its activities to the economic, cultural, and social spheres with respect to collective security; it was mentioned that the proposed organization of Arab states should deal with conflicts of an intra-Arab nature, coordinate the Arab states' "political plans," and safeguard their sovereignty.

The Alexandria Conference finished its work in October after issuing the Alexandria Protocol. The protocol set out Arab perspectives on the League of Arab States, opportunities for its establishment, and the benefits and advantages the Arab countries could gain from such an organization. In March 1945, the seven founding members signed the final version of the LAS Charter in Cairo, officially launching the regional organization and taking Cairo as its headquarters.

Charter of the LAS

The LAS Charter includes twenty articles and the three annexes. The first annex discusses Palestine, and the second annex addresses cooperation with Arab states that are not LAS member states. The principles contained in the second annex have not, however, always been carried out as envisioned. The last annex established the appointment of Abdel Rahman Azzam as the first secretary general of the league.

According to the charter's articles, any independent Arab state has the right to join the League of Arab States. The league is to act as a mediator in disputes between members or between a member state and a nonmember state. Other articles deal with the duties of the secretary general, the functions of the League Council, preparation of the LAS budget, and so on. The charter also established a mechanism to amend the charter, which is by a two-thirds vote of the member states.

The purposes of the League of Arab States are also enumerated in the charter. They include strengthening relations between and among member states, coordinating their policies in order to further cooperation and to safeguard their independence and sovereignty, and engaging in other activities that arise out of a general concern for the affairs and interests of the Arab countries. Four principles are to govern the league, namely, nonintervention in the policies of member states, equality among member states, peaceful resolution of conflicts, and mutual support.

Principal Organs

The League of Arab States consists of three main organs: the League Council, the Arab Specialized Organizations (which replaced the earlier Permanent Committees), and the General Secretariat. Some additional bodies were established by resolution of the League Council to promote the Joint Arab Defense Treaty in 1950. Arab Unions were established at the founding of the LAS to deal with labor and industrial concerns.

The League Council, the supreme authority of the Arab League, has representatives from all LAS member states. The council determines how to implement agreements ratified by the member states, works to reduce or prevent actual or expected aggression against any member state, attempts to ensure peaceful settlement of conflicts, establishes channels of cooperation with international organizations, appoints the secretary general of the LAS, determines the budget, and lays down the basic internal statutes of the council and the other bodies within the LAS.

The Permanent Committees dealt with all forms of cooperation between and among member states. Committees established included the Political Committee, the Cultural Committee, the Transportation Committee, and the Social Committee, all established in 1946; the Economy Committee, established in 1945; the Law Committee, established in 1947, in part to deal with issues concerning visas and passports; and the Military Committee, the Health Committee, the Arab Media Committee, the Petrol Exports Committee, the Arab Committee for Human Rights, and the Finance and Administrative Affairs Committee, established in 1971. Because of the large role these committees played and their many duties, they were replaced by the Arab Specialized Organizations.

Eighteen Arab Specialized Organizations were established: the Arab States Broadcasting Union; the Arab League Educational, Cultural and Scientific Organization; the Arab Center for the Study of Arid Zones; the Arab Organization for Agricultural Development; the Arab Industrial Development and Mining Organization; the Arab Administrative Organization; the Arab Labor Organization; the Arab Atomic Energy Board; the Arab Interior Ministers Council; the Arab Satellite Communications Organization; the Arab Civil Aviation Association; the Council of Arab Economic Unity; the Organization of Arab Petroleum Exporting Countries; the Arab Academy for Science and Technology; the Inter-Arab Investment Guarantee Corporation; the Arab Monetary Fund; the Arab Fund for Economic and Social Development; the Arab Bank for Economic Development in Africa; and the Arab Authority for Agriculture, Agricultural Investment and Development.

There are twenty-three Arab Unions: the Arab Association of Medical and Drug Equipment Manufactures; the Arab Association of Fish Producers; the Arab Association of Cement and Construction Materials; the Arab Association of Leather Works; the Arab Association of Iron and Steel; the Arab Association of Railroad Authorities; the Arab Association of Food Industries; the Arab Association of Maritime and Port Authorities; the Arab Association of Chemical Fertilizer Producers; the Arab Association of Maritime Carriers; the Arab Association of Textile Industries; the Arab Over-Land Transport Association; the Arab Association of Engineering Industries; the Arab Association of Printing and Paper Industries; the Arab Association of Air Transport; the Arab Association of International Airports; the Arab Banks Association; the Arab Association of Electric Power Producers and Distributors; the Arab Insurance Association; the Arab Association of Commerce, Industry and Agriculture; the Arab Accountants Association; the Arab Association of Accountants and Auditors; and the Arab Engineering Association.

The secretary general and assistant secretary general are appointed by a two-thirds majority of the votes of the member states for five-year renewable terms. From the founding of the LAS in 1945 to the present, six secretaries general have been appointed: Abdul Rahman Azzam, Mohamed Abdul Khalek Hassouna, Mohamed Riyad, Al-Shazly Al-Kaleiby, Esmat Abdul Maguid, and Amre Moussa. Amre Moussa, the present secretary general, was appointed in 2001.

The secretary general has a variety of responsibilities, including administrative, technical, and political duties. He determines the dates of Arab League Council sessions, organizes related secretarial work, prepares the Arab League budget, speaks on behalf of the league, attends to League Council matters and other matters concerning the member states, and attends the League Council sessions.

The league's headquarters were moved from Cairo to Tunis in 1979, when Egypt's membership in the LAS was suspended as a result of its peace treaty with Israel, signed that year by Egyptian President Anwar al-Sadat and Israeli Prime Minister Menachem Begin. Arab leaders renewed diplomatic ties with Egypt in 1987; it was readmitted to the league in 1989. Cairo again became the site of LAS headquarters, though some Specialized Organizations remained in Tunis.

In addition to the seven founding member states (Egypt, Iraq, Jordan, Lebanon, Saudi Arabia, Syria, Yemen), there are now fifteen additional member states: Algeria, Bahrain, Comoros, Djibouti, Kuwait, Libya, Mauritania, Morocco, Oman, Palestine, Qatar, Somalia, Sudan, Tunisia, and the United Arab Emirates.

Before 2000, the LAS held Arab Summit meetings upon request by member states or in response to other needs that arose. The Cairo Summit, held in October 2000, adopted a resolution to hold regular conventions to discuss economic and other issues. Arab leaders are confident that these periodic conventions will play an active role in consolidating and enhancing joint Arab actions in all spheres, especially those affecting economics.

The first Arab Summit was held in Cairo in January 1964 to address a dispute with Israel over diversion of the Jordan River. The second summit was held in Alexandria in September of the same year.

Programs and Activities

The LAS plays a multidimensional role as its activities cover a variety of fields and interests, including economic affairs, conflict management, cultural and educational affairs, mass communications and the media, dialogue between and among cultures and peoples, Arab African cooperation, and human rights. These activities have involved the LAS in cultural exchange programs, youth and sports programs, programs pertaining to the role of women in Arab societies, and child welfare programs.

The LAS has played an important role in several areas of Arab development: In its early years, it took part in efforts by Arab countries to gain independence, especially in consolidating the liberation movements in Algeria, Oman, South Yemen (before Yemen unity), and Sudan. It also has advanced the peaceful settlement of intra-Arab conflicts, such as the Egyptian-Sudanese conflict in 1958, the Moroccan-Algerian conflict in 1963, and the Yemeni-Yemeni conflict in 1987. It has promoted Arab-Arab cooperation in the Specialized Organizations, and it has represented the Arab countries in various international organizations, such as the United Nations and the African Union (the organization that replaced the Organization of African Unity in 2002).

In summit conferences, the LAS has affirmed the importance of dealing with the main issues confronting Arab states: the ongoing Arab-Israeli conflict, nonproliferation of weapons, Arab consolidation, Emirates island occupation, water issues, the Iraqi-Kuwaiti problem, Arab-Chinese relations, and Arab-African relations. From its first phases, it has made the Arab-Israeli conflict a top priority, as demonstrated by the annex in the LAS Charter dealing with Palestine and the fact that it held its first Arab Summit in response to problems

with Israel over diversion of the Jordan River. The variety of areas covered by the Arab Specialized Organizations also demonstrate the organization's relevance to current affairs affecting the region.

Cooperation between the LAS and the UN

Cooperation between the LAS and United Nations was initially a manifestation of the league's emphasis on a functional approach to peace and regional security. The founders of the Arab League understood the significance of fruitful mutual cooperation with the United Nations, especially in the economic, social, and cultural realms. This cooperation is in the context of adherence to the principles and purposes of the UN Charter for the benefit of the region and the member states.

Both the UN Charter and the LAS Charter assured the cooperation between the two organizations. The cooperation has taken place in a variety of ways—for example, through consultations and exchanges of information, through followup action on proposals agreed to at general meetings between the UN system and the League of Arab States, through programs and specialized organizations such as the UN Development Programme (UNDP), and through the league's associated agencies on specific initiatives. The two organizations together have implemented programs to combat desertification and increase the green area of the LAS region, to combat industrial pollution, to promote environmental education, to conserve the biodiversity of the region, and to establish a network of environmental information.

The LAS has cooperated with the UN Population Fund through its population research unit, a permanent structure of the league. The league's cooperation with the United Nations Relief and Works Agency (UNRWA) for Palestine Refugees in the Near East has been very close, as the latter has benefited from the league's support for its program and its efforts to urge member states to increase voluntary contributions to UNRWA's budget.

There has also been cooperation between the United Nations Industrial Development Organization (UNIDO) and the league's Arab Industrial Development and Mining Organization (AIDMO). Moreover, the League of Arab States has some cooperative programs with the United Nations Environmental Programme, the World Health Organization (WHO), and the International Monetary Fund (IMF). In 1995, the World Bank joined the dialogue, initiated by the league in Cairo, on ways to mount joint activities in the region.

Nilly Kamal El-Amir

See Also Economic Integration; Council of Arab Economic Unity (CAEU); Gulf Cooperation Council (GCC)

References

Abdel-Maguid, Esmat. 2003. *Situations and Challenges of the Arab World.* Cairo: Dar-El-Sherouk.

Al-Ibraheemy, Al-Akhdar. 2003. *The Arab Diplomacy in a Changing World.* Beirut: Center for Arab Unity Studies.

Ghali, Boutros. 1977. *The League of Arab States and Arab Conflicts Management.* Cairo: Arab Researches and Studies Institute.

Helal, Aley El-Din, and Nivine Mosaad. 2000. *Arab Political System: Causes of Continuation and Change.* Beirut: Center for Arab Unity Studies.

Macdonald, Robert. 1965. *The League of Arab States: A Study in the Dynamics of Regional Organization.* Princeton, NJ: Princeton University Press.

Matar, Gamil. 1993. *League of Arab States: The Historic Experience and Development Projects.* Cairo: Arab Center for Development and Future Studies, and Center for Political Researches and Studies.

Matar, Gamil, and Aley El-Din Helal. 1988. *The Arab Regional Regime: A Study on Arab Political Relations.* Beirut: Center for Arab Unity Studies.

Mekky, Youssif. 2003. *Causes of Arab Nationalism Failure.* Beirut : Center for Arab Unity Studies.

Mozahem, Ghassan. 1976. *The Arab Specialized Organizations at the League of Arab States.* Cairo: Arab Researches and Studies Institute.

Sarhan, Abdel Aziz. 1976. *The Principles of the International Organization.* Cairo: Dar El-Nahda.

Shalabi, Ibrahim. 1992. *International Organization: The International Regional and Specialized Organizations.* Beirut: El-Dar El-Gamaa.

Shehab, Mofid. 1978. *League of Arab States, Charter and Accomplishments.* Cairo: Arab Researches and Studies Institute.

———. 1978. *The International Organization.* Cairo: Dar El-Nahda.

Youssif, Ahmed. 2001. "Amman Summit and the Arab League Development: A Competitive Criticizing Vision." *Arab Affairs,* no. 106 (June): 15–22.

Youssry, Ahmed. 1999. "Development of Institutions in the Escwa Region." Pp. 135–176 in Riyadh Tabbara, ed, *Escwa and Social Developments.* Beirut: Economic and Social Council for West Asia.

Zacher, Mark. 1979. *International Conflicts and Collective Security, 1946–1977: The United Nations, Organization of American States, Organization of African Unity and Arab League.* New York: Praeger.

North American Free Trade Agreement (NAFTA)

The purpose of the North American Free Trade Agreement (NAFTA) is to remove most barriers to trade and investment between Canada, Mexico, and the United States by January 1, 2008. Formal trade negotiations began on June 12, 1991, in Toronto, and ended on August 12, 1993, in Ottawa. In addition, two side agreements on labor and the environment were negotiated between March and August 1993 and implemented parallel to NAFTA. NAFTA was ratified by the Canadian Parliament on June 23; by the U.S. Congress on November 20; and by the Mexican Senate on November 23, 1993. It entered into force on January 1, 1994.

The NAFTA Negotiations

One of the challenges in negotiating the agreement had to do with the fact that NAFTA was the first free trade agreement between a developing country on one side and two industrialized countries on the other (Robert 2000; Cameron and Tomlin 2000). Another challenge arose from the asymmetry in terms of country size: The economies of Canada and Mexico are relatively small, whereas the U.S. economy is the largest in the world. Negotiation outcome has two determinants: structure (that is, power) and process (Robert 2000). Power is typically a function of resources, a fact that tends to favor larger and richer economies in international negotiations. However, in explaining success in negotiations, overall or aggregate resources appear to be less important than issue-specific power—that is, the amount of resources a country is willing to dedicate to a specific issue that is being negotiated. The concept of issue-specific power can explain why smaller countries may be able to "win" in trade negotiations with larger countries where winning is defined as "achieving a preferred outcome" (ibid., 7). By focusing their limited resources on a specific issue of great national importance, smaller countries can outspend larger ones whose governments spread their resources more evenly over a wide range of issues. Furthermore, it is possible that power is issue-specific and does not translate easily from one area to another (Keohane and Nye 1989). A powerful country able to win the "cold war," for example, may not be as successful in the "war on drugs."

The second important factor in explaining negotiation outcome is process. Process encompasses two components—bargaining skills and use of tactics. These components constitute a type of resource known as behavioral resources, which differ from economic resources in one important dimension: Whereas the latter are static, at least in the short run, the former are dynamic. Judging from four case studies of contentious NAFTA issues, Maryse Robert (2000, 21) concluded that small countries can "win" in negotiations if they have "both issue-specific power and strong tactics." He showed that Canada "won" on the issues of *culture,* where the country sought exemptions similar to the ones granted in the Canada-U.S. Free Trade Area (CUSFTA), and on *automotives,* where Canada fought successfully for a new rule of origin and its retroactive application. In contrast, Canada "lost" in the case of the pharmaceutical industry, by agreeing to abolish its system of compulsory licensing, and in the case of the textile and apparel industry, where Canada accepted more restrictive rules of origin than existed under the CUSFTA.

The Content of NAFTA

NAFTA is divided into twenty-two chapters followed by seven annexes. It covers seven major issues: trade in goods, including rules of origin (chapters 3 to 7, 7A, and 8); trade in services (chapters 12 to 14); standards (chapters 7B and 9); government procurement (chapter 10); foreign investment (chapter 11); intellectual property rights (chapter 17); and dispute settlement (chapters 18 to 20). The agreement also contains stipulations on competition policy (chapter 15), temporary visas for business persons (chapter 16), and exceptions (chapter 21).

With regard to goods trade, the agreement stipulates that barriers must be eliminated for some products immediately, and for others over a five-, ten-, or fifteen-year schedule. However, only goods produced predominantly within North America are tariff-exempt. To fall into this category, a product must have 60 percent North American content (62.5 percent for vehicles). Whether a product meets this requirement is determined by precise rules of origin, and the process of obtaining this status is known as "NAFTA certification." Though the above specifications are generic, there are a number of industry-specific regulations and exemptions. With regard to trade in energy and related products, proportional export restrictions apply to the United States and Canada but not to Mexico. For example, if—for conservation reasons—Canada decided to reduce its energy export to the United States, domestic energy sales would have to be lowered proportionately. However, the same rule would not apply to Mexican energy exports to either the United States or Canada. Similarly, although the United States and Canada are constrained

in their abilities to use national security as an argument to restrict energy exports or imports, the same does not apply to Mexico. Regarding agricultural tariffs, countries are allowed to impose temporary tariffs for up to ten years on certain products. With regard to nontariff barriers (NTBs), the agreement forces the United States to increase its quotas for textiles and non-wool apparel, but not for wool suits. In addition, all countries must convert their quantitative restrictions on certain agricultural imports to tariff rate equivalents. It is noteworthy that Canadian cultural industries are exempt from the agreement altogether.

NAFTA's main stipulations with regard to trade in services are the national treatment and the most-favored-nation (MFN) principle. The first principle states that suppliers of services from other NAFTA countries must receive the same treatment as domestic suppliers, whereas the second principle is simply the application of the General Agreement on Tariffs and Trade (GATT) MFN principle to trade in services. Another stipulation concerns the location of service providers: In order to supply a service, neither the establishment of an office nor residency in the foreign country is required. Two service-sector industries are given special considerations. Although the agreement requires that reasonable access and use of public telecommunication networks must be guaranteed, it does not cover radio and television broadcast or cable distributions. Due to the differences in market structure and government regulation of financial services between NAFTA countries, the scope of trade in financial services is limited (Hufbauer and Schott 1993). For example, due to U.S. restrictions on branch banking by foreign banks, and the subordination of NAFTA under U.S. state law, Mexico and Canada do not allow U.S. banks to establish branches, only subsidiaries. In addition, exceptions to free trade in financial services are allowed for prudential reasons such as the stability of the financial system.

NAFTA separates the issue of sanitary and phytosanitary (SPS) measures from all other standards-related measures. With both standards, the agreement appears to take a precautionary approach (IISD 2004). All countries have the right to establish the level of protection they find appropriate, although scientific evidence should be used to determine the risks associated with an imported product, and in the case of SPS measures on nonhuman health issues, a type of cost-benefit analysis must be conducted and countries must choose the most cost-effective solution.

NAFTA also contains rules for government procurement. Above a threshold of $50,000 for federal government entities ($250,000 for federal government enterprises), government contracts for purchases of goods and services are open to competition. The U.S. Buy American Act can no longer be applied, except for small- and minority-owned businesses.

In terms of foreign investment, NAFTA stipulates that performance requirements, such as domestic content requirements, are prohibited both at the national and subnational government level. In addition, foreign investors are protected against losses through expropriation since they are entitled to adequate financial compensation. As the main exception to the principle of free international capital flows, Mexico is allowed to maintain certain restrictions on foreign investment in its petrochemical industries.

With regard to intellectual property right protection, the agreement defines specific protection for patent and copyright holders. Furthermore, countries are not allowed to issue compulsory licenses (that is, authorize a third party to make or sell a patented invention without the patent owner's consent), a practice frequently used by Mexico and Canada to promote development of generic pharmaceutical products.

The implementation and operation of the agreement is guaranteed through a number of institutions that provide dispute settlement procedures similar to those adopted by the World Trade Organization (WTO). Foremost, binational panels have the authority to determine whether countervailing duties and antidumping restrictions are applied appropriately, that is, that they are consistent with NAFTA and other trade agreements. Furthermore, the Free Trade Commission, which consists of cabinet-level representatives from each country and convenes only as required, supervises the implementation and further development of the agreement and oversees the work of NAFTA's more than thirty committees, working groups, and other subsidiary bodies. Finally, each country maintains a section of the NAFTA Secretariat, which is responsible for the administration of the dispute settlement provision.

The NAFTA Side Agreements

The purpose of the North American Agreement on Labor Cooperation (NAALC) is to stimulate a dialogue between the parties on labor issues and to promote the enforcement of existing labor laws in each member country. To implement the agreement, the parties agreed to establish the Commission for Labor Cooperation in 1994. The commission consists of an NAALC Council, composed of the ministers of labor, and the Secretariat, located in Washington, DC. The Secretariat provides technical and operational support for the commission's work. From 1994 to 1999, twenty-two public communications were received under the NAALC, of which fourteen were directed at Mexico, six at the United States, and two at Canada. Public communications are typically submitted by unions or other labor organizations and concern allegations relating to work conditions, occupational safety issues, freedom of association, and similar problems.

The goal of the North American Agreement on Environmental Cooperation (NAAEC) is to promote the enforcement of existing environmental laws, to help prevent conflicts relating to trade and the environment, and to ensure that member countries do not lower their environmental standards in order to attract foreign investment. The implementation of the agreement is overseen by the Commission for Environmental Cooperation, created in 1994. The commission consists of an NAAEC Council composed of the environment ministers (or the equivalent) of each country, a Joint Public Advisory Committee, and a Secretariat located in Montreal, Quebec, Canada, that provides technical and operational support. Among other things, the commission reviews public submissions on cases where governments appeared to have failed to enforce environmental laws effectively. After a thorough investigation, it may publish a factual record of its findings.

NAFTA and the Canada-U.S. Free Trade Agreement

The Canada-U.S. Free Trade Agreement constituted an important predecessor to NAFTA as far as trade between the United States and Canada was concerned. In many ways, the composition and content of NAFTA were modeled after the CUSFTA, which was negotiated between June 17, 1986, and December 9, 1987, and went into effect on January 1, 1989. The agreement's main provisions were to eliminate all tariff barriers on merchandise trade over a period of ten years, to remove most NTBs over the same time period, and to end most restrictions on cross-border investments. In addition, the accord established basic rules concerning trade in services, such as the elimination of discrimination in services, forcing each country to treat foreign and domestic services equally—the so-called "national treatment" provision. Also, national preferences on government contracts in excess of $25,000 were eliminated (see Kreinin 2000).

The Public Debate about NAFTA

In the wake of the trilateral negotiations on the creation of NAFTA, a vigorous public debate ensued between supporters and foes of the agreement. U.S. opponents to NAFTA included political columnist Pat Buchanan, Green Party leader Ralph Nader, Texas businessman Ross Perot, organized labor (AFL-CIO), some research think tanks such as the Economic Policy Institute, some environmental groups such as Public Citizen, Greenpeace USA, and Friends of the Earth, and a large number of Democrats in Congress, including House Majority Leader Richard Gephardt. The proponents of NAFTA included most academic and business economists, business leaders, college-educated journalists, key political figures such as Presidents George H. W. Bush and Bill Clinton, and the vast majority of Republicans in Congress.

A central issue in the debates during the negotiations on NAFTA and in subsequent years has been the economic, environmental, and social effects of the agreement. Critics have argued that the agreement would destroy jobs in the United States because U.S. manufacturers would be unable to resist dollar-an-hour wages in Mexico. They have also predicted that American high-wage manufacturing workers would be the biggest losers in terms of job losses and/or reductions in wage income; that NAFTA would change the structure of Mexican industry, turning the country into one big maquiladora; that NAFTA would be a sort of Trojan Horse, giving Japanese firms unrestricted access to the U.S. market via Mexican-based production facilities; and that the agreement would trigger a migration of dirty industries from Canada and the United States to Mexico, where environmental standards are less stringent or not as effectively enforced (see Orme 1996).

Proponents of the agreement, in contrast, have insisted that NAFTA would create jobs on both sides of each border, with a net gain of up to 150,000 additional jobs in the United States alone over a period of five years (Hufbauer and Schott 1993). They expect NAFTA to increase exports, income, and productivity in each member country and say the increased prosperity in Mexico will weaken the urge for Mexican workers to migrate north. Furthermore, they claim that NAFTA will protect existing U.S. investments in Mexico and stimulate additional investments (*Wall Street Journal* 1993). They also expect NAFTA to have attractive social consequences by demonstrating that industrialized and developing countries can not only coexist but also reduce standard-of-living gaps (Negroponte 1991).

Impact of NAFTA

Methodological Issues

A common approach in evaluating the economic effects of NAFTA ex ante is based on computational general equilibrium (CGE) models. These computer-based models simulate a certain number of national economies (or regions) that are connected through international trade and/or international capital flows. Each economy comprises various industries (or sectors). The sum of net supplies across all sectors within a country determines gross domestic product (GDP), which in turn is used for consumption, investment, and exports. Tariffs and NTBs can alter the international flow of goods, services, or capital across countries. Trade agreements such as NAFTA are modeled as a reduction in those barriers.

Early CGE models were static in nature and thus did not take account of the evolution of regions and sectors over time (see USITC 2003). More recent CGE models typically have a dynamic structure that allows the identification of trade-barrier effects (or the removal thereof) over time, such as changes in the growth rate of GDP (Young and Romero 1994; Kehoe 1994). In contrast to CGE models, econometric studies typically examine the ex post economic impact of trade agreements (Frankel 1997; Gould 1998; Krueger 1999, 2000; Baier and Bergstrand 2001; Romalis 2001). These studies estimate models that relate trade measures (such as the growth in the volume of trade) to a set of explanatory factors that vary from model to model. However, all specifications have in common that they include some direct or indirect measure of barriers to trade. The estimated coefficient on the trade-barrier variable can then be used to gauge the impact of a specific trade agreement on the selected trade measure.

Ex Ante Assessments

Aggregate Impact. Static CGE models of NAFTA calibrated to a pre-1994 base year (Brown et al. 1992a, 1992b; Roland-Holst et al. 1994; Trela and Whalley 1994) have found that the agreement should have a positive but modest effect on U.S. output and trade, with an average expected increase in exports and imports of 4 percent and 4.4 percent, respectively. In addition, these studies indicate that economic welfare should improve as well, with a change of about 0.7 percent on average. Comparable CGE studies for Mexico (Sobarzo 1994; Young and Romero 1994) and Canada (Cox 1994) have come to similar conclusions: Both countries should experience a rise in the overall volume of North American trade, with larger percentage increases for Mexico than for Canada.

Sector-Specific Impact. Some NAFTA-CGE studies have focused on the expected sectoral rather than the expected aggregate effects of the agreement. The main advantage of the sectoral approach is that it generates estimates of NAFTA-induced changes that can vary from industry to industry. However, the results from these studies have been quite varied and sometimes contradictory. For example, Drusilla Brown (1994, Table 5.3) reported U.S. production gains in textiles of 0.6 percent, whereas Irene Trela and John Whalley (1994, Table 9.6) expected U.S. textile production to decrease by 0.1 percent. Some studies predicted strong increases in output levels for certain industries due to NAFTA. For example, Mary E. Burfisher et al. (1994, Table 7.5) estimated an increase in production of U.S. corn of close to 7 percent, whereas David W. Roland-Holst et al. (1994, Tables 2.9–2.11) predicted production gains in the U.S., Canadian, and Mexican transport equipment sectors of 17.6 percent, 63.1 percent, and 10.5 percent, respectively. In contrast,

Florencio Lopez-de-Silanes et al. (1994, Table 8.12) predicted output gains of only 1 percent or less for North American auto and engine producers. Although most studies predict at least modest growth for the vast majority of U.S. industries as a result of NAFTA, some studies have identified industries likely to be adversely affected by NAFTA. Trela and Whalley (1994, Table 9.6), for example, predicted negative growth of 5 percent and 10.7 percent for apparel and steel, respectively.

With regard to NAFTA's impact on Mexican sectors, Horacio E. Sobarzo (1994, Table 3.5) estimated the largest positive effects for construction (+55 percent), nonelectronic machinery (+48 percent), and steel (+39 percent). Furthermore, with the exception of agriculture (−8 percent), all sectors were predicted to expand as the result of lower tariffs and NTBs. Using a dynamic CGE model to assess the impact of NAFTA on the Mexican economy, Leslie Young and Jose Romero (1994, Table 10.7) identified Mexico's automobile vehicles and parts industry as the winner with regard to long-term output growth (+25.8 percent) and estimated the strongest decline in growth for textiles and apparel (−48.3 percent). David J. Cox (1994, Table 4.6) estimated that most Canadian sectors would experience a modest increase in output levels, ranging from 0.17 percent for textiles and leather to 0.58 percent for machines and appliances. The only Canadian sectors expected to have negative output growth due to NAFTA were woods and paper (−0.03 percent) and forestry (−0.04 percent).

Ex Post Assessments

Aggregate Impact. Empirical ex post studies of NAFTA have produced more mixed results than CGE-based approaches. Although some have shown gains in the volume of regional trade (Romalis 2001; Burfisher et al. 2001), others have found little evidence that NAFTA has increased North American trade at the aggregate level (Krueger 1999, 2000). In between these extremes are studies that have found NAFTA to be effective in stimulating U.S.-Mexico trade in both directions, while leaving Canada-U.S. and Mexico-Canada trade essentially unchanged (USITC 1997, 2003; Gould 1998). The finding that NAFTA has had little impact on Canada-U.S. trade may not be that surprising given that the two countries had already lowered or even eliminated many trade barriers before NAFTA became effective with their bilateral free trade agreement (CUSFTA).

James F. Hollifield and Thomas Osang (2004, Table 2) showed that from the U.S. perspective, NAFTA's total trade share (that is, the sum of U.S. exports and imports to and from Mexico and Canada relative to exports and imports with all countries, including NAFTA partners) grew at an annual rate of 0.2 percent in the pre-NAFTA period 1986–1993, compared to a rate of 1.4 percent for the NAFTA period 1994–2003. This represents a sevenfold increase in the annual growth rate of the NAFTA trade share. Clearly, other factors, such as the devaluation of the Mexican peso, declining transport costs, and trade diversion effects (Romalis 2001), also contributed to this increase. Another study (USITC 2003, Table 6-2) estimated that the removal of trade barriers between the United States and Mexico due to NAFTA explains 16.8 percent of the observed 63 percent increase in Mexico's share of U.S. imports of manufactured products over the period from 1990–2001. Tariff reductions prior to NAFTA explain an additional 4.2 percent, and the devaluation of the Mexican peso and the reduction in transport costs explain 23 percent and 4.7 percent, respectively.

From Mexico's perspective, the impact of NAFTA on its U.S. trade share was equally significant. Hollifield and Osang (2004, Table 5) showed that from 1985 to 1993, the share of Mexico's trade with the United States relative to total trade with all countries was essentially flat, whereas the same share grew at an annual rate of 1.1 percent between 1994 and 2002 (the NAFTA period). A U.S. International Trade Commission (USITC) study (2003, Table 6-4) shows that the removal of Mexican trade barriers (before and after NAFTA) on manufactured imports from the United States contributed to an estimated 13.7 percent increase in the import share, while the devaluation of the peso caused an estimated 11.5 percent decline. The two factors together can thus fully explain the observed 2.5 percent increase in the U.S. share of manufactured goods imported by Mexico between 1991 and 1999.

Finally, from the Canadian perspective, the impact of NAFTA on its trade share with Mexico and the United States was expected to be moderate, given the fact that CUSFTA preceded NAFTA and the relatively small volume of trade between Canada and Mexico. As shown in Hollifield and Osang (2004, Table 4), the share of total trade with Canada's NAFTA partners grew at an annual rate of 1.1 percent between 1988 and 1993 (pre-NAFTA period), compared to a rate of only 0.6 percent between 1994 and 2001 (NAFTA period). However, this surprising decline in the annual growth rate was largely driven by a steep decline in Canada's trade with the United States in 2001, which was caused to a large extent by the downturn in U.S. economic activity that year. Without this "outlier" year, the average annual growth rate of Canada's NAFTA trade share was 1 percent over the NAFTA period, nearly identical to the 1.1 percent pre-NAFTA growth rate.

Sector-Specific Impact. Since the level of tariff protection varies across industries, the impact of trade agreements such as NAFTA changes from industry to industry. Unless exemptions are granted, industries with high levels of protection prior to the agreement are likely to experience the most dramatic change in trade flows, value added, and employment as the result of an agreement.

Impact on Selected U.S. Industries. Among the ten U.S. sectors studied by the USITC (2003), forestry and fisheries, energy and fuel products, and transport equipment had the highest NAFTA exposure in 2001 (70 percent, 51.6 percent, and 43.6 percent, respectively; these and subsequent figures are calculated from USITC

2003, Tables 5-3 to 5-39). Sectoral NAFTA exposure is defined as the ratio of total sector trade with Mexico and Canada relative to total sector trade with all countries including NAFTA partners. U.S. sectors with low NAFTA total trade ratios include services, miscellaneous products, and textiles and apparel (14.8 percent, 18.1 percent, and 23 percent, respectively). In terms of NAFTA import penetration (defined as the ratio of U.S. imports from Mexico and Canada relative to all U.S. imports), the U.S. sectors most exposed to competition from Mexico and Canada are the same as those for total trade. With regard to NAFTA export dependence (defined as the ratio of sector exports to Mexico and Canada relative to total sector exports), the leading U.S. sectors are textiles and apparel, minerals and metals, and energy and fuel products (50.1 percent, 49.3 percent, and 48.5 percent, respectively).

Between 1993 and 2001, NAFTA exposure in terms of total trade shares increased for all but one of the ten industries studied by the USITC: Only services had a NAFTA total trade share that was smaller in 2001 (14.8 percent) than in 1993 (15.8 percent), a decline of 1 percent. Total trade shares grew fastest for textiles and apparel, forest and fisheries, and energy and fuel products (+63.7 percent, +59.1 percent, and +55.9 percent, respectively). On the other end, transport equipment (+10.2 percent), minerals and metals (+11 percent), and chemical and allied products (+11.2 percent) are among the sectors that were least affected by NAFTA. In terms of changes in import penetration, NAFTA had the biggest impact on textiles and apparel (+96.2 percent), forestry and fisheries (+52.5 percent), and machinery and electronics (+52.2 percent), and NAFTA export dependence increased the most for energy and fuel products (+116.5 percent), forestry and fisheries (+42.8 percent), and agriculture (+45.1 percent).

With respect to exports, the U.S. textile and apparel industry is strongly NAFTA dependent, with about half of total exports going to either Canada or Mexico in 2001. The picture is different for imports: Less than one-fifth of sector imports come from NAFTA countries. However, imports from NAFTA partners grew at more than twice the rate of exports to NAFTA partners between 1993 and 2001, mostly as a result of strong increases in apparel imports from Mexico. In contrast, the U.S. textile industry has benefited from NAFTA by expanding exports to both Mexico and Canada, especially of high-quality textiles.

NAFTA trade, in particular with Canada, accounts for a substantial fraction of overall trade in U.S. forestry and fishery products. In 2001, more than four-fifths of U.S. sector imports came from Canada and Mexico, and more than two-fifths of U.S. exports went to NAFTA partners. In comparison, U.S. sector exports to Canada and Mexico accounted for slightly more than half of total exports in 1993, while sector imports from the two countries made up less than one-third of total imports. This strong growth in sector trade with NAFTA partners stands in contrast to a decline in trade with non-NAFTA countries. Between 1993 and 2001, U.S. sector exports to non-NAFTA countries declined by more than 50 percent, and imports fell by more than 20 percent. This diversion of trade flows cannot be explained by a change in U.S. tariff rates because rates were close to zero before NAFTA came into effect.

U.S. exports in energy and fuel products to NAFTA partners more than doubled between 1993 and 2001, while exports to non-NAFTA countries fell by one-third. Sector imports from NAFTA partners also more than doubled. In comparison, sector imports from non-NAFTA countries increased by less than a third. Most of the change in U.S. sector trade was driven by a large increase in imported crude petroleum from both Canada and Mexico, followed by a substantial increase in U.S. exports of refined petroleum to Mexico. Overall, half of U.S. sector imports and exports occurred with NAFTA partners in 2001, compared to about one-third in 1993.

For U.S. chemicals and allied products, there was a modest positive effect of NAFTA on U.S.-Canada total sector trade, which increased

by 84.5 percent between 1993 and 2001 compared to an increase of 70 percent with all non-NAFTA countries. NAFTA had a more pronounced impact on U.S.-Mexico sector trade, increasing bilateral trade volume by 140.6 percent over the 1993–2001 period. As with other sectors, such as machinery and electronics, transport equipment, and miscellaneous products, the change in U.S. sector imports from Mexico (+192.1 percent) was stronger than U.S. sector exports to Mexico (+125.2 percent).

For U.S. machinery and electronics, NAFTA had a significant impact on U.S.-Mexican bilateral trade. The impact on U.S.-Canada trade has been less pronounced. Overall, total U.S. trade in machinery and electronics with non-NAFTA countries increased by 44.2 percent in 1993–2001. While total trade in sector products with Canada increased proportionately (+39 percent), total trade with Mexico increased by 162 percent (USITC 2003, Table 5-7). Although the reduction of Mexican tariffs is one reason for the increase in U.S.-Mexico sector trade, the other, more important explanation has to do with substantial sector-specific U.S. foreign direct investment in Mexico. Since NAFTA lowered the risk associated with investment in Mexico, the rise in U.S.-owned production facilities in Mexico has triggered a drastic increase in U.S. imports of machinery and electronics from Mexico.

U.S. agricultural trade with Mexico and Canada has grown rapidly: Between 1993 and 2001, total trade with Canada and Mexico increased by 48.5 percent and 71.8 percent, respectively (ibid., Table 5-11). In comparison, U.S. total agricultural trade with non-NAFTA countries increased by merely 2.1 percent over the same period. NAFTA had only a small impact for most agricultural commodities. Products with high rates of protection prior to 1994—rice, cotton, apples, and pears in Mexico; cotton in Canada; and sugar in the United States—have seen the most dramatic increase in trade, with a gain in volume of trade of 15 percent or more directly attributable to NAFTA (USITC 2003).

Impact on Mexican Agriculture. Contrary to conventional wisdom, NAFTA did not have a detrimental effect on Mexico's agriculture (Lederman et al. 2003). Both the value of Mexico's agricultural production and the share of agricultural products in total trade were higher in the post-NAFTA period than in the pre-NAFTA period (ibid., Fig. 6). Explanations for this outcome include strong overall economic growth in both Mexico and the United States since 1995; productivity gains in Mexico's agricultural production; and a more efficient use of agricultural subsidies in Mexico.

Conclusions

Though the debate on the economic and social ramifications and merits of NAFTA continues in all three member countries, it is clear by now that NAFTA achieved its primary goal, to increase the volume of trade among member countries, with two notable exceptions: Canada's total trade share with NAFTA partners declined, as did the U.S. service sector trade share. As far as other effects, such as changes in income, employment, investment, migration, and unionization, are concerned, the verdict is still out, though there is strong evidence that NAFTA contributed heavily to the observed increase in U.S. capital flows to Mexico in general, and to the rise in Mexico's maquiladora industrial production, in particular.

Two final observations are noteworthy. First, despite NAFTA and its dispute settlement mechanism, some trade conflicts between NAFTA partners are being settled by the WTO instead, either because they involve WTO but not NAFTA rules—as in the case of the U.S.-Mexican dispute over Mexican taxes on products containing high-fructose corn syrup imported from the United States—or because one of the parties decided to defend its interests through both institutions in cases involving both NAFTA and WTO rules—as in the case of the U.S.-Canada softwood lumber dis-

pute. Second, some aspects of NAFTA's implementation have been tied up in the court system for years. Under NAFTA, Mexican trucks should have gained access to U.S. roadways beginning in 2000. But owing to a legal challenge from consumer groups, unions, and others who sued on safety and environmental grounds, entry was never granted. In June 2004, a U.S. Supreme Court ruling gave the U.S. president the right to immediately open U.S. highways to Mexican trucks. Nevertheless, Mexican trucks are not yet allowed to roll on U.S. roads, and it is unclear how long it will take for them to gain full access.

The author would like to thank Farrah Jamal for excellent assistance in reviewing the literature.

Thomas Osang

See Also Economic Integration; Australia New Zealand Closer Economic Relations Trade Agreement (ANZCERTA); The Central American Common Market (CACM); European Union; Latin American Free Trade Association (LAFTA)

References

Baier, Scott L., and Jeffrey H. Bergstrand. 2001. "The Growth of World Trade: Tariffs, Transport Costs and Income Similarity." *Journal of International Economics* 53: 1–27.

Brown, Drusilla K. 1994. "Properties of Applied General Equilibrium Trade Models with Monopolistic Competition and Foreign Direct Investment." In Joseph F. Francois and Clinton R. Shiells, eds., *Modeling Trade Policy.* Cambridge: Cambridge University Press.

Brown, Drusilla K., Alan V. Deardorff, and Robert M. Stern. 1992a. "The North American Free Trade Agreement: Analytical Issues and a Computational Assessment." *World Economy* 15, no. 1: 15–29.

———. 1992b. "North American Integration." *Economic Journal* 102: 1507–1518.

Burfisher, Mary E., Sherman Robinson, and Karen Theirfelder. 1994. "Wage Changes in a U.S.-Mexico Free Trade Area: Migration versus Stolper-Samuelson Effects." In Joseph F. Francois and Clinton R. Shiells, eds., *Modeling Trade Policy.* Cambridge: Cambridge University Press.

———. 2001. "The Impact of NAFTA on the United States." *Journal of Economic Perspectives* 15, no. 1: 125–144.

Cameron, Maxwell A., and Brian W. Tomlin. 2000. *The Making of NAFTA.* Ithaca, NY: Cornell University Press.

Cox, David J. 1994. "Some Applied General Equilibrium Estimates of the Impact of a North American Free Trade Agreement on Canada." In Joseph F. Francois and Clinton R. Shiells, eds., *Modeling Trade Policy.* Cambridge: Cambridge University Press.

Frankel, Jeffrey. 1997. *Regional Trading Blocs in the World Economic System.* Washington, DC: Institute for International Economics.

Gould, David M. 1998. "Has NAFTA Changed North American Trade?" *Federal Reserve Bank of Dallas Economic Review.* First quarter.

Hollifield, James F, and Thomas Osang. 2004. "Trade and Migration in North America: The Role of NAFTA." Manuscript.

Hufbauer, Gary C., and Jeffrey Schott. 1993. *An Evaluation of NAFTA.* Washington, DC: Institute for International Economics.

International Institute for Sustainable Development. 2004. "Environmental Aspects of Regional Trade Agreements," http://www.iisd.org/trade/handbook/ 7_1_2.htm (cited January 28, 2004).

Kehoe, Timothy J. 1994. "Toward a Dynamic General Equilibrium Model of North American Trade." In Joseph F. Francois and Clinton R. Shiells, eds., *Modeling Trade Policy.* Cambridge: Cambridge University Press.

Keohane, R. O., and Joseph Nye. 1989. *Power and Interdependence.* 2d ed. Glenview, IL: Scott Foresman.

Kreinin, Mordechai. 2000. "The Canada-U.S. Free Trade Agreement: An Overview." In Mordechai Kreinin, ed., *Building a Partnership—The Canada–United States Free Trade Agreement.* East Lansing: Michigan State University Press.

Krueger, Anne. 1999. "Trade Creation and Trade Diversion under NAFTA." National Bureau of Economic Research Working Paper 7429. Cambridge, MA.

———. 2000. "NAFTA's Effects: A Preliminary Assessment." *World Economy* 23, no. 6: 761–775.

Lederman, Daniel, William F. Maloney, and Luis Serven. 2003. *Lessons from NAFTA for Latin America and the Caribbean Countries: A Summary of Research Findings.* Washington, DC: World Bank.

Lopez-de-Silanes, Florencio, James R. Markusen, and Thomas Rutherford. 1994. "The Auto Industry and the North American Free Trade Agreement." In Joseph F. Francois and Clinton R. Shiells, eds., *Modeling Trade Policy.* Cambridge: Cambridge University Press.

Negroponte, John D. 1991. "Continuity and Change in U.S.-Mexico Relations." *Columbia Journal of World Business* 26, no. 2: 5–11.

North American Free Trade Agreement. 1994. Text of Agreement, http://www.dfait-maeci.gc.ca/trade/ nafta-alena/agree-en.asp (cited January 28, 2004).

Orme, William A. 1996. *Understanding NAFTA—Mexico, Free Trade, and the New North America.* Austin: University of Texas Press.

Robert, Maryse. 2000. *Negotiating NAFTA.* Toronto: University of Toronto Press.

Roland-Holst, David W., Kenneth A. Reinert, and Clinton R. Shiells. 1994. "A General Equilibrium Analysis of North American Integration." In Joseph F. Francois and Clinton R. Shiells, eds., *Modeling Trade Policy.* Cambridge: Cambridge University Press.

Romalis, John. 2001. "NAFTA's Impact on North American Trade." University of Chicago Graduate School of Business Working Paper.

Sobarzo, Horacio E. 1994. "The Gains for Mexico from a North American Free Trade Agreement—An Applied General Equilibrium Assessment." In Joseph F. Francois and Clinton R. Shiells, eds., *Modeling Trade Policy.* Cambridge: Cambridge University Press.

Trela, Irene, and John Whalley. 1994. "Trade Liberalization in Quota-Restricted Items: The United States and Mexico in Textiles and Steel." In Joseph F. Francois and Clinton R. Shiells, eds., *Modeling Trade Policies.* Cambridge: Cambridge University Press.

U.S. International Trade Commission. 1997. *The Impact of the North American Free Trade Agreement on the U.S. Economy and Industries: A Three-Year Review.* Publication 3045. Washington, DC: USITC.

———. 2003. *The Impact of Trade Agreements: Effect of the Tokyo Round, U.S.-Israel FTA, U.S.-Canada FTA, NAFTA, and the Uruguay Round on the U.S. Economy.* Publication 3621. Washington, DC: USITC.

Wall Street Journal. 1993. "Foreign Investment in Mexico." September 28, A14.

Young, Leslie, and Jose Romero. 1994. "A Dynamic Dual Model of the North American Free Trade Agreement." In Joseph F. Francois and Clinton R. Shiells, eds., *Modeling Trade Policy.* Cambridge: Cambridge University Press.

Organisation for Economic Co-operation and Development (OECD)

The Organisation for Economic Co-operation and Development (OECD) is the modern successor to the Organisation for European Economic Co-operation (OEEC). Its thirty members are advanced market democracies producing some two-thirds of the world's annual economic output. The OECD's activities include gathering statistical information on economic performance to help member states cooperate in economic policy planning, coordinating development assistance to less developed countries (LDCs), and providing a forum for members to negotiate both legal and nonbinding policy agreements. Over the past decade, its efforts have grown to include outreach programs to LDCs and other nonmembers on governance and economic management.

Historical Overview

The current OECD is the product of a long organizational evolution. In the aftermath of World War II, the United States provided some $12 billion in reconstruction aid to Western Europe through the European Recovery Program (known as the Marshall Plan). One major condition of this aid was that funded projects should benefit more than one country and involve cooperation among recipients. Accordingly, recipients formed the Conference for European Economic Co-operation (CEEC), which was quickly institutionalized into the Organisation for European Economic Co-operation. When the OEEC was officially inaugurated on April 16, 1948, it had sixteen member states: Austria, Belgium, Denmark, France, Greece, Iceland, Ireland, Italy, Luxembourg, the Netherlands, Norway, Portugal, Sweden, Switzerland, Turkey, and the United Kingdom. A portion of Italy under Anglo-American control; the Free Territory of Trieste; and the American-, French-, and British-controlled sections of West Germany were also involved. The OEEC played a major role in the implementation of the American-funded European Recovery Program in the distribution of aid, and, after 1950, in the operation of an intra-European payment union designed to function until currencies returned to convertibility. In the last two years of the Marshall Plan, under American pressure, OEEC member states negotiated their first reductions in trade barriers. This resulted in a substantial freeing of private interstate trade by the end of the decade on a mutually agreed list of products, even prior to the negotiation of the Treaty of Rome founding the European Economic Community (EEC).

By 1960, Western Europe was firmly back on its feet, and the organization's focus steadily shifted from internal economic development to external development assistance. Even in the latter part of the 1950s, pressures from the Cold War ideological conflict between the United States and the Soviet Union had led

Western Europe and the United States to unite in providing development funding, often as a thinly disguised reward or bribe, to strategic or key LDCs. As former European colonial holdings became independent during the 1960s, this trend became even stronger. In 1961, the United States and Canada joined, along with Spain, and the OEEC was transformed into the Organisation for Economic Co-operation and Development to reflect this new global orientation. Japan joined three years later, in 1964, bringing total membership up to twenty-two.

Organizational growth and activities slowed in the late 1960s and 1970s, as the Cold War constrained the number of possible market democracies that could join. Economic difficulties mounted in developed countries, spurred on by U.S. abandonment of the dollar-gold parity in August 1971 and the oil shocks of 1973 and 1979. Nevertheless, several new members did join: Australia (1966) and New Zealand (1973).

The end of the Cold War and the economic boom of the 1990s saw a wave of new members from previously unrepresented parts of the world. Mexico joined in 1994, and South Korea in 1996; the former Soviet bloc was represented by Czechoslovakia (1995, succeeded by the Czech Republic), Hungary (1996), Poland (1996), and after the "Velvet Divorce," the Slovak Republic (2000). These latest additions brought the OECD's total membership to thirty countries. Membership is still heavily dominated by Western European and North American states, but the increasing inclusion of other nations, such as South Korea, Mexico, and the Central European states, bodes well for future expansion. Potential candidates in the first decade of the new century could well include South Africa and Brazil; Argentina may be considered shortly after that, depending on its recovery trajectory from its financial crisis of the late 1990s. Russia applied for membership in May 1996; its application is still pending.

Member Accession and Nonmember Partnership

Formally, membership in the OECD is limited only by commitment to pluralistic democracy and a market economy, though increasingly respect for human rights has become a third fundamental principle required for membership. In practice, accession is by invitation only and occurs after a lengthy series of negotiations in which the current members ascertain the candidate's willingness and capability to implement the organization's binding agreements. Of particular concern are the agreements on capital movement, international investment, and cross-border trade in services. These agreements are founded on the principles of equal treatment of nationals and foreigners, and nondiscrimination between members; together, equal treatment and nondiscrimination help provide a "level playing field" for international economic competition.

Sometimes, candidates may be reluctant or unable to implement some policies or agreements, whether from physical incapacity (lack of facilities to monitor such a policy, for example) or from political unwillingness (protection of certain strategically important or "infant industries," or specific concerns of a leader's key constituents). Candidate countries may submit reservations about agreements or parts of agreements that they will not or cannot implement. Requests for such reservations must be approved by the OECD's member states, meeting in the organization's chief governing body, the Council; these requests can often cause major delays in the accession process, since most decisions in the Council are by unanimity or consensus (lack of objections as opposed to unanimity's active approval).

More than seventy other nonmember countries cooperate with the OECD on various projects and initiatives through the Centre for Co-operation with Non-Members. These projects range from technical assistance provided by OECD directorates to consultation on proposed

OECD agreements, inclusion on select working committees, policy dialogues with the organization and its directorates, and various types of observer status at the organization itself. Cooperating nonmembers are often invited to sign binding agreements and adhere to voluntary principles devised and agreed upon by organization members. Middle-income developing countries have found this type of cooperation to be very beneficial; gradual but increasing adherence to the organization's rules and policies can help to prepare a country for future membership candidacy as well as increasing the compatibility of its regulatory system with those of larger economic powers, which promotes trade and investment.

Organizational Structure

The OECD's central decisionmaking body is the Council, which consists of an ambassador from each member state, a nonvoting representative from the Commission of the European Union, and the organization's secretary-general, who chairs the Council but has no official vote. The full Council meets regularly to monitor the work of the organization's directorates and committees, but between regular meetings it may delegate authority for routine decisions to an Executive Committee of members. The Council also meets at the ministerial level (member-state ministers of finance and foreign ministers, plus others as needed) at least once per year to set organizational priorities and settle unresolved disputes.

Policy work is spread over twelve functional directorates that study and help coordinate policy in specific sectors (see "Organization Activities" below for list and functions). These directorates are staffed by approximately 2,300 professionals, including some 700 lawyers, economists, scientists, and social scientists, recruited from the member states, who serve as international civil servants for the duration of their OECD posting (OECD Web site). From its

Parisian headquarters in the Château de la Muette, this international secretariat has an annual budget of some US$200 million that it uses to provide research and analysis about member-state policies in order to help members to identify best practices, promising alternative policies, and emergent crises across a wide range of policy fields. Funding for organization activities comes from member-state contributions; the United States normally contributes around 25 percent of the annual secretariat budget, with Japan providing the next largest contribution. The organization's two official working languages are English and French.

Directorate staff provide research and analysis in broad policy areas and manage information exchanges between members. They also support the more than 200 specialized committees and working groups of member-state officials who meet regularly to discuss policy in narrow and particular policy areas. These officials review, discuss, and often contribute to ongoing organization research or work in a particular area. The OECD has also created an electronic information exchange network for these officials, so that even between committee meetings they can continue to share information and data.

Organization Activities

OECD organization activity at the start of the twenty-first century is spread over twelve functional directorates, each of which provides research and analysis in its particular policy area of expertise. With the rise of globalization and increased understanding of policy interconnectedness, however, OECD efforts at policy analysis are more and more frequently cutting across directorate lines. This is reflected in the OECD's reorganization of its work into "themes," which often include the work of more than one directorate. This capability for multidisciplinary analysis is one of the OECD's strengths as a policy analysis organization. This section will provide more in-depth summaries of several key policy areas of OECD involvement, and then conclude with brief overviews of other sectors and programs.

Development Assistance Committee

The Development Assistance Committee (DAC) traces its roots back to the tumultuous period when the OEEC became the OECD. As Western Europe's economies stabilized and the Cold War intensified, the United States and European colonial powers became increasingly eager to assert or reestablish their influence in the rest of the world. The primary instrument under consideration was official development assistance (ODA), which takes the forms of loans, grants, or credits from one state to another state. This issue was so contentious, and seen as such a vital component of security policy, that it sparked a major debate over the appropriate forum for coordination of such aid, with the two major contenders being the OEEC and the North Atlantic Treaty Organization (NATO), under Article 2 of NATO's founding Treaty of Washington. The United Nations was also considered and rejected because of its inclusion of Communist states. NATO was ultimately rejected because it was too militarily focused, and use of it as the primary ODA coordination instrument risked alienating Western-leaning but technically neutral states such as Austria, Switzerland, Sweden, and Ireland.

Talks among the "Four Wise Men" representing the United States, Great Britain, West Germany, and France led in 1961 to the creation of the OECD, in which the OEEC's original seventeen members (including the new state of West Germany), Spain (which had joined in 1959), and the United States and Canada were members. Japan joined soon after, in 1964, and Australia in 1966. Continuing developments in the Cold War led to nominally Communist but Moscow-defiant Yugoslavia obtaining "observer status" at the OEEC and then the OECD; Finland, which was technically neutral but had

a Soviet-friendly foreign policy (resulting from the geopolitical imperative of a long common border), was eventually listed as "participating in certain activities."

The DAC was created in 1960 as part of that initial reorganization, and its purposes and functions have remained generally the same throughout its existence. Unlike the World Bank and the International Monetary Fund (IMF), the DAC does not dispense aid funds directly. Instead, it serves to coordinate member-state funding efforts for maximum effect, as well as evaluating the effectiveness of various aid programs. The DAC also helps to identify best practices on the part of both donors and recipients, and then works to promote those practices to maximize growth and aid effectiveness.

Member states have also used the DAC as a forum to set target goals for ODA giving. Currently, the target is 0.7 percent of gross domestic product (GDP). Since the mid-1970s, the Scandinavian states of Norway, Sweden, Denmark, and Finland have regularly met, and have often exceeded, this target, giving an average of over 1 percent of GDP per year as official development assistance; very few others do. In 2001, the average across the DAC's twenty-two members was 0.46 percent of GDP given as ODA. The DAC's membership includes Austria, Australia, Belgium, Canada, Denmark, Finland, France, Germany, Greece, Ireland, Italy, Japan, Luxembourg, the Netherlands, New Zealand, Norway, Portugal (which left the DAC and actually applied for aid-recipient status during the 1970s and 1980s, before rejoining in 1991), Spain, Sweden, Switzerland, the United Kingdom, and the United States. In addition, Mexico obtained observer status at the DAC in 1994, and the Commission of the European Union is also a member.

Finance and Investment

The finance and investment theme of OECD activity deals with capital and capital movements broadly conceived. It studies banking systems and banking regulation, financial services liberalization, and best practices in both of these fields. Financial market practices and regulation, by securities firms as well as private and institutional investors, also fall under this category, with the OECD studying regulatory practices and reforms in these critical areas. The Asian financial crisis of 1997–1999 demonstrated vividly the importance of sound banking regulation combined with careful attention to investment practices in providing stable environments that are conducive to economic development. OECD work in this field seeks to understand the linkages among these issues and to provide states with guidance on effective ways to prevent similar crises.

Other special fields of interest include measuring and monitoring capital flows, with a special emphasis on the relationship between capital movements and economic development. In this vein, the OECD is particularly interested in foreign direct investment (FDI), both within member countries and by member-state firms in less developed countries. The OECD also works on issues related to the liberalization of investment in developed and developing countries that came out of the World Trade Organization's Doha Round, in 2001, with a focus on the benefits of transparency in international investment policies as well as on how bilateral and regional investment arrangements can be integrated into multilateral structures.

The OECD has monitored member-state behaviors in export credit finance since the late 1980s. After a rather serious row over state subsidies to exporting industries, which serve as a competitive boost by allowing a company to sell abroad at prices lower than its domestic production costs, OECD states negotiated a "gentlemen's agreement" on the most generous permissible terms for export credit. Though the agreement has no legal standing, the organization's monitoring of state behavior, and its publication of violations, provide an incentive for states to comply, if only to avoid damaging their reputations.

Countering Money Laundering and Corruption

The OECD's emphasis on good governance and sound economic policy makes the fight against money laundering and corruption a natural target for organization activity. Member states formed the Financial Action Task Force on Money Laundering in 1989. This body is housed within the OECD's secretariat and has a small support staff of its own. In 1990, the task force published forty nonbinding recommendations for member states and developing countries to combat money laundering. These recommendations were revised in 1997, when the first list of fifteen "uncooperative" countries—that is, countries that had not taken steps to prevent money laundering—was published, and again in 2003.

In December 1997, OECD members and five nonmembers (thirty-five states in all) signed an antibribery convention in an effort to reduce corruption. This convention, which entered into force on February 15, 1999, requires signatories to criminalize the offering of bribes for the purpose of retaining or gaining international business. In addition, such bribes are no longer tax-deductible. The goal of the agreement is to reduce corruption by eliminating the supply of bribes, since efforts to reduce the demand for bribes would place serious strain on the administrative structures of developing countries, where such demand is usually highest. An OECD working group is charged with monitoring implementation and issuing reports on signatory compliance. As of February 2003, thirty-four states, including several nonmember signatories (Chile, Brazil, Argentina, Bulgaria, and Slovenia), had ratified the convention and were at varying points in the implementation process.

Economics and Statistics

Since the OECD defines its primary mission as promoting economic growth, both in member states and nonmember states, it is no surprise that a substantial directorate has as its primary function economic reporting and forecasting.

The OECD publishes an economic outlook report twice a year, using current trends to forecast economic conditions. It also tracks general trends across member states in areas such as taxation and inflation rates, unemployment, growth rates, and overall GDP. These forecasts are quite influential and can help states and firms shape policy by providing an independent, third-party estimate of likely short- to medium-run economic conditions.

Indeed, the OECD is widely known for its excellent statistical services. Its statistics unit compiles data from members' national statistics agencies related to many facets of economic activity, and also collects data independently. Most substantive directorates also collect data and develop measurable indicators of relevant policy issues in their sectors for use in their own research and analysis reporting; much of this data, and a substantial amount of the resulting analysis, are made available to the general public via the organization's Internet site (www.oecd.org).

Governance and Management

The OECD works to analyze and promote principles of good governance and public management, namely democratic policymaking, the rule of law, efficient provision of public services, ethics, and transparency. This program is another where collaboration between members and nonmembers is high. Members work with nonmembers, providing technical assistance and coordination, to implement basic reforms toward better governance and public management. Recent innovations in this field have also included efforts to study and identify best practices in "e-government" and electronic provision of government services, work to integrate good governance into sustainable development, regulatory reform, and public-sector budgeting.

Other Policies

OECD officials have moved beyond studying purely economic factors contributing to development and economic growth. Other areas receiving attention include social issues such as health care, education, and labor practices. Issues of gender equality and child labor have been prominent in recent years. In education policy, the OECD has helped states compare educational practices by collecting a wealth of detailed statistical data and working to develop comparable indicators of educational progress and instructor competence and qualifications.

The OECD has also branched off from its traditional macroeconomic and firm-level microeconomic analysis to look at areas where these two fields meet. The OECD's directorates study issues of insurance and pensions, helping states examine their taxation and health care policies to provide for aging populations, because increased longevity threatens many member states with potentially bankrupt social-insurance and old-age schemes, while increased global competition pressures firms to minimize formerly generous pension schemes. These two contradictory forces represent a serious challenge to existing social welfare policies in a number of member states. A forum has been established to examine harmful tax practices, particularly tax havens and other offshore arrangements. These practices provide firms with incentives to establish operations in certain jurisdictions in order to evade taxation in other jurisdictions.

Efforts have been made to coordinate policy on electronic commerce (e-commerce), particularly with regard to transborder commerce taxation policy. E-commerce is seen as part of a viable strategy of sustainable development and also as part of a larger trend toward commercial reorganization, and so the organization works to facilitate international trade conducted via the Internet. Likewise, efforts in the traditional area of enterprise and industrial policy have shifted toward identifying best practices and offering practical advice for industrial restructuring at the local, national, and global levels in both manufacturing and service industries.

Among the more innovative and proactive areas of OECD work is the so-called "future studies" theme, which examines emerging policy problems. By looking at nascent public policy issues and working to coordinate policy responses from the initial onset of the problem, the OECD hopes to help states avoid conflicting policy responses that exacerbate the problem, or policies that address only the surface symptoms rather than the underlying causes of the problem.

In line with the OECD's emphasis on economic growth are its efforts to study and promote sustainable development, which involves economic growth coupled with regard for social structures and needs, environmental considerations, and demographic trends. Integration into the global economy can be incredibly disruptive for a formerly protected society; efforts to transition to sustainable development hope to minimize the disruption, or at least make it more predictable, so that public support for growth is maintained. Sustainable development involves attention to issues of drinking water supply, sanitation, pollution, soil erosion, and forest protection. All of this must occur alongside the traditional issues of generating economic growth from an usually large, young, and poorly educated population.

Both future studies and sustainable development programs are excellent examples of the types of interdisciplinary work the OECD has begun to undertake in recent years. Both combine issues of economic analysis with social policy, pure science, and political analysis in ways that are not widely duplicated elsewhere.

In addition to these, the OECD is the home of the International Energy Agency (IEA), an autonomous agency created during the first oil crisis of 1973. The IEA pools national oil reserves and, in time of crisis, can help ensure that states get the minimum energy supply they need to stabilize their economies and prevent massive inflation or economic collapse.

Leanne C. Powner

See Also European Union; Group of 8 (G8)

References

Aubrey, Henry. 1967. *Atlantic Economic Cooperation: The Case of the OECD.* New York: Praeger.

Esman, Milton, and Daniel Cheever. 1967. *The Common Aid Effort.* Columbus: Ohio State University Press.

Jolly, Adam, ed. 2003. *OECD Economies and the World Today: Trends, Prospects, and OECD Statistics, 2003.* London: Kogan Page.

Keesing's Record of World Events. Various issues. London: Longman.

Moravcsik, Andrew M. 1989. "Disciplining Trade Finance: The OECD Export Credit Arrangement." *International Organization* 43, no. 1 (Winter): 173–205.

Organisation for Economic Co-operation and Development, http://www.oecd.org.

South Asian Association for Regional Cooperation (SAARC)

An intergovernmental organization (IGO) consisting of seven states across South Asia, the South Asian Association for Regional Cooperation (SAARC) officially sprang into existence with a summit of regional heads of state in December 1985 held in the Bangladeshi capital, Dhaka. Founded with a view toward mitigating socioeconomic and developmental problems common to the states of South Asia, the organization has often been criticized for failing to live up to the goals set forth in its charter. SAARC is presently composed of representatives from the member states of India, Pakistan, Nepal, Bangladesh, Bhutan, Sri Lanka, and the Republic of the Maldives. Member states meet at the head of government/state level for annual summit meetings. Overall coordination of organization activities is achieved by the SAARC Secretariat, based in Kathmandu, Nepal.

Historical Overview

The states collectively constituting SAARC by and large share a common British colonial experience and administrative traditions. Regional cooperation, however, was delayed for decades following decolonization owing to a variety of factors, including persistent enmity and territorial conflict between the two largest states of the region, India and Pakistan. Also tending to delay the onset of interstate collaborative efforts across South Asia was the asymmetry in power relations between the aforementioned larger states and the smaller countries of the region (Gonsalves 1995, 34). Mutual distrust among South Asian states thus ensured that regional cooperation would obtain long after such projects had been launched in Europe (with the creation of the European Economic Community and, later, the European Union), Southeast Asia (under the Association of Southeast Asian Nations, ASEAN), and other sectors of the globe.

Although the actual establishment of SAARC was thus chronologically late compared with equivalent regionalist tendencies in other parts of the world, the idea of Asian or South Asian cooperation is of a relatively early vintage. Indeed, future Indian leader Jawaharlal Nehru expressed as early as 1945 the desire to someday form some sort of federation comprising India (which then included Pakistan), Iran, Iraq, Afghanistan, and Burma (Kumar 2002, 7). Political turmoil during the preceding independence era, as well as the establishment of regional alliances in the Middle East, prevented this dream from becoming reality. Heightened tensions between India and Pakistan, exacerbated by overarching Cold War conflict, limited cooperation between South Asian states throughout the 1950s and 1960s.

Conditions began to change during the 1970s as tensions eased between India and Pakistan (temporarily, as it turned out), and a new generation of South Asian leaders came to power. Such heads of state and government proved more committed to achieving the aim of regional cooperation than previous ones had been. Chief among such advocates of collaboration was the Bangladeshi leader during this period, General Zia ur-Rahman. During a tour of South Asian capitals in the late 1970s, Rahman floated the idea of forming a cooperative body composed of the countries of the region (Kashikar 2000, 53–54). The idea was given a further boost by the proven effectiveness of such bodies as the European Economic Community and ASEAN (ibid., 54). The early efforts of Prime Minister Rahman culminated in the 1983 Declaration of South Asian Regional Cooperation (SARC), which paved the way for the official launch of SAARC two years later. In an era of growing international interdependence (a trend now termed "globalization"), it was believed that a collective approach to problem solving, as well as a means for the region to speak with one voice, could reap vast dividends.

The foundation of SAARC in 1985 also coincided with initial efforts to liberalize the economies of the individual member states. Throughout much of the postindependence era, many of the states across the area had established highly protective economic regimes under the broader rubric of import-substitution industrialization (ISI), which sought to decrease dependence on imports and correspondingly foster the growth of domestic industries. The (relatively) backward state of economies across the region increasingly impinged on the credibility of ISI regimes and led to gradual liberalization, a project that could be best pursued within a broader framework of regional cooperation (Hossain 1995, 117).

Structure and Operation

SAARC was designed with the intention of treating key issue areas such as poverty, meteorology, science and technology, and agricultural policy. Deliberately avoided were issues of bilateral conflict (chief among which, of course, was the ongoing Indo-Pakistani ri-

valry). Framers of the SAARC Charter operated under the assumption that the overall spirit of regional cooperation could be severely weakened unless outstanding diplomatic issues were left out of association discussions (Hussain 2000, 75).

The organization was thus geared toward dealing with some of the chief causes of underdevelopment in the region, with the hope that cooperation among states would lead to the socioeconomic advancement of all states of the region. A subsidiary goal was to lessen conflict among nations through cooperation on multiple fronts. The sources of bilateral conflict were thus to be avoided by the organization, and it was believed social and cultural cooperation would gradually bind all South Asian nations closer together. Article 10 of the SAARC Charter set down the principle of unanimity in all association decisions, a means by which issues pertaining to bilateral conflict could be largely (if not entirely) avoided (Kashikar 2000, 63).

Since the organization's founding, much debate has developed around the question of whether the avoidance of issues relating to bilateral conflict represents a help or hindrance when it comes to the overall efficacy of SAARC. Some, including the current president of Pakistan, Pervez Musharraf, claim the strategy serves to effectively "cripple" the regional body (Lawson 2002). Others, including the original framers of the founding charters, maintain that diplomatic conflict avoidance allows progress to be made across many other policy areas. Both agree that bilateral conflict has played a large role in the politics of the region since independence. Long-simmering tensions between India and Pakistan were recently (1998) punctuated by tit-for-tat nuclear weapons tests on the part of the two countries.

Though perhaps the most prominent among South Asian conflicts on the world stage, the ongoing Indo-Pakistani enmity is not the only such bilateral conflict between states of the region. Relations between India and Bangladesh, for example, have long been strained over the issue of cross-border migration. Another dispute has pitted India against Nepal, and India and Sri Lanka have fought wars of words over the latter's civil war and India's alleged role in it. The conflict led to the cancellation of the 1989 SAARC summit slated to be held in Colombo, the Sri Lankan capital (Kashikar 2000, 82).

Conflict between states has thus proven to be a formidable obstacle to closer regional integration. For several years, SAARC summitry has been overshadowed by speculations regarding the diplomatic activities of representatives from India and Pakistan. Indeed, although SAARC was not itself designed to handle such bilateral conflicts, summit meetings have provided an opportunity for South Asian leaders to meet informally, thus raising hopes of eventual conflict resolution. Leading officials continue to hope, moreover, that great social and cultural integration could lead to greater mutual understanding among nations, thereby reducing diplomatic tensions that have long paralyzed the region.

The functions of SAARC are carried out through several bodies, including a permanent Secretariat based in Kathmandu, the Nepalese capital, and regular meetings of heads of state and government and foreign ministers (Singh 1989, 149–150). The SAARC Charter calls for summit meetings at the heads of state and government level to be held at least once a year. Several years, however, have passed since the founding of the organization during which no such meetings were convened. Summit meetings occurred in Dhaka, Bangladesh, in 1985; Bangalore, India, in 1986; Kathmandu, Nepal, in 1987; Islamabad, Pakistan, in 1988; Male, Maldives, in 1990; Colombo, Sri Lanka, in 1991; Dhaka in 1993; New Delhi, India, in 1995; Male in 1997; Colombo in 1998; Kathmandu in 2002, and Islamabad in 2004 (SAARC Web site).

Controversy has often arisen from failures to hold summit meetings in a given year, but bilateral conflict is often the cause of such failure. A notable example was the failure of leaders to meet in 1989, an event (or nonevent) that nearly occurred again the following year in an atmosphere of controversy and mutual recriminations among states (Kashikar 2000, 82–83). Over three years elapsed following nuclear tests in the region in 1998 before another SAARC summit could be convened. The last summit meeting was held in January 2004. Meetings of foreign ministers and foreign secretaries have tended to be held at slightly more frequent intervals, and the SAARC Secretariat tends to day-to-day association activities between meetings of the region's heads of state and government.

The annual summit meetings set down under the SAARC Charter represent the highest tier of the organization's structure. Immediately below the heads of state level stands the Council of Ministers (composed of the foreign ministers of member states) and the Standing Committee (composed of foreign secretaries from the seven states of SAARC). Whereas the Council of Ministers makes policies under the broader grouping of goals set forth by successive summit meetings, the Standing Committee actually supervises the programs that the council creates while also coordinating these various programs. SAARC also sponsors other meetings of various groupings of top-level officials and government advisers. Some of the issues tackled by annual meetings at the ministerial level include housing, poverty, youth, information, and international economic issues (SAARC Web site).

In addition to the policymaking and monitoring bodies mentioned above, the SAARC Secretariat brings together the activities of technical committees. These currently include committees dedicated to agriculture and rural development; communications and transport; social development; the environment, meteorology, and forestry; science and technology; human resources development; and energy. The number of committees was brought down to seven, out of eleven original bodies, following the adoption of a revised SAARC Integrated Program of Action in 1999.

Regional centers are currently composed of an Agricultural Information Center, a Tuberculosis Center, a Documentation Center, a Meteorological Research Center, and a Human Resources Development Center. Regional apex bodies form another part of the overarching SAARC organizational structure. These groups foster contact between members of various professions across the region. Occupations currently represented by regional apex bodies include legal professionals, accountants, and leaders of commerce (through a regional chamber of commerce). Just below regional apex bodies in the SAARC hierarchy are SAARC-recognized organizations. These organizations, which are also composed largely of representatives from various professions, currently include the SAARC Cardiac Society, the SAARC Federation of University Women, and the SAARC Association of Town Planners, among others.

SAARC hosts a variety of programs designed to engender cultural unity across the diverse population of South Asia. Current cultural programs include an annual film festival (inaugurated in Sri Lanka in 1999), an awards program for aspiring young scientists, and a youth volunteer program. Working to coordinate communications policy across the region, SAARC hosts meetings of member state communications ministers. The organization also publishes various media materials, including those offered on its Web site (ibid.).

Programs and Accomplishments

After Dhaka, the first SAARC summit meetings were held in Bangalore, India, in November 1986 and Kathmandu in October 1987. These early summit meetings focused mainly on organizational and procedural issues. Declarations, issued at the end of each summit, always opened with a vast array of goals and ideals, including the aim of quickening the pace of development across the region and reducing the problem of poverty that faced (and, indeed, continues to face) each member state. Activities were given some structure through the early formulation of an Integrated Program for Action (IPA), revised in 1999, which set forth

broad areas in which cooperation among member states might be achieved. Policy areas in which SAARC claimed some jurisdiction included rural development; health; gender; transportation and telecommunications; postal service; meteorology; science and technology; sports, arts, and culture; and drug trafficking and abuse.

A departure from this state of affairs occurred during the course of the 1990 Male summit. There SAARC members published a declaration outlining five "core areas" in which the organization sought to achieve progress. These included poverty alleviation, a goal partially addressed through the establishment of a regional foodgrain reserve, for which contributions were sought from each member state (Rieger 1995, 125). In the late 1980s and early 1990s, moreover, SAARC leaders sought an unprecedented level of involvement from members of civil society and nongovernmental organizations (NGOs) when they convened the South Asian Commission on Poverty Alleviation, following the submission of technical advice from the Independent Group of South Asian Scholars and Professionals (IGSAC) (Wignaraja 1995, 218).

The resulting declaration called on member states to work toward the eradication of poverty by 2002 (Hossain et al. 1999, 222). Member states were encouraged to radically change policies on poverty, replacing a state-centric approach with one that fostered greater involvement of the poor and their representatives. The development of mediating institutions was another focus of the declaration. Assumed in the document was continued economic growth among member states—the target of eradicating poverty within a decade was explicitly tied to a substantial expansion of gross domestic product (GDP) across the seven SAARC members (Wignaraja 1995, 224).

Among other notable activities on the part of the organization has been the development of a South Asian Preferred Trade Area (SAPTA) in 1993, followed by calls for a South Asian Free Trade Area (SAFTA) during the 1995 summit (Hossain et al. 1999, 149). Representing the first step toward regional economic integration, SAPTA dictated reduction of tariffs between member states across hundreds of commodities (Bhalla and Bhalla 1997, 83). Various obstacles to closer trade relations have largely prevented further economic cooperation from taking place, even as successive SAARC summit declarations enunciate the desire of regional leaders to work toward this ideal.

The SAARC region has yet to come close to the level of economic integration achieved in Europe, or even across the states of Southeast Asia, where regional institutions have been in place for considerably longer periods of time (Mehrotra 1995, 24–25). Free and extensive trade among the nations of South Asia remains hobbled by a variety of factors, including the remnants of ISI regimes, a dearth of import financing mechanisms, and mismatched economic specialization (that is, many of the products imported from outside South Asia are simply not produced within the region) (Hossain 1995, 117).

The latter state of affairs is partly a holdover of the colonial era, when economies of the region were designed so as to promote the export of raw materials to Great Britain. There is, however, a considerable degree of variation in trade relations across the region. India and Pakistan, for example, trade only in very small quantities with other SAARC nations, whereas some of the smaller states of the region, such as Nepal, are closely tied to the larger regional powers economically (Bhalla and Bhalla 1997, 89). Nonetheless, the overall level of trade between SAARC member states remains very low in comparison to the amount attained by ASEAN and members of the European Union.

Scholars are split as to the steps SAARC and its constituent nations might take to most effectively deepen economic integration, with some pointing to a gradualist, step-by-step approach and others advocating a "leapfrog" method along the lines of that employed by the members of the European Common Market (Rieger 1995, 23). Others, also having compared the economic position of SAARC nations to that of other regional trade blocs, recommend that states of the region focus on building reserves of foreign direct investment (FDI) and continue to liberalize domestically before taking further steps toward regional economic integration.

Although SAARC has been faced with significant shortcomings with regard to economic integration and trade relations among member states, it has taken action across a wide array of functional areas. SAARC first took on the issue of terrorism in 1987 with association approval of a regional convention on the issue (Singh 1989, 155). Controversy surrounded the convention, with the issue of violence in Kashmir factoring into the debate surrounding it. Further tension marked more recent efforts to strengthen the protocol on suppression of terrorism in the wake of the terrorist attacks against the United States on September 11, 2001, and the attack on the Indian Parliament in December of that year. The issue of terrorism represents the area of SAARC activity tending to most closely touch on the issue of bilateral conflicts, with both India and Pakistan claiming that agents and surrogates of the other should be held accountable for what they perceive as acts of terrorism, particularly in the disputed region of Kashmir.

Heightened bilateral conflicts, as well as heightened global tensions over the past several years, have together tended to dampen the spirit of regional cooperation established with the founding of SAARC nearly two decades ago ("Unmagnificent Seven" 2002). Whereas the European Union and its forerunners were developed (and deepened) in the wake of two devastating world wars, and under the resulting assumption that unchecked national independence and ambition could prove dangerous in the long run, such sentiment is still lacking across many areas of South Asia (Elsenhans 1995, 238).

Future Directions

After failing to meet for over three years, South Asian leaders met for the eleventh SAARC summit January 4–6, 2002, in Kathmandu. The declaration arising from the meeting set several goals, including the "harmonization" of national development programs across the region. Also discussed was the ongoing effort to stem (if not entirely eradicate) poverty, as well as the need for global cooperation toward the formulation of a Comprehensive Convention on Combating Terrorism. The body also took a moment to note certain of SAARC's recent achievements, which included efforts to encourage free and fair elections through meetings of the chief election commissioners of SAARC countries, last convened in February 1999 (Zia et al. 2001).

The last SAARC summit meeting was held in Pakistan in January 2004.. Tensions between India and Pakistan, particularly over the contested region of Kashmir, continue to overshadow any significant progress toward greater regional integration. Critics of SAARC continue to question the worth of the organization, pointing to the lack of progress in fostering freer trade across the region or in significantly improving the quality of life for the people of South Asia. Defenders, however, make reference to the many important contacts being fostered behind the scenes between notable figures of the region, as well as the more abstract spirit of cooperation the organization is designed to foster (but which is difficult to measure).

Dan Ehlke

See Also Economic Integration; Association of Southeast Asian Nations (ASEAN)

References

Bhalla, A. S., and P. Bhalla. 1997. *Regional Blocs: Building Blocks or Stumbling Blocks?* New York: St. Martin's.

Elsenhans, Hartmut. 1995. "Neofunctionalist Integration Approach to Strengthening the European Union and Raising Global Industrial Competitiveness of Its Member States." In H. S. Chopra, Gert W. Kueck, and L. L. Mehrotra, eds., *SAARC 2000 and Beyond.* New Delhi: Omega Scientific.

Gonsalves, Eric. 1995. "South Asian Cooperation: An Agenda and a Vision for the Future." In H. S. Chopra, Gert W. Kueck, and L. L. Mehrotra, eds., *SAARC 2000 and Beyond.* New Delhi: Omega Scientific.

Gonsalves, Eric and Nancy Jetly, Editors. 1999. The Dynamics of South Asia: Regional Cooperation and Saarc. Thousand Oaks, CA. Sage Publications.

Hossain, Kamal. 1995. "Towards a Single Market for South Asia." In H. S. Chopra, Gert W. Kueck, and L. L. Mehrotra, eds., *SAARC 2000 and Beyond.* New Delhi: Omega Scientific.

Hossain, Moazzem, Iyanatul Islam, and Reza Kibria. 1999. *South Asian Economic Development: Transformation, Opportunities and Challenges.* New York: Routledge.

Hussain, Akmal. 2000. "The Imperative of a Political Agenda for SAARC." In B. C. Upreti, ed., *SAARC: Dynamics of Regional Cooperation in South Asia.* Vol. 1. New Delhi: Kalinga.

Kashikar, Mohan. 2000. *SAARC: Its Genesis, Development and Prospects.* Mumbai: Himalaya.

Kumar, A. Prasanna. 2002. "SAARC: Retrospect and Prospect." In K. C. Reddy and T. Nirmala Devi, eds., *Regional Cooperation in South Asia.* New Delhi: Kanishka.

Lawson, Alastair. 2002. "South Asia's Crippled Regional Body." *BBC News Online,* January 4, http://news.bbc. co.uk/2/hi/south_asia/1741449.stm.

Mehrotra, L. L. 1995. "Why Regional Cooperation?" In H. S. Chopra, Gert W. Kueck, and L. L. Mehrotra, eds., *SAARC 2000 and Beyond.* New Delhi: Omega Scientific.

Rieger, Hans Christoph. 1995. "Winners and Losers in International Economic Cooperation: With Special Reference to SAARC." In H. S. Chopra, Gert W. Kueck, and L. L. Mehrotra, eds., *SAARC 2000 and Beyond.* New Delhi: Omega Scientific.

Singh, Tarlok. 1989. "Perspective after the Third Summit." In Bimal Prasad, ed., *Regional Cooperation in South Asia.* New Delhi: Vikas.

South Asian Association for Regional Cooperation, http://www.saarc-sec.org.

"The Unmagnificent Seven." 2002. *Economist,* January 24.

Wignaraja, P. 1995. "Poverty Eradication: The 'Entry Point' for Recapturing a South Asian Economic Community." In H. S. Chopra, Gert W. Kueck, and L. L. Mehrotra, eds. *SAARC 2000 and Beyond.* New Delhi: Omega Scientific.

Zia, Khaleda, et al. 2001. "Declaration of the South Asian Association for Regional Cooperation." *Presidents & Prime Ministers* 10, no. 6 (November/December).

Southern African Development Community (SADC)

In 1980, nine members of the frontline, black-ruled southern African nations joined together to establish the Southern African Development Coordination Conference (SADCC), which evolved into the Southern African Development Community (SADC) in August 1992 at a meeting in Windhoek, Namibia. The stated goals of the organization were to promote economic cooperation and integration and to encourage growth in Southern Africa while reducing dependence on a South Africa rampant with apartheid. Once apartheid was eradicated, South Africa joined the Southern African Development Community. The architects of SADC realized that such an organization was needed to motivate southern African countries to realize the full potential of the region and to gain some measure of independence from international entities that were eager to help or to exploit the developing southern African nations.

Cooperation among southern African nations was sorely needed in this region, which suffers from periodic droughts and floods, rampant political unrest, a lack of clean water, high infant mortality and HIV/AIDS infection rates, low life expectancy, and a shortage of reliable transportation systems. The common practice of trading with countries outside the region rather than with other southern African nations had seriously depleted the resources of the region. Although there is little doubt that SADC has had some successes, many critics argue that the organization has done little to alleviate the vast economic inequalities among member nations.

Historical Overview

The SADCC met for the first time in Arusha, Tanzania, in July 1979. The meeting was attended by Angola, Botswana, Mozambique, Tanzania, and Zambia. At that time, attendees agreed to open membership in the SADCC to all independent southern African states. A subsequent meeting, held in Lusaka, Zambia, in April 1980, was attended by nine countries who became the founding members, including Angola, Botswana, Lesotho, Malawi, Mozambique, Swaziland, Tanzania, Zambia, and Zimbabwe. In Lusaka, the SADCC announced that it was determined to "free the peoples of Southern Africa from misery, hunger, and chronic dependency" (Nsekela 1981, xii).

During the course of its development, the SADC has created a number of internal sectors designed to deal with issues common to its members. These sectors include energy; tourism; environment and land management; water; mining; employment and labor; culture; information and sport; transport and communications; finance and investment, human resource development; food, agriculture, and natural resources; legal affairs; and health. Each sector has been charged with accomplishing particular SADC goals. For example, the Food,

Agriculture, and Natural Resources (FANR) Development Unit coordinates SADC efforts toward food security policies and programs and promotes agricultural development and the utilization of natural resources while working to promote biodiversity and free trade. Much of the efforts of FANR have been directed toward reducing hunger and famine within poorer SADC countries.

The Treaty of Windhoek that established the SADC identified five guiding principles for member states to follow: sovereign equality of all member nations; solidarity, peace, and security for southern Africa; respect for human rights, democracy, and the rule of law throughout the region; equity, balance, and mutual benefit among member nations; and peaceful settlement of disputes. In order to put these guiding principles into practice, the treaty identified eight specific objectives: achieving development and economic growth by alleviating poverty and improving the quality of life for southern Africans; generating common political values, systems, and institutions among SADC members; promoting and defending national and regional peace and security; promoting self-sustaining development that encourages self-reliance and interdependence of SADC members; coordinating national and regional strategies and programs; promoting maximum employment and utilization of member resources; promoting the utilization of natural resources and the protection of the environment; and strengthening historical, social, and cultural ties among member nations. (SADC 2003).

Governance of SADC

SADC operations are guided by the SADC Summit, which is made up of the heads of state of the various member nations. The purpose of the summit is to establish policy and set overall SADC goals. The Council of Ministers, which is made up of the foreign ministers of each member state, oversees the day-to-day activities of

the SADC. The Secretariat was given the responsibility for strategic planning and coordinating and managing SADC programs. Various commissions and sectoral committees have been periodically created to further cooperation among member states and to determine the impact of SADC policies within particular sectors. Sectoral committees of ministers oversee the work of the various commissions and sectoral committees. SADC established the Standing Committee of Officials to serve in a technical advisory capacity. Finally, the SADC Tribunal interprets the treaty as it applies to SADC activities and mediates disputes that arise among member nations. All tribunal decisions are final and binding.

SADC Challenges

Producing healthy economies within SADC countries is complicated by the fact that some members experience prolonged dry spells with accompanying drought, while others are victims of flooding. In Malawi, Zambia, and Zimbabwe, for example, serious food shortages have resulted from weather-related conditions, leading to the necessity of importing food from other countries. Overall, drought and the resulting famine in 1982–1983 cost members of SADCC over $154 million and the loss of more than 100,000 lives. Inconsistent and impractical government policies and inefficient and sometimes corrupt private sectors, in conjunction with political insurgency, have further crippled the economies of SADC members.

Heavily dependent on agricultural resources for its economic growth and survival, southern Africa has experienced a number of other debilitating problems in addition to weather-related crises. For instance, foot and mouth disease has decimated livestock among member nations. As a result of the many problems related to agriculture, the SADC has devoted a good deal of its resources to bringing knowledge of agricultural practices and processes up to date. These efforts include advanced research into ways that make the area more productive and independent and improved training of agriculturalists and their workers.

Internal problems have also plagued the SADC, including staffing and economic problems and a lack of enforcement capability. While maintaining membership in SADC, individual members have sometimes neglected to sign particular SADC protocols, making it harder for the SADC to implement policies and carry on its activities. For example, South Africa refused to ratify the Immunities and Privileges Protocol that gives SADC officials freedom of movement within the various SADC countries as they conduct SADC business. Several members have also threatened to withdraw their support for SADC.

SADC Members

Although members of the SADC have much in common, each member state is unique and has strengths and weaknesses. This very uniqueness has often allowed inequalities to flourish among SADC member nations. The poorest SADC nations are heavily dependent on agriculture for survival, whereas middle-range SADC nations have been successful in exporting various metals and materials. Only the most developed nations have achieved viability on a global scale.

The founding member states are: Angola, Botswana, Lesotho, Malawi, Mozambique, Swaziland, United Republic of Tanzania, Zambia and Zimbabwe. South Africa joined SADC in 1994 followed by Mauritius (1995), the Democratic Republic of Congo–DRC (1997), and Seychelles (1997). The Seychelles subsequently pulled out of the SADC in 2004. Uganda's application for membership in the SADC, submitted in the fall of 2000, currently is awaiting SADC approval. In August 2004, Madagascar was granted candidate membership status, which may be upgraded to full membership in August 2005. As the twentieth

century drew to a close, members of the Southern African Development Community had thus increased to twelve active members that, with varying degrees of success, attempted to eradicate all obstacles to trade among member nations. In September 1997, the SADC approved the membership applications of the Democratic Republic of Congo (formerly Zaire) and the Seychelles.

Angola
Although it is the second largest of the countries within sub-Saharan Africa, Angola is sparsely populated, in part because the country is subject to severe droughts that may last over several decades. Since agriculture is an important element of the Angolan economy, drought leads to suffering and food deficits throughout the population. Poor agricultural practices, such as overuse of pastures, which leads to soil erosion and extensive desertification and deforestation, have further damaged Angola's economic outlook. The lack of clean water has also continued to create major health problems in Angola. Life expectancy in Angola is only 36.96 years, and infant mortality is high, at 193.92 deaths per 1,000 live births. The U.S. Central Intelligence Agency (CIA) estimates that more than 1 million Angolan lives were lost in the internal fighting that took place during the last quarter of the twentieth century.

Botswana
Formerly known as the British protectorate of Bechuanaland, Botswana established its new identity in 1966. Since its independence, Botswana has developed a robust economy that has resulted in one of the highest growth rates in the world, partially because of its successful diamond export and tourism businesses. However, Botswana suffers from overgrazing, desertification, and a scarcity of fresh water. It also suffers from a low life expectancy rate of 36.26 years and a high infant mortality rate of 67.34 deaths per 1,000 live births. Botswana's HIV/AIDS infection rate of 38.8 percent is the highest in the world, with serious implications

for national health. The economic security of Botswana is threatened by the fact that the incomes of 47 percent of its people fall below the poverty line and by an unemployment rate of 40 percent.

Lesotho

Known as Basutoland until 1966 when the country won its independence from Great Britain, Lesotho established constitutional government in 1993 after more than twenty years of military rule. During the early 1980s, the drought in Lesotho was so severe that conservative estimates placed economic losses at over $123 million. Without the frequent contributions from citizens of Lesotho who work in South Africa to their family members in Lesotho, the economic outlook for Lesotho would be even worse than it is. Agricultural success in Lesotho is heavily dependent on eradicating the problems of overgrazing and soil erosion and depletion. Life expectancy in Lesotho is only 36.94 years, and the infant mortality rate is high, at 86.21 deaths per 1,000 live births. Like many other African nations, Lesotho is also experiencing an HIV/AIDS epidemic. Almost half of the residents of Lesotho live below the poverty line, and 45 percent of the nation's residents are unemployed.

Malawi

Established in 1891 as the British protectorate of Nyasaland, Malawi achieved its independence in 1964. Although it has the potential to be self-sufficient, Malawi has much work to accomplish before achieving that status. Approximately 90 percent of the population of Malawi lives in rural areas. Malawi's major crop is maize, but weather conditions sometimes result in maize deficits that threaten the overall economy. Because of these problems, Malawi is heavily dependent on funding from the International Monetary Fund (IMF) and the International Bank for Reconstruction and Development (IBRD). Malawi also suffers from deforestation, land degradation, water pollution, inadequate sewage facilities, and siltation

of the spawning grounds of various species of endangered fish. The life expectancy for residents of Malawi is 37.98 years, and the infant mortality rate is high, at 105.15 deaths per 1,000 live births.

Mauritius

In 1968, Mauritius won its independence from Great Britain, establishing a democratic system that placed high priority on respect for human rights. With one of the highest per capita incomes among SADC members, Mauritius has a sufficiency of arable land and the capability of exporting sugar and fish products. Unfortunately, the country suffers from water pollution and degradation of its coral reefs. The progressive status of Mauritius among SADC countries is illustrated by a high life-expectancy rate of 71.8 years and a low infant mortality rate of 16.11 deaths per 1,000 life births. In recent years, Mauritius has attracted almost 10,000 offshore entities, resulting in a banking sector that generates an income of approximately $1 billion per year. Partly because of this, only 10 percent of the population of Mauritius lives below the poverty line, and the unemployment rate is only 8.8 percent.

Mozambique

After achieving relative independence from Portugal in the mid-1970s, Mozambique suffered a major loss in human resources as large numbers of whites emigrated, leaving the country heavily dependent on South Africa and vulnerable to civil war and a socialist government. Like many of its neighbors, Mozambique falls short of its potential for self-sufficiency, failing to sufficiently utilize its natural resources of coal, titanium, natural gas, hydropower, tantalum, and graphite. The country also suffers from problems with deforestation, pollution of surface and coastal water, and elephant piracy. The life expectancy in Mozambique is only 31.3 years, and the high infant mortality rate of 199 deaths per 1,000 live births further depletes Mozambique's human resources. The country is one of the poorest nations in the world: Seventy percent of the inhabitants live below the poverty line, and approximately one-fifth of the nation's population is unemployed.

Namibia

In the mid-1960s, the Marxist South-West African People's Organization (SWAPO) initiated a guerrilla war that eventually led to independence from South Africa and the emergence of Namibia in 1990. Although Namibia has been forced to cope with the problems of limited freshwater resources, desertification, wildlife piracy, and land depletion, the country made history by incorporating environmental protection into its constitution. Namibia suffers from a low life expectancy of 42.77 years, a high infant mortality rate of 68.44 deaths per 1,000 live births, and an HIV/AIDS infection rate of 22.5 percent. Around one-half of the population of Namibia lives below the poverty line, and unemployment hovers around 35 percent.

South Africa

Once apartheid ended and free democratic elections were held in 1994, South Africa became a member of the SADC. Even though the country normally exports a good deal of maize, severe periodic droughts are a problem. Excellent transportation facilities give South Africa a distinct advantage among SADC nations. Like most of its neighbors, South Africa has a low life expectancy, at 46.56 years. The high infant mortality rate of 60.84 deaths per 1,000 live births and an HIV/AIDS infection rate of 20.1 percent also demonstrate a continued need for improved health conditions. Economically, the 50 percent poverty rate and the 37.9 percent unemployment rate also signal the need for improvement.

The inclusion of South Africa in SADC has proved to be a mixed blessing. South Africa maintains close ties with the West, including close relationships with the European Union and the United States. Western interests at times come into direct conflict with the perceived interests of southern Africa. There has also been a strong tendency for other SADC members to depend too heavily on South Africa's healthy economy rather than developing their own internal resources.

Swaziland

Although Swaziland was technically granted independence from Great Britain in the late nineteenth century, it was not until 1968 that the country achieved true independence. Agriculture continues to dominate Swaziland's economy; and the country continues to cope with problems that develop as a result of insufficient clean water supplies, wildlife depletion, overgrazing, and soil depletion and erosion. Weather-related problems are frequent in Swaziland, and in 2002 around one-fourth of Swaziland's residents received emergency food aid. Nine-tenths of Swaziland's imports are received from South Africa, leaving Swaziland heavily dependent on its larger neighbor. Persistent health problems have resulted in a life expectancy of 39.47 years, an infant mortality rate of 67.44 deaths per 1,000 live births, and an HIV/AIDS infection rate of 33.4 percent. Economically, 40 percent of Swaziland's people live below the poverty line, and the unemployment rate remains around 34 percent.

Tanzania

The nation of Tanzania was created from the merger of Tanganyika and Zanzibar in 1964. Tanzania has a wealth of natural resources that include hydropower, tin, phosphates, iron ore, coal, diamonds, and gold. Unfortunately, like many of its neighboring countries, Tanzania suffers from periodic flooding and droughts. These problems are intensified by environmental problems such as soil degradation, deforestation, desertification, destruction of coral reefs, and wildlife piracy. Health resources in Tanzania have repeatedly been depleted by the low life expectancy of 44.56 years, the high infant mortality rate of 103.68 deaths per 1,000 live births, and an HIV/AIDS infection rate of 7.8 percent. As one of the world's poorest countries, Tanzania is heavily dependent on agriculture. It supplements its income with funds from the World Bank, the International Monetary Fund, and various other donors.

Zambia

Although Zambia, formerly known as Rhodesia, is more self-sufficient than many other southern African nations, the country is landlocked and suffers from internal food distribution problems. The country prospered after its independence from Great Britain in 1964; however, declining copper prices and prolonged drought in the 1990s set Zambia back economically. In addition to periodic droughts, Zambia suffers from heavy tropical storms that regularly assail the country each year from November to April, leading to air pollution, acid rain, and chemical runoff. Zambia also faces problems with wildlife poaching, deforestation, soil erosion, desertification, and a lack of clean water. Health problems in Zambia result in a low life expectancy of 35.25 years, a high infant mortality rate of 99.20 deaths per 1,000 live births, and an HIV/AIDS infection rate of 21.5 percent. Approximately 86 percent of Zambia's population lives below the poverty line, and 85 percent of the country's population is employed in the agricultural sector.

Zimbabwe

Formerly Southern Rhodesia, Zimbabwe unilaterally announced its independence from South Africa in 1965. However, it took a guerrilla uprising and interference from the United Nations before true independence was achieved in 1980. Zimbabwe continues to be a major exporter of maize, and this export capability has made the economy of Zimbabwe second only to South Africa among SADC countries. Like its neighbors, Zimbabwe suffers from deforestation, soil erosion, land degradation, air and water pollution, and wildlife poaching. Zimbabwe is also held back by a life expectancy rate of 39.01 years, a high infant mortality rate of 66.47 deaths per 1,000 life births, and an HIV/AIDS infection rate of 33.7

percent. Seventy percent of Zimbabwe's population lives below the poverty line, and the unemployment rate has also settled at 70 percent.

Contemporary Outlook

The SADC has been most successful in achieving cooperation on a bilateral scale. For example, Tanzania and Malawi worked together to create a road that provided Malawi with much-desired access to the port of Dar es Saleem. In another cooperative effort, Zambia granted Mozambique access to a rail link that provided the latter country with access to port facilities. Tanzania has worked with other SADC countries to improve interregional rail transport aimed at stimulating agricultural production and processing.

Overall, the SADC has also helped to promote a sense of regional identity within southern Africa that was not present before 1980. Some member states have achieved a measure of financial independence from outside forces, while others remain heavily dependent on more developed nations. Tariffs in the region have fallen by 70 percent, and trading among member nations has grown at a rate of approximately 10 percent per year. The gross domestic product (GDP) of the region has risen to nearly 60 percent of that of sub-Saharan Africa, with around 80 percent of the total GDP of SADC countries deriving from South Africa. Per capita incomes of SADC countries are roughly double those of other sub-Saharan countries. Furthermore, more than half of all foreign trade in this region is conducted with SADC countries.

The SADC has established goals for the twenty-first century that include a major restructuring of the organization, an emphasis on technological development, and the development of subregional trading blocs. The SADC also created its first two directorates, which began operation at the turn of the century: the Trade, Finance, Industry, and Investment Directorate and the Food, Agriculture, and Natural Resources Directorate. Plans were also in place to establish southern Africa as a free trade area by 2008.

In addition to participation by individual SADC members in other regional organizations, in February 1998 the SADC signed a formal agreement with the Economic Community for West African States (ECOWAS), the Intergovernmental Authority on Development (IGAD), and the Common Market for Eastern and Southern Africa (COMESA). The agreement among the four African organizations was designed to coordinate efforts to deal with Africa's national debt and to promote actions that would speed up the process of establishing an African Economic Community that would benefit the member nations of all four groups.

Before it can achieve its own full potential, however, the Southern African Development Community must come to terms with what globalization means for southern Africa. Outside interest in the area offers greater potential for development in some countries than in others, with an accompanying increase in the already existing inequalities among SADC member nations. The SADC may also be forced to determine the role that the region will play in the developing global economy.

Elizabeth Purdy

See Also Economic Integration; Common Market for Eastern and Southern Africa (COMESA); East African Community (EAC); Economic Community of Central African States (CEEAC); Franc Zone

References

Central Intelligence Agency. 2003. "The World Factbook," January, http://www.cia.gov/cia/publications/factbook/index.html (cited December 29, 2003).

El-Agraa, Ali M. 1997. *Economic Integration Worldwide.* London: Macmillan.

Kell, Sue, and Troy Dyer. 2000. "Economic Integration in Southern Africa." Pp. 363–393 in York Bradshaw and Stephen N. Ndegwa, eds., *The Uncertain Promise of Southern Africa.* Bloomington and Indianapolis: Indiana University Press.

Legum, Colin. 2000. "Balance of Power in Southern Africa." Pp. 12–23 in York Bradshaw and Stephen N. Ndegwa, eds., *The Uncertain Promise of Southern Africa.* Bloomington and Indianapolis: Indiana University Press.

Libby, Ronald T. 1987. *The Politics of Economic Power in Southern Africa.* Princeton, NJ: Princeton University Press.

Mazur, Robert E., ed. 1990. *Breaking the Links: Development Theory and Practice in Southern Africa.* Trenton, NJ: Africa World Press.

Moyo, Sam, Phil O'Keefe, and Michael Sill. 1993. *The Southern African Environment: Profiles of the SADC Countries.* London: Earthscan.

Nsekela, Amon J., ed. 1981. *Southern Africa: Toward Economic Liberation.* London: Rex Collings.

Peet, Richard. 1984. *Manufacturing Industry and Economic Development in the SADCC Countries.* Stockholm: Beijer Institute.

Sklair, Leslie. 2002. *Globalization: Capitalism and Its Alternatives.* Oxford: Oxford University Press.

Southern Africa Development Community, http://www.sadc.int/index.php?lang=english&path=&page=index (cited December 29, 2003).

———. 2003. SADC Treaty, http://www.sadc.int/index.php?lang=english&path=about/background&page=objectives (cited December 29, 2003).

United Nations Conference on Trade and Development (UNCTAD)

Established in 1964 as a permanent intergovernmental body, the United Nations Conference on Trade and Development (UNCTAD) is the UN's focal point for issues pertaining to trade, investment, and development. The main goal of UNCTAD, as laid out in its mandate, is to maximize trade, investment, and development opportunities for developing countries—in particular, to assist them in their efforts to face the challenges and reap the benefits of globalization. UNCTAD has 191 member states and its headquarters are in Geneva, Switzerland.

Based on such a wide membership and on its all-encompassing mandate, UNCTAD has maintained over the years a leading role as a forum for intergovernmental deliberations on trade and development and as a contributor to the policy research and analysis conducted on globalization and development, international trade, competition policy, investment, enterprise development and technology transfer, transport and infrastructure, and so on. All UNCTAD activities take into account the issues of sustainable development, gender equality, and economic cooperation among developing countries. From the very beginning, UNCTAD's philosophy (as expressed by its first secretary general, Raul Prebisch) has been based on compromise and cooperation among developed and developing countries. UNCTAD's activities and policy advice needed, nevertheless, to evolve constantly and respond to the changing needs of its member states and to the rapid transformations within the international economic environment. The UNCTAD conferences held every four years provide regular forums to refocus UNCTAD's approaches, recommendations, and actions.

UNCTAD's role since 1964 has been a difficult one, as the tasks lying ahead have become even more challenging. Despite its intellectual contribution and sustained intergovernmental efforts, UNCTAD as an institution, and developing countries as a group, have not seen their efforts matched with substantial changes in the course of the world economy (UN 1985). There is no doubt, however, that UNCTAD (along with other multilateral agencies, such as the General Agreement on Tariffs and Trade [GATT], the World Bank, and the International Monetary Fund [IMF]) has introduced new actions, concepts, and approaches to the development debate through its research, policy analysis, technical assistance, capacity building, negotiations, and consensus building (UNCTAD 1994).

UNCTAD's work has prompted or facilitated a number of policy initiatives at the international level. Among them, notable achievements are the introduction of the special and differential (S&D) treatment principle and the Generalized System of Preferences (GSP). Since 1971, more than US$70 billion in exports from developing countries have received preferential treatment in developed markets annually

The Principle of Special and Differential Treatment for Developing Countries: Background and Evolution in the Context of the Multilateral Trading System

The principle of S&D treatment was first formulated in the context of interstate trade relations as a result of coordinated efforts by developing countries to correct the perceived inequalities of the trading system by introducing preferential treatment in their favor across the spectrum of international economic relations. The principle found expression in a succession of articles and instruments associated with the multilateral trading system created by the GATT, notably Article XVIII, "Governmental Assistance to Economic Development," which enabled developing countries to maintain a certain flexibility in their tariff structures in order to develop their industrial base (and to apply quantitative restrictions for balance-of-payments reasons), and Part IV of GATT, Article XXXVI, adopted in 1964, in which, among other things, the developed-country parties declared that they did "not expect reciprocity for commitments made by them in trade negotiations to reduce or remove tariffs and other barriers to the trade of less-developed contracting parties." The Generalized System of Preferences (GSP) accorded by developed countries to developing countries in international trade—introduced at the UNCTAD II Conference in New Delhi, 1968—was a further manifestation of the principle. The 1994 Uruguay Round agreements provided for special and differential treatment mainly in the form of time-limited derogations, greater flexibility with regard to certain obligations, and other more favorable clauses. The S&D principles are a major negotiating element in the current WTO negotiations.

At the regional level, preferential treatment for developing countries was also embodied in the provisions of the First ACP-EEC Lomé Convention regulating nonreciprocal trade preferences granted by the European Union.

through the GSP schemes. A number of international commodity agreements, for instance on cacao, coffee, sugar, jute products, tropical timber, olive oil, and grains, have been negotiated under the aegis of UNCTAD. A Common Fund for Commodities was also set up to provide financial assistance for price stabilization mechanisms and research and development (R&D) projects in the field of commodities. In the area of maritime transport, UNCTAD played an active role in the adoption of the UN Convention on a Code of Conduct for Liner Conferences (1974) and the UN Convention on the Carriage of Goods by Sea (1978). UNCTAD has also contributed to the elaboration of guidelines in the area of debt rescheduling (1980), to agreements reached on aid targets as a percentage of gross national product (GNP), and to the creation of Special Drawing Rights (SDRs) by the IMF.

Historical Overview

In the aftermath of World War II, developing countries were not recognized as a special category of countries with specific characteristics and needs. However, the increasing economic interdependence and the increased number of newly independent states in the developing world during the 1950s and 1960s led to an intensified debate on economic development. Therefore, during the Conference on the Problems of Developing Countries, held in 1962 in Cairo, the idea of an international forum dealing with vital questions relating to trade and development received wide support that was reiterated in the Cairo Declaration.

In December 1962, the UN General Assembly adopted Resolution 1785 (XVII) calling for the establishment of UNCTAD as a permanent institution, with the first conference to be held in 1964. The significance of UNCTAD I was universally acknowledged at the time. The UN secretary general, U Thant, described it as one of the most important events since the establishment of the United Nations. The Final Act marked a major step forward in multilateral economic diplomacy (Cordovez 1967) and contained a number of goals and basic orientations, adopted by consensus, that remain at the core of UNCTAD's mandate in the twenty-first century.

Eleven UNCTAD conferences have been held so far: UNCTAD I, Geneva, Switzerland (1964); UNCTAD II, New Delhi, India (1968); UNCTAD III, Santiago, Chile (1972); UNCTAD IV, Nairobi, Kenya (1976); UNCTAD V, Manila, Philippines (1979); UNCTAD VI, Belgrade, Yugoslavia (1983); UNCTAD VII, Geneva, Switzerland (1987); UNCTAD VIII, Cartagena de Indias, Colombia (1992); UNCTAD IX, Midrand, South Africa (1996); UNCTAD X, Bangkok, Thailand (2000); and Sau Paolo, Brazil (2004).

UNCTAD VIII represented a major turning point in cooperation for development and revitalized UNCTAD as an institution following a deadlock in economic cooperation dialogue during the 1980s. In the Cartagena Commitment adopted at UNCTAD VIII, the participants pledged to form a new partnership for development, expressing their political will to translate best endeavors into reality. The international community acknowledged that UNCTAD was the most appropriate institutional focal point within the United Nations for an integrated approach on key issues of sustainable development, including trade, finance, investment, services, and technology (see sidebar, "The Spirit of Cartagena").

UNCTAD X played a crucial role in international economic diplomacy. It came after the failure of the World Trade Organization (WTO) to launch a new round of negotiations in Seattle and managed to reestablish a more consensual approach among developed and developing countries. The Bangkok Declaration adopted at the end of the conference emphasized the commitment of the international community to a multilateral trading system that is fair, equitable, and rules-based and that operates in a nondiscriminatory and transparent manner and in a way that provides benefits for all countries, especially developing ones.

Among other things, countries agreed to find ways to improve market access for goods and services of particular interest to developing countries, to resolve issues relating to the implementation of WTO agreements, to fully implement special and differential treatment, to facilitate accession to the WTO, and to provide technical assistance to developing countries. The conference reiterated that all countries and international organizations should do their utmost to ensure that the multilateral trading system fulfills its potential in terms of promoting the integration of all countries, in particular the least developed countries (LDCs), into the global economy. It was also agreed that a new WTO round of multilateral trade negotiations should take account of the development dimension.

Structure of UNCTAD

As of 2005, UNCTAD is composed of 192 members. Its intergovernmental machinery is comprised of the conference (held every four years), the Trade and Development Board (TDB), and its subsidiary bodies, serviced by a permanent Secretariat. The conference, the organization's highest policymaking body, formulates major policy guidelines and decides on the work program for the following four years. The TDB, the executive body of UNCTAD, meets once a year in Geneva and up to three times a year in executive session to deal with urgent policy issues as well as management and institutional matters.

The TDB reports to the UN General Assembly through the Economic and Social Council (ECOSOC). The annual *Trade and Development Report,* published by the UNCTAD Secretariat, serves as a basis for the board's deliberations. The board is directly involved in all policy is-

---

The Spirit of Cartagena

The General Assembly,

Reaffirming the importance and continued validity of the Declaration on International Economic Cooperation, in particular the Revitalization of Economic Growth and Development of the Developing Countries, the International Development Strategy for the Fourth United Nations Development Decade, the United Nations New Agenda for the Development of Africa in the 1990s, the Programme of Action for the Least Developed Countries for the 1990s, and the various agreements, especially Agenda 21, that were adopted during the process of the United Nations Conference on Environment and Development

[...]

Having considered the final documents adopted by the United Nations Conference on Trade and Development at its eighth session, in particular the Declaration and the document entitled 'A New Partnership for Development: The Cartagena Commitment', and noting with satisfaction the highly successful outcome of the eighth session of the Conference and the spirit of genuine cooperation and solidarity—the Spirit of Cartagena—that emerged therefrom

[...]

Reaffirms the important role of the United Nations Conference on Trade and Development, as a principal organ of the General Assembly in the field of trade and development and as the most appropriate focal point within the United Nations proper for the integrated treatment of development and interrelated issues in key areas, including trade, commodities, finance, investment, services and technology, in the interests of all countries, particularly those of developing countries;

[...]

Urges all countries to fulfil their commitments to halt and reverse protectionism and to reach a final agreement on the remaining issues of the Uruguay Round, and reaffirms that the balanced and comprehensive conclusion of the multilateral trade negotiations is crucial and is needed in order to strengthen the rules and disciplines of the international trading system and significantly enhance the prospects for trade, economic growth and development of all countries, especially developing countries.

Source: Excerpts from the Declaration of the eighth session of the United Nations Conference on Trade and Development (Cartagena de Indias, Colombia, February 8–25, 1992), adopted by the UN General Assembly at its 93rd plenary meeting, Document Symbol A/RES/47/183, December 22, 1992.

---

sues that the UNCTAD Secretariat covers and overviews the output and priorities of the work program for each subsidiary body of the Secretariat. The subsidiary machinery of the TDB is composed of three commissions that meet once a year in regular session and may convene up to ten "expert meetings" a year on specific issues. A fourth commission, the Commission on Science and Technology for Development, reports directly to ECOSOC.

Apart from these formal linkages, UNCTAD remains in close cooperation with the WTO and the World Bank, the United Nations Development Programme (UNDP), UN regional commissions, and other international organizations. Notable in this regard is the partnership between UNCTAD, the World Bank, the IMF, and the UNDP in the Integrated Framework for Technical Assistance to the Least Developed Countries (LDCs) and in the International Task Force on Commodity Risk Management in Developing Countries (UNCTAD 2001a). UNCTAD has also maintained a strategic partnership with the WTO, as is evident from the work of the joint UNCTAD-WTO International Trade Center. Since UNCTAD IX,

UNCTAD has been seeking increasingly to involve civil society in its work, and a significant feature of UNCTAD's work is the participation of nongovernmental organizations (NGOs) in the execution of its main activities and during intergovernmental consultations.

Technical Assistance Activities

UNCTAD's technical cooperation encompasses almost all of its areas of responsibility. The emphasis of UNCTAD's programs is on capacity building and human resources in developing countries and economies in transition. Technical assistance activities on trade-related issues include, for instance, support for negotiations, trade policy formulation, commodity policy and commodity risk management, and customs reform. Technical assistance is also provided on the links between trade and other policies, such as environmental and competition policy. Other areas of competence include debt management, insurance, investment, technology issues, and multimodal transport and shipping.

UNCTAD is involved in more than 300 technical assistance projects in over 100 countries. Its activities are aimed at enhancing the capacity of developing countries and countries in transition to strengthen their institutions and to better adjust the economic policies to their development needs. More than half of UNCTAD's technical assistance expenditures are interregional. Large shares of the technical assistance resources are devoted to Africa (21.6 percent) and the Asia and Pacific region (18.8 percent). The remainder is allocated to Latin America (5.7 percent), Eastern Europe, the former Soviet Union (3.4 percent), and other countries.

Trade Policy

In the field of trade, UNCTAD helps governments to formulate and implement trade poli-

cies aimed to encourage the business sector to adapt products to a dynamic international trading system. UNCTAD's trade agenda contains three main areas of work: multilateral trade negotiations; regional economic integration involving developing countries; and unilateral trade preferences for developing countries. Since its establishment, UNCTAD has been a major resource for developing countries in terms of capacity building and in the development of analytical tools with regard to the impact of the multilateral trading system on development. For instance, UNCTAD has designed the SMART model (used to quantify ex ante the effects of trade negotiations) and several databases on tariffs (such as the *Trade Analysis and Information System,* or TRAINS) and nontariff measures (the UNCTAD Coding System of Trade Control Measures) to assist negotiators in better identifying areas of common concern.

UNCTAD remains a leading authority in all these areas. This role was explicitly acknowledged during the UNCTAD III Conference, for instance, when the UNCTAD Secretariat was specifically assigned the responsibility of assisting developing countries during the GATT Tokyo Round. A similar role was assigned to the UNCTAD Secretariat at the Doha 2001 round of WTO negotiations on specific trade-related issues such as competition, environmental policies, and investment policies. Parallel to the attention given to the multilateral trading system, UNCTAD's considerable analytical work and recommendations have been a useful input for many regional trading arrangements implemented by developing countries, in particular in Africa and Latin America. In addition, as the major architect of the GSP system, UNCTAD reviews, monitors, and works to improve the many GSP schemes implemented by developed countries.

One particular set of trade-related policies that UNCTAD has been promoting over the past twenty-five years encompasses competition and consumer protection policies at national, regional, and international levels. UNCTAD has been promoting the elimination of anticompetitive practices affecting the trade interests of developing countries since the early 1970s. After the adoption in 1980 by the UN General Assembly of the Set of Multilaterally Agreed Equitable Principles and Rules for the Control of Restrictive Practices, UNCTAD has become a focal point for multilateral discussions on anticompetitive practices.

A long-standing issue central to UNCTAD's work has been the diversification of production and trade structures of developing countries, often reliant on a small number of products with declining terms of trade. Other major new areas of focus include the study of trade in services, e-commerce, and trade and environment issues (climate change, carbon emissions, conservation, sustainable biological diversity, and so on).

Investment and Enterprise Development

UNCTAD provides a wide range of technical assistance activities to developing countries and economies in transition in order to attract foreign direct investment and enhance the contribution it can make to the domestic economy. It is implementing a work program on international investment agreements, with a view toward assisting developing countries to participate as effectively as possible in international investment rule-making at the bilateral, regional, plurilateral, and multilateral levels. The program embraces capacity-building seminars, regional symposia, training courses, and dialogues between negotiators and civil society groups.

One area of investment-related activities involves the creation of sustainable support structures that help promising entrepreneurs to build innovative and internationally competitive small and medium-sized enterprises (SMEs), thereby contributing to the development of a dynamic private sector. The main UNCTAD "business incubator" is the EMPRETEC program. EMPRETEC is a program that provides developing countries with training in entrepreneurship. Its activities involve the delivery of motivational and technical seminars, the provision of advisory services, and the development of national and international networks serving the needs of entrepreneurs. Since its inception in 1988, the EMPRETEC program has been initiated in twenty-three countries, assisting more than 42,000 entrepreneurs through local market-driven business support centers (UNCTAD 2000a). EMPRETEC identifies promising entrepreneurs, conducts training aimed at developing entrepreneurial traits and business skills, assists companies in accessing financial and nonfinancial services, encourages the exchange of experiences and networking among program participants locally and internationally, and puts in place long-term support systems to facilitate the growth and internationalization of their companies.

Since the early 1980s, UNCTAD has been involved in the development of international standards of corporate accounting and reporting. With the increased globalization of financial flows, the need for reliable, comparable, and transparent financial information in financial statements of enterprises became crucial for the efficient functioning of stock markets, banks, and foreign direct investment. UNCTAD has serviced the Intergovernmental Working Group of Experts on International Standards of Accounting and Reporting (ISAR), a major international forum in this field. ISAR accomplishes its mandate through an integrated program of research, intergovernmental dialogue, consensus building, and technical cooperation.

Macroeconomic Policies, Debt, and Development Financing

The provision of adequate financial aid on satisfactory terms and conditions to developing and least developed countries, as well as the reform of the international monetary system, have been among UNCTAD's central objectives from the very beginning. Although the various elements of the two areas have shifted in importance over time, the many challenges facing UNCTAD today remain broadly similar to those in the early 1960s, which provided impetus for the establishment of UNCTAD. UNCTAD has used its analytical capacity to warn against the increased vulnerability of developing countries during financial crises. As early as 1990, UNCTAD's *Trade and Development Report* has warned about the potential for an extremely costly financial crisis to occur that would affect, in particular, the most dynamic developing countries, especially those that implemented ambitious financial liberalization and deregulation programs (UNCTAD 1990). Similar early-warning signals were triggered with regard to the external debt crises, and support and technical assistance was provided to the intergovernmental group of developing countries (G-24) during their discussions with the World Bank and the IMF, as well as with the Paris Club of creditors.

Based on this experience, UNCTAD has developed a computer-based Debt Management Financial and Analysis System (DMFAS) that was especially designed to assist developing countries in managing their participation in the globalized world of international finance. Having provided assistance in debt management for over twenty years, DMFAS is the world's major provider of technical assistance and advisory services in debt management (UNCTAD 2000b). At the end of 2000, more than 34 percent of outstanding public and publicly guaranteed long-term debt for all developing countries and economies in transition—totalling $514 billion—was managed using DMFAS. At the end of December 2001, the program was collaborating with more than sixty countries, including seventy-six institutions. DMFAS is fully integrated with World Bank tools that are designed to assist country officials in formulating debt strategies and in incorporating debt relief or new borrowing alternatives that are sustainable and consistent with long-term macroeconomic policies (UNCTAD 2001b).

Other Programs

One area in which UNCTAD has been particularly active since its establishment is international transport, especially shipping, with complementary work in customs systems. The Automated SYstem for CUstoms Data (ASYCUDA), a major UNCTAD program, helps developing countries to reform and modernize their customs procedures and management. Implemented in more than eighty countries, it has become the internationally accepted standard for customs automation. Another UNCTAD initiative, the ACIS program, a computer-based cargo tracking system, is now operational in twenty developing countries in Africa and Asia.

UNCTAD has also launched a Science and Technology Diplomacy Initiative with the aim of mobilizing scientific and technological expertise to enable developing-country diplomats and representatives to make informed decisions on emerging issues where science and technology play an important role, particularly in the aftermath of the 2001 Doha WTO ministerial meeting. The Science and Technology Diplomacy Initiative seeks to provide training and workshops for diplomats, scientists, and policymakers to assist them in international negotiations, particularly those that take place at the WTO TRIPS Council (for the Agreement on Trade-Related Aspects of Intellectual Property Rights) and with respect to the UN Convention on Biological Diversity covering aspects of biotechnology and transfer of technology.

UNCTAD's program on least developed, landlocked, and island countries is also central to its mandate. UNCTAD analyzes the effects of major international initiatives on LDCs and supports LDCs in key areas such as trade, investment, and services. It has also played a leading role in organizing the three United Nations conferences on LDCs (Paris in 1981 and 1990, Brussels in 2001). UNCTAD's work led to the creation of the list of LDCs and has subsequently increased awareness of the special needs of these countries.

This awareness has changed the policies of countries and multilateral agencies in several important ways. First, there has been a shift in the share of official assistance going to LDCs. Several donor countries have not only increased their assistance but have also canceled the debt of LDCs or taken other debt-relief measures in their favor. Second, a shift in favor of LDCs has been particularly noticeable for major multilateral organizations, which are now providing a major share of assistance to the least developed countries. This awareness has also led to a few innovations in commercial policy measures on behalf of these countries. Third, the creation of a special subcommittee for least developed countries within the WTO (previously within the GATT) should be noted, as should the WTO Plan of Action for the Least Developed Countries. Fourth, trade preferences, including provisions in the Lomé Conventions and within the generalized system of preferences, have also resulted. Finally, the European Union has provided the LDCs with duty- and quota-free access for their products, creating an important precedent (Bora et al. 2002).

UNCTAD Reports and Publications

In addition to studies and analyses prepared for meetings in various committees and working groups, UNCTAD issues numerous useful publications. Many of these are annual publications. The *Trade and Development Report,* for example, contains analyses of the current global economic situation, regional trends, and the interaction between trade, investment, and financial flows, with a particular focus on the strategies and policy issues of interest to developing countries. *The Least Developed Countries Report* is a comprehensive and authoritative source of socioeconomic analysis and data on the forty-nine least developed countries.

The *World Investment Report* provides a thorough analysis of trends in foreign direct investment and proposes policy recommenda-

tions to further the FDI contribution to development. The *Review of Maritime Transport* examines recent developments in seaborne trade and analyzes the performance of different geographic regions in maritime transport. The *Handbook of International Trade and Development Statistics* is a comprehensive collection of statistics relevant to the analysis of world trade and development. It also is available in CD-ROM format. And *Trade Analysis and Information System (TRAINS)* is the most comprehensive computerized information system at the tariff-line level. It covers tariff, para-tariff and nontariff measures and provides data on import flows by origin for more than 140 countries.

UNCTAD also publishes a number of research papers in series, such as UNCTAD Policy Issues in International Trade and Commodities, the G-24 Discussion Paper Series, and others. For further information on all these resources, see UNCTAD's Web page at www. unctad.org.

Lucian Cernat

See Also Inequality; Economic and Social Council (ECOSOC); Sustainable Development

Note

The views expressed herein are those of the author and do not necessarily reflect the views of the United Nations or its member states.

References

Bora, B., L. Cernat, and A. Turrini. 2002. "Duty and Quota-Free Access for LDCs: Further Evidence from CGE Modelling." *UNCTAD Policy Issues in International Trade and Commodities Study Series*, no. 14. New York and Geneva: United Nations.
Cordovez, D. 1967. "The Making of UNCTAD: Institutional Background and Legislative History." *Journal of World Trade Law* (May): 243–328.
United Nations. 1985. *The History of UNCTAD, 1964–1984.* New York: United Nations.
United Nations Conference on Trade and Development. 1990. *Trade and Development Report.* New York and Geneva: United Nations.
———. 1994. *A Guide to UNCTAD: 30 Years and Beyond.* Geneva: UNCTAD.

———. 2000a. *Evaluation of UNCTAD EMPRETEC Programme*. Document TD/B/WP.129. New York and Geneva: United Nations.

———. 2000b. *The DMFAS Programme—A Brief Description*. Geneva: UNCTAD.

———. 2001a. *United Nations Conference on Trade and Development: Trade, Investment and Development*. Geneva and London: UNCTAD and International Systems and Communications.

———. 2001b. *DMFAS 2001 Annual Report*. New York and Geneva: United Nations.

World Health Organization (WHO)

Globalization in the nineteenth century made health an international issue requiring greater cooperation among states. This cooperation occurred first through ad-hoc conferences and later through permanent health organizations. Institutionalization of international cooperation on public health led eventually to the establishment of the World Health Organization (WHO) in 1948. The importance and relevance of this organization has been proven and strengthened over the past half century through its active participation in the fight against major infections.

A continuing rapid pace of globalization in the 1980s and 1990s underscored the need for a more global action against the rapid spread of disease, particularly communicable epidemics. The complex nature of the measures that needed to be taken in order to successfully contain or treat diseases compelled WHO in these decades to refocus its activities. Instead of concentrating on intergovernmental cooperation, it began to spearhead more globally driven campaigns and action plans, increasingly relying on partnerships with a wide range of international institutions and governmental and societal actors, including commercial groups. The force of globalization in the late twentieth century made diseases more widespread and potentially more lethal to a greater number of people. Simultaneously, however, the same globalization processes compelled and allowed WHO to enmesh its activities with a global network of multiactor partnerships that could confront challenges related to international public health more effectively.

Historical Overview

The first wave of globalization took place during the nineteenth century as significant improvements in transportation and communication took place. This wave was characterized by rapid growth in both trade and travel, not only among nations within particular regions, but also across continents, particularly Asia, the Americas, and Europe. As the number of interactions between peoples increased, infectious diseases, such as cholera, the plague, and yellow fewer, among others, began propagating much more rapidly than ever before, both across time and geographical space. These changes raised significant concerns about public health and sparked continual debates among state officials about the sorts of international cooperation needed to contain the spread of epidemics and the kinds of measures that could protect populations without hindering international commerce.

In 1851, the representatives of twelve European states gathered in Paris at the first International Sanitary Conference. There, they adopted the International Sanitary Convention, which envisaged international harmonization of diverse requirements for conducting national inspections and imposing quarantines in order to halt the spread of epidemic diseases. The convention, however, did not gain the required ratifications and therefore never came into force. The failure of the ratification process showed the difficulty of finding a proper balance between the need for firmer national measures to stop the spread of disease, on the one hand, and the desire to maintain a free flow of people and international trade, on the other. It took five more international conferences (Paris in 1859; Constantinople in 1866; Vienna in 1874; Washington, DC, in 1881; and Rome in 1885) before the European states could agree on another International Sanitary Convention, which occurred at the seventh International Sanitary Conference in Venice in 1892. This convention was limited, however, to quarantine measures for cholera. During the tenth International Sanitary Conference, in 1897, and again in Venice (two previous conferences were in Dresden in 1893 and in Paris in 1894), the countries adopted an International Sanitary Convention covering the plague. Six years later, in 1903, the eleventh International Sanitary Conference, held in Paris, agreed on a single consolidated International Sanitary Convention that regulated protective measures against both cholera and the plague. This convention was subsequently amended in 1926 to cover two other diseases: smallpox and typhus.

While participating in these ad-hoc international meetings, the states tightened their regional cooperation, which resulted, among other things, in the creation of the first permanent international health organization, the International Sanitary Bureau (ISB), in Washington, DC, in 1902, and another one, the Office International d'Hygiène Publique (which translates as International Office of Public Health), in Paris in 1907. The fundamental goals of these early organizations were to collect and disseminate information about epidemics and to regulate international efforts in fighting them. The ISB was subsequently renamed the Pan American Sanitary Bureau (PASB) in 1923. Since 1949, the PASB has served as the World Health Organization Regional Office for the Americas. PASB is also the secretariat of the Pan American Health Organization (PAHO), which emerged from the International Sanitary Conferences (the Pan American Sanitary Conferences from 1923 and PAHO after 1958).

The next step in institutionalization of international cooperation on health issues was the creation of the League of Nations Health Organization in 1923, which was responsible for hygiene- and health-related issues as well as the establishment and operation of epidemiological information systems for malaria, tuberculosis, syphilis, cancer, and other diseases. In 1943, the United Nations Relief and Rehabilitation Administration was set up to prevent humanitarian and epidemiological catastrophes in countries devastated by war. The administration was eventually dissolved in 1946. In the same year, the International Health Conference was convened. It drafted the constitution for an international health organization and set up an Interim Commission to assist in the preparation for the first meeting of the World Health Assembly (WHA). The constitution came into force in April 1948, and the WHA meeting took place on June 24, 1948. At this meeting, delegations from fifty-three member states officially established the World Health Organization (WHO) as a United Nations specialized agency.

WHO Functions

WHO conducts various types of activities that aim at the "attainment by all peoples of the highest possible level of health" (Article 1, WHO Constitution), where "health" is defined as "not merely the absence of disease or infirmity" but "a state of complete physical, mental and social well-being" (Preamble). Because of this broad mandate, WHO performs several functions that can be grouped into four major task roles:

1. A standard-setting role based on setting guidelines, codes, recommendations, and regulations and establishing monitoring and validating mechanisms to ensure their proper implementation (WHO as a *normative agency*).
2. An operational role based on prevention, treatment, and eradication of communi-

cable and noncommunicable diseases, which requires coordination and harmonization of the work of various governmental and nongovernmental actors with the aim of facilitating, building, and sustaining global partnerships (WHO as an *action agency*).

3. A technical role based on providing assistance to WHO member states through technical and policy support, education, and training in order to strengthen the institutional capacities of their national health systems (WHO as a *service agency*).

4. A research role based on storing, managing, and disseminating information on public health and supporting tests and diagnoses of new technologies and health-related inventions (WHO as an *epistemic agency,* serving as a repository of knowledge on public health).

WHO Governing System

WHO is composed of several governing bodies linked through a web of formal interactions that constitute the WHO governing system. These bodies include WHA, an Executive Board, and regional offices. A director general serves as the chief administrative officer.

World Health Assembly

The World Health Assembly, composed of delegates from 192 member states, is the central political organ of WHO. Although no more than three delegates can officially represent a particular state during WHA meetings, in practice country delegations are often larger because alternates and advisers accompany official delegates. The WHO Constitution (Article 11) recommends that the delegates have a high level of technical competence in a health-related field and, if possible, that they come from the national health administrations of the member states. WHA sessions are also attended by the representatives of multilateral institutions and

nongovernmental organizations (NGOs) that have official relationships with WHO. These representatives may make statements, but they do not vote at WHA sessions.

At the sessions, each member state has one vote, and the decisions are taken either by a qualified majority of two-thirds (for example, in the adoption of regulations or of amendments to the WHO Constitution or in the admittance of new members) or by a simple majority. WHA has one regular session a year and may hold special sessions as requested by the Executive Board (see below).

Two procedural and two substantive committees assist WHA. One of the procedural committees, the Committee on Nominations, is responsible for nominating people to serve in various official positions, such as chairmanships for other committees and the WHA president and vice president. The other, the Committee on Credentials, is responsible for determining whether the country delegations have appropriate authorization from their respective governments to participate in WHA or to be elected to its organs. The substantive committees are Committee A and Committee B. Committee A deals with technical programs and policy-oriented issues, and Committee B focuses on administrative and financial matters.

WHA is both a guidance and supervisory body. As such, it makes decisions about the general direction of WHO activities, scrutinizes WHO spending, approves the organization's regular budget (almost $856 million in the 2002–2003 biannual budget), and monitors other extra-budgetary resources (assessed at about $1.4 billion in 2002–2003). WHA adopts regulations, proposes recommendations, and makes agreements with other UN agencies or intergovernmental organizations. It also appoints the director general (DG), who would already have been nominated earlier by the Executive Board. WHA may ask the DG and the Secretariat, as well as the Executive Board, to bring health-related matters to the attention of the delegates of the member states. At its discretion, WHA may also establish committees or ad-hoc bodies as deemed necessary to facilitate and improve the work of the organization.

The Executive Board

The Executive Board (EB) meets at least twice a year and brings together thirty-two persons designated by their state to fill positions on the board, which are three-year appointments. The states authorized to appoint a representative to this board are elected by the WHA. Each of the delegates must have a specific qualification in the field of health. In order to maintain a balanced geographical distribution of seats, the EB must have no less than three delegates representing each of the WHO's six regions. By informal arrangement, the five permanent members of the UN Security Council—China, France, Russia, the United Kingdom, and the United States—have their representatives to the EB seated for three consecutive years interrupted by a one-year intermission (so-called "semi-permanent memberships"). EB meetings are also attended by the representatives of multilateral institutions and nongovernmental organizations that have official relationships with WHO. These representatives have the right to speak but not to vote at EB sessions.

The EB executes the tasks that WHA delegates to it and supervises the implementation of WHA decisions and the provisions of WHO regulations and recommendations. It adopts the agenda for WHA sessions; supervises financial and budgetary assessments prepared by the director general; and sets up, changes, or closes its committees. The EB is composed of five substantive committees: (1) a Programme Development Committee, which is responsible for reviewing all aspects related to planning, budgeting, and evaluation of WHO activities; (2) an Administration, Budget and Finance committee, charged with supervision of WHO's activities in these areas; (3) an Audit Committee, which conducts internal audits of all WHO financial operations with the aim of enhancing their accountability and transparency; (4) a Coordinating Committee on Health, which

aims to increase coordination on the health-related policies and programs carried out by WHO, the United Nations Children's Fund (UNICEF), and the United Nations Population Fund (UNFPA); and (5) a Standing Committee on Nongovernmental Organizations, which evaluates the work conducted jointly by WHO and other nongovernmental organizations and considers requests for admittance of new nongovernmental organizations into official relations with the organization. Additionally, the EB runs committees on nonsubstantive issues. Its foundation committees (for the Darling Foundation, the Leon Bernard Foundation, the Jacques Parisot Foundation Fellowship, the Ihsan Dogramaci Family Health Foundation, Sasakawa Health Price, and the United Arab Emirates Health Foundation), for example, consider the nomination and selection of individuals for WHO awards and fellowships.

The Director General and WHO Secretariat

The director general (DG) is nominated by the EB and elected by the WHA. The DG is "the chief technical and administrative officer of the Organization" (WHO Constitution, Article 31). Throughout its history, WHO has had six DGs: Brock Chisholm (Canada),1948–1953; Marcolino Gomes Candau (Brazil), 1953–1973; Halfdan Mahler (Denmark), 1973–1988; Hiroshi Nakajima (Japan), 1988–1998; Gro Harlem Brundtland (Finland), 1998–2003; and Jong Wook Lee (Korea), 2003 to the present. Since the end of the 1980s, the DG has been limited to a five-year term, renewable only once. The DG heads the WHO Secretariat, located in Geneva, a permanent administrative and operational organ of WHO.

The Secretariat is composed of nine clusters, seven of which deal with substantive technical issues and research on various aspects of health care. One of the two remaining clusters is responsible for the Secretariat's contacts with WHA and the EB and its external relations with UN bodies. The last cluster is charged with administrative support and internal management of the Secretariat itself. The DG and

Secretariat are responsible for the day-to-day activities of the organization, implementation of technical programs, coordination of work on health-related matters among various governmental and nongovernmental actors, management of information and expertise on public health, and preparation of the organization's budget.

The DG appoints the staff of the Secretariat, which in the performance of its duties is expected to maintain independence and integrity and not to seek any instructions from the member governments. In accordance with the United Nations common system of grades and salaries, the WHO staff is divided into two general categories: professional and general services. Professional service staff (from P1 to P6 and D2) is responsible for the substantive and policy-oriented work of the organization, whereas general service staff (from G1 to G7) performs administrative and Secretariat support duties. The Secretariat staff also includes nongraded high-level officials such as the deputy director general and assistant directors general. At the end of 2002, the total WHO professional and general staff numbered 3,510, including 1,411 professionals and 2,099 general service personnel, according to WHO human resources reports.

Regional Offices

WHO has six regional health organizations around the world headed by regional directors and regional executive committees assisted by subcommittees. The Pan American Health Organization, mentioned above, is an exception and has a complex structure that includes a directing council, an executive committee, the Pan American Sanitary Conference acting as the WHO regional committee, and the Pan American Sanitary Bureau, with headquarters in Washington, DC, serving as the WHO Regional Office for the Americas. The other regional offices (ROs) are as follows: the Regional Office for Europe, with headquarters in Copenhagen; the Regional Office for the Western Pacific, with headquarters in New Delhi; the Re-

gional Office for Africa, with headquarters in Brazzaville; the Regional Office for the Eastern Mediterranean, with headquarters in Cairo; and the Regional Office for South-East Asia, with headquarters in Manila.

Regional directors (RDs) are nominated by the regional committees and appointed by the WHO EB for a five-year term that is renewable once. Since the RDs are not appointed by the DG and have a strong affiliation with their regional constituents, they enjoy a considerable degree of autonomy vis-à-vis the DG. The regional committees, with their subcommittees, are regional assemblies that are responsible, among other things, for formulating and implementing policies that have an exclusively regional character; supervising the work of their administrative and executive organs, namely the ROs and RDs; nominating the RDs; and providing advice to the DG on health issues that have both regional and international impacts.

WHO Programs

The Fight against Communicable Diseases

From its inception, most of WHO's institutional energies and financial resources were committed to the fight against communicable diseases. In 1951, WHA adopted the International Sanitary Regulations, which were legally binding upon WHO member states. They were revised, consolidated, and renamed the International Health Regulations (IHRs) in 1969. The purpose of the IHRs was to facilitate the establishment of effective control and monitoring measures against the spread of four infectious diseases: smallpox, cholera, plague, and yellow fever. The IHRs set up a global notification system; installed certain types of disease surveillance at the maritime ports, airports, and border control posts; and specified health certificate requirements for people who traveled from infected to noninfected states. In order to maintain free trade and travel while strengthening provisions against disease proliferation, the IHRs enumerated permissible sanitation and disinfection measures allowed to be implemented at arrival and departure points to protect national populations. Since 1995, the IHRs have been under revision with the purpose of expanding their legal scope. Since the eradication of smallpox in 1980, the regulations have covered only three communicable diseases; they do not apply to new important epidemics such as AIDS or Serious Acute Respiratory Syndrome (SARS). The revision process is to be concluded in May 2005.

At the end of the 1990s, the fight against communicable diseases gained renewed importance with international recognition that diseases are both caused by poverty and also in many cases the reason for poverty. In order to increase its institutional capacity to deal with communicable diseases, WHO set up a Global Outbreak Alert and Response Network in 1998, which became fully operational two years later. This global network brings together various governmental and nongovernmental actors to facilitate compilation of information about various diseases and to aid in the verification of epidemics and the coordination of the international response toward confirmed epidemic outbreaks. The network proved its effectiveness in containing the spread of SARS and was further strengthened in June 2003 with the adoption of two WHA resolutions. The resolutions, though not legally binding, officially conferred onto the Secretariat and the DG the power to issue global alerts regarding public health threats. They emphasized the duty of states to report infectious diseases promptly and to cooperate in good faith with other states and WHO on disease-related matters. These resolutions also acknowledged the increasing role of nongovernmental organizations as significant data-gathering and data-disseminating sources.

The Campaign against Smallpox. The eradication of smallpox is a WHO success story in the fight against communicable diseases. WHO embarked on its efforts to eliminate smallpox

in 1967, when the twentieth meeting of the World Health Assembly charged the Secretariat with the implementation of the Intensified Smallpox Eradication Programme. At this time, smallpox accounted for almost 2 million deaths annually. The fight against the disease was two-pronged and included both a mass vaccination campaign and the establishment of a sound surveillance system to track new outbreaks of the disease.

In 1980, the Global Commission for Certification of Smallpox Eradication announced that smallpox had been eradicated and recommended ending routine vaccinations against the disease. The success of the smallpox campaign is usually attributed to several factors: an effective vaccine; good management of vaccine delivery; clear diagnostic and epidemic-identification tools; and relatively straightforward methods of controlling disease transmission. Still, WHO involvement, which greatly facilitated international cooperation and, more notably, contributed to sustaining that cooperation over a long period of time, was a significant if not essential factor in the eradication of the disease. Given the possibility that smallpox could be reintroduced, WHO has begun the process of stockpiling the smallpox vaccine in the event of an emergency since May 2005.

Work to Eradicate Malaria. In 1955, WHA directed the Secretariat to embark on the Malaria Eradication Program and to establish proper verification mechanisms in this program. Despite important achievements in scaling back malaria in the 1950s and at the beginning of the 1960s, WHO faced technical, administrative, and financial difficulties that had significant implications for the effectiveness of these efforts. By the end of the 1960s, the campaign had lost its initial momentum, and the program implementation strategy was substantially changed in favor of a greater involvement of the national health services. Such a shift of emphasis was partly a confirmation of the enormous complexity of malaria prevention and treatment as well as an acknowledgment of failure for WHO's centrally led campaign against the disease.

Since then the WHO position has evolved from its initial desire to eradicate malaria toward a more feasible approach focusing on controlling the disease. This shift occurred in the background of a significant rise in reported malaria cases in the 1980s and the first half of the 1990s. In response to the increase, in 1992 WHO adopted the Global Malaria Control Strategy, which stressed decreasing the burden of the disease and reducing its geographical scope through better diagnosis, stronger national research capacities, and enhanced monitoring and preventive measures. In order to improve global coordination and involve a greater number of actors in the fight against malaria, WHO, in partnership with the United Nations Children's Fund (UNICEF), the United Nations Development Programme (UNDP), and the World Bank, launched Roll Back Malaria (RBM) at the end of 1998. This campaign was soon joined by other multilateral institutions, donor governments, representatives of affected nations, NGOs, academic centers, and private enterprises, turning it into a global partnership. The goal of the RBM is to scale back the "malaria burden" by 50 percent by the end of 2010. Although significant political commitments to reduce the malaria burden were made at the first ever summit on malaria, held in 2000 in Abuja, Nigeria, it is too early to judge whether a broad-based effort to fight the disease will reach its 2010 objective.

Polio Immunization. Although polio was a long-standing concern for WHO, the organization did not have a centrally coordinated policy for polio eradication until the end of the 1980s. In 1985, the Pan American Health Organization announced an initiative to eradicate polio in both Americas by 1990. This goal was eventually achieved in 1994 when the Americas were certified to be polio-free. Subsequently, in 1988, the World Health Assembly adopted the Global Polio Eradication Initiative, which called for elimination of the disease by the year

2000. Though the goal of complete eradication of the disease has not been reached, significant progress has been made.

Today, the initiative brings together various donor governments, governments of countries affected by the disease, development banks, private foundations, research centers (including the U.S. Centers for Disease Control and Prevention), and international and nongovernmental partners such as UNICEF and Rotary International. In 1992, the Global Polio Laboratory Network, consisting of more than 140 national and regional laboratories, was set up to assist in establishing a worldwide surveillance network of polio outbreaks. WHO's efforts included massive and well-coordinated immunization campaigns throughout the 1990s, which brought about a substantial decrease in reported polio cases. During 2004 there was the most significant progress towards polio eradication with a 99 percent reduction in polio incidence over the previous year. There were only 1264 cases in 2004, which were limited to six countries: Nigeria, Niger, India, Pakistan, Afghanistan, and Egypt.

Poliovirus, for which there is no cure, has a tendency to reemerge unexpectedly and infect unimmunized populations. The most recent example was the polio outbreak in Nigeria in the second half of 2003, which spread quickly to neighboring areas that were previously declared polio-free. As a result of this tendency, WHO set a new goal of eradicating the disease by the end of 2005.

Control of Tuberculosis. WHO has been in the forefront of the fight against tuberculosis. In 1982, with the International Union Against Tuberculosis and Lung Disease (IUATLD), WHO announced the first World TB Day, which has been held each year since then on March 24 to commemorate Robert Koch's discovery of the TB bacillus in 1882. This event is aimed at raising public awareness of the destructive impact of TB on the health and lives of millions of people.

The fight against TB gained a new importance in the 1990s when the spread of HIV infections, combined with a further deterioration of national health systems, particularly in developing countries, contributed to a rapid increase in TB cases. TB has become one of the most lethal infectious diseases worldwide. According to WHO statistics, it claims the lives of approximately 2 million people each year. In 1991, WHO recommended that member states strengthen the institutional capacities of their national tuberculosis-control programs, which were seen as essential tools in the speedy detection and cure of TB.

In 1993, the effort to fight tuberculosis was again given a new urgency when TB became the first disease ever to be declared "a global emergency" requiring a quick and coordinated worldwide response. This declaration was followed by the establishment in 1995 of a worldwide TB surveillance and monitoring program. Its aim was to provide a comprehensive measurement of the effectiveness of TB control on the global level. In 1997, WHO released its first global tuberculosis control report, which has been published on an annual basis since then. Finally, in 2001 WHO launched a new campaign, "Stop TB," which has rapidly developed the global partnership to stop TB. The aim of this partnership is to decrease morbidity and mortality resulting from TB by half by the end of the decade.

Response to the HIV/AIDS Pandemic. The identification of Acquired Immunodeficiency Syndrome (AIDS) in 1981, which is caused by the Human Immunodeficiency Virus (HIV), led initially to the establishment of a small program on AIDS within the Secretariat of WHO. Because there was no effective vaccine against HIV/AIDS, this program was focused on containment rather than treatment of the disease and aimed at coordinating national research on cure development, the dissemination of information about the disease, and its causes and patterns of development. In 1987, the WHO DG began to take a much more robust approach to the rapidly spreading disease and created the

Global Program on AIDS, accompanied by the Global AIDS Strategy.

The strategy, like the previous program on AIDS, relied more on preventive measures than on treatment and focused mainly on improving dissemination of information about disease transmission, with educational campaigns addressing safe sexual conduct in the forefront, and on strengthening international research and political cooperation in the fight against the pandemic. World AIDS Day was commenced on December 1, 1988, and has been held on that date every year thereafter. Progress in strengthening multilateral cooperation among international institutions led WHO and UNDP to form in 1988 a common initiative, the Alliance to Combat AIDS. Later, in 1996, the Joint UN Program on HIV/AIDS (UNAIDS) was set up to bring together UNICEF, UNDP, UNFPA, WHO, the World Bank, donor governments, the most HIV/AIDS-affected states, and various NGOs in the fight against HIV/AIDS. This global advocacy coalition adopted the main objectives of the previous WHO Global Program on AIDS and rallied behind two main principles: prevention of HIV transmission through educational campaigns and offers of technical assistance to communities affected the most by the pandemic. In order to fight HIV/AIDS more effectively, WHO introduced internal changes within its Secretariat, consolidated its human and financial resources, and transformed its small unit on HIV/AIDS and sexually transmitted diseases in 2002 into a new HIV/AIDS department within the HIV/AIDS, Tuberculosis and Malaria (HTM) Cluster of the Secretariat. The new department was made responsible for enhancing WHO's overall strategic approach in dealing with the disease by expanding and improving the coverage as well as the impact of WHO technical support in the countries most affected by HIV/AIDS.

From the mid-1990s onward, medical advances such as antiretroviral (ARV) drugs have been slowly shifting the fight against AIDS toward treatment of people infected with HIV. Although ARV drugs do not provide a cure, they have significantly reduced death rates, prolonging the lives of many and turning this lethal disease into a sickness that people can have and live with for a longer period of time than used to be possible. The shift toward HIV treatment has placed greater emphasis on better distribution and access to affordable ARV medicines, leading WHO to announce, in September 2003, the "3 by 5" target plan—the goal of enabling 3 million out of 6 million people in urgent need of anti-HIV treatment to receive access to ARV therapy by 2005. The "3 by 5 " target required stepped-up efforts to train national medical workers to implement the measures, with a goal of having at least 100,000 trained HIV/AIDS medical professionals worldwide. The plan is viewed as a significant step toward an overall objective of universal access to ARV therapy for all who need it.

The Fight against Noncommunicable Diseases

The Case of Tobacco Control. In recent years, WHO has given strong attention to the campaign to control tobacco use. In 1996, WHA requested the DG to draft a framework convention on tobacco. In May 2003, WHA adopted the Framework Convention on Tobacco Control (FCTC), the first legally binding international treaty negotiated under Article 19 of the WHO Constitution.

The FCTC set a framework to facilitate the development of national tobacco-control legislation. It enumerates measures to decrease both the demand for and the supply of tobacco by stipulating information/awareness-raising campaigns about the dangers of tobacco, encouraging states and others to take criminal and civil liability actions against tobacco industries, and calling for worldwide cooperation against tobacco use, along with support for the development of tobacco-control research and surveillance involving governments and civil society groups. The success of the FCTC may have important ramifications for WHO work, leading the organization to rely more than in the past on international, legally binding instruments in order to enhance the effectiveness of its fight against both communicable and noncommunicable diseases.

WHO Research Activities

WHO as a scientific organization has been in the forefront of research on public health. Its research responsibilities were written into the organization's constitution, where Article 2 stipulated that WHO would promote and conduct research in the field of public health. The constitutional provision became operationalized only in 1959 with the establishment of the Advisory Committee on Medical Research (ACMR), which was renamed the Advisory Committee on Health Research (ACHR) in 1986. ACHR has provided guidance for national and international biomedical research, evaluated and identified new technologies and scientific knowledge that could be utilized in the fight against disease, and exercised control over various research policies carried out by WHO to enhance coordination among different entities.

WHO research activities have been carried out primarily within the framework of two programs: The Special Programme for Research, Development and Research Training in Human Reproduction, established in 1972, and the Special Programme for Research and Training in Tropical Diseases, set up in 1975. These initiatives, though concentrating on different areas of health care, are based on common objectives aimed at broadening scientific knowledge, enhancing the institutional capacities of national health systems, and developing instruments that are more effective in dealing with the identified problems. The strategies to reach these objectives have relied on education, training, and publication of pertinent materials.

Over the years, WHO research activities have also been given impetus by expert committees and study groups run by eminent academic specialists and practitioners from various medical fields. Examples include expert committees on biological standardization, food additives, malaria, and SARS. The importance of WHO as a research-driven organization was further enhanced in 1998 when the former director general, Dr. Brundtland, established a separate Cluster on Evidence and Information for Policy within the Secretariat. This cluster is responsible for collecting and analyzing data and managing information and research on the performance of health systems as well as studying ways to improve services and delivery mechanisms of health systems. One result of the work of this cluster was a major study on the Global Burden of Disease published in 2000.

The complexity and magnitude of health-related problems that easily crisscross national boundaries has compelled WHO to shift from simple intergovernmental and interstate-based cooperation on research toward global networks. In its research activities, WHO started increasingly relying on global partnerships and networking involving numerous actors, such as policymakers, scientists, health-care providers, clinicians, multilateral institutions, international health research NGOs, and other civil society groups and coalitions engaged in public health studies.

Cooperation with International Groups

Because of the intricacy of health issues, WHO has had to expand its cooperation not only to other multilateral organizations, governments, and coalitions of nongovernmental organizations but also to universities, research institutes, and other societal groups, such as consumer associations, human rights advocacy organizations, and nonprofit international charity foundations (for example, the Rockefeller Foundation and the Bill and Melinda Gates Foundation). During the 1980s and the 1990s, WHO gradually transformed itself from an interministerial and intergovernmental organization to an entity whose global policy agendas are driven as much by governments as

by diverse coalitions of private-sector and societal actors. WHO is still de jure an intergovernmental organization, but de facto it communicates, designs, and implements its policies through worldwide, complex, multiactor networks that stretch both vertically, cutting across international, regional, national, and local levels, and horizontally, involving simultaneously various different aspects of public health and forming networks or coalitions of diverse interest groups around each of these concerns.

With a progressing globalization of WHO activities, the organization is entering into closer collaboration with the private sector through public-private partnerships (PPPs). PPPs are seen as providing WHO with specific benefits, such as facilitating universal access to medicine and health services based on substantial reductions in costs; enabling WHO and private-sector entities to share expertise and knowledge on health-related issues; and stimulating research leading to discoveries of new vaccines. At the same time, WHO needs to maintain its integrity and guard itself against partnerships dominated by wealthy corporations that could dictate its priorities and strategies. With WHO policies that increasingly promote reliance on private-sector involvement in the organization's work, WHO needs to find a healthy balance between its public-driven programs and the commercial interests of powerful companies.

WHO's New Objectives

For many years, WHO's guiding principle was "Health for All by the Year 2000," as stated in the Alma Ata Declaration of 1978. In practice, this objective meant that all people should have reached a level of health allowing them to lead socially and economically viable lives by the end of the twentieth century. The goal was to be reached through the coordination of international and national efforts to establish more effective primary health care, particularly in the developing states. Although health for all was not achieved by 2000, and the phrase ceased to be the organization's main slogan, the principle of health for all continues to be a powerful notion as viewed from a long-term perspective.

WHO draws its new objectives from the United Nations Millennium Development Goals, which call for halving poverty among 1.2 billion of the world's poorest people—those living on less than a dollar per day—by 2015. The UN and WHO see the WHO's work to improve health standards as a cornerstone in this battle. WHO, however, faces a dilemma over what direction it should take to address poverty. By narrowing its focus to the fight against major communicable diseases, WHO seems to have adopted the view and expectations of its major donors. There is, however, a danger that in taking on this agenda WHO could disregard more important instruments of poverty alleviation that, in the long run, could better serve the interests of the world's poorest, such as building effective public health systems, a strategy viewed by many as the key to sustainable improvement and maintenance of appropriate health standards and thus, to progressive eradication of poverty. WHO will therefore need to strike a fine balance in the strategies it uses to realize its new objectives.

Maciej Bartkowski

See Also Pharmaceuticals; Food Safety; Population Growth; Public Health

References

Beigbeder, Yves. 1998. *The World Health Organization.* The Hague: Martinus Nijhoff.

Berkov, Robert. 1957. *The World Health Organization: A Study in Decentralized International Administration.* Geneva: Droz.

Bulletin of the World Health Organization, http://www.who.int/bulletin/en.

Fidler, David. 2001. "The Globalization of Public Health: The First 100 Years of International Health Diplomacy." *Bulletin of the World Health Organization* 79: 842–849.

———. 2003. "Developments Involving SARS, International Law, and Infectious Disease Control at the Fifty-Sixty Meeting of the World Health Assembly." *The American Society of International Law* (June).

Gezairy. Hussein. 1998. "Fifty Years of the World Health Organization." *Eastern Mediterranean Health Journal* 4 (Supplement): 6–30.

Goodman, Neville. 1952. *International Health Organizations and Their Work.* London: J&A Churchill.

Horton, Richard. 2002. "WHO: The Casualties and Compromises of Renewal." *The Lancet* 359 (May 4): 1605–1611.

McCarthy, Mark. "Special Report. What's Going On at the World Health Organization." *The Lancet* 360 (October 12): 1108–1110.

Nielsen, Henrik. 1999. *The World Health Organization. Implementing the Right to Health.* Copenhagen: Europublishers.

Robbins, Anthony. 1999. "Brundtland's World Health Organization: A Test Case for United Nations Reform." *Public Health Reports* 114 (January/February): 30–39.

Sterky, Göran, Kim Forss, and Bo Stenson. 1996. *Tomorrow's Global Health Organization: Ideas and Options.* Stockholm: Ministry of Foreign Affairs.

Talyor, Allyn. 1992. "Making the World Health Organization Work: A Legal Framework for Universal Access to the Conditions for Health." *American Journal of Law and Medicine* 18: 301–346.

Talyor, Allyn, and Douglas Bettcher. 2000. "WHO Framework Convention on Tobacco Control: A Global Good for Public Health." *Bulletin of the World Health Organization* 78: 920–929.

Wood, Patricia. 1988. *World Health Organization. A Brief Summary of Its Work.* Canberra: Australian Government Publishing Service.

World Health Organization. 1952. *The First Ten Years of the World Health Organization.* Geneva: WHO.

———. 1968. *The Second Ten Years of the World Health Organization, 1958–1967.* Geneva: WHO.

———. 2004. "WHO Proposed Programme Budget, 2004–2005."

———. "WHO Human Resources: Annual Reports," www.who.int.

———, www.who.int.

Yamey, Gavin. 2002. "WHO's Management: Struggling to Transform a 'Fossilised Bureaucracy.'" *British Medical Journal* 325 (November 16): 1170–1173.

World Trade Organization (WTO)

The World Trade Organization (WTO) is an international organization that administers the international trade rules embodied in the Uruguay Round Agreement, including the General Agreement on Tariffs and Trade (GATT). In 2004, the WTO counted 148 countries and customs territories as members, making it the largest organization in the world dealing with issues of trading relations among countries. In addition to administering the WTO and GATT rules, it acts as a forum for negotiating more liberal trade among its members, arbitrates trade disputes, monitors and reports on the national trade policies of its members, and provides technical assistance and training for developing countries to bring them into full compliance with its rules.

The WTO is headquartered in Geneva, Switzerland, and has a small staff of approximately 600 people. Relative to other international organizations, such as the World Bank and the United Nations, the WTO is a young organization, having been established on January 1, 1995. However, its historical roots go back to the post–World War II era when its sister organizations, the International Monetary Fund (IMF) and the International Bank for Reconstruction and Development (World Bank), were founded. The WTO's predecessor, the GATT Secretariat, was an ad-hoc organization that oversaw the smooth functioning of the world trading system between 1947 and 1994.

The WTO is a growing organization that regularly negotiates the entry of new countries into the multilateral trading system. Most of the world's major economies, including the United States and Japan, are members. Its membership spans the spectrum of countries' sizes and stages of development. Recent additions to the WTO have included Albania in 2000, the People's Republic of China in 2001, and Cambodia in 2004. Membership is not limited to traditional nation-states but also includes customs territories such as the European Communities, Hong Kong, and Chinese Taipei (Taiwan) (see WTO 2003).

History of the WTO

The WTO's beginnings can be traced to 1947 when twenty-three countries became the contracting parties, or, in layman's terms, members, to the GATT, a treaty that stipulated global trading rules and reduced import tariffs among its members. Over the next forty years, the expanding world trading system outgrew the original GATT treaty—its dispute resolution system had become ineffective; many rules were vague or imprecise, leading to different implementation schemes in different countries; and the scope of issues covered—trade in goods other than textiles, agriculture, and civil aircraft—was too narrowly defined. Beginning in 1986, members of the GATT negotiated a new global trade treaty, the Uruguay Round Agreement, that would overcome the original treaty's deficiencies and be poised to tackle the future challenges of the multilateral trading system. The Uruguay Round Agreement, signed by 128 countries in 1995, created the WTO in 1995 to oversee the smooth operation of the revamped world trading system.

The origins of the GATT itself are more complex. At the Bretton Woods Conference in 1944, the finance ministers from the Allied nations gathered to discuss the failings of World War I's Versailles Treaty and the creation of a new international monetary system that would support postwar reconstruction, economic stability, and peace. The conference produced two of the most important international economic institutions of the postwar period: the IMF and the World Bank. In the 1930s, "beggar thy neighbor" tariff policies—import tariffs that pushed down the price that exporters would receive for the goods they sold, thus benefiting importing countries at the expense of exporting countries—had proliferated. Recognizing that these policies had contributed to an environment that had led to war, the ministers discussed the need for a third postwar institution, an International Trade Organization (ITO), but left the problem of designing it to their colleagues in government ministries with responsibility for trade.

By the late 1940s, representatives of the U.S. government had met several times with representatives of other major nations to design a postwar international trading system that would parallel the international monetary system. These meetings had two objectives: (1) to draft a charter for the ITO, and (2) to negotiate the substance of an ITO agreement, specifically, rules governing international trade and reductions in tariffs. Ultimately, although a charter was drafted, the ITO never came into being. By 1948, support for yet another international organization had waned in the U.S. Congress. Without American participation, the institution would have been powerless, and thus the effort to create an organization to manage problems relating to international trade was abandoned.

However, although the U.S. Congress wouldn't support another international institu-

tion, in 1945 it had given the U.S. president the authority to negotiate a treaty governing international trade by extending the 1934 Reciprocal Trade Agreements Act. Thus, the General Agreement on Tariffs and Trade—a treaty whereby twenty-three countries agreed to a set of rules to govern trade with one another and maintained reduced import tariffs for other members—was established in 1947 as the arbiter of the world trading system. The GATT did not provide for a formal institution, but a small GATT Secretariat, with a limited institutional apparatus, was eventually headquartered in Geneva to administer various problems and complaints that might arise among members.

Over the next forty years, the GATT grew in membership, and its success in reducing barriers to trade also grew. GATT members regularly met in what came to be known as negotiating "rounds." These rounds were primarily focused on negotiating further reductions in the maximum tariffs that countries could impose on imports from other GATT members. The success of these rounds was evident: Tariffs on manufactured products fell from a weighted average of roughly 35 percent before the creation of the GATT in 1947 to about 6.4 percent at the start of the Uruguay Round in 1986 (Hoekman and Kostecki 1995). At the same time, the volume of trade among GATT members surged: In 2000 the volume of trade among WTO members stood at twenty-five times its 1950 volume (WTO 2001).

Despite this success, by the 1980s several problems had surfaced with the GATT apparatus. First, the dispute resolution mechanism of the GATT was barely functioning. Countries with long-standing disagreements were unable to reach any sort of resolution on a number of issues ranging from government subsidies for exports to regulations regarding foreign direct investment. Second, a number of commodities—most important, agricultural products and textiles—were not subject to GATT disciplines. Third, it was widely believed that cer-

Table 1: WTO Members as of October 2004

Member	Date of Entry	Member	Date of Entry
Albania	September 8, 2000	Djibouti	May 31, 1995
Angola	November 23, 1996	Dominica	January 1, 1995
Antigua and Barbuda	January 1, 1995	Dominican	
Argentina	January 1, 1995	Republic	March 9, 1995
Armenia	February5, 2003	Ecuador	January 21, 1996
Australia	January 1, 1995	Egypt	June 30, 1995
Austria	January 1, 1995	El Salvador	May 7, 1995
Bahrain	January 1, 1995	Estonia	November 13, 1999
Bangladesh	January 1, 1995	European Communities	January 1, 1995
Barbados	January 1, 1995	Fiji	January 14, 1996
Belgium	January 1, 1995	Finland	January 1, 1995
Belize	January 1, 1995	Former Yugoslav	
Benin	February 22, 1996	Republic of	
Bolivia	September 12, 1995	Macedonia	April 4, 2003
Botswana	May 31, 1995	France	January 1, 1995
Brazil	January 1, 1995	Gabon	January 1, 1995
Brunei Darussalam	January 1, 1995	Gambia	October 23, 1996
Bulgaria	December 1, 1996	Georgia	June 14, 2000
Burkina Faso	June 3, 1995	Germany	January 1, 1995
Burundi	July 23, 1995	Ghana	January 1, 1995
Cambodia	October 13, 2004	Greece	January 1, 1995
Cameroon	December 13, 1995	Grenada	February 22, 1996
Canada	January 1, 1995	Guatemala	July 21, 1995
Central African		Guinea	October 25, 1995
Republic	May 31, 1995	Guinea Bissau	May 31, 1995
Chad	October 19, 1996	Guyana	January 1, 1995
Chile	January 1, 1995	Haiti	January 30, 1996
China	December 11, 2001	Honduras	January 1, 1995
Colombia	April 30, 1995	Hong Kong, China	January 1, 1995
Congo	March 27, 1997	Hungary	January 1, 1995
Costa Rica	January 1, 1995	Iceland	January 1, 1995
Côte d'Ivoire	January 1, 1995	India	January 1, 1995
Croatia	November 30, 2000	Indonesia	January 1, 1995
Cuba	April 20, 1995	Ireland	January 1, 1995
Cyprus	July 30, 1995	Israel	April 21, 1995
Czech Republic	January 1, 1995	Italy	January 1, 1995
Democratic Republic		Jamaica	March 9, 1995
of the Congo	January 1, 1997	Japan	January 1, 1995
Denmark	January 1, 1995		*continues*

tain forms of administered trade protection—especially antidumping duties, voluntary export restraints, and countervailing duties—were restricting trade and distorting trade patterns in many important sectors. Fourth, trade in services was expanding rapidly, and the GATT had no rules regarding trade in ser-

vices. Fifth, countries that produced intellectual property—movies, computer programs, and patented pharmaceuticals, for example—were becoming increasingly frustrated by the lack of intellectual property protection in many developing nations. Finally, the rules regarding trade-related investment measures—for ex-

Table 1: WTO Members as of October 2004 *continued*

Member	Date of Entry	Member	Date of Entry
Jordan	April 11, 2000	Philippines	January 1, 1995
Kenya	January 1, 1995	Poland	July 1, 1995
Korea, Republic of	January 1, 1995	Portugal	January 1, 1995
Kuwait	January 1, 1995	Qatar	January 13, 1996
Kyrgyz Republic	December 20, 1998	Romania	January 1, 1995
Latvia	February 10, 1999	Rwanda	May 22, 1996
Lesotho	May 31, 1995	Saint Kitts and Nevis	February 21, 1996
Liechtenstein	September 1, 1995	Saint Lucia	January 1, 1995
Lithuania	May 31, 2001	Saint Vincent	
Luxembourg	January 1, 1995	and the Grenadines	January 1, 1995
Macao, China	January 1, 1995	Senegal	January 1, 1995
Madagascar	November 17, 1995	Sierra Leone	July 23, 1995
Malawi	May 31, 1995	Singapore	January 1, 1995
Malaysia	January 1, 1995	Slovak Republic	January 1, 1995
Maldives	May 31, 1995	Slovenia	July 30, 1995
Mali	May 31, 1995	Solomon Islands	July 26, 1996
Malta	January 1, 1995	South Africa	January 1, 1995
Mauritania	May 31, 1995	Spain	January 1, 1995
Mauritius	January 1, 1995	Sri Lanka	January 1, 1995
Mexico	January 1, 1995	Suriname	January 1, 1995
Moldova	July 26, 2001	Swaziland	January 1, 1995
Mongolia	January 29, 1997	Sweden	January 1, 1995
Morocco	January 1, 1995	Switzerland	July 1, 1995
Mozambique	August 26, 1995	Taipei, China	January 1, 2002
Myanmar	January 1, 1995	Tanzania	January 1, 1995
Namibia	January 1, 1995	Thailand	January 1, 1995
Nepal	April 23, 2004	Togo	May 31, 1995
Netherlands	January 1, 1995	Trinidad and Tobago	March 1, 1995
New Zealand	January 1, 1995	Tunisia	March 29, 1995
Nicaragua	September 3, 1995	Turkey	March 26, 1995
Niger	December 13, 1996	Uganda	January 1, 1995
Nigeria	January 1, 1995	United Arab Emirates	April 10, 1996
Norway	January 1, 1995	United Kingdom	January 1, 1995
Oman	November 9, 2000	United States	January 1, 1995
Pakistan	January 1995	Uruguay	January 1, 1995
Panama	September 1997	Venezuela	January 1, 1995
Papua New Guinea	June 1996	Zambia	January 1, 1995
Paraguay	January 1, 1995	Zimbabwe	March 5, 1995
Peru	January 1, 1995		

ample, domestic purchase requirements for plants built from foreign direct investment—were hotly disputed.

To address these problems, a new round of trade negotiations—the Uruguay Round—was launched in 1986. The goals of the Uruguay Round were far more ambitious than those of any previous round. It sought to introduce major reforms into how the world trading system would function. The treaty negotiated during the Uruguay Round, the Uruguay Round Agreement, established the WTO—the international institution to govern trade that was first visualized by the attendees of the

Bretton Woods Conference fifty years earlier. The new agreements provided for an entirely new and different dispute resolution mechanism to eliminate the gridlock of the old system under which serious disagreements between countries had gone unresolved for years. Furthermore, the Uruguay Round expanded the WTO's authority to new areas—agreements regarding trade in textiles, agriculture, services, and intellectual property were major achievements (see Hoekman and Kostecki 1995 and Jackson 1997 for good brief histories of the GATT and WTO).

Over the past ten years, the WTO has functioned effectively, although at times it has become highly controversial. From the standpoint of developed countries that desired a more responsive, rules-based trading regime, the WTO has been a great success. Trade disputes are resolved in a timely manner today. However, because some party, either a country, industry, group of workers, or other agent, is the losing party when the WTO resolves a dispute, WTO decisions and the organization itself are often severely criticized. Although many grievances are legitimate, many analysts believe that some of the sharp criticism of the WTO seems misplaced. Possibly because few people know very much about the WTO and what it does, the WTO has served as a focal point for the anger and frustration of those who have suffered or perceive themselves to have suffered from any change that can be associated with the process of globalization.

This anger against the WTO culminated during the Seattle Ministerial Conference of WTO members in 1999. At this biannual meeting of high-ranking officials from all WTO member countries, thousands of protesters took to the streets of Seattle to object to the negative consequences of globalization. Participating groups included representatives of labor unions, environmentalists, human rights activists, members of nongovernmental organizations (NGOs), and anarchists. In response to this massive display, the WTO increased its ef-

forts to educate the public about what it does and does not do and allowed many NGOs to have an observer status at its meetings.

Statement of Purpose

The WTO's purpose is to promote the economic health of all its members through their economic and trade relations. The preamble to the Uruguay Round Agreement Establishing the World Trade Organization clearly states the members' goals, preferred method for achieving these goals, and organizing principles. In addition to defining the specific economic criteria to be improved in all countries, the preamble highlights the need for efforts to fully incorporate developing countries into the world trading system.

Specifically, in the Preamble to the agreement, the members of the WTO recognized that:

> their relations in the field of trade and economic endeavor should be conducted with a view to raising standards of living, ensuring full employment and a large and steadily growing volume of real income and effective demand, and expanding the production of and trade in goods and services, while allowing for the optimal use of the world's resources in accordance with the objective of sustainable development, seeking both to protect and preserve the environment and to enhance the means for doing so in a manner consistent with their respective needs and concerns at different levels of economic development. (WTO 1995b)

To achieve these goals, the members of the WTO agreed to enter into "reciprocal and mutually advantageous arrangements directed to the substantial reduction of tariffs and other barriers to trade and to the elimination of discriminatory treatment in international trade relations." More specifically, the members resolved to create a new multilateral trading system based on the original GATT treaty, embodying the substantial revisions created in the Uruguay Round Agreement, and overseen by the WTO (see WTO 2003).

Organizational Structure

The WTO is run by its members, the countries and customs territories that comprise it. Historically, decisions within the WTO have been made by consensus. Although the WTO's agreements allow for a majority vote, this procedure has never been used. The WTO's organizational structure consists of three levels of decisionmaking bodies.

At the top of the hierarchy, the Ministerial Conference has supreme decisionmaking authority. It meets once every two years and consists of all WTO members. Unlike other international organizations, the WTO does not delegate authority to a board of directors or professional bureaucracy. All members participate directly in decisionmaking.

Below the Ministerial Conference, the next level of decisionmaking in the WTO is the General Council. As with the Ministerial Conference, all WTO members are members of the General Council. The General Council, while one group, serves three functions and meets under three different names. In addition to the General Council, this group also meets as the Trade Policy Review Body and as the Dispute Settlement Body.

Below the General Council are the various special councils—the Council for Trade in Goods, the Council for Trade in Services, and the Council for Trade-Related Aspects of Intellectual Property Rights. As with the higher levels of organization, all WTO members belong to all councils.

With close to 150 members, meetings of the WTO's organizational bodies at all levels are large. On a practical level, although every country is a member of every council and committee, countries usually send different individuals to represent them at these meetings. For example, a high-ranking official, such as a country's minister of trade, would typically represent it at the Ministerial Conference; an ambassador or head-of-delegation in Geneva would serve as its representative at the General Council; and a lower-ranking official with technical expertise may serve as its representative at a lower-level council or committee meeting.

Outside of the decisionmaking structure of the WTO, administrative and technical support is provided by the WTO Secretariat, which has a permanent staff of approximately 600 based in Geneva. At the head of the Secretariat is the director general. Perhaps the most important responsibility of the director general is to facilitate and organize new rounds of trade negotiations. He also provides important administrative help to countries that wish to negotiate trade disputes. Below the director general are a number of deputy directors general, each with responsibility for a specific administrative or support function. For example, one deputy has responsibility for trade policy reviews, another for economic research, and another for legal affairs.

The Secretariat staff provides technical support to the WTO's councils and committees, both toward the implementation of the agreement and toward the resolution of trade disputes. Economists and statisticians provide economic analysis of trade patterns and policies. Finally, the staff provides technical support to help developing countries garner the full benefits of the multilateral trading system.

Fundamental Rules Governing Trade in the WTO

The success of the WTO as a dynamic institution that has fostered dramatic increases in worldwide trade lies in its founding principles of reciprocity and nondiscrimination. These principles lie at the heart of the General Agreement on Tariffs and Trade and are present, to a lesser extent, in the General Agreement on Trade in Services (GATS) and the Agreement on Trade-Related Aspects of Intellectual Property Rights (TRIPS).

"Reciprocity" refers to the practice that occurs in GATT negotiating rounds whereby one country offers to reduce a barrier to trade and a second country "reciprocates" by offering to reduce one of its own trade barriers. Reciprocity, the practice of swapping tariff concessions, facilitates the reduction of trade barriers. "Nondiscrimination," or equal treatment, means that if one WTO member offers a benefit or a tariff concession to another WTO member, for example, a reduction in its import tariff for bicycles, it must offer the same tariff reduction to all WTO members. Thus, nondiscrimination extends the benefits of a reciprocal tariff reduction beyond the two parties that initially negotiated it to all WTO members. Economists Kyle Bagwell and Robert W. Staiger (2002) argued that, together, these principles work toward increasing the efficiency of the world trading system.

But why is reciprocity important in reducing barriers to trade? Don't countries benefit by unilaterally reducing their tariffs because lower tariffs lead to lower domestic prices? They may, but economic theory teaches that it depends on the size of the country (see Caves et al. 2002; Krugman and Obstfeld 2000). Import tariffs are, by definition, a tax. As a tax, tariffs raise the price that consumers must pay for a good, provide tax revenue to the government, and have the potential to create distortions, or inefficiencies, in consumption and production decisions.

If a country is very small, it will benefit by unilaterally lowering its tariffs and "reciprocity" is not an important consideration. This is because small countries are unable to affect the prices of goods on the world market. For example, if a small country in Africa suddenly decided to impose a 25 percent tariff on imports of automobiles, this would not affect the worldwide price at which automobiles trade. The tiny decrease in worldwide demand caused by this

country's new tariff would be minuscule compared to the demand for automobiles in large markets such as the United States, the European Union, and Japan. However, this tariff would make the small African country worse off. Although the country's government would now collect more tariff revenue, consumers would have to pay a higher price, resulting in a loss of welfare to consumers, and there would be an inefficiency loss owing to the "consumption distortion" of the tariff—fewer cars would be purchased overall. Thus, the optimal trade policy for small countries is to charge no import tariff. Regardless of the trade policies of its trading partners, a small country should engage in free trade.

The story is a bit more complicated for large countries and trading blocs. "Reciprocity" is an important consideration for leaders of large countries who are thinking about changing their trade policies. Because import demand in a large country will comprise a large share of worldwide demand, any change in a large country's demand for a good will have an effect on that good's price on the world market. Specifically, when a large country's government imposes a tariff, this reduces the quantity of imports demanded and consequently causes the world price to fall. When the price of a country's import good falls on the world market relative to the price of the goods it exports, this is called a "terms-of-trade" improvement. A terms-of-trade improvement makes a country better off because it can now buy more on the world market.

Another way to think about a large country's use of tariffs is to focus on the question of who bears the cost of this tax. Although the consumers in a large country must pay a higher final price for the imported good when their government imposes a tariff, they do not bear the full tax burden of the tariff. A tariff that causes the world price of a good to fall hurts the foreign exporters who produce that good. As a whole, the exporting country loses some of its purchasing power on the world market in this worsening of its terms of trade.

In this way, some of the cost of the tariff is pushed onto the foreign producers of the good in the form of the lower price they receive for their product than they would receive under free trade. Because foreign producers lose out under this import tariff, it is sometimes called a "beggar-thy-neighbor" policy.

The use of a beggar-thy-neighbor tariff by a large country not only makes the importing country strictly better off and the exporting country strictly worse off, it introduces inefficiencies into the world trading system that cause the net effect of the tariff to be negative. The import tariff induces inefficient production distortions in both countries. The level of production is too high in the importing country and too low in the exporting country relative to what they would be under free trade. However, although the tariff is bad for the world as a whole, it remains a desirable and beneficial policy for the importing country. Thus, at the end of World War II, the large countries that became the original members of the GATT had high tariffs. They found themselves in what economists call a terms-of-trade–driven prisoner's dilemma. The prisoner's dilemma is a famous problem in the field of game theory that describes a situation in which two parties can improve their situations by acting cooperatively, but the individual incentives they face lead them to act noncooperatively.

The problem facing countries at the end of World War II was that they knew they would collectively be better off under free trade. Although each country benefited from its own import tariff, it also suffered at the hands of its trading partners' import tariffs. What was needed was a mechanism by which countries could jointly commit to tariff reductions that would reduce the losses due to production and consumption distortions and, through gains in efficiency, make all countries better off.

The GATT, through its practice of reciprocal tariff reductions, provided the necessary mechanism for countries to commit to freer trade. Under the GATT, large countries that re-duced their import tariffs would experience a net gain because their trading partners would simultaneously reduce their import tariffs. In all countries, the reallocation of labor and capital away from protected import-competing firms and toward export sectors would generate real efficiency gains.

It is evident that reciprocity is necessary for two large countries to engage in trade liberalization, but this could have been achieved with a network of bilateral treaties. Why was a multilateral approach with a strict requirement for nondiscrimination adopted by the WTO?

Nondiscrimination is a convenient way to reduce the complexity of international trading relations. On a purely practical level, it may be easier to negotiate one set of import tariffs than to engage in dozens of bilateral agreements. In fact, John Jackson (1997) speculated that when nondiscrimination, or "most-favored-nation," clauses were originally introduced into trade treaties in the sixteenth century, they had a practical benefit—drafters did not have to copy large sections of treaties again and again.

However, while convenience and practicality are important, nondiscrimination would not have become a central feature of the multilateral trading system if it did not yield real economic benefits. Nondiscrimination in tariff policy, that is, setting the same tariff on imports from all countries, ensures that resources are allocated to their most productive use. On the import side, nondiscrimination ensures that countries purchase imports from the lowest-cost source country. Further, nondiscrimination prevents trade "rerouting" in which goods are moved through third countries in order to circumvent high tariffs. Lastly, Bagwell and Staiger (2003) argued that, on the export side, nondiscrimination protects exporting countries from "bilateral opportunism."

As an importer, a country can charge a single "nondiscriminatory" tariff on imports from all countries, or it can set different tariffs on imports from different countries. Under a nondiscriminatory tariff, imports will be sourced from the lowest-cost producer in the world. Compare this to a system of discriminatory tariffs in which, for example, the United States sets a lower "preferential" tariff on T-shirts from Mexico than on T-shirts from China. If China can produce T-shirts more cheaply than Mexico, but the tariff on Chinese T-shirts is so much larger than the tariff on Mexican T-shirts that it is cheaper for Americans to buy T-shirts from Mexico, there is a real loss due to the production distortions caused by the discriminatory tariffs of the United States. Resources in Mexico that could have been better employed in some other sector are utilized in its relatively high-cost T-shirt industry. Resources in China that could have been efficiently used to make T-shirts are allocated to another industry. When a country uses a nondiscriminatory tariff, this facilitates the allocation of resources worldwide to their most productive uses.

Trade rerouting is a costly practice whereby an exporter ships its goods to a third country, repackages it, and then ships it to a final destination where it will qualify for the third country's lower, preferential tariff rate. In some cases, in order to qualify for the preferential tariff, the product must undergo a "substantial transformation" in the third country. This sometimes leads firms to move a stage of the production process to the third country. When an importing country utilizes a single nondiscriminatory tariff for all imports, there is no need for exporters to engage in the costly process of rerouting.

When two countries bilaterally negotiate tariff concessions, the principle of reciprocity ensures that the terms of trade between the two countries remain unchanged (that is, neither country is "beggaring" the other) while the volume of trade increases to a more efficient level. However, in a world in which both countries remain free to go on and negotiate an additional trade agreement with a third country, the problem of "bilateral opportunism" arises. For example, if one country were to later offer a lower tariff rate to the third country, this could

erode the value of the original tariff concession to the first trading partner. Bagwell and Staiger (2003) have shown that when negotiations utilize the practices of reciprocity and nondiscrimination, the problem of bilateral opportunism is eliminated.

In summary, the GATT's founding principles of reciprocity and nondiscrimination facilitate increases in well-being for the countries that belong to the WTO. By coordinating tariff reductions among large countries, efficiency gains from trade become a reality. By requiring that countries set nondiscriminatory tariffs, the WTO ensures that goods are produced in the most efficient location.

GATT Rules

Rules regarding the trade of physical goods are embodied in the revised GATT of 1994, one annex to the Uruguay Round Agreement. Institutionally, the GATT of 1994 is the oldest of the agreements, having originated in the GATT of 1947, the predecessor and model for the WTO. As such, its fundamental rules of reciprocity and nondiscrimination, described above, are its bedrock. In brief, the GATT's rules-based system for the trade of goods lies at the heart of the WTO. It regulates the trade of all goods except agricultural products, textiles and apparel, and civil aircraft. The trade of each of these goods is regulated in a separate agreement.

GATS Rules

The General Agreement on Trade in Services (GATS), created during the Uruguay Round, establishes a limited set of rules on access to foreign markets for the purpose of providing services. In developed economies, trade in services —for example, banking, travel, and education—represents over half of gross domestic product (GDP). Services trade differs from goods trade in that it involves the exchange of something intangible. Moreover, the mode of exchange varies dramatically by service. For example, medical services require that the seller and purchaser meet together in one location, whereas telecommunications services can be bought and sold by agents in remote locations who never meet in person. Similarly, barriers to services trade differ from barriers to trade in goods in that they are not usually incremental and graduated, like tariffs, but generally take the form of government prohibitions or regulations.

Because both the nature of services trade and the barriers to services trade differ so dramatically from goods trade, the GATS treaty is markedly different from the GATT. Rather than following the WTO's broad general rules of reciprocity and nondiscrimination in all sectors, the emphasis in the GATS has been for countries to make reciprocal market access commitments in specific sectors. Although nondiscrimination is nominally a core principle of the GATS, the number of exemptions allowed can make it appear that nondiscrimination is the exception rather than the rule. In essence, whereas the GATT may be regarded as a set of general rules regarding all goods trade that incorporates commitments to liberalize trade for specific goods, the GATS is the opposite, a list of specific commitments to liberalize trade that may or may not (depending on the country) also be combined with some general rules. The creation of the GATS brought services trade into the oversight of the WTO. This is perhaps best understood as the first important step in creating a multilateral trading system for services rather than as a system itself. The GATS offers a forum and framework in which a rules-based system for services trade can be negotiated in the future (see Hoekman and Kostecki 1995 for a brief overview of the GATS).

TRIPS Agreement

The final major agreement overseen by the WTO is the Agreement on Trade-Related Aspects of Intellectual Property Rights. The TRIPS Agreement differs from the GATT and the GATS in that it calls for all WTO members to follow specific policies to ensure the protection of intellectual property. Intellectual property includes products as varied as movies, pharmaceuticals, literary works, and computer circuit design. The TRIPS Agreement requires all WTO members to provide minimum standards of protection for intellectual property, prescribes remedies that should be available to help enforce intellectual property rights, and makes the WTO's dispute settlement mechanism available to resolve disputes that arise between members.

Intellectual property rights are covered in a number of international conventions that date back to the nineteenth century and are administered by a UN body, the World Intellectual Property Organization (WIPO), that is based in Geneva, Switzerland. Previous conventions on intellectual property did not require that all countries follow the same policies and did not provide a strong international forum in which to present disputes. During the Uruguay Round, developed countries that produce a great deal of the world's intellectual property lobbied hard for the TRIPS Agreement as a way to safeguard their intellectual property in less developed countries that provided weak intellectual property protection. Moreover, developed countries favored including intellectual property rights issues under the umbrella of the WTO so that they could have access to the WTO's dispute settlement mechanism to resolve disputes on such matters (see Hoekman and Kostecki 1995 for a brief overview of the TRIPS Agreement).

Internal Relations among WTO Members

When a trade dispute arises between countries that belong to the WTO, the WTO mediates and resolves the dispute through well-defined dispute settlement mechanisms.

Under the Uruguay Round Agreement, which is an international treaty, the WTO has no authority over individuals, private firms, or public corporations. Rather, it merely governs the interactions of countries that voluntarily agree to abide by its rules. This means that when the WTO has to intervene in a trade dispute, its authority is limited to deciding two things: (1) Are the national laws of an "accused" country consistent with the treaty obligations that the country assumed by signing the GATT? and (2) Is the "accused" country following its own trade rules? Is it implementing its own laws fairly and consistently? In other words, the WTO does not decide the merit of individual cases in which disputes arise—it simply evaluates whether existing national laws are consistent with the GATT treaty and whether they have been properly applied.

Traditionally, a mutually agreeable negotiated settlement to a dispute has been preferred to a more contentious or acrimonious legal proceeding. However, because mutually agreeable settlements are not always easy to come by, the WTO has a a legal forum for handling trade disputes. Disputes that cannot be resolved among the members themselves are referred to a panel of three persons who act as judges in determining the answers to the two questions mentioned above. When a country is found to be in violation of its WTO obligations, it has two choices. It can amend its laws to bring them in line with the Uruguay Round Agreement, or it can keep its laws as they are and face "measured retaliation" from its aggrieved trading partners. Measured retaliation is the WTO's main enforcement mechanism. In the simplest case, if one country were to violate its GATT obligations by raising its tariff on some good, its trading partners could respond by raising their own tariffs on something. This retaliation is "measured" in the sense that it should reduce trade from the offending first country by roughly the same value as the first country's tariff increase.

The practice of measured retaliation is extremely useful in maintaining the smooth functioning of the world trading system. Historically—that is, before measured retaliation became the common practice—when one party to a treaty violated one of its terms, the other party could either accept the violation or withdraw from the treaty entirely. Measured retaliation essentially allows both parties to jointly withdraw from some of their treaty obligations while still enjoying the benefits of the rest of the treaty.

External Relations

Although nondiscrimination is an ideal in the GATT, in practice a number of exceptions to this general rule exist. Regional trade agreements—both free trade areas and customs unions—are allowed. In 1947 when negotiators drafted the original GATT treaty, they recognized that from time to time, some countries might want to push ahead with greater trade liberalization. Although the GATT preferred nondiscriminatory tariffs, it did not wish to impede the gains from trade that could be had if only a few members were willing to reduce their tariffs even further. Therefore, it allowed the formation of two types of regional trade agreements—free trade areas and customs unions. In a free trade area, the members maintain their original external tariffs with the rest of the world but engage in free trade with one another. In a customs union, all member countries set the same external tariff for imports from nonmembers and eliminate the tariffs on imports from members. When GATT members form a customs union, the common external tariff can be no higher than a weighted average of the tariffs of the member countries before the customs union was formed.

From the beginning, the decision to allow regional trade agreements within the GATT was controversial. Jacob Viner (1950) framed the question as an essentially empirical one: Were regional trade agreements "trade creating" or "trade diverting"? He coined the terms "trade creation" and "trade diversion" to describe what happens when several countries join together to form a regional trade agreement (RTA). The reduction in tariffs among RTA members leads to "trade creation" among members. The problem is that the trade that develops between RTA members may not reflect an overall expansion of a country's imports, but rather a diversion of trade away from a non-RTA country to an RTA member. In this case, there may be no worldwide efficiency gains from trade if the non-RTA country is the lowest-cost producer of some good.

Today, the question of whether regional trade agreements are trade creating or trade diverting remains unresolved. In fact, it is almost impossible to answer this question definitively because economists never observe the appropriate benchmark for estimating the amount of trade creation and trade diversion associated with a regional trade agreement. Because economies and trade are always growing, it is hard to construct a counterfactual estimate of how much trade would have grown among RTA members if these countries had not actually formed a regional trade agreement.

Gary Sampson (1996) argued that the question of trade creation and trade diversion is much less important today than it was fifty years ago because tariffs are now much lower. For the United States and the European Union, for example, most products face import tariffs of less than 5 percent. Therefore, Sampson argued, although RTA members with these countries do benefit from a 0 percent tariff rate, the size of this tariff preference—the difference between the tariff for RTA members and the tariffs of other countries—is so small that it cannot possibly induce much trade diversion. Overall, the empirical literature in economics finds evidence that trade diversion occurs. However, the debate over the relative magnitude of trade creation and trade diversion continues.

Meredith Crowley

See Also Antidumping and Countervailing Duties; Nontariff Barriers; Protectionism; Subsidies; Tariffs; Technical Barriers to Trade; Pharmaceuticals; General Agreement on Tariffs and Trade (GATT); Copyrights and Intellectual Property

References

Bagwell, Kyle, and Robert W. Staiger. 2002. *The Economics of the World Trading System.* Cambridge: MIT Press.

———. 2003. "Multilateral Trade Negotiations, Bilateral Opportunism and the Rules of GATT/WTO." *Journal of International Economics* 63, iss. 1, pp. 1–29.

Bhala, Raj. 1996. *International Trade Law: Cases and Materials.* Charlottesville: Michie Law Publishers.

Caves, Richard E., Jeffrey A. Frankel, and Ronald W. Jones. 2002. *World Trade and Payments: An Introduction.* 9th ed. Boston: Addison-Wesley.

Hoekman, Bernard, and Michel Kostecki. 1995. *The Political Economy of the World Trading System.* Oxford: Oxford University Press.

Jackson, John H. 1997. *The World Trading System: Law and Policy of International Economic Relations.* 2d ed. Cambridge: MIT Press.

Krugman, Paul R., and Maurice Obstfeld. 2000. *International Economics: Theory and Policy.* 5th ed. Reading, MA: Addison-Wesley.

Sampson, Gary P. 1996. "Compatibility of Regional and Multilateral Trading Agreements: Reforming the WTO Process." *American Economic Review* 86: 88–92.

Viner, Jacob. 1950. *The Customs Union Issue.* New York: Carnegie Endowment for International Peace.

World Trade Organization. 1995a. *Analytical Index: Guide to GATT Law and Practice,* vol. 2. Geneva: WTO.

———. 1995b. "Uruguay Round Agreement Establishing the World Trade Organization." Geneva: WTO.

———. 2001. *International Trade Statistics.* Geneva: WTO.

———. 2003. *Understanding the WTO.* 3d ed. Geneva: WTO.

PART FOUR

Other Issues

Conflict, Cooperation, and Security

Globalization, and its lineal development, stems from the concerns, crises, and diplomacy of the Cold War epoch. The birth and evolution of globalization has engaged and vexed the minds of scholars of all academic disciplines, not least the scholars of economic history. Whereas political philosophers may focus on globalization from the perspective of, for example, Hegelian determinism, or engage in a game of "what-might-have-been," the economic historian focuses instead on such questions as whether world historical, political, and economic occurrences are globalizing or tend to create fragmentation.

The recession of bipolarity and the power politics involved in territorial, economic, and cultural issues is the delineated framework in which many commentators have located the process of globalization, not least of all Ian Clark in his 1997 book *Globalization and Fragmentation: International Relations in the Twentieth Century.* Clark's work portrays globalization as a phenomenon that has gradually revealed itself in a cumulative fashion. He offered abstract explanations for its development, emphasizing his own interpretation that it has derived from power politics. Consequently, Clark drew upon neo-functional integration theorists to explain how cultures, through state systems and apparatuses, are beginning to resemble each other. This homogenizing effect also embodies economic structures of production, which are indicated by the global transition to post-Fordist methods of production and Taylorism.

Although Clark stated that ulterior interpretations, including world systems and international sociological explanations, do have important explanatory characteristics, he also noted that such explanations fail to accurately depict the influence of power politics and state relations. Clark criticized these normative theories for placing "value judgments" on these areas of state structures and relations, a sentiment echoed by John Baylis and Steve Smith (2004). In explaining the factors influencing globalization, Clark viewed the period of détente, the transmutation of the United States from a "benign" to a "predatory" hegemony, as the inaugural step in the fragmentation of nations from the Western bloc alliance. The U.S. policy of "linkage," where Western nations were to ensure their own security and share the burden with the United States, provided an indication of this direction, according to Clark. He thus views détente and linkage as a period of fragmentation of nation-states. He ignored, however, the globalizing aspect of détente, whereby it facilitated new ties and new bilateral and multilateral agreements among nations to ensure security and economic prosperity. Therefore, Clark drew upon differing and diverse interpretations, ranging from sociological theory to Marxism, to reinforce his power politics explanation. Other economic and political analysts have had different takes on the subject of the globalizing forces of the twentieth century and the tension between these and forces of fragmentation.

Conception, Process, and Theory

It has been asserted that globalization was the only major political and economic force to survive most of the twentieth century, and more important, that the concept of globalization was the only one to retain some coherence at the end of the long boom. This scenario occurred because the globalizing nature of world culture, economics, and politics has evolved into an entity that grows and develops from its own conception. Globalization itself has developed and fostered its own momentum, in other words, and all other aspects of society, including other aspects of economics and culture, are symbiotically linked to globalization and parasitical in nature. This concept of "momentum" and the growing strength of globalization as a force unable to be tamed by the nation-state is supported by Robert Keohane (1984). Keohane argued that conditions created by the United States were conducive to a global economy and have allowed the economy and other symbiotically linked areas, especially international institutions, to conjure their own momentum. Global industries and institutions have thus been able to thrive and gain momentum with U.S. guidance and subsidizing.

Therefore, according to Keohane the U.S. move to a more malignant form of hegemony has been ignored because the global institutions created in the post–World War II setting, including the International Monetary Fund (IMF) and the North Atlantic Treaty Organization (NATO), undertook the role of global watchdog, whereas the United States was often less ostensibly involved in the global arena, in terms of regulation over the flow of global finance, military intervention, and even the "virtuous and moral action" of attempting to stop communism. The international bodies were conceived and imbued with a life of their own. But the control of global affairs is no longer as demarcated as it was in the pre-détente era. Globalization has not, and cannot, be isolated to a postdétente explanation, as Kevin Cox

(1997) and others have contended, nor has it been contained to a post-1945 environment.

Globalization received perhaps its greatest early boost by the commencement of World War I and the resulting involvement of the U.S. military. The U.S. involvement in the Spring Offensive, and the allied victory over Germany, provided a sign of the potential for the United States to become the next major world power. However, the United States chose not to wield this hegemony and instead pursued an isolationist policy during the interwar years. It was concerned more with specific "spheres of influence," as reflected in the Monroe Doctrine, proclaiming this as the most effective path to ensuring international peace and security, than with world dominance. Nonetheless, under the mandate of President Woodrow Wilson, the United States pushed for the establishment of the League of Nations, a forerunner to the United Nations, and under the Lend-Lease Act became the world's altruistic financier, aiding, for example, Germany in its reparations program and devising the Dawes and Young plans to assist Germany in its rebuilding. The United States also made loans to allied nations in the interwar period. These were the initial steps toward globalization, the rebuilding of the world order under the auspices of the United States, even though it was officially pursuing a policy of isolation. It took the rest of the century for these globalizing effects to filter through.

International Momentum

The institutions that the United States created during the first half of the century have mutated and taken on an agenda of their own, attaining momentum and experiencing a form of governed interdependence that has detracted from the international career of the United States. When the United States realized that its international obligations had been seized by these institutions, it began its orientation toward a more predatory form of hegemony, allowing international institutions to gain momentum and supersede the United States, while most of the benefits of these institutions still gravitated to the United States. For this reason, Ian Clark still refers to the United States as possessing the persona of a hegemon and exhibiting hegemonic characteristics, without being burdened with all the associated hegemonic obligations. Although it is Clark's contention that these international institutions perpetually maintain the status quo, thus preventing the United States from suffering any dramatic decline, they did not initially possess the power to do so; indeed, they did not obtain this momentum until the Cold War period was in full swing. Clark stated: "What the evidence suggests is that a transnational economic order has been sustained since 1970—despite the appearance of American decline—because the economic forces realized during the Cold War period have now themselves become a kind of self-reinforcing structural political condition" (Clark 1997).

Thus, bipolarity and the security concerns generated during the Cold War were influential and conducive to the globalization process because they allowed the economic preconditions of a global economy and international institutions to flourish, as attention was diverted to the security threat that each bloc faced from the other. Power politics then inadvertently allowed trade, economics, and international institutions to become global forces capable of seizing the national power of states.

It was the security concerns of the twentieth century, particularly in the Cold War period, that eventuated in the global nature of economics and production orientation. Clark alluded that economics, politics, and culture are all parasitical in nature. The gregarious nature of warfare, especially once the Iron Curtain descended, allowing capital to be devoted to international institutions, coupled with changes in trade and finance, including the revolution in production methods to a post-Fordist orientation, enabled globalization to occur unhin-

dered. The capital allocated to the transition to mass production was supported and supplied by the public, whose taxes were increased to finance this additional unquestioned spending, owing to a collective consensus that there was a perennial security threat from the other bloc. Spending and Keynesian pump-priming was also encouraged by national government leaders who perceived not only a perennial security threat but also an opportunity to fine-tune their skills in diplomacy and increase the wealth of their constituents.

Subsequently, Immanuel Wallerstein's (1976) "grand periphery" was dissolving owing to the international export of post-Fordist mass production as well as the scientific restructuring of the workplace under Taylorism in the United States. The "three worlds" were gradually becoming one, especially during détente, when the effects of the inconspicuous investment made during the Cold War were beginning to be realized.

It was the recycling of petrodollars from the Organization of Petroleum Exporting Countries (OPEC) that provided the capital for Second World and Third World nations to invest in First World production techniques. This resulted in a convergence of economic systems, even though some were more advanced than others; as a result, the "grand periphery" was obscured and could not be detected in such a demarcated way.

Ironically, the recycling of these petrodollars through First World banks, and their reallocation to Third World nations, also combined with budget deficits in advanced industrialized nations throughout the 1970s to produce a liquidity squeeze. The squeeze forced the United States to raise interest rates and to issue Treasury Bonds to attract capital to finance its budget deficit and foreign liabilities. Interest rates were raised to an extraordinary level in the late 1970s and early 1980s, and Third World nations defaulted on their repayments to First World banks, plunging the world into recession on a global scale not seen since the early 1930s.

Clark linked power politics, especially the U.S. ability to bring about a dramatic rise in global interest rates, to the period of stagnation in which we still remain. That is, he posited that the United States made a conscious effort to raise interest rates in order to keep Third World states subordinate to its whims and maintain its control of global capital. Predatory hegemony can be seen most blatantly in the U.S. government's ambivalent approach to globalization. The United States wanted Third World nations to transform, or converge, economically to the same system that was dominant in the West, yet it imposed exogenous shocks—namely, interest rates and inflation, as well as an exponentially increasing foreign debt—to keep these nations tied to democracy and prevent the transition to communism. Clark believes that the United States was still trying to impose imperialistic controls over nations as late as the early 1980s, even though international institutions were by then promoting most of its interests overseas. U.S. President Ronald Reagan emphasized the bipolar nature of world politics with his "evil empire" sentiments.

The period of détente, commencing in the early 1970s and lasting until the beginning of revived tensions in the early 1980s, had somewhat ameliorative characteristics. The level of power politics changed over time, decreasing in the détente period, reestablishing itself in the Reagan years, and relaxing again with the gradual decline of communism starting in 1989. Regardless of this political ambivalence, however, the globalizing nature of world financial markets and international institutions not only continued, they came to life and derived their own momentum and culture. Clark neglected the fact that although the relative hegemony of nations could change over time, along with relations among and between aligned and enemy nations, globalization itself continued unabated. Power politics may inaugurate some forms of globalization and encourage their diffusion, but globalization itself appears subliminal; it cannot be controlled by any obvious or steadfast measure. For this reason, although in-

ternational institutions do essentially have an allegiance to the United States, this allegiance is dramatically diminishing, and although the United States in the past has relied upon these institutions heavily to promote its foreign policy and to provide a facade of hegemonic legitimacy, it has by now lost all control of them. These institutions are beginning to fulfill their original function, that is, to act globally, unfettered by the agenda of any particular nation-state. Hence, globalization seems to be out of control, and definitely out of the scope of power politics on an international level.

Globalization's rampant growth has many commentators concerned. Theoretically, power politics and the diplomacy resulting from bipolarity and the Cold War essentially created the framework for globalization to emerge, but globalization has now grown out of proportion to the power of the nation-states and capital markets that created it. Globalization may be viewed as impenetrable, and frankly, unstoppable, according to this view. Although Clark did not blatantly assert that this was the case, he accurately described a world that has continued to globalize in many facets and domains over the past century. He indicated that power politics, and specifically the relationship among alliance members of each bloc, shifted during the détente period, providing an example of global fragmentation; although he did not see this as a transition to greater globalization, that is essentially what it has turned out to be. The détente period eroded barriers between the First and Second Worlds and increased contact between the two, primarily through summits, a trademark of President Richard Nixon's secretary of state, Henry Kissinger. It also expanded the social contact between East and West by allowing the movement of civilizations, however minimal, and signaled a period of greater cultural and economic reciprocity, and hence globalization on a larger scale. Clark stated, "Détente must then be understood to be as much about relations within the western bloc as about the antagonistic relationship between the two superpowers." He asserted that Western nations were then asked to contribute to regional and global security, that the United States adopted a policy of geopolitics, and that this linkage was also endorsed by the United States under the behest of Kissinger.

This process of "linkage" on a geopolitical level was promoted by Kissinger as the best response to Nixon's Vietnamization policy and the gradual withdrawal of the United States from the Vietnam War. Kissinger saw that the most effective and least confrontational way of closing this policy was to embark on a process of "triangular politics," whereby the two superpowers would talk, and hopefully cooperate, on the Vietnam issue, and the Soviets would stop supplying the North Vietnamese army with weapons and training, while the United States and its allies would gradually retreat from the South and only provide minimal military support. While the two superpowers arrogantly decided upon the future of Vietnam, the Vietnamese were supposed to submissively cooperate like any other subordinate state. Stephen Ambrose hinted at Kissinger's megalomania when he wrote: "Kissinger regarded North Vietnam, South Vietnam, Cambodia and Laos as pawns to be moved around the board by great powers"(1991). Thus, the linkage ideal, derived from the earlier process of triangular politics, is seen as almost exclusively concerned with the transition of security issues from the United States to Western-bloc nations.

Hence, although "détente" was concerned with relations between the two superpowers, the term was essentially a euphemism for the delegation of regional security to nations of the Western bloc. If they could play their part, share the moral burden—and, more important, the financial burden—and relieve the United States from the pressures it was experiencing, then the United States could concentrate on where the real "action" was—the East Asian economies and the rise of the Eurodollar market.

Linkage was thus utilized as a subterfuge for deregulating the whole power and security issue and assisted in the delegation and demarcation of security issues to aligned nations so they could form their own spheres of influence. Ambrose concurred with this view, reiterating the notion that linkage was an ambiguous concept: "Kissinger [strove] to seek the broadest possible agreement with Russia. Everything was linked—the industrial nations' oil shortage, the Vietnam War, wheat sales to Russia, China's military capacity, etc. Kissinger sought nothing less than an all encompassing agreement that would bring worldwide, permanent peace. Through linkage Kissinger would out 'Mettemich Mettemich'" (1991).

Clark agreed with Ambrose to an extent, relating the whole détente period to power politics and the emergence of geopolitics, as opposed to bipolarity. Interestingly, he saw this divergence from the hegemonically closely intertwined blocs as a process of fragmentation, not globalization, as nations now had to secure their own security and, consequently, economic interdependence. This point is intrinsic to Clark's thesis. That is, although he attributed most globalizing and fragmentizing scenarios to power politics throughout the twentieth century, he failed to comprehend the consequences or aftereffects. Clark interpreted these events from a historical perspective, where their immediate influence is the correct one, and relegated later permutations or factors stemming from this immediate outcome to an unimportant level. His writings could be interpreted as somewhat absolutist in their nature because they do not give much credence to the influence of norms or constructivist theory. His view that détente heralded a period of fragmentation, when it actually encouraged globalization, was a serious oversight. In reality, nations had to make independent alliances and forums to safeguard themselves from hostile external threats. Clark also failed to address the notion that international institutions promoted globalization and allowed it to develop unfettered, because he was consumed by the proposition that power politics instigated fragmentation and did not recognize the subliminal preponderance of globalization.

Clark criticized constructivist and normative writers for the value judgments they make about historical events. These value judgments, he said, are potentially fatal because they often contradict the facets of world historical developments and take little account of uncontrollable areas such as economics and some aspects of culture. He granted little credence to normative aspects of globalization, although in all fairness, he alluded to these competing theories of globalization in his initial chapter and conceded that some are relevant to explanations of globalization and world affairs.

Nevertheless, Clark utilized the writings of neo-functional integration theorists to explain globalization in terms of power politics and Cold War bipolarity, citing Sean Jones (1991) and his discussion of the impact of interdependence, which emerged during the 1970s. This functionalist literature on globalization was influenced by the export of production orientation, including post-Fordism and Taylorism, by Western nations to those on the development periphery, as well as later processes such as deregulation and privatization. Technical cooperation and scientific management led many normative and constructivist theorists to deduce that nation-states, regardless of their political or social structure, were beginning to resemble each other. This was occurring in areas most susceptible to the onslaught of globalization—culture and market production; hence, nation-states were becoming homogenized, a blatant indication that globalization was occurring. Clark drew upon this thesis quite comprehensively to develop his own argument, despite its functionalist and constructivist traits. He concluded that it was this transition of production techniques, finance, and consumer culture that would instigate a demonstrative effect and "yield a superstructure of political behaviour in which the sovereignty of the nation state would be steadily eroded and circumvented."

Thus, Clark adapted the neo-functional integration thesis to complement his argument. The fact that these theorists talked of the ho-

mogenizing effect of globalization on the political framework of nations, and thus power politics, helped to reinforce Clark's argument. Clark thus appears to have exploited the neo-functional integrationist argument in order to appease his normative and constructivist critics. Clark and others have agreed on the globalizing and detrimental effect of the Gulf War on those nation-states that were homogenized and classified by their dependency on oil, a factor that caused the war to have a greater impact on the global society. Colleagues suggested the impact that globalization can have by looking at the example of Kuwait, where the Iraqi invasion of 1990 led to short-term instabilities in world oil and financial markets, which in turn had an impact upon other nations and their ability to maintain their existing level of welfare provisions. Clark utilized these normative aspects as a subversive measure to inject some diversity and appeasement into his thesis, while not compromising its integrity and primary focus—that of the effects of globalization on power politics, and vice versa, over the past century.

Clark then emphasized that in this era of diminishing nationalism, globalism has emerged to fill the void. Nationalism, in its extreme guise, was one of the contributing factors in the outbreak of World War I, and it reappeared in a mutated form known as fascism, whereby nations were led by dictators, during the global depression of the 1930s, then played a major role in the outbreak of World War II. Nationalism thus led to two devastating global wars during the first half of the twentieth century, and there existed no real international institution to provide any impediment to this, even in the interwar period. The utopian notion of collective security and the League of Nations failed dismally.

It was the Cold War, and various other "brush fires" that emerged, including Korea, Suez, and Cuba, that ensured the stability of the world in its bipolar orientation. "Brinkmanship" and the constant security concerns of the Cold War quelled nationalism, as only two blocs essentially existed, which meant that conformity and subordination, deriving from the benevolence of each power within their respective blocs, were prerequisites to national security and economic growth. Fukuyama acknowledged this but explained that nationalism was only necessary in the early stages of capitalism because it provided a guarantee that the benefits of initiatives undertaken in a nation to provide growth, including economic transformation and evolution, would remain in that nation, thus allowing early capitalist and industrializing nations a chance to attain a comparative advantage over other competing nations. Once the developmental process was over for the most powerful nations, the same governmental and societal forces that in the past required nationalistic controls now demanded a desegregation of these policies and institutions, as well as the reversal of cultural values, in a transition to the diametrically opposed principle of globalization. Those groups that have encouraged this transition realize the potential benefits that global culture, capital, and security encompass, and the correspondingly decreased emphasis on national governments.

Clark's discussion of nationalism incorporates important empirical evidence for the notion that globalization is not a phenomenon that was isolated to the post-1945 or the post-1970 era, but rather the current incarnation of a gradual transition that has been occurring throughout the century. Nationalism has not disappeared: It has now become manifest as global market nationalism, whereby nation-states and other powerful and influential "actors" in the global arena are competing for their own spheres of influence and, in the case of business, their own personal markets, a quest that often transcends national boundaries, culture, and ideology. This new market nationalism exists on a global scale, where everybody is a potential consumer, and spheres of influence within society are determined by what commodity is produced for that particular market. Traditional nationalism has been disbanded,

and globalism endorsed, in order to facilitate the mobility of capital and the ability of markets to accommodate intercultural and societal consumers.

In this new global environment, the ambiguity of power has ensured the inability of analysts to define hegemonic relationships in any clear and demarcated manner. Rather, the new pluralism, redefined as fragmentation, harbors many facets of power, where all its variants can be exhibited. Power politics—strategic and economic power as well as other kinds, including religious power and the power of ideological beliefs—takes different forms with multiple leaders, is not necessarily defined by nation-states, and is more transitory at present than ever before. Indeed, Clark asserted that "there is no single balance of power but multiple barriers within separate issue areas, and possibly in various regional settings."

Hence, the world has entered into a period in which strength and influence are not measured by economic or military might, but rather by the harm that one "actor" can impose on another. Power politics, the development of international institutions, and the decline in nationalism over the past century have together created this environment and allowed it to develop unfettered. Clark explained the rise of globalization in terms of his own framework, which is comprehensive. From this structure, and his emphasis on détente as a process that sparked interest in and acknowledgment of the globalizing nature of nation-states and international finance, he traced the ascendancy of nongovernmental "actors" in the power game as their share of influence increased, at a time when the monopoly of the nation-states was declining. Clark acknowledged this process when he wrote of the "desegregation of political and strategic developments at the center from those on the periphery," stating that "the sum no longer had a significance greater than its parts" (1997).

Power does have ambiguity in this increasingly globalized system, and it is multidimensional as well, emanating from various sources.

Nevertheless, Clark views these various power structures as possessing one core characteristic: that they all developed from and directly benefited from the lack of attention given to many issues during the Cold War period, when the flow of capital was unregulated and capitalist nation-states were allocated various spheres and industries for security purposes. This Cold War–era system had unintended advantages and disadvantages for the world.

Therefore, globalization cannot be attributed to any particular influence, occurrence, or "actors" in the global arena; rather, it is a multi-dimensional phenomenon. Globalization can only be interpreted through a delineated framework and agenda, as Clark has done, focusing on power politics and the security concerns of the Cold War. Though this analysis is plausible, it does not necessarily explain the rise of globalism fully—further critique and analysis are called for. There is one certainty that may be deduced from Clark's thesis: Globalization continues to grow and evolve exponentially, and it has managed to supplant a way of life. The cultural global norm that existed during the Cold War period is no longer.

It is also clear that it was the Cold War and détente period that fostered globalization. It developed international institutions and allowed different cultures to emerge and become powerful. It allowed "linkage" policies to demolish barriers to a global society. All of this was presaged by the U.S. decline and transition to a more predatory form of hegemony, which thrust Western bloc nations into the international arena to form their own relations and interdependence links.

David Brennan

See Also Group of 8 (G8); Political Systems and Governance; Social Policy

References

Ambrose, Stephen. 1991. *Nixon: Ruin and Recovery 1973–1990.* New York: Simon & Schuster.

Baylis, John and Steve Smith (ed). 2004. *The Globalization of World Politics.* 3rd Ed. London: Oxford University Press.

Clark, Ian. 1997. *Globalization and Fragmentation: International Relations in the Twentieth Century.* London: Oxford University Press.

Cox, Kevin (ed). 1997. *Spaces of Globalization: Reasserting the Power of the Local.* Guilford Press.

Keohane, Robert O. 1984. *After Hegemony: Cooperation and Discord in the World Political Economy.* Princeton: Princeton University Press.

Lynn-Jones, Sean (ed). 1991. *The Cold War and After: Prospects for Peace.* Cambridge, MA: MIT Press.

Wallerstein, Immanuel. 1976. *The Modern World-System: Capitalist Agriculture and the Origins of the European World-Economy in the Sixteenth Century.* New York: Academic Press.

Copyrights and Intellectual Property

Copyright forms a part of a larger body of law known as "intellectual property." Intellectual property can be thought of as creations of the human mind and intellect, and intellectual property law in general recognizes, and attempts to protect, the property rights of creators in their creations. It also serves, indirectly, as a means under which human creativity may be stimulated, and under which the fruits of such creation can be made available to the public in general via transactions involving intellectual property. It is widely recognized that without some sort of recognition and protection of intellectual property rights, economic systems (including international trade) would be significantly adversely affected, with corresponding negative effects on economic growth in general.

Although Latin-based languages have always used the term "intellectual property" to refer only to the property of creators of works with some cultural value, internationally the same term is generally taken to refer to both cultural and industrial property. Initially, industrial property was protected by the Paris Union (created by the Paris Convention for the Protection of Industrial Property of 1883), whereas the Berne Union (established under the Berne Convention for the Protection of Literary and Artistic Works of 1886) dealt with issues regarding copyright. The secretariats of the two unions were combined in 1893, forming what is now known as the World Intellectual Property Organization (WIPO).

The document that was written to establish WIPO does not define "intellectual property" directly, but it does clearly state the subject matter that is protected by intellectual property rights, including (among others) literary, artistic, and scientific works; inventions in all fields of human endeavor; and industrial designs and trademarks. Intellectual property law therefore can be divided into two branches, patent law (which refers principally to inventions and other industrial property) and copyright law (which refers principally to literary and artistic creations, typically considered goods with cultural value).

Inventions can be thought of as new solutions to technical problems, but they need not be represented in a physical embodiment to be protected under patent law; that is, it is sufficient that the inventor fully describes the nature and working of the invention in a written document. However, the patent protects the invention itself, and not the form of expression that may have been used to describe it. Creations with cultural value (for example, books, musical compositions, paintings and other works of art, and technology-based works such as computer programs and electronic databases), in contrast, are protected by copyright law, which only provides protection for the form of expression and not the ideas expressed.

Copyright and Cultural Markets

All economies, both developed and developing, have an important dependence on culture and cultural activity in general. "Cultural activity" is that part of the "culture and leisure industry" in general that comprises all activities that produce and distribute goods and services with cultural content, that are products of creative work, and that are destined for consumption via reproductive mechanisms. The intellectual property in such cultural goods is both recognized by, and protected by, copyright law. For the purposes of copyright, this would include every work of original authorship, irrespective of its literary or artistic merit; that is, the recognition of a property right via copyright should always be independent of the true cultural value of the work in question.

A "cultural creation" is any work with any degree of cultural content. As soon as the exact identity of the owner of this creation is determined, it is considered intellectual property. The initial owner of the intellectual property is usually simply the creator of the work, though there may be exceptions to this rule—for example, in cases of patronage, or in other cases where a creator cedes his or her rights before the act of creation takes place (for example, when an employee authors a company report, any intellectual property thus created usually belongs to the employer). Copyright law recognizes and protects the property right in the cultural creation.

The rights granted under copyright law to the owner of the copyright in a protected work are the exclusive rights to use, in any way or form, the work, subject to the legally recognized rights and interests of others. Basically, these rights can be divided into "economic rights" (the right to derive financial reward from the use of the work) and "moral rights" (the right to preserve the authorship of the work).

Under copyright law, the owner of the copyright has the legally recognized right to prevent certain uses of the protected work, and also the right to authorize use. Naturally, authorized use normally occurs in exchange for a monetary recompense, which is known as a copyright "royalty." The types of use that are usually of concern are the right to reproduce the work on a physical support (for example, photocopies of written works, or electronic copies of musical compositions), the right of public performance (broadcasting and public communication), and the right of translation and adaptation. However, under the right to reproduce there are several related issues, some of which are designed to ensure the right of reproduction, and others to ensure the best interests of other members of society. Within the first type, there is the right to authorize distribution of copies (including the right to import and export) and the right to authorize rental of copies. The second type of right (encompassing those rights ensuring the best interests of other members of society), generally known as "fair use," sets a limitation on the rights of the copyright holder. Under fair use, a small part of most protected works can be reproduced without prior authorization when it is generally accepted that such reproduction is in the public interest, or that it is simply economically inefficient to request formal authorization for the reproduction. An excellent example of fair use is when a particular amount of an academic journal may be reproduced at no cost for research or teaching purposes.

Aside from fair use, a further limitation occurs in that copyright has, in all countries, a limited duration, after which the copyright expires and the entire set of rights is effectively shifted into the public domain. In most countries, copyright is established upon the creation of the work and lasts until at least fifty years after the death of the author in order that the author's immediate successors may benefit from the exploitation of the work.

In spite of limitations, the exploitation of copyrights forms a very large part of most developed economies. Recent studies suggest that between 4 and 5 percent of gross domestic product (GDP) can be attributed to the culture and leisure industry. Between 65 percent (in the case of books) and 85 percent (in the case of recorded music) of the general public are users of cultural intellectual property protected under copyright. Also, as a very rough estimate, each individual member of society (assuming a developed economy) contributes close to $10 annually to total copyright royalty income (about $6 for music-related royalties and about $4 for written creations).[1] Finally, total copyright royalty revenue is growing at between 10 and 40 percent per annum around the world (depending on the source of the income and the particular country of reference). Clearly, if copyright can be properly managed and protected, the recent advances in digital technologies that permit greater distribution opportunities for cultural products could lead to even more impressive figures into the future.

Transactions Involving Copyright

Although a copyright is the property right in a creation of a cultural nature, it is also an asset in itself because it has value and can be transacted. Indeed, one of the principal reasons why copyright exists is to allow the general public to gain access to the fruits of creative endeavor— that is, to allow certain rights to be transacted in market settings.

In transactions involving cultural intellectual property, the seller grants the buyer the right to use, or to have access to, intellectual property of a cultural nature. That is, the intellectual property itself is not transacted, only the right to have access to it. Clearly, there is a wide range of options, depending on the degree of access that is granted under the transaction contract. In this sense, the complete set of all possible rights included under copyright law can be subdivided into different independent subsets. The copyright holder involved in a transaction to sell some of these rights can thus decide on different degrees of access by specifying exactly which subrights are included in the access list, and the time period during which access is granted. One particular right that should be included in the total set of rights is the exclusive right to grant access at a price. If this right was retained by the copyright holder (and even if it was the only right that

was retained), one would say that only incomplete access had been granted. A short list of options is:

1. Complete access that is unlimited in time (the outright sale of the copyright).
2. Complete access that is limited in time (an exclusive rental contract with a limit, or an end date).
3. Incomplete access that is unlimited in time (the outright sale of a properly defined subset of rights).[2]
4. Incomplete access that is limited in time (a restricted rental contract).

An important aspect of copyright transactions is the fact that intellectual property is a public good. This means that there can be, simultaneously, many users, and no particular user's access is negatively affected in any way by the existence of the others. Therefore, so long as the right to grant access has not been ceded, the initial copyright holder can grant access to many users. Even if the right to grant access has been sold, then the new holder of this particular right can grant different degrees of access to many users simultaneously.

Once cultural intellectual property has been exposed via some type of authorization to access, it becomes necessary to protect it from unauthorized use or access. To be effective, copyright protection requires monitoring of use. Clearly this is prohibitively expensive for individual copyright holders, since the transaction costs involved in monitoring the use of all possible consumers would be enormous. For this reason, almost all copyrights are administered by copyright collectives, which are simply associations to whom authors transfer copyrights for purposes of exploitation. A copyright collective is essentially a large group of copyright holders acting together.

Since the activity of dealing with copyrights presents many aspects of a natural monopoly, in most countries there is only one copyright collective for each general type of creation (musical compositions, written works, and so on), with the notable exception of the United

States, where two principal collectives administer copyrights in musical compositions—AS-CAP (American Society of Composers, Authors & Publishers) and BMI (Broadcast Music, Inc.). Copyright collectives grant licenses to access the works in their repertory; negotiate and collect royalties, which are then distributed to the members; and take legal action against copyright infringements. Typically, copyright collectives sell what is known as a "blanket license," that is, the right to limited access of all of the individual copyrights contained in its repertory, rather than the right to use each copyright individually.

The economic theory literature concerning optimal regulation of natural monopolies is very clear. The socially optimal way to regulate a natural monopoly is to set prices equal to marginal cost, and then to subsidize the fixed costs so that the business may continue. The collective administration of copyrights is an excellent example of a natural monopoly, since adding new, independent copyrights to an existing repertory will not, in general, increase average costs as repertory size increases. Collective administration is the only way that the high transaction costs of copyright administration (in particular, the costs of monitoring use and of charging the access price) can be overcome. However, since the marginal cost of adding a user to a blanket license is basically zero, one can formulate a good argument for setting the price of access to a copyright at precisely zero.[3]

If one assumes that the demand for access to intellectual property is negatively sloped (that is, intellectual property is an ordinary good), then a price of zero will maximize the demand, and consequentially the distribution, of the intellectual property, assuming this property exists. However, a price of zero would minimize the revenue of the copyright holder, and if the copyright holder is the initial creator, then that price would eliminate the economic incentive to create in the first place.[4] Hence, if the creator foresees a price of zero, then it is possible that he or she will not have sufficient

incentive to dedicate time to the creative process, and as a result the entire market will collapse, since no intellectual property will exist. A strictly positive price, however, will imply less demand (and so less distribution), but will generally imply that there exists an economic incentive for the creator, thereby providing a greater guarantee that creators will dedicate their time to the creative process. However, in most cases, there will exist a price that is so high that demand is reduced to nothing, which once again eliminates the economic incentive for creators.

It is practically indisputable that it is important and valuable that cultural intellectual property exists, and that it is shared among members of society. The second of these objectives can be attained using a low price of access. However, for intellectual property to be distributed, there must exist a stock of intellectual property in the first place (and it may well be the case that it is interesting for this stock to be expanding over time), which requires a price that is sufficiently positive to guarantee the economic incentive in creators. Copyright law is designed to balance these two opposing effects. In general, it can be concluded that in almost all cases, the socially optimal price will be relatively low but strictly positive.

Current Concerns
Surrounding Copyright

Although copyright transactions are flourishing worldwide, there are several aspects of copyright markets that are causing a certain degree of worry for copyright holders. Two of the most important concerns have to do with the establishment of the correct price of access and the effects of piracy (unauthorized access).

Strictly speaking, there is no such thing as a "correct price"; rather, economists are interested in "equilibrium prices," which are the prices such that no demander at that price is left unsupplied, and no supplier is left without a demander. The equilibrium price of access will occur at the intersection of the particular supply and demand curves for the degree of access under consideration. But what factors determine the shapes and positions of these curves? One aspect has typically been dealt with in an ad-hoc manner—the dependence of the final price on the final market value of the copyright being accessed.

In order to take this aspect of copyright transactions into account, one must consider the environment of uncertainty in which such transactions are typically carried out. Between the creation phase and the final consumption of intellectual property, there will exist several contracts under which access to the intellectual property is distributed. In the first place, the initial copyright holder (the creator) will usually cede his commercial rights to a distributor[5] (normally a copyright collection society). Second, the distributor will then grant access to final users, generally via a second, more specialized level of distribution. At each transaction level, there will exist a total surplus that must be distributed between the two parties to the contract, and over the entire range of contracts, the final value of the access being contracted (the total value of this degree of access to final users) must be allocated among all participants in the creation-distribution-consumption chain.

The problem is that the final value of the access under consideration is effectively a random variable (it may take on any one of many values, depending upon a great many influencing factors), and yet the contracts that specify how this value must be shared must be written and agreed upon before this uncertainty is resolved, since it is precisely via these contracts that the uncertainty can be resolved. The question is, how should the price of access in each moment of the distribution chain depend upon each possible contingency of the final value?

In practice, this aspect of access contracts is solved in the simplest possible way—there is a constant proportional price, that is, the final value of the copyright being accessed is divided among the participants to the contract according to proportional splits that do not depend on the value being shared (for example, author royalties are often set at 10 percent of final sales revenue, independently of how much that sales revenue turns out to be). However, although this rule is simple and thereby certainly saves on other transaction costs, it can be shown that it is in general an inefficient manner in which to distribute inherent risk among the parties to the contracts. Pricing access efficiently, at all levels of the distribution chain, is certainly one of the most important questions facing copyright collectives today.

The second important concern for copyright collectives is the presence of piracy of intellectual property, that is, unauthorized use of copyrights. When a legal copyright exists, it is necessary to pay the copyright holder the access price in order to gain access to the intellectual property in question. When a user takes access without paying the price, an act of piracy has occurred. Piracy of intellectual property is equivalent to the outright theft of any other type of good.

Copyright holder lobby groups often present arguments to the effect that piracy is so rampant that it is threatening the very existence of legal transactions involving intellectual property. Indeed, in some countries, it is argued that the proportion of consumers using pirated copies of certain items of intellectual property is almost as great as the proportion using legitimate copies. Statistics implying that piracy is costing immense amounts of money in lost legitimate trade are often cited. However, such statistics must be treated with a certain degree of doubt, since they are typically based upon the assumption that each pirated copy that is transacted represents the loss of a legitimate sale. This is obviously an incorrect foundation upon which to base an estimate of the loss of legitimate trade, simply because pirated copies are always transacted at a lower price than legitimate copies. Eliminating the pirated copies would not necessarily mean that users would then purchase the more expensive legitimate copies.[6] Indeed, recent studies based on more correct economic theory suggest that only about 10 percent of pirated-copy transactions represent lost sales of originals (compared to the figures that multinational record companies cite, often between 40 and 60 percent).[7]

Even though piracy occurs for all types of intellectual property, the most worrying area today is certainly piracy of musical compositions. Software piracy is also a worry, but it can be more easily controlled using programming techniques that limit the number of copies that can be produced from an original. However, on this point it should also be noted that the technology race that ensues as software producers attempt to outwit pirates, and pirates attempt to outwit producers, amounts to a costly waste of resources with no final productivity. Piracy of literary works also exists (photocopying of books), but given the generally low price of original formats, the high cost of copying (photocopying an entire book is a time-consuming activity), and the fact that the pirated version is often a poor substitute for an original, it is generally considered to be less rampant than piracy of musical compositions. Indeed, given new technologies (for example, CD burners and digital data-transfer mechanisms over the Internet), a pirated copy of a CD containing music is very close to a perfect substitute for an original, and yet can be obtained for a fraction of the price.

One method of ensuring that copyright royalties are paid in spite of piracy is to charge a tax on blank supports and copy technology, which can be used to finance lost copyright royalty income. This is done in many countries, for example, on photocopy machines, where a small fraction of the price of the machine is passed on to copyright collectives that deal with authors' rights to cover any royalties that may have been lost through illegal photocopying of books. Along the same lines, in some countries a tax is set on blank tapes (both video and audio), and these revenues are passed on to copyright holders. In Spain, a court decided that the producer of blank CD ROMs should pay the local music-related copy-

right collective a tax on each unit produced since 1997 to make up for lost royalty income on copies of prerecorded music using this media. However, this type of solution is really no more than a shift of the economic costs of piracy from copyright holders to consumers who use blank supports (and copy technologies) for purposes other than reproducing protected works. Indeed, in some countries (for example, Australia), this type of tax-based solution has been declared anticonstitutional.

Although piracy can take many forms, depending on the type of access (and the type of intellectual property), in principle it is relatively easy to pirate a work (that is, it can be done at a relatively low cost), whereas it is relatively difficult (that is, costly) to prevent piracy via the legal system. The higher the price at which legal access is granted, the greater the incentive for users to resort to piracy as a substitute for legal access. There are basically two ways to attack the problem of piracy, one based upon the introduction of legal regulations, and the other based upon incentives provided by pricing systems. The first is the domain of the legal profession, whereas the second is the domain of economists. Both imply the need for a consistent definition and recognition of copyright, but whereas legal solutions are exogenous barriers to behavior, incentive-based solutions are totally endogenous manners in which to curb behavior. It is not clear which of the two is likely to be more effective, but what is obvious is that the introduction of artificial rules will always require maintenance costs (behavior will need to be monitored and verified for the rules to have any real effect, since otherwise parallel markets in which the rules are not observed will always be established[8]), and that incentive-based mechanisms can never be avoided.

Naturally, the legal system will generally provide a disincentive for piracy—for example, by stipulating fines and other penalties for pirates once discovered. However, whenever the probability of piracy being detected is quite low, as is the case in practice, then the legal system can turn out to be rather ineffective as a mechanism against piracy. In general, the greater the equilibrium price of access, and the less effective the legal system in monitoring use, the greater will be the threat of piracy. If the copyright holder considers that the existence of piracy is damaging to him,[9] then he may well find it beneficial to reduce the price at which legal access is granted, since this should provide a direct, and significant, disincentive to piracy activity.

However, copyright holders are typically unwilling to admit that a solution, even though partial, to the problem of piracy lies in their own pricing policies. The main reason for this reluctance is that legitimate production costs are high and profits generally low. The costs of production include not only the marginal cost of producing the physical support units, but also the fixed costs of producing the original unit (the master tape, for example, in the case of music) and the costs of promotion. On top of this, legitimate units are obviously subject to the copyright royalty that units produced by pirates save. Consequently, pirated copies are a means of supply of a perfect substitute item at a lower fixed and marginal cost, and thus can be sold profitably at a lower price. Although theoretical solutions, based on the economic theory of incentives, do exist, they typically involve business strategies that imply moving in completely new directions, with corresponding uncertainty as to the final outcome. It is much less risky, and overall less costly, for copyright holders to attempt to invoke stronger legal protection, effectively passing the economic costs of controlling piracy onto the legal system, and hence onto society in general. Much theoretical work remains to be done in this area so that real working solutions that are socially efficient can be established.

Conclusions

Legal recognition of copyright is undoubtedly a necessary ingredient for transactions involving cultural intellectual property to take place—transactions that have an obvious importance within developed economic systems. In the twenty-first century, copyright will need to evolve to account for new technological developments. Traditionally, copyright has been dealt with through legal mechanisms; more recently, a good deal of effort has been devoted to searching for less costly, more efficient alternatives. However, copyright holders have not yet been convinced of the efficacy of such systems, and so the emphasis on the legal system has remained.

Only time will tell whether a copyright system based on purely legal mechanisms can be upheld in the age of the Internet and in an era in which technological methods of reproduction are continually improving. Some experts believe that the future of music will involve a return to original values in which music held a purely cultural role in society, attracting musicians who are not motivated by financial gain. Others have a bleaker outlook, and foresee the end of the prerecorded music industry as we know it, as musicians who cannot protect their property rights effectively become insufficiently motivated to dedicate their time to creative activities. However, many musicians themselves have other opinions and are willing to look into more innovative solutions, viewing the options that distribution via the Internet can offer as more constructive than destructive.

Richard Watt

See Also Technology and Technical Change; Pharmaceuticals; General Agreement on Tariffs and Trade (GATT); World Trade Organization (WTO)

Endnotes

1. Figures based upon Spanish economic data.

2. For example, the doctrine of "fair use" is tantamount to the outright sale of the right to access a small part of some intellectual property to the general public at a price of zero.

3. An access price of zero for any given degree of access is formally equivalent to not recognizing this particular degree of access in the initial set of rights covered by

the copyright, since it means that any user can freely access the intellectual property in this degree.

4. Naturally, there may exist other, noneconomic, incentives that creators take into account.

5. This relationship is founded on the theory of comparative advantage and specialization and is made possible by the existence of high transaction costs in the management of intellectual property rights.

6. On top of this, eliminating the option of pirated copies would certainly affect the price at which legitimate copies are sold, presumably increasing it further since legitimate trade would be facing less competition. Hence, there is reason to believe that eliminating the option of piracy may even reduce the number of legitimate copies sold.

7. In any case, the economic harm that piracy inflicts upon copyright holders should not be measured in terms of lost income, but rather lost profit. Given that profit

margins may be as low as 5 percent of sales, the true economic harm is far less than what is often cited.

8. Outside of the realm of piracy of copyright and cultural markets, but clearly very related, are smuggling and other trade in illegal goods (drugs, arms, and the like), activities that are established when legitimate trade in these goods is made illegal.

9. Surprisingly, it is not true that piracy will always be damaging to copyright holders. See, for example, "Copying and Indirect Appropriability," by Stan Liebowitz, in *Journal of Political Economy* 93 (1985): 945–957; "The Welfare Implications of Unauthorised Reproduction of Intellectual Property in the Presence of Demand Network Externalities," by Lisa Takeyama, in *Journal of Industrial Economics* 17 (1994): 155–166; and "The Intertemporal Consequences of Unauthorised Reproduction of Intellectual Property," by Lisa Takeyama, in *Journal of Law and Economics* 40 (1997): 511–522.

Corruption and the Underground Economy

Corruption, the misuse of public power for private benefit, has repercussions on international flows of goods, services, and capital by leading to the misallocation of resources and by adversely influencing investors' confidence. Corruption is commonly defined as the misuse of public power for private benefit. Public power is exercised by bureaucrats, who are appointed to their office, and by politicians, who are elected to their position. The term "misuse" can relate to a behavior that deviates from the formal duties of a public role (elective or appointive), to a behavior that is in contrast to informal rules (public expectations or codes of conduct), or, more generally, to a behavior that promotes the interests of a particular group or groups at the expense of those of the public at large. "Private benefit" relates to receiving money or valuable assets, but it may also encompass increases in power or status. Receiving promises of future favors or benefits for relatives and friends may also be considered a private benefit. With regard to favors for relatives and friends, the terms nepotism and favoritism are also used.

A world free of corruption would be one that incorporated three ideals. First, pertinent arguments in public decisionmaking would not be overshadowed by personal or other relationships (the arm's-length principle), and equality of treatment for all economic agents would be achieved. Second, citizen participation and involvement would be encouraged, giving people a say in public decisionmaking. Third, transparent procedures would be in place with regard to public decisionmaking, limiting discretion of officeholders.

Corruption, certainly, is sometimes defined differently in different regions of the world. What changes are the public expectations with regard to how officials should serve the public. The three principles mentioned above may be given different weight in different countries. Equality of treatment may be less relevant in societies characterized by strong personal relations, where relatives and friends expect officeholders to provide favorable treatment. Transparency and participation may be given less significance in societies where people trust that pertinent arguments are only relevant for bureaucrats. What seems to be universal, though, is that the public commonly considers self-seeking behavior by politicians and bureaucrats as corrupt when this goes along with a blunt neglect of their expectations and interests.

Corrupt Actors

Corruption is an exchange of favors between two actors, an agent and a client. The agent is entrusted with power by his superior, the principal. The principal delegates a task to the agent and sets up the rules for how this task is supposed to be fulfilled. The agent is supposed to serve the client in accordance to these rules. Bribery, extortion, embezzlement, and fraud in the public sector are variants of corrupt behavior where an agent defects. In the case of bribery, the client acts as a briber and makes a payment (also called kickback, baksheesh, sweetener, payoff, speed-money, or grease-money) to the agent, who then is called a bribee. In return, the briber obtains an advantage, such as a service or license he is not entitled to obtain (for example, a tax rebate or a public contract). In the case of extortion, the agent uses his power to extract money or other benefits from the client. The client may have to pay for a service, although he is legally entitled to obtain it without such payment. The agent uses coercion, violence, or threats to use force in order to obtain this payment. Embezzlement, in contrast, is a simple theft of public resources by the agent and does not involve the client.

In bribery, extortion, and embezzlement, the principal's rules are trespassed and his interests are hurt. The opportunity for corruption exists because the agent is commonly better informed about the details of his daily tasks and his efforts to fulfill them than the principal is; that is, he benefits from informational advantages. The agent can also actively conceal information from the principal (committing fraud) with the help of trickery, swindling, deceit, manipulation, or distortion of information, facts, and expertise.

Corruption must be distinguished from forms of criminal conduct that involve only private parties. Tax evasion, smuggling, black-market activity, insider dealings at the stock exchange, production of counterfeit money, and subsidy fraud can be carried out without misusing public power. Actors involved in such activities are private businesspeople and others—for example, taxpayers—who are not entrusted with public power. Nonetheless, these activities may accompany corruption when public officeholders are paid to refrain from prosecution, to grant impunity, or to provide inside information on criminal opportunities. At the same time, these activities are equally likely to create an uncertain environment that deters all those economic actors, in particular

investors, who are not insiders to the criminal peculiarities of a country.

Forms of Corruption

In distinguishing among various forms of corruption, one issue is whether the briber or the bribee obtains the larger benefit from a corrupt deal, which depends largely on which side has the stronger bargaining power. "Clientilist" corruption takes place if the briber obtains the higher benefit, whereas "patrimonial" corruption occurs when the bribee obtains the higher share. One may also distinguish between petty and grand corruption, where the former involves frequent, small payments to public servants lower in a hierarchy, whereas the latter involves large, one-shot payments to higher ranks. The terms "political" and "administrative" corruption are defined according to the key actors and whether they are politicians or bureaucrats.

In addition to these clear-cut, well-defined areas of corruption, controversy exists over whether certain acts in a gray area should be regarded as corrupt. Lobbying is one such area. Although lobbying involves decisions in the public sector about benefits that are, so to speak, up for sale, it is often legal, is often carried out in a transparent and competitive manner, and often involves not the narrow interests of an individual but the interests of business or even nonprofit sectors. This distinguishes it from ordinary types of corruption. Gift giving to public servants is another such gray area. It involves the danger of dependency and reciprocity by the receiver, but it may not require obfuscation, which is a characteristic of corruption. Gifts, in contrast to bribes, can always be given in an open, transparent manner. Bribing of private firm employees—for example, the payment of kickbacks to sales managers—is another gray area. This involves the misuse of entrusted power, suggesting that it constitutes a case of corruption. But the position of power was not provided by the public but by a private firm, suggesting differences from common corruption.

Any public sector seems to be vulnerable to corruption. Corruption can particularly flourish in sectors where the private and the public interact, such as the judiciary, public procurement, business regulations and granting of permits, privatization, foreign exchange (including customs, trade permits, and international financial transactions), taxes (including the granting of tax exemptions), police, subsidies, public utilities (water, electricity, telephone, garbage collection, and health care), and government services (health, education, and the like).

Corruption and the Unofficial Economy

Corruption is observed to accompany a variety of related economic distortions and societal malfunctions. Some managers prefer to go "underground" with their firms, that is, to carry out their transactions unofficially. This frees them from paying taxes and obeying government regulation, but disallows them from use of public services and utilities. One important such service, for example, is justice, created by courts that settle disputes impartially. Public services are not available to the underground economy. Underground operations do not produce official documentation, which must be provided to courts in order to substantiate claims. When corruption is rampant, this makes it more favorable for managers to go underground. Moreover, taxes and government regulation become arbitrary when officials take bribes, increasing the costs of operating officially. Where judges take bribes instead of providing justice, there are fewer benefits to engaging in transparent and official transactions. Corruption therefore induces firms to prefer the unofficial economy. As a result, in countries with high levels of corruption there is also a large share of the unofficial economy. These two economic

activities are also often caused by similar policies: Excessive, vague, and arbitrarily enforced government regulation makes it more costly to operate officially and provides a basis for corrupt officials to ask for bribes.

A related topic is tax evasion. Tax evasion is not corruption, because it does not per se involve the misuse of public power. But as soon as tax collectors are bribed in exchange for lowering the tax burden, there emerges an overlap between the two activities. Related issues are tax privileges, granted by politicians in exchange for political support, party donations, or bribes. Although this lowers the tax burden in some cases, tax collectors may also obtain the position to extort bribes in excess of the true tax burden by threatening harassment. Tax systems, once open to such hidden payments, become opaque. No equal and impartial fiscal treatment is available, but rather privileges are provided to those who are best connected.

Criminal organizations can operate without having contact with bureaucrats or politicians, and their activity is not per se corrupt in this sense. Smuggling, counterfeiting, money laundering, subsidy fraud, and extortion rackets can operate without misusing public power. However, criminal organizations are often in a prime position to use corrupt means for their operation. Inside information on forthcoming police raids or reduced penalties for their members might be obtained with the help of bribes. Above that, criminal organizations can complement bribery with threats of violence so as to have a better bargaining position vis-à-vis corrupt public servants.

Measuring Corruption

Quantitative estimates of the extent of corruption are usually difficult to provide, owing to the opaque nature of corruption. Objective data are therefore irretrievable. A plausible approach to collecting data has been taken by gathering the subjective perceptions of well-informed people. These are commonly senior businesspeople and political country analysts. The perceptions provided by such people tend to correlate well with each other, irrespective of whether they are residents or expatriates. This suggests that the perceptions are invariant to cultural preconditions. Although perceptions should never be confused with reality, the given consensus provides some confidence that the perceptions gathered are informative on actual levels of corruption.

Most prominent in recent years has been the Transparency International Corruption Perceptions Index (CPI). The CPI is a composite index. Fifteen data sources were used in the 2002 CPI from nine different institutions, such as the World Economic Forum, the World Bank, and the Institute of Management Development. These data provide a ranking of nations according to the overall level of corruption. The strength of the CPI lies in the combination of multiple data sources in a single index, which increases the reliability of each individual score. The benefit of combining data in this manner is that erratic findings from one source can be balanced by the inclusion of other sources, and the probability of misrepresenting a country's level of corruption is lowered. The official list by Transparency International includes only those countries where more than three reliable sources of data were available in an effort to guarantee that the results provide a high level of precision. Table 1 reports data for 102 countries.

Perceptions can vary from one source to another. This is dealt with by publishing the standard deviation of the assessments. In case of a large value, the sources tend to differ with regard to a country's score. In case of small values, there is agreement. Together with the number of sources, the list provides a comprehensive picture of perceptions of corruption in these countries. This type of data has been helpful in facilitating empirical research because it allows the causes and consequences of corruption to be investigated for a cross-section of countries. This has increased ana-

lysts' knowledge in an area where research was long considered impossible.

Corruption and the Costs of Doing Business

There now exists plenty of evidence that countries riddled by corruption exhibit poor government institutions. These, in turn, deter foreign investors and affect trade. For example, corruption leads managers to waste more time negotiating with bureaucrats. There is therefore consensus nowadays that corruption does not "grease the wheels," as suggested in the literature formerly. Corruption does not help to overcome cumbersome regulation but acts as an inducement to public servants to create artificial bottlenecks. It therefore "sands the wheels."

Countries with high levels of corruption are characterized by vague and lax regulation and hidden import barriers. Entry regulation is equally distorted by corruption. The number of procedures required to start a new business may be very high, and it may be time consuming and expensive to work through all the official and unofficial requirements. Politicians and bureaucrats who impose excessive and cumbersome regulation ultimately cause the distortions. Once such bottlenecks have been created, private firms face the dilemma of whether to pay the bribes to work around the impediments, or to abandon business objectives that would require this. There emerges a vicious circle because excessive regulation, once in place, provides opportunities for future corrupt transactions. Once corruption becomes the rule, corrupt politicians and bureaucrats attempt to increase their cut by imposing more troublesome impediments on the private sector. Not surprisingly, trade and foreign direct investments suffer from corruption. An increase in corruption has adverse effects on foreign direct investment similar to those that result from an increase in the tax rate.

Investments are particularly hurt by corruption. Investments are often sunk and can-

Table 1: Transparency International, Corruption Perceptions Index, 2002

Country Rank	Country	2002 CPI Score	Number of Surveys	Standard Deviation
1	Finland	9.7	8	0.4
2	Denmark	9.5	8	0.3
	New Zealand	9.5	8	0.2
4	Iceland	9.4	6	0.4
5	Singapore	9.3	13	0.2
	Sweden	9.3	10	0.2
7	Canada	9.0	10	0.2
	Luxembourg	9.0	5	0.5
	Netherlands	9.0	9	0.3
10	United Kingdom	8.7	11	0.5
11	Australia	8.6	11	1.0
12	Norway	8.5	8	0.9
	Switzerland	8.5	9	0.9
14	Hong Kong	8.2	11	0.8
15	Austria	7.8	8	0.5
16	United States	7.7	12	0.8
17	Chile	7.5	10	0.9
18	Germany	7.3	10	1.0
	Israel	7.3	9	0.9
20	Belgium	7.1	8	0.9
	Japan	7.1	12	0.9
	Spain	7.1	10	1.0
23	Ireland	6.9	8	0.9
24	Botswana	6.4	5	1.5
25	France	6.3	10	0.9
	Portugal	6.3	9	1.0
27	Slovenia	6.0	9	1.4
28	Namibia	5.7	5	2.2
29	Estonia	5.6	8	0.6
	Taiwan	5.6	12	0.8
31	Italy	5.2	11	1.1
32	Uruguay	5.1	5	0.7
33	Hungary	4.9	11	0.5
	Malaysia	4.9	11	0.6
	Trinidad and Tobago	4.9	4	1.5
36	Belarus	4.8	3	1.3
	Lithuania	4.8	7	1.9
	South Africa	4.8	11	0.5
	Tunisia	4.8	5	0.8
40	Costa Rica	4.5	6	0.9
	Jordan	4.5	5	0.7
	Mauritius	4.5	6	0.8
	South Korea	4.5	12	1.3
44	Greece	4.2	8	0.7
45	Brazil	4.0	10	0.4
	Bulgaria	4.0	7	0.9
	Jamaica	4.0	3	0.4

continues

Table 1: Transparency International, Corruption Perceptions Index, 2002
continued

Country Rank	Country	2002 CPI Score	Number of Surveys	Standard Deviation
	Peru	4.0	7	0.6
	Poland	4.0	11	1.1
50	Ghana	3.9	4	1.4
51	Croatia	3.8	4	0.2
52	Czech Republic	3.7	10	0.8
	Latvia	3.7	4	0.2
	Morocco	3.7	4	1.8
	Slovak Republic	3.7	8	0.6
	Sri Lanka	3.7	4	0.4
57	Colombia	3.6	10	0.7
	Mexico	3.6	10	0.6
59	China	3.5	11	1.0
	Dominican Rep.	3.5	4	0.4
	Ethiopia	3.5	3	0.5
62	Egypt	3.4	7	1.3
	El Salvador	3.4	6	0.8
64	Thailand	3.2	11	0.7
	Turkey	3.2	10	0.9
66	Senegal	3.1	4	1.7
67	Panama	3.0	5	0.8
68	Malawi	2.9	4	0.9
	Uzbekistan	2.9	4	1.0
70	Argentina	2.8	10	0.6
71	Côte d'Ivoire	2.7	4	0.8
	Honduras	2.7	5	0.6
	India	2.7	12	0.4
	Russia	2.7	12	1.0
	Tanzania	2.7	4	0.7
	Zimbabwe	2.7	6	0.5
77	Pakistan	2.6	3	1.2
	Philippines	2.6	11	0.6
	Romania	2.6	7	0.8
	Zambia	2.6	4	0.5
81	Albania	2.5	3	0.8
	Guatemala	2.5	6	0.6
	Nicaragua	2.5	5	0.7
	Venezuela	2.5	10	0.5
85	Georgia	2.4	3	0.7
	Ukraine	2.4	6	0.7
	Vietnam	2.4	7	0.8
88	Kazakhstan	2.3	4	1.1
89	Bolivia	2.2	6	0.4
	Cameroon	2.2	4	0.7
	Ecuador	2.2	7	0.3
	Haiti	2.2	3	1.7
93	Moldova	2.1	4	0.6
	Uganda	2.1	4	0.3

Table 1: Transparency International, Corruption Perceptions Index, 2002
continued

Country Rank	Country	2002 CPI Score	Number of Surveys	Standard Deviation
95	Azerbaijan	2.0	4	0.3
96	Indonesia	1.9	12	0.6
	Kenya	1.9	5	0.3
98	Angola	1.7	3	0.2
	Madagascar	1.7	3	0.7
	Paraguay	1.7	3	0.2
101	Nigeria	1.6	6	0.6
102	Bangladesh	1.2	5	0.7

Notes: 1. The 2002 CPI Score ranges between 10 (highly clean) and 0 (highly corrupt).
2. "Standard Deviation" indicates differences in the values given by the sources. As indicated by shading, values below 0.5 indicate agreement (no shading); values between 0.5 and 0.9 indicate some agreement (pale shading); and values greater than or equal to 1 indicate disagreement (dark shading).

not be redeployed if investors are frustrated and disillusioned about the institutional environment of a country. Railroads cannot be redeployed, pipelines cannot be located elsewhere, and real estate cannot possibly be used in a different region. Also, human capital can sometimes be specific to a certain society—for example, when it is of value only for a specific institutional framework. After sinking investments, investors' capital becomes locked into a certain country. Politicians and bureaucrats may misuse their position once investments are sunk. For example, they can delay necessary permits and hold up investors until they are offered a bribe.

Societies with widespread public corruption face the challenge of how to commit themselves to honoring such investments and how to disallow a holdup by public servants. They have to establish transparent procedures and allow for legal recourse where investors' confidence is hurt. Corruption seriously undermines this confidence. Instead of providing transparent procedures, corrupt courts often make rulings that are arbitrary. Corrupt bureaucrats may develop capricious regulations so as to increase their own turf, and corrupt politicians can hold up investors by threatening to seize sunk investments or by imposing excessive taxation. In a corrupt environment, investors have no reason to be confident that public officials will honor sunk investments. Investors therefore tend to prefer safe havens to countries with an unreliable institutional framework. Governments with a reputation for corruption find it difficult to commit to effective policies and may not be able to convince investors of their achievements. As a result of such failures, investment ratios deteriorate as the level of corruption rises. Evidence across countries reveals that countries with high levels of perceived corruption are characterized by a low ratio of investment to gross domestic product (GDP), by low inflows of foreign direct investment, and by low levels of persistent capital inflows.

But establishing confidence among investors can also backfire when investors themselves engage in paying bribes. For example, large contracts for public utilities in less developed countries are sometimes awarded to bribe-paying investors. On the one hand, if a newly elected regime challenges these old contracts, it faces a dilemma. If old contracts are declared void due to the bribe payments, investors' confidence may be hurt. The World

Bank and the International Monetary Fund (IMF) have particularly emphasized this position. On the other hand, honoring such contracts could be regarded as an encouragement to carry out corrupt deals in the future. Avoiding this encouragement becomes more compelling if corruption has more adverse economic consequences besides damaging investors' confidence.

Economic Consequences of Corruption

Corruption is not a riskless activity. The risk associated with corruption increases with the number of transactions, the number of people involved, the duration of the transaction, and the simplicity and standardization of the procedure. Since the risk does not clearly increase with the value of a transaction, large, one-shot purchases create a more efficient base for a bribe. This biases the decisions made by corrupt politicians and bureaucrats in favor of capital-intensive, technologically sophisticated, custom-built products and technologies. It is therefore no surprise that empirical evidence links corrupt countries with those that spend excessively on the military and little on education. The quality of investments suffers from corruption because supervisors can be bribed to turn a blind eye to the use of substandard material or poor work. There will be a distortion also with regard to trade. It is not those products that best serve the public at large that are imported, but those that allow for maximum bribes.

Corruption within the public sector of a country often forces private competitors to offer bribes. It may be difficult for private firms to resist such offers because they are in a prisoner's dilemma: Although all would jointly profit from reducing corruption, paying bribes is the dominant strategy for each single competitor. Though paying bribes is regarded to be immoral, it may increase profits. It is sometimes assumed that striving for maximum profit induces all competitors to behave

Table 2: Transparency International, Bribe Payers Index, 2002 (incomplete)

Rank	Country	Score
1	Australia	8.5
2	Sweden	8.4
	Switzerland	8.4
4	Austria	8.2
5	Canada	8.1
6	Netherlands	7.8
	Belgium	7.8
8	United Kingdom	6.9
9	Germany	6.3
11	Spain	5.8
12	France	5.5
13	United States	5.3
17	Italy	4.1
21	Russia	3.2

Note: The scores range between 10 (highly clean exporter) and 0 (highly corrupt exporter).

equally. This position was challenged by empirical evidence claiming differences in moral standards across leading exporting nations. A 2002 survey by Gallup International on behalf of Transparency International produced the Bribe Payer's Index (BPI). Businesspeople in fifteen emerging markets were asked whether companies from particular exporting countries were very likely or unlikely to pay bribes to win or retain business in their country. As shown in Table 2, the results indicated remarkable differences: Although moral considerations were perceived for some exporters, others were regarded as unscrupulous.

The willingness of exporters to offer bribes is likely to affect trade. The most obvious kind of influence relates to goods that are imported by the public sector. The extent of corruption among public officials and politicians influences which competitor is most likely to win a contract. Tendering procedures can be falsified and contracts awarded in favor of those competitors who offer the highest bribes. Also, private-sector imports—and even trade between headquarters and subsidiaries of multinational companies—can be influenced by the extent of corruption prevalent in a country. On the one hand, the extent of corruption at all state levels that regulate and control external trade—such as customs, trade ministry, and trade regulation authorities—has an effect on this kind of business. A plausible assumption is that those exporting countries that are prone to offering bribes can obtain a competitive advantage in corrupt import markets. On the other hand, in the case of clean import markets such a competitive advantage cannot be achieved by means of paying bribes. Thus, there will be no level playing field.

Whether competitors are in a prisoner's dilemma with regard to paying bribes is still a controversial question. Some argue that honesty, under certain conditions, can be more profitable and less risky, particularly for large multinational firms. Given the opacity of corrupt deals, a firm's own employees may attempt to divert part of the bribe money back into their private accounts. Allowing employees to engage in bribery may therefore backfire. A firm engaging in bribery might also be exposed to denunciation and extortion and fear for its reputation. Furthermore, corrupt agreements cannot usually be legally enforced. A potential risk is that public servants may fail to deliver after receiving a bribe. Finally, the level of bribes requested may rise with the propensity of an exporter to pay. A reputation for honesty can constitute a safeguard against excessive demands for bribes by public servants. Therefore, forbidding employees to pay bribes may sometimes be in line with profit-maximizing behavior.

Corruption Reform

Given the global character of corruption, reform has often focused on requests to include all global players. Poor developing countries, often among those most affected by high levels of corruption, may not have the capacity to contain corruption by themselves. Sometimes, their local efforts are impeded by multinational firms and donor institutions that do not sufficiently fight corruption within their own ranks and tolerate bribes to be paid to public servants. The industrial countries have come to accept their responsibility through a variety of international agreements. An Organisation for Economic Co-operation and Development (OECD) convention signed by all OECD member countries in 1997 now prohibits the payment of bribes to foreign public officials and prohibits such payments from being tax deductible. International organizations such as the World Bank and the IMF have revised their lending policies so as to inhibit corruption within their own institutions. How effective these initiatives have been remains to be determined.

Whether countries perceived to be corrupt should be barred from receiving financial aid from the donor community is a current concern. In the past, a variety of projects have been canceled and funds barred owing to allegations of corruption. The risk of misuse may have appeared too high in these cases. However, countries with high levels of corruption are often those where donor aid is most needed. Instead of eliminating aid, a better alternative would be to help in the fight against corruption and to support appropriate local initiatives.

Johann Graf Lambsdorff

See Also Organisation for Economic Co-operation and Development (OECD)

References

Ades, Alberto, and Rafael Di Tella. 1999. "Rents, Competition, and Corruption." *American Economic Review* 89: 1023–1042.

Andvig, Jens C., and Odd-Helge Fjeldstadt. 2000. "Research on Corruption: A Policy Oriented Survey." Chr. Michelsen Institute and Norwegian Institute for International Affairs, http://www.gwdg.de/~uwvw/research.htm.

Bardhan, Pranab. 1997. "Corruption and Development: A Review of Issues." *Journal of Economic Literature* 35: 1320–1346.

Heidenheimer, Arnold, and Michael Johnston. 2002. *Political Corruption: Concepts and Contexts.* 3d ed. New Brunswick, NJ: Transaction.

Lambsdorff, Johann Graf. 2002a. "Corruption and Rent-Seeking." *Public Choice* 113, nos. 1/2 (October).

———. 2002b. "Making Corrupt Deals—Contracting in the Shadow of the Law." *Journal of Economic Behavior and Organization* 48, no. 3: 221–241.

———. 2003. "How Corruption Affects Persistent Capital Flows." *Economics of Governance.* vol 4, Issue 3, pages 229-243.

Mauro, Paolo. 1995. "Corruption and Growth." *Quarterly Journal of Economics* 110, no. 3: 681–712.

Moody-Stuart, George. 1997. *Grand Corruption: How Business Bribes Damage Developing Countries.* Oxford, UK: WorldView.

Pope, Jeremy. 2000. *The Transparency International Source Book 2000—Confronting Corruption: The Elements of a National Integrity System.* Berlin: Transparency International. Online version at http://www.transparency.org/sourcebook.

Rose-Ackerman, Susan. 1999. *Corruption and Government: Causes, Consequences and Reform.* Cambridge: Cambridge University Press.

Shleifer, Andrei, and Robert W. Vishny. 1993. "Corruption." *Quarterly Journal of Economics* 108: 599–617.

Wei, Shang–Jin. 2000. "How Taxing Is Corruption on International Investors." *Review of Economics and Statistics* 82, no. 1: 1–11.

Culture and Globalization

Globalization can be defined from a cultural perspective as the attribution of meaning to global communities created through many different types of interactions. Why do people today care about what they see on the world news? Usually it is because they have some understanding of how the news affects their own lives, an understanding based on a conceptualization of linkages between their local concerns and the concerns of these far-off places. This new understanding of the world through a global perspective has helped scholars involved in the study of culture reevaluate traditional concepts of culture and opened up new ways of studying culture. Global communities are studied closely to understand the ways in which individuals experience globalization. Studies of global culture have necessitated an awareness of methodological issues such as field site choices. Anthropologists have begun to expand their focus through multi-sited research or to define communities through the use of technologies, such as groups in Internet chat rooms.

One of the common debates about the cultural aspects of globalization is concerned with whether globalization inherently fosters a homogenization of culture, establishing "global culture" at the cost of local cultural heritage. Cultural studies of globalization have shown a number of different ways in which meanings flow between regions and are reinterpreted through cultural exchange. Therefore, the flow of meaning in global exchange cannot be characterized as simply a one-way exchange. Although globalization today is often discussed in terms of its relationship to capitalism, from a cultural standpoint financial transactions are only one part of a complex web of interactions and must be understood within a specific historical setting.

Historical Background of Scholarly Approaches

The study of globalization as a cultural issue has its roots in the theoretical approaches of social scientists working within both the world system and culture history paradigms. These theoretical frameworks provide a model of the modern world that emphasizes global influences on local cultures and share a concern for how historical processes affect individual communities.

World system theory has grown largely out of the work of sociologist Immanuel Wallerstein in his book *The Modern World System: Capitalist Agriculture and the Origins of the European World Economy in the Sixteenth Century* (1974). Wallerstein's work provided an understanding of how global historical trends since the sixteenth century have contributed to the formation of the modern world. His model was primarily concerned with the role of capitalism as a vehicle for European hegemony. The world system approach fostered a comparative view of regional participation in global systems. The theory also contributed a specific vocabulary to the study of global interactions, especially terms for categories of regions based on their economic interactions in global capitalism as well as internal economics and politics. Wallerstein's "core," "semi-periphery," "periphery," and "external" areas are terms still used today by many authors writing about global trends. In numerous subsequent publications, Wallerstein applied his own work to the case of Africa, examining the role of African regions in the world capitalist economy. Critics of world system theory have raised a number of concerns with this approach to world history, which is primarily concerned with the global expansion of Western capitalism. World system theory can become the intellectual expression of the type of imperialism that its authors often denounce. This can occur when authors focus on the European "core" areas and interpret world events solely through the lens of Western capitalism.

One way of reconciling these concerns within the theoretical framework of world system theory is suggested by Janet L. Abu-Lughod in her book *Before European Hegemony: The World System, AD 1250–1350* (1989). Abu-Lughod pointed out that historical studies of global trends do not need to conceptualize a single world system. Instead, scholars can understand history as comprising a series of multiple world system models through time. Her book takes a world system perspective but focuses on an earlier world system that involved trade across the "Old World" from East Asia to Europe and included Africa. World system theory has similarly been applied to studies of the role of global processes in world cultures by social scientists from many different disciplines. Whether discussing the role of Bronze Age societies in a world system or the role of world systems in modern terrorism, the perspective is now commonly used to understand the historical depth of global connections in human society.

Culture history was introduced in works by authors such as Sidney Mintz and Eric Wolf, who postulated that local and regional communities are fundamentally shaped by larger global processes such as colonialism and capitalist expansion. The culture history approach to global trends concentrates on how the histo-

ries of individual cultures or regions have been shaped by global processes. Mintz's book *Sweetness and Power: The Place of Sugar in Modern History* (1987) provided an anthropological perspective on sugar consumption and the place of sugar in world history. Mintz discussed the role of sugar in the world market, contextualized in the specific regional experiences of sugar plantations in the Caribbean region. This perspective offers readers a finely detailed view of the impact of sugar as a global commodity from a distinctly regional perspective. From this point of view, material culture, the objects that humans produce, is both economic and symbolic. Material culture is economic because the objects are commodities that fuel economic systems. It is symbolic because of the significance of the objects on other levels. This symbolism includes the social meaning of objects as well as historically specific social relations surrounding the transactions of the objects as commodities.

Defining Globalization from a Cultural Perspective

Globalization literature has taken a different approach to the discussion of global issues in modern life. Rather than focus on the conceptualization of global connections from a systemic approach or a primarily historical view of regionally centered interactions, scholars interested in the role of culture in globalization often focus on the ways in which specific cultural identities interact with larger global trends.

Anthropologist Jonathan Friedman, in his book *Cultural Identity and Global Process* (1994), provided a sound definition of globalization for scholars working with cultural issues. According to Friedman, globalization can be defined as the consciousness and attribution of meaning by individuals to the global arena. This approach can be distinguished from that of world system theory and culture history in three ways: (1) it deemphasizes capitalism as a process; (2) it necessitates a critical examination of the specific historical setting; and (3) it conceptualizes global cultural exchange as horizontal flows of meaning.

The first aspect of this definition, the deemphasis of capitalism as a process, is an important part of the overall definition. Globalization depends upon the existence of a global arena, which is an "interest community" on a global level. These interest communities can be based on activities, such as "people around the world who watch British Broadcasting Corporation (BBC) news." They can be based on ethnicity, such as "Asian Americans," or even on placement within a world system, such as "consumers of petroleum products." These global arenas must be formed by specific sets of dynamic global systems and processes. The international BBC news watchers have been formed in part by access to global cable television; Asian American group formation is linked to conceptualizations of cultural connections related to global human migration; and the petroleum products consumer group has been formed through consumption patterns and participation in global capitalist systems. Capitalist interactions are simply one among many types of processes that can contribute to the formation of the global arena.

In *Modernity at Large: Cultural Dimensions of Globalization* (1996), Arjun Appadurai proposed terms for five different "scapes" of global interaction, the sites of global processes, which reflect the diversity of processes inherent in globalization. These terms reflect the places for flow in global systems: the ethno-scape (people and communities), the media-scape (medias), the techno-scape (technologies), the finance-scape (financial and economic), and the ideo-scape (ideologies and information). These aspects of global process overlap; for example, the "BBC news watcher" community has certain cultural aspects (such as language use), is formed by the presence of the media, and is enabled by technology (television, radio, or Internet), access to which is often fueled by economics. Therefore, capitalism is inherently

deemphasized, as the financial interactions in what is termed the global economy necessarily include all of these other processes. Discussions of financial processes in globalization literature concerned with cultural issues are thus not only concerned with production, but also with the attribution of meaning. This can be in the form of studies of the effect of labor migration on production in global cities, or even about topics not normally relegated to the sphere of global economics, such as the spread of global music.

The second aspect of the definition of globalization, as a phenomenon that must be located within specific historical settings, can be seen clearly in the popular modern characterization of globalization as the intensification of communication and/or flows of knowledge through the use of new media such as the television and Internet. This common understanding of globalization highlights the necessity of defining relevant technologies within all discussions, as the modes of these linkages change with each historical context.

Globalization studies on this subject have focused on a variety of technological forums, including electronic communications and television. New media technologies play a significant role in modern human cultures. Unofficial numbers based on national reports estimate that there are currently 21,500 television stations and more than 44,000 radio stations worldwide. The cultural impact of this technology is immeasurable; each of these stations broadcasts its own selection of cultural programming, news that is perceived to be relevant to its audience, and advertising directed at target groups.

In her article "The Global and the Local in International Communications" (1991), Annabelle Sreberny-Mohammadi discussed the role of mass communications in cultural issues in terms of oral, literary, and visual traditions. The historical specificity of the role of technology in global issues is not simply an issue of the development of the relevant scientific knowledge (that is, the scientific knowledge and production ability to make a television), but also an issue of the specific roles that the technology plays in relation to the historical time period. The original spread of radio and communication technologies such as the telegraph was intimately linked to colonial and nationalist projects. The original uses of radios and telegraph systems must be studied within this context; however, their roles today have new cultural meanings. As new technologies appear on the global scene, they do not simply take the place of older technologies, but fundamentally change their functions.

Another interesting source on this topic is *Media Worlds: Anthropology on New Terrain* (2002), a book edited by Faye D. Ginsburg, Lila Abu-Lughod, and Brian Larkin. *Media Worlds* brings together a series of essays on the cultural roles of diverse media technologies from Indian cinema to Zambian radio. These essays examine regional media from new theoretical perspectives, expanding readers' understanding of the role of technology in both global and local arenas. The authors explain multiple roles of new media technology through the different case studies about international media such as television shows, films, advertising campaigns, radio programs, and mechanical reproduction. These forms of communication technology can be used to give voice to minority community interests, provide new forms for traditional arts, expand popular access to cultural icons, and represent national and ethnic interests.

The final point in this definition of globalization from a culture perspective focuses on the ways in which meaning is attributed to the global arena. Unlike both previous models of global interaction, cultural globalization literature forwards the idea of a horizontal and reciprocal (though not necessarily always egalitarian) global forum. Global meanings can be horizontal and reciprocal because ideas, objects, and situations are reinterpreted in new cultural settings; these new meanings will sometimes then help to redefine the cultural source. In Wallerstein's terms of "core" and "periphery" regions, theories of the cultural as-

pects of globalization allow us to recognize that cultural meanings do not simply flow from a core cultural region to a periphery; new ideas on the periphery can help to redefine cultural meanings in core areas.

The American image of a "cowboy" in the western movies is a good example of one such flow of cultural meaning. The American western frontier was considered to be on the periphery of mainstream American culture in the mid–nineteenth century. Cowboys, hired by ranch owners to drive cattle across the plains, were a peripheral labor community. Yet the cultural meaning of the cowboy as an independent spirit has become central to American popular images of core cultural values. Furthermore, today in many cultures around the world American culture is represented by media images of a western frontier cowboy, and the meanings of this cultural icon are being reinterpreted in very different ways.

The reciprocal nature of cultural globalization necessitates an understanding of cultural plurality and multiculturalism within new cultural settings. For example, Sreberny-Mohammadi (1991) pointed out that studies of global trends in television programming that examine the effect of the worldwide distribution of American programs must also take into account the global spread of television programming from non-Western countries.

It is also important to note that this flow of meanings exists with a system of inequality, which is why it is nonegalitarian. Flows of cultural meaning are controlled to some degree by economic and political systems. Communities with better access to technology, increased representation in political venues, or other such advantages have more opportunity to define cultural meaning in global arenas.

Redefining Culture in Relation to Globalization

Studies of cultural aspects of globalization have affected the theoretical concerns in studies of culture in a number ways. The nature of a "complex" society and the role of ethnicity in human experience are two important cultural concepts that have undergone significant change in recent decades.

The study of cultural aspects of globalization has challenged the notion of what were once thought of as "simple" societies. Late nineteenth-century anthropological studies of culture expressed complexity in terms of social evolution from "savagery" to "civilization" or as a direct dichotomy between complex and simple societies. The study of migration in anthropology has been a key component in challenging these concepts of cultural complexity. The concept of globalization provides the opportunity to understand how migrants' culture interacts with larger national and international systems. The implications of studying immigrant or refugee communities are many—moving with migrant communities can create a field site without borders (or at least a field site that challenges traditional notions of borders), the opportunity to observe the processes of globalization within a discrete community, and the chance to challenge traditional notions of cultural communities. Migration studies therefore represent a combination of the study of local cultures and global influences, while locating culture within larger systems.

Studies of ethnicity have also benefited from an understanding of culture in global arenas. Ethnicity, as a unit of social organization that has shared cultural meaning between group members and group boundaries, has been studied in a variety of ways. Many social scientists have focused on boundary maintenance as the most important aspect of ethnic identity. From this point of view, ethnicity is a tool that is used, and even manipulated, based on self and group interests. The cultural practices of ethnic groups are shared patterns of normative behavior, part of the way that groups situate themselves within larger frameworks.

Other studies emphasize that ethnicity is defined by distinct cultural traits, a collective identity that is bounded and self-replicating.

Multiple authors have written about the role of ethnicity in the global arena, and understandings of globalization have refined the debate about ethnicity in the social sciences. In the 1970s, many anthropologists began writing about how globalization affected the use of the term "ethnicity." These scholars saw focusing on ethnicity as a way of adapting their work to the breakdown of more traditional notions of isolated "village" cultures as the impact of global communications and cultural flows became more apparent. By studying culture as expressed in ethnicity, social scientists could look at how cultural groups expressed their identity at local, national, and international levels. Anthropologist Ronald Cohen (1978) used such a perspective to discuss the ways in which the ethnic identity of Sikh diasporic communities in England and Australia interacted with national and international interests.

Global Communities

There are many different arenas in which individuals experience the globalization of culture in their daily lives, or live in global communities. One of the most common ways to address this topic is through the study of transnational communities. This includes communities such as immigrants, transnational workers, refugees, and international nongovernmental organizations (NGOs).

In the book *Workers without Frontiers: The Impact of Globalization on International Migration* (Stalker and ILO 2000) the International Labour Office (ILO) reported that worldwide immigration involved approximately 120 million people in 2000. The ILO argued that global movements toward economic restructuring can result in social disruption that breaks apart communities. Once community cohesion is weakened, workers feel encouraged to look abroad for employment. Other authors have argued that the economic pressures necessitate migration for jobs and that social disruption occurs after migration. Having migrated, immigrant communities experience cultural change in many forms, such as cultural hybridity, the radicalization of cultural politics, and movements toward cultural conservatism.

Diasporic communities, communities with a common cultural heritage that are spread around the globe, experience the globalization of culture in other ways. These communities are not marked by national boundaries. Cultural changes in diasporic communities can occur globally in relation to world economic and political trends, but most often are reactions to local interactions. This creates a global community with a shared cultural heritage and regionally specific cultural differences. Being of African descent has a certain associated heritage and cultural meaning. But what it means to be African American in the United States has a different set of culturally associated meanings than being of African descent in Mauritius or Haiti.

Transnational workers, groups of people who migrate for labor-related reasons, experience modern global labor flows in yet another way. Many pre–twentieth century economies, especially agricultural economies, organized in plantation systems and depended on inexpensive immigrant labor. The global labor systems associated with plantations were the basis of these economic systems as well as the basis of the gross social injustices underlying multiple social issues today. The contemporary transnational worker is often a temporary migrant who will return to his or her country of origin after a specified amount of time. Technology booms have created a new class of migrant workers, a highly skilled workforce from countries such as India, China, and the Philippines who work in centers of technological industry. In the United States, the H-1B visa program allows such temporary guestworkers into the country for a limited amount of time. The fact that temporary guestworkers are dependent on their jobs for their continued presence in the United States highlights a new set of issues about the role of corporate culture in global communities. The linkages between fitting into corporate culture and adjusting to American culture can provide anthropologists with a better understanding of American subcultures.

According to the *World Refugee Survey* published by the United States Committee for Refugees (2003), there are 13 million refugees and asylum seekers worldwide who have been compelled to leave their homeland for economic or political reasons. The largest numbers of refugees currently come from Afghanistan, the Middle East (Palestinians), Burma, Angola, Congo-Kinshasa, Burundi, and Vietnam. Refugee communities often experience a high degree of cultural disruption because of family separation, lack of preparation for migration, and the inability to return home regardless of the ability to adjust to new cultural settings. The study of global movements of refugee communities has highlighted the relationship between identity and memory in culture. Studies of the cultural aspects of the refugee ask questions that position meaning in culture directly within the political arena, focusing on the incongruities of the concept of a "national identity." For example, what does it mean to be Tibetan for an individual living in Tibet, and what does it mean to be a Tibetan born in India, and living there as a member of the Tibetan refugee community?

Nongovernmental organizations provide another vantage point for understanding culture in global communities. NGOs such as the World Bank, the World Health Organization, the United Nations, and the International Red Cross have their own corporate culture that includes expectations of behavior and beliefs about social roles and value systems. The global culture of NGOs is embodied in their workers stationed around the world, but it has a separate expression in the institutions themselves. Red Cross workers from the United States who are stationed in Afghanistan to aid in relief work deal with cultural difference in their daily lives. The intercultural experiences of international aid workers are expressed in specific ways, such as their choices in food, clothing, and language.

However, the full import of the global nature of the Red Cross is not represented by these individual experiences, but rather in the Red Cross institutional guidelines and agendas that have been drafted to pursue the organization's goals on a global level. It is through such work that one finds the idea of global movements, such as the Millennium Development Goals of the United Nations. These goals are listed as: (1) to eradicate extreme poverty and hunger; (2) to achieve universal primary education; (3) to promote gender equality and empower women; (4) to reduce child mortality; (5) to improve maternal health; (6) to combat HIV/AIDS, malaria, and other diseases; (7) to ensure environmental sustainability; and (8) to develop a global partnership for development (see the United Nations Web page at http://www.un.org/millenniumgoals). Although each of these goals represents a critical development issue, the eight points for NGO action also reflect a global development culture with its own set of behaviors, beliefs, and values. Such agendas can be problematic when questions arise about the relationship between a global agenda, such as the promotion of gender equality, and the best way to pursue that agenda in specific cultures. Can the promotion of gender equality take the same form in France, Iran, and Fiji? In fact, development workers often find that the very existence of the issue as a global agenda will have differing significance in these nations.

Other NGOs with global interests focus on raising awareness about global connections in modern life. Many people today are aware that the clothing they wear could be made in another country. Few people ponder the social implications of the fact that their shirt may have been designed in France for an American retail business, manufactured in China with raw materials from Egypt and Bangladesh, and shipped by multinational freighting corporations. Organizations such as the National Labor Committee for Worker and Human Rights, which represents international workers' interests, seek to educate consumers of such products about the lives of

the people who produce them. This goal means that the organization seeks to turn global consumers into individuals participating in globalization. People who may be participating in this system only in the economic arena are prompted to ascribe meaning to their participation, to conceptualize their relations to others around the world, and in so doing, to become a part of cultural globalization.

But global communities are not only formed through the movement of people. They can also be interest groups that cross national boundaries (again, such as those who watch BBC news programs, or international consumers of petroleum products). Global interest groups share cultural information, commodities, behavior, or concerns. The worldwide interest in the Harry Potter book series in the early years of the twenty-first century is a good example of a global interest group. J. K. Rowling's books were sold in more than 200 countries and available in at least 60 languages. But what does it mean to create such a global interest group? What do we know about the culture of the readers of these books? The problem with asking such a question is that a global interest group does not necessarily experience their shared interest in identical ways.

These issues are discussed in relation to global music trends in essays from *Global Pop, Local Language* (2003), a book edited by Harris M. Berger and Michael Thomas Carroll. The book looks at diverse types of music in many different cultures, such as hip-hop in East Africa, alternative music in Indonesia, pop music in France, and traditional music in Hawaii. The language choices in the music industry reflect the changing cultural significance of worldwide musical forms. World fans of "heavy metal" music, for example, may enjoy listening to the same music and admire the same musicians. Perhaps, although not necessarily, heavy metal music may even have similar connotations of rebellion against authority for listeners both in England and Indonesia. However, the aspects of social life to which that rebellion is applied may be quite different.

Localized responses to global culture thus come in many different forms. The import of this statement on our understanding of the role of local cultures in an increasingly economic and technologically globalized world is a topic that deserves particular attention.

Globalization: Toward Cultural Homogeneity or Heterogeneity?

Popular concepts of globalization view the global movement of information, ideas, and cultural expression as a movement to increase cultural homogeneity. This conceptualization of cultural globalization is important to consider seriously. One of the most popularly cited examples of how globalization creates not just a single, homogenized global culture, but often a specifically Americanized global culture, is the existence and impact of official McDonald's franchises in more than fifty-six countries. This excludes the existence of equally (or perhaps even more) significant unofficial McDonald's restaurants or international restaurants with names designed to invoke McDonald's to the public. A book edited by James Watson, *Golden Arches East: McDonald's in East Asia* (1997), examines the cultural role of McDonald's restaurants in five East Asian countries: China, Hong Kong, Japan, Taiwan, and South Korea.

The five authors who contributed to the book discuss ways in which the global corporate culture of McDonald's has changed local methods of restaurant management, placing a decidedly American stress on concepts of orderly queuing to order food and bathroom cleanliness. At the same time, these McDonald's restaurants have become localized in a number of ways. The types of food offered on the menu vary to reflect local tastes, employees view their role in the workplace with more pride than the average American McDonald's employee, and the pricing of menu items means that McDonald's cuisine is often for special occasions. These localization examples reveal one of the basic truths about the horizontal flows of global meaning: Cultural objects and movements may circulate on a global level, but they are often interpreted through largely local criteria.

Additional commentary on the strength of the role of McDonald's as a symbol of globalization is provided by Benjamin R. Barber's book *Jihad vs. McWorld: How Globalism and Tribalism Are Reshaping the World* (1995). The reference to McDonald's is simply an analogous one; the book is not about McDonald's or *jihad* but uses the terms to evoke popular conceptualizations of particular contemporary debates on global cultural movements. The book examines the adverse impact of global capitalism in the form of transnational corporations on nationalism and argues for the strengthening of local civil society to counteract these perceived effects. Curiously, the title's metaphor does not always translate cross-culturally; the two German editions of Barber's book are entitled *Coca Cola und Heiligeic Krieg* (1996) and *Demokratie Im Wurgegriff* (2000), which roughly translate as *Coca-Cola and Holy War* and *Democracy in a Stranglehold*. One can only conclude that this particular meaning of McDonald's as an analogy for cultural homogeneity through global capitalism is not an effective metaphor on a global level.

The plurality of culture in the global arena does not have to be studied simply in terms of its relationship to global capitalism. *The Challenge of Local Feminisms: Women's Movements in Global Perspective* (1995), essays edited by Amrita Basu, examine the academic and political contexts of global feminism in Asia, Africa, the Middle East, Latin America, Europe, and the United States. The authors discuss the levels at which women's movements are shaped, showing how national agendas often play a more significant role in shaping women's movements than what are perceived as global ideologies. Whereas in China the political history of the Communist Party has become most significant, in Brazil the role of the Catholic Church is central to an understanding of the national women's movement. Each region has its own particular interests, relevant history, and social issues of key importance to women. Thus, in addition to the global culture of NGOs and global dialogues about women in meetings such as the United Nations World Conference on Women, global feminism is also part of local and national processes.

As culture moves with information, ideas, commodities, and people around the globe, a proliferation of forms and forums for cultural expression can be observed. Globalization does not have to be a product of the global process where the world becomes smaller; rather, it can familiarize all with greater diversity (see Featherstone 1996), thereby creating new kinds of sites of diversity and difference.

Researching the Cultural Aspects of Globalization

Situating the global in the local is an important task in the study of globalization that is of special interest to social scientists. The idea of situating studies refers to the fact that all research must be done in a particular place. A broad topic such as globalization can be studied all over the world, and scholars need to choose the best sites to study the issue in which they are interested. Where is the best place to study globalization? Cities are obvious choices for locating processes of globalization. In a city, globalization is often expressed in very obvious and concrete terms. Globalization is everywhere in cities; there are international newspapers in the newsstands, many different cuisines to choose from in restaurants, multiple languages being spoken in the streets, and constant interactions between diverse individuals from different cultural backgrounds (see Hannerz 1993 and Sassen 1996).

However, anthropologists studying globalization in urban areas must avoid making assumptions about the role of the local in the global. Locating global processes in urban areas is a valid perspective; however, globaliza-

tion does not only occur in large cities. The anthropological study of the effects of globalization on both urban and rural communities has the potential to provide a more complex understanding of globalization. For example, the globally varied essays in Basu's (1995) book show how studies of globalization and feminism concentrating on only urban locals can distort one's understanding of the situation by denying the heterogeneity of women's experience and the different ways in which women of various communities resist forms of dominance. Studying cultural issues related to globalization in small towns, villages, and rural settings can lead to an understanding of the full range of human experience in the modern global world.

Another important aspect of studying the cultural aspects of globalization is the need for new sites of ethnographic research. Traditionally, anthropologists have located their study in one place, often a small village or neighborhood of a city. Recent attempts to study global issues have prompted them to consider studying in multiple places for a more holistic understanding, an approach called multi-sited ethnography. One of the leading scholars writing about multi-sited ethnography is George Marcus. His article "Ethnography in/of the World System: The Emergence of Multi-Sited Ethnography" (1995) provided anthropologists, historians, political scientists, and sociologists with ideas about working in multiple research areas.

Multi-sited ethnography yields information about the ways in which people in many different communities experience globalization in their lives. There are many different ways of framing multi-sited research. One topic can be examined cross-culturally, such as the role of McDonald's in Watson's 1997 book *Golden Arches East*. A chain of global connections can be followed around the world—for example, tracing the trade routes of goods through multiple villages. Or, to understand immigrant experiences, one person's life can be researched in multiple places to provide a new perspective in a traditional life-history format. Researchers in the corporate world have been quick to see the usefulness of multi-sited ethnography for market research, and corporate anthropologists are using the approach to understand the global meanings of commodities.

Jacqueline Fewkes

See Also Gender and Globalization; Human Rights and Globalization; Social Policy; Sustainable Development; Urbanization

References

Abu-Lughod, Janet L. 1989. *Before European Hegemony: The World System, AD 1250–1350.* New York: Oxford University Press.

Appadurai, Arjun. 1996. *Modernity at Large: Cultural Dimensions of Globalization,* vol. 1. London: Minnesota Press.

Barber, Benjamin R. 1995. *Jihad vs. McWorld: How Globalism and Tribalism Are Reshaping the World.* New York: Times Books.

Basu, Amrita, ed. 1995. *The Challenge of Local Feminisms: Women's Movements in Global Perspective.* Boulder: Westview.

Berger, Harris M., and Michael Thomas Carroll, eds. 2003. *Global Pop, Local Language.* Jackson: University Press of Mississippi.

Cohen, Ronald. 1978. "Ethnicity: Problems and Focus in Anthropology." *Annual Review of Anthropology* 7: 379–403.

Featherstone, Mike. 1996. "Localism, Globalism, and Cultural Identity." Pp. 46–77 in R. Wilson and W. Dissanayake, eds., *Global/Local: Cultural Production and the Transnational Imaginary.* Durham, NC: Duke University Press.

Friedman, Jonathan. 1994. *Cultural Identity and Global Process.* London: Thousand Oaks.

Ginsburg, Faye D., Lila Abu-Lughod, and Brian Larkin, eds. 2002. *Media Worlds: Anthropology on New Terrain.* Berkeley: University of California Press.

Hannerz, Ulf. 1993. "The Cultural Role of World Cities." Pp. 67–84 in A. P. Cohen and K. Fukui, eds., *Humanizing the City?* Edinburgh: Edinburgh University Press.

Marcus, George. 1995. "Ethnography in/of the World System: The Emergence of Multi-Sited Ethnography." *Annual Review of Anthropology* 24: 95–117.

Mintz, Sidney. 1987. *Sweetness and Power: The Place of Sugar in Modern History.* New York: Penguin.

Sassen, Saskia. 1996. "Whose City Is It? Globalization and the Formation of New Claims." *Public Culture* 8: 205–223.

Sreberny-Mohammadi, Annabelle. 1991. "The Global and the Local in International Communications." Pp. 177–203 in J. Curran and M. Gurexitch, eds., *Mass Media and Society.* London: E. Arnold.

Stalker, Peter, and International Labour Office. 2000. *Workers without Frontiers: The Impact of Globalization on International Migration.* Geneva: ILO; Boulder: Lynne Rienner.

United States Committee for Refugees. 2003. *World Refugee Survey.* New York: USCR.

Wallerstein, Immanuel. 1974. *The Modern World System: Capitalist Agriculture and the Origins of the European World Economy in the Sixteenth Century.* New York: Academic Press.

Watson, James, ed. 1997. *Golden Arches East: McDonald's in East Asia.* Stanford: Stanford University Press.

Environmental Impacts of Globalization

There is growing concern among environmentalists, nongovernmental organizations, and some governments that globalization—the lifting of economic barriers and opening of national borders to commerce, financial capital, and human movements across the world—will have substantive influence on the environment at local, regional, and global scales. A key concern is ensuring that sustainable development—improving and maintaining the well-being of humans and the ecological systems on which they depend—is linked to the global economy such that international economic systems promote growth without environmental degradation. The issue of sustainable development is especially relevant to developing countries, mostly in the Southern Hemisphere, which are rich in natural capital (air, water, forests, seas, and the like) but economically poor, lacking many basic human needs and services.

Despite a plethora of writings and media coverage over the past few years, globalization is not a new issue, and environmental impacts due to economic integration have occurred over centuries. But the tempo and modes of globalization have increased dramatically since the 1980s, with the rise of global transportation networks and electronic communication systems, such that environmental change now occurs at unprecedented rates. J.R. McNeill (2000) summarized the history of economic integration in the twentieth century and identified four environmental consequences of globalization, beyond mass consumption. First, globalization made nature a sudden commodity. Groups of consumers, faced with a previously unavailable commodity such as rhino horn or elephant ivory, demanded natural products in quantities exceeding natural rates of renewal or reproduction. Thus, consumer demand could affect the environment of remote regions by exhausting populations of valuable species, resulting in potentially undesirable changes in ecosystem structure and function as well as loss of economic livelihood. Second, globalization focused the demand of millions of dispersed consumers on limited supply zones. Often these supply zones were sparsely populated frontiers with limited human impact and few regulations on resource extraction or environmental pollution. Rapid resource depletion, often by destructive extraction practices, resulted in degradation and transformation of many frontier supply zones. Third, sudden globalization disrupted common property regimes that once prevented environmental degradation—a "tragedy of the commons." Ages-old land use practices by small-scale social systems—for example, grazing rotations and protection of fish spawning grounds by local peoples—were overwhelmed by demands from distant markets and by large-scale extraction by bigger, more efficient operators. Lastly, globalization promoted a rapid "financialization" of the world economy such that by 1980, investment in finance dwarfed that of trade and manufacturing, enriching the world's banking systems. Much of this money passed through development banks such as the World Bank that lent money to poor countries for infrastructure development and energy projects. Many of these projects proceeded without environmental review, often with disastrous ecological effects. Thus, the recent history of globalization appears to be one that maximizes economic gain with little concern for environmental issues.

There are two fundamental views of the effects of globalization and economic growth on the environment: one positive, the other negative. Some environmentalists argue that unsuitable production and consumption patterns may arise as a result of trade liberalization, leading to environmental damage through overexploitation of natural capital—"the environmental depletion argument." Environmental damage may be further exacerbated by lack of environmental regulations, particularly in developing countries. Others, primarily economists but also some environmentalists, argue that though there may be negative aspects to economic growth, a portion of the revenue generated by growth can be used to improve the environment—"the environmental reinvestment argument." A corollary to this argument—"the poverty gap argument"—suggests that improving the basic human condition through health, welfare, and economic reform, thus increasing the affluence of the populace, will stem environmental degradation, as poverty often leads to overcrowding, social and political unrest, pollution, and the plundering of natural capital. However, it can be argued that rising affluence may increase mass consumption and the "ecological footprint" of a population, resulting in further environmental degradation. Ultimately, the scope of environmental degradation due to globalization will be determined by the economic, social, and environmental policies of individual nations and the policies and programs of international bodies such as the United Nations Environmental Programme and the World Trade Organization (WTO).

The specific ways in which globalization may impact the environment are complex and can vary in scale from local to global. Global-change drivers—those capable of changing ecological systems on a large scale—include climate change, land cover changes, and biotic changes caused by invasive plant, animal, and microbe species (biological invasions). Global-change drivers are of particular concern to environmentalists and scientists as they can have a cascade effect in ecological systems: reverberating changes in ecosystem structure and function that alter the abundance and interaction of species and the basic physical and chemical processes on which life depends (for example, energy and matter cycles). By altering ecosystem structure and function, global-change drivers can disrupt or deplete the basic ecological goods and services necessary for human welfare and economic livelihood: clean air and water, soil, fiber, fuel, and food. Thus, they can create "poverty gap" conditions that can lead to further environmental degradation.

Debate continues among environmentalists, economists, planners, and others on the mode and tempo of global change associated with trade liberalization and economic growth. Proponents of globalization argue that the link between economic growth and environmental degradation is tenuous and with little supportive data, whereas opponents argue that enough empirical and theoretical information exists to suggest that a precautionary approach to globalization is warranted. Environmentalists contend that, in the absence of strong scientific data, the uncertainty associated with environmental impacts of globalization should be addressed by application of the "precautionary principle"—if there is significant risk that an action will result in environmental degradation, then that action should not be undertaken. Proponents of globalization counter that the precautionary principle is arbitrary and divisive, deepening the divide between trade and the environment without substantive data. Ultimately, development of specific risk-assessment and management tools, such as benefit-cost models that incorporate consumptive and nonconsumptive direct-use, indirect-use, and nonuse values of a resource, is needed to better gauge the impact of trade liberalization on the balance between economic growth and environmental degradation.

Today three major categories of global-change drivers—biological invasions, land use changes, and climate change—are of central concern to environmentalists and others focused on the issue of sustainable development in a globalizing world. A key issue is identifying the potential links between globalization and environmental degradation for each global-change driver such that development policies have contingencies to limit or mitigate potentially negative environmental effects.

Biological Invasions

Biological invasions result from the accidental or intentional introduction of an organism to an environment in which it was previously absent. These nonnative, nonindigenous, or alien species—freed from the predators, competitors, and pathogens that may have limited their abundance in their native habitats—can become wildly successful once naturalized, displacing native species, altering the structure and function of the ecosystems that they invade, and causing economic damage to natural resources. In the United States alone, more than 50,000 species of plants, animals, and microbes have been introduced. The economic damage incurred by invasive alien species—pests of natural and human-dominated ecosystems—and the cost of controlling them is estimated at US$138 billion yearly.

Not all introductions of alien species are problematic: Some alien species are innocuous and ecologically benign. However, in some instances the ecological and economic effects of alien species can be devastating. Environmentalists are concerned that the breakdown of natural barriers due to globalization will cause the invasive species threat to proliferate, making classic cases such as those of the chestnut blight, the brown tree snake, and the Nile perch more common and widespread. The chestnut blight fungus (*Cryphonectria parasitica*), a pathogen introduced into North America on Asian chestnuts (*Castanea mollissima*) in the early twentieth century, destroyed 3.6 million hectares of American chestnut (*Castanea dentata*) forest within fifty years, disrupting both forest ecosystems and the forest product industry focused on this species. The brown tree snake (*Boiga irregularis*), introduced to Guam from the Philippines—probably as a shipping stowaway—caused the extinction of nine bird species, four lizard species, and two bat species, all of which were endemic to Guam. The brown tree snake is also an economic pest, causing agricultural losses—particularly to the poultry industry—and losses of US$1 million to US$4 million yearly owing to electrical outages that result from the snake's penchant for climbing utility poles and electrical wires, short-circuiting electrical power systems. The predaceous Nile perch (*Lates niloticus*)—introduced to Lake Victoria in 1958 to enhance local fisheries—caused the extinction of 200 of the nearly 600 species of cichlid fish endemic to the lake. This wave of vertebrate extinction, the most massive and rapid ever recorded, occurred within a ten-year period in the late 1970s and early 1980s when the Nile perch population was increasing. Today, the Nile perch fishery in Lake Victoria is worth approximately US$220 million and employs thousands in a region with little economic opportunity. However, this prosperity has come at a cost: loss of a unique, native biota that was the source of a productive and potentially sustainable fishery for local peoples.

Trade liberalization and more efficient modes of product transport may increase the speed and intensity of biological invasions. Biological invasion of freshwater and marine habitats is increasing worldwide, and the prime mode of transport of alien aquatic organisms is ship ballast water. Ballast provides stability and maneuverability to a ship after its cargo is unloaded. Once in port, ballast water is usually pumped into the local water body as cargo is taken on. Since World War II, the average size of ships has increased from around 10,000 tons to between 150,000 and 250,000 tons today, with some vessels surpassing 600,000 tons. Ballast volume has risen with ship tonnage, increasing the probability that alien species may be contained in ballast and that a large innoculum of certain species may be transported to new habitats. It is estimated that the United States alone receives 21 billion gallons of ballast yearly from worldwide sources.

Ballast water was the source of introduction for the Eurasian zebra mussel (*Dreissena polymorpha*) into the Great Lakes in the 1980s. The mussel spread rapidly through the Great Lakes and now occurs in most major river systems in the eastern and Midwestern United States. Zebra mussels have displaced native mussel species, altered food webs, and clogged water intakes and delivery systems from southern Canada to New Orleans. Control efforts for zebra mussels in the Great Lakes alone are expected to exceed US$5 billion. In response to the invasive threat of ballast-dispersed organisms, development of ballast-water treatment methods is progressing, including research in ballast-water exchange, chemical biocides, filtration, and irradiation with ultraviolet light. To date, no one treatment has proven cost effective for removing all organisms from ballast water.

Speed of product transport has increased dramatically since World War II with the advent of global air travel and the rise of efficient transport infrastructures in developed countries. Shorter transport time favors biological invasions, including disease transfer, by limiting the time that organisms may be exposed to unfavorable conditions and the time in which they may be detected. In addition to rapid transport, increasing use of containerized freight to transport materials by air, ship, and rail may also promote biological invasions. Containers are difficult to inspect, are rarely cleaned, and may be stored in railways and shipyards for extended periods, increasing the potential for pest entry.

The Asian tiger mosquito (*Aedes albopictus*) is thought to have spread from the Indo-Pacific region to North and South America, Europe, Africa, New Zealand, and Australia in containers of used tires slated for recycling, traveling as larvae in pools of water contained within the tires. The tiger mosquito—an active, aggressive species—is the main vector for dengue or break-bone fever in Asia and a potential vector for eastern equine encephalitis, LaCross encephalitis, yellow fever, and dog heartworm in the United States. Tiger mosquitoes inhabit both urban and rural areas. In the Caribbean—where dengue is primarily an urban disease—there is concern that the species could become an efficient rural vector of the disease, spreading it region-wide and possibly to the southern United States. Dengue was eradicated from the United States in the 1940s but could possibly reemerge in this way.

Globalization, along with land use change (see below), has been linked to the rise of emerging infectious diseases—previously unknown diseases that may be transmitted to humans via other vertebrate species through incidental contact—in many parts of the world. Emerging infectious diseases may be spread to new regions by travelers, military personal, or immigrants. Recent examples of emerging infectious diseases that have spread beyond their original foci through human movements include HIV/AIDS (human immunodeficiency virus/acquired immunodeficiency syndrome), SARS (sudden acute respiratory syndrome), and the West Nile virus. Transmigration and frontier colonization and development schemes that expose humans to new pathogens, in conjunction with rapid global transportation, will increase the probability that outbreaks of emergent diseases will continue in the future.

In the post-9/11 world, there is increasing concern that biological agents—diseases, food contaminants, and the like—could be used by extremists to intentionally harm human health, the environment, or the economy of a region or nation. In the United States, the specter of bioterrorism has spawned considerable interest in the field of biosecurity—a comprehensive approach to minimizing negative impacts of alien organisms, intentionally or unintentionally introduced, on the economy, human health, and the environment of the nation. The island nations of Australia and New Zealand have developed and implemented comprehensive biosecurity programs, but the large size, shared borders, high trade volume, and large movements of people via tourism and immigration complicate development of a biosecurity program for the United States.

In 2000 alone, 489 million passengers crossed U.S. borders in 140 million vehicles for travel and trade, and 38,000 animals were imported daily. With trade liberalization, these numbers are likely to climb along with the potential for alien species introductions, making biosecurity a vital national and global issue. At a minimum, an effective biosecurity program should include measures to prevent species introductions, to provide for early detection of invasion, and to facilitate rapid alert and response to contain, control, or eradicate a pest. Multidisciplinary teams will implement biosecurity programs; thus personnel training, information exchange, coordination and management, and policy and regulation will be important components for success, along with research on how species spread and become established in new areas and outreach programs to garner public support for prevention, eradication, and control efforts for alien species. Where relevant, trade liberalization efforts should consider biosecurity threats early in the planning process.

Land Use Changes

As individual and national economic wealth increases as a result of trade liberalization, investment, and infrastructure development, the size and density of human populations, and their consumption levels, will likely increase, resulting in changes in the use, structure, and function of rural and urban landscapes. Major categories of change in predominantly rural landscapes include deforestation, habitat conversion, urbanization, ecosystem fragmentation, and agricultural expansion or loss. In urban landscapes, changes in land use can include redevelopment and revitalization, sprawl, and abandonment and decay of structures, neighborhoods, and districts. The issue of sustainable development is central to land use and landscape change, as the landscape is the matrix in which virtually all natural capital is embedded.

Land use change as a result of globalization may have both intended and unintended effects. Often, it is the unintended effects that have significant impacts on the environment. The intent of land use change is usually to increase the capacity for human enterprise in a region in the form of economic growth. For example, clearing forest for crop land or pasture may have the intended effect of increasing crop or livestock production, and therefore increasing economic gain, from a region in the short term. But in the long term, unintended effects, such as increased soil erosion, decreased rainfall, and siltation of water supplies, may degrade ecosystems, deplete natural capital, and result in economic costs or losses that exceed the profits initially gained from forest clearing and land conversion. This is of special concern in regions where the pressure for economic development is heavy, land use change is rapid, and the unintended effects of land use change are not adequately considered or addressed, such as in many developing nations.

Global patterns of land use change within the past decade show that the greatest rates of change are occurring in developing countries, particularly in the tropics of the Southern Hemisphere. Deforestation in tropical regions is the main category of land use change, with forest converted principally to agricultural use, especially crop land and pasture. Latin America and Southeast Asia contain the largest expanses of tropical humid forest, followed by West and Central Africa. The proximate causes of deforestation in these three regions are generally similar—agricultural conversion of forests and extractive logging—although specific issues vary. Land transfer policies, in-migration of impoverished settlers, transmigration and other frontier colonization projects, corruption, and poor law enforcement are the underlying factors driving deforestation across the three regions.

In the late 1980s, the United Nations Food and Agriculture Organization (FAO) estimated that cropland expansion accounted for 27 percent of worldwide tropical deforestation, whereas pasture expansion accounted for an additional 18 percent of deforestation. The remaining 55 percent of deforestation was attributed to increases in "other land," principally urban land, residential land, and roads. Recent reassessment of the FAO data suggests that much of this "other land" is abandoned, degraded crop land and pastures that do not easily revert back to forest. At issue is sustainability of agricultural practices in the tropics. The current model of land use appears to be one of conversion of forest to agriculture and then to degraded land as pastures and crop lands are worn out, resembling large-scale, shifting cultivation. There are concerns that as globalization proceeds, land degradation will increase in the tropics, particularly as urban areas, and their ecological footprints, grow rapidly. Moreover, rapid development of urban areas within the tropics may be accompanied by poor environmental conditions—air and water pollution, sanitation—influenced by globalization flows, increasing wealth, and national and local policies toward urban growth.

Land use change also plays a role in the resurgence and emergence of infectious disease. Deforestation in the tropics has altered habitats and put humans in close proximity to diseases and disease vectors that remained isolated when forest habitats were intact. In their natural habitat, these diseases—mostly viral—cycle through rodent, primate, or avian hosts and are usually spread by insects such as mosquitoes and biting flies. Conversion of forest or grassland to agriculture may increase the food supply for local host populations, especially rodents, thus increasing the disease reservoir and potential for transmission to humans. In South America, several viral hemorrhagic diseases have emerged in human populations in regions of agricultural expansion. Argentine hemorrhagic fever—caused by the Junin virus—was endemic to wild rodents such as the mouse *Callomys callosus*. When grasslands were converted to cornfields, the mouse increased in number with abundant food, exposing farm workers to the novel virus. In Africa, the deadly ebola virus—whose animal reservoirs and potential vectors are unknown—is thought to have initially infected humans engaged in logging and forest clearing. In the Sudan, water projects, such as the Gezira Scheme, to irrigate dry-land cotton caused an emergence in schistosomiasis and the reemergence of malaria, a result of the increased availability of the aquatic habitats needed by the larvae of mosquito vectors.

Climate Change

Climate change, or global warming, is due to the excess release of so-called greenhouse gases, such as carbon dioxide, methane, and ozone, which trap heat within the Earth's atmosphere, causing global temperatures to rise: the greenhouse effect. The average surface temperature of the Earth rose between $0.3°C$ and $0.6°C$ between 1890 and 1990 in two surges: one that occurred between 1910 and 1940, the other after 1975. Warming, however, has not been equal across the globe. High latitudes in the Northern Hemisphere—above 40° North—and Antarctica have generally experienced the greatest warming, while other areas have cooled.

Although the anthropogenic basis of climate change continues to be debated, it can be hypothetically linked to globalization in two ways. First, it is caused in part by a change in land use that diminishes the size and capacity of regional carbon sinks—such as forests—to absorb and store greenhouse gases. The continued agricultural conversion of forests in the

Southern Hemisphere, and the recently intensified logging of boreal forests in the Northern Hemisphere, may cause more carbon dioxide to be released to the atmosphere, exacerbating the greenhouse effect. Second, an increase in the atmospheric pool of carbon dioxide and other greenhouse gases may result from increased burning of fossil fuels and other activities associated with industrialization or urbanization. Thus, the extent of climate change caused by globalization will be a function of the extent and intensity of land use changes that affect regional carbon sinks, the reliance on fossil fuels for economic development, and the degree to which anthropogenic effects may synergize periodic natural events—such as El Niño or the Southern Oscillation—that can greatly influence regional and global climate patterns.

Charles E. Williams

See Also Energy and Utilities; World Health Organization (WHO); Food Safety; Natural Resources; Public Health; Sustainable Development; Urbanization

References

Baskin, Y. 1997. *The Work of Nature: How the Diversity of Life Sustains Us.* Washington, DC: Island Press.

Bright, C. 1998. *Life Out of Bounds: Bioinvasion in a Borderless World.* New York: W. W. Norton.

Carew-Reid, J., R. Prescott-Allen, S. Bass, and B. Dalal-Clayton. 1994. *Strategies for National Sustainable Development: A Handbook for Planning and Implementation.* London: Earthscan.

DiCastri, F. 2000. "Ecology in a Context of Economic Globalization." *BioScience* 50: 321–332.

Epstein, P. R. 1995. "Emerging Diseases and Ecosystem Instability: New Threats to Public Health." *American Journal of Public Health* 85: 168–172.

Fidler, D. P. 1996. "Globalization, International Law, and Emerging Infectious Diseases." *Emerging Infectious Diseases* 2: 77–84.

Hollander, J. M. 2003. *The Real Environmental Crisis: Why Poverty, Not Affluence, Is the Environment's Number One Enemy.* Berkeley: University of California Press.

Houghton, R. A. 1994. "The Worldwide Extent of Land-Use Change." *BioScience* 44: 305–313.

Lambin, E. F., and H. J. Geist. 2003. "Regional Differences in Tropical Deforestation." *Environment* (July/August): 22–36.

Marcotullio, P. J. 2003. "Globalisation, Urban Form and Environmental Conditions in Asia-Pacific Cities." *Urban Studies* 40: 219–247.

McMichael, A. J. 1999. "Globalization and the Sustainability of Human Health." *BioScience* 49: 205–210.

McNeill, J. R. 2000. *Something New under the Sun: An Environmental History of the Twentieth-Century World.* New York: W. W. Norton.

Meyerson, L. A., and J. K. Reaser. 2002. "Biosecurity: Moving toward a Comprehensive Approach." *BioScience* 52: 593–600.

Mooney, H. A., and R. J. Hobbs, eds. 2000. *Invasive Species in a Changing World.* Washington, DC: Island Press.

Pimentel, D., I. Lach, R. Zuniga, and D. Morrison. 2000. "Environmental and Economic Costs of Nonindigenous Species in the United States." *BioScience* 50:53–65.

Sampson, G. P. 2002. "The Environmentalist Paradox: The World Trade Organization's Challenges." *Harvard International Review* (Winter): 56–61.

Speth, J. G., ed. 2003. *Worlds Apart: Globalization and the Environment.* Washington, DC: Island Press.

Food Safety

Food trade has been expanding in step with the expansion of global trade in general. As a result, many countries find a growing share of their food supply coming from an increasingly diverse set of international sources. Assuring the safety of these imported products is a major concern of governments and companies. At the same time, exporting governments and companies have a large stake in assuring safety in order to protect their continued access to markets and the viability of their domestic industries.

Global Food Trade

Global trade in agricultural and food products has been growing over time. For example, from 1980 to the late 1990s the value of world agricultural exports more than doubled from just more than US$200 billion to more than US$450 billion. Over the two decades of the 1980s and 1990s, there was also a decided shift in the composition of agricultural and food trade. Bulk commodities such as raw grains and oilseeds declined from over 40 percent of all world trade to less than 30 percent by 1997. Processed consumer products such as beverages, snack foods, and fresh and frozen meat increased in their share of total trade over the same period from less than 20 percent to around 30 percent. As a result of this shift, by the late 1990s world trade in pastry, prepared foods, and chocolates combined exceeded the value of the world wheat trade. Similarly, the world wine trade is contending in size with the

world trade in maize (corn). Two other categories of trade, intermediate processed goods (for example, flours, meals, and oils) and fresh horticultural products (such as unprocessed fruits and vegetables) maintained their shares of total trade from 1980 up to the late 1990s. Within countries, dependence on imports can vary greatly by food categories. In the United States, for example, imports account for about 9 percent of total food consumption, whereas nearly 70 percent of fish and shellfish and only about 6 percent of grain cereals are imported.

These trends suggest both an increasing volume of trade and a growing emphasis on trade in food products that will be consumed with minimal or no further processing within the importing country. In addition, the demand for food safety is increasing in developed countries particularly, but also in developing countries. This has led to stricter regulations aimed at a broader range of food safety–related attributes (for example, microbial pathogens, environmental contaminants, animal drug and pesticide residues, and possible presence of Bovine Spongiform Encephalopathy [BSE]). Thus, food safety assurance is an increasingly important issue in public health, international trade, and international relations.

Assuring Food Safety in a Global Economy

The growing volume and increasing diversity of food trade puts extra demands on government regulatory systems and company and supply-chain quality assurance systems. On the export side, countries and companies know that their markets can be devastated overnight by a food safety incident that is traced to them. For example, in the mid-1990s a linkage to a cyclosporiasis outbreak in the United States wiped out the Guatemalan fresh raspberry export market. Similarly, the fish export business from the Lake Victoria region of Africa was crippled in the late 1990s by the European Union's refusal to import due to safety concerns. On the import side, countries and companies face major challenges in assuring the safety of food products that are flowing in from multiple suppliers in multiple countries. Concerns about food biosecurity have added to these challenges. The central issue is selecting which safety attributes to devote resources to controlling and at what levels.

Governments may choose among three generic approaches to controlling food safety. First, they can employ process standards that specify how the product is produced. For example, Good Agricultural Practices rules may specify the cleanliness of water sources and worker hygiene practices in fields producing fruits and vegetables for the fresh market. Similarly, processing plants may be directed to implement certain practices believed to assure production of safe products. Second, governments can focus on product (or performance) standards that specify the characteristics of the finished product. For example, the standard could specify a maximum incidence for a microbial pathogen in a processed meat product. Third, governments can establish information standards for food products that dictate the types of safety information that must accompany a product. An example is the inclusion of safe handling instructions on packages of fresh meat. Governments frequently use these three approaches in combination.

The choice of regulatory approach has a strong influence over how food safety is assured in the global food trade. On one hand, process standards may require the certification of facilities in foreign countries if imported products are to be held to the same standards as domestically produced products. On the other hand, product or information standards may only require testing or inspection of the imported product at the port of entry. In either case, the sheer volume of processing locations or of products makes food safety assurance a challenging task in the global market.

Regulatory Trends

Developed countries are the regulatory pace setters, largely because their high incomes create both demand for food safety and the resources to assure it. Regulatory trends in these countries include:

- *Stronger public health and consumer welfare emphasis in decisions by regulatory agencies.* This trend is leading to a supply chain or "farm to fork" approach that stresses identifying where hazards are introduced and how they can be most effectively controlled.
- *Adoption of more stringent safety standards, with a broader scope of standards.* Examples of more stringency include specific load standards for *Escherichia coli, Salmonella,* or other pathogens in meat products. Examples of a broadening scope of regulations include new feeding restrictions to avoid the spread of BSE in cattle and tolerances for dioxin in feeds and foods.
- *Adoption of the HACCP approach to assuring safety.* Under the Hazard Analysis Critical Control Point (HACCP) approach, companies are responsible for analyzing entry points for hazards such as foodborne pathogens, establishing effective control points, and monitoring and revising the system to assure continuing high levels of food safety. HACCP is primarily a process standard but specifies an approach to safe operation rather than prescribing operating actions.

- *Adoption of hybrid regulatory systems.* Some countries are combining mandatory HACCP measures with product standards measures (on, for example, the incidence of pathogens) in order to provide assurance that HACCP programs are working effectively.
- *Increased reliance on certification, including traceability.* Requirements for documentation of safety assurance, including the ability to trace back to the origin of products and forward to their disposition, are increasingly being built into regulatory systems.

Many developing countries are also placing an increased emphasis on food safety assurance both in order to promote domestic public health and to develop and sustain export markets.

Means of Assuring Import Safety

Importing countries employ a variety of means to assure the safety of products entering their food supplies. At one end of the spectrum, countries may ban imports from countries that are not deemed to produce safe products. The recognition of competent authorities in exporting countries, and/or the direct oversight of production facilities in those countries, provide another means of safety assurance for imports. This approach is frequently employed where standards are process-based and thus require oversight of the actions of parties in the supply chain to verify compliance. The importing country may require that the exporting country establish a regulatory authority that the importer judges to be competent to assure that exported products meet the importer's standards. Under this approach, the importing country certifies the certifier (that is, the exporting country's regulatory agency). In addition, or as a substitute, the importing country may directly inspect plants or a sample of plants to certify them. The degree to which the judgment

of whether a plant produces products that meet the importing country's standards is devolved to authorities in the exporting country varies across importing countries and even across imported products within a single country.

The major alternative means of assuring import safety is port-of-entry inspection—for example, at ocean ports, border crossings, and airfreight facilities. This approach is suited to enforcement of performance or information standards that can be tested for or monitored in the final product. Port-of-entry inspection is extensively used for assuring the safety of imported products. The success of this approach depends on the quality of the targeting and sampling techniques used, because trade volume assures that only a small fraction of imports will be inspected.

A final alternative for assuring import safety is for the government to delegate the responsibility for verifying that safety standards have been met to the importing company. The government may provide varying degrees of oversight to the companies, for example, through an audit or spot testing program. In practice, many countries use a mix of all these means to assure import safety in a global economy.

Means of Assuring Export Safety

Exports of agricultural and food products are an important element in the economies of many countries. To support these exports and develop new ones, countries have become increasingly active in promoting the types of safety assurance infrastructure that will allow continuing entry into world food markets. Many countries, especially developing countries, find meeting the varied standards of importing countries to be a major obstacle to success.

Establishing a competent authority to oversee safety is usually a necessary first step in encouraging food exports, particularly if required by the importing country. This can necessitate new laws, new agencies, extensive training of personnel, new or overhauled enforcement systems, and the hosting of visiting delegations from importing countries. Maintaining this competency over time also requires substantial investment on the part of the exporting country.

Many countries have also been making significant investments to help exporting companies make the changes in facilities, procedures, and training necessary to compete in international trade. An example is the training programs instituted by countries, frequently aided by international organizations such as the United Nations Food and Agriculture Organization, to help companies comply with HACCP requirements for seafood and meat products. Industry and government may also cooperate to respond to crisis situations. For example, in the mid-1990s producers and the Guatemalan government cooperated to try to reestablish exports of raspberries to the United States after sales were cut off when the product was implicated in an outbreak.

Food Safety and Equity Issues

Rising food safety standards, particularly in developed countries, raise equity and distributional issues between the richer and poorer countries of the world. One aspect of these issues is the disproportionate share of government and company resources that may be commanded for producing safe products for the export market, while domestic food safety remains low. The World Health Organization has identified food safety as a key public health issue for the twenty-first century for developing countries. Process standards frequently result in the export of some regulatory responsibility and costs from the importing to the exporting country. Resources to improve safety are woefully inadequate. Technical assistance to poorer countries has not been adequate to address this aspect of rising food safety standards in developed countries.

A related concern is that rising food standards in developed countries may secure only minor health improvements in the adopting country while exporting significant costs to other countries. For example, one study showed that a proposed stringent aflatoxin standard for cereals, dried fruits, and nuts in the European Union would save only 1.4 deaths per billion people per year, while resulting in a decrease in African exports of these products to the EU of 64 percent, or US$670 million (Otsuki et al. 2001). Very small benefits in one country group would be gained at the expense of large costs elsewhere in the world, where those costs would likely translate into significant overall reductions in human well-being.

Food Safety under Trade Agreements

Food safety, and more generally sanitary (human or animal health or life) and phytosanitary (plant health or life) regulations, are a continuing source of friction among trading partners. Although the right of countries to provide this type of protection is unchallenged, there is the potential for safety-related regulations to be subverted to protectionist purposes. For example, a country could impose a standard for a particular contaminant in a food product arguing that it is doing so to protect consumer health, when it may be the case that the contaminant does not have any adverse health consequences, and that domestic producers can meet the standard, whereas international producers cannot. In this situation, the standard would provide no health benefit but instead be a cover for protectionist actions that would not otherwise be admissible under existing trade rules. The concern is that countries will use nontariff barriers to trade, such as food safety regulations, to replace banned or restricted tariff and quota barriers to trade.

The major challenge for trade agreements is to set rules for deciding disputes among trading partners over what is a legitimate regulation and what is not. The Uruguay Round of the General Agreement on Tariffs and Trade (GATT) set these rules under the Agreement on the Application of Sanitary and Phytosanitary Measures (SPS Agreement), now administered by the World Trade Organization (WTO). The SPS Agreement has been in force since January 1995.

The SPS Agreement recognizes the desirability of harmonized standards and encourages countries to adopt international food safety standards developed by the Codex Alimentarius Commission. However, it also recognizes national sovereignty in retaining the ability to choose a risk standard that is different from international standards. If a country wishes to set standards that are stricter than Codex standards, those standards should be based on a scientific risk assessment. In addition, a country should be able to clearly link its risk assessment to its targeted level of protection, to its regulatory goals, and to its standards and inspection systems. The risk-management options chosen should be as least trade restrictive as possible. National treatment is required under which the same standards for health protection are applied to domestic and imported products. The agreement also supports the recognition of equivalence; that is, countries should accept the SPS measures of other countries as equivalent to their own, even if they differ in the particulars of how they operate, if they result in the same level of protection.

The SPS Agreement has resulted in greater and more consistent use of risk assessment in regulatory decisionmaking. It has also resulted in greater transparency for national-level regulation of food safety. Countries are required to notify the WTO of new regulations and to provide a means for trading partners to receive answers to questions they may have about the regulations. Countries must provide an explanation of the rationale for the regulation, a clear statement of the requirements, and information on the timing and methods of enforcement. In several cases, this notification process has resulted in changes in proposed regulations in response to questions and concerns raised by trading partners.

Trade Conflicts

The WTO provides a dispute settlement process for use when trading partners disagree. Formal complaints about the legitimacy of a food safety regulation can be filed with the WTO. If the complaint is not resolved through consultations between the trading partners, a panel will be appointed to hear the dispute and issue a decision. This decision may be appealed to the Appellate Body, whose decision is final. If a country's regulation is found to be inconsistent with WTO rules, the country may change its measure to come into compliance, or keep the regulation but negotiate a deal with the affected trading partners to compensate them by providing trade concessions on other products. If these approaches to resolution fail, the WTO General Council may authorize the affected trading partners to retaliate with increased tariffs against the products of the noncompliant country.

To date, three major SPS cases have progressed through the entire dispute settlement process. Two of these cases, by the United States against Japanese requirements for testing the effectiveness of horticultural treatments, and by Canada against an Australian ban on salmon imports, had to do with plant and animal health. The third, by the United States and Canada against the European Union's ban on the use of growth hormones in beef production, directly relates to human health and food safety. In that case, the Appellate Body decision against the European Union hinged on the finding that the EU's ban was not based on an objective risk assessment. This dispute has not been finally resolved, however, because the EU was not willing to lift its ban, and the parties could not negotiate a mutually acceptable alternative regulatory approach or compensation package. The United States and Canada were authorized to retaliate, and the

European Union continues to pursue additional evidence to support its risk assessment.

The introduction of biotechnology to agriculture may provide the next major challenge to the ability of the SPS Agreement to manage disputes between trading partners. The European Union and other countries have adopted policies that have greatly slowed the introduction of biotech crops into production and that require strict labeling of the presence of biotech ingredients in finished food products. In the United States, the introduction of biotech has been rapid, and labeling of final products is voluntary and infrequent. The European Union defends its policy as prudent, given uncertainties about the rapid introduction of biotechnology, and as consistent with the desires of its citizens. The United States attacks the policy as a lightly veiled effort to protect European markets from competition from U.S. agriculture. A dispute in this area would be a major test for the SPS Agreement, particularly because defining what constitutes a sound risk assessment is difficult for newly introduced technologies.

To date, the broad history of the operation of the SPS Agreement is one of success, as increased trade has been generally supported by the adoption of a common set of rules for judging tradeoffs between regulatory goals and trade impacts. However, major disputes underline that important differences persist in countries' approaches to food safety regulation.

Enforcement Issues

Regulations set the groundwork for the terms of trade in the food safety area, but enforcement determines their day-to-day impact. In developed as well as developing countries, newly issued regulations and those already on the books are outstripping enforcement resources and capabilities. This is largely because enforcement is detail-oriented and resource-intensive in terms of personnel, laboratory capacity, and other needs. In addition, new risk-based approaches to regulation often require complete overhauls of old regulatory structures. For example, HACCP measures may be required for all food-processing operations, but the country may not have a broadly effective program of monitoring compliance. Reliance on voluntary compliance is likely to generate uneven effects where some companies comply in good faith and others do not.

Problems with inadequate enforcement are often exacerbated for imported food products. On the one hand, imports may be even less adequately controlled for safety, so that imports contribute unequally to health problems. On the other hand, imports may be regulated more strictly than domestic products because limited points of entry make monitoring easier and more effective. In either case, domestic and imported products do not receive equal treatment, resulting in trade conflicts. The efficiency of the regulatory structure is particularly important for imports owing to the perishable nature of many food products. Long or unexpected delays upon entry to the country may result in a ruined shipment. The existence of enforcement overhang introduces uncertainty, as companies must try to gauge which regulations will be enforced, at what level, and when.

Company Incentives

Regulations and country-to-country trading relationships are only a part of the international food safety story. Companies have strong incentives to institute food safety assurance systems, including the desire to protect brand or store reputation, to attract customers based on quality, and to avoid liability for inadequate systems. These incentives have resulted in a very active private market for food safety whose standards may exceed those set by governments. These systems usually involve self-certification by the selling company or certification by the buyer or a third-party organization. Market-based forces, particularly consumers' willingness to pay for these services, support private food-safety assurance. For domestic as well as international producers, market success depends increasingly on meeting government standards as a minimum and then complying with the additional requirements of buyers in the supply chain.

Broader Food Quality Issues

Food safety may be the most prominent issue in international food trade, but it is far from the only one. The demand for quality is increasing across a broad spectrum of food attributes, including nutrition, taste, compositional integrity, and process attributes. The term "process attributes" refers to aspects of how the product was produced rather than qualities inherent in the final product. These process attributes are becoming particularly important. They include such attributes as organic production, ecofriendly production, fair trade, worker protection, animal welfare, authenticity of methods of production, and support of artisan or local production systems. A particular characteristic of a food product may relate to food safety and other attributes at the same time. For example, the use of biotechnology can be a process attribute, if its main impact is at the production level, or a food safety issue, if it affects human health. Since process attributes are usually not detectable in the final product (that is, they are credence attributes), regulation focuses on setting up monitoring and certification systems to support the labeling of these attributes on final products.

The WTO's Agreement on Technical Barriers to Trade (TBT Agreement) and Agreement on Trade-Related Aspects of Intellectual Property Rights (TRIPS Agreement) manage trade conflicts related to regulation of quality attributes other than food safety. As with food safety, disputes arise over whether regulation of these attributes serves legitimate governmental purposes or is predominantly a means of disadvantaging imported products relative to do-

mestic ones. For example, do regulations to protect the use of the term "Parma ham" serve a legitimate purpose of protecting consumers from fraudulent products and supporting authentic producers, or do they primarily protect a certain group of producers against competition from others? Dispute cases under the TBT Agreement are only beginning to sort out these tradeoffs. In the meantime, regulations and private systems related to the certification and labeling of other attributes, particularly process attributes, are rapidly proliferating.

Overall, countries are placing an increased emphasis on quality, especially safety, for food products. This is reflected in more stringent and more far-reaching regulatory systems. At the same time, market demand for quality is resulting in higher requirements being enforced privately within the supply chain. As trade in food products increases, the challenge for importing countries and companies is to set up fair systems to assure quality for both domestic and imported products. For exporting countries and companies, the challenge is to respond to escalating standards.

Julie A. Caswell

See Also Agriculture; Food and Beverages; World Health Organization (WHO); Public Health

References

Calvin, Linda, et al. 2002. "Response to a Food Safety Problem in Produce: A Case Study of a Cyclosporiasis Outbreak." Pp. 101–127 in Barry Krissoff et al., eds., *Global Trade and Consumer Demand for Quality.* New York: Kluwer Academic/Plenum.

Caswell, Julie A. 2003. "Food Safety Standards and Regulation." In Laurian Unnevehr, ed., *Collection of Policy Briefs: Food Safety in Food Security and Food Trade.* Washington, DC: International Food Policy Research Institute.

———. 2003. "International Food Inspection." In *Encyclopedia of Life Support Systems,* Article 5.18.3.5. Paris: United Nations Educational, Scientific and Cultural Organization.

Gehlhar, Mark, and William Coyle. 2001. "Global Food Consumption and Impacts on Trade Patterns." Pp. 4–13 in Anita Regmi, ed., *Changing Structure of Global Food Consumption and Trade,* ERS WRS No.

01–1. Washington, DC: U.S. Department of Agriculture, Economic Research Service, http://www.ers.usda.gov/publications/wrs011 (cited April 28, 2003).

Henson, Spencer, Ann-Marie Brouder, and Winnie Mitullah. 2000. "Food Safety Requirements and Food Exports from Developing Countries: The Case of Fish Exports from Kenya to the European Union." *American Journal of Agricultural Economics* 82, no. 5: 1159–1169.

Hensen, Spencer, et al. 2000. *Impact of Sanitary and Phytosanitary Measures on Developing Countries.* Reading, UK: Department of Agricultural and Food Economics, University of Reading.

Henson, Spencer J., and Julie A. Caswell. 1999. "Food Safety Regulation: An Overview of Contemporary Issues." *Food Policy* 24, no. 6: 589–603.

Otsuki, Tsunehiro, John S. Wilson, and Mirvat Sewadeh. 2001. "Saving Two in a Billion: Quantifying the Trade Effect of European Food Safety Standards on African Exports." *Food Policy* 26, no. 5: 495–514.

Roberts, Donna, et al. 2001. "The Role of Product Attributes in the Agricultural Negotiations." Commissioned Paper 19. Presented at the International Agricultural Trade Research Consortium (IATRC) conference on Agriculture in the WTO, Washington, DC, http://agecon.lib.umn.edu/cgi-bin/pdf_view.pl?paperid=3022 (cited April 28, 2003).

Unnevehr, Laurian, and Nancy Hirschhorn. 1999. "Food Safety Issues in the Developing World." World Bank Technical Paper No. 469. Washington, DC: World Bank.

World Health Organization. 2002. *WHO Global Strategy for Food Safety: Safer Food for Better Health,* http://www.who.int/fsf/Documents/fos_strategy_en.pdf (cited April 28, 2003).

Foreign Aid

Foreign aid refers to the noncommercial flow of grants or loans to a country from another country or some international entity, characterized by concessional interest rates and long repayment periods. Sometimes these loans can be paid back in recipients' domestic currencies. Foreign aid is generally given to less developed countries (LDCs) by more developed countries (MDCs) at an intergovernmental level. The aid can be bilateral (given by one country to another) or multilateral (channeled though an institution such as the World Bank). In addition to financial aid, technical help (for various investment projects), food aid, and other commodity aid may also be part of an overall aid package. Direct military aid is generally not regarded as foreign aid, but in a number of situations it becomes difficult to distinguish between military aid and nonmilitary aid.

The World Bank breaks down total foreign aid into two regional categories: net official development assistance (ODA) and net official aid (OA). ODA refers to loan disbursements (net of repayments of principal) made on concessional terms (including grants) to low-income countries. The grant element must be at least 25 percent (calculated at a rate of discount of 10 percent) to qualify as ODA. OA refers to aid flows (net of amortized repayments) made by MDCs to East and Central European countries. In 2001, total foreign aid (ODA plus OA) amounted to approximately $58 billion, or about $10 per capita in recipient countries in the less developed world. Between 1996 and 2001, there was a $4 billion decline in absolute amount of aid disbursed. Some of the countries of sub-Saharan Africa, however, became more dependent on foreign aid during this time.

Concessional loans are given in various forms and for different purposes. Loans are often given for specific projects (for example, for construction of a highway) or general programs (for example, women's literacy programs in a country). At the multilateral level, the International Monetary Fund (IMF) provides relatively short-term loans (not classified as ODA or OA) to tide over balance of payments difficulties. The World Bank gives longer-term loans, usually for specific projects. The International Development Association (IDA), an affiliate of the World Bank, provides concessional loans to the poorest and least developed countries. The United Nations Development Programme (UNDP) coordinates much of the technical assistance provided by various UN agencies. These include the United Nations Children's Fund (UNICEF), which works in the area of education and health for children, and the United Nations Food and Agriculture Organization (FAO), which focuses on food security and eradication of hunger. Also, the World Health Organization (WHO) focuses on health in general, and the International Labour Organization (ILO) works on labor rights. These multilateral and other official government-sponsored organizations provide foreign aid to a large number of less developed countries.

History of Foreign Aid

For much of the nineteenth century and the early part of the twentieth century, global economic relations were characterized by colonial domination, not foreign aid. Many authors have argued that during this time, a large resource outflow took place from poor countries to rich countries. The idea that there should be a reverse flow of resources—that richer countries should actually provide economic and technical assistance to poorer countries—reflected a surprising change of attitude in international relations. The change occurred as a response to international political events in the aftermath of World War II.

World War II dealt a major blow to much of the global economy. It was clear that world peace could not be achieved and that the economic and strategic interests of developed countries would not be served if fundamental global inequities remained. Although foreign aid was on the agenda of the United Nations from its inception in 1946, the organization had limited resources to carry out this economic function. Several colonial powers began providing limited economic assistance to their former colonies after World War II. But foreign aid only became a significant international event in 1948, when the United States introduced the Marshall Plan. The Marshall Plan was aimed at the postwar reconstruction of Europe. During 1948–1951, the United States provided more than $13 billion for the reconstruction of war-ravaged Europe. It was the largest government-to-government aid in history at that time. In subsequent years, international financial institutions such as the World Bank and the IMF, established during this time, took active roles in channeling funds from developed countries to underdeveloped countries. The era of foreign aid had begun.

Motivations for Giving Aid

Humanitarian or altruistic concerns do not explain a large part of the foreign aid disbursed over the past fifty years. National interests, economic interests, geopolitical aims, and sometimes goals of refugee repatriation have played important roles in establishing donor interest in giving foreign aid. The Marshall Plan itself grew out of an American fear of Soviet expansion. Fear of Soviet communism was also a factor in subsequent American and West European aid for developing countries. The famous Truman Doctrine of U.S. President Harry S. Truman was essentially formulated to help the nations threatened by the expansion of communism. Officially, the Truman Doctrine made it a U.S. policy to "aid the efforts of economically underdeveloped areas to develop their resources and improve their living conditions." In reality, however, Truman's program focused on a handful of developing countries considered important for their strategic alliances with the United States. The Soviet Union also provided aid (including technical and military expertise) to its allies. Both of the superpowers used foreign aid to buy influence and to contain each other's global hegemony.

In a sense, foreign aid has worked like economic sanctions. Donor countries at different periods of time have found that it is useful to encourage certain international allegiances and discourage certain others. Cold War concerns dominated much of foreign aid during the post–World War II period. Following Jan P. Pronk (2001), one can describe the foreign aid focus of developed market economies over time in terms shown in Table 1.

The strategic game of foreign aid is not only played by the donor; it is also played by the recipient country. Since resources from foreign aid are often spent on purchasing goods and services from firms in the donor country (when such purchases are required as a part of aid conditionality, it is known as "tied aid"), recipient countries are also able to influence aid decisions. During the foreign aid negotiation process, the recipient countries are sometimes able to tilt aid in their favor by promising lucrative private contracts to favored private firms in the donor country. As Table 1 shows, although *realpolitik* has been an important factor behind foreign aid, peace-building efforts and

Table 1: Evolution of Foreign Aid: Implicit Goals of OECD Countries

Years	Purpose of Foreign Aid
1940s	Technical assistance
1950s	Community development and containment of communism
1960s	Trade and investment gaps and containment of communism
1970s	Basic human needs and containment of communism
1980s	Structural adjustment/debt relief and containment of communism
1990s	Rehabilitation and humanitarian assistance
2001 and later	Prevention of violent conflicts and establishment of democracy

Source: Adapted from Jan P. Pronk, "Aid as a Catalyst," *Development and Change* 32, no. 4 (2001): 611–629.

humanitarian concerns did assume higher importance in the 1990s.

Amounts and Allocations of Foreign Aid

Foreign aid has grown substantially since the Truman years. Direct foreign aid to developing countries has grown from a negligible amount in 1950 to more than US$58 billion in 2001. Aid has been disbursed under various categories: humanitarian aid, project-based aid, program aid, aid to overcome an imminent balance of payments problem, and hidden military aid. The most charitable aid, as defined above, is ODA. As a percentage of a recipient's gross national income (GNI), ODA has always been relatively high in sub-Saharan countries and very low in South Asian and East Asian countries (Table 2). In per capita terms, sub-Saharan African countries and the Middle Eastern/ North African countries receive higher ODA (approximately $21 and $16 per person, respectively, per year). The West Bank and Gaza areas (under Israeli occupation) receive the maximum ODA per capita ($280). A large amount of foreign aid is also given at less concessional terms. Some calculations use a related concept, effective development assistance (EDA), to calculate the true value of concessional aid. EDA calculations are not significantly different from ODA calculations, however, and are omitted here.

Data presented in Table 2 show that the absolute value of aid has declined in middle-income, lower-middle-income, East Asian, Latin American, sub-Saharan, and Middle Eastern countries. Sub-Saharan Africa, however, still depends significantly on aid (almost a quarter of sub-Saharan capital formation comes from foreign aid). A large part of aid given to sub-Saharan Africa is earmarked for humanitarian purposes (such as prevention of famine, HIV/AIDS, and the like).

As stated earlier, an overwhelming amount of foreign aid is given for political and strategic reasons. In the 1990s, Bosnia and Herzegovina received a large amount of foreign aid after their civil war and after the member countries of the North Atlantic Treaty Organization (NATO) carried out military operations in that region. The U.S. preoccupation with the conflict in the Middle East explains why Israel and Egypt, not sub-Saharan Africa, receive very high amounts of foreign aid. Although a large part of foreign aid has always been politically motivated, project-specific humanitarian aid is also popular. In recent years, for example, the United States has pledged a significant increase in aid to contain the HIV/AIDS epidemic in sub-Saharan Africa.

On the donor side, there is also considerable variation with regard to quality and quantity of foreign aid. Assistance is sometimes given at a bilateral level and sometimes at a multilateral level (often channeled via international organizations such as the World Bank, the IMF, the

Table 2: Foreign Aid Recipients

Region/Country	Net Official Development Assistance (in millions of US dollars))		Aid per Capita ($)		Aid as Percentage of Gross National Income		Aid as Percentage of Gross Capital Formation		Aid as Percentage of Imports of Goods and Services	
	1996	2001	1996	2001	1996	2001	1996	2001	1996	2001
Low income	25,309	25,342	11	10	2.5	2.4	10.2	11.0	8.9	8.1
Middle income	21,799	20,284	9	8	0.5	0.4	1.7	1.6	1.6	1.2
Lower middle income	17,598	16,086	9	7	0.7	0.6	2.3	2.1	2.5	1.9
Upper middle income	3,532	3,672	7	7	0.2	0.2	0.7	0.8	0.6	0.5
East Asia and Pacific	8,040	7,394	5	4	0.6	0.5	1.4	1.3	1.6	1.2
Europe and Central Asia	8,670	9,783	18	21	0.8	1.0	3.3	4.4	1.6	2.3
Latin America and the Caribbean	7,446	5,992	15	11	0.4	0.3	1.9	1.6	3.2	1.2
Middle East and North Africa	5,956	4,838	22	16	1.0	0.7	5.0	3.2	4.4	2.7
South Asia	5,169	5,871	4	4	1.0	1.0	4.6	4.4	23.4	5.1
Sub-Saharan Africa	16,552	13,933	28	21	5.2	4.6	27.3	23.4		10.9
Bosnia and Herzegovina	845	639	239	157	33.5	12.8	73.6	—	33.8	23.8
Israel	2,217	172	389	27	2.3	0.2	9.4	—	5.2	0.3
West Bank and Gaza	550	865	218	280	13.2	19.6	42.9			
China	2,646	1,460	2	1	0.3	0.1	0.8	0.3	1.5	0.5
India	1,897	1,705	2	2	0.5	0.4	2.2	1.6	3.2	2.2
World	62,264	58,244	11	10	0.2	0.2	0.9	0.9	0.8	0.6

Source: World Bank, *World Development Report* (New York: Oxford University Press, 2003).

UN-affiliated bodies, and other organizations). All Organisation for Economic Co-operation and Development (OECD) countries have provided foreign aid to poorer countries. But there is a great variation between OECD donors. Denmark, Norway, the Netherlands, Luxembourg, and Sweden have the distinction of being the largest donors when foreign aid is measured as a percentage of the donors' gross national product (GNP). These countries have provided more than 0.7 percent of their GNP in foreign aid. The United States ranks very high ($12.9 billion in 2002) in terms of absolute aid, but ranks at the bottom on a relative scale (0.12 percent of GNP). Table 3 shows the overwhelming importance of the OECD as a global source of foreign aid. The table also shows that in

terms of absolute value of foreign aid, the Netherlands, France, the United Kingdom, Germany, Japan, and the United States are major donors of foreign aid annually (more than $3 billion each).

The relative size of foreign aid (as a percentage of gross national income or as a percentage of gross domestic capital formation) has declined in most developing countries (Table 2). In the 1970s, bilateral, multilateral, and other official aid flows were sometimes close to 70 percent of all capital inflows to developing countries (the rest of the capital inflows were flows of privately owned foreign direct investment, or FDI). FDI to LDCs has increased in recent years, and the ratio of aid to total capital flow has now declined to less

Table 3: Official Development Assistance (ODA), 1999 to 2002

	Country	ODA (in millions of U.S. dollars)				ODA (as percentage of gross national product)			
		1999	2000	2001	2002	1999	2000	2001	2002
1.	Denmark	1,733	1,664	1,599	1,632	1.01	1.06	1.01	0.96
2.	Norway	1,370	1,264	1,346	1,746	0.91	0.8	0.83	0.91
3.	Netherlands	3,134	3,075	3,155	3,377	0.79	0.82	0.82	0.82
4.	Luxembourg	119	116	142	143	0.66	0.7	0.8	0.78
5.	Sweden	1,630	1,813	1,576	1,754	0.7	0.81	0.76	0.74
6.	Belgium	760	812	866	1,061	0.3	0.36	0.37	0.42
7.	Ireland	245	239	285	397	0.31	0.3	0.33	0.41
8.	France	5,637	4,221	4,293	5,182	0.39	0.33	0.34	0.36
9.	Finland	416	371	389	466	0.33	0.31	0.33	0.35
10.	Switzerland	969	888	908	933	0.35	0.34	0.34	0.32
11.	United Kingdom	3,401	4,458	4,659	4,749	0.23	0.31	0.32	0.3
12.	Canada	1,699	1,722	1,572	2,013	0.28	0.25	0.23	0.28
13.	Germany	5,515	5,034	4,879	5,359	0.26	0.27	0.27	0.27
14.	Spain	1,363	1,321	1,748	1,608	0.23	0.24	0.3	0.25
15.	Australia	982	995	852	962	0.26	0.27	0.25	0.25
16.	Portugal	276	261	267	282	0.26	0.26	0.25	0.24
17.	New Zealand	134	116	111	124	0.27	0.26	0.25	0.23
18.	Japan	15,323	13,062	9,678	9,220	0.35	0.27	0.23	0.23
19.	Austria	527	461	457	475	0.26	0.25	0.25	0.23
20.	Greece	194	216	194	295	0.15	0.19	0.19	0.22
21.	Italy	1,806	1,368	1,493	2,313	0.15	0.13	0.14	0.2
22.	United States	9,145	9,581	10,884	12,900	0.1	0.1	0.11	0.12

Note: The ODA target set by the UN is at 0.7 percent of GNP. Most nations do not meet this target.
Source: Organisation for Economic Co-operation and Development (OECD) data.

than 10 percent. This decline is much less dramatic if China, which attracts a very large amount of FDI every year, is excluded. It is, however, important to realize that while overall aid has gone down in absolute value, the proportion of direct military aid (which, according to some estimates, was about 20 percent of all aid) has also gone down in the post–Cold War era. The nonmilitary component of aid, therefore, may have increased. There is some indication that as an aftermath of the 2003 Iraqi war, overall foreign aid may go up. Much of the increase may be used for reconstruction projects in Iraq.

Theories of Foreign Aid

There is a voluminous body of literature on the theoretical aspects of foreign trade. Why do countries need foreign aid? Opinions are sharply divided regarding the purpose and role of foreign aid. Many conservative economists think that foreign aid really does not help the recipient countries and may actually make the situation worse. For example, famous economists such as Milton Friedman, Peter Bauer, and many others have opposed foreign aid as a policy instrument because they think that availability of cheap foreign aid interferes with market mechanisms and allows the recipient country governments to postpone tough policy reforms. These economists claim that establishment of property rights and a facilitating, capitalism-friendly institutional structure is more important than foreign aid for economic development. Economists on the left of the ideological spectrum do not like foreign aid either; they think that aid accentuates the existing rural-urban, traditional-modern, and rich-poor income divide in less developing countries. According to these economists, aid is used mostly as an instrument to further the global hegemony of rich industrial countries. It caters to the interests of a limited number of large firms and individuals located in the donor countries, and it obstructs the development of indigenous capital. There are also a large number of economists who think the truth lies somewhere between these two extremes.

A Macroeconomic Identity

Foreign aid also raises less controversial macroeconomic issues. Economists have always emphasized the important role of capital formation in economic growth. All theories of growth place a great emphasis on the role of capital formation in developing countries. Capital-starved less developed countries clearly need financial resources to grow. These resources can come from either domestic (private and government) sources or from foreign sources. The relevant basic macroeconomic identity can be represented as follows:

$$I = S + (T - G) + (M - X)$$

Where the symbol I refers to gross investment, S is private savings, T is taxes collected by the government, G is government expenditure, M is imports, and X is exports. The identity says that gross domestic investment, which is an indicator of future productivity and growth, depends on three factors: private savings (S), public savings (T − G), and foreign savings (M − X). Capital inflow from abroad

would generally increase foreign savings (M − X). If foreign aid goes up, capital inflow from abroad will go up and will contribute to gross investment in the country. Note that higher capital import allows a country to buy more importable goods, including capital goods from abroad.

A related literature, focusing on what is known as the "two-gap model," assumes that there are two constraints as far as investable resources are concerned: the domestic savings gap (that is, S + [T − G]) and the foreign trade/foreign exchange gap (which would affect M − X). According to the two-gap model, domestic and foreign savings are not perfect substitutes for investment. On one hand, if a country has a foreign exchange gap, that is, if it is not able to export enough to earn valuable foreign exchange to import critical capital goods, this will affect domestic investment negatively. On the other hand, if foreign exchange is plentiful, inadequate domestic savings may still turn out to be the binding constraint on domestic investment. In terms of the identity above, in order to increase capital formation and growth, S + (T − G), (M − X), or both must increase. According to this theory, therefore, countries that suffer from a foreign exchange gap will benefit the most from an inflow of foreign private capital or foreign aid. In these countries, it is more important to raise (M − X), financed by capital inflows or foreign aid.

Returning again to the basic macroeconomic identity above, the question is, when (M − X) goes up as a result of foreign aid inflow, will all other variables on the right-hand side of the basic macroeconomic identity remain constant? If all other variables on the right-hand side are constant, investment (I) will increase and stimulate growth. The controversy regarding foreign aid can be understood with reference to this basic question. To put it differently, will an increased inflow of capital or foreign aid simply replace domestic savings? That is, will S fall? Will it reduce the incentive for governments to collect appropriate taxes? That is, will T fall? Will it encourage corrupt government officials to increase unproductive and wasteful government expenditure? That is, will G rise? Is it going to increase imports of luxurious consumer goods (part of M)? Is it going to crowd out exports (X)? These questions are analyzed below.

How Foreign Aid Helps a Poor Economy

According to the economists on the right, the *availability* of resources for investment is not a critical problem in less developed countries. Investors seek the highest return for their money. So if existing projects in developing countries promise profitable returns, investors will borrow, and resources will be available for investment. The real issue, these economists argue, is that in these countries, the existing investment projects are not profitable because of misguided policies of the government at the microeconomic and macroeconomic levels. These policies impede the forces of the free market and encourage rent-seeking behavior. In addition, aid tends to be "fungible." For example, if aid is given to enhance the quality of primary education in a country, the aid money may divert previously invested funds in education to other less desirable uses. As a result, total investment in education may not rise. The correct policy, according to these economists, is to ensure that property rights are protected and that the basic laws of the free market are adhered to. Given property rights and free markets, the profit potentials of all investment should reflect their true social opportunity costs, and therefore, foreign aid is not needed. A well-known conservative think tank, the Cato Institute, has gone one step forward and recommended that the United States "abolish the U.S. Agency for International Development and end government-to-government aid programs; withdraw from the World Bank and the five regional multilateral development banks; not use foreign aid to encourage or reward market reforms in the developing world; eliminate programs, such as enterprise funds, that provide loans to the private sector in developing countries and oppose schemes that guarantee private-sector investments abroad" (Cato Institute 2002).

The Cato Institute's view implicitly assumes that capital market imperfections (credit constraints, asymmetric information, moral hazards, and the like) cannot be corrected by government policy. This view contrasts with the view of development theorists, who believe that a "big push" is needed to get a poor country out of a low-level equilibrium trap, and that capital market imperfections such as credit constraints, asymmetric information, and moral hazard need to be addressed with the help of an efficient, fair, balanced, and impartial public policy. Much of the development literature stresses the need to create an "enabling environment" in developing countries in terms of infrastructure projects such as national and regional road networks, electricity generation, and telecommunication links. An efficient infrastructure (in addition to a transparent and corruption-free legal and institutional framework) is a necessary precondition for the private sector to flourish. But would foreign capital or an indigenous private sector on their own invest in massive infrastructure projects? The theory of public finance can be used to show that more often than not, large investment projects have to be financed by public funds, because private provisions of large investments may not be adequate. In other words, if the government needs to fund an expensive infrastructure project, it must raise taxes to pay for it.

One of the basic problems with respect to taxation is that the less developed countries have an inadequate tax base. People are poor, so most do not pay income tax. Domestic resource mobilization becomes a difficult task. Many governments thus depend on foreign aid as one of the few sources for investment in infrastructure (this is especially true for sub-Saharan Africa; see Table 2). A significant amount of foreign aid is also sought in the form of technical expertise, since many of these countries also lack skilled labor to implement infrastructure projects.

This is not to say that all such investments are worthwhile or that governments are not vulnerable to special-interest groups and corruption. Many developing countries simply lack the ability and the political will to reduce fiscal deficits, curb government consumption, and increase taxes for infrastructure investments. Very often, vested interests make it harder to raise taxes on the rich rent-seeking landlords, and consequently, these governments find it difficult to cut subsidies doled out to various constituencies. Given these difficulties, developing countries may find it easier to mobilize foreign resources than domestic ones. But there is also a genuine need for external funding when market imperfections prevent private capital from flowing to labor-abundant developing countries. Although one must be wary of government failure, one must also be cognizant of extensive capital market failures in these countries. A number of economists thus disagree with the Cato Institute's premise and argue that in a great many cases, the developing countries must be taught "how to fish" before they can catch fish themselves.

It needs to be pointed out that economists on both the right and the left of the ideological spectrum agree that a "debt overhang" is a serious problem in poor countries, and that foreign aid should be used judiciously for debt relief. The debt-overhang problem arises when a highly indebted country gets into a vicious cycle: The country cannot borrow because it has a "bad credit history," and it cannot grow to pay off its debt because it cannot borrow for the right projects. Consequently, foreign aid in the form of one-time debt forgiveness will break the vicious cycle of stagnation due to the debt burden. In 1996, the World Bank and the IMF proposed the Heavily Indebted Poor Countries (HIPC) Initiative to forgive appropriate amounts of debts of very poor sub-Saharan countries. By 2003, approximately $36 billion in debt had been forgiven under this program.

Consequences of Foreign Aid

Foreign Aid and Economic Slowdowns

From the basic macroeconomic identity, $I = S + (T - G) + (M - X)$, it has been shown that a higher foreign aid will increase $(M - X)$. But will it reduce national savings, $S + (T - G)$? If it does, the effect of foreign aid on investment (I) will be small, zero, or may even reduce gross investment.

The theoretical literature has shown that under certain conditions, foreign aid may create "immiserizing growth," that is, economic growth that makes a country worse off, and a "transfer problem" to exist. A large transfer of resources may adversely affect the exchange rate of the aid recipient's currency and change traded and nontraded good prices. These effects may make the recipient countries worse off after aid transfer. This result, however, cannot be generalized, and considerable theoretical doubt exists regarding the immiserization argument (see Basu 1997, 93–98).

One way to address the issue of effectiveness of foreign aid, therefore, is to study the existing empirical evidence. At an empirical level, the hypothesis that foreign aid "crowds out" national savings has been tested. The results are not encouraging. Robert Cassen (1994) found that a "significant portion of aid does not succeed." Peter Boone (1994) showed that in eighty-two developing economies where foreign aid was less than 15 percent of gross domestic product (GDP), foreign aid was consumed entirely and added nothing to total savings. Boone also found that aid money is often used to fund the relatively well-off population in poorer countries. It seems that "poor people in rich countries" give foreign aid to help the "rich people in poor countries!" (*The Economist* 1994).

Some authors, however, have found problems with Boone's method. Henrik Hansen and Finn Tarp (2000), for example, found that Boone's complete crowding-out hypothesis can only be supported under rare circumstances (this is the case where elasticity substitution of domestic savings with respect to foreign aid is equal to −1). But their results also suggest that some crowding out does occur and that there is wide variation among countries.

Political Climate in the Recipient Country

The nature of the government in a country is an important factor in how foreign aid is used. Presumably, a repressive and dictatorial regime will be less inclined to use foreign aid for the right purposes. Alberto Alesina and Beatrice Weder (1999), however, found that dictatorial regimes have received as much foreign aid as democratic ones. There is also some evidence that corrupt governments have received more foreign aid than ones that are not corrupt. Other researchers have found that foreign aid has been successful in improving quality of life in the recipient countries when it was given to democratic countries (Kosack 2003), and that bilateral aid is more successful in promoting growth than multilateral aid (Ram 2003). Kosack also found that foreign aid given to democratic countries enhances "state capacity for reaching out to citizens," strengthens state-society institutions, and empowers the civil society organizations. When democratic states with vibrant civil societies receive foreign aid, their growth rates go up.

Misallocation of Foreign Aid

A common thread in empirical studies is that the donors regularly misallocate aid. In other words, the same amount of aid money could be reallocated in a more efficient manner. In an ideal world, foreign aid should be used to finance the *marginal* project that cannot be financed by the developing country for lack of funds. But given the predominance of strategic and military interests of the donors, needless to say, an economically rational allocation rule is rarely followed.

Paul Collier and David Dollar (2002) studied this issue directly. They found that much foreign aid has been misallocated away from deserving recipients. If aid were reallocated ap-

propriately, about 20 million people could be moved out of poverty every year (as opposed to about 10 million every year currently). David Dollar and Jacob Svensson (1998) also found that when a country starts implementing necessary economic reforms, foreign aid is often withdrawn, and when the country does not implement necessary reforms, aid is often increased. This creates a perverse incentive for the developing countries not to implement good economic policies. Dollar argued that the civil and political environment in a developing country should be an important consideration for all donors.

Several researchers have also pointed out that the type of aid (food aid, technical help, or financial aid) matters a great deal. Other studies have found that international coordination of foreign aid is a very important concern. Project aid, program aid, technical assistance, food aid, and other aid need to be coordinated by the donors to create the correct facilitating environment.

Table 1 and Table 2 point to the fact that foreign aid has indeed been used arbitrarily. It should come as no surprise that the empirical studies have not found significant effects of aid on growth. The donors did not really use aid to increase economic growth, so aid failed to increase economic growth! Gus Edgren (2002), commenting on this issue, said that the aid industry is "very fragmented" and that it is characterized by market imperfections. Politically motivated donor agencies distort the market because they are powerful and because they can pick and choose the recipients. The activities of large aid agencies change the shadow prices of various developmental projects and distort the markets. "If one looks at the industry as a global mechanism for transferring resources from rich countries to poor," wrote Edgren, "one could be excused for thinking that the Devil himself could not have created a more infernal system. . . . When all agents are simultaneously trying to get the most out of the system for themselves, the results produced by the system as a whole are bound to be less than effective. It is particularly counter-productive that the system allows individual agencies to boast of good results for their own projects while these 'successes' are being achieved at the expense of the total outcome" (Edgren 2002).

Agency Problems

When governments of less developed countries turn to multilateral institutions for financial and technical resources, it immediately opens up possibilities for rent-seeking behavior *on both sides*. As discussed earlier, a less developed country may genuinely need infrastructure investments, but the politicians and special interest groups in the government may have a different agenda. The LDC government may not represent the true priorities of the people, and the government bureaucrats may be subject to corruption. But this problem, to a lesser extent, can also occur in a multilateral institution such as the World Bank. Bureaucrats in the World Bank may have their own rent-seeking agenda. Since the World Bank officials are usually not rewarded for withholding aid, they may have an incentive to lend to not-so-deserving governments, for example.

James K. Boyce (2002) argued that the policies of these institutions do not "fit well with an incentive structure that puts a premium on aid disbursements. If institutions face penalties for withholding aid, but not for disbursing it, they naturally make every effort to 'move the money' to their favored projects." Although the funds for the multilateral organizations come from donor-country taxpayers, the officials of these organizations are hardly ever penalized for funding incorrect foreign aid projects. The multilateral institutions are supranational organizations, and unlike private firms, they are not directly accountable to their "shareholders." These "agency" problems may make both recipient governments and officials of the donor organizations ineffective and self-seeking players in a game ostensibly played for the welfare of poor countries.

Even if the multilateral agencies do not suffer from agency problems, doubts remain about the effectiveness of aid when potential recipients compete for aid and each recipient country wants to prove that it has the most compelling case for aid. There is a body of theoretical work that shows that even if the donors are altruistic and care about reducing poverty in the recipient countries, foreign aid may actually increase poverty in the developing countries. This is because the governments of developing countries may consciously follow a perverse income-distribution policy in order to be eligible for foreign aid. Indeed, many economists argue that a number of developing countries now have a dependency syndrome with respect to foreign aid. This dependency did not exist before.

Foreign Aid, Conditionality, and Structural Adjustment

When a less developed country approaches the multilateral institutions for aid, these institutions routinely examine the fiscal and monetary policies of the developing country. The IMF has regularly required stringent macroeconomic policies as a condition for giving loans. The World Bank also provides structural/sectoral adjustment (concessional) loans in tandem with the IMF. The World Bank and IMF "conditionalities" are a strict set of macroeconomic rules that typically require reductions in government budget deficits and cuts in various government subsidies in recipient countries. These restrictions have become a sore and contentious point for the developing countries. Stringent conditions associated with IMF/World Bank loans and aid, at least in the short run, increase prices of essential goods, create unemployment, and increase income inequality. The conditionalites are very unpopular in the less developed countries and have proven to be politically damaging for the aid-recipient governments. Ajit Singh (2002) has argued that conditionalities actually reduce policy autonomy in the less developed countries and that a lack of autonomy probably reduces growth in developing countries.

The fact that the less developed countries find traditional conditionalities unpalatable must strike some as curious. Paul Streeten (1987) called this a double paradox: Why do the developing countries complain about conditionalities attached to foreign aid if conditionalities are supposedly good for them, and why do the donor countries donate money in the first place if they do not trust the governments in these countries? The answer, of course, is that much aid is misallocated and tends to be politically motivated (on both sides). Aid does not really flow to countries; it flows to particular groups within countries. Sometimes obvious human rights violations are ignored. Very often aid is misplaced and directed to the wrong people. Rwanda is a classic example. In 1993–1994, although some organizations criticized the human rights record of the government in Rwanda, foreign aid to that country was not reduced. In fact, aid to the Rwandan Hutu government actually increased before the government-supported groups in that country committed the 1994 genocide.

Economists at the IMF and the World Bank respond to these criticisms by saying that although some mistakes have been made, one must remember that the countries that seek foreign aid from these multilateral organizations are a "self-selected" group. Most countries seek help from the World Bank and the IMF when they already have their houses on fire. They come to the World Bank and the IMF only as a last resort when unsustainable monetary and fiscal policies have already brought them to the brink of economic disaster. In general, these countries would perform even worse if they did not receive concessional and other loans.

Jan P. Pronk (2001) mediated this interesting controversy, arguing that the *policy stance* of a country's government should be an important consideration before aid is approved. One should recognize that: (1) a good policy should be oriented toward broad-based sustainable economic growth, with poverty reduction as an objective; (2) a one-size-fits-all precondition for aid approval is a prescription for disaster because what works in one country may not (yet) work in another; (3) even if the macroeconomic policy of a particular country is on the wrong track, focused, goal-oriented, welfare-enhancing projects on, say, health care, education, or water management might be considered worthy of support; and (4) what really matters is the marginal impact of aid, and therefore the aid agencies should focus on "better policies" rather than perfect policies. Many development economists have started taking Pronk's valuable comments seriously. The IMF and the World Bank have started to reconsider their aid policy: There is now an emerging consensus that aid-related conditionalities should have a "human face."

The problems associated with foreign aid do not mean that all foreign aid should be abandoned. It is true that empirically, the aid-growth relationship is not a strong one. There are serious concerns about many aspects of foreign aid, including concerns about the true intentions of donors, agency problems, the bureaucratic inefficiencies of multinational institutions, the rent-seeking behavior of governments, coordination problems among donors, perverse games between donors and recipients, damaging competition between recipients, and last but not least, the effects of corruption, all of which cast doubts on the usefulness of foreign aid. But resource mobilization for productive investment, including investments for health, education, and infrastructure, are critically important for economic growth. There is clearly a crying need for a "big push" and more productive investment in developing countries. The question is whether the problems associated with foreign aid are serious enough to merit a policy of actual aid reduction or complete elimination of foreign aid. Once again, most economists would rather attempt to correct the problems associated with foreign aid than throw the proverbial baby out with the bathwater.

Nongovernmental and Governmental Organizations

Although foreign aid refers to government grants and concessional loans, nongovernmental organizations (NGOs) have played increasingly important roles in economic development. Nonprofit NGOs work in selected geographical locations in developing countries, typically in relatively small areas, to promote activist policies that emphasize education, health, women's and children's welfare, and the like at local levels. In recent years, a large amount of official foreign aid has been siphoned off to NGOs. In the Copenhagen summit on NGOs (1995), the United States pledged that it would direct 50 percent of all foreign aid through NGOs. This has not yet happened. But the statement shows the emerging importance of NGOs. International NGOs such as CARE, Oxfam, Child Relief and You (CRY), Save the Children, and many others now actively seek donations and have a visible presence in developed counties. Local NGOs such as Esperança (Mozambique), Grameen Bank (Bangladesh), Swanirvar (India), Casa Alianza (Latin America), and many others have been partially funded by private foreign donors.

The Changing Face of Foreign Aid

There are some indications that enormous changes are taking place in the area of foreign aid. The foreign aid program was kick-started by the United States when it introduced the famous Marshall Plan; there are probably equally significant changes taking place today.

There are both negative and positive changes taking place in foreign aid today. Although U.S. assistance to poor countries did decline in absolute value as well as in percentage terms (from 0.2 percent to 0.1 percent) during the 1990s, the United States repeatedly responded to international humanitarian concerns with generous offers of foreign aid. In the 1990s, famines in Sudan and Ethiopia would

have been much worse without U.S. food aid. The new U.S. preoccupation with terrorism will probably politicize the flow of foreign aid (as was the case during the Cold War), and aid may not flow to the most deserving countries. However, in 2002 the George W. Bush administration set up the Millennium Challenge Account to address the scourge of HIV/AIDS in Africa and pledged to increase development aid by 50 percent in the next few years, resulting in a $5 billion annual increase over current levels by 2006. More important, although current U.S. official donations are still relatively low, U.S. private individuals, and unexpectedly, many private corporations, have decided to lend a helping hand. U.S. private individual donations and corporate donations are substantial and growing. U.S. citizens donate generously to nongovernmental humanitarian and charitable organizations such as the Red Cross, Oxfam, and CARE and to other local NGOs in less developed countries. These donations are mostly humanitarian and issue-oriented and not overtly political. Some estimates suggest that U.S. individual private donations earmarked for developing countries may amount to some $30 billion per year, which is far more than the amount of U.S. official aid.

An interesting development in recent years is the growth of corporate charitable donations. Corporate charities such as the Bill and Melinda Gates Foundation, the David and Lucille Packard Foundation, and other corporate entities have donated significant amounts of money in recent years.

Conclusion

Foreign aid has been a part of North-South relations for more than fifty years now. The record of aid activity has been less predictable than one would have hoped. Too often, both the donors and the recipients have had conflicting priorities, or their priorities were not consistent with economic growth and poverty alleviation. In terms of its effectiveness, it would appear that foreign aid has been neither necessary nor sufficient for higher economic growth to occur in less developed countries. Countries such as India and China have progressed with minimal foreign aid; therefore the aid is not necessary for growth to occur. And there are many examples of countries in Africa where foreign aid has failed to stimulate economic growth; therefore the aid is not sufficient for growth to occur. An empirical survey of the literature shows that foreign aid can be a catalyst for growth, however, if it is targeted well. An appropriately coordinated allocation of growth-enhancing foreign aid is a critical element in the economics of foreign aid. Rosenstein Rodan's (1969) comment, "Aid should be allocated where it will have the maximum catalytic effect in mobilizing additional national effort," seems as true today as it was when he first wrote it.

Foreign aid accounted for a large amount of capital flow from developed countries to underdeveloped countries in the second half of the twentieth century. The contribution of foreign aid as a percentage of capital formation has now declined in most developing countries. Many of these countries have now started receiving significant amounts of private capital flows. China has attracted a very large amount of foreign direct investment in the 1990–2003 period. Sub-Saharan Africa, however, still depends heavily on foreign aid. If aid dependency declined in importance, economists would be the first to celebrate the event. Economic theory predicts that private long-term capital should flow from developed countries to less developed countries, and that a free flow of long-term capital would enhance world welfare. A decline of foreign aid and a rise of private capital flows would usher in a new era in global economic growth.

Dipankar Purkayastha

See Also International Indebtedness; International Bank for Reconstruction and Development (IBRD)

References

Alesina, Alberto, and Beatrice Weder. 1999. "Do Corrupt Governments Receive Less Foreign Aid?" NBER (National Bureau of Economic Research) Working Paper W7108, May.

Basu, Kaushik. 1997. *Analytical Development Economics.* Cambridge: MIT Press.

Boone, Peter. 1994. *The Impact of Foreign Aid on Savings and Growth.* Mimeo. London: London School of Economics.

Boyce, James K. 2002. "Aid Conditionality as a Tool for Peacebuilding: Opportunities and Constraints." *Development and Change* 33, no. 5: 1025–1048.

Burnside, Craig, and David Dollar. 2000. "Aid, Policies and Growth." *American Economic Review* 90, no. 4: 848.

Cassen, Robert. 1994. Does Aid Work, Second Edition. Oxford: Clarendon Press.

Cato Institute. 2002. Cato Handbook for 108th Congress, http://www.cato.org/pubs/handbook/handbook106.html.

Collier, Paul, and David Dollar. 2002. "Aid Allocation and Poverty Reduction." *European Economic Review* 46: 1475–1500.

Dollar, David, and Jacob Svensson. 1998. *What Explains the Success or Failure of Structural Adjustment Programs.* World Bank Working Paper No. 1938. Washington, DC: World Bank.

The Economist. 1994. "Foreign Aid, the Kindness of Strangers." May 7, p. 22.

Edgren, Gus. 2002. "Aid Is an Unreliable Joystick." *Development and Change* 33, no. 2: 261–267.

Hansen, Henrik, and Finn Tarp. 2000. "Aid Effectiveness Disputed." *Journal of International Development* 12, no. 3: 375–398.

Kosack, Stephen. 2003. "Effective Aid: How Democracy Allows Development Aid to Improve the Quality of Life." *World Development* 31, no. 1: 1–22.

Pronk, Jan P. 2001. "Aid as a Catalyst." *Development and Change* 32, no. 4: 611–629.

Ram, Rati. 2003. "Roles of Bilateral and Multilateral Aid in Economic Growth of Developing Countries." *Kyklos* 56, no. 1: 95–110.

Robert Cassen and Associates. 1994. *Does Aid Work? Report to an Intergovernmental Task Force.* Oxford: Clarendon.

Rosenstein-Rodan, P. N. 1969. "Criteria for Evaluation of National Development Effort." *UN Journal for Development Planning* 1, no. 1: 19–21.

Singh, Ajit. 2002. "Aid, Conditionality and Development." *Development and Change* 33, no. 2: 295–305.

Streeten, Paul. 1987. "Structural Adjustment: A Survey of the Issues and Options." *World Development* 15, no. 12: 1469–1482.

World Bank. 1998. *Assessing Aid: What Works, What Doesn't and Why.* New York: Oxford University Press.

———. 2003. *The World Development Report.* New York: Oxford University Press.

Gender and Globalization

Gender Impacts of Trade and Financial Liberalization

Studies focusing on the gendered processes and outcomes of globalization have highlighted how trade liberalization has led to feminization of the labor force, feminization of work (low-paid, flexible/insecure, and unorganized work), and feminization of poverty. The development toward the feminization of labor has been accompanied by a shift in employment from manufacturing to services in developed countries, and from agriculture to manufacturing and services in developing countries. Although greater trade openness is associated with increased participation of women in paid employment, women are still being assigned to low-paid jobs, and they continue to have the main responsibility for unpaid work and care in families. Feminist scholars have emphasized the different experiences of globalization across time, countries, and groups of women. Some women (in the South) have been able to find new jobs, while others (in the North) have lost jobs. At the same time, many women have seen their wages decline, their working conditions deteriorate, or their workloads increase as a result of deregulation of labor markets and cuts in social services.

Feminization of Manufacturing Employment

The gendered impacts of economic liberalization and export-oriented growth in the manufacturing industries of the developing countries are well documented, whereas the implications of trade for small-scale agriculture, informal-sector work, and unpaid household labor are less well understood (see Carr et al. 2000). Labor-intensive manufacturing, such as the industries in textiles, electronics, and toys, have relocated to developing countries as a result of low female labor costs and national policies promoting liberation of trade and foreign investment as well as deregulation of labor markets (for example, reduced minimum wage levels, lifted controls over working hours, and reduced workers' rights to social security coverage). Many women in developing countries have been able to find new employment opportunities in export-oriented manufacturing, which has in turn contributed to economic growth and to the feminization of the labor force in the these countries (Kanji and Menon-Sen 2001).

One popular policy measure to promote foreign investment in developing countries has been the construction of Export Processing Zones (EPZs). EPZs are small areas that offer tax incentives and tariff concessions for foreign transnational corporations (TNCs) specializing in export-oriented manufacturing production. Studies of the working conditions in EPZs have found that wages are often so low that workers are barely able to cover their living costs. The hazards of working in many of the zones are enormous, and the majority of the workers are young women from rural areas. The low tariff incentives offered by EPZs are now being eroded as trade and investment is increasingly liberalized. Subcontracting or homeworking involving a flexible and cheap form of production has become the most popular route for TNCs to reduce costs. Studies have found that the majority of homeworkers are women, and that these flexible work arrangements pay low wages and provide no benefits. Furthermore, homeworkers find themselves excluded from social security and minimum labor standards as well as from labor legislation and collective bargaining agreements (Meyer 2001).

The trend toward the rise in the female share of employment appears to have been stalled or reversed in the few countries such as Taiwan that have moved beyond labor-intensive export manufacturing. Studies undertaken during the 1990s found that rising capital intensity, technological upgrading, and improvement in the quality of export products were accompanied by a secular decline in women's share of manufacturing employment in the developing countries. Employers' discrimination against hiring women in the new, higher-paid, skill-intensive jobs and capital-intensive production processes has been used to explain this unfavorable trend. The demand for women's labor declines as some production jobs disappear while others are redefined as "technical" and become "men's" jobs. There is evidence that the diffusion of just-in-time organizational innovations is leading to a defeminization of manufacturing employment as men emerge as the more flexible, cost-effective workers compared to women (Berik 2000).

Feminization of Manufacturing Work

Informal work, part-time work, subcontracting, home-based work, and low pay associated with women's employment has become widespread for both men and women around the world (see Standing 1999). The newly created manufacturing jobs in developing countries have in most cases been low skilled and low paid, characteristics associated with jobs performed by women. Labor-intensive manufacturing export industries have been attracted to the developing countries by the low labor costs, especially for women. Women in these coun-

tries have accepted low wages because of their responsibility for caregiving and domestic work, norms assigning them the role of secondary wage earners, and because of their lack of access to resources (land, capital, and technology) and services (education and child care). In other words, employers, especially in manufacturing, have taken advantage of women's disadvantage. The low labor cost of women workers has crowded them into limited numbers of industries and occupations, which in turn has perpetuated gender wage inequality in many developing countries (see Berik 2000; Kanji and Menon-Sen 2001).

The long-term development and effects of women's low pay is debated. Linda Lim (1990) reasoned in her study of East Asia that once multinational assembly plants reach majority, they will improve the labor market for women by increasing demand and raising wages throughout the labor market. She also argued that multinational assembly plants improve women's position in the local labor market by providing better-paid alternatives than those traditionally available to women. Other researchers stress that women's employment in export manufacturing firms is a double-edged sword. The wages paid for these jobs improve women's bargaining positions within the household, but at the same time they are insufficient to enable women to support themselves or their dependents. There is also little hope of advancement (see, for example, Elson 1995).

In her study of textile, electronics, and machinery-assembly factories in Mexico, Elizabeth Fussell (2000) found that employers employ women with few other employment opportunities, low levels of human capital, and a great need for stable employment, all of which forces them to accept low wages. Hence, these manufacturing employers have not provided women with significantly better employment than other local employers would have been able to provide. Instead, they are increasingly providing employment to the least-skilled women who have few other options in the local labor force. This development is reflecting a race to the bottom in manufacturing wages as a result of globalization of production.

Agriculture and Services

Trade liberalization in agriculture has led to greater use of land for cash crops such as horticultural products in Africa and aquacultural products in Asia. Women have provided producers of horticulture with flexible and seasonal labor, while men predominantly occupy permanent and more secure work (Barrientos 1999). Moreover, studies of women in Africa who are engaged in cash crops show that they have less time for food production and preparation. The aquaculture has required large tracts of land, in some cases reducing land for food production and making it difficult for women to secure enough food for the household (Wichterich 2000). Reductions in public investment and expenditures in food and fertilizer subsidies, and the promotion of foreign, capital-intensive production, have contributed to increased urbanization and fewer job opportunities for women in the formal sector in countries such as India. To escape poverty, many women have moved to the cities, where they are often forced into sex work due to lack of job opportunities (Upadhyay 2000).

The low wages of women in developing countries have also induced labor-intensive service firms to relocate their data-processing, tele-work, and call-center work to these areas (Wichterich 2000). Women have played an important role in the expansion of services, particularly in Latin America and the Caribbean, northern Africa, and western Asia. Evidence from Malaysia indicates that preference for female labor in manufacturing carries over into new trade-related services (see Joekes and Weston 1994). Increased trade in services has, in most cases, expanded employment opportunities for women. However, many women working in the service sector have found themselves concentrated at the low-skilled and clerical levels. They carry the burden of work both inside and outside the home, and they face sexual harassment in the workplace. Moreover, men in the service sector refuse to accept women as colleagues or seniors, women often need to work twice as hard as men to gain recognition, and there is a lack of solidarity among women (Meyer 2001). In her study of women in high-tech information jobs in foreign-owned offshore data entry companies in Barbados, Carla Freeman (2000) revealed how these women have created a new "pink-collar" identity that is associated with increased consumption patterns and certain gender ideologies in order to distinguish themselves from women working in the export manufacturing sector. Many of these women in high-tech jobs supplemented their formal employment with participation in informal economic trade activities in order to sustain this new identity.

In recent years, feminization of migration has taken place as more and more women have moved from the poor developing countries to the more affluent countries in Europe and North America to work as cleaners, housemaids, entertainers, and sex workers. The jobs of most migrant women are low paid and low skilled as well as outside the formal economy. The Philippines has, for example, an estimated 7 million people working abroad, 60 percent of them women (Wichterich 2000).

Financial Liberalization

Globalization of finance has brought certain advantages for women, such as greater supply of credit, greater access to the foreign exchange market (to receive remittances from partners or relatives abroad, for example), and increased employment opportunities. As customers of financial institutions, women have less property and lower earnings and are therefore less likely to save than men. Moreover, women tend to borrow more irregularly and in smaller amounts than men. Women therefore need more flexible services and credit terms when borrowing money, which credit institutions have not always been willing to provide because of the administrative costs involved. At the same time, women in most cases are more likely than men to repay their loans. The inability of financial institutions to adapt to these gender differences when allocating funds is believed to have contributed to low savings rates, low investment rates, and distorted interest rates (Staverene 2000).

Studies of the financial crisis in East Asia during the late 1990s revealed that the economic and social impacts were more negative for women than for men. In his study of the employment of women and men in the Philippines before and after the financial crisis, Joseph Y. Lim (2000) found that women's employment and hours of work increased after the crisis, whereas men experienced greater unemployment and shorter working hours. Hence, women were the provisioners of last resort in societies that lacked social safety nets. Based on this and other evidence, one may conclude that reductions in the volatility and instability of the global financial system would be in women's interest (Grown et al. 2000).

(De)Feminization in the North

Feminist research on developed countries has focused on the implications of trade growth in manufacturing for women's employment opportunities and working conditions. In her study of North-South trade, Adrian Wood (1991) did not find strong evidence of a fall in northern women's employment in manufacturing as a result of trade liberalization. David Kucera and William Milberg (2000), however, found in their study of industrialized countries (Australia, Canada, Japan, the Netherlands, and the United States) that the expansion of manufacturing trade with countries that were not members of the Organisation for Economic Co-operation and Development (OECD) between 1987 and 1995 reduced female manufacturing employment relatively more than male employment in the industrialized countries.

The gender impacts of globalization in Eastern Europe differ somewhat from the gender impacts found in developing countries. In the former, more privatized market economies have reduced women's labor force participation such that it has become closer to the rising

level of participation found in Western Europe. Moreover, Eastern European women have been relegated to temporary and low-paying jobs or forced to migrate to more affluent European countries, where they have found themselves sold into prostitution (see Standing 1999; Wichterich 2000).

The threat of outsourcing and capital relocation has put a downward pressure on wages in the high-income countries, particularly for unskilled labor. This pressure has contributed to the growing inequality in income distribution between highly skilled and less-skilled labor within and across countries (see Standing 1999). There has been a rapid growth of informal work in most of the major cities of the developed world. Scholars do not agree on the effects of the informal economy on women. One group stresses that informal employment empowers women by providing autonomy, control over production, and the ability to work and care for children. Others have found that informal employment often constrains women's options through isolation and intensifies the shift toward a greater workload for women (see Meyer 2001). According to Guy Standing (1999), employment characterized by low pay, insecurity, and flexibility, and associated with women, has grown faster across the world than employment traditionally associated with men, which typically offers higher pay, more stability, and union protections.

Feminization of Poverty

Poverty is linked to the inability of economies to generate a sufficient number of jobs. There is a gender dimension to poverty, as women are more likely to suffer the loss of their jobs than men and to become engaged in the informal sector to secure the livelihood of their families. Loss of jobs often leads to greater informalization of work or the shifting of jobs from the formal to the informal sector. Jobs in the informal sector do not offer regular wages, benefits, employment protections, and so on. Informal workers are therefore more subject to poverty than workers in the formal labor market. The withdrawal of states from their responsibilities for social services and the redistribution of wealth has also led to a transfer of social services and obligations to the informal sector, where women have taken them over, either individually, in the household, or collectively, in the community (Wichterich 2000). Women's increased engagement in paid work has therefore not led to a significant reduction in poor women's share of unpaid work. Globalization, involving greater reliance on markets, tends to devalue nonmarket goods and services and shift resources such as land from nontradable to tradable goods. This means that a significant proportion of women's contributions to the economy are relegated to a position of little or no importance, enhancing women's vulnerability to poverty (see Elson 1995).

The feminization of poverty refers not only to the increasing number of women among the poor, but also to the connection between women's social and economic subordination. An increase in women's employment does not necessarily lead to poverty reduction or increases in household welfare. Women in some parts of the world have almost total control over their own income (for example, in parts of West Africa). In other parts of the world, women hand over their income to men or to older women (parts of South Asia). Whether women or men have control over the household income has implications for the well-being of women and children, as studies have shown that men tend to prioritize items for personal use for investment, whereas women emphasize food and basic goods for households (Kanji and Menon-Sen 2001).

Studies of the debt crisis in developing countries found that women gained less when stabilization and structural adjustment programs (SAPs) were successfully implemented and lost more when these policies did not produce the desired results. Women were more likely to lose their jobs than men, and they were less likely to benefit from the privatization of business and granting of property rights. Moreover, women were overrepresented among the poor and disproportionately affected by cuts in health care and education expenditures, and they had to work harder and longer than before to provide for their families when real wages fell (see Aslanbeigui and Summerfield 2000). Austerity measures such as fees for health care, water supply, and education, as well as increased prices for food and medicine connected with SAPs supported by the International Monetary Fund (IMF) and the World Bank, also affect women more than men, as women are the ones usually responsible for maintaining consumption levels. Moreover, SAPs tend to substitute public services with home-provided services that often fall on the shoulders of women, such as health care, child care, education, and public utilities, including energy, transportation, and drinking water (Elson 1995).

The Trafficking in Women

The effects of economic globalization and structural adjustment are most severely felt by poor women, leading greater numbers of them to migrate in search of work. There is no internationally agreed definition of "trafficking." The term has been used to refer to a wide range of situations, usually involving the movement of persons through the threat or use of force, coercion, or violence for certain exploitative purposes, such as prostitution. The term has sometimes been used to refer to voluntary migration, but according to the UN Special Rapporteur on Violence Against Women, trafficking is never consensual. It is the nonconsensual, exploitative, or servile nature of the trafficking, together with elements involving the brokering of human beings, that distinguish trafficking from other forms of migration (United Nations 2000).

The most widely accepted definition is found in the United Nations Protocol to Prevent, Suppress and Punish Trafficking in Persons, Especially Women and Children, signed in December 2000 in Palermo, Italy (the

Palermo Protocol). It includes any recruitment, transportation, and receipt of persons, by means of threat, force, deception, or abduction for the purpose of exploitation, where exploitation includes prostitution or sexual exploitation, forced labor or services. The protocol defines the trafficking of children similarly, and "child" means any person under eighteen years of age.

The Scale of Trafficking

Even though definitions of trafficking vary considerably, there is a consensus that it is a rapidly increasing global problem that has to be addressed through a global response. At the same time, the scope of trafficking is difficult to estimate. The U.S. government has estimated that between 1 million and 2 million people are trafficked each year worldwide (IOM 2001), and the United Nations has estimated that 4 million persons are trafficked each year (United Nations 2000). Indeed, all these figures are uncertain. Reliable statistics are difficult to collect owing to the underground nature of trafficking.

Migrant Domestic Workers

Until recently, the issue of trafficking has revolved around trafficking in women for sexual exploitation. However, more and more attention is being paid to legal and illegal migrant domestic workers, that is, women from developing countries who have migrated voluntarily to the United States and Europe to earn a living. Some of these women have left their own families behind to do the mothering and caretaking work of the global economy in other countries. A special focus has been on the emergence of the parallel lives of migrant Filipina domestic workers, who experience exclusion from their host society as well as downward mobility from their professional jobs in the Philippines (Parrenas 2001). Furthermore, studies of migrant domestic workers in northern and southern Europe have revealed the racial and class aspects of paid domestic work (Anderson 2000). This phenomenon has been

conceptualized as "the global care chains of domestic labor," implying that women are tied to each other by a series of personal dependencies of paid and unpaid service. Women from developing countries, looking after families in Europe and North America, employ carers to tend to their own families, and these carers, in turn, have other women to care for their dependents, and so on (Adam 2002).

Sexual Exploitation

As the Palermo Protocol acknowledged, trafficking often involves sexual exploitation. The focus has been on those who end up in prostitution or as victims of trafficking, mostly women and children.

According to the International Organization for Migration (IOM), trafficking for sexual exploitation is a growing problem of increasing complexity (*Trafficking in Migrants* 2001). The U.S. State Department has estimated that 50,000 women are trafficked into the United States each year (Miko 2000). More than 225,000 victims of trafficking each year are taken from Southeast Asia, bound for various destinations, and more than 150,000 from South Asia; meanwhile, an estimated 100,000 each year come from the former Soviet Union, and 75,000 or more from Eastern Europe. More than 100,000 are estimated to come from Latin America and the Caribbean, and 50,000 more from Africa. Most of the victims are sent to Asia, the Middle East, Western Europe, and North America (ibid.).

Trafficking routes have traditionally been from South to North, although these routes continue to change. Originally, the focus was on the trafficking from Asia to Western Europe. Increasingly, however, the focus is on the trafficking of women from Russia and the newly independent states (NIS) of Eastern Europe to Western Europe, the United States, and Asia (GSN 1997; Weijers and Lap-Chew 1997).

Information on trafficking in Asia is more readily available than data on trafficking elsewhere. There are widely documented trafficking routes from South Asia and within the region, such as from Nepal to India; from Burma to Taiwan (HRW 1995); and from Bangladesh, Nepal, and Pakistan to India.

Thailand has also long been a central country of origin for the trafficking of women. More of the young rural population is now being trafficked to Thailand from neighboring countries such as Burma, Laos, and Vietnam (Biemann, 2002). Moreover, women and girls from the People's Democratic Republic of Korea are being trafficked to China for forced marriages to Chinese farmers and laborers (United Nations 2000), and trafficking occurs within China as well as into China from bordering countries.

Indeed, trafficking within the country borders of Asia is also on the rise. Extensive trafficking is reported within India itself, particularly to the cities of Calcutta and Bombay (United Nations 2000). India's New Economic Policy has resulted in increased poverty for women, forcing many of them into sex work and trafficking. Approximately 200 Indian women and girls go into prostitution each day, and the number of sex workers is increasing rapidly (see Upadhyay 2000). Now trafficking is also increasing within other Asian countries—especially from rural to urban areas (Weijers and Lap-Chew 1997).

There is a growing concern as well about the growth in trafficking within and from Africa. Although it has been difficult for researchers to gather any reliable information on the subject, the existence of trafficking networks in Africa is gradually being revealed. For example, some 25,000 Kenyans are reported to be living in inhumane conditions in the Middle East as a result of trafficking (United Nations 2000).

Eastern Europe is a growing area of concern as well. After the fall of the Berlin Wall, trafficking from Eastern Europe and the former Soviet Union increased dramatically. In a similar manner, the Balkan War contributed to an increase in trafficking in the area (United Nations 2000).

Trafficking is not limited to developing countries or newly liberalized socialist coun-

tries, however. The problem affects the developed countries as well, mainly because they are the major receiving countries. The United Nations, relying on data from the International Organization for Migration (United Nations 2000), has estimated that approximately 500,000 women are trafficked into Western Europe alone. Somewhere between 200,000 and 400,000 prostitutes are thought to be in Germany, the majority of whom are foreigners (De Stoop 1992). The Netherlands has the contradictory policy of having normalized prostitution with legislation but at the same time having a specific policy against trafficking (Raymond 1998).

Antitrafficking Movements

In some cases, a distinction is made between forced and free prostitution as regards the issue of trafficking (Doezema 2000). However, the dominant opinion is that trafficking includes sex work that is to a large extent forced, and that it is violence against women (Raymond 1998).

Over the past decade, international opinion against trafficking has resulted in national and transnational efforts and cooperation. Many international women's organizations and networks have been created to fight trafficking. The two most widely known are the Coalition Against Trafficking in Women (CATW) and the Global Alliance Against Traffic in Women (GAATW). The GAATW distinguishes between forced and free prostitution, which the CATW does not (ibid.).

Global Feminism

Global feminism is a multifaceted phenomenon that is not easy to demarcate. It can be said to consist of everything from world bodies acting on behalf of women to local grassroots movements, alliances, and networks. The aims, objectives, and methods of these organizations are as diverse as their institutional forms and ideological underpinnings. A common denominator, however, is a collective effort to improve the situation of women.

The United Nations, Nongovernmental Organizations, and Lobbies

Since the 1970s, a large number of grassroots women's organizations have sprung up to work on a local level as well as globally to improve women's social and economic conditions, raise consciousness, challenge patriarchal structures, and end sexual harassment and violence (Meyer 2001). These nongovernmental organizations (NGOs) have operated as a third force apart from government and private businesses. They have established international networks and instituted lobbying efforts around world bodies such as the United Nations. A number of tribunals have been held in and around UN conferences to break the silence surrounding human rights violations against women (Wichterich 2000).

In 1975, the United Nations announced the International Women's Year, and the World Conference of the International Women's Year was arranged that same year in Mexico City. The conference designated the decade 1976–1985 as the UN Decade for Women. The women's decade coincided with the Second United Nations Development Decade, which made the discourse of women's rights a main feature of the discussion on development. Within this framework, the status of women was linked to the development of their countries. Promoting women's rights and equality between men and women were seen as necessary for economic and social development, and women's issues became a central focus of many development documents and projects. This impelled the governments of the world to promote women's issues (Berkovitch 2000).

Three UN conferences were held in the wake of the first one. The next was the Copenhagen conference in 1980. The third conference was held in Nairobi in 1985, and its aim was to review and appraise the achievements of the UN decade for women. The latest conference was the Beijing conference in 1995, which adopted

the Beijing Declaration and Platform for Action.

Since the first UN conference on women in Mexico in 1975, networks have been created among women's groups. Although very extensive around the globe, the movement is decentralized and lacks an organizational umbrella. It was the NGO Forum at the Third International Women's Conference in Nairobi in 1985 that helped to crystallize the newly forming international women's movement. New alliances were established between South and North, along with a broadening of the issues from the earlier emphasis on women's reproductive rights and mortality in childbirth to include world political and economic questions (Wichterich 2000).

The spread of Information and Communication Technologies (ICT), as well as deepening links among national economies through the formation of regional trading groups and common markets, have created new opportunities for women's groups struggling for gender equality (Meyer 2001). These technologies have made it possible for women's groups from both the developed and developing world to share information, resources, and strategies in their efforts to promote gender equity (Wichterich 2000).

Perspectives on Women and Development

In the 1970s, an approach called Women in Development (WID) emerged that emphasized the need to integrate women into the development process. This approach was not only adopted by feminists, but also by organizations such as the United Nations, the World Bank, and the IMF. As a part of this approach, programs for women's integration into development were implemented in the area of technology transfers, credit facilities, technologies that would lighten women's workloads, and the like. WID programs soon came under criticism for an implicit acceptance of industrialization as beneficial and inevitable, and for not offering a framework to analyze power structures and women's subordination. In response to the shortcomings of the WID approach, a new approach, Women and Development (WAD), gained in popularity. As opposed to WID's emphasis on integrating women into the development process, the WAD approach highlighted the ways in which women have always participated in economic activity, although these roles are often invisible and ignored because of patriarchal structures. The WAD approach was criticized, in turn, for not producing programs that were significantly different from WID programs and for not challenging the fundamental social relations of gender (Meyer 2001).

In the 1980s, the WID/WAD approaches were replaced with the Gender and Development (GAD) position. GAD focuses on the social construction of gender relations and how women have systematically been assigned inferior and secondary roles. In order to understand and transform gender inequalities, GAD includes analysis on the micro-, meso- (community and social institutions), and macro-levels. Postmodern feminists have pointed out that mainstream development agencies have not fully accepted the implications of GAD to focus on empowering and encouraging women to challenge established structures, as they reject social transformation as a development strategy. From this postmodern perspective, GAD policy recommendations have been too similar to those made by WID and WAD proponents (Marchand and Parpart 1995).

Mainstreaming Gender Equality

A new approach in accordance with GAD is the concept of gender mainstreaming (GM), now generally adopted by government and policy-making bodies. GM is the (re)organization, improvement, development, and evaluation of policy processes so that a gender equality perspective is incorporated in all policies at all levels and at all stages by actors normally involved in policymaking (Council of Europe 1998). GM was introduced into the European Employment Strategy (EES) in 1999 in order to promote gender equality, and recently the World Bank has been mainstreaming gender into its

activities rather than targeting women as a group, moving from Women in Development (WID) to Gender and Development (GAD).

Feminist scholars have claimed that although mainstreaming gender issues is essential, new institutions focusing especially on women's and gender issues are needed. They hold that the mainstreamed gender approach appears safer and less political than a women's approach. Although the recognition of gender disparities is a potentially progressive step, both women and gender are necessary concepts in development analysis and policies (Aslanbeigui and Summerfield 2000). In an echo of the tension between WID and GAD, it is now debated whether GM is "integrationist" (that is, introduces a gender perspective into prevailing policy processes without challenging existing policy paradigms) or "revolutionary" (leading to a fundamental change in structures, processes, and outcomes; see, for example, Pollock and Hafner-Burton 2000; Verloo 2001).

Women's Organizations Today

Today there is neither a united women's political front nor a global unified feminism, but rather decentralized organizations connected through networking. Women in the South claim their own "indigenous" feminism independent of Western feminism. East European women have been inspired by Western feminism but find it too centered on the United States and Europe. New groupings, initiatives, projects, and nonstate organizations are continuously taking shape, developing along various paths of institutionalization and professionalization (Wichterich 2000).

There are many examples of the new international women's politics. Among these are Development Alternatives with Women for a New Era (DAWN), a South-South network of women academics and activists; Network Women in Development Europe (WIDE); and the Women's Environment and Development Organization (WEDO) (Moghadam 1996). Another well-known example is WEDO, an international network established 1990, with headquarters in New York. The acronym WEDO is itself a program: We Do. The Center for Global Leadership in New Jersey is another important networking organization and attempts to influence and gain a foothold in negotiating structures (Wichterich 2000).

Local grassroots movements are also numerous. Examples of these are the Self-Employed Women's Association and the Working Women's Forum in India, the Grassroots Women Workers Center in Taiwan, the National Commission on Working Women in Tunisia, the Caribbean Association for Feminist Research and Action (Meyer 2001), and the Society for the Promotion of Area Resource Centres (SPARC), operating in India and South Africa (Wichterich 2000).

Perspectives within the women's international movement today have an implicit tension between autonomy and adaptation as well as between transformation and participation. The women's movement has to balance the integration of women's issues into the negotiating framework of world political institutions with the vision of radical and global structural change. Thus, DAWN focuses on transformation, while WEDO stresses participation, especially in international institutions such as the United Nations, the World Bank, the IMF, and the World Trade Organization (WTO). WEDO has initiated extensive analyses of the IMF, the World Bank, the General Agreement on Tariffs and Trade (GATT), and the WTO (Meyer 2001).

Lilja Mósesdóttir
Porgedur Einarsdóttir

See Also Media and Entertainment; Culture and Globalization; Human Rights and Globalization; Social Policy

References

Adam, Barbara. 2002. "The Gendered Time Politics of Globalization: Of Shadowlands and Elusive Justice." *Feminist Review* 70: 3–29.

Anderson, Bridget. 2000. *Doing the Dirty Work? The Global Politics of Domestic Labour.* London: Zed.

Aslanbeigui, Nahid, and Gale Summerfield. 2000. "The Asian Crisis, Gender, and the International Financial Architecture." *Feminist Economics* 6, no. 3: 81–103.

Barrientos, Stephanie Ware. 1999. "Gender and Employment Relations in Global Horticulture: The Anomaly of Change in Chile and South Africa." Mimeo.

Benería, Lourdes, et al. 2000. "Globalization and Gender." *Feminist Economics* 6, no. 3:7–18.

Berik, Günseli. 2000. "Mature Export-Led Growth and Gender Wage Inequality in Taiwan." *Feminist Economics* 6, no. 3: 1–26.

Berkovitch, Nitza. 2000. "The Emergence and Transformation of the International Women's Movement." In F. J. Lechner and J. Boli, eds. *The Globalization Reader.* Oxford, UK: Blackwell.

Biemann, Ursula. 2002. "Remotely Sensed: A Topography of the Global Sex Trade." *Feminist Review* 70: 75–88.

Carr, Marily, Martha Alter Chen, and Jane Tate. 2000. "Globalization and Home-Based Workers." *Feminist Economics* 6, no. 3: 123–142.

Council of Europe. 1998. *Gender Mainstreaming: Conceptual Framework, Methodology and Presentation of Good Practices.* EG-S-MS (98) 2. Strasbourg: Council of Europe.

De Stoop, Chris. 1992. *They Are So Sweet, Sir: The Cruel World of Traffickers in Filipinas and Other Women.* Limitless Asia. English Trans.

Development Alternatives with Women for a New Era. 1995. "Securing Our Gains and Moving Forward to the 21st Century." Position paper for the Fourth World Conference on Women.

Doezema, Jo. 2000. "Loose Women or Lost Women? The Re-emergence of the Myth of 'White Slavery' in Contemporary Discourses of 'Trafficking in Women.'" *Gender Issues* 18, no. 1 (Winter): 23–50.

Elson, Diane. 1995. "Gender Awareness in Modeling Structural Adjustment." *World Development* 23, no. 11: 1851–1868.

Elson, Diane, ed. 2000. *Progress of the World's Women 2000.* New York: UN Development Fund for Women (UNIFEM).

Freeman, Carla. 2000. *High Tech and High Heels in the Global Economy: Women, Work, and Pink-Collar Identities in the Caribbean.* Durham, NC: Duke University Press.

Fussel, Elizabeth. 2000. "Making Labor Flexible: The Recomposition of Tijuana's Maquiladora Female Labor Force in Taiwan." *Feminist Economics* 6, no. 3: 1–26.

Global Survival Network. 1997. *Crime and Servitude.* Washington, DC: GSN.

Grown, Caren, Diane Elson, and Nilufer Cagatay. 2000. "Introduction." *World Development* 28, no. 7: 1145–1156.

Human Rights Watch. 1995. *Human Rights Watch Global Report on Women's Human Rights*. New York: Human Rights Watch.

Joekes, Susan, and Ann Weston. 1994. *Women and the New Trade Agenda*. New York: UN Development Fund for Women.

Kanji, Nazneen, and Kalyani Menon-Sen. 2001. "What Does the Feminisation of Labor Mean for Sustainable Livelihoods?" *IIED Opinion: World Summit on Sustainable Development*. August.

Kucera, David, and William Milberg. 2000. "Gender Segregation and Gender Bias in Manufacturing Trade Expansion: Revisiting the 'Wood Asymmetry.'" *World Development* 28, no. 7: 1191–1210.

Lim, Joseph. 2000. "The Effects of the East Asian Crisis on the Employment of Women and Men: The Philippine Case." In *World Development* 28, Issue 7, 1285–1306.

Lim, Linda. 1990. "Women's Work in Export Factories: The Politics of a Cause." In Eirene Tinker, ed., *Persistent Inequalities: Women and World Development*. New York: State University of New York Press.

Marchand, Marianne, and Jane Parpart. 1995. *Feminism/Postmodernism/Development*. London: Routledge.

Meyer, Lisa B. 2001. *International Trade Liberalization and Gender Relations in Labor Markets: A Cross-National Analysis, 1970–1998*. Ph.D. dissertation, Emory University.

Miko, Francis T. 2000. "Trafficking in Women and Children: The U.S. and International Response." Congressional Research Service Report 98–649 C. U.S. Department of State. May 10.

Moghadam, Valentine M. 1996. "Feminist Networks North and South: DAWN, WIDE and WLUML." *Journal of International Communication* 3: 111–112.

"New IOM Figures on the Global Scale of Trafficking." 2001. *Trafficking in Migrants Quarterly Bulletin*, International Organisation for Migration, no. 23, April.

Parrenas, Rhacel Salazar, ed. 2001. *Servants of Globalization: Women, Migration and Domestic Work*. Stanford, CA: Stanford University Press.

Pollock, Mark A., and Emilie Hafner-Burton. 2000. "Mainstreaming Gender in the European Union." *Journal of European Public Policy* 7, no. 3: 432–456.

Raymond, Janice G. 1998. "Prostitution as Violence against Women: NGO Stonewalling in Beijing and Elsewhere." *Women's Studies International Forum* 21, no. 1: 1–9.

Seguino, Stephanie. 2000. "Accounting for Gender in Asian Economic Growth in Taiwan." *Feminist Economics* 6, no. 3: 1–26.

Standing, Guy. 1999. "Global Feminization through Flexible Labor: A Theme Revisited." *World Development* 27, no. 3: 583–602.

Staverne, Irene van. 2000. "Global Finance and Gender," http://www.eurosur.org/wide/Globalisation/Global%20Finance.htm (cited April 15, 2002).

Trafficking in Migrants Quarterly Bulletin. 2001. International Organisation for Migration. Special Issue, no. 23 (April).

The United Nations Protocol to Prevent, Suppress and Punish Trafficking in Persons, Especially Women and Children. 2000. Supplement to the United Nations Convention against Transnational Organized Crime, Palermo, Italy, December 12–15.

Upadhyay, Ushma D. 2000. "India's New Economic Policy of 1991 and Its Impact on Women's Poverty and AIDS." *Feminist Economics* 6, no. 3: 105–122.

Verloo, Mieke. 2001. *Another Velvet Revolution? Gender Mainstreaming and the Politics of Implementation*. IWM Working Paper No. 5/2001. Vienna: Institute for Human Sciences.

Weijers, M., and L. Lap-Chew. 1997. "Trafficking in Women: Forced Labour and Slavery-like Practices in Marriage, Domestic Labor and Prostitution." In *Marriage, Domestic Labour and Prostitution*. Utrecht and Bangkok: Foundation Against Trafficking in Women (STV)/Global Alliance Against Trafficking in Women (GAATW).

Wichterich, Christa. 2000. *The Globalized Women: Reports from a Future of Inequality*. London: Zed.

Wood, Adrian. 1991. "North-South Trade and Female Labor in Manufacturing: An Asymmetry." *Journal of Development Studies* 27, no. 2: 168–118.

Global Climate Change

Global climate change generally refers to long-term fluctuations in average global weather patterns. Some of these fluctuations, especially those that seem to be recent developments, are thought to be caused by human activities. Global climate change has been a particularly intractable problem in both domestic and international forums for several reasons. First, there is a great deal of conflicting scientific evidence about the causes, effects, and even existence of global warming. Some, but not all, of this disagreement is due to the fact that global climate trends can only be fully understood in the context of very long-term climate patterns, reaching back much further than comparable data have been collected.

As a result, policy debates have been somewhat muddled, with politicians, bureaucrats, activists, and corporate entities citing whatever evidence best suits their political and economic ends. Like all environmental problems, global climate change, if it is to be addressed effectively at all, will by definition require a truly transnational approach. It will also require states to weigh the potential environmental costs of pursuing their own particularistic economic gain and maintaining their commitment to an abstract concept of state sovereignty.

The Scientific Evidence and Debates

The History of the Concept of the Greenhouse

The first scientist to posit the reasons for the earth's temperature to remain warm despite the earth's vast distance from the sun was Jean-Baptiste Joseph Fourier. A scholar of heat and its diffusion, he posited a speculative "bell jar" model in 1827. According to this model, rather than bouncing off the surface of the earth, at least some of the sun's heat that reached the earth was trapped by clouds and other components of the atmosphere. Since this work was more theoretical than some of Fourier's earlier publications, it received less attention at the time than did his more concrete contributions to thermodynamic theory (Christianson 1999, 11–12). John Tyndall in England in about 1860 recognized the role of carbon dioxide and water vapor in absorbing radiation and posited that past ice ages might have been caused by a decrease of one or both of these gases in the air (Houghton 1997, 12). With the advent of the Industrial Revolution, the work of Fourier and Tyndall attracted renewed interest.

Scientists now know that these models are essentially accurate. Fourier and Tyndall had both hit upon key factors that function to keep the earth's climate habitable—that is, on average, about 20° Celsius higher than it would otherwise be (ibid., 18). Water vapor, carbon dioxide, and other naturally occurring gases in the earth's atmosphere function as a sort of a blanket, trapping a proportion of solar heat rather than allowing it to bounce back into space. This effect is potentially rather unstable, however, because the more heat is trapped, the greater the amount of water vapor that stays trapped in the atmosphere, and this water vapor, in turn, captures even more solar radiation (ibid., 8).

Other self-perpetuating cycles occur in climate change as well. For instance, some parts of the earth's surface, such as snow and ice, reflect more heat back into space than others. But it is those most reflective parts that are the ones most quickly disappearing in recent decades as a result of warmer temperatures. For instance, the "perennial sea ice," those areas near the poles that never thaw, have shrunk up to 10 percent in each of the past two decades, according to National Aeronautics and Space Administration (NASA) researcher Josefino Comiso, who was cited in an October 24, 2003, Associated Press (AP) article. It has also been recently posited that even the snow and ice that is left is less reflective than it otherwise would be owing to soot from diesel engines and other sources, according to a NASA study cited in a December 23, 2003, AP article.

Certain other kinds of naturally occurring emissions affect the greenhouse functions of the earth's atmosphere as well, such as volcanic ash. For instance, when Mt. Pinutubo in the Philippines erupted in the early 1990s, enough ash accumulated in the upper regions of the atmosphere to cut solar radiation reaching the earth's surface by an average of 2 percent, suppressing average global temperatures by a quarter of a degree Celsius for the next two years. This kind of ash usually hangs in the upper regions of the atmosphere for up to a decade, after which it falls to lower layers and is quickly washed out by rain (Houghton 1997, 6).

A related problem is the emission of gases from manmade sources that deplete the ozone layer. Ozone is a naturally occurring form of oxygen that filters out a substantial amount of the sun's ultraviolet (UV) rays. Ironically, the ozone layer also contributes (naturally) to the greenhouse effect, so as it is repaired, it may exacerbate the greenhouse effect (Manchester Metropolitan University).

The Role of the Seas in Moderating Climate
Some areas of the planet are kept much warmer than they would otherwise be due to the influence of a system of ocean currents

called the North Atlantic Meridional Overturning Circulation (NAMOC), of which the Gulf Stream is the best known. The Gulf Stream brings warm water from the Caribbean up to the seas surrounding Britain and northern Europe. This keeps these areas on average about 5° Celsius warmer than comparable latitudes in Greenland and Canada, greatly affecting agricultural productivity in the region, among other things, according to a November 12, 2003, article in *The Guardian*. This "conveyer belt" of warm water is kept going, in part, by the fact that it cools as it moves northward; by the time it reaches the Arctic, much of it has sunk back down and started to head south again (like cold air, cold water sinks).

But global warming is nevertheless melting the polar ice packs and thus causing large amounts of cold, fresh water to be dumped into the North Atlantic. An August 13, 2003, AP article cited Swedish climatologist Ola Johannessen, who warned that the entirety of the polar ice caps could melt over the next century. Since scientists first started taking reliable measurements of the Arctic ice cap, it has shrunk by about a million square kilometers, and it now extends over an area of only 6 million square kilometers in the summertime. According to Bogi Hansen at the Faroese fisheries laboratory, cited in a November 13, 2003, article in *The Guardian*, this change could disrupt, slow down, or possibly even *stop* the ocean conveyer belt. Some scientists have estimated that the conveyor belt may have slowed by up to 20 percent over the past fifty years. This effect could lead to much colder temperatures in Europe.

In addition, the higher the temperature of the surface of the ocean, the more water vapor in the air, so rising average ocean surface temperatures could increase the greenhouse effect even further (Houghton 1997, 8).

The Extent of Temperature Change
Short-term trends indicate that global temperatures are indeed rising. They have steadily increased over the course of the past three

decades (Christianson 1999, ix), and based on current trends, scientists have predicted that the average global temperature will rise 2.5° Celsius over the course of the next century, probably a faster rate than at any time in the past 10,000 years. Although this sounds like a very small amount, it may be put into perspective by the fact that the average global temperature difference between ice age and non–ice age periods is estimated to be only 6° Celsius (Houghton 1997, 8).

How much of this change in average temperatures is due to human activity? This is a hotly debated question. Scientists know that the kinds of fluctuations that ice ages represent have occurred over and over again in the course of the earth's history. Thus, there is only limited evidence on how unusual current trends actually are. This evidence includes ice cores, tree rings, and sedimentary deposit patterns, and though such evidence does seem to suggest that current warming patterns are unusual, it has not been enough to satisfy all researchers in the field.

The Role of Manmade Emissions

The Swedish chemist Svante August Arrhenius warned in 1896 that increasing amounts of carbon dioxide in the atmosphere could increase the average global temperature by 5 to 6 percent. In the 1940s, Englishman John Callendar was able to more precisely estimate the amount of this increase due to the burning of fossil fuels (Houghton 1997, 12). Current research indicates an increase of about 30 percent in carbon dioxide since the start of the Industrial Revolution, and this percentage may double again in the next century (ibid., 18). The first scientists to voice serious concern about the climate change that might result from increased carbon dioxide in the atmosphere were Roger Ravelle and Hans Suess of the Scripps Institute, in 1957. The first consistent measurements of greenhouse gases in the atmosphere date to this period (ibid.,12).

There are certain greenhouse effect–enhancing gases whose occurrence in the atmosphere is significantly affected by human activity. The most important of these are carbon dioxide, methane, nitrous oxide, and chlorofluorocarbons (CFCs). Concentrations of the first three are easiest to identify; carbon dioxide contributes about 70 percent of the enhanced greenhouse effect from this group, methane 24 percent, and nitrous oxide 6 percent (ibid., 22). Carbon dioxide, though a naturally occurring gas, has come to represent a greater and greater proportion of the gases in the atmosphere as a result of certain kinds of industrial processes and because of increasing deforestation. (Green plants remove carbon dioxide from the air and put oxygen into the air). Methane gases are primarily released by cattle, and as global (especially northern) demand for beef has continued to increase, so have methane emissions. Finally, CFCs, originally introduced as a refrigerant (Christianson 1999, xii), became popular in the mid–twentieth century as propellants for aerosols of all kinds, and they also served as an important component of Styrofoam.

Industrialization and the burning of fossil fuels have borne the brunt of blame for atmospheric changes that enhance the greenhouse effect. But new evidence seems to suggest that humans have been altering the composition of the atmosphere, and thus global climate trends, for at least 8,000 years. It was at about that time that the advent of large-scale rice farming and raising of livestock in Asia led to deforestation, and therefore to an increase in carbon dioxide and methane in the atmosphere, according to a paper presented at a meeting of the American Geophysical Union in San Francisco (cited in a December, 10, 2003, article in *Nature*).

The Effects of Climate Change

Estimations of the effects of global warming, should it persist, range from the cataclysmic to the benificent.

Rising Sea Levels. The earliest estimates of the predicted rise in sea levels due to the melting of the polar ice caps topped 10 feet, meaning that many of the most populated parts of the planet would become largely uninhabitable. Other evidence points to a rise of only a few inches (Michaels and Balling 2000, 3). Even this amount, however, could threaten many marshy and brackish areas, which serve many purposes for coastal regions. They are refuges and/or nurseries for many species, and they restrict the flow of tides during floods. They also act as natural filters for drinking water. Overdevelopment along coastlines (such as that in the New York City area's Jamaica Bay) exacerbates these problems, according to a January 1, 2004, article in the *New York Post*.

Rising Rates of Extinction. The World Wildlife Fund reported that a million species may be at risk in coming decades due to global climate change, according to a press release carried January 8, 2004, by U.S. Newswire. Even short of extinction, just depletion of some species could have severe effects. For instance, an article in *The Guardian* on August 13, 2003, reported that warmer air and water temperatures in huge Lake Tanganyika in Africa have led to less mixing of surface-level and deeper water. This means that fewer nutrients from the bottom get to the surface, leading to lower concentrations of the algae that feed important fish populations. These populations are key components of the food supply for several developing nations on the continent.

More Violent Weather. Warmer water temperatures could also fuel greater numbers of typhoons and other kinds of storms (Houghton 1997, 3). In addition, some areas, such as the Great Lakes region of the United States, could experience increases in snowfall. This effect would occur as overall air temperatures rose, leading to an increase in the differential between air temperatures and water temperatures. It is this differential that causes lake-effect snow. If more vehicles were deployed to deal with the snow, these additional vehicles would emit still more fossil-fuel exhaust, as pointed out in a November 5, 2003, Reuters article.

Global Cooling? Because of the role of ocean currents such as the Gulf Stream in regulating global temperatures, if currents are disrupted some areas could experience severe global *cooling*, as suggested in a November 12, 2003, article in *The Guardian*. The places most likely for this to happen would be those currently most warmed by heated Caribbean air in the Gulf Stream, such as Britain and Western Europe.

Melting of Polar Icecaps. Though this phenomenon could have negative effects on ocean currents, as discussed above, Ola Johannessen, the Swedish climatologist cited in the August 13, 2003, AP article, pointed out that there could also be positive effects. New, more efficient northern shipping routes would open up, for example, and the additional water would help to absorb the excess carbon dioxide that had led to warming and melting in the first place.

Greening of the Planet. Other scientists point to the fact that the temperature change would mostly affect winter in the coldest parts of the inhabited world, namely Siberia and northwestern North America. This could lead to an increase in the growing season, suggesting to these optimists that a moderate rise in average global temperatures could be beneficial for most inhabitants and actually increase the carrying capacity of the planet (Michaels and Balling 2000, 2–4).

The Political Realm

Action Internationally

The most important international action with regard to investigating evidence of global warming, the role of humans therein, and the best possible ways to address it have come in the form of the establishment of the International Panel on Climate Change, an organization commissioned by the UN Environmental Programme and the World Meteorological Organization to research the issue. Three UN conferences on the environment have also addressed global warming issues, including the Montreal Summit on Substances that Deplete the Ozone Layer in 1987, the UN Conference on Environment and Development (Rio Summit) in 1992, and the Kyoto Summit in 1997. All of these summits led to protocols that called for reductions in greenhouse gases by at least some members of the international community.

In the Montreal Protocol, which was based on the 1985 Vienna Convention (establishing guidelines for nations to conduct research into the ozone layer and ozone-depleting substances), developed nations agreed to cut their emissions of CFCs and other ozone-depleting substances entirely by 2000 (2005 for one subcategory, methyl chloroform). The protocol was signed by twenty-four countries and the European Economic Community (EEC). Two later amendments, the London Amendment and the Copenhagen Amendment (and additional minor amendments) substantially clarified and refined the protocol's objectives. These goals have largely been met.

With the United Nations Framework Convention on Climate Change (UNFCCC) (opened for signature at the 1992 Rio Summit and therefore known as the Rio Protocol), signatories agreed to "stabilize greenhouse gas concentrations in the atmosphere at a level that [prevents] dangerous anthropogenic interference in the climate system." The Rio Protocol was signed by President George H. W. Bush and ratified by the U.S. Senate, and it went into effect on March 21, 1994, following ratification by the requisite forty-nine other countries (UNFCCC 2003).

At the Kyoto conference, developed nations (known officially in the UNFCCC as Annex I nations, those that have historically contributed the most to greenhouse gas emissions and therefore have more stringent reduction goals and more detailed reporting requirements) agreed to either cut or limit their increases of greenhouse gas emissions (depending on the country). These commitments were codified in the Kyoto Protocol to the UNFCCC. For example, the United States agreed to cut its emissions by 7 percent (from 1990 levels) by 2012, and the European Union pledged to cut

emissions by 8 percent. Globally, these cuts would add up to a total reduction of at least 5 percent from 1995 levels (UNFCCC 2003).

These limits cover the six main kinds of greenhouse gases that have been demonstrated to be the greatest contributors to the greenhouse effect, including carbon dioxide, methane, nitrous oxide, hydrofluorocarbons, perfluorocarbons, and sulfur hexafluoride. Besides cutting emissions actually produced, nations could lower total emissions by engaging in activities that remove greenhouse gases from the atmosphere, such as reforestation. These kinds of activities provide states with credits (called "removal units") that they can either apply to their own targets or sell to other states (UNFCCC 2003).

Such limits are legally binding on Annex I developed nations that have ratified the protocol, meaning that failing to meet them could draw UN sanctions. Most developing nations are exempt from any limits. Those exempt include large, rapidly industrializing nations such as India and Mexico. These exemptions have led to a great deal of criticism by some parties in the United States and other developed nations.

The Kyoto Protocol was signed by President Bill Clinton but has yet to be ratified by the U.S. Senate, largely because of perceived unfairness due to the differential restrictions, and also because of projected domestic costs of limiting emissions. Some argue these costs would make the U.S. economy less competitive vis-à-vis the economies of those countries on whom no restrictions were placed (see, for instance, Michaels and Balling 2000).

The UNFCCC has been updated through a series of annual meetings (Conferences of Parties, or COPs) that have served as vehicles for the 186 signatory states to determine strategies for working toward the goals outlined in the protocols. The tenth and most recent of these meetings took place in December 2004 in Buenos Aires, Argentina. Signatories must report progress toward their goals on an annual basis.

International Debates

There have been three main barriers to progress on the goals of the UNFCCC. One is the inconclusiveness of scientific evidence. Another is the perceived unfairness of the differential restrictions by some developed states. A third barrier is the lack of enforcement mechanisms built into the UNFCCC itself.

In response to the first two barriers, proponents of more proactive approaches argue that if progress is too long delayed, the problem will have expanded beyond the realm of human control (Philander 1998, 10).

U.S. Action

Although the United States did ratify the Montreal and Rio protocols, it has yet to ratify the Kyoto Protocol, largely because of the kinds of objections expressed by other industrialized nations. Under the George W. Bush administration and a Republican-dominated Congress, it seems unlikely the Kyoto Protocol will be ratified any time in the foreseeable future.

Bethany A. Barratt

See Also Energy and Utilities; Environmental Impacts of Globalization; Natural Resources; Sustainable Development

References

Christianson, Gale E. 1999. *Greenhouse: The 200 Year Story of Global Warming.* New York: Walker.

Houghton, John. 1997. *Global Warming: The Complete Briefing.* 2d ed. Cambridge: Cambridge University Press.

Manchester Metropolitan University, Department of Computing and Mathematics. "Global Climate," http://www.doc.mmu.ac.uk/aric/eae/Ozone_Depletion/Older/Global_Climate.html (cited February 8, 2003).

Mason, Betsy. "Man Has Been Changing Climate for 8,000 Years," http://www.nature.com/nsu/031208/031208-7.html (cited February 9, 2003).

Michaels, Patrick J., and Robert C. Balling, Jr. 2000. *The Satanic Gases: Clearing the Air about Global Warming.* Washington, DC: Cato Institute.

National Research Council. 2002. *Abrupt Climate Change.* Washington, DC: National Academy Press.

Philander, S. George. 1998. *Is the Temperature Rising? The Uncertain Science of Global Warming.* Princeton, NJ: Princeton University Press.

United Nations. "United Nations Framework Convention on Climate Change," http://unfccc.int (cited February 9, 2003).

Human Rights and Globalization

The term "human rights" constitutes a claim that there exist basic rights enjoyed by individual human beings based solely on the fact of their humanity and not on their citizenship in a particular nation-state. The universal nature of this claim generates two forces for globalization. First, the claim has resulted in the creation of positive laws and accompanying institutions that challenge traditional international relations. Second, the claim engenders a human rights culture that acts as a source of moral pressure on global political and economic relations.

Origins of the Modern Human Rights Movement

World War II was the catalyst for the modern human rights movement. The devastation of the war encouraged a successful second attempt by nations of the world to forge global mechanisms for peace and security. The creation of the League of Nations in 1919 was the first attempt to construct a political architecture of conflict resolution, but it failed for want of widespread participation and because of the animosities of post–World War I politics. As the outcome of World War II grew clearer, the Allies, especially Great Britain, the Soviet Union, and the United States, met in 1944 to set the groundwork for institutions that would eliminate sources of global insecurity responsible for war. It was within these institutions that core struggles for human rights would occur.

At a conference at Bretton Woods, New Hampshire, in 1944, the Allies addressed the causes of international economic conflict. To promote currency stability and provide development assistance to poorer nations, new financial organizations were envisioned, including the International Bank for Reconstruction and Development (the World Bank), the International Monetary Fund (IMF), and an International Trade Organization that ultimately failed to emerge. Later, at Dumbarton Oaks in Washington, D.C., plans were furthered to enable the United Nations to take over where the League of Nations had left off as a vehicle to mediate political conflicts among states.

In 1945, the horrific specter of the Holocaust mobilized forces that would promote international recognition that fundamental human rights transcend the sovereignty of the nation-state. The shocking picture of human barbarism that emerged upon the opening of the Nazi concentration camps engendered worldwide revulsion and strengthened the resolve that the principle of sovereignty not be allowed to provide cover for a state to abuse its own citizens with impunity. When the UN General Assembly subsequently endorsed the prosecution of Nazi and Japanese war criminals in the Nuremberg and Tokyo trials (1945–1946), it defined for itself a new mandate—the protection of individuals throughout the world from "crimes against humanity." In 1945, persistent lobbying by several nations and international organizations led to the inclusion of "human rights" in the UN Charter and the creation of a special Human Rights Commission, chaired by Eleanor Roosevelt, widow of the wartime president. The commission was charged with developing the basic documents of the proposed new human rights regime.

Creation of a
Human Rights Framework

The Universal Declaration of Human Rights (UDHR) was crafted over a period of nearly two years and adopted by the UN General Assembly on December 10, 1948. In its preamble, it succinctly captured a broad international consensus, proclaiming that "recognition of the inherent dignity and of the equal and inalienable rights of the members of the human family is the foundation of freedom, justice and peace in the world."

The UDHR's thirty articles include statements about the right to life, civil and political rights, and economic and social rights. A declaration of standards, the UDHR would become the springboard for subsequent conventions that spell out binding legal obligations of states to respect specific rights of their citizens. The most important of these treaties include the International Covenant on Civil and Political Rights (ICCPR); the International Covenant on Economic, Social, and Cultural Rights (ICESCR); the Convention on the Prevention and Punishment of the Crime of Genocide (CPPCG); the International Convention on the Elimination of All Forms of Racial Discrimination (CERD); the Convention on the Elimination of All Forms of Discrimination Against Women (CEDAW); and the Convention on the Rights of the Child (CRC).

The total body of rights has been described in terms of three "generations": (1) those rights relating the individual to the state, so-called "civil and political rights"; (2) those rights providing for the economic and social well-being of the individual; and (3) so-called "solidarity" rights that provide for the individual's ability to participate in general human progress. The first has been associated with the liberal tradition emanating from the West in the seventeenth and eighteenth centuries; the second with the widespread social democracy and labor rights movements of the nineteenth and twentieth centuries; and the third with the rise of globalization in the late twentieth century.

This body of human rights norms, conventions, and laws has been realized in overlapping stages. The first stage was marked by an initial "articulation of standards" that occurred between the signing of the UDHR and the adoption of the ICCPR and the ICESCR in 1966. This stage was characterized by little actual reporting of violations and virtually no attempt at enforcement. The second stage was preoccupied with "reporting of violations" and was characterized by the rise of human rights nongovernmental agencies such as Amnesty International (founded in 1961; Nobel Peace Prize recipient in 1977). Reporting was further encouraged by the 1975 Helsinki Accords among thirty-five major states, including the principal Cold War nations, and by the Country Reports on Human Rights Practices produced by the U.S. Department of State beginning in 1977. The third stage has increasingly focused on "enforcement." It developed from the imposition of UN embargoes against the former white-dominated English colony of Rhodesia in 1966 and against South Africa in 1977 and continued to assume an important role with the UN's ad-hoc tribunals in the former Yugoslavia and in Rwanda in the 1990s. The creation of the International Criminal Court (ICC) in 2002 augurs new enforcement capabilities in line with this third stage of human rights activity.

The human rights movement is now a global undertaking that involves the United Nations, individual countries, and thousands of nongovernmental organizations (NGOs) that monitor, report, lobby, and at times enforce more than 100 human rights treaties, conventions, proclamations, and declarations.

Laws and Institutions

Though universal human rights as an idea has existed in a variety of forms since ancient times and was propelled forward by both the eighteenth-century French Revolution and the twentieth-century crisis of two world wars, the formal and legal institutions that implement human rights law derive primarily from the United Nations and related institutions in the post–World War II era. Because the United Nations acts through concurrence of its member states, national sovereignty poses the greatest hurdle to the emerging body of human rights law that claims universal jurisdiction. Strong governments, particularly that of the United States, initially opposed the idea that the UDHR should immediately produce enforceable rights. Over time, UN covenants and conventions, regional and multilateral treaties, and domestic institutions and procedures have increased enforcement capacity as states bind themselves to uphold particular provisions of the UDHR or elaborate upon them. The European Union, for example, has made the realization of human rights a condition of membership.

Human rights law ultimately rests on a series of more than thirty multilateral treaties that are legally binding on those countries that have signed and ratified them according to their own domestic procedures of treaty ratification. The most well known of these treaties are the UDHR, the ICCPR, and the ICESCR; but the Convention on the Prevention and Punishment of the Crime of Genocide (1951), the Convention against Torture and Other Cruel, Inhuman or Degrading Treatment or Punishment (1987), the Convention on the Rights of the Child (1990), the Convention on the Elimination of All Forms of Discrimination against Women (1981), and the International Convention on the Elimination of All Forms of Racial Discrimination (1969) also now play a prominent role in international law.

There exists also a large body of so-called "soft law"—declarations, standards, principles, and norms—that has been articulated and endorsed by a majority of nations and is therefore available to legal proceedings. Although soft law is regarded more as a cultural phenomenon than a strictly legal one, nonetheless judges may—as in U.S. negligence law—discern standards by which appropriate practice may be judged using recognized authorities. Within human rights legal practice, standards espoused by the UDHR have gained widespread acceptance among the nations of the world, which has led to their limited acceptance under the rubric of "customary law." Soft law, however, does not normally prevail against competing positive law.

The major institutions that attempt to implement human rights law can be divided geographically into three arenas: international, regional, and domestic. The United Nations itself is the major international institution accepting responsibility for promoting and ensuring human rights, as its charter mandates. There are four bodies within the UN that carry out this responsibility: the Security Council, composed of five permanent and ten rotating members; the General Assembly; the special and thematic committees and commissions with particular jurisdictions; and the permanent International Criminal Court (playing a role similar to that formerly carried out by the ad-hoc tribunals).

The Security Council has the authority to intervene, economically or militarily, in conflicts where, in addition to open hostilities, widespread human rights abuses have occurred or threaten to occur. It has done so in Korea, the Congo, Southern Rhodesia, South Africa, Haiti, Somalia, Iraq, Liberia, Libya, Angola, and the former Yugoslavia. The General Assembly, led by the secretary general of the United Nations, has used its public platform to make and publicize resolutions and declarations that expose human rights abuses throughout the world.

Enforcement Bodies

The UN Commission on Human Rights was established in 1946 with the founding charter of the Economic and Social Council. It oversaw the creation of the UDHR, and its members now meet yearly to hear complaints about human rights abuses and to recommend actions. In 1993, the UN created the related Office of the High Commissioner for Human Rights with overall responsibility for promoting human rights inside and outside of the UN. The Human Rights Committee is a body of eighteen human rights experts that investigates cases of abuse and recommends actions under the jurisdiction of the Covenant on Civil and Political Rights. Special committees are established from time to time—for example, on apartheid in South Africa or the Israeli-Palestinian conflict—to address the particular issues raised by specific conflicts or patterns of abuse.

In response to the atrocities that occurred in Bosnia-Herzegovina as a result of the breakup of the former Yugoslavia, including genocide, "ethnic cleansing," and systematic rape, in 1994 the UN Security Council created the International Criminal Tribunal for the former Yugoslavia (ICTY) and the Criminal Tribunal for Rwanda (CTR). Based on the model of the Nuremburg and Tokyo tribunals, these ad-hoc tribunals led to suggestions for additional courts in the aftermath of hostilities in Cambodia, Sierra Leone, and Iraq. The most dramatic development in the implementation of human rights law has been the creation in 2002 of the International Criminal Court. The court was established by the Rome Statute in 1998 and came into force in 2002 after the requisite sixty countries had ratified the treaty. Its jurisdiction is "universal," that is, it operates across national boundaries, a concept first adopted in the UN Charter and affirmed in the four Geneva conventions of 1949. The ICC will prosecute major violations—genocide, crimes against humanity, and war crimes—committed by individuals in or from countries signatory to the treaty. The ICC has not been ratified by major powers such as the United States, China, or Russia, however, which have attempted to protect themselves from the court's reach. For example, in 2002, the United States asked for and received a twelve-

month postponement from ICC prosecutions as its price for continued assistance in UN peacekeeping missions.

Regional bodies created by multilateral treaties also implement international human rights law. These include the African Union (formerly the Organization of African Unity), the Organization of American States, and the European Union. The latter two have permanent courts devoted to hearing human rights cases—the Inter-American Court of Human Rights and the European Court of Human Rights, respectively.

At the same time that international and regional courts try cases of human rights abuse, domestic courts and institutions at times use international human rights law in their proceedings. For example, the United States is required by its domestic law to report the human rights conditions of countries with which it has economic relations and to use those reports in determining whether the economic relations should continue or be suspended. In its post-apartheid constitution, South Africa has built human rights into its national legal system.

Tensions in Human Rights Implementation

The increasing popularity of the claim that rights are universal makes them a normative force with a global reach. This role within the larger process of globalization creates three major tensions. Like other forms of globalization, human rights must contend with the power of the nation-state in world relations. To the extent that the human rights movement permits or encourages governments to interpret and enforce human rights on their own, its universality is compromised and its impact as a global force is limited. A second key tension is posed by the existence of other global institutions whose purposes may conflict with human rights. This tension is felt most acutely in attempts to promote and enforce economic and development rights at odds with actions taken by global economic and financial institutions such as the IMF and the World Trade Organization (WTO). The charters of such organizations direct them to pursue economic goals and do not explicitly authorize them to consider human rights. A third tension is internal to the human rights discourse. Because human rights constitute broad claims that involve divergent fields such as politics, economics, culture, and science, the exercise of a right specific to one field may come at the expense of another right specific to a different field. When implementation of a right is contingent upon the enforcement of other rights, the claim of universality is harder to make.

The value of the human rights movement does not arise solely from its claim to universality, however, and consequently globalization is not the sole measure of its success. However, universality is a building block by which human rights achieve moral authority. How the tensions inherent in these claims are resolved will be central to the nature and progress of globalization.

Universality and the Nation-State

The most unmistakable challenge to human rights, and indeed to globalization itself, is the assertion of sovereignty by nation-states. In natural law theory, upon which human rights are often predicated, the state provides the foundation of social order. To be legitimate, this order hinges upon a social compact in which a people surrenders some rights over their own persons and property to secure that order. The surrender of rights is limited, however, and governments are assumed to protect the individual by ensuring that the rights not surrendered are free from government usurpation or violation by others. The nation-state exercises a unique place in human rights theory because its police powers make it both the guarantor of individual rights and a potential source of their abuse.

If a nation's internal agencies fail to protect a people's rights, abuses can only be checked through the exercise of a countervailing force. One such force involves insurrections by an abused populace against their government. Alternatively, an oppressed people may call for external assistance. However, the sovereignty of the nation-state to do as it wishes inside its borders has, until recently, largely provided the operating principle of international relations. Tensions within international relations typically produce no shortage of states ready to proclaim that their enemies violate the rights of their citizens, yet actions taken on behalf of another nation's inhabitants possess dubious legitimacy, subject as they are to interpretations of self-interest or opportunism. Within the political and legal processes of globalization, the crowning achievement for human rights has been the surrender, however limited, of state sovereignty to transnational bodies empowered to enforce human rights against the will of ruling governments.

That achievement is not without its own concerns. Members within global enforcement bodies typically represent the nation-states and may be expected to possess a bias toward the principle of sovereignty. Forcible interventions remain contingent upon multinational coalitions and will not be settled merely by application of a uniform standard. For example, UN Security Council intervention can be vetoed by any of the five permanent members, suggesting that enforcement of universal human rights indirectly depends ultimately upon the will of strong nation-states. Furthermore, the major nation-state powers continue to exercise disproportionate influence by virtue of size, military capacity, or contributions to organizational budgets. The use of force, whether through global institutions, through multilateral agreement, or by unilateral action, is conditioned by a "realist" global politics by which nations assess interventions in terms of their own costs and benefits. During the 1990s, in the cause of human rights, the United Nations, the North Atlantic Treaty Organization (NATO), and the United States all intervened to halt abuses of sovereign power by Iraq against Kuwait or against domestic abuses of human rights in Haiti, Somalia, and Bosnia. The choice and timing of interventions reflects political realities faced by member states who are unwilling or unable to enforce all gross violations of human rights, making questionable the degree to which enforcement of human rights is either neutral or universal. For example, in 1994 the UN removed itself from Rwanda at the very moment when a genocide that may have claimed as many as 800,000 lives was beginning.

To secure human rights objectives, one alternative to military power is the use of economic sanctions. However, not only is the power to coerce recalcitrant governments unreliable, but the results of economic sanctions have been mixed, particularly because it is difficult to coordinate actions among nations having diverse interests. Coalitions are stressed by the costs that loss of trade and investment opportunities imposes upon those who boycott and by the rewards to competitors who do not. The twelve-year-long economic blockade against Iraq is indicative of all these problems. The loss of food and medicine, either directly from the boycott or indirectly through the corruption of the ruling Iraqi elite, made Iraqi citizens the victims, while sanctioning states were threatened with a loss of oil supplies and other investment opportunities. A food-for-oil provision implemented in 1996 allowed some countries to seize economic advantages that otherwise would not have been present.

Unilateral action is easier to implement, but generally less effective. The United States has unilaterally undertaken more than seventy economic sanctions against countries—of which the most notable is Cuba. Although not all such actions were undertaken in the cause of human rights, when they are, unilateralism risks the interpretation that human rights are a screen for Western hegemony.

Universality and Global Institutions

The emergence of multiple global organizations charged with technocratic supervision over a variety of overlapping world concerns requires some determination of priorities among them. Although universal rights and fundamental freedoms might be expected to dominate more material concerns, so far this has not always been the case.

UN agencies generally weigh the effects of their actions on human rights, whereas the WTO and the IMF have historically resisted pleas to subordinate their tasks to these concerns. Though the actions these agencies conduct may secondarily promote specific human rights, their primary mandate is to promote economic stability and development as distinct from second-generation economic rights such as an adequate standard of living, or freedom of association and the right to collective bargaining.

On January 1, 1995, the World Trade Organization succeeded the General Agreement on Tariffs and Trade (GATT). Unlike the failed plans for a post–World War II International Trade Organization that promoted employment rights and standards, the WTO has so far persevered with a narrower charter designed to reduce and resolve trade-based disputes by decreasing barriers to trade. WTO members enjoy most-favored-nation (MFN) status. The WTO also provides a mechanism to resolve trade disputes and, where necessary, to penalize violators. In late 1999, international attention was focused on the WTO as protesters in Seattle obstructed its meeting, arguing that environmental, labor, and human rights be included among the criteria used to regulate trade. Although President Bill Clinton made public overtures in support of their concerns, the subsequent accession of China to the WTO, despite its problematic human rights record, was generally presumed to constitute defeat for the protesters' argument.

The WTO's rules commit member nations to abide by principles of nondiscrimination among member economies but do not appeal or respond to more general human rights. Governments strongly influenced by an economic elite frequently oppose the enforcement of human rights standards where these might conflict with economic growth generally or with their own self-interest in particular. Equally, however, many governments of developing nations argue that moves to impose labor and human rights standards place their nations at a disadvantage and serve as protectionist measures for rich nations. Their position echoes the 1993 Bangkok Declaration, in which Asian leaders argued in favor of national sovereignty to protect less developed nations against Western values disguised as universal human rights. Nonetheless, in at least one instance, the WTO has been forced to consider a decision in light of human rights concerns. Specifically, it has given a tentative green light for developed nations to manufacture inexpensive versions of anti-HIV/AIDS drugs despite patent rights held by multinational pharmaceutical companies. In this case, protection of human rights was deemed to take priority over protection of intellectual property rights.

For the enforcement of labor rights and standards, advocates will either have to turn to the International Labour Organization (ILO) or to other voluntary mechanisms. Drawing its membership from labor organizations, privately owned companies, and states, the ILO has been active in defining and promoting labor standards since its inception in 1919. However, other than the moral suasion it can bring to bear on abusive labor practices, the ILO has very limited enforcement powers. To date, its principal work has been to publicize labor standards, to hear disputes regarding violations of its standards, and to provide technical assistance to remedy abuses. The ILO exercised a right granted under Article 33 for the first time in June 2000 when it requested that ILO and UN members review their trade relations with Myanmar to stop the forced labor prac-

tices of its military government. This action suggests that the ILO may become more active in enforcing human rights, although its ability to require member states to abide by its decisions remains, so far, limited. Effective economic power to regulate national behavior more clearly resides with the WTO and the IMF.

The IMF has been involved in a number of controversies concerning human rights in very poor countries. It has been especially criticized for the effects it has had on the rights of self-determination, the right of development, environmental rights, and the rights of indigenous peoples. Along with the World Bank, the IMF was designed in 1944 to secure global economic and financial stability. In particular, it was charged with responsibility to maintain stable international exchange rates by providing reserves to countries facing severe balance of payments problems.

Particularly since the post–Cold War era, IMF and World Bank aid to developing countries has imposed structural adjustments on beneficiary nations. The conditions for loans typically require governments to reduce expenditures, privatize nationally held industries, increase interest rates, reduce public services, and/or devalue their currencies. Such requirements invariably impose hardships upon the majority of citizens in already poor countries. Critics assert that IMF policies frequently fail to achieve even their immediate goals, which are to stabilize currencies and to improve the position of the debtor so that repayment is possible.

The IMF is not primarily an aid institution and instead attempts to act as a banker, refusing to commit resources where it fails to see prospects for repayment. Liberal economists argue that if the IMF offers relief without requiring fiscal prudence, it invites the moral hazard that governments will not take sufficient precautions against their own default. At present, the economic concerns of core global financial institutions outweigh human rights concerns. Poor nations are faced with ratcheting demands for human rights accountability, especially in the economic arena, at the same time that structural adjustment diminishes their short-term capacity to respond.

Universality and Internal Consistency

The sets of rights agreed upon through human rights declarations, covenants, and conventions can at times seem contradictory, requiring some prioritization to reduce the tension in reconciling competing claims. To dissolve this tension, advocates suggest that human rights not only define what "is," but also what "ought" to be. In addition, authorities such as Burns H. Weston argue that it is counterproductive to think of rights in absolutist terms. So understood, human rights inform globalization by creating a "human rights culture" that sustains a global conversation about moral standards.

Although rights claims gain authority through the assertion that they are indivisible and universal, it is recognized that some rights will only be realized progressively. For example, the ICESCR recognizes that its standards can be promoted only to the extent that resources become available. Thus, the right to work, trade union rights, and the right to an adequate standard of living might be called goals rather than rights, though to do so would clearly weaken their force.

A major challenge has arisen over the so-called third-generation solidarity rights, which include the right to self-determination, the right to control over national resources, and the right to participate in all the fruits of human progress. For example, despite the reluctance of some, the willingness of developing nations to collaborate to reduce drug prices to less-developed HIV/AIDS-inflicted countries suggests that humane concerns may yet prevail over economic interests. As of 2002, major pharmaceutical companies have begun to reduce HIV/AIDS drug prices to some nations. Such ad-hoc solutions to human rights set precedents with broader consequences, though they may not have the force of law.

Increasingly, human rights advocates leverage public indignation to produce economic results on a situation-by-situation basis. Whether and how these precedents can be reconciled and prioritized will constitute the story of human rights in the near future.

Daniel Jacoby, Bruce Kochis

See Also International Labour Organization (ILO); Culture and Globalization; Gender and Globalization; Labor Rights and Standards; Social Policy

References

Claude, Richard Pierre, and Burns H. Weston. 1992. *Human Rights in the World Community: Issues and Action.* 2d ed. Philadelphia: University of Pennsylvania Press.

Donnelly, Jack. 1998. *International Human Rights.* 2d ed. Boulder: Westview.

Forsythe, David P. 1989. *Human Rights and World Politics,* 2d ed. Omaha: University of Nebraska Press.

Hannum, Hurst. 1999. *Guide to International Human Rights Practice.* 3d ed. Ardsley, NY: Transnational.

Henkin, Louis, et al. 1999. *Human Rights.* New York: Foundation Press.

Lauren, Paul Gordon. 1998. *The Evolution of International Human Rights: Visions Seen.* Philadelphia: University of Pennsylvania Press.

Sen, Amartya. 1999. *Development as Freedom.* New York: Knopf.

Shue, Henry. 1996. *Basic Rights: Subsistence, Affluence, and U.S Foreign Policy.* 2d ed. Princeton, NJ: Princeton University Press.

Steiner, Henry J., and Philip Alston. 1996. *International Human Rights in Context: Law, Politics, Morals.* Oxford: Clarendon.

United Nations Center for Human Rights. 1994. *Human Rights: A Compilation of International Instruments.* 5th ed., 2 vols. New York: UN.

Labor Rights and Standards

Labor standards are laws and regulations governing the relationship between workers and employers. They include labor-market conditions, such as wages and work hours; workplace conditions relating to health and safety and the elimination of hazards; and agreements between workers and employers, including procedures for forming unions, bargaining, and hiring and firing. Labor rights are those human rights applied to the work setting to which all individuals are justly entitled, regardless of cultural, political, and economic circumstances.

Globalization has increased awareness of labor conditions around the world, leading to the creation of *international* labor standards. The International Labour Organization (ILO) was formed in 1919 to advance a broad range of social and labor issues, which today include industrial relations, conditions of work, social security, forced and child labor, and employment discrimination. Through a tripartite structure of dialogue between governments, workers' organizations, and employers' representatives, the ILO creates international labor standards, supervising and supporting their implementation in member states. Two rationales for harmonizing labor standards across countries are to protect human rights and to prevent unfair competitive advantage from harming the economies of high-standard nations. Recently, debate has arisen over whether the World Trade Organization (WTO) should enforce labor standards by using trade sanctions on its members.

History of Labor Standards

Rules governing the relationship between employer and worker are as old as the nation-state. Basic regulations for factory workers in Russia (1719), apprentices in Austria (1780s), and chimney sweeps in England (1788) are early examples. However, many historians trace the genesis of labor standards to the English Factory Act of 1802, which was introduced by Sir Robert Peel. More extensive than earlier regulations, this act improved conditions for pauper apprentices by limiting their workday to twelve hours, prohibiting them from night work, and allowing them to participate in educational and religious organizations. Having emerged first in the textile industry, early labor standards spread to nontextile factories by 1845 and finally to the mining sector. In 1842, women and children were banned from working in mines in England in a law that reflected the focus of most early standards on female and underage populations. Legislation of standards governing men's work were viewed as unnecessary as well as inconsistent with the constitutional ideal that men should be free to perform contract work.

Early laws were frequently revised and expanded to include new classes of workers, both within and across nations. Having taken root in England, the introduction of labor standards spread to Western Europe, North America, Eastern Europe, Latin America, and finally Africa and Asia. The activists tended to be from the middle class and argued that labor standards were not only necessary on moral grounds, but also beneficial for economic growth. Dissenters made a common objection: Labor standards would raise wages too much and cause job loss, further obfuscating conditions.

The emergence and expansion of labor standards internationally took place in three periods (Engerman 2003). Early labor standards were legislated first at the national level and were intended only for citizens of the country, but by the mid–nineteenth century, the notion emerged that labor standards could apply internationally. In 1818, the Welsh social worker and philanthropist Robert Owen first proposed the idea to a meeting of European statesmen. Owen argued that labor conditions constituted basic human rights, whereas many other proponents identified the harmful impact of low standards in some countries on the trade competitiveness of nations with higher labor standards. They also argued that international cooperation could reduce the cost of making standards domestically.

In 1833, Charles Hindley wrote about specific mechanisms for state cooperation on labor standards. The Brussels Congress of Benevolent Societies (1856) began a series of European, unilaterally organized conferences in which two major bilateral agreements were created, one limiting night work of children and women and the other banning the use of white phosphorus in the production of matches. These agreements were not truly universal, however, because participants were limited to developed Western nations and the laws did not apply to colonies or native populations. Of the twenty bilateral agreements signed between 1904 and 1915, as well as the few that preceded them, only one—the French-Italian treaty of 1904—was intended to actually change any national laws in the signatory states.

The creation of the ILO in 1919 began a new phase of more inclusive, multilateral cooperation. The provisions of the Paris Peace Conference (and later the Treaty of Versailles) created the ILO as the body of the League of Nations charged by its original forty-four members with the task of defining and promoting universal labor standards. Following World War II, the League of Nations was replaced by the United Nations, and the ILO became the only surviving agency incorporated into its system. With UN membership expanding to 54 in 1924, 121 in 1969, and 176 in 2003, new challenges emerged for multilateral agreement on the definition and interpretation of standards, and the focus increased on the provision of technical assistance to improve standards in developing countries.

Defining Labor Rights and Standards

Labor standards are national and international laws and regulations governing labor-market conditions as well as a range of agreements between workers and employers. Laws regulating minimum wage, workplace health and safety conditions, and the formation of unions are examples of labor standards. Labor rights are the most fundamental aspects of working conditions to which all human beings are justly entitled and which transcend all cultural, political, and economic situations (OECD 1996). Some generally accepted labor rights are reflected in bans on slavery and forced labor; on the use of prisoners in the production of market-competing goods; on employment discrimination on the basis of sex, religion, race, or nationality; and on sexual harassment in the workplace. Limits on work performed by children are another important area of labor-standards concerns.

Labor rights, or human rights more generally, are important justifications for creating labor standards. For example, people have the right to be fairly compensated for work. A minimum wage is a standard corresponding to this right. Often, the terms "labor rights" and "labor standards" are used interchangeably; ILO standards are considered international labor standards and are based on human rights.

Labor conditions and laws vary considerably across nations, reflecting the fact that there is no single, universally agreed formulation of labor standards. Mita Aggrewal (1995) distinguished between labor standard *outcomes,* such as specific wages and benefits guaranteed in higher standard countries, and basic *procedural* rights and standards, which reflect progress in lower standard countries toward outcomes.

Numerous formulations of basic labor standards exist worldwide. The rights and standards that are considered basic international labor standards under U.S. trade law are as follows (as cited in Singh 2003, 112; see also Brown et al. 2003, Appendix 1):

1. Freedom of association
2. The right to organize and bargain collectively
3. Prohibition of forced labor
4. A minimum age for the employment of children
5. A guarantee of acceptable working conditions, possibly including guarantees of maximum work hours, vacation or rest periods, adequate health and safety standards in the workplace, elimination of employment discrimination, and other employment benefits

The five basic international labor standards proposed by the Organisation for Economic Cooperation and Development (OECD) (1996) are very similar to those from U.S. trade law, except that they include only rights and not specific benefits. Similarly, consensus was renewed at the World Social Summit in 1995 to limit fundamental labor standards to those derived from the 1948 Universal Declaration of Human Rights and to exclude hours, wages, or other benefits. The Governing Body of the ILO has selected from its 180 conventions and 185 recommendations four fundamental labor standards, each with two supporting conventions.

ILO core labor standards are considered universal and are intended for ratification by all member states, regardless of development level, culture, political or economic institutions, industrial conditions, or climate. Through the consensus-building format of the ILO's tripartite structure, they are deemed viable for implementation in any nation. The four fundamental international labor standards are flexible, however, allowing states with special development constraints to demonstrate progress in lieu of immediate implementation. Also, they are adaptable over time to changing global labor patterns.

Formation and Adoption of Standards

The ILO is the UN agency mandated with the task of building consensus on and improving labor rights in its member states, as well as with a host of other research, statistical, and technical support functions. A major part of this mandate is the formation and adoption of international labor standards, tasks carried out each June in Geneva by the International Labour Conference. The ILO's Governing Body sets the agenda for the conference according to suggestions made by governments and other organizations. Each member country sends two delegates, one representing workers and the other employers, who participate on equal footing in the unique three-way, or tripartite, format established under Convention 144 (1976). After two successive discussion periods designed to create a broad consensus, the conference concludes with a vote that determines whether the proposed conventions and recommendations will be adopted.

Two classes of formal international labor standards—conventions and recommendations—are created by the ILO. Conventions are treaties intended to be ratified by the legislatures of member states, entering into force as binding international law. By ratifying a convention, a state makes a solemn agreement to abide in good faith, *pacta sunt servande,* by its provisions and to alter national policies accordingly. Many international treaties allow states to enter reservations signifying that they do not wish to be bound by certain provisions; however, reservations are not allowed on ILO conventions. Recommendations, although not intended for ratification, provide additional information to augment the principles found in the conventions. The Governing Body classifies conventions and recommendations as follows: basic human rights, employment, social policy, labor administration, industrial relations, working conditions, social security, employment of women and children, migrant workers, indigenous and tribal peoples, and special categories such as fishermen, sharecroppers, and nursing personnel.

In addition, informal instruments, including resolutions, conclusions, codes of practice, and guidelines, are made by technical or other ILO bodies to provide specific technical guidelines for implementation of conventions or recommendations. One example is the Governing Body's Tripartite Declaration of Principles concerning Multinational Enterprises and Social Policy (1977) encouraging self-regulation of multinational firms.

Ratification and Compliance

Conventions adopted by the International Labour Conference must be ratified by all member states; however, this obligation is not enforced. Although the ratification rate has improved in the past decade, it remains low—at about 86 percent for fundamental conventions and 20 percent for the other conventions. Convention 143, concerning the elimination of forced labor, is the one most widely ratified (by 143 of 176 member states), and Convention 138, which sets the minimum age of work to fifteen years, is least ratified (51 member states).

More than half of the member states have ratified all eight fundamental conventions. The states that have ratified the fewest are Armenia,

Myanmar, Oman, and the United States (two ratified); Laos and the Solomon Islands (one ratified); and Vanuatu (none ratified). Ratification of conventions does not necessarily correspond with the actual rights and standards enjoyed by workers in a given state, as some high-standard countries have ratified very few core standards, while some low-standard countries have ratified all eight conventions.

Almost no state summarily denies labor rights, but noncompliance with ILO conventions, even when ratified, is widespread, particularly in developing countries. Although ratification may at times reflect empty rhetoric, most violations are explained by two causes: failure to observe standards in specific sectors, or weak and nonexistent monitoring and enforcement mechanisms. Since poverty and underdevelopment contribute to poor standards, the ILO has increased technical support to assist developing states in improving and complying with standards.

In addition to resource and other constraints within nations, there are severe limits on the ILO's ability to enforce labor standards. The nation-state is sovereign, meaning that no other national or international body has the right to impose restrictions within its territory. By becoming members of the ILO, and in particular by ratifying conventions, states delegate part of their sovereignty over labor issues to the ILO, agreeing to come under the supervisory mechanisms embodied in it.

Although the ILO cannot enforce standards through punishment (member states have not created an institution within the ILO to do so), it supervises labor standards in several ways. First, under the representation provisions of the ILO Constitution (Article 24), any national or international organization of workers or employers can make a claim against a member state that has failed to comply with a ratified convention. Under this procedure, the International Labour Office acknowledges receipt of the complaint and informs the state's government of the issue, which brings the matter to the Governing Body. If it accepts the complaint for consideration, the Governing Body presents it to a relevant ad-hoc committee that investigates the claim and prepares a report. The results may be published as a representation or a complaint under Article 26. A Committee of Experts on the Application of Conventions and Recommendations follows up on the state's response to the violation, and governments may refer the complaint to the International Court of Justice for a final decision.

Furthermore, even if member states have not ratified a convention, they are required under the provisions of Article 19 of the ILO Constitution to report at intervals specified by the Governing Body on the extent to which they intend to undertake the provisions. States that have ratified conventions may be required under Article 22 to present a similar report on implementation. The Labour Inspection (Agriculture) Convention of 1969 (No. 129) and the Labour Inspection Convention of 1947 (No. 81) require member governments to provide the level of industrial inspection required to adequately enforce standards.

In addition to its supervisory role, the ILO also promotes labor standards through international norm-building, publicity of noncompliant policies of signatory governments, and provision of technical and financial assistance for developing states.

Child Labor

Noncompliance with child labor conventions, in addition to those dealing with freedom of association, is among the most common labor standard issues addressed by the ILO. The Minimum Age Convention of 1973 (No. 138) defines child labor as work before the end of compulsory schooling or before the age of fifteen (previously fourteen under the Minimum Age [Industry] Convention of 1919 [No. 5]). For work involving health, safety, or moral hazards, Convention 138 sets the minimum age at

eighteen years, and for light work, thirteen to fifteen years, depending on certain conditions. In 1989, the UN Convention on the Rights of the Child identified the right to be free from economic exploitation and work that is hazardous, interferes with schooling, or hinders physical, mental, or moral development.

By 1999, the Prohibition and Immediate Action for the Elimination of the Worst Forms of Child Labour Convention (No. 182) had been adopted. It became the most rapidly ratified convention in ILO history, amplifying earlier commitments embodied in the Forced Labour Convention of 1930 (No. 29). Along with Recommendation 190, Convention 182 banned the worst forms of child labor, labeled "unconditional worst forms," including slavery, trafficking, debt bondage, recruitment into armed forces, prostitution, pornography, and illicit activities. Both the 1989 and 1999 conventions recognize that not all forms of work are equally detrimental to child development and distinguish between economically active "child workers" and those "child laborers" in the most harmful forms of work.

The legal framework addressing child labor includes the following rights and standards (ILO 2003):

1. The setting of a minimum age for admission to employment or work
2. The immediate suppression of the worst forms of child labor as the priority of national and international action
3. The prohibition of young persons from working at night
4. The requirement that a working young person under the age of eighteen be found fit to work by undergoing medical examination
5. Recommendations for the allowable conditions of employment of persons under the age of eighteen in underground work situations

Labor force participation rates of children between the ages five and fourteen have declined in all regions from an estimated 28 percent worldwide in 1950 to 18 percent in 2000. The rates of child labor are highest in Africa, where 29 percent of the total child population is engaged in work activities.

Of the 1.2 billion children in the world between the ages of five and seventeen in 2000, 180 million—or one in six—are believed to be in the worst forms of work, including 8 million in the unconditional worst forms (ILO 2002). Among children in developing countries, three-quarters work at least six days a week, and half work more than nine hours per day. Seventy-one percent work in the fishing and agricultural industries operating machinery, handling agrochemicals, picking produce, and loading. Eight percent of child workers manufacture items such as matches and small glass objects; many in these jobs are exposed to toxic fumes, excessive heat, broken glass, and hazardous chemicals.

Empirical evidence suggests that families with resources—a mother with a marketable skill, older children, or household enterprise assets, for example—are more likely to choose education. Providing financial incentives to parents for children's school attendance, as well as improving school quality and access to capital markets, are important steps in reducing child labor. The high rate of child labor in England during the Industrial Revolution (about 36.9 percent for boys and 20.5 percent for girls in 1861), along with its subsequent decline there, suggests the importance of both legislation and economic growth, as well as the development of social norms, in ending child labor (Humphries 2003).

Labor Standard Harmonization

Harmonization is the process of making labor standards, such as those limiting child labor, more alike across countries, and effectively raising them in low-standard countries to levels closer to those in high-standard countries.

Two main theoretical and empirical questions are associated with the desirability of harmonization: Is harmonization consistent with free trade, and what is the impact of labor standard harmonization on the economic and social welfare of individual states and the individuals within them?

Harmonization and Free Trade

There is general consensus that diversity of labor standards across countries is consistent with free trade and that there are economic benefits for the world economy as a whole when a diversity of standards exists. Like differences in factor endowments, technology, and preferences, variation in labor standards creates comparative advantage and allows gains from trade. Hence, multilateral interventions, such as proposed WTO trade sanctions against low-standard countries, cannot be justified on the grounds that lower standards violate conditions of free trade.

Harmonization and Welfare of Individual States

Even if lower labor standards do not make world trade less free, several ethical, social, and economic rationales exist for improving work conditions. The arguments may be divided into two categories: those aimed at preventing erosion of standards in developing countries, and those intended to circumvent damage to the economies of high-standard countries that might result from an unfair trade advantage in low-standard countries. A recent body of research focuses on what, if any, are the effects of diversity in labor standards on the economic well-being of individual countries and whether these effects support the use of trade sanctions against trading partners with low standards.

Human Rights, Welfare, and the "Race to the Bottom"

Concern for human rights and welfare generally motivates arguments for improving standards in developing states or for preventing their erosion. Moral arguments for labor standards suggest that individuals are imbued with human rights and therefore deserve fair and humane treatment. The welfarist approach, by contrast, considers the desirability of a given set of rights or standards by evaluating their effect on the happiness, or utility, of an individual. Labor rights themselves hold no value apart from their ability to increase utility. The human rights and welfarist approaches are usually consistent and may both be used to advocate intervention in the market in the form of labor standards.

Both human rights and welfarist approaches suggest that intervention in the form of labor standards might also be necessary if market failure or unequal bargaining arise, or if positive externalities, such as improved education or health, are undersupplied. A human rights or welfarist approach suggests further that even if a labor market is perfectly competitive and efficient according to economic models, that is, even if under conditions such as slave or child labor no resources could be reallocated in a way that makes an individual better off without hurting another individual, improvement in labor standards might be desirable to achieve equity or improve human rights. T. N. Srinivasan (1998) asserted that low standards, with the exception of the most egregious forms such as slave labor, are not unfair so long as they are consistent efficient resource use. He argued that if harmonization occurred, international income transfers and domestic taxes or subsidies would be necessary to maintain free and fair trade.

Finally, preventing a "race-to-the-bottom" or "regulatory-chill" is a potential human rights or welfarist motivation for promoting labor standards. Through arbitrage, capital might flow to countries with the lowest labor standards, allowing workers to be paid less and firms to earn higher profits. A "regulatory chill" effect might occur if governments, because of pressure to keep standards low, removed existing protection from workers.

Empirical Evidence for the "Race to the Bottom"

In its survey of the literature, the OECD (1996) concluded that there was little theoretical or empirical evidence for the "race-to-the-bottom" effect occurring. Rather, evidence suggests that labor standards are rarely among the factors that multinational enterprises (MNEs) consider when locating operations, and that the presence of multinational firms is associated with improvements of worker rights and benefits in low-standard countries. Hence, multilateral trade sanctions against low-standard countries may not be justifiable on the grounds that they will prevent a "race-to-the-bottom" effect.

Labor Standards, Wages, and Trade Competitiveness

The second set of arguments for harmonization is motivated by efforts to prevent any deleterious effects in the economies of high-standard countries due to unfair competitive advantage in low-standard countries. The issue of the possible linkage between trade and labor conditions, addressed as early as the nineteenth century, has grown in importance in recent decades. Chapter II, Article 7, of the 1948 Charter of the International Trade Organization (ITO) alleged unfair comparative advantage, but the General Agreement on Tariffs and Trade (GATT) that replaced unsuccessful efforts to inaugurate the ITO did not address the issue except for in Article XX(e) banning the sale of goods produced by prisoners. In 1953, the United States made unsuccessful efforts to add labor standards to the GATT's Article XXIII, followed by further abortive attempts to introduce them in the negotiations of the Tokyo and Uruguay rounds in the mid-1970s and 1980s, and in the mid-1994 final draft agreements of the Uruguay Round in Marrakech. Although numerous states, including the United States, the European Union, Canada, and Japan, continue to raise the issue at WTO Ministerial Conferences of the WTO, multilateral negation of the issue is unlikely to occur during the current Doha Rounds.

The enforcement of labor standards through trade privileges continues to be most successful in bilateral and regional, rather than multilateral, agreements. For example, the U.S. Generalized System of Preferences (GSP), which allows sanctions under Section 301 of the 1988 Trade Act, and the European Union's special preferences system employ both incentives and punishments to pressure governments to improve labor standards.

Effect of Labor Standards on Wages and Trade Competitiveness

According to a meta-analysis conducted by the OECD (1996), there is no compelling evidence that lower labor standards improve trade competitiveness or that they have a downward effect on the wages of unskilled workers in higher standard countries. The following points summarize the evidence.

Low labor standards and trade competitiveness. There is little evidence that low labor standards improve export performance; rather, factor endowments, technology, and economies of scale predict the competitiveness of states and firms in the global economy (OECD 1996; Raynauld and Vidal 1998). Of U.S. textile imports, for example, a significant number are produced in high-standard countries; as a whole, these imports do not appear to correlate with enforcement of child labor standards.

Low labor standards and wages. Dani Rodrik (1996) concluded that low labor standards do not have a significant downward effect on the wages of unskilled laborers in high-standard countries, except in some sectors where unskilled labor is particularly plentiful (Brown et al. 2003). Drusilla K. Brown (2000) found that although it may be difficult to gauge the precise impact of labor-standard diversity on wages in high-standard countries, the decreasing wages of unskilled labor in the United States is due to biased technical change, not lower standards of trading partners.

The argument that low standards create unfair trade advantage and thus justify sanctions on these grounds is not supported by empirical evidence. Instead, research suggests that improvement of labor standards in low-standard countries may be more beneficial than maintaining low standards because it has the potential to promote economic development by raising wages and improving human capital.

Strategies for Improving Labor Conditions

At least five strategies are suggested for improving international labor standards. These include not only enforcing core labor standards through WTO trade sanctions, but also improving the capabilities of the ILO, promoting labor-standard provisions in bilateral and regional trade agreements, increasing the activity of private monitoring agencies and self-regulation of firms, and augmenting the awareness and responsibility of individual consumers.

Proposals to enforce minimum labor standards on WTO members through the use of trade sanctions have attracted considerable debate in recent years. In the past, trade sanctions have been used unilaterally, but never multilaterally under the WTO. For example, unilateral sanctions were instrumental in ending the policy of apartheid that institutionalized racial discrimination in employment and other practices in South Africa. Under Section 502(b)(8) of the 1984 Trade Act and Section 301 of the 1988 U.S. Trade Act, the president is authorized to remove GSP benefits to induce compliance with labor and other human rights. In April 1999, for example, provisions were withheld from Sudan. This followed earlier measures against Burma, Chile, Romania, and other states.

Many developing countries and regional organizations express opposition to allowing the WTO to use trade sanctions for punishing noncompliance with labor rights, arguing that it could be misused by powerful states. Further, almost all scholars argue that WTO authorization of trade sanctions is unlikely to improve conditions for workers. Trade sanctions would likely be particularly ineffective at improving the welfare of child laborers, for example, because they would *decrease* the demand for unskilled labor where unemployment is already high. Evidence from complaints filed under the National Administrative Organizations (NAOs) of North American Free Trade Agreement (NAFTA) member states, as well as technical and financial support programs initiated by the United Nations Children's Fund (UNICEF), the ILO, and other international organizations, suggest that consultation and support for alternatives to poor labor conditions are plausible and effective alternatives to trade sanctions.

Second, the ILO, as the only effective and directly relevant supervising mechanism for labor standards, could be strengthened in its abilities to promote them. Its efficacy might be improved if financial and institutional changes were made, thus allowing it to monitor state behavior more directly, devote more resources and expertise to convincing governments of the economic desirability of standards, and provide technical and financial assistance to developing countries. In 1994, the ILO began a research project designed to analyze the possible integration of social and trade policies and to enhance its ability to enforce labor standards through trade relationships between countries. However, the Work Party on the Social Dimensions of the Liberalization of International Trade terminated dialogue on the issue because of disagreements among member states.

A third set of solutions includes more fully integrating labor-standard clauses into bilateral and regional trade agreements such as those within the U.S. and EU systems of preferences for trading partners with improved standards and the NAO consultation mechanism within NAFTA.

Fourth, efforts could be made to promote the growing trend toward privately developed codes of conduct created in consultation with the ILO. Private advocacy and monitoring groups also play an important role by exposing violating firms and by serving as independent monitors contracted by firms to certify conditions in supplier plants. For example, in May 1998, monitoring and reputation concerns played a role in Nike's announcement that it would ensure that no children under sixteen years of age were hired by the company and that it would implement American health and safety standards in its foreign plants. Other major companies, such as Mattel, use independent monitoring agencies to ensure compliance with labor standards in the factories of its suppliers.

Finally, private-sector approaches might induce consumers to base their purchasing decisions on knowledge about the conditions under which products are produced. "Social labeling" of products and "socially responsible investment schemes" are important components to this strategy.

Summary

Labor rights and standards are increasingly important areas of international concern in a globalizing world economy. The highly institutionalized nature of the ILO's international lawmaking and supervision mechanisms make it an important advocate for labor standard improvements; however, action at the regional, national, and private-sector levels are also important components of labor-standard development. Careful consideration of empirical evidence is essential for evaluating the effectiveness and appropriateness of new approaches, such as the institutionalization of WTO trade sanctions, to enforce core standards. This evidence suggests the relative success of incentives, consultation, and assistance over punitive approaches to improving conditions for workers in developing countries.

Lindsay J. Benstead

See Also Labor Markets and Wage Effects; International Labour Organization (ILO); World Trade Organization (WTO); Human Rights and Globalization

References

Aggrewal, Mita. 1995. "International Trade, Labor Standards, and Labor Market Conditions: An Evaluation of the Linkages." U.S. International Trade Commission, Office of Economics Working Paper No. 95-06-C (June).

Alcock, Antony. 1971. *History of the International Labor Organization.* New York: Octagon.

Basu, Kaushik. 1999. "Child Labor: Cause, Consequence, and Cure, with Remarks on International Labor Standards." *Journal of Economic Literature* 37: 1083–1119.

Brown, Drusilla K. 2000. "International Trade and Core Labour Standards: A Survey of the Recent Literature." Labour Market and Social Policy, Occasional Papers No. 43 (October). Paris: Organisation for Economic Co-operation and Development.

Brown, Drusilla K., Alan V. Deardorff, and Robert M. Stern. 2003. "Child Labor: Theory, Evidence, and Policy." Pp. 195–247 in Kaushik Basu et al., eds., *International Labor Standards.* Malden, MA: Blackwell.

Engerman, Stanley L. 2003. "History and Political Economy of International Labor Standards." Pp. 9–83 in Kaushik Basu et al., eds., *International Labor Standards.* Malden, MA: Blackwell.

Fields, Gary S. 2000. "The Role of Labor Standards in U.S. Trade Policies." Pp. 167–188 in Alan V. Deardorff and Robert M. Stern, eds., *Social Dimensions of U.S. Trade Polices.* Ann Arbor: University of Michigan Press.

Humphries, Jane. 2003. "The Parallels between the Past and the Present." Pp. 84–98 in Kaushik Basu et al., eds., *International Labor Standards.* Malden, MA: Blackwell.

International Labour Organization. 2002. *A Future without Child Labor.* Geneva: ILO.

———, http://www.ilo.org (cited June 29, 2003).

Lowe, Boutelle Ellsworth. 1918. *International Aspects of the Labor Problem.* New York: W. D. Gray.

Organisation for Economic Co-operation and Development. 1996. *Trade, Employment and Labour Standards: A Study of Core Workers' Rights and International Trade.* Paris: OECD.

Raynauld, Andre, and Jean-Pierre Vidal. 1998. *Labour Standards and International Competitiveness: A Comparative Analysis of Developing and Industrialized Countries.* Northampton, MA: Edward Elgar.

Rodrik, Dani. 1996. "Labor Standards in International Trade: Do They Matter and What Do We Do About Them?" in R. Lawrence et al., *Emerging Agenda for Global Trade: High Stakes for Developing Countries,* Washington, DC: Overseas Development Council.

Singh, Nirvikar. 2003. "The Impact of International Labor Standards: A Survey of Economic Theory." Pp. 107–181 in Kaushik Basu et al., eds., *International Labor Standards.* Malden, MA: Blackwell.

Srinivasan, T. N. 1998. "Trade and Human Rights." Pp. 225–253 in Alan V. Deardorff and Robert M. Stern, eds., *Constituent Interests and U.S. Trade Policies.* Ann Arbor: University of Michigan Press.

Natural Resources

Globalization, that is, the increasing international integration of peoples, cultures, and economies, has had a variety of negative impacts on the environment and important natural resources. International trade, foreign investment, economic development, and increased travel are among the direct causes of these environmental impacts. An increasing number of nonnative species of animals, plants, and microbes, for example, have been introduced into the environment, causing damage to native ecosystems. Some of these impacts have been addressed by a growing number of treaties and other international agreements that help assure the sustainability of the global commons. Others will require further cooperation among states if sustainable use of the earth's resources is to be achieved.

Protecting the Global Commons

Common-pool resources are either natural or constructed resource systems that are sufficiently large that it is costly, though perhaps not impossible, to exclude those wishing to harvest from the resource system. A common-pool resource should be thought of as a stock from which is generated a flow of resource units. For example, healthy fishery stocks can produce a harvestable flow for commercial and recreational fishermen. Common-pool resources have the additional characteristic of subtractability, meaning that resource units harvested or withdrawn by one user subtract from what is available to other potential users.

Continuing the fishery example, fish harvested by one fisherman are not available for capture by other fishermen.

Some common-pool resource systems are renewable, meaning that under favorable conditions they are capable of self-replenishment, though excessive harvest of some resources can overwhelm the self-replenishment process and result in depletion of the resource stock. Examples include fish and game populations, rivers, aquifers, forests, and the stratospheric ozone layer. Infrastructure such as roads, bridges, and telecommunications networks may also have renewable common-pool resource characteristics when the services that they provide suffer from periodic congestion, at which time use by one reduces the capacity of the system to provide services to others. Other common-pool resource systems are not renewable within a normal human timeframe, and continued harvest from these systems will result in depletion. Some important examples of nonrenewable common-pool resources include oil and natural gas fields and coal beds.

If the use of common-pool resources is not adequately managed, rivalry among users could damage the productive capacity of the resource systems, thereby harming all users. Incentives for overuse occur because individual resource users receive all of the benefits from the resource units that they harvest, but share any damage that they cause to the productive capacity of the overall resource system among all the users. Examples include the decline of fish and wildlife populations due to excessive fishing or hunting, the depletion of aquifers drawn down by excessive water pumping, and travel and time delays caused by excessive use of congested roads, bridges, and telecommunications networks. Garrett Hardin (1968) coined the term "tragedy of the commons" in reference to resource users who see the damage resulting from their actions but nevertheless continue their dysfunctional behavior because any resource that they save will simply be gathered by another.

As Elinor Ostrom (1990) and others since have observed, the tragedy of the commons can be averted if resource use can be properly managed through a well-defined and enforced system of property rights for the resource system. These may be private property (property owned by individuals, families, or businesses), state property (property owned by various levels of government), or common property (property owned collectively by a group of individuals, families, or other entities). Many common-pool resources, such as groundwater basins and migratory fish and wildlife, are fugitive in nature and cannot easily be partitioned into private property. Common property regimes have been successful at managing small-scale common-pool resources when the participants have successfully implemented formal and informal norms and rules, collectively known as an institutional structure, to align individual incentives with the good of the group, enforce agreements, resolve disputes, and facilitate necessary change. One example is the common-property tradition in the Swiss Alps, where a large fraction of the land has been managed as the common property of various Swiss alpine villages. Such collective choice arrangements are increasingly difficult to sustain as common-pool resources become larger in scope, necessitating that government assert state property rights and regulatory management.

Many of the earth's important common-pool resources are international or global in scale. Examples include transboundary groundwater basins and rivers, populations of certain boundary-straddling or highly migratory fish and wildlife, the earth's stratospheric ozone layer, and the health of the earth's oceans and atmosphere. Other global natural systems that share some characteristics with common-pool resources include biological and genetic diversity as well as global ecosystem services such as climate regulation and oxygen–carbon dioxide exchange. Factors related to globalization, such as economic development, technological change, and population growth, have placed increasing pressure on many vital global commons. Although sovereign nations have the capacity to provide for and enforce property rights to regulate user impacts on common-pool resources within their sovereign boundaries, international action is required to protect transboundary and global common-pool resources.

Treaties provide a legal framework and institutional structure for international regulation of transboundary and global common-pool resources, as well as of local resources that are the subject of global concern. There are more than 140 international treaties designed to protect the environment and natural resources. (A full-text listing of these treaties is available on the Internet from the Center for International Earth Science Information Network [CIESIN], which operates the Socioeconomic Data and Applications Center [SEDAC] for the U.S. National Aeronautics and Space Administration [NASA], at http://sedac.ciesin. org/entri/texts-home.html.) A summary of several important treaties is given below, with the date on which they entered into force given in parentheses.

United Nations Convention on the Law of the Sea (UNCLOS) (1994)

This treaty established a comprehensive new legal regime for the sea and oceans, including a 200-mile exclusive economic zone and continental-shelf development rights for coastal states. All states are acknowledged to have navigational, fishing, and other rights on the high seas, as well as an obligation to cooperate in international management and conservation efforts. The treaty established liability for damage due to marine pollution, as well as an International Tribunal for resolving disputes (see http://www.un.org/Depts/los/index.htm).

United Nations Framework Convention on Climate Change (UNFCCC) (1994)

The UNFCCC seeks the stabilization of greenhouse gas concentrations in the atmosphere at a level that would prevent dangerous anthropogenic interference with the climate system. It also established the Conference of Parties to implement the convention. The Kyoto Protocol to the convention, adopted in 1997 and in force since February 2005, called for industrialized countries to reduce their overall emissions of greenhouse gases by at least 5 percent below 1990 levels in the commitment period 2008 to 2012 (see http://www.unfccc.de).

United Nations Agreement on the Conservation and Management of Straddling Fish Stocks and Highly Migratory Fish Stocks (adopted in 1995 and in force since 2001)

Straddling fish stocks are stocks of fish that occur both within the exclusive economic zone (EEZ) of a coastal state and in the adjacent high seas. Highly migratory fish stocks migrate through the high seas and in some cases through the EEZs of coastal states. Both categories of fish stocks have been subject to unregulated overfishing on the high seas. This agreement was adopted because UNCLOS is not clear about the legal rights and obligations of states regarding management and conservation of highly migratory and straddling fish stocks (see http://sedac.ciesin.org/entri/texts/acrc/fish95.txt.html).

Montreal Protocol on Substances that Deplete the Ozone Layer (1988)

This international agreement was established to protect human health and the environment against adverse effects resulting from modifications of the ozone layer. It called for 50 percent reductions in the production and consumption of ozone-depleting chemicals (relative to 1986 levels) by 1999. The agreement was revised in London in 1990 to totally phase out production and consumption by 2000 for industrialized countries, and by 2010 for developing countries (see http://www.unep.ch/ozone/treaties.shtml).

Convention on International Trade in Endangered Species of Wild Fauna and Flora (CITES) (1975)

CITES provides a framework to ensure that international trade in specimens of wild animals and plants does not threaten the survival of the species. Enforcement includes trade bans. Each of the more than 150 parties must adopt their own domestic legislation to implement CITES at the national level (see http://www.cites.org).

Convention on Biological Diversity (adopted in 1992 and as of 1998 more than 170 countries have signed to become participants)

This convention was established to conserve biological diversity, promote the sustainable use of its components, and encourage equitable sharing of the benefits arising out of the utilization of genetic resources. It places an obligation on the parties to provide for environmental impact assessment of projects that are likely to have significant adverse effects on biological diversity and provides for both technology transfer and provision of financial assistance (see http://www.biodiv.org).

International Convention for the Regulation of Whaling (1948)

This convention, established to formulate, adopt, and revise measures to conserve whales, created the International Whaling Commission, which is given the authority to regulate and ban the harvest of whales. Changes in regulation, including bans, require a three-fourths majority of the commission (see http://www.oceanlaw.net/texts/iwc.htm).

Globalized Trade and the Environment

One important economic dimension of globalization is the international commercial exchange of natural resource and agricultural commodities. This section summarizes a more extensive treatment of the topic that is given in Steven Hackett's book *Environmental and Natural Resources Economics: Theory, Policy, and the Sustainable Society* (2001). The classical argument in favor of free and unimpeded international trade, which goes back to Adam Smith and David Ricardo, is that free trade allows for regions and countries to specialize in those activities that they do best. In particular, the law of comparative advantage states that total material wealth can be increased when production is specialized based on cost, with the preference for a more diverse bundle of consumption goods met through trade among these specialized producers.

To see how the law of comparative advantage works, consider the potential for wealth-enhancing trade between a mountainous area with abundant mineral resources and lower-elevation areas with abundant agricultural resources. In the absence of trade, agricultural goods are scarce and expensive in the mountainous area, whereas mineral resources are scarce and expensive in the lower-elevation area. Specialization and trade would reduce the cost of mineral resources in the lower-elevation region and the cost of agricultural goods in the mountainous region, providing for increased consumption with the given stock of resources. As a consequence, specialization and trade creates material wealth and reduced consumer prices. Therefore, international trade has the potential for raising people out of poverty. By exposing people to different cultures, it can also foster increased understanding and tolerance of diversity.

The social, cultural, and economic displacements caused by international trade make it very difficult for all members of society to benefit from trade. In the example given above, free trade created a flow of cheaper imports that displaced those people in the mountains engaged in relatively unproductive agriculture, and those people from the lower-elevation regions who specialized in mining. Workers at risk of displacement can be expected to oppose increased international trade, along with those who value the social and cultural bonds associated with traditional production.

Free trade can also contribute to a more rapid pace of environmental degradation when the governments that are engaged in the trade, or the trade agreements they create, lack adequate democratic institutions and processes. Graciela Chichilnisky (1994), for example, modeled trade between a high-income country with well-defined and enforced property rights to environmental resources and a low-income country with poorly defined and enforced property rights. The difference in the level of property rights enforcement is sufficient by itself to motivate bilateral trade. In the case of poorly defined and enforced property rights to the environmental resource, tragedy of the commons leads to excessive resource harvest, which reduces the price of these resources. Thus, the environmental resource is relatively cheaper in the low-income country owing to excessive rates of harvest. Chichilnisky showed that under free trade the tragedy-of-the-commons effect in the low-income country is worsened. Overproduction of the environmental resource in the low-income country is matched by overconsumption of the resource in the high-income country.

There is also the concern that comparative advantage can be created from lax environmental and other regulations. Producers in more heavily regulated countries are placed at a competitive disadvantage in the global marketplace by these so-called "pollution havens." If the threat of job loss due to production shifting to pollution havens is credible and politically compelling, free trade can lead to a "race to the bottom" in which countries relax their environmental regulations in order to protect domestic jobs and income. Similarly, relatively cheap land and limited opportunities in poor regions of the world give them a comparative advantage in providing waste disposal services. The result is a flourishing trade in garbage and other wastes.

Environmentalists are concerned that international trade agreements such as the World Trade Organization (WTO) limit the power of signatory countries to enforce process standards on imports from countries with more lax environmental standards. WTO rules incorporate environmental protections. For example, Article XX of the WTO states that WTO rules shall not be construed as preventing the adoption or enforcement of measures (1) necessary to protect human, animal, or plant life or health, or (2) relating to the conservation of exhaustible natural resources, if such measures are made effective in conjunction with restrictions on domestic production. The scope of this article has been tested in a number of disputes lodged against the United States.

For example, Mexico filed a trade complaint against the United States in 1991 over provisions of the Marine Mammal Protection Act that required the United States to ban imports of tuna from countries that could not prove that adequate dolphin protection measures were being utilized. A panel determined that Article XX did not allow for unilateral trade bans or tariffs based on the method used to produce goods in foreign countries. This interpretation was upheld in a more recent dispute between the United States and India, Malaysia, Pakistan, the Philippines, and Thailand challenging a U.S. ban on imports of shrimp caught without using turtle-excluding devices in their nets. Consequently, one country cannot use trade restrictions to reach out beyond its own territory to impose its standards on another country. The WTO requires international environmental treaties rather than unilateral action by a single country. Therefore, in the absence of international environmental treaties, a WTO member country's markets are forced to be open to foreign products produced in an environmentally harmful manner, even if domestic producers are banned from such practices.

Taken together, it is clear that the WTO position has restricted the tools available for assuring environmental protection.

Nevertheless, most human cultures over thousands of years have engaged in some degree of trade, driven by the age-old incentive to buy goods where they are abundant and cheap, and transport them to where they are scarce and expensive. Attempts to heavily regulate or eliminate trade usually result in the development of black markets. As economist Paul Krugman has stated, "If there were an Economist's Creed it would surely contain the affirmations, 'I believe in the Principle of Comparative Advantage,' and 'I believe in free trade'" (1987, 131).

Globalization and Economic Development

In the years following World War II, many European colonies in Africa, Asia, and South America became independent states. Many of these newly independent states pursued an "inward-looking" import-substitution development strategy designed to protect fledgling domestic industries from international competition. This strategy included the use of tariffs and other barriers to foreign imports; restrictions on foreign direct investment, such as minimum local content requirements; and limited currency convertibility. Industrial investment was focused on production of domestic goods and services rather than on the production of exports. State ownership of key industrial enterprises kept the focus on these and other social goals. Import substitution is a development strategy designed to limit the loss of income out of the domestic economy due to the purchase of imports, in much the same way that a plug in a bathtub prevents the leakage of water down the drain.

From the standpoint of economic development, globalization can be thought of as an "outward-looking" process of liberalizing trade and investment. Examples include the promotion of investment in export-producing industries, reduction of tariffs and other barriers to imports, removal of restrictions on foreign direct investment, increased currency convertibility, and privatization of industry. Globalization strategies were seen by many Western economists as being more likely to promote economic growth. Globalization had displaced import substitution in many low- and middle-income countries by the 1980s. The rise of globalization is partially a consequence of international-development lending programs. As described in Hackett (2001) and summarized below, globalization strategies were used to help resolve problems associated with international-development lending programs, and in the process created social and environmental problems that in turn spurred the sustainable development movement.

The World Bank played a key role in designing development projects and in pooling loan funds from donor countries such as Germany, Japan, and the United States. Many large commercial banks in the United States and elsewhere also participated in financing large-scale development projects. These loans tended to be focused on large-scale infrastructure projects such as the construction of hydroelectric and other power plants, mines, irrigation networks, road systems, and port facilities. Unfortunately, many of these debt-financed projects were economically, socially, and environmentally inappropriate.

For example, loans were used to fund large-scale resettlement of the urban poor in rainforests in Brazil and Indonesia, resulting in the displacement of indigenous peoples and massive deforestation. Loans were used to fund large coal-fired power plants and open-pit coal mines in India, leading to massive sulfur dioxide and heavy metals pollution problems and the uncompensated displacement of thousands of local people. Loans were used to fund large dam projects in Thailand, displacing numerous small, locally self-governed irrigation common-pool resource systems in which local people used sustainable methods to manage

the community forests that served as watersheds for the community rice-paddy irrigation systems. As Ostrom remarked, "The failure . . . to develop an effective set of rules for organizing their irrigation system is not unusual for large-scale, donor-funded irrigation systems in Third World settings" (1990, 166).

Many World Bank–financed programs were also poorly designed, as revealed by the World Bank's own Wapenhans Report in 1992 (World Bank Vice President Willi Wapenhans et al. 1992). The report found that World Bank staff used project appraisals as marketing devices to advocate loan approval rather than as unbiased assessments of project viability. Moreover, developing countries that borrowed from the World Bank saw the negotiation stage of a project as a largely coercive exercise in imposing the World Bank philosophy on the borrower. Confidential surveys of World Bank staff indicated that substantial pressure was being exerted on staffers to meet lending targets, and that this pressure overwhelmed all other considerations. The report stated that only 17 percent of the staff in the survey believed that their project analysis was compatible with achieving project quality.

Other problems with international-development lending programs included a lack of democratic political institutions in debtor countries, where national leaders were able to appropriate development funds or project revenues, further weakening project performance. Those projects that were successful in producing export commodities contributed to rapid growth in world commodity supplies that outpaced demand, resulting in a downward trajectory in commodity prices and repayment capability, as described below. Thus, the overall performance of large-scale international economic development lending was mixed and led to a crisis in which developing countries were faced with staggering external debt and inadequate income for repayment.

Because many development loans were provided by large commercial banks, there was fear of a collapse of the international financial system if developing countries were to default on their loans. The International Monetary Fund (IMF) responded to this debt crisis by offering debtor countries an opportunity to restructure their debt through structural adjustment loan (SAL) programs. Accepting a SAL also implied that the debtor country accepted structural adjustment plans (SAPs). SAPs promoted globalization strategies such as privatization of government-owned industrial enterprises, reduction of import/export tariffs, restrictions on foreign direct investment, and reorganization of economic activity. Economic reorganization was focused on promotion of export-oriented production designed to generate income from trade with rich countries.

Developing countries operating under a SAP had little to export beyond their natural resources. Natural resource–based export earnings in the early 1980s were 59 percent or more of the overall economy in countries such as the Central African Republic, Ethiopia, Indonesia, Nepal, Costa Rica, Mexico, and Paraguay. The increased supply of raw commodity exports resulted in a substantial decline in the price of these commodities, as would be suggested by simple supply-and-demand analysis. This is revealed in the "barter terms of trade," or the ratio of export prices to import prices for low-income countries. According to the World Bank (1991), the barter terms of trade for low-income countries declined by 50 percent during the period between 1965 and 1988.

The decline in the value of commodity exports relative to finished goods imports reduced the income that developing countries gained from commodity exports. In the case of Africa, for example, where a majority of export earnings came from basic commodities such as cocoa, coffee, palm oil, and minerals, analyst Tore Rose observed that "prices [fell] so rapidly with increased production and supply that increases in export volume actually result in a decrease in earnings" (1985, 178). In order to maintain adequate incomes to support both the national economy and SAL repayment

schemes, more raw commodities would have to be harvested and exported.

The World Commission on Environment and Development (better known as the Brundtland Commission) argued that the promotion of commodity exports in the manner described above led to unsustainable overuse of the natural resource base for commodities such as forestry, beef ranching, ocean fishing, and some cash crops (World Commission on Environment and Development 1987, 80–81). There is some evidence supporting the Brundtland Commission's argument. For example, Malawi has had ten SALs since 1979, and the Overseas Development Institute found negative outcomes resulting from those SALs. Similarly, Ghana's SAP called for export-oriented cocoa production, which failed as an income-generating strategy following the collapse of world cocoa prices. In the Philippines, the World Resources Institute found that SALs encouraged overexploitation of natural resources, increased pollution, and urban decay.

Recent analysis of tropical deforestation data by Kamaljit Bawa and S. Dayanandan (1997) uncovered a statistically significant and relatively large positive correlation between per capita external debt levels and annual tropical deforestation rates. In particular, Bawa and Dayanandan used World Resources Institute data for seventy tropical countries and looked at fourteen socioeconomic factors thought to be related to deforestation. Their multiple regression analysis of the relative magnitude of direct effects indicated that per capita external debt is the single most important factor explaining deforestation rates in Latin America and Asia, while in Africa the debt measure is ranked behind population density in importance. Interestingly, per capita gross national product (GNP) was not found to be a significant factor in explaining deforestation.

The sustainable development movement calls for the recognition that improving human well-being requires development strategies to be crafted that take into account social and environmental factors in addition to the traditional goal of economic growth. The World Bank has incorporated some aspects of sustainability in its development program. Its new environmental strategy, Making Sustainable Commitments, adopted in 2001, has three objectives: improving quality of life, improving the quality of growth, and protecting the quality of the regional and global commons. In a press release dated October 25, 2001, Kristalina Georgieva, World Bank director of the Environment Department, stated, "The strategy will ensure economic growth does not come at the expense of people's health and future opportunities because of pollution and degraded natural resources and ecosystems. It calls for a full and coherent mainstreaming of environmental concerns into poverty reduction strategies, and in Bank lending and non-lending activities."

Structural adjustment can also be attacked on humanitarian grounds for the impacts of transferring income from very poor to rich countries. For example, the World Bank (1991) indicated that interest payments on external debt in Latin America consumed up to 40 percent of the national export earnings of these countries, leaving little money available for necessary imports, let alone health care, low-income assistance, job-creation programs, education, or the promotion of more pollution-efficient technologies. Oxfam International estimated that Uganda spent $17 per person on debt repayment annually but only $3 on health care. Overall, expenditures on health in IMF/World Bank–programmed countries in Africa declined by 50 percent while these countries were under SAL programs in the 1980s, and education expenditures declined by 25 percent.

The process of debt repayment by heavily indebted poor countries is widely seen as fostering serious health, developmental, and environmental problems and has led to calls for debt forgiveness. The IMF and the World Bank have responded by developing the Heavily Indebted Poor Countries (HIPC) Initiative, a program to help such countries with IMF- and World Bank–supported adjustment programs. The HIPC Initiative entails coordinated action by the international financial community, including multilateral institutions, to reduce the external debt burden of these countries to sustainable levels. By 2001, the IMF and the World Bank had approved debt-reduction packages for twenty-four countries, twenty of them in Africa. According to the IMF, these packages will remove $36 billion in debt, and together with other initiatives, these countries will see their debts fall, on average, by about two-thirds.

Globalization and the Spread of Nonnative Species

The expansion of travel, migration, and trade that is associated with globalization entails the more rapid spread of nonnative species of plants, animals, and microbes, with various positive and negative economic impacts. In their authoritative survey of the literature, David Pimental et al. (2000) estimated that approximately 50,000 nonnative species have been introduced into the United States. The introduction of valuable and productive agricultural plants and animals has often had positive impacts. For example, nonnative cultivars such as corn, rice, wheat, and other food crops, and Old World livestock such as cattle and poultry, have been estimated by the U.S. Bureau of the Census (1998) to provide more than 98 percent of the food produced in the United States, with an estimated annual value of $800 billion.

The intentional and unintentional introduction of other nonnative species, however, has sometimes had negative impacts on the environment, including direct losses and damages. Pimental et al. estimated that introduced species of animals, plants, and microbes impose costs of $123 billion a year in damage and control costs in the United States. The unintentional introduction of the Norway rat (*Rattus norvegicus*), for example, has cost some $19 billion a year. Other examples of destructive introduced pests include the tree-killing diseases known as chestnut blight, Dutch elm disease, and the more recent sudden oak death syndrome, which struck California trees in 1995. According to the National Research Council (2002), nonindigenous plants and plant pests that (intentionally or unintentionally) find their way into the United States and become invasive can often cause problems. The council estimated that plants and plant pests impose more than $100 billion per year in crop and timber losses, as well as the added costs of herbicide and pesticide control treatments. Its report is conservative in that it does not include the costs of invasions in less intensively managed ecosystems, such as wetlands.

Fortunately, the growing impact of nonnative species in the United States is gaining the attention of policymakers. On February 2, 1999, President Bill Clinton issued Executive Order 13112, which allocated $28 million to combat nonnative species invasions and created the Interagency Invasive Species Council. The goal of the council was to produce a plan within eighteen months to mobilize the federal government to defend again nonindigenous species invasions. The council's plan was implemented but the drive to deal with nonnative species and other environmental problems faded with the George W. Bush administration and the shift to a focus on other global problems that took center stage.

Steven C. Hackett

See Also Environmental Impacts of Globalization; Sustainable Development

Note

Portions of this entry are adapted from Steven C. Hackett, *Environmental and Natural Resources Economics: Theory,* *Policy, and the Sustainable Society.* Armonk, NY: M. E. Sharpe, 2001, pp. 298–304, 328–332. Copyright © 2001 by M. E. Sharpe, Inc. Published with permission.

References

Bawa, K., and S. Dayanandan. 1997. "Socioeconomic Factors and Tropical Deforestation." *Nature* 386 (April 10): 562–563.

Chichilnisky, G. 1994. "NorthSouth Trade and the Global Environment." *American Economic Review* 84 (September): 851–874.

Hackett, S. 2001. *Environmental and Natural Resources Economics: Theory, Policy, and the Sustainable Society.* 2d ed. New York: M. E. Sharpe.

Hardin, G. 1968. "The Tragedy of the Commons." *Science* 162 (December 13): 1243–1248.

Krugman, P. 1987. "Is Free Trade Passé?" *Journal of Economic Perspectives* 1 (Fall): 131–144.

National Research Council. 2002. *Predicting Invasions of Nonindigenous Plants and Plant Pests.* Washington, DC: National Academy Press.

Ostrom, E. 1990. *Governing the Commons: The Evolution of Institutions for Collective Action.* Cambridge: Cambridge University Press.

Pimentel, D., et al. 2000. "Environmental and Economic Costs Associated with Non-Indigenous Species in the United States." *BioScience* 50: 53–65.

Rose, T., ed. 1985. *Crisis and Recovery in Sub-Saharan Africa.* Paris: Organisation for Economic Co-operation and Development.

U.S. Bureau of the Census. 1998. *Statistical Abstract of the United States, 1996.* 200th ed. Washington, DC: U.S. Bureau of the Census, U.S. Government Printing Office.

Wapenhans, W., et al. 1992. "Report of the Portfolio Management Task Force, July 1, 1992." Internal World Bank document.

World Bank. 1991. *World Development 1991: The Challenge of Development.* Oxford: Oxford University Press.

World Commission on Environment and Development. 1987. *Our Common Future.* Oxford: Oxford University Press.

Political Systems and Governance

Globalization, defined here as the increasing volume of commercial, financial, cultural, informational, and political links among states and peoples, has had a diverse set of influences on national political systems and governance. The effects of each of these factors on political systems and governance methods and tools depends, to a very large degree, on a state's initial position or condition at the outset of the recent globalization wave. States with democratic political systems and good governance processes have experienced some stress, but states whose institutional structures were less robust have often experienced serious challenges as they have adapted. Most particularly, although critics contend that globalization is a severe constraint on governments' policy choices and behaviors through effects such as the "race to the bottom" and increasing political ties, evidence that this is actually the case is mixed.

Defining Political Systems and Governance

Governance can generally, though inexactly, be defined as the process by which social problems are identified, potential solutions proposed and examined, and selected policies implemented. It also includes obtaining feedback from the implemented policies and making adjustments in response to such feedback. Issues of governance include which and whose demands receive attention, who has access to the policymaking process, who decides on issues and policies to be addressed, how solutions are proposed and decisions made, how efficiently implementation and decisionmaking institutions proceed, and how policymakers collect information and evaluate policies.

Political systems are the forums in which governance occurs. These can be national, subnational (where state structure allows for this, as in federal countries such as Brazil, Mexico, and the United States), or, in a relatively prominent feature of modern globalization, international (regional or global). Issues of political systems include who is an actor in the system, patterns in or characteristics of actor behavior, and institutions (broadly defined) that structure, shape, contain, or constrain actor behavior.

Commercial Ties

Most prominent among the arguments about the role of commercial ties in governance and political system changes is a variant of the Kantian democratic peace argument; that is, that increased trade between states will decrease the potential for war between them. For democratic states, in particular, the argument is that citizens will not wish to start wars with trading partners because wars disrupt trade by removing the adversary as both a potential export market and a potential source of inputs. Domestic firms doing business with the adversary will agitate against conflict and press for peaceful resolution to minimize economic disruption, whereas workers will support peace because war disrupts production and can lead to lower incomes, both from reduced production and a higher tax burden to finance the war.

Arguments about trade and democracy are highly salient because, while a substantial fraction of all trade is still conducted between countries that share a common border or are in reasonable geographic proximity to one another, almost all interstate conflicts are also fought between adjacent or nearby states. Added to this, the proportion of democracies in the international system has skyrocketed in the past thirty years. States that gained independence in the "third wave" (Huntington 1991) of democratization in the 1960s and 1970s often backslid into a period of authoritarianism, but many have redemocratized in the "fourth wave" of democratization that followed the end of the Cold War. Combining the trade-promotes-peace argument with both increasing levels of trade (on both the global and regional scales) and increased democratization suggests that interstate conflict should continue to decline as a result. Interstate violence is already quite rare, particularly in the global North, but the argument suggests that state-to-state violence in the global South will also become rarer.

Closely related to this argument is the suggestion that democratic governance is beneficial to states' economic growth rates. States governed democratically tend to have lower tariff rates than autocratically governed states; democracies experience economic growth of 4 percent a year, on average, whereas autocracies grow only 3 percent a year. Over two decades, this difference compounds and produces an enormous divergence in economic trajectories (Bueno de Mesquita and Root 2000).

The role of mass economic satisfaction in democratic elections is well-demonstrated: Economic conditions in the year preceding an election provide one of the strongest predictors of an incumbent's reelection success. Trade helps to boost the national economy by providing imports that are cheaper than domestically produced goods and also providing an outlet for surplus domestically produced goods. Ed-

ward Mansfield, Helen Milner, and B. Peter Rosendorff (2002) found that a pair of democracies is twice as likely to sign a trade agreement as a pair consisting of one democracy and one autocracy, and the democratic dyad is four times as likely as an autocratic dyad to sign a trade agreement. This finding compounds the trade-and-democracy argument presented above as well as arguments presented below about international agreements and policy commitment and about the increasing frequency of political agreements as the number of democracies increases.

One final caution should be added that relates more directly to globalization's effects on political systems. Ronald Inglehart (1997) found that many of the countries thought to be most globalized, that is, those of Western Europe, Scandinavia, and North America, display a pattern of (often emergent rather than salient) political cleavages that he described as "postmodern." Modern cultures form political cleavages around traditional income-based left-right issues such as free enterprise, labor unionism, and incomes and industrial policy; postmodern cultures form cleavages over issues such as environmental protection, abortion, and human rights, which do not directly affect income. Much of the rest of the world is still in a "modern" culture where income-affecting policies are key contentious political issues, so trade liberalization and increased commercial ties will have much more political salience in these states than in the highly globalized states of Western Europe and North America.

These diverging trends in salient political cleavages could, if not properly considered in policy formation, result in misunderstandings that could contribute to a renewed globalization "backlash." Although trade policy and commercial openness will still have some political salience from directly affected groups, their decline in importance relative to other issues is quite evident in the pro–free trade approach of almost every serious contender for the American presidency, Republican or Democrat, since 1980, and similar trends in many other advanced countries. Trade policymaking in industrial or postindustrial democracies is increasingly contested by individuals whose concerns with trade are not related to the income effects of trade at all; instead, their concerns are over the treatment and wages of labor, human rights observance in potential trading partners, or the environmental consequences of industrial development.

Moreover, trade issues mobilize individuals who occupy different positions in their domestic political systems. Particularly with the advent of the Internet, groups that favor or (more frequently) oppose trade for any reason have been able to collaborate relatively cheaply, thus amplifying the effect of their positions by coordinating approaches to national leaders. State leaders have been faced with coordinated opposition to policies, which makes achieving further cooperation difficult (see below.) In other states, trade has presented a different problem for political systems. Because trade reinforces income divergence between owners of the locally scarce and locally abundant economic factors, political systems premised on egalitarian values have faced pressure to mitigate the effects of trade on social structures. The People's Republic of China is a prominent example. As a Communist country, China provides employment for all citizens in the state-run economy; opening to trade unconditionally would cause the decline of inefficient sectors and mass unemployment. As a consequence, the government has embraced a policy of "controlled openness," in which exports are promoted, but imports that would compete directly with domestically produced goods are strictly limited. Government-sponsored programs to transform less competitive sectors through privatization or retraining have been only moderately successful. Rising unemployment is a serious concern for the regime, since any peasant protest effort might well turn into a repeat of the 1989 Tiananmen Square incident. The brutal repression of that event tarnished the government's credibility (and desir-

ability as a political partner) for several years afterward.

In developed democracies, particularly those of Western Europe, which have high provision of social services and insurance, governments have experienced pressures to reduce social expenditures, and make business more competitive, by decreasing taxes on profits and capital, and to reduce government deficits incurred on social services and transfers. Although it cannot be denied that reductions in social services have taken place, they cannot necessarily be attributed to the pressures of international trade and competitiveness. Nonetheless, such a decline is troubling; scholarship generally agrees that social insurance schemes allow small states to maximize welfare by remaining open to trade while satisfying political pressures for social stability (Katzenstein 1985; Garrett 1998).

Financial Ties

One of the primary differences between the first wave of globalization (c. 1880–1914) and the second one (1970–present) lies in the nature of cross-border financial ties. The earlier wave saw large capital flows, primarily into long-term, fixed investments such as railroads, municipal transportation, and sanitation improvements. In contrast, the present wave is characterized not so much by the *volume* of transactions (as a proportion of gross domestic product [GDP], 1914 levels have only been surpassed in the past handful of years) as by the *speed* of transactions. Improvements in communications technology and financial instruments have created profit opportunities in short-term investment and speculation. The Organisation for Economic Co-operation and Development (OECD) estimated that almost $1.5 *trillion* dollars a day crosses borders—a value several times the world money supply, implying that a substantial amount of money crosses several borders in different transactions on any given day.

Capital openness ties states into this web of high-speed, high-volume flows. When industrializing states are tied into global capital networks, and are dependent on the world market for developmental capital, domestic instability or capital-hostile policies can provoke disastrous capital flight. Since most capital is in short-term stocks and bonds, the resulting stock-market crash can create enormous social disruptions with far-reaching political implications. Integration into world capital markets also affects a state's ability to use monetarist or neo-Keynesian policies to achieve domestic economic or political goals such as reduced unemployment or reflation. Perceived social, political, or economic instability can deter capital investments, even with the lure of a higher interest rate. For both developed and developing countries, attempts to tax capital, restrict its mobility, or impose labor standards or other regulations that substantially increase the cost of doing business may benefit domestic political or economic interests, but in a global capital market, potential investment will simply look elsewhere for lower costs and higher returns. In theory, then, a world of integrated capital markets and forward-looking states will result in a "race to the bottom" where labor, which is substantially less internationally mobile than capital, will have to bear all of the costs. States are predicted to engage in competitive reductions of health and labor standards, capital taxes, and the like to attract the most capital possible.

This scenario—a world where capital from the global North exploits labor in the developing global South—is the fear of many anti-globalization activists. Quite unfortunately for both the activists and the theorists, there is very little evidence of such convergence. In fact, OECD research has found the complete opposite to be the case: Countries having the most success in opening to trade and investment have also shown improvement in achieving core labor standards. Since companies invest abroad to tap into new markets, host governments actually retain considerable influence over the multinational's behavior and

can effectively resist pressures to reduce regulation (Dresner 2000, 65–66).

Another important consequence of financial integration—on governance, in particular—is that financial integration can often lead to financial crisis contagion. Large flows between a pair of countries mean that a crisis in one will disrupt expected flows to the other, possibly triggering crisis or collapse there as well. In other cases, states with similar structural or policy conditions will experience similar shocks sequentially or simultaneously, as in the 1997 Asian financial crisis. The overvalued Thai baht was the target of speculation, which eventually drove the collapse of both the baht and the Thai banking system. The resulting panic and inflation required massive intervention by the International Monetary Fund (IMF) to restore stability. More important, the attack on the baht prompted similar attacks on other regional currencies that were fixed at overvalued rates. Combined with the weak banking systems in many of these states, and especially the large role of inadequately regulated private banks in corporate investments and the stock market, the speculative attack spread very easily. The only policy response that was even moderately successful at preventing contagion was Malaysia's immediate imposition of capital controls, which was in direct opposition to the prevailing economic wisdom about crisis management and capital behavior.

In tightly integrated or trade-interdependent countries, both financial and nonfinancial crises can be highly contagious. In the 1995 Mexican peso crisis, U.S. policymakers defended their immediate use of a credit facility intended for defense of the dollar to shore up the peso on the grounds that if the peso had been allowed to continue to fall, the dollar would have fallen with it because of the large amount of trade between the two countries. If the Mexican economy had collapsed when the peso was devalued, U.S. officials argued, American businesses would have lost such a large export market that the U.S. economy would likely contract in reaction. Even nonfinancial crises can spread through financial ties: The 2002 Sudden Acute Respiratory Syndrome (SARS) crisis, which started in China, spread not only the disease but also economic slowdowns through most of East Asia as consumers chose to refrain from going out to eat, shop, and spend money.

Foreign direct investment (FDI) also affects both governance and political systems. States with mineral resources but no domestic capital to exploit those resources often must turn to foreign companies to achieve any benefit. For developing countries with high capital needs, large incentives exist to cut capital taxes and provide only minimal regulation to attract as much capital as possible. Companies are often willing to provide bribes, kickbacks, and other incentives in return for minimal government interference and exclusive rights to mineral exploitation or monopoly of the domestic market. In both cases, the foreign-owned (and often foreign-managed) industry normally accounts for a notable percentage of national income; mineral extraction alone can account for a large part of the hard currency earnings in a less developed country (LDC). Some sources estimate that in Angola in the late 1980s and early 1990s, at the height of a civil war, oil production off the Cabinda coast accounted for over half of Angolan GDP. Quite often, this status as "primary breadwinner" allows these companies to obtain a disproportionate influence in policymaking. As democratization progresses in many of these states, the state's need to placate capital conflicts with the need for leaders to placate their constituents.

According to the OECD, FDI was down by 20 percent in 2002 among developed countries, and it declined again overall in 2003. In contrast, developed countries exported more than $600 billion in capital, largely to developing countries; the People's Republic of China was the single largest recipient in 2002, with US$53 billion in inflows (OECD 2003). In general, FDI accounts for a substantially smaller portion of cross-border flows in this second wave of globalization than in the previous wave, largely be-cause financial ties have shifted into short-term investments rather than long-term projects such as factory construction. What is most important about FDI and capital flows in general, though, is that states have not managed to resist the lure of international capital. Even (nominally) socialist countries such as China allow foreign direct investment; in the Chinese case, the investment must contain a Chinese ownership component, and often the firm must be located in one of the Special Economic Zones in which capitalist industry is permitted.

Cultural Links

One of the more prominent concerns expressed by non-Western globalization foes is the fear that "globalization" really means "westernization." Almost all of the phenomena associated with globalization—the growth of capitalist economies, democratization, the "jeans and T-shirts" lifestyle—were perfected first in the West and then exported to the rest of the world. The erosion of traditional lifestyles, or at least their perceived erosion, is a major concern that could contribute to globalization backlash in the future, changing political systems not by changing the structure of the systems themselves but by changing the nature of inputs into the system. McDonald's franchises are in some 118 countries; the so-called "Golden Arches' thesis," that no two countries with McDonald's have ever fought each other, held until the 1995 U.S. bombing of Sarajevo, in the former Yugoslavia. *National Geographic* magazine photographers have spotted University of Michigan–blazoned apparel in places as remote as rural Tibet and Arctic Eskimo settlements, suggesting that both Western modes of dress as well as American commercialism have spread beyond their initial borders.

Hollywood movies are viewed around the world (in fact, there is such a demand for American films in China that a major trade dispute exists between the United States and the Chinese government over pirated copies of

American films and intellectual property rights). Through most of the 1990s, the world's most-watched television show was *Baywatch* (*Guinness World Records* 2000). Some countries have reacted more negatively to this spread of Western (read "American") culture than others, arguing that barriers to free trade in intellectual property are appropriate when issues of national culture are at stake: France has blocked numerous moves to liberalize broadcasting and telecommunications media in the European Union to preserve a role for French-produced francophone film. Recently, though, non-Western cultures have begun to make headway in cultural exports. Indian film, known colloquially as "Bollywood," has become increasingly popular in Western countries, even those without large Indian expatriate or émigré communities.

Even democratization, with all its economic benefits and normative associations, is often perceived as a Western cultural phenomenon deemed inappropriate for some societies. King Hassan II of Morocco explicitly stated during a 1996 round of constitutional revisions that although he agreed that political life needed more public participation, he did not feel that a Western-style democracy was appropriate for Morocco. Despite this, developing countries very often look explicitly at Western constitutions as models and import institutional designs wholesale, with little regard for the finer points of why those institutions were designed and selected in the first place. France's 1958 ("Fifth Republic") constitution is a common model. Because it provides for two top-level political figures, a president and a prime minister, countries trying to settle a civil war or other dispute between two rival factions often select it to allow both factions major roles in government. In 1991, Russia opted for a semi-presidential system to placate the hard-liner Communists, reduce the sense among them that their ways were under threat, and allow them to influence the speed of change. The 1994 Angolan constitution, produced after the Bicesse Peace Accords, followed this pattern as

well. Needless to say, this institutional configuration has not been as successful at creating political stability and the necessary conditions for economic growth in any of these cases as it was in France under Charles de Gaulle, who designed it and also served as the first president under the new system.

Human Rights

Human rights are another "Western" concept that has become part of the "cultural globalization" debate. Human rights as a concept and practice have transformed the international political system as well as many domestic ones. Only Western societies have comparatively long-standing traditions of state respect for persons, lives, and property; customary law in many parts of Africa and the Middle East frequently includes the death penalty, and many repressive regimes rely on intimidation, torture, and large security forces to maintain power. Gender equality as a right is even less widely held, even in the West; Swiss women did not receive the right to vote until 1971. Developing states often resent Western governments' efforts to condition developmental aid on respect for human rights; many of them are so dependent on outside aid and trade concessions, however, that they begrudgingly accept human rights treaties, even if implementation is weak. Nonetheless, even minimal observance of human rights has empowered previously repressed groups. Formerly suppressed women in India (and many other parts of the world) have joined literacy initiatives, and microcredit lending circles now allow women to start their own businesses, for example. Both of these practices contradict long-standing rural social norms about the role of women. Former Moroccan detainees and torture victims and their heirs, using human rights principles, have protested government secrecy about their fates and succeeded in forcing the government to create a Truth and Reconciliation Commission to investigate claims of torture, involuntary imprisonment, and "disappearances," and to pay victims compensation.

Since the seventeenth century, international relations have been based on the doctrine of sovereignty, but some have argued that sovereignty is eroding because of the application of human rights concepts internationally. In theory at least, sovereignty is what allows a state government to behave as it pleases within its own territory, and all other states are forbidden to interfere in that state's domestic policies. The idea of universal human rights violates this fundamental concept. Under human rights theory, other states claim the right to interfere in a state's domestic policies, and even to violate its territorial integrity by invading, if the outside states determine that the state is violating its citizens' human rights. States even claim these rights to interfere if the domestic government of the country in violation has not formally accepted these principles. In an even larger theoretical violation of sovereignty, states have willingly ceded the right to treat their citizens as they choose to the broader international community by signing treaties that give human rights the status of international law. By signing the treaties, leaders essentially cede the rights of their government to determine their internal policies independently and agree to be bound by the international agreements. Many have thus argued that the foundations of sovereignty itself are being undermined and that sovereignty will eventually be replaced as the organizing principle of the international system.

Cultural Linkage and Change

A number of schools of thought suggest that increased exposure to other cultures will enhance tolerance and reduce the likelihood of war. Increasing frequency of interactions via international travel, television programming, people-to-people exchanges, international educational opportunities, and arts and cultural exchanges can contribute to better understanding of other peoples and their cultures and values. Though there is some evidence to the contrary, that too much exposure to other cultures can make individuals feel that their own culture is being invaded and provoke a de-

fensive reaction, there are some grounds for hope on a smaller scale. Several programs send Israeli and Palestinian youths on extended camping retreats, for example; the teens frequently start the program holding antagonistic views of the other group, but conclude the program with much more moderate opinions.

More important for both critics and proponents of cultural globalization arguments, cultural products, cultural practices, and culturally based opinions are not absorbed blindly and in their entirety. Recipients take in new values, customs, and habits in small pieces and in a selective manner, normally working to minimize dissonance between their existing value set and the new information, and translate the messages they receive through their own values and culture. Even if human rights, Hollywood, McDonald's, and democracy are observed around the world with increasing frequency, the cultural meaning of *Baywatch,* or an election, or government renunciation of torture will vary from society to society. Global availability of a cultural product does not mean that it will have global acceptance, or even acceptance in different ways all over the globe. Advertisers and marketing agencies are among the first to acknowledge this and regularly adapt the way they market the same product to different cultural circumstances. This suggests that global culture is not yet truly global: Significant differences remain across societies, regions, and even countries within regions.

Information Flows

Information flows do not normally touch political systems directly but instead affect them in distinct but indirect ways through their influence on governance. The rise of the Internet as a cheap and effective means of disseminating information, for example, has both allowed governments to provide more information to citizens and facilitated the organization of a cross-border opposition to various international policy issues.

Informed citizens are better equipped to make demands on their governments, and in repressive societies these demands often include democratization. At a minimum, many modern authoritarian governments fear what would happen if their citizens obtained accurate information about the rest of the world. China, the People's Democratic Republic of Korea (North Korea), and many other similar states routinely block citizen access to the Internet as well as global media sources such as CNN and BSkyB. They do so with good reason—the 2003 debacle surrounding the emergence and spread of SARS in China is an excellent case in point. Under normal operating circumstances, the Chinese government would have continued to suppress information about the true scope of the illness's spread. When the severity of the illness finally brought the World Health Organization into the picture, Western journalists began investigating. Publication of their discoveries through Western media channels brought international pressure to bear on the Chinese government to provide the truth. More important, Chinese citizens gained access to Western media reports. Fury over the government's decision to deceive citizens in order to maintain its public façade of having the infection under control led to street demonstrations and other forms of protest, resulting in the first known case in which the Chinese government explicitly responded to public opinion when two government ministers were dismissed for their complicity in the scheme.

Even prior to the Internet, though, information was considered dangerous to repressive states. The Soviet Union and many other Communist states frequently censored mail, publishing, and international news media, fearing what could happen if their citizens learned the true disparity between life in the West and what they experienced. The most notable example of the effect of information on political systems occurred in 1975 with the Helsinki Accords, which called for, among other things, unimpeded access for journalists and free circulation of information. Over the next fifteen years, public dissatisfaction with the standard of living under Communist regimes grew as the public learned about lifestyles in the West. Governments were forced to increase expenditures on social and private goods, and both are widely acknowledged contributions to the relative ease with which the Communist regimes of Central and Eastern Europe were dismantled.

International organizations also play a major role in facilitating the exchange of information among states. Many international organizations, which themselves are the products of cooperation among states, provide forums for states to exchange information about policy sectors within that institution's jurisdiction. Within the Association of Southeast Asian Nations (ASEAN), there is an ASEAN Regional Forum (ARF), for example, that enables member states to gather twice a year to discuss their views on current regional political and security issues and to share their thoughts on each other's policies. Many international organizations also provide independent information and monitoring services. The World Health Organization (WHO) disseminates information on potential public health threats and publishes travel advisories; the World Trade Organization (WTO) and the OECD provide annual reviews of members' policies in their areas of competence, highlighting deviations from policies agreed upon under the auspices of the WTO and OECD, respectively.

In many ways, information flows are critical to the other facets of globalization examined here. The rise of modern telecommunications technology permits round-the-clock, round-the-world financial trading and increasing levels of short-term investment. With easier access to information about market conditions, and the ability to monitor behavior more closely than when sailboats took several months to cross the Atlantic, investors are more willing to invest in intangible assets such as stocks and bonds, and they learn about downturns or bad news fast enough to sell. Political actors in one state can make overtures to or try to influence political actors in other states.

Political Ties

Overall, the feature that most distinguishes modern globalization from prewar globalization is the level of interstate political cooperation, and particularly the institutionalization of this cooperation in international organizations. The distinctive feature of prewar globalization was laissez-faire capitalism, where governments were unwilling (and in many ways generally unable) to interfere in economic affairs, domestic or international. The enormous expansion of trade and investment in the late nineteenth century was subject to hardly any regulation or government control; no Gold Standard Monitoring Organization existed to manage the international currency regime. Globalization in that era was primarily economic, featuring a remarkable convergence in factor prices and living standards in the central Atlantic economies, though with little effect on peripheral economies.

In contrast, modern globalization has been supported and, many argue, promoted by a dense network of interlocking agreements between and among states. Chief among these are agreements signed at Bretton Woods, New Hampshire, at the end of World War II that attempted to regularize the conditions for international trade and exchange rate changes and make them more predictable. The Bretton Woods Agreements created the World Bank (known then as the International Bank for Reconstruction and Development, or IBRD), the General Agreement on Tariffs and Trade (GATT, the institutional precursor to today's World Trade Organization), and the International Monetary Fund. By stabilizing the political components of international economics, Bretton Woods facilitated the rapid postwar expansion in trade between developed countries that continues to this day and created the structures needed to bring developing countries into the international trading system. This cooperation and coordination in the economic arena were facilitated and complemented by similar efforts in the political arena (the United Nations), the military arena (the Western European Union, and later, the North Atlantic Treaty Organization, NATO), and a variety of other fields.

Since then, the number of agreements signed each year has grown almost exponentially. International treaties and other agreements govern an incredible range of topics, from the rights of international air travel companies and their passengers (the Warsaw Convention on International Air Carriage, 1929), to permissible catches of certain whales (International Convention for the Prevention of Whaling, 1946), and even what constitutes a treaty (the Vienna Convention on the Law of Treaties, 1980). Many of these treaties are supported by organizations or secretariats of varying sizes that help states carry out their treaty obligations. The densest network of such treaties and organizations is in Western Europe, where twenty-seven states have delegated substantial governance powers to the institutions of the European Union. Members of the EU no longer have the right to make such regulatory decisions as determining who is a dentist, for example, or what colors refrigerator wiring should be, or what percentage milk content is required for a drink to be a called a "milkshake." These powers are shared with the (appointed) European Commission, seated in Brussels, Belgium.

Global Governance

Many authors argue that, taken together, these international agreements and organizations represent a fundamental change in the nature of governance, but opinion is still divided over whether these changes are good. Supporters argue that efforts at "global governance" allow states to find collective solutions to problems in ways that are more efficient than if each state tried to resolve their problems separately. They point to the numerous environmental agreements of the 1990s: One state reducing emissions is not likely to affect global warming, but all states working together may have an impact. Likewise, international efforts to establish telecommunications standards and consistent e-commerce policies facilitate international trade and investment, making all states better off.

Critics argue that democratic governance processes are being short-circuited because much of the negotiations that occur at the international level go on behind closed doors. The public usually does not have any input on whether action on a particular issue even needs to be taken at this level, and the highly technical nature of the agreements and programs often obscures who the real domestic winners and losers are. The critics also point to the incredible number of major trade liberalization agreements signed in the 1990s, including the formation of the WTO itself. Many of these trade agreements were signed by governments led by those on the left of the political spectrum (Social Democrats, American Democrats, Socialists, and the like), which is more often associated with labor and thus protectionist policies than with free trade. Critics charge that the surrender of sovereignty inherent in agreements of any type restricts national policy choices and constrains the ability to pursue national goals by prohibiting tariff increases or other protectionist measures, in the case of most trade agreements, or by ignoring alternative approaches to reducing global warming, in the case of the Kyoto Protocol, for example.

International Organizations and Political Behavior

International organizations increasingly make policy on behalf of states; they also provide constraints on current and future policy behavior, particularly in democracies. States may seek to join, create, or otherwise make use of international organizations for these reasons. In other words, sovereignty is ceded for capacity. States trade the ability to set policy independently for some policy capacity they lack, such as the ability to formulate or implement a policy to solve the problem or the ability to pay for the solution.

States facing serious currency crises or balance of payment problems can turn to the IMF for loans to help them weather the crisis. These loans come with strings attached: Countries accepting IMF aid normally must accept a structural adjustment agreement that includes specific policy measures that the government must take to fix whatever the IMF has identified as the "cause" of the country's economic problem. These measures are usually quite politically painful, involving cuts to state subsidies for food, child care, social insurance, and industry, along with regulatory restructuring for banks, insurance, and sometimes other sectors. Since most IMF-assisted bailouts occur after a boom-and-bust cycle, economic deflation resulting directly from the crisis increases unemployment (and raises demand for social insurance), causing additional political pain just as the government is facing the difficult task of reorganizing the economy to fit the vision of the IMF's economists. Without the conditionality of the IMF agreement, which effectively commits a government to the reform policies as a condition of further assistance (and implicitly to enable the country to avoid further disaster or backslide), many developing states with weak or underdeveloped political institutions would not be able to muster the political will to implement these sweeping reforms. Such externally imposed reforms, however, are often thought to undercut democratic governance because voiced popular opinions for enhanced social insurance and government efforts to alleviate suffering and create employment are often ignored in favor of the appointed IMF economists' preferences.

Developed democracies also use international agreements and institutions to commit themselves to policy positions, but for a more sophisticated reason. In a mature developed democracy, international agreements and organizations allow parties of a particular ideology or political preference to commit themselves—and their successors, who will likely be of a different political ideology or preference— to a particular policy or to use or nonuse of a particular policy instrument. The treaty creates an additional hurdle for future governments, should they wish to deviate from the current incumbent's preferences, and helps to ensure that current preferences will remain national policy well after the incumbent and his or her party lose office. Pro-EU British Prime Minister Tony Blair (Labour Party, 1997–), for example, signed the EU's Social Charter as part of the Treaty of Amsterdam, which his Conservative predecessor John Major (1991–1997) had refused to do. Future British prime ministers, Labour or Conservative, will have to contend with social policy obligations that are not only enshrined in domestic law but also part of a binding international agreement as well as part of a larger package of agreements. The same rationale can also be used by developing states. Mexican leaders followed Central European leaders in admitting very bluntly that their major goal for signing free trade agreements with their larger, democratic neighbors (and in the Central European case, applying for EU membership) was to lock in reforms and help deter or prevent backslides into authoritarianism. In these cases, politics and economics have become thoroughly intertwined so that developments in one almost automatically affect the other.

The EU deserves special mention here for its demonstration of multilevel governance. Policy is made there on several levels: the European level, the national level, the subnational level (for federal states), and the local level. The EU practices *subsidiarity,* a policy that argues for decisions to be taken at the closest possible level to the citizen. Issues are only taken up at the European level if national policies have been insufficient and if national political leaders consent to its consideration at the European level. For the past several decades, the EU has been held up as a model of postterritorial or postsovereignty governance. Recently, however, some arguments have been made suggesting that this practice of taking nationally unresolvable issues to the European level will put incredible strain on EU institutions. The EU's in-

stitutions were not designed for direct governance over the range of issues now considered regularly at the Union level. Eventually, the institutions may be confronted with a severe crisis imperiling the entire political structure of the European Union. Given the level of integration achieved by EU members, if the Union institutions prove unable to respond to such a crisis in a manner that is satisfactory to the general public, the resulting collapse could become the basis of an unprecedented economic and political disaster (see also James 2001, chap. 6).

New Actors in the International Political System

In the traditional model of Westphalian international relations, which forms the dominant paradigm for most scholarly work, the primary if not sole actors were states. It is now incredibly difficult to argue that states are the only actors in world politics, and it is increasingly a challenge even to argue that states are the major actors in world politics. States now compete with multinational corporations (many of whom have annual revenues greater than states' GDPs), international organizations, transnational pressure groups, and international governmental networks. The rise of new actors, which is largely attributable to globalization's different facets presented here, represents a fundamental shift in the nature of the international system.

These new actors also affect the concept of governance at the national and international levels insofar as these groups and individuals have the ability to raise issues for policy consideration and action. Sometimes, nonstate actors are directly involved in the implementation of the policies they help design. International organizations fill the many roles discussed above. Transnational pressure groups include environmental activist groups such as Greenpeace, human rights groups such as Amnesty International and Médecins Sans Frontières (Doctors Without Borders, which won the 1999 Nobel Peace Prize for its work in war-torn areas), and a variety of other groups in different fields of work. Some individuals are increasingly able to manipulate policy attention on the global level through their high-profile personal involvement: South Africa's Nelson Mandela, Britain's late Princess Diana, and former U.S. president Jimmy Carter are all examples of people advancing particular causes through individual action. Policy networks—consisting of national officials with expertise in particular areas meeting with their foreign counterparts to discuss issues of concern—are also a little-known facet of global governance. These networks of central bankers, bank examiners, constitutional judges, police officials, health officers, and so on come to a consensus on a preferred policy, return home, and implement the policy through their own national policymaking processes (Slaughter 1997).

Democracy and Globalization

Those who believe that globalization undermines democratic governance also contend that the shift in policymaking from the national to the global level relaxes many of the constraints that normally operate in democratic societies. Mass publics around the world are notoriously uninformed about international politics, even in Western societies, where information is plentiful and access is relatively easy. Treaty politics differs from domestic politics in that the legislature, the people's elected representatives, did not formulate the policy they vote on, and unlike domestic politics, treaty ratification votes rarely permit amendment. Whatever the executive branch submitted is either approved or rejected in entirety. Domestic interests may be compromised in search of a draft with a net gain. Moreover, the treaty negotiation was most likely secret, and the length and highly technical nature of the resulting document means that most legislators will not have time to study the entire draft, determine its likely effects, and weigh their votes. State leaders go over the heads of their own legislators, sometimes using complex international package deals to obtain policies and programs that would otherwise be unachievable in the domestic context. The EU is often criticized for having a "democratic deficit," where policymaking is subject to insufficient popular control. The directly elected European Parliament has very little ability to stop a policy that national leaders want; on many sensitive policy issues, it has no role at all. For policies where competence is solely at the European level, national parliaments are then given no chance to consent to the policy or hold their leadership responsible for its behavior at the European level.

Global governance therefore provides a new set of democratic accountability problems. Policy and regulations made by international organizations in many ways lack democratic legitimacy. The bureaucrats who staff the secretariats are sometimes seconded from national governments, but many of the more policymaking-oriented organizations, such as the World Bank, the International Monetary Fund, and the European Union, recruit their own staff through open competition in all member countries. International staff have no political or national affiliation; they are supposed to be technocrats in every sense of the word, appointed rather than elected to their posts, accountable only to their own (often appointed) superiors. They are often alleged to act without any regard for the political, social, or environmental implications of their proposed policies. In a sense, this is what lies behind many of the WTO, World Bank, and IMF protesters' calls for representation of labor, environmental organizations, or other interests on institution boards. If representation of national interests is not possible or appropriate, at least policy would then contain some direct input from the affected parties. However, many advocates of the protesters' ideas fail to realize that democracy, or at least popular legitimacy, would not ultimately be better served by the appointment of self-appointed issue advocates to these boards.

Leanne C. Powner

See Also Monopolies and Antitrust Legislation;
International Monetary Fund (IMF); Conflict,
Cooperation, and Security; Culture and Globalization;
Human Rights and Globalization; Labor Rights and
Standards

References

Bueno de Mesquita, Bruce, and Hilton L. Root, eds. 2000.
   Governing for Prosperity. New Haven, CT: Yale
   University Press.
Dresner, Daniel W. 2000. "Bottom Feeders." *Foreign Policy*
   121 (November/December): 64–70.
Garrett, Geoffrey. 1998. *Partisan Politics in the Global
   Economy.* Cambridge: Cambridge University Press.
Guinness World Records. 2000. London: Guinness World
   Records.
Held, David, et al. 1999. *Global Transformations: Politics,
   Economics and Culture.* Stanford: Stanford University
   Press.
Huntington, Samuel. 1991. *The Third Wave:
   Democratization in the Late Twentieth Century.*
   Norman: University of Oklahoma Press.
Inglehart, Ronald. 1997. *Modernization and
   Postmodernization: Cultural, Economic, and Political
   Change in 43 Societies.* Princeton, NJ: Princeton
   University Press.
Jacobson, Harold K. 2000. "International Institutions and
   System Transformations." *Annual Review of Political
   Science* 3: 149–166.

James, Harold. 2001. *The End of Globalization: Lessons
   from the Great Depression.* Cambridge: Harvard
   University Press.
Katzenstein, Peter J. 1985. *Small States in World Markets:
   Industrial Policy in Europe.* Ithaca, NY: Cornell
   University Press.
Mansfield, Edward, Helen Milner, and B. Peter
   Rosendorff. 2002. "Why Democracies Cooperate
   More: Electoral Control and International Trade
   Agreements." *International Organization* 56, no. 3
   (Summer): 477–513.
Olson, Mancur. 2000. *Power and Prosperity.* New York:
   Basic.
Organisation for Economic Co-operation and
   Development. 2003. "Foreign Direct Investment
   Continues Downward Slide." Press release, June 19.
Rodrik, Dani. 1997. *Has Globalization Gone too Far?*
   Washington, DC: Institute of International
   Economics.
———. 1999. *The New Global Economy and Developing
   Countries: Making Openness Work.* Washington, DC:
   Overseas Development Council.
Ruggie, John Gerard. 1982. "International Regimes,
   Transactions, and Change: Embedded Liberalism in
   the Postwar Economic Order." *International
   Organization* 36, no. 2 (Spring): 379–415.
Slaughter, Anne-Marie. 1997. "The Real New World
   Order." *Foreign Affairs* 76, no. 5 (September/October):
   183–197.
Walt, Stephen M. 2000. "Fads, Fevers, and Firestorms."
   Foreign Policy 121 (November/December): 34–42.

Population Growth

The twentieth century witnessed unprecedented population growth rates resulting in large population sizes worldwide. Currently the world population has reached 6,414,378,456 people, according to The U.S. Bureau of the Census (Census 2004). Every second, 4.1 babies are born and 1.8 deaths occur, thus contributing to a net increase of 2.3 people. Each successive billion has been added to the world population in a shorter time span over the course of history (see Table 1).

The timeline in Table 1 shows that within a span of sixty-nine years, from 1930 to 1999, the population of planet Earth grew by 4 billion people, and approximately 200,000 people are currently added every day (Weeks 2001, 5).

Historical demographers claim that sizable population growth took place after the agricultural revolution between 1750 and 1900. However, wars, territorial invasions, plagues, and pestilence kept the population size small. It is only after the Industrial Revolution in Europe that population growth accelerated, surpassing previous growth rates. For instance, the annual world population growth rate in 1750 was 0.34 percent; it gradually increased to 0.53 percent in 1850 and reached 1.07 percent in 1930. Since 1930, the growth rate has steadily increased, peaking in 1970 at 2.07 percent (Census 2001). Some of the highest population growth rates occurred following World War II owing to the temporary "baby boom" experienced by the developed countries of North America and Europe during 1946–1964 and high birthrates in the developing countries of Asia, Latin America, and Africa. At the same time, the world experienced a medical revolution that curtailed infant mortality rates and increased life expectancy. Together, fertility increase and mortality reduction led to substantial additions to the world population.

Although the current population growth rate has decreased over time to 1.26 percent per annum, the world population will keep growing into the future because of "population momentum," that is, the tendency of the population to continue growing despite low growth rates because of a relatively high concentration of women in their childbearing years. An easy way to gauge the population growth potential is to calculate the doubling time, the time required for a population to double its size given the current rate of population growth. Since human populations grow exponentially, the "rule of 69" (natural logarithm of 2) can be applied to population estimation. The doubling time is approximately equal to 69 divided by the growth rate. The world population will double in fifty-five years at the current growth rate of 1.26 percent per year.

The Demographic Divide

A focus on the world population size and growth rates conceals the international regional variation in such rates. More than 80 percent of the world's population lives in the less developed regions. In 2004, developed regions contained 1.206 billion people, whereas the less developed regions contained 5.190 billion people. Within the less developed regions,

Table 1: World Population Landmarks

1st billion reached in 1800
2nd billion reached in 1930 after a period of 130 years
3rd billion reached in 1960 after a period of 30 years
4th billion reached in 1974 after a period of 14 years
5th billion reached in 1987 after a period of 13 years
6th billion reached in 1999 after a period of 12 years
7th billion projected by 2013 after a period of 14 years
8th billion projected by 2028 after a period of 15 years
9th billion projected by 2054 after a period of 26 years

Source: United Nations, World Population Prospects (New York: United Nations, 2004).

Figure 1: World Population Growth Rate: 1950–2050

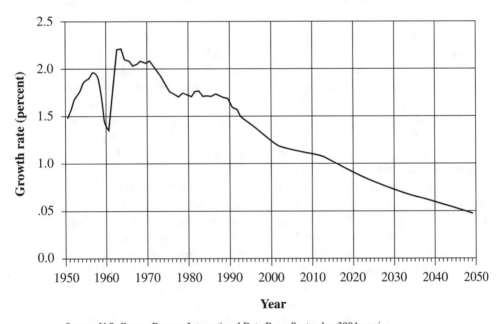

Source: U.S. Census Bureau, International Data Base, September 2004 version.

China, with 1.3 billion people, and India, with 1.087 billion people, accounted for 37 percent of the world's 6.4 billion population. Table 2 presents the world's ten most populous countries in 2004 and projected in 2050.

In 2004, only two of the ten most populated countries, namely the United States and Japan, were from the developed regions. The projected estimates for 2050 show the United States, with a population of 420 million people, to be the only developed country included in the top ten countries of the world. By that time, 90 percent of the global population will be living in the less developed regions, and Asia and Africa will contain the most populated countries of the future.

Table 2: World's Ten Most Populous Countries in 2004 and Projected in 2050

	2004			2050	
Rank	*Country*	*Population (millions)*	*Rank*	*Country*	*Population (millions)*
1	China	1,300	1	India	1,628
2	India	1,087	2	China	1,437
3	United States	294	3	United States	420
4	Indonesia	219	4	Indonesia	308
5	Brazil	179	5	Nigeria	307
6	Pakistan	159	6	Pakistan	295
7	Russia	144	7	Bangladesh	280
8	Bangladesh	141	8	Brazil	221
9	Nigeria	137	9	Congo, Dem. Rep.	181
10	Japan	128	10	Ethiopia	173

Source: Population Reference Bureau, World Population Data Sheet (Washington, DC: PRB, 2004).

The African continent, with a population of 885 million, is growing at an annual rate of 2.4 percent. Within this region, the growth rates vary from 1 percent in South Africa and 1.2 percent in Zimbabwe to 2.4 percent in Libya and Ethiopia and a high of 3.1 percent in Congo and Malawi. Much of the future projected increase in population will take place in this region. Countries with a growth of 3 percent will double in twenty-three years. Another region that has a high growth rate is Western Asia, where Saudi Arabia and the Palestinian territory have growth rates of 3 percent and 3.5 percent, respectively. In contrast, Turkey and the United Arab Emirates have a growth rate of only 1.4 percent. Within Latin America, Guatemala and Honduras are the rapidly growing countries, at a rate of 2.8 percent. Mexico, the most populous country in the region with 106.2 million people, is currently growing at a rate of 2.1 percent. In South America, Argentina, Chile, and Brazil have reduced their growth rates to 1.1 percent, 1.2 percent, and 1.3 percent, respectively. Bolivia, Paraguay, and Ecuador have growth rates above 2 percent. In South Central Asia, India is the most populated country, with 1.086 billion people and a growth rate of 1.7 percent. Currently Afghanistan, Pakistan, and Bangladesh have growth rates above 2.3 percent. In Southeast Asia, Cambodia and the Philippines have growth rates above 2 percent, whereas Indonesia, Myanmar, and Vietnam are growing at a rate of between 1.3 and 1.6 percent. The most significant statistic has been in the region of East Asia, where China has a growth rate of 0.6 percent. South Korea and Taiwan have growth rates between 0.4 and 0.5 percent.

The European region has the lowest growth rates in the world. Most of Eastern Europe is experiencing a negative growth rate. Russia, Belarus, and Bulgaria combined have a growth rate of –0.6 percent. The United Kingdom, Sweden, and Denmark are growing at a rate of 0.1 percent. In Western Europe, Germany has a negative growth rate, whereas France and the Netherlands share a growth rate of 0.4 percent. The "demographic divide" refers to the fact that some countries are growing quickly while others are experiencing net losses. Nigeria is expected to double its population to 53 million by 2050, for example, whereas Bulgaria should see its current population of 7.5 million decline to 5 million by that same date.

Such fluctuations in growth rates necessitate a deeper understanding of the demographic processes of fertility and mortality. Changes in fertility and mortality influence the

Figure 2: World Population 1950–2050

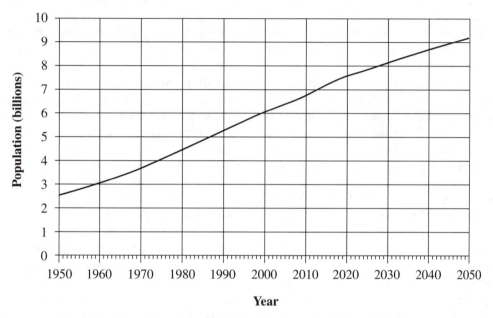

Source: U.S. Census Bureau, International Data Base, September 2004 version.

demographic transition of nations from high growth rates to low growth rates and vice versa.

Fertility Transition

Population changes are directly affected by the demographic processes of fertility and mortality and indirectly by net migration. The relationship between these variables is best expressed in the "Balancing Equation," a simple calculation of population change over time.

Population Size$_t$ = Population Size$_{t-1}$ +
(B − D) + (I − E), where
Population Size$_t$ = population at time t
B = total number of births between the time t − 1 and t
D = total number of deaths between the time t − 1 and t
I = total number of immigrants entering a country between t −1 and t

E = total number of emigrants leaving the country between t − 1 and t

"Natural increase" is said to take place when births outnumber deaths. The current natural increase of world population consists of an addition of 77 million people annually (132 million babies will be born in the world while 55 million people will die, resulting in a net addition of 77 million people) (Population Reference Bureau 2004, 3).

"Fertility" refers to the actual reproductive performance of a population. It differs from "fecundity," the physiological capability of couples to reproduce. Fertility thus encompasses fecundity and the other social attributes, such as age at marriage or cohabitation, availability and use of contraceptives, economic development, the status of women, the desire for children and the age-sex structure desired, that will eventually influence the number of children born to women.

The Crude Birth Rate (CBR) calculates the

number of live births per 1,000 population in a given year. For instance, in 2004 the world CBR was 22 births per 1,000 population. Niger, with 55 births per 1,000 population, had the highest CBR, Pakistan had a CBR of 39, Spain and Italy a CBR of 9, and China a CBR of 7 per 1,000 population. This is a useful but crude measure of a region's fertility because it ignores the age and sex structure of the population, which can immensely affect the number of children born in a given year. Hence, improved measures take into account the number of live births per 1,000 women aged fifteen to forty-nine years in a given year. For international comparative purposes, for example, most demographers focus on the Total Fertility Rate (TFR) of a given year. The TFR is a synthetic measure that calculates the average number of children a woman would have if she were to follow the age-specific fertility rates of women in a given age group from fifteen to forty-nine years. It is a useful indicator that answers the question of how many children women are having. A TFR of 7, for example, implies that a typical woman will have seven live births in her reproductive years. TFRs today vary from 1.2 in Eastern Europe to 1.7 in China, 2 in the United States, 3.1 in India, 5.7 in the Palestinian territory, and 6.9 in Uganda. A TFR of 2.1 is considered to be fertility at replacement level such that one generation can be replaced by the next generation, resulting in a stable population. Most European countries have a TFR that is below replacement levels, whereas most countries in Africa, West Asia, and South Asia are above replacement levels.

Correlates of Fertility

Historically, very high fertility in premodern societies was a response to the high infant and maternal mortality rates of the regions. Over time, certain institutional structures and ideological systems were created such that people were encouraged to have large families to offset the high death rates in the interest of reproduc-

tion. Europe was the first to experience a decline in mortality levels with improvements in sanitation and personal hygiene. As more infants survived to adulthood, large families became unnecessary, and small family sizes became more common (Davis 1963). Rapid industrialization and urbanization created further disincentives for couples to have large families, thus setting up an attitudinal change toward desire for children. As the conditions of the supply of children and the demand for children were modified, couples chose options that further delayed childbearing or reduced the number of children ever born. For instance, as the supply of children increased owing to improvements in rates of infant survivorship, it exceeded the actual demand, thus producing a response from couples to use some method of fertility regulation (Easterlin 1978). In post–World War II, Japan made fertility reduction its national goal and encouraged women to delay marriage or use contraception or abortion to limit their family size. As the costs of childbearing and childrearing increased, placing greater demands on the quality rather than the quantity of children, couples used various means of fertility regulation.

With industrialization, urbanization, and mass education, the status of women in European nations was challenged by many feminist movements demanding equal rights in the areas of education, work, property ownership, and reproductive rights. As these rights were accomplished, the opportunity cost of children increased for women, lowering fertility. Based on the European experience, one can identify a set of factors that can produce lower fertility levels.

However, such factors may not lead to lower fertility levels in the less developed regions of the world, where the transition is taking place in a different economic, political, and social context. The biggest challenge facing the less developed countries in their fertility transition is that mortality rates are rapidly declining, but without concomitant changes in economic development, educational achievement, and the status of women. Many countries in Africa, South Asia, and some parts of Latin America are predominantly agrarian. They have a history of colonization, face capital scarcity and high levels of poverty, and still hold traditional value systems promoting large family size ideals and a low status for women. As long as these structures remain intact, the motivation for couples to reduce family size will be weak or absent in the less developed world.

The birth of children, especially sons, is perceived to bring prestige, power, and social security in old age to parents (Cain 1981). Such androcentric beliefs and traditions of patriarchy pressure parents to desire sons that will survive into adulthood. Traditions of patriarchy, supported by fundamental religious beliefs in the countries of Asia and Africa, hinder the reduction of fertility rates in such regions.

Mortality Transition

World population growth is taking place because mortality rates decreased dramatically in the twentieth century. "Mortality" refers to both the biological and the social components of death. Variations in the death rate and its incidence reveal much about a population's quality of life and health care. "Life span" refers to the maximum number of years human beings can survive. Different estimates all place the limit at 122 years. "Longevity," however, refers to the age to which one actually survives, based on given social, cultural, political, and economic conditions.

Mortality can be measured through the Crude Death Rate (CDR), which is the total number of deaths in a year per 1,000 population. The world has a CDR of 9 per 1,000 population. The more developed regions have CDRs of 10 per 1,000 population, whereas the less developed regions have a CDR of 8 per 1,000.

The "life expectancy" is an estimate of the average number of years a person can expect to live, given certain age-specific death rates for a given year. It is an index that sums up the mortality experience of a population in a hypothetical case while taking into account the age and sex structure of the population. The life expectancy at birth in the world as a whole is 67 years, which is approximately half of the human life span. Measures of life expectancy display tremendous regional variations. Sub-Saharan Africa, for example, has one of the lowest life expectancies in the world, at 49 years, with Sierra Leone at 35 years. Some African nations, such as Nigeria, Sudan, and Ghana, have made recent improvements, reaching life expectancies of 52, 57, and 58, respectively. Low life expectancies reflect higher infant and child mortality rates. Much of Latin and South America have life expectancies in the mid-70s, although in Nicaragua and Guatemala the figure is lower. In South Asia, India, Pakistan, and Bangladesh have life expectancies of 62, 61, and 60, respectively. China and South Korea have life expectancies of 71 and 77 years, respectively. Japan has the world's highest life expectancy, 82 years. Japan is closely followed by northern and Western European countries such as Switzerland, Sweden, Denmark, and the Netherlands, all with a life expectancy of 80 years. Relative to other industrialized countries, the United States has a lower life expectancy, 77 years.

Life expectancies can also be calculated separately for males and females. Differences in male and female expectancies reflect biological and social differences. Females are born with a biological advantage over males where female infants have lower infant mortality rates. However, social disadvantages due to the preference for sons in traditional societies can even this gap. For instance, women outlive men by seven years in Japan, by six years in Germany, and by five years in the United States. However, this gap is narrowed to three years in China, two years in India, and one year in Saudi Arabia. In Afghanistan, Bangladesh, and Nepal, males outlive females by a slim margin of a year. Such regional variations can be understood by examining the epidemiological transition experienced worldwide.

Epidemiological Transition

The term "epidemiological transition" refers to the shifts in health and morbidity conditions that have resulted in lower death rates, primarily the decline in infectious diseases in the general population and in degenerative diseases among the elderly.

Control of communicable diseases has resulted in mortality declines worldwide. However, less developed nations, unlike more developed nations, have experienced such declines through transfer of medical technology and public health knowledge without the necessary socioeconomic development. Less developed countries have achieved low mortality levels in just fifty years, whereas European countries took five centuries to reach those levels. However, major economic obstacles hinder further successes in lowering mortality rates. Lack of economic development limits public health delivery systems and provision of potable water, sewage systems, and electricity. John Caldwell (1982, 1986) also identified education for women as a critical variable in the reduction of infant and child mortality rates. As caregivers, women play a crucial link to such improvements in the overall health of the nations. On one hand, for example, in Kerala, Sri Lanka, and Costa Rica, higher than expected life expectancies, despite low levels of development, are thought to be due to a more egalitarian attitude toward women and a commitment to education in those countries. On the other hand, the low status of women in some wealthier nations, such as Saudi Arabia, Oman, and Iran, may be largely responsible for the lower than expected life expectancies in those regions.

As nations around the world are confronting their health challenges and conquering some traditional infectious diseases, new viruses, such as HIV/AIDS, and preventable diseases, such as cancer, strokes, diabetes, and heart risks, are becoming the leading causes of death in the advanced and less developed nations.

One 2004 United Nations report estimated that between 2001 and 2003, the incidence of HIV/AIDS increased from 35 million to 38 million worldwide. Two-thirds of the HIV/AIDS-affected individuals were concentrated in sub-Saharan Africa. Of the 6.5 million cases of HIV/AIDS in Southeast Asia, 5 million cases were from India. AIDS is now the leading cause of death in Africa. The Joint United Nations Programme on HIV/AIDS (UNAIDS) estimated that 2.9 million adults and children worldwide died of symptoms associated with AIDS in 2003. The number of children orphaned has increased from 12 million to 15 million in two years.

UNAIDS has identified six sociobehavioral risk factors that promote HIV/AIDS: (1) infrequent or no condom use; (2) large proportion of population with multiple sexual partners; (3) overlapping sexual partnerships; (4) large sexual networks, as seen in migrant workers; (5) age mixing, as in older men with younger females; and (6) women's economic dependence on marriage or prostitution. HIV/AIDS in less developed nations is spread through heterosexual intercourse. A high incidence of premarital and extramarital sexual relations, along with extensive sexual networking and polygyny and a low status for women, which forces women to submit to sex without condom use, thus contribute to a higher incidence of HIV transmission in sub-Saharan Africa.

Changing Age Structure

Increasing life expectancies have contributed to another demographic shift: an aging world population. The changing age structure has created a further regional divide. Whereas more developed nations are facing an increasingly older population that is nearing death, the less developed nations are beset with younger populations that will be in their reproductive prime in the future.

A population is considered relatively "young" if 35 percent of its population is under age fifteen, and relatively "old" if 12 percent of its population is over the age sixty-five. An ag-

Table 3: Prevalence of HIV/AIDS, Top Fifteen Countries, Within Africa and Excluding Africa (2003)

Africa			Out of Africa		
Rank	*Country of Population*	*Percent*	*Rank*	*Country of Population*	*Percent*
1	Swaziland	38.8	1	Haiti	5.6
2	Botswana	37.3	2	Trinidad and Tobago	3.2
3	Lesotho	28.9	3	Bahamas	3.0
4	Zimbabwe	24.6	4	Cambodia	2.6
5	South Africa	21.5	5	Guyana	2.5
6	Namibia	21.3	6	Belize	2.4
7	Zambia	16.5	7	Honduras	1.8
8	Malawi	14.2	8	Dominican Republic	1.7
9	Central African Rep.	13.5	9	Suriname	1.7
10	Mozambique	12.2	10	Thailand	1.5
11	Tanzania	8.8	11	Barbados	1.5
12	Gabon	8.1	12	Ukraine	1.4
13	Côte d'Ivoire	7.0	13	Myanmar	1.2
14	Cameroon	6.9	14	Jamaica	1.2
15	Kenya	6.7	15	Estonia	1.1

Source: Population Reference Bureau, World Population Data Sheet (Washington, DC: PRB, 2004).

ing population is one where the proportion of the older population to the total population is increasing. As mortality rates are controlled and a larger percentage of infants survive into adulthood, the percentage of population aged sixty-five years an up is expected to double over the next fifty years, increasing from 7 percent to 16 percent. In Japan, only 14 percent of the population is below age fifteen, while 19 percent is above age sixty-five. Nearly half of Nigeria's population is below age fifteen, and only 3 percent is above age sixty-five (Population Reference Bureau 2004, 2). Many of the European countries that are experiencing declining population growth rates are also experiencing an aging population structure. This presents another set of challenges, a growing demand for better provision of health and social services geared toward those over eighty-five, as more than 50 percent of the baby boomers in Europe and North America are expected to survive into their eighties. Management of more debilitative and degenerative diseases, such as Alzheimer's, arthritis, various

forms of cancer, diabetes, and osteoporosis, will become the focus of future research in the attempt to achieve compression of morbidity in the older age groups.

A related phenomenon is the feminization of old age. As people survive into the later years, females have a better chance of surviving than males, and this has resulted in an imbalance of the sex ratio in old age. For the United States, between the ages of sixty-five and seventy-four, there are 84 males per 100 females; this ratio drops to 54 males per 100 females in the age category for those seventy-five and up (Census 2001).

The less developed countries will also soon encounter the challenges of an increasing elderly population. Indeed, large increases in elderly populations are expected to be found in developing countries by 2020. China already has a sizable population of older people, at 89 million, and this figure is projected to increase to 198 million by 2025. China already contains 20 percent of the world's older population; however, this group (those sixty-five and up) represents only 7 percent of China's total population. China is already beset with an imbalance in its sex ratio in the younger age groups due to its rigorous population policies, which favor the birth of sons.

Population Policies

An understanding of factors influencing demographic causes and consequences can be utilized to shape and improve the human condition through the policymaking process. Population policies are strategies and procedural guidelines used to achieve a certain population goal. The specific development needs of a nation and its endowment of natural and human resources will influence a nation's population goals. Political ideologies—conservative, liberal, or radical—will influence policy formulation. Policies aiming to reduce mortality and expand longevity rarely encounter much opposition; however, the availability of resources may severely hinder attainment of such goals. It is in the area of fertility and migration that policymaking bodies encounter many moral dilemmas and challenges. Governments may take a pro-natalist or an anti-natalist position, for example, on population goals.

Pro-natalist policies encourage births to increase population growth. European countries faced with declining populations into the future and aging populations have adopted variations of policies that provide incentives to have larger family sizes. France has adopted a social policy that provides monthly allowances to couples that have more than two children. To reduce the opportunity cost of having children, working families have access to nursery school placement by age three, so that mothers can return to work. In 1985, to ensure the vitality of the population in European countries, the European Parliament passed a resolution promoting higher birthrates through subsidized childcare and extended maternity and paternity leave.

Anti-natalist policies focus on providing incentives and the means to reduce reproduction with the overall goal of slowing population growth. These approaches present moral challenges to fundamental religions that may oppose use of contraceptives, legal access to abortions, increases in the age at marriage for women, and improvements in the status of women within a patriarchal society.

Despite its traditional patriarchal roots, for example, India introduced the Family Planning Program in 1952, soon after gaining its independence, to limit its galloping population growth through fertility reduction (Visaria and Chari 1998). The program was geared toward providing education about reproduction, birth prevention, and infant and child care and increasing access to birth control. The initial program, however, did not educate men about their reproductive responsibilities and failed to challenge the traditional link of sexual performance with virility and manhood. As a result, it was not successful in promoting the use of condoms or male sterilization as a means of reducing fertility. Nor has the Family Planning Program succeeded in changing attitudes, beliefs, and values that promote the desire for sons or large families. Those changes must occur through cultural transformation and economic development and are unlikely to occur without increases in the status of women and improvements in per capita income. It took India fifty-two years to reduce its fertility rate from five children per woman in 1952 to three children per woman in 2004.

China did not take its population growth seriously as a crisis to its future development until the 1970s. Before then, it had adopted a Marxist view on population as a vast human resource with the potential of increasing the wealth and prosperity of the nation. Attempts to reduce fertility began in 1971 with education campaigns to introduce the masses to a new concept: *wan xi shao,* which means "later, longer, fewer" (that is, later marriage, longer intervals between births, and fewer children). By 1979, the government strongly advocated birth planning and set a target of reaching a stable population of 1.2 billion people by the year 2000 (Chen 1979).

To achieve this goal, the government adopted the "one child policy" in 1979. This program uses incentives and disincentives to limit family size. Implementation occurs at the local level, where urban families that pledge to have only one child receive a monthly support allowance until the child reaches the age of fourteen, a higher pension in their retirement years, and housing and school enrollment preferences. The program also discourages higher birthrates in the rural areas. Couples with more than one child are expected to cover the additional maternity costs, must pay higher taxes, and receive the same grain ration and plot size for cultivation as those with one child. The policy has resulted in lower rural fertility rates within a short span of time. China exceeded its initial target of 1.2 billion, but in 2004 it reached a population of 1.3 billion, with a below-replacement fertility rate of 1.7 per woman and a population growth rate of 0.6 percent per annum. Although this appears to be a remarkable achievement, many critics feel that the cost of this success is too high. The consequence has been female neglect and abortion of female fetuses, resulting in a severely imbalanced sex structure consisting of 133 males for every 100 females. The sex imbalance will have social, intergenerational, and care-giving consequences for many years to come.

There are other demographic policies concerning international migration, retirement benefits to an aging population, health-care delivery, human rights of women, provision of education to the future workers of the society, and ecological preservation that may or may not be incorporated by nations based on their ideologies, competing interests, and resources.

Conclusion

The twentieth century experienced historic demographic shifts in its size, composition, and distribution worldwide. Currently the world is experiencing a major demographic divide. The developed nations are encountering slow population growth or declining populations, and have an aging population that is facing financial security issues and the possibility of degenerative diseases, whereas the less developed nations are struggling to reduce their high population growth rates and improve life expectancies, and have a younger population facing the challenges of obtaining education, jobs, and opportunities to realize their human potential. This divide has resulted in differences among nations in the specific population policies that they implement to achieve their goals. It has also resulted in divergent interests among nations. Historically, when population pressures in one land increased, people migrated to other regions to find new opportunities, but since the formation of nation-states, crossing international boundaries has become more difficult. Migrants are now facing even more restrictive policies in some cases as nations confront issues of national security.

Meanwhile, the population increases that are occurring today are putting increased stress on the earth's resources and ecosystems. Despite some losses and gains in population sizes by region, globally nations will have to address issues concerning the preservation of ecological diversity and focus on pursuing a more equitable and sustainable development of natural resources for the future well-being of current and future populations.

Nivedita Vaidya

See Also International Migration; Economic and Social Council (ECOSOC); World Health Organization (WHO); Sustainable Development; Urbanization

References

Becker, Gary. 1960. "An Economic Analysis of Fertility." In National Bureau of Economic Research, ed., *Demographic Change and Economic Change in Developed Countries.* Princeton, NJ: Princeton University Press.

Bongaarts, John. 1978. "A Framework for Analyzing the Proximate Determinants of Fertility." *Population and Development Review* 4: 105–132.

Brown, Lester. 1998. "The Future of Growth." In L. Brown, C. Flavin, and H. French, eds. *State of the World, 1998.* New York: W. W. Norton.

Bulatao, Ronald, and R. Lee. 1983. *Determinants of Fertility in Developing Countries.* Vol. 1, *Supply and Demand for Children.* New York: Academic Press.

Cain, Michael. 1981. "Risk and Fertility in India and Bangladesh." *Population and Development Review* 7: 435–474.

Caldwell, John. 1982. *Theory of Fertility Decline.* New York: Academic Press.

———. 1986. "Routes to Low Mortality in Poor Countries." *Population and Development Review* 12: 171–220.

Chen, Muhua. 1979. "Birth Planning in China." *International Family Planning Perspectives* 5: 92:101.

Cipolla, Carlo. 1981. *Fighting the Plague in 17th Century Italy.* Madison: University of Wisconsin Press.

Coale, Ansley, and Judith Banister. 1994. "Five Decades of Missing Females in China." *Demography* 31: 459–480.

Cohen, Joel. 1995. *How Many People Can the Earth Support?* New York: W. W. Norton.

Davis, Kingsley. 1963. "The Theory of Change and Response in Modern Demographic History." *Population Index* 29: 345–366.

Easterlin, Richard A. 1978. "The Economics and Sociology of Fertility: A Synthesis." In Charles Tilly, ed., *Historical Studies of Changing Fertility.* Princeton, NJ: Princeton University Press.

Ehrlich, Paul. 1990. *The Population Explosion.* New York: Simon and Schuster.

Population Reference Bureau. 2004. *World Population Data Sheet.* Washington, DC: PRB.

Preston, Samuel, and M. R. Haines. 1991. *Fatal Year: Child Mortality in Late Nineteenth Century America.* Princeton, NJ: Princeton University Press.

United Nations. 1989. *Trends in Population Policy.* New York: United Nations.

———. 2001. *World Population Prospects: The 2000 Revision, Highlights.* New York: United Nations.

———. 2002. *Demographic Yearbook.* New York: United Nations.

United Nations, Joint United Nations Programme on HIV/AIDS (UNAIDS)/World Health Organization. 2004. "AIDS Epidemic Update: December 2000." Geneva: WHO.

Upadhyay, U. D., and B. Robey. 1999. "Why Family Planning Matters." *Population Reports,* Johns Hopkins University, Series J.

U.S. Census Bureau. 1975. *Historical Statistics of the United States.* Washington, DC: Government Printing Office.

———. 1998. *World Population Profile, 1998.* Report WP/98. Washington, DC: Government Printing Office.

———. 2001. *Statistical Abstract of the United States, 2000.* Washington, DC: Government Printing Office.

U.S. Census Bureau, International Programs Center. 2004. *Global Population Profile, 2002.* Washington, DC: Government Printing Office.

Visaria, Pravin, and Vijaylaxmi Chari. 1998. "India's Population Policy and Family Planning Program: Yesterday, Today and Tomorrow." In Anirudh Jain, ed., *Do Population Policies Matter? Fertility and Politics in Egypt, India, Kenya and Mexico.* New York: Population Council.

Weeks, John. 2001. *Population: An Introduction to Concepts and Issues.* Belmont, CA: Wadsworth.

Public Health

Health-care issues are inherently global issues. Disease and pollution are not contained by national borders, and knowledge gained about healthy living in one locale may be shared and at least partly applicable in another. The hallmarks of globalization—the movement of peoples, goods, information, and ideologies—all inform and are in turn informed by notions of public health.

Globalization presents new challenges for public health, as the movement of people and goods allows for a more rapid spread of communicable disease than occurred in the past and may also contribute to the dissemination of concepts related to unhealthy ways of life. Modern medical knowledge, medicines, and technologies have risen to face the challenges of globalization, such as the growth of diseases encouraged by urban sprawl and the spread of HIV/AIDS. Global institutions such as the World Health Organization (WHO) have taken it upon themselves to aid in coordinating global efforts to combat disease and provide a healthy living environment for all. But in some cases, modern medicines have actually created problems—overuse of antibiotics, for example, has contributed to the growth of stronger, more drug-resistant viruses—and the challenge faced by many nations to fund comprehensive health programs inhibits full-scale attempts to put public health at the top of national priorities.

What Is Public Health?

Definitions of public health and its goals vary according to the beliefs and ideals of those who practice it. Most public health officials agree, however, that they are concerned with improving the health of a particular population (whether at the national, regional, or social level), not simply providing health care for individuals (Baum 2002, 14; Walley et al. 2001, 2).

Providing health care to individuals, whether in clinics, hospitals, or doctors' offices, is a *part* of public health, alongside larger issues that may affect a population's well-being, such as sanitation issues, hygiene, the general structure of medical services, the control of communicable infections, and the importance of health care within the concerns of a community (Gebbie et al. 2003, 29). But although all public health practitioners would agree that their concern is with the health of a particular population, they might differ in terms of the focus of that concern. For example, some public health workers are concerned with making primary health-care accessible to all, whereas others focus on the eradication of communicable diseases. Some health-care workers may be concerned with the economic health of populations as an underlying indicator of people's physical health, while others may want to target environmental pollutants as the biggest threat to populations. Because many populations have limited funds to spend on their health programs, however, these goals must be prioritized. The ideological underpinnings of the choices themselves may or may not be in harmony with other choices that a population has made. For instance, placing heavy restrictions on the actions of companies that are environmental polluters may drive industry away from a population that depends on it for income. Such a move could ultimately undermine health goals, as money gained from that industry would not be available to provide primary health care for all.

Definitions of public health, and indeed, of health itself, have varied over time and from one place to another. Differences in beliefs about human health can make it difficult to assess or implement a public health program in a particular area. Thus, public health agencies often adopt a standardized means of seeing and understanding health that can help them to identify the areas of greatest crisis as well as the greatest health successes, and to allocate funds or share important health knowledge as needed. In surveying a particular population's public health situation, theorists about public health consider such questions as, What is health, and why are some people considered healthy and others not? There have been many attempts in various times and places to measure the health of a particular population, often through statistics displaying the causes of death or disease, or compiling various multidimensional health profiles. By collecting this information, it is possible for public health officials to consider the health trends of specific populations over time and to compare the health status of one population with that of other populations. This is an imprecise exercise at best, however, as such recordkeeping is neither globally standardized nor uniformly or completely fulfilled. As part of an overall public health infrastructure, recordkeeping becomes one of many priorities for funding and resource allocation, and it may not get all of the attention that health professionals would like.

It is especially important to consider financial and ideological constraints and differences in public health priorities and concepts when addressing public health issues within a global context. Political borders are not effective deterrents to the spread of disease, and yet how different populations choose to address their own health issues will have consequences for them all.

The World Health Organization (WHO) represents the most extensive effort to date in the international community to coordinate a global public health campaign. WHO has spearheaded various public health initiatives at various times throughout its history, including attempts to eradicate diseases such as polio and malaria, and adopted the goal of ensuring primary health care for the entire world population (WHO 1988, 23). The goals of the WHO initiatives have been difficult to meet, however, often simply because of the enormity of coordinating such projects on a global scale. These are challenges faced by all public health workers within the globalization of health issues, but they are not wholly unique to modern times. Epidemics, environmental changes, and new approaches to understanding health care have a history as long and varied as that of populations themselves.

Public Health
in Historical Perspective

The modern conception of public health is about 200 years old and can be traced to Europe and the United States, where groups of professionals such as scientists, social workers, and statisticians began to study the way people lived in correlation with their health, longevity, and rates of infectious diseases in the late 1700s. Eventually, these studies allowed people to draw connections between the hygiene and sanitation practices of particular populations and their health status (Raeburn and Macfarlane 2003, 244). These early connections were the beginning of the discipline or movement of modern public health, but most societies have always had some consideration for the health of their populations. The Roman baths are one famous example of this, and whenever and wherever there was an outbreak of disease or a perceived threat to the well-being of individuals, regulatory measures were taken. Prostitution was regulated in ancient Greece and Rome, for example, and in Venice ships were quarantined in an effort to prevent the spread of disease (Baum 2002, 18).

Consideration of public health as a formal discipline that needed to be taught, however, is a fairly modern invention. In the United States in 1918, the Johns Hopkins University School of Hygiene and Public Health opened and helped to solidify the discipline in the country (Gebbie et al. 2003, 60). Throughout the twentieth century, public health improved as death rates declined, particularly thanks to improvements in sanitation and hygiene, but also in terms of food and workplace safety (ibid., 27).

How people understand health has also altered over time: Although the health of a population continues to be measured in terms of rates of death and disease, in the 1950s WHO promoted a view of health that embraced the mental and social aspects of health, not just the physical. This idea was set out in an influential Canadian white paper by Marc Lalonde, Canada's minister of national health and welfare, in 1974. The Lalonde report encouraged populations to consider health as an overall state that took into account not just physical well-being but environment, lifestyle, healthcare organization, and other considerations (ibid., 31). Entitled *A New Perspective on the Health of Canadians,* this paper went beyond health as something diagnosed by a physician to encompass a larger concept of health, one that was embraced by health-care professionals around the world as well as by WHO (Health Promotion Agency of Northern Ireland 2004).

Public Health in Global Perspective

As people, money, goods, services, and information continue to become more connected and less impeded by geographical distance, the importance of public health as a concern that crosses political borders increases. Indeed, public health decisions have potential consequences for all populations. Communicable diseases such as HIV/AIDS have spread to all corners of the globe, and travelers in one country may spread epidemics to others. As well, decisions to over-prescribe and misuse antibi-

otics by health-care workers in some populations have led to the emergence of drug-resistant strains of bacteria that may threaten a number of populations (Gebbie et al. 2003, 35–36). Unlike most national or state policies, health concerns and decisions in one locality have consequences for other populations far beyond those borders.

The Global Spread of Disease

From the plagues that spread across Europe via trade routes to the transatlantic jump of measles and smallpox carried by European explorers and colonists to the Americas, the movement of peoples has long been a transmitter of exotic disease (ibid., 34). These historical examples were the precursors to contemporary epidemics such as HIV/AIDS, which in Africa has tended to spread along major road transport routes (Brower and Chalk 2003, 16; Walley et al. 2001, 224). As people make contact with each other, the risk of transmitting infection runs high. Although the process of globalization has caused new health concerns to arise, the spread of disease through the movement of people and goods through travel and trade is not a new phenomenon, and there are global institutions in place to help coordinate resistance to global health problems.

Contemporary Issues

Historical plagues that spread across regions have their contemporary versions in today's deadly crop of infectious diseases: HIV/AIDS, Ebola, Creutzfeldt-Jakob disease, and Legionnaires' disease, to name a few. Even some diseases that were believed to be either eradicated or under control have reemerged in modern times in newer, stronger, forms. Tuberculosis, for instance, has reemerged in a form that is resistant to past methods of treatment and must now be treated with daily doses of medication (Brower and Chalk 2003, 13). These health concerns are spread in part by the greater movement of, and contact between, populations, but concerns about health safety do not begin and end with human interaction.

As animals are moved from country to country and region to region as a commodity to be bought, sold, and often eventually consumed, health concerns move with them. For instance, Creutzfeldt-Jakob disease emerged in Europe owing to the consumption of British beef derived from cattle afflicted with bovine spongiform encephalopathy, or "Mad Cow Disease." In this case, a disease carried by an animal is later passed on to human populations through the consumption of that animal. There is also concern over the method of movement as a means of spreading disease. Both animals and humans often travel in cramped, unsanitary conditions. As people travel together in crowded, poorly ventilated vehicles, such as airplanes, they may transmit viruses and bacteria indigenous to one locale to people traveling to and from others (ibid., 15–16). In such a scenario, individuals may contract and then disseminate a disease that is indigenous to a part of the world they have never visited.

Contemporary public health issues have widened the scope of health beyond the challenge of simply combating disease, and in some cases embraces a notion of total population well-being. The post–September 11, 2001, War on Terror by the United States has widened notions of public health as a concept linked to concerns with terrorist activity. Concerns with biological warfare following the American anthrax scare have caused political officials to consider the possibility of contaminated food and water supplies and to tighten measures to protect America's resources (Beaglehole 2003, vii–viii). Public health in this regard has become entwined with notions of national security, although it is a particular definition of health that is being used here, and as these particular policy effects are still quite recent, it is too soon to tell what the ramifications will be of understanding certain kinds of health as important to national security.

Even some more contentious aspects of globalization, such as global warming, could pose future public health concerns. For instance, warmer weather could mean that dis-

ease-carrying insects, such as mosquitoes, could survive for longer periods of time in geographical areas that were not normally hospitable to them, exposing new populations to dangers such as malaria or yellow fever (Brower and Chalk 2003, 24). These health issues may not be considered a priority, however, until the effects of global warming become more apparent, unless the debate surrounding global warming is resolved before that point is reached.

All of these contemporary global challenges faced by public health workers are also compounded by another more mundane, but equally important, consideration: financing. As national political entities consider which health concerns they will prioritize and what approaches and recommendations they will take, one major concern will be to consider what they can and cannot afford. Or, put another way, health considerations will have to be weighed against other needs that compete for financial resources, such as development initiatives, education, the military, or national infrastructure (Baum 2002, 46). Societies will also have to determine how costs for global health problems should be levied in a global arena. Although efforts have been made to create institutions that will coordinate global responses to many public health concerns, the challenges involved go beyond getting a majority to agree on how health concerns should be addressed to encompass how they should be paid for.

The Globalization of Health and Health-Mandated Institutions

As such epidemic diseases as cholera, the plague, and yellow fever continued to spread through Europe in the 1800s, accelerated by the increase of trade and commerce among nations, the first international coordination of public health was born (Beigbeder et al. 1998, 1). Initially a scattering of international public health institutions followed by international sanitary conferences and conventions, this first attempt at international public health coordination was transformed into a global Health Organization by the post–World War I creation of the League of Nations (WHO 1988, 2). The organization was composed of member nations, which it would aid, at their request, in dealing with public health issues. These concerns ranged from improving health services to reducing infant mortality rates or fighting epidemic diseases (Beigbeder et al. 1998, 5). The collapse of the League of Nations, and the creation of a new global body, the United Nations, resulted in a new global health organization, WHO, which took up and expanded its predecessor's mandate.

With the adoption of its constitution in 1948, WHO was officially created and given a mandate as a global agency in charge of organizing and directing international health (WHO 1988, v). Although the methods WHO has chosen to fulfill this mandate have changed over the ensuing decades depending on the priorities and goals of its member nations, the organization has consistently attempted to conceive of health as more than just the physical well-being of individuals within a population and to include concerns of mental and social health as well.

WHO's annual budget is not large enough to fund large-scale disease-eradication programs or to set up major health infrastructures in localities that need it. Rather, WHO is a coordinating body with access to information and experts in various areas of health care that can advise member states on how to best allocate their health resources to accomplish their public health objectives. WHO can also propose and coordinate global health initiatives funded by money donated by its member states. An example of WHO's capacity as a global health organizer would be its creation of a central health database whereby members facing a particular health situation can study how other states have tackled similar issues and learn from their successes and mistakes. WHO also has helped nations with a dearth of well-trained health professionals to develop training programs for their citizens. The agency has provided fellowships so that individuals without financial means can attend this training (ibid., 8). WHO has also helped to lead initiatives to provide sanitary water supplies for people around the globe and to establish the correlation of certain diseases with unclean drinking-water and lack of hygiene in order to promote healthier living practices in various localities.

Although WHO's medical authorities may have knowledge of how diseases are spread and what constitutes a healthy lifestyle, however, those ideas are not universally shared or even understood. Attempting to create a change in behavior in one locale—practicing safer sex by using condoms in order to stem the spread of HIV/AIDS, for example—may lead to fear, anxiety, or social mishaps if it is introduced in a way that runs counter to local beliefs and customs or explained by people who hold no local authority (Walley et al. 2001, 224). WHO's task is not only to promote concerns regarding global public health, but to do so in a way that may become locally translatable.

Because WHO's concerns are transnational, it was created as a global institution that must consider the viewpoints and problems of all of its members. However, WHO's members are representatives of national entities that must contend with their own local, cultural beliefs about the nature and form of health and sickness, as well as their own ambitions and financial abilities, to create a comprehensive health-care program (Beigbeder et al. 1998, 187). These global-national tensions, which are often political in nature, are in play in any discussion of global health mediated through the institution of WHO or through any other multilateral organization.

Looking Ahead

Public health as both a discipline and a policy area continues to affect and be affected by the process of globalization, and although it is making great strides in creating a healthier environment for all, it still faces great challenges.

On the one hand, advances in medicine, technology, and health-related knowledge have prolonged life and general physical well-being in most parts of the world. In addition, concern that health is an international as well as a national issue has prompted greater global cooperation in how public health should be considered and protected. On the other hand, globalization has brought challenges, resulting from increased travel, trade, and urbanization, that may affect public health in negative ways, especially if a locality does not have the financial or social resources to combat them.

Urban sprawl can lead to poor housing, overcrowding, and poor sanitation if not adequately maintained, and this in turn can lead to more rapid spread of infectious diseases. The modern diet, a lack of exercise, smoking, and urban pollution can lead to heart and lung diseases and asthma, and a lack of education and prevention methods have contributed to the spread of HIV/AIDS (Walley et al. 2001, 252). Lack of oversight and study into the overprescription and misuse of antibiotics have contributed to the rise of drug-resistant bacteria. These challenges for global public health must also be considered in the future in light of the U.S.-led global War on Terror, which combines issues of public health with concerns about biological warfare and contaminated food and water supplies.

Christiana Gauger

See Also Pharmaceuticals; World Health Organization (WHO); Food Safety

References

Baum, Fran. 2002. *The New Public Health.* 2d ed. Oxford: Oxford University Press.

Beaglehole, Robert. 2003. "Preface." Pp. vii–ix in Robert Beaglehole, ed., *Global Public Health: A New Era.* Oxford: Oxford University Press.

Beigbeder, Yves, with Mahyar Nashat, Marie-Antoinette Orsini, and Jean-François Tiercy. 1998. *International Organization and the Evolution of World Society.* Vol. 4, *The World Health Organization.* The Hague: Martinus Nijhoff.

Brower, Jennifer, and Peter Chalk. 2003. *The Global Threat of New and Reemerging Infectious Diseases: Reconciling U.S. National Security and Public Health Policy.* Santa Monica, CA: RAND.

Gebbie, Kristine, Linda Rosenstock, and Lyla M. Hernandez, eds. 2003. *Who Will Keep the Public Healthy? Educating Public Health Professionals for the 21st Century.* Washington, DC: National Academies Press.

Health Promotion Agency of Northern Ireland. "1974. Lalonde Report," http://www.healthpromotionagency. org.uk/Healthpromotion/Health/section6a.htm (cited December 22, 2004).

Raeburn, John, and Sarah Macfarlane. 2003. "Putting the Public into Public Health: Towards a More People-Centred Approach." Pp. 243–252 in Robert Beaglehole, ed., *Global Public Health: A New Era.* Oxford: Oxford University Press.

Walley, John, John Wright, and John Hubley, eds. 2001. *Public Health: An Action Guide to Improving Health in Developing Countries.* Oxford: Oxford University Press.

World Health Organization. 1988. *Four Decades of Achievement: Highlights of the Work of WHO.* Geneva: WHO.

Social Policy

Social policy may be defined broadly as that set of public policies that aim to improve the social and economic well-being of the population. Social policy objectives often include the provision of an adequate income, sufficient education, affordable housing, and decent healthcare, although governments have historically also seen such redistributive policies as a political tradeoff to counter popular resistance to their rule and as a practical means to secure a healthy and competent workforce.

Governments in market economies have traditionally affected the distribution of incomes and benefits in two ways: (1) by topping up wages or improving access to employment; and (2) by transferring income or lowering taxes to those disadvantaged in the labor market or unable to work. Unemployment insurance, pensions, welfare, education, and health care constitute the most common components of modern social programs in most countries. Social policy is thus intimately related to and affected by wider economic and political structures and forces. In recent decades, the increasingly global nature of economies and societies—the accelerated internationalization of trade and financial markets and the establishment of a set of international political rules governing economic policies—has helped to shape a new social policy context. Although observers are sharply divided over its exact nature and impact, there is convincing evidence that globalization, coupled with the widespread adoption of market-friendly policies by national governments, has set definite limits to and even weakened social policies.

Social Policies and the Economy in Historical Context

Social policies have varied enormously across time and distance. In preindustrial Europe and Asia, all societies relied on limited forms of family or community welfare. Comprehensive states in the modern sense did not exist, and the limited political structures that did focused almost exclusively on military matters. Economies were geared mostly toward subsistence agriculture for family consumption or expropriation by feudal rulers and small-scale production for local markets. In Europe, the eighteenth-century development and spread of capitalism—an economic system based on production for profit in the market with a wage labor force—gradually altered the role of the state in society. On both an international and national scale, economic activities became much more complex owing to the increasing volume of international trade, the establishment of a colonial system by the great European powers such as Britain and France, technological innovations, and expanded domestic industrial development. States enlarged their military activities to protect and further their spheres of influence around the world. They also took initial steps to regulate conditions of trade and work in an attempt to tame the largely anarchic process of capitalist development.

The massing of large groups of workers in urban factory settings, for instance, necessitated government regulation to ensure health, efficiency, and stability. Evidence mounted that unregulated industrial capitalism led to extremely poor health conditions among European workers and therefore reduced competitive efficiency and the ability to wage effective wars. The state needed to systematically support and control the healthy reproduction of the workforce through regulation of the employment relationship and wider social benefits. Gradually, governments passed legislation to govern working hours and employment benefits, prohibit child labor, manage the growing poor of the urban centers, and establish rudimentary forms of public education, social assistance, and health care. Working populations themselves were also changing as a result of international migration. Immigration policies and citizenship regulations would form part of the emerging social policy apparatus. Finally, the imperialist state system of the nineteenth century led to increasing military and economic competition among the major nations, which provided a clear incentive for social policy development. By the late nineteenth century, broad agreement existed among most politicians, employers, and the general public that a modern society needed healthy and educated workers to ensure a competitive national economy and military. As British Prime Minister Lloyd George quipped in the early twentieth century: "You can't have an A1 army on a C3 population." Social policy thus evolved into a conscious state strategy to gain competitive advantage over economic and military rivals.

Perceived threats to the social order from below were also central to the establishment of social programs in this period. Working-class organizations used strikes, demonstrations, and other forms of political struggle to demand better economic benefits from employers and political rights from the state. The right to vote was extended through these struggles, and governments soon had to contend with the wishes of a much larger section of the working population. A layer of increasingly influential voices—trade unions, progressive churches, social reform groups, academics, and sympathetic members of the middle and upper classes—developed theories of and advocated for more active government intervention on behalf of the poor and working class. Governments themselves were worried about rebellion by the masses and sometimes adopted social policies as a preemptive measure to undercut political challenges.

Families, religious institutions, and private charities continued to be the main forms of social assistance until the twentieth century even in industrial societies, but by the World War I period, many European, North and South American, and some Asian states had begun to build a basic social safety net that included workers' compensation, state schools and hospitals, and some forms of public welfare. Quite limited and highly controlling of those in need, early social policies were nevertheless increasingly regarded as essential to maintain economic growth and promote social peace.

The first half of the twentieth century witnessed an acceleration of the social, economic, and political developments—inter-imperialist economic and military rivalry, class and popular struggles, socioeconomic deprivation, and increased migrations—that had sparked the first social policy interventions in the preceding century. The devastating impacts of World War I and World War II, the Great Depression of the 1930s, and general economic instability encouraged economic theorists and policymakers to embrace interventionist social policies in a wide range of areas. Many industrial societies began to construct what would later be called "welfare states" with sustained government financial and political support in family policy, housing, education, social care, and social security.

With secure economic growth and full employment, the post–World War II era would witness unprecedented state intervention in the market, the workplace, and the home. In the state Communist regimes of Russia, Eastern Europe, and China, a commitment to a full-fledged welfare state was, in theory at least, a founding principle of these societies. Even in many underdeveloped nations and those still

Table 1: Four Social Policy Regime Types in Europe and North America

Model	Liberal	Conservative	Social Democratic	Catholic
Principles of welfare provision	Minimal assistance aimed only at the most needy in society	Insurance-based, funded by employee and employer contributions	Universal social rights linked with citizenship	Minimal, but a strong religious focus on family solidarity
Degree of inter-vention	Low: Social security regarded as the responsibility of the individual	Medium: Welfare benefits based on paid work	High: The state intervenes to reduce dependency on the market and social inequality	Low: Social benefits focused on the most needy and accumulated through labor-market participation
Typical receiving unit	Individual	Family	Individual	Family
Gender variations	"Male breadwinner model": Women's standard of living and social protection derive primarily from the husband	"Parental model": Women are seen as wives, mothers, and workers and men solely as workers. The state, however, makes significant contributions to child-care facilities	"Dual breadwinner model": Formal equality between men and women is recognized and the state socializes family care	"Male breadwinner model," but with generous benefits in pensions and healthcare
Represen-tative nations	Ireland, the United Kingdom, the United States, Canada	Germany, Belgium, France, the Netherlands	Sweden, Finland, Norway, Denmark	Italy, Greece, Portugal, Spain

Source: Adapted and revised from Esping-Andersen, Hillmert, Le Feuvre and Andriocci.

under the yoke of European colonial powers, there were steps taken toward the provision of basic social services. There was widespread popular, intellectual, and government support for social policies that aimed to reduce inequality. Despite a generalized move toward welfare-state policies around the world, however, the timing, nature, and extent still varied greatly by nation.

Current Social Policy Regimes

Gosta Esping-Andersen (1990), the leading scholar of the European welfare state, has provided a useful general schema to classify what he calls the social policy regimes of Europe and North America. He focused on three different empirical indicators to distinguish different "ideal types" of welfare states: (1) the nature and extent of social rights; (2) the concrete effects of public policies on the redistribution of income; and (3) the kinds of interactions among the state, the market, and families. Incorporating recent critiques of Esping-Andersen's schema, especially by feminist scholars who have criticized his neglect of how women have historically been responsible for much of the unpaid domestic labor involved in caring for family members, Table 1 summarizes four ideal types of welfare states.

There has inevitably been some overlapping among these ideal types and even variations in the details within particular models. For instance, Australia and Canada may be reasonably classified as liberal social policy regimes. Yet Canada has a national unemployment insurance program based on earnings that is delivered on a local level, and Australia has only a single flat-rate benefit. Canada has a publicly provided, universal health-care system, whereas health care in Australia is provided through a mixed public-private system. Indeed, in some programs, Canada and the Netherlands approximate the social democratic model. In several of the catholic and conservative social policy regimes, local particularities have resulted in extremely generous benefits in some programs.

Nations outside of Europe and North America have also constructed social programs that do not easily fit into these ideal types. Japan and South Korea have extensive national pension and health-care systems based on participation in the labor market, but few welfare policies for those who do not work. Personal investments, savings, and family support still constitute a significant part of the social safety net in Asia. Regionally significant and populous nations such as Brazil have also introduced various social security programs in recent decades. All legally registered Brazilian workers, for example, enjoy an extra "thirteenth salary" paid at the end of the year and one full month of paid holidays. However, salaries for most occupations are extremely low. Moreover, almost half the workforce relies on employment in the informal sector of street trading and various forms of casual labor and therefore are not eligible for any benefits. Other developing nations, such as India, suffer from similar obstacles. In general, deep poverty and inequality have prevented many developing nations in Africa, Latin America, and Asia from instituting public policies to better the social and economic situation of their peoples.

The schema of ideal types has proved useful, however, for comparative analysis and illustrates the great diversity of social policies around the world. It is essential to emphasize this diversity because economic pressures, po-litical changes, and social policy developments in response to globalization have differed considerably around the world according to the general health of economies, historical traditions, and the level of social struggle.

Globalization and Its Impact on Social Policies

In broad outline, the globalization of trade and finances has opened up economies around the world, resulting in much greater competition, deregulation of key economic sectors, and growing sensitivity to international economic fluctuations. Global financial markets that lend money to governments and buy and sell their currencies and bonds have imposed an external financial discipline that has induced governments to adopt more market-friendly policies. Powerful multinational companies have been able to negotiate favorable investment, production, and taxation benefits from states. The resulting shift in labor-market, macroeconomic, and industrial policies has certainly favored corporations and contributed to the end of full employment; caused downward pressures on wages, working conditions, and benefits; and affected changes in the labor market resulting in less stable and secure jobs. Traditional unionized industries that offered high wages and benefits have restructured, leading to contracting out of production and services to low-wage companies or sometimes even the transfer of production to other countries with lower wages and benefits. The jobs that have been created have tended to be in low-paid, insecure positions, often in the services sector, that offer few opportunities for long-term advancement.

By and large, the global economic pressures levied by corporations have been undertaken not in opposition to but in alliance with political strategies determined by national domestic concerns. A strong ideological transformation among economists, political parties, and policymakers in favor of the corporate agenda, along with the weakening of traditional social movements and trade unions, has prompted governments to lessen income redistribution and social investment. With some exceptions, governments now routinely accept the existence of income inequality and high unemployment, reject structural causes of poverty, and promote a more or less socially conservative social policy agenda that stresses individual morality.

Studies of income distribution over an extended period in the richest countries belonging to the Organisation of Economic Cooperation and Development (OECD) have demonstrated clearly that there has been an increase in income inequality in almost all member countries. In the most powerful economy in the world, the United States, average real income was only slightly higher in 1993 than in 1973, largely because more married women entered the workforce. In the same twenty years, there was even what Karl Marx called "absolute impoverishment": The working year increased in the United States by up to a week and a half.

During the 1990s, some developing countries enjoyed rises in average incomes, but many groups, such as women, ethnic minorities, and rural workers, benefited slowly, while wealthy segments of these countries surged ahead. According to the 2003 United Nations *Human Development Report* (UNHDR), fifty-four countries, mostly in Africa, are poorer now than they were in 1990. The Russian Federation saw the fastest rise in income inequality ever, and the entire continent of Latin America stagnated. Needless to say, on a global level the gap between the richest and poorest has increased substantially. The ratio of income of the richest fifth of the population to that of the poorest fifth rose from 30 to 1 in 1960 to 60 to 1 in 1990. By 1997, the ratio had widened to 74 to 1.

A general reduction in labor-market equality has had negative impacts on social policies. The erosion of employment prospects and political support for improved labor-market conditions for workers has placed a higher burden on unemployment insurance and welfare. This has had the effect of undermining the political potential for continued maintenance or expansion of unemployment benefits, and in several advanced countries it has led to outright cutbacks and restrictions in coverage. There has also been a shift from what has been termed "passive" to "active" social policies in the OECD countries. Passive schemes refer to policies such as unemployment insurance and welfare that mitigate the effects of job losses on family incomes. Historically, such policies have had positive effects in leveling out regional inequalities within countries and cushioning the workforce from the cyclical instability inherent to capitalist economies. Nowadays, the advanced countries prefer more flexible social policies, such as the subsidization of a factory's operations through wage or training assistance to ensure that firms remain competitive and maintain employment. Yet there is a clear contradiction in these reforms. At the same time as governments shift their priorities toward active social policies, there is increasing pressure under new international trade agreements, such as the World Trade Organization (WTO), to end all interventionist policies that give certain companies a competitive advantage.

Countries such as Canada, the United States, and Britain also introduced "workfare" programs in the mid-1990s that forced social assistance recipients to work for their welfare benefits. In addition to potentially undermining the jobs of other better-paid workers, workfare resolutely cuts against traditionally accepted notions of social equality: A poorly paid job chosen by somebody else is not really a right, and there is no convincing evidence that workfare has truly improved workers' long-term chances of employment success. Indeed, workfare represents a reversal back to a highly moralistic social policy orientation that subjectively separates out "deserving" from "undeserving" workers. Moreover, it has particularly penalized single mothers and visible minorities who are already the most disadvantaged in the labor market.

Not all national governments have responded to globalization by worsening employment programs and labor-market conditions. In the realm of unemployment and job training, institutional variations, levels of benefits, and the percentage of beneficiaries differ greatly across European nations, for example. France introduced a shortened work week in the late 1990s without a loss of pay for a large percentage of workers. Belgium, France, and Germany continue to administer extensive vocational training schemes and unemployment insurance.

Despite the worsening labor market for many workers, the intense pressures resulting from the adoption of decidedly pro-business government policies, and the relentless competition of the global economy, specific impacts on social expenditures and income redistribution programs as a whole have so far been mixed. On the one hand, governments in the Anglo-Saxon countries (Canada, the United States, Britain, Australia, and New Zealand) began to cut social programs and introduce harsh rules in the 1980s. There is abundant evidence that universal-type welfare programs and comprehensive public provision are slowly being whittled away in favor of selective policies targeted to smaller groups, a greater reliance on the private sector, and a consciously moralistic emphasis on individual responsibility. Governments reduced funding for a range of programs in these countries, including public housing, social assistance (welfare), public education, health care, and a wide variety of other social services.

Under the New Labour government in Britain, for instance, funding for welfare, disabled people, education, pensions, single parents, and refugees has come under new and highly moralistic rules that have resulted in reductions in benefits and beneficiaries. Moreover, numerous government programs were farmed out to the private sector under new public-private arrangements. In Canada, the funding formulas for public health and education were reformed in the mid-1990s, resulting

in substantial reductions in per capita spending. In several Canadian provinces, welfare payments were slashed significantly and eligibility rules were tightened. In the United States, the 1996 Personal Responsibility and Work Opportunity Reconciliation Act abolished universal entitlement to aid and introduced a five-year limit of state support. Many individual states have followed suit with social service reductions.

Yet it is dangerous to generalize from the experience of the Anglo-Saxon countries alone. Statistics show that in terms of expenditures and beneficiaries, the welfare states of Western Europe continued to grow in the 1980s and 1990s. There has been no uniform pattern of cutbacks. Popular support for established social policy rights and entitlements have remained constant in Europe, and attempts to implement radical cutbacks have been met with widespread and largely successful resistance by trade unions and popular organizations. Some positive reforms to European welfare states have allowed the public sector to successfully meet new and growing needs, especially in health care and unemployment. The Scandinavian countries, in particular, have generally maintained their welfare systems largely intact.

The experience has also been mixed in the so-called Third World. A context of deep poverty and inequality, weak industry, and the inability to compete in world markets has handicapped many developing nations. Most countries in Africa have largely been unable to maintain the already limited structures of social assistance established in the postcolonial era. Yet some poor nations have recently established and increased social policy commitments. In several Indian states, for instance, comprehensive state-mediated social security systems were established in the 1990s. The end of the military dictatorships and other forms of authoritarian governments in Latin America sometimes saw new initiatives in social policy emerging, even though many redistributive policies have faced crises and political shifts since the late 1990s that have put all social programs in peril. It is symptomatic that the first legislation passed by the Workers' Party government in Brazil in 2003 was a substantial cutback in the national pension program.

Social Policy Futures

In conclusion, there is a diverse range of social policies around the world. Political traditions, types of economies, dominant ideas, and social struggles have all determined the nature and extent of social policies. Social policy futures will undoubtedly vary. There are, however, certain observable trends. The internationalization of trade and finance will continue unabated. Sweeping reforms intended to restrict social policies remain a stated commitment of the business community and most political parties in many countries. Although not all governments have been able to implement radical changes to date, rising public debt levels and continued global economic integration will continue to put social policies under intense pressure for restructuring in most of the world. Yet traditional political principles, such as redistribution, equality, and solidarity, have not died, as witnessed in the significant rise of the anticapitalist movement that has recently confronted the corporate globalization agenda. The outcome of these ongoing struggles will largely determine social policy in the decades to come.

Sean Purdy

See Also Conflict, Cooperation, and Security; Culture and Globalization; Gender and Globalization; Human Rights and Globalization

References

Arjona, R., M. Laidaique, and M. Pearson. 2001. "Growth, Inequality and Social Protection." Occasional Paper No. 51, Directorate for Education, Employment, Labour and Social Affairs. Paris: Organisation for Economic Co-operation and Development.

Callinicos, Alex. 2000. *Equality.* Cambridge: Polity Press.

Carroll, Eero. 2000. "Globalization and Social Policy: Social Insurance Quality, Institutions, Trade Exposure and Deregulation in 18 OECD Nations, 1965–1995." Paper presented at the Year 2000 International Research Conference on Social Security in Helsinki, September 25–27.

Esping-Andersen, Gosta. 1990. *The Three Worlds of Welfare Capitalism.* Princeton, NJ: Princeton University Press.

Ferguson, Iain, Michael Lavalette, and Gerry Mooney. 2002. *Rethinking Welfare: A Critical Perspective.* London: Sage.

Goodman, R., and I. Peng. 1996. "The East Asian Welfare States: Peripatetic Learning, Adaptive Change and Nation Building." In Gosta Esping-Andersen, ed., *Welfare States in Transition: National Adaptations and Global Economies.* London: Sage.

Held, David, et al. 1999. *Global Transformations.* Cambridge: Polity Press.

Hillmert, Steffen. 2000. "Welfare State Regimes and Life-Course Patterns: An Introduction." Unpublished paper, Max-Planck-Institut für Bildungsforschung, Berlin.

Kuhle, Stein. 2001. "Reform and Consolidation of Scandinavian Welfare States." Paper presented at the First Congress of the Hellenic Social Policy Association, Athens, May.

Le Feuvre, Nicky, and Muriel Andriocci. 2003. "Comparative Data Report 3: Employment Opportunities for Women in Europe." A Report of the EU-funded project "Employment and Women's Studies: The Impact of Women's Studies Training on Women's Employment in Europe," HPSE-CT2001–00082, April.

Mishra, Ramesh. 1999. *Globalization and the Welfare State.* Cheltenham, UK: Edward Elgar.

Osberg, Lars. 2002. "Room for Differences? Social Policy in a Global Economy." Working Papers of Institute of Social and Economic Research, paper 2002-xx. Colchester, UK: University of Essex.

Yeates, Nicola. 2001. *Globalisation and Social Policy.* London: Sage.

United Nations Development Programme. 1999. *Human Development Report 1999.* New York: United Nations.

———. 2003. *Human Development Report 2003.* New York: United Nations.

United Nations Research Institute for Development. 2000. *Social Policy in a Development Context.* Report of the UNRID Conference, Tammsvik, Sweden, September.

Sustainable Development

In the broadest sense of the term, "sustainable development" refers to meeting the needs of present generations without reducing the options of future generations for meeting their own needs. In its general as well as its more specific formulation, it is an approach to development that is increasingly recognized to be one of the most important legacies of the twentieth century, and it is expected to shape development concepts and theory, as well as policy and strategy, for decades to come. Indeed, the sustainable development approach calls for a fundamental reformulation of conventional perspectives on economic development, social change, international relations, and private as well as public policy, nationally and internationally.

Context and Concept

To a large extent, the origins of sustainable development theory can be traced to the early years of environmental awareness during the second part of the twentieth century. As such, it was often considered a by-product of environmentalism, and the initial formulation of "eco-development" at the Stockholm Environment Conference in 1972 clearly connected environmental concerns and development. But these early linkages were undermined by the emphasis on industrialization and wealth-maximization as the main goals of social change, most notably in developing countries, which assumed that their own development should emulate the economic growth process of the in-

dustrial countries. This basic assumption set the stage for a major reframing of the notion of development, the goals of development strategies, and the management of social change.

It is commonly recognized that the World Economic Commission of the United Nations General Assembly and its final report of 1987 provided the first general statement about the sustainable development concept. The report was somewhat vague, however, and avoided specific definitions and recommendations. In many ways, its genius lay in this very lack of precision. The commission was thus able to avoid stirring up powerful contentions, conceptual as well as political. Development theorists began to identify what sustainable development is not, rather than stipulating what it is. As it turned out, appreciating the former is an important prerequisite for reaching an understanding of the latter.

Gradually, the concept of sustainable development assumed some specific features. It came to include intergenerational and international equity, intertemporal considerations, environmental valuation, recognition of irreversibilities, and other ideas, but these ideas remained to be integrated into an overall conceptual framework. Moreover, the initial formulation, outlined in broad terms, was dominated by the state-centric view of international relations and did not address the sustainability of other entities, such as social systems, firms and corporations, subnational unities, economic sectors, and so forth. Invariably, this oversight obscured inquiry into a seemingly fundamental matter, namely, the possibility that the quest for sustainable development on the aggregate might imply little, if anything, about the potential sustainability of individual components or constituent elements of the society.

Elements of Consensus

Defining sustainable development has become something of a cottage industry—perhaps even a large-scale enterprise. The term is used in a variety of often contradictory and sometimes mutually exclusive ways. There is, however, something of a general consensus about what sustainable development is *not*. Sustainability is *not*, for example, unrestricted growth; nor does it include activities that entail pollution of the environment, poverty, or deprivation. It is not about the accumulation of wealth per se; it is not about material well-being as such; it is not about meeting targets for economic performance; and above all, it is not about maintaining the traditional economic growth model, which is rooted in the historical development of the industrial West over the past several centuries. It does not accept unlimited expansion, exploitation of resources, unabated population growth, or wasteful energy use. And the list goes on.

More recently, the term "sustainable growth" has been used to amend the initial concept, or perhaps to reintroduce the very concept that *sustainability* was designed to avoid, namely *growth* per se. The debates continue, as do the contentions, conflicts, and conceptual clashes —and their attendant policy implications. In this connection, the 1992 United Nations Conference on Environment and Development left a significant impact on both policymaking and strategic thinking, to one degree or another, and at all levels of development. Especially notable are the new organizational developments that have occurred within the framework of international institutions in order to help support states as well as civil societies in their anticipated transitions toward sustainable development. The Global Conference on Oceans and Coasts at Rio+10, for instance, convened in 2002 in Rio de Janeiro, with the aim of assessing the present status of oceans and coasts and progress achieved over the last decade, addressing continuing and new challenges, and laying the groundwork for the inclusion of an oceans perspective at the 2002 World Summit on Sustainable Development (WSSD). Although critics and cynics alike argue that the Rio+10 review showed that *plus ca change, plus c'est la meme chose* (the more things change, the more they stay the same), there is nonetheless a general sense that the intervening years were significant because during this time development theorists and policymakers were able to begin to chart new ways of thinking about and acting on matters of sustainability.

Transcending the "Market"

Much of the development process throughout the second part of the twentieth century was shaped by neoclassical economic approaches to growth. This traditional view grounds the notion of development in the context of the market economy and sets the system boundary for the entire domain at issue (or discourse of relevance) as the market, with the implication that the effects will spill over into other social domains. In other words, the relevant "world" is that of the marketplace; everything else is outside the bounds of relevance, and most of the potentially relevant factors are, at most, in the nature of "externalities."

Notions of sustainable development provide powerful criticism of neoclassical economics that sees (and defines) social and biological interactions at one level of analysis, that of market exchange disembedded from its contextual conditions, with social preference functions based on individual choices made in markets, and individual choices having no adverse effects on other individuals. Even when the limits of the market are recognized, the economist's tendency is to expand the scope of market valuation and proceed *as if* the basic precepts held. This conceptual edifice is especially problematic to social scientists and others who recognize the necessity of addressing the role of economics in the quest for development but at the same time realize the serious limitations of the market-focused orientation of compartmentalized mainstream thinking. The challenge for sustainability thinking, therefore, is to provide some alternative to the neoclassical approach.

Critical Drivers

Although the roots of sustainability debates are generally to be found in environmental concerns, the critical factors shaping the quest for sustainable development are to be found in population dynamics (including expected dangers of rapid population growth), persistent growth in energy use (and attendant reliance on fossil fuels), and the imperatives of technological change (with the distortions embedded in the technological trajectories of the industrial West). Individually and collectively, these factors constitute the basic variables, the fundamental building blocks, or critical drivers of social interactions (and of human activity at the roots of these interactions) and contribute directly to specific patterns of environmental degradation.

Thus, at a fundamental level, the critical drivers of sustainable development (and at the same time the core challenges to sustainability) are to be found in the levels, composition, distribution, and changes in population, resources, and technology—and in the interactions among these factors—all embedded in the context of the natural environment. Indeed, recognition of the dual and interactive context within which all human activities are embedded—namely, the natural environment, on the one hand, and the social environment, on the other—is one of the most critical features of sustainable development. Humans are part of nature, not separate from it, and social activities are anchored in environmental, ecological, atmospheric, terrestrial, and other modalities of nature's dimensionalities.

Theory Matters

On theoretical grounds alone, the concept of sustainability is not just a major departure from conventional economic growth and development theory; it is an explicit effort to reject traditional premises and assumptions about the nature of economic and social systems and to reformulate the entire model. This reformulation is currently in the making. It is fair to say that the nascent theory of sustainable development is at its earliest stages, as are its rejection of economic growth as a desirable model of social change and its rejection of traditional economic assumptions as viable anchors for thinking about the future.

For the most part, the early interdisciplinary formulation of sustainability-related concerns has been centered on linkages between ecological and economic variables. "Ecological-economics" thus took shape as an addition to the knowledge strategies of the social sciences.

A common distinction is made between "weak" and "strong" sustainability. Whether sustainability is weak or strong depends upon the degree of "substitutability"(the ability to substitute one commodity for another) that can be assumed. To simplify a complex part of sustainability theory, weak sustainability assumes that there are no constraints on substitutability—an example would be the weak sustainability of oil since it has low substitution possibilities—whereas strong sustainability recognizes some critical differences between, for example, renewable and nonrenewable resources. In this connection, for strong sustainability to take place, the stock of nonrenewable resources should be sufficient to last indefinitely at the current rate of technological change and/or with the rate of savings through conservation. Roughly in the same vein, rates of use of renewable resources should be kept equal to or less than the rates of their

Table 1: The Quest for Sustainable Development

Issue Areas	Critical Questions
Key dimensions	What is it that must become "sustainable"?
Core processes	How is it that the quest for sustainability might proceed?
Behavior principles	Which norms (conceptual and computational) could facilitate transitions toward sustainability?
Performance goals	What would be the generic, society-wide outcomes desired?
Implementation conditions	What conditions would facilitate the implementation of sustainability strategies?
Decisions and policy	What decisions must be made, and what are the available choices?

Source: Adapted from Nazli Choucri, "The Political Logic of Sustainability," in Egon Becker and Thomas Jahn, eds., *Sustainability and the Social Sciences* (New York: Zed, 1999), 147.

regeneration. Resources, in other words, should be maintained.

Framing the Fundamentals

Efforts to extend the notion of sustainability beyond ecology and economy have raised a new set of questions, many of which are summed up in Table 1. The left-hand side of the table identifies the key elements (or components) of interest, and the right-hand side lists the corresponding questions that need to be answered. This table is largely for schematic purposes to help articulate an internally consistent and more dynamic conception of sustainability that takes both contextual variations and socioeconomic differences into account.

Integrative Definition

Since there is very little that is formally "recognized" about sustainability or sustainable development, there is no formally understood set over which this function is defined. There may well be as many definitions of "sustainable development" as there are theorists attempting to pin down a definition. Thus, the fundamental challenge is to put in place systems or methods that enable theorists and others to "recognize"

sustainable development as a "defined function."

Drawing on a wide range of literatures, it is useful to formulate a coherent conception of sustainable development as a process associated with variable initial conditions, and to extend this conception into an operational approach to the representation of sustainable development as a knowledge domain. The sustainable development view centers on human activities and places human beings in social systems at its core, while taking into account and respecting the imperatives of nature and natural systems. Most notable among the social sciences are concepts derived from political science (comparative and international politics, public policy); economics (neoclassical, development, and ecological economics); business and management (system dynamics and decision theory); law and new legal reasoning (including new instruments for sustainable development); science and engineering (global change science, ecology, and technology applied to social needs); and complexity, as reflected in emerging understandings of adaptive systems and innovative computational techniques to facilitate access to electronic networks (and improve uses of communication technologies). Also relevant, clearly, are evolving trends in international law seeking to respond to challenges.

Sustainable development may thus be defined as *the process of meeting the needs of current and future generations without undermining the resilience of the life-supporting properties or the integrity and cohesion of social systems.* In this connection, it is useful to follow the overall thrust of Table 1. Accordingly, the key *dimensions* of sustainable development include: (1) ecology, (2) economy, (3) governance, and (4) institutions, with the understanding that society as a whole is the underlying system encompassing these dimensions.

The processes shaping propensities toward sustainability emerge from this general definition. The notion of sustainable development can thus be classified further in terms of: (1) ecological conditions, in terms of ecological resilience and balances; (2) economic activity that involves less polluting and supports "cleaner" types and forms of production and consumption; (3) governance modes and political processes that involve some consideration of representation and respect for equity; and (4) institutional performance that involves or incorporates mechanisms for adaptation and responsiveness.

These essential processes that are required for shaping propensities toward sustainable development lead, in turn, to some decision principles. The intersections of ecology and economy (and their derivative elements) yield the principle of "eco-efficiency," one of the most widely cited principles or norms in sustainable development discourse. By the same token, the intersection of governance and institutions yields a companion principle, namely that of "accountability."

On this basis, sustainable development proponents put forth the proposition that, to become sustainable, a system must meet four "conditions"—that is, processes, not discrete outcomes. More specifically, they define these processes as consisting of: (1) *ecological systems* exhibiting balance and resilience; (2) *economic production and consumption* protecting the resilience of ecological systems; (3) *governance modes* reflecting participation and re-sponsiveness; and (4) *institutional performance* demonstrating adaptation and feedback. Overall, if, and only if, these conditions hold will a system be disposed toward sustainability. The degree of sustainability, therefore, is a function of the above processes, and invariably, these must bear directly on implications for overall security.

If these are the dimensions, processes, principles, and expected "output," so to speak, what is next? Clearly, the step that follows pertains to determining the *implementation* conditions that facilitate decisions and choices supporting sustainability—in all contexts and at all levels of social aggregation. What are the most fundamental decisions? Completing this logic, the most fundamental decisions are those that bear upon and influence each of the four dimensions of sustainable development—ecology, economy, governance, and institutions—by facilitating their core processes, as defined above. And the operational principles to help guide these decisions would then be eco-efficiency and accountability.

Dilemmas of definition aside, there is a mounting international consensus that some form of "sustainability" must be devised for the peoples of this world—in all political entities and in all geographical localities. This conception of sustainable development is commonly cast in the context of social systems, countries, economies, or states. Yet its fundamentals are relevant and applicable to other units and other levels of abstraction and with other forms of aggregation around various organizing principles.

The definition of sustainable development and the views presented above provide an important point of departure—but only a point of departure. They enable development workers and researchers to focus on matters of knowledge and knowledge management about human activities broadly defined, that is, those that both include and transcend models of economic growth, persistent deprivation, and related dilemmas, and to look at "sustainable development" as a domain of knowledge.

Generic Dilemma

This brings us back to an issue hinted at above—namely, *whose* sustainability is being promoted? Or, alternatively, the sustainability of *what*? There is currently little that can be agreed upon as constituting the "political economy" of sustainable development. However, there are some important advances pertaining to economic concepts of sustainability, on the one hand, and the political logic thereof, on the other. Jointly, these may well provide the foundations for the "political economy" of sustainable development.

What might be considered sustainable development from the perspective of the state or its society, or even adjacent areas, may not necessarily be viewed as such by other entities. Increasingly, people may speak of the sustainability of such entities as firms, organizations, social units, and the like. Debates about "sustainability," however, have not yet entered the domain of corporate strategy. Indeed, the notion of "sustainable corporate activity" remains beyond the acceptable discourse in most executive boardrooms. Nonetheless, the corporate community is beginning to recognize the ubiquity of environment and sustainability issues. It might be foolhardy indeed for any self-respecting national leader or chief executive officer to express indifference to environmental conditions, or even to proclaim their irrelevance to corporate goals. At a minimum, it would be rather poor public relations; at most, it could serve as a magnet for litigation.

The relation between state and firm is especially thorny in the context of sustainable development. Indeed, the proposition that the firm's own sustainability does not require taking into account the sustainability of the home state, the host community, or even the attendant markets is certainly one that requires systematic inquiry. Since, by definition, the corporation seeks to maximize profits and/or maximize its control over its own organization and operations, depending on the theoretical precepts at hand, there seems to be no built-in

logic for the pursuit of sustainable development as a prime goal. However, if sustainability were to be viewed in light of the long-term survival (hence profitability) of the firm itself, then the gap between profitability and sustainability would be considerably reduced.

Sustainable Development as a Knowledge Domain

Against this background, the next major challenge is to chart sustainable development as a domain of knowledge. This can be done by starting with the critical drivers—that is, the critical variables underlying the types of human activities (organized patterns of behavior), on the one hand, and the commensurate environmental, social, economic, and other disturbances that invariably result, on the other. This is not to say that all activity is detrimental, far from it, but rather to stress that all activity does leave an impact and that, with the best of intentions, actions designed to solve one set of problems will, more often than not, bring added and sometimes novel and unintended impacts. All of this points to new and emergent efforts to provide multidimensional perspectives to help further develop, or map out, the meanings and realities of perhaps the single most important issue for the twenty-first century, the quest for sustainable development.

Nazli Choucri

See Also Economic and Social Council (ECOSOC); Culture and Globalization; Environmental Impacts of Globalization; Global Climate Change; Natural Resources; Population Growth

References

Becker, Egon, and Thomas Jahn. 1999. *Sustainability and the Social Sciences.* New York: Zed.

Choucri, Nazli. 1994. "Corporate Strategies toward Sustainability." Pp. 189–201 in Winifried Lang, ed., *Sustainable Development and International Law.* Boston: Graham and Trotman/Martinus Nijhoff.

———. 1999. "The Political Logic of Sustainability." In Egon Becker and Thomas Jahn, eds., *Sustainability and the Social Sciences.* New York: Zed.

Holdren, J. P., G. C. Daily, and P. R. Ehrlich. 1995. *The Meaning of Sustainability: Biogeophysical Aspects.* Edited by M. Munasinghe and W. Shearer. Washington, DC: United Nations University (distributed by the World Bank).

Lang, Winifried. 1994. *Sustainable Development and International Law.* Boston: Graham and Trotman/Martinus Nijhoff.

Moldan, Bedrich, Suzanne Billharz, and Robyn Matravers. 1997. *Sustainability Indicators: A Report on the Project on Indicators of Sustainable Development.* New York: John Wiley and Sons.

World Commission on Environment and Development. 1987. *Our Common Future.* Oxford: Oxford University Press.

Urbanization

Urbanization was an important feature of human life in a limited number of regions by about 5,000 years ago, but it became the dominant mode of existence for the first time in parts of Western Europe during the construction of the current world system. By the early seventeenth century, when the Netherlands came to play a dominant role in transcontinental commerce, 60 percent of its population lived in cities. After Great Britain came to dominate the world system, the proportion of urban dwellers there reached 54 percent by 1851, and 78 percent by 1901 (Geyer 2002, 88, 186).

During the subsequent process that created the conditions for "modernization" in country after country around the world, the growth of cities has always been a crucial component. During the early phases of this process, there was a tendency for migrants to crowd into a limited number of "primate" cities that dominate the urban spaces of entire regions or nations, as in the examples of London, New York, or Tokyo. Later phases have witnessed movements toward deconcentration of population, through the spreading of suburbs into the countryside around major centers and through the growth of regional or national networks of small- and mid-sized cities. This process of urbanization, exhibiting common features in many countries, is a truly global experience.

The transition from a primarily agricultural economy and rural habitation for most people occurred in Europe and North America by the early twentieth century, but at the current scale of city formation, soon most of the human race will be involved. In the year 2000, 2.9 billion people already lived in cities out of a total world population of about 6 billion, but projections indicate that the world's urban population in 2030 will encompass 60 percent of the total population, amounting to some 5 billion people. The annual increase in city dwellers at the end of the twentieth century was 43 million; by 2020–2025 this figure is expected to peak at 75 million new urbanites every year. During the first three decades of the twenty-first century, cities will absorb nearly all of the world's population increase (UN 2002, 5, 15).

The vast majority of new city dwellers will be citizens of what the United Nations calls "developing" countries, where urban population is projected to double in twenty-nine years. Inhabitants of cities in "developed" countries already amounted to 75.4 percent of their nations' populations in 2000 and are projected to reach 83 percent in 2030. In developing countries, 40 percent of the population lived in cities in 2000, but 56 percent will live there in 2030 (a level reached by developed countries in the 1950s), and 70 percent by the year 2054. The absolute numbers of people involved is staggering. In the 1950s, 447 million people were living in cities within developed countries, and only 304 million in developing nations. By 2000, those figures had already grown to 898 million and 1.9 billion, respectively; by 2030, when urban population in developed countries will just exceed 1 billion (including 335 million in North America), almost 4 billion people will be living in the cities of the currently developing world. Absorbing over 80 percent of average annual urban growth, Asia (2.8 billion) and

Africa (787 million) are each expected to have more urban dwellers than any other world region by 2030, even though they will still be the least urbanized continents (UN 2002).

Urbanization can be understood through an analysis of "global cities," or "global city-regions," that sees urban sites as nodes within a worldwide network of economic control. At the highest level of the global hierarchy, three cities—London, New York, and Tokyo—support the largest concentrations of institutions that coordinate the flow of capital throughout the world, grouped around their stock markets. The headquarters of finance, insurance, and real estate firms aggregate in these cities because of the ready availability of producer services—the consulting, advertising, and accounting firms that support decisionmaking. Although other cities might demonstrate the characteristics of these truly "world" cities, they remain at a second level within the global urban hierarchy, specializing in particular types of coordinating functions. One example is Hong Kong, serving as a financial center oriented specifically toward the Chinese economy; another example is Washington, DC, serving as the node for articulation of the national and transnational economy of the U.S. government and its military apparatus.

Lower levels in the urban hierarchy provide central-place services for smaller hinterlands, supporting regional and local organizations that connect finance to the world system. A standard feature of the contemporary city, therefore, is its central business district, anchored by a collection of financial institutions providing links to regional, national, and ultimately transnational credit, aided by the nearby offices of companies that provide producer services. An urban center with a higher rank within the global financial hierarchy exhibits a more extensive high-rise environment housing its financial offices and associated service firms and exhibits more complex interactions within these firms and with organizations outside the metropolitan region (Friedman 1986; Sassen 2000, 2002; Scott 2001).

Changes in transportation and in information and communication technologies, supported by massive investment or financial subsidies by governments, have made possible the global mobilization of capital and a continuous alteration of the physical contours of cities. Suburban growth around rail transit lines was already a feature of major cities in the early twentieth century, but the increasing affordability of automobiles, combined with the construction of superhighways linking central business districts to the suburbs, has allowed a massive deconcentration of population and workplaces. The driving force behind this movement is the globalized petroleum industry, dominated by some of the world's largest transnational corporations, which in turn have benefited from advances in shipbuilding technology allowing the construction of supertankers. Investing in cars fueled by the petroleum industry, and seeking affordable housing and space for the family, a large percentage of the middle class throughout the world has headed to the suburbs. This migration has brought with it the phenomenon of the beltway (alias bypass or ring road), which allows long-distance traffic to avoid the city and also enables suburb-to-suburb commuting.

The result, immediately visible in North America, is the proliferation of the "edge city" (Garreau 1991), or a low-rise sprawl, that reaches far into the surrounding countryside. Commuters from more than 100 kilometers away travel to work in offices near the beltways, completely avoiding the central city. Firms looking for cheaper office space and skilled labor similarly migrate to the peripheries around beltways or even farther into rural communities. In this way, the city of Atlanta, Georgia, for example, has generated a sprawl extending many kilometers north toward the foothills of the Appalachian Mountains, and only 20 percent of the metropolitan region's population lives within the city limits. Washington, DC, is surrounded by high-rise business centers in such outlying areas as Silver Spring, Maryland, or Falls Church, Virginia, which are home to hundreds of consulting firms nicknamed the "beltway bandits" at the intersections of ribbon development, rapid transit lines, and interstate highways. In countries such as Taiwan or Thailand, where superhighways to and through the suburbs have developed more slowly, the neighborhoods of the central city experience sometimes continuous traffic jams. In North America, where the interstate highway system facilitates suburb-to-suburb commuting and peripheral concentration of workplaces, traffic jams have relocated to metropolitan beltways.

Changes in global transportation networks have had additional impacts on port cities. The shift to containers for the movement of sea freight (allowing ready interface with road transport systems) has resulted in the relative decline of many ocean ports, such as San Francisco in the United States or Amsterdam in the Netherlands, which originally owed their rise to waterborne trade. Meanwhile, other ports that have significantly upgraded their container-handling facilities have been able to position themselves as major transit points. Thus, Oakland, California, and Rotterdam in the Netherlands have been able to take over leading regional roles as centers for land-sea freight processing.

Simultaneously, the shift from ships to airplanes for long-distance passenger traffic has led to the development of large international airports that have become a necessity for urban primacy. Schiphol Airport near Amsterdam, for example, has allowed the city to retain its character as a major coordinating and entry point for northwestern Europe. Hartsfield Airport, in becoming one of the largest passenger transit centers in North America, has been a major factor in the explosive growth of the Atlanta metropolitan region, making the inland city a port for transoceanic travel and immigration. The growing volume of air freight has reinforced these tendencies.

Cities have experienced major impacts from the rapid development of computer technology and its integration with communications for the construction of global digital networks.

The survival of central city business districts with their financial institutions and producer service firms rests on their connectivity with national and global finance through high-speed data lines. The clustering of the headquarters of the world's transnational corporations in urban regions depends on access to high-bandwidth data networks. The continued viability of major urban centers thus requires their appearance as points of presence within a global telecommunications system including transcontinental cables and satellites. Within metropolitan regions, the same networks allow for a reorganization of space: the transfer of back-office functions to campuses in suburbs or in smaller cities; the relocation of corporate offices beyond the beltways; and the opportunity for managerial control of production and service activities in multiple locations.

The shift in the regional profile of national employment (for example, from the northeastern United States to the south, or from northern to southeastern Britain), affecting primarily the suburban rings of older cities, follows the location of service industries relying heavily on telecommunications infrastructure. The hollowing-out of older industrial regions through the relocation of factories to low-wage regions globally also relies on the ability of transnational corporations to monitor activities in multiple locations and in multiple outsourcing arrangements supported by telecommunications systems. Early commentators on the Internet suggested that these technologies would contribute to the dissolution of cities as more people within the service economy worked from home. Although this phenomenon has affected a minority of workers globally, the dominant trend has been a strengthening of central places through the clustering of service firms or through rapid industrialization in the vicinity of older settlements.

Science and technology play their roles in the globalization of cities in regions described by Manuel Castells and Peter Hall (1994) as "milieus of innovation" or "technopoles." These urban forms have been evolving since the early twentieth century in areas where a concentration of research and industrial development establishments has produced next-generation innovations using advanced electronics. Emerging either from market-driven product development or from state-sponsored projects, and manifested as sprawling agglomerations of private enterprises or as industrial parks, these urban spaces have became planned or unplanned cities employing thousands of highly paid specialists and generating thousands of semiskilled factory jobs.

The prototype of the innovative milieu, Silicon Valley (an extended suburban sprawl southeast of San Francisco), originated in entrepreneurial startups and early forms of venture capital that interacted with electronic engineering faculty from Stanford University. The Route 128 phenomenon in the suburbs of Boston displayed similar dynamics, including significant stimulation by the central government in the form of defense contracts (Kenney 2000). Standard descriptions of Silicon Valley society picture a predominantly middle-class, professional workforce, with little patience for hierarchy, putting in long hours in pleasant surroundings. The problems of traffic jams, pollution, the rising cost of living, and the growth of a large proletarian workforce in low-skilled manufacturing jobs have not detracted from the allure of a unique Silicon Valley cultural ethos (Fainstein and Campbell 2002, 57–91).

Technopoles have become a global phenomenon because national governments view their presence as necessary for the development of indigenous high-technology capacity, and local governments view them as the centerpiece of economic rejuvenation. Many cities in the United States have spent considerable effort to duplicate the initial conditions for growing their own Silicon Valleys; although most of these endeavors have yielded mixed results, some cities, including Austin, Minneapolis, and Phoenix, and regions in northern Virginia or North Carolina, have created smaller concentra-

tions of high-technology firms. Similar efforts have produced technopoles in other countries. Many of these initiatives have resulted in the relocation of branch facilities of transnational corporations. They have also facilitated numerous startups of small- and medium-sized businesses (Markusen et al. 1999, 223–266).

In France, a national-level technopole program built on the success of Sophia-Antipolis in the Riviera, a large industrial park initiated in the 1960s as a scheme to help remedy the hyper-centralization of research around Paris. By the end of the millennium, Sophia-Antipolis had become the site of one of the largest concentrations of information and communication industries in Europe, employing about 20,000 people directly and ultimately generating employment for 120,000 people. Known locally as "Telecom Valley," it is now an advanced telecommunications zone with an optical fiber backbone and a heavy concentration of nationalized French communications facilities, government-funded university and research departments, and offices of transnational corporations.

The Japanese technopolis program took off in the 1980s. Designed to redistribute high-technology facilities away from Tokyo, it involved several dozen medium-sized cities in major upgrades of transportation and telecommunications infrastructure, the expansion of education facilities, and the construction of extensive industrial parks. In India, the city of Bangalore became a major national center for technology firms, the site of the Indian Institute of Science, and the headquarters of the Indian Space Research Organisation. By the 1990s, benefiting from high-speed data communications facilities and intense entrepreneurial activity, the city was gaining a transnational reputation as the "Silicon Valley of India," specializing in software production and consulting (Heitzman 2004). Similar tales of technology appeared wherever national efforts at infrastructure development and local initiative intersected with the programs of transnational corporations—for example, Cambridge in the United Kingdom, Munich in Germany, and Shanghai in China.

Technopoles are magnets not only for national and transnational investment, but also for the migration of well-educated scientists, technologists, and managers from throughout the world. Silicon Valley itself has come to be the home base for large numbers of foreign telecommunications experts, especially from India and China (Saxenian 1999), and the global shortage of skilled programmers has prompted similar movements of personnel from developing countries into high-tech clusters from Munich to Sydney. This migration of personnel at the high end of the education spectrum is only the edge of a truly massive transfer of populations across political borders in search of employment that, in turn, often emerges as the result of technological innovations. Most of this migration, once rural-to-urban, now involves moving from one city to another.

The United States has long been familiar with the immigration of laborers from Mexico and other Central American countries in search of agricultural jobs, but most immigrants from those sources are now targeting urban centers ranging from Los Angeles to Miami as their final destinations. Similar movements of workers from southern Europe, the Caribbean, or Africa into northern Europe have resulted in highly visible minority groups who often end up in ghettoized urban neighborhoods. Large numbers of migrants from northeastern Africa and South Asia have headed toward opportunities for mostly manual labor in Saudi Arabia and other Persian Gulf countries, where they help to produce the world's fastest rates of urbanization. In Saudi Arabia, for example, where the urban population has soared from 16 to 93 percent in only two generations, they typically occupy specified neighborhoods for guestworkers in Riyadh or Jidda (where annual growth rates after 1975 reached 7.4 and 6.7 percent, respectively). In Southeast Asia

and the Pacific Rim, the Chinese diaspora has been important at least since the fourteenth century, but recent liberalization initiatives, and the reunion of Hong Kong with the People's Republic, have produced a new wave of emigration affecting cities from Singapore to Vancouver (Ong and Nonini 1996).

The extent of transnational migration to cities pales in comparison to the domestic migration occurring in response to the penetration of global capital. Perhaps the most striking example is the Pearl River Delta in southern China, where investment funneled through the Chinese diaspora and financial institutions in Hong Kong has been creating a multicity cluster of perhaps 20 million people. Many thousands of workers (including a large percentage of women) from all over China have moved to this region in search of low-paying but steady employment in production facilities, many oriented toward export. The case of Malaysia, where 37 percent of the population was urban in 1975, and 67 percent in 2000, shows a similar impact of national openness to foreign direct investment in the low-paying production facilities of transnational investors.

But even when the climate for global investment worsens, massive migration can continue, leading to the extensive slums associated with the urban peripheries of many cities in South America, Africa, and South Asia. The situation in Lagos, Nigeria, is an example. Until the 1980s, supported by the dynamic exploitation of fossil fuels, the economy of this capital city was developing rapidly, but deterioration in the world market for oil resulted in a dramatic downturn. The population of the city nonetheless continues to grow at a rate of 300,000 people per year, a path that could lead to a population of over 20 million in 2020, making it one of the world's largest cities. The resulting expansion of slums, traffic congestion, and failures of water and sewerage systems are signs of a population that cannot find enough jobs and an urban government that cannot find adequate funds. In such circumstances, the "informal" economy, operating outside the taxation system of the state, provides subsistence employment for over 50 percent of the urban population.

Thus, the global city, the site of transnational finance and corporate headquarters closely linked to high-technology productivity in the milieu of innovation, is also the site of gigantic economic disparities. In almost every country, the gap between the highest tier and the lowest tier of earners has widened in recent decades. In almost every major city, gated communities with security systems for well-to-do citizens stand in stark contrast with street people commanding few resources. Edward Fowler (1996) described the depressing underside of the city even in Japan at the height of its prosperity when he worked with temporary day laborers in Tokyo, demonstrating that the most advanced infrastructure and the fullest array of personal services depend, paradoxically, on the labor of the poor. The very construction of the infrastructure for globalized finance and transnational corporations may in fact create the conditions for a radical displacement of the poor and the working class.

One of the most well-known cases exemplifying the relationship between globalized development and humble citizens is the renovation of the Docklands area in the east of London during the late twentieth century. Here a combination of government intervention and private investment eliminated an obsolete industrial landscape and created a high-rise office and residential complex that attracted many transnational companies. The success of this well-publicized project also involved social costs, including the disruption of communities of longtime residents who could not afford the new housing, and the establishment of new communities sharply divided along class and racial lines (Foster 1999). The situation at the Docklands highlights, within one of the world's global cities, the creative and divisive processes visible in every major city of the world, as the established poor and the immigrant poor confront the investment priorities of global capital.

To fully examine urban environments, it is necessary to position the metropolis within a more complete perspective on urban hierarchies. The world's 16 megacities, that is, agglomerations including more than 10 million people, were home to only 4.4 percent of the world's urban population in 2000, a proportion expected to rise to only 8.8 percent by 2015, when the number of such places will increase to 21. Additional cities with populations between 5 million and 10 million (numbering 23 in 2000, with 37 projected for 2030) accounted for 5.9 percent of the world's urban population in 2000, and will include only 6.8 percent in 2030. A more important demographic phenomenon consists of cities with between 1 million and 5 million inhabitants (numbering 348 in 2000, with 496 projected for 2030), encompassing almost one-quarter of global urbanites. But it is the small- and medium-sized settlements that continue to absorb the greatest share of urban demographic growth; throughout the early twenty-first century, 50 to 55 percent of the world's urban population will live in cities with less than 500,000 people. This last category is already the most important one in Europe, encompassing nearly two-thirds of the urban population (UN 2002, 7, 77, 82). For most people, therefore, the confrontation with globalization occurs within the fourth- or fifth-level nodes of a global urban hierarchy.

One of the most well-known phenomena demonstrating the rapid formation of small- and medium-sized cities is the development of northern Brazil, which has been destroying the world's largest remaining rain forests. This epochal process is related to programs of the Brazilian government designed to shift industry and population away from the southern part of the country, and especially away from São Paolo, which alone contained almost 18 million people in 2000 (the world's third largest city). In the northern region of the country that includes the Amazon River Basin, an area as large as the eastern United States, the population rose from less than 2 million in 1950 to almost 13 million in 2001 (changing from 3.5 to

7.6 percent of the country's total population). The rate of urbanization in the northern region grew from 32 percent to almost 70 percent (in a nation 81 percent urbanized). In the 1960s, just 22 cities in the northern region had populations of more than 5,000; by the early 1990s, the number of such cities already had grown to 133, with 8 exceeding 100,000 residents. Well over half of the residences in these new cities stood within self-built shantytowns.

The case of the Amazon demonstrates the intersecting personal and institutional arenas linked to the transnational economy that are simultaneously altering ecosystems while generating fast urbanization. A number of Amazonian cities have sprung up around major projects promoted by the state but funded or constructed through transnational organizations, aiming primarily at extractive industries (such as rubber, gold, and timber) or at tapping the huge hydroelectric potential of the Amazon watershed. Even the hundreds of thousands of poor farmers who are destroying the rainforest while attempting to survive on their own lands are linked to the projects or financing of institutions linked back through the bigger cities to national and transnational finance.

The port of Belém (population 1.4 million in 2003) at the mouth of the river has long served as the import-export center for the region, but the city of Manaus (population 1.6 million in 2003), 1,300 kilometers (800 miles) inland, has grown rapidly as a coordinating center for regional growth. The Manaus Free Trade Zone, established in 1967, was originally conceived as an attraction for branch plants of transnational corporations. By 2003, its "industrial pole" employed 50,000 people, with mature electrical and electronics industries accounting for 55 percent of a US$10 billion income and exports valued at US$851 million. In practice, however, the free trade zone has functioned primarily as a transit point for the import of foreign-produced goods to the Amazon Basin (Browder and Godfrey 1997; Markusen et al. 1999, 97–145; Superintendent of the Manaus Free Trade Zone, http://www.suframa.gov.br).

Cities, the gateways for economic exchange, are also the sites for the display of cultural artifacts and behavior affected by globalization. Perhaps the most visible phenomenon is Americanization, or the diffusion of commercial products and styles originating in the United States. The U.S. core copyright industries, for example, exported US$88.97 billion worth of goods and services in 2001, including a large percentage contributed by the film industry, consumed primarily by moneyed people in cities throughout the world. When one combines this massive cultural load with the exported output of other sectors, such as the fashion industry and retail franchises such as McDonald's, Pizza Hut, or Kentucky Fried Chicken, one quickly gains the impression of a one-way transmission of signs and organizational forms.

Two perspectives may serve to qualify this perception. First, the diffusion of cultural products to an urbane public is creating a global "metropolitan" culture that includes contributions from many sources. Consider just a few examples: India's "Bollywood" film industry (based in Bombay/Mumbai), which produces more titles annually than Hollywood, not only dominates South Asia but reaches audiences from Russia to Cairo, with increasing visibility in Europe and North America; East Asian martial arts have found global audiences in schools and theaters globally; and a "world" music form is evolving with inputs from the four Atlantic continents and spreading in cities throughout the world. Second, the diffusion of cultural attributes is not simply the reception of a unitary message, but involves the agency of social groups who adopt artifacts or ideas and adapt them to specific urban environments. For example, in western Africa one may encounter among the fashion-conscious a distinct preference for the "Italian" style that includes a particular brand of shoe made in the United States. The choice of footware does not result from aggressive U.S. marketing, but from the self-conscious choices of Senegalese transnational migrants interacting with urbanites at home who are constructing class markers connected to a perception of global chic (Scheld 2003). In this way, one may see in the ubiquitous urban accessibility of MTV the acculturation of a young global elite, or one may notice in the regional shifts of its presentation the marks of identity formation.

The city is thus the most conspicuous sphere for the construction and manifestation of identity, an arena for often conflicting claims on the definition of citizenship, now defined not only at the national level, but also at the level of the urban node. If one looks at citizenship through the urban lens, a space appears between the legal definition of the citizen and the cultural or social definitions of the city dweller. One of the most potent sources for social definition is urban religiosity. One can view its more destructive forms in the recurring "communal" riots (mostly pitting Hindus against Muslims) in South Asian cities. But many of its forms are subtle, following the paths of transnational migrants but spinning off regional or national variations on common themes. For example, more than 10 million people worldwide (mostly middle-class urbanites) are devotees of the Indian spiritual leader Sathya Sai Baba (b. 1926). His original messages and devotional practices in the Telugu language have been translated to a wide variety of regional styles in Indian cities and worldwide among nonresident Indians alongside a large percentage of non-Indian adherents.

But perhaps the most dynamic contemporary examples of transnational urban religiosity come from Islam. The veneration of the sufi saint Amadou Bamba (1853–1927) has deeply affected the visual culture of his native Senegal. But it also has followed the migrations of trading communities to become a feature of city life throughout Muslim communities in Africa and also in North America and Europe (Diouf 2000; Roberts and Roberts 2003). In Istanbul, a global city for the past seventeen centuries, one can experience a full array of transnational influences: Women in miniskirts and men in black business suits, conjuring the image of 1920s secular nationalism, jostle in the streets with women in the *tesuttür* fashion of long coats and large headscarves, the "traditional" style of Islam. In the 1990s, when the Islamicist Welfare Party took control of the city government in Istanbul, the capital of a nation promoting modernist and globalizing credentials, the world witnessed the power of a different kind of globalization proclaiming Islamic cultural principles. A closer look at the language used by the Islamicists reveals Arabic terms blended with distinctly Ottomon Turkish elements, and a closer look at "traditional" garb reveals embellishments constituting a new "Islamic chic" that signals class differences (Keyder 1999). As in other spheres, therefore, global cultural phenomena express a variety of particularistic social affiliations and class cleavages within the city.

James Heitzman

See Also Natural Resources; Population Growth

References

Browder, John O., and Brian J. Godfrey. 1997. *Rainforest Cities: The Urban Transformation of Amazonia.* New York: Columbia University Press.

Castells, Manuel, and Peter Hall. 1994. *Technopoles of the World: The Making of 21st Century Industrial Complexes.* New York: Routledge.

Diouf, Mamadou. 2000. "The Senegalese Murid Trade Diaspora and the Making of a Vernacular Cosmopolitanism." *Public Culture* 12, no. 3: 679–702.

Fainstein, Susan S., and Scott Campbell, ed. 2002. *Readings in Urban Theory.* 2d ed. Oxford, UK: Blackwell.

Foster, Janet. 1999. *Docklands: Urban Change and Conflict in a Community in Transition.* Philadelphia: Taylor and Francis.

Fowler, Edward. 1996. *San'ya Blues: Laboring Life in Contemporary Tokyo.* Ithaca, NY: Cornell University Press.

Friedmann, John. 1986. "The World City Hypothesis." *Development and Change* 17: 69–83.

Garreau, Joel. 1991. *Edge City: Life on the New Frontier.* New York: Doubleday.

Geyer, H. S., ed. 2002. *International Handbook of Urban Systems: Studies of Urbanization and Migration in Advanced and Developing Countries.* Cheltenham, UK: Edward Elgar.

Heitzman, James. 2004. *Network City: Information Systems and Planning in India's Silicon Valley.* New Delhi: Oxford University Press.

Kenney, Martin, ed. 2000. *Understanding Silicon Valley: The Anatomy of an Entrepreneurial Region.* Stanford, CA: Stanford University Press.

Keydar, Caglar. 1999. *Istanbul: Between the Global and the Local.* Lanham, MD: Rowman and Littlefield.

Markusen, Ann R., Yong-Sook Lee, and Sean DiGiovanna, eds. 1999. *Second Tier Cities: Rapid Growth beyond the Metropolis.* Minneapolis: University of Minnesota Press.

Ong, Aihwa, and Donald Nonini, ed. 1996. *Ungrounded Empires: The Cultural Politics of Modern Chinese Transnationalism.* New York: Routledge.

Roberts, Allen F., and Mary Nooter Roberts. 2003. *A Saint in the City: Sufi Arts of Urban Senegal.* Los Angeles: University of California at Los Angeles, Fowler Museum of Cultural History.

Sassen, Saskia. 2000. *Cities in a World Economy.* 2d ed. Thousand Oaks, CA: Pine Forge.

Sassen, Saskia, ed. 2002. *Global Networks, Linked Cities.* New York: Routledge.

Saxenian, AnnaLee. 1999. *Silicon Valley's New Immigrant Entrepreneurs.* San Francisco: Public Policy Institute of California.

Scheld, Suzanne. 2003. "The City in a Shoe: Redefining Urban Africa through Sebago Footwear Consumption." *City and Society* 15, no. 1: 109–130.

Scott, Allen J., ed. 2001. *Global City-Regions: Trends, Theory, Policy.* Oxford: Oxford University Press.

United Nations. 2002. *World Urbanization Prospects: The 2001 Revision.* New York: United Nations Department of Economic and Social Affairs, Population Division (ST/ESA/SER.A/216).

U.S. Trade Laws

The U.S. Constitution provides the foundation of the nation's trade laws and remained the primary instrument of trade regulation for many years. The term "commerce" is synonymous with "trade" in the U.S. Constitution and refers to the business of buying and selling goods. Through the Commerce Clause, the constitution grants power over trade activities, both between the states and between the United States and foreign countries, to the U.S. Congress. The states are allowed to regulate trade that occurs within the confines of their own jurisdiction, however. Today, trade that occurs within a single state is almost nonexistent, as more reliance is placed on other states and countries for goods and services in the global economy.

Early Trade Laws

The Fordney-McCumber Tariff Act

President Warren G. Harding signed the Fordney-McCumber Tariff Act into law on September 21, 1922. Many tariff acts had been passed before this date; however, this tariff initiated a new stance attempting to take account of changing international conditions after World War I. Early in its history, the United States had been forced to rely on other countries for certain goods that it could not produce itself, and it could not rely on the goods of certain countries because of the difficulty in transporting items. Most U.S. international trade before World War I had been conducted with the European nations that had colonized the United States. During World War I, the United States was the only nation still capable of engaging in significant international trade. International trade had gained in importance with the Industrial Revolution, which made the production and transport of goods easier. The United States had been seeking to protect its domestic interests through tariffs since the 1800s, and this concept also gained importance during World War I.

The Fordney-McCumber tariff was created as a protectionist measure, and the tariff on goods that it established was high. With its passage, the United States had the highest tariff rate of any nation of the time, which posed many problems. The act granted the president the power to raise or lower the tariff by as much as 50 percent on items that were recommended for adjustment by the Tariff Commission. It used an "American selling price" as a means of protecting the higher prices of American goods. During World War I, when there was a high demand for goods, but few countries capable of providing any goods, these high prices had been justified. However, the tariff did not have the beneficial effects that had been expected, and soon a movement was afoot to change the tariff, as many blamed it for their economic woes. In effect, the Fordney-McCumber tariff created an artificial barrier around the country, restricting both imports and exports. U.S. citizens were forced to pay higher prices for many goods because they could not reap the comparative advantage effect that is essential to creating a thriving capitalistic society.

American agriculture reaped many profits during World War I because, in addition to supplying products to U.S. residents, it was called upon to supply many of the agricultural needs of war-torn Europe. To match a rising demand, American farmers increased production acres. After the war, however, they were left with a lowered demand as European farmers began to recover. The surplus of products led to lower prices for agricultural products and introduced farmers to a depression that would spread to the rest of the nation ten years later. Many farmers blamed these problems on the high tariffs because they were stuck with overpriced goods that no one wanted or could afford to purchase, and the tariff did nothing to solve this problem.

The high tariff rates also hurt bankers, who were seeking repayment of wartime loans. Europe's economic resources were drained during the war, and many American institutions had made loans to Europe. These were calculated to amount to about $10 billion. Lenders wanted their money back, and Europe was struggling to repay them. The tariff was applied to debt repayments, however, which made it even more difficult for lenders to recover their money.

Hawley-Smoot Tariff Act

The Hawley-Smoot Tariff Act of 1930 was a response to the Fordney-McCumber tariff and followed a decade-long agricultural depression. Created by House Ways and Means Committee Chairman Willis Hawley and Senate Finance Committee Chairman Reed Smoot, it was signed into law on June 17, 1930, by President Herbert Hoover. A compromise between the Senate and House leaders, it increased the protectionist efforts of the United States through tariffs on farm products and manufactured goods. Although the act did not comply with Hoover's recommendations, he signed it into law in an attempt to deal with the worsening economic state of the nation at the time. The country was already beginning to feel the effects of the Great Depression.

The tariff rates were higher under the Hawley-Smoot Tariff Act than they had been under the Fordney-McCumber Act. Most products had tariff rates twice as high in 1930 than ten years prior, especially agricultural products. Tariffs were placed on some items, such as bricks, leather, and shoes, for the first time. Import duties were 50 to 100 percent higher on raw materials in 1930 than in 1920. One of the few exceptions to the increased tariff rates was a decrease on the automobile tariff, which went from 25 percent to 10 percent.

Foreign governments expressed their opposition to the Hawley-Smoot Tariff Act by directing protests to the U.S. government, by publishing articles criticizing the new tariff, and though tariff retaliation. Thirty-eight countries sent protest letters to Congress urging its members not to pass the bill. Countries hurt by World War I needed markets for revenue and a favorable trade balance. European countries instituted favored-nation trading status with each other and discontinued trade with the United States. French Foreign Minister Aristide Briand proposed the idea of a European Federation that would give Europe a market of its own and leave out the United States entirely. Without the support of all of Europe for such a federation, France established a quota system in retaliation to the United States. The quotas placed limitations on the number of goods that could be imported into the country and were applied to coal, flax, wines, woods, meats, eggs, and poultry.

Italy reacted to the Hawley-Smoot Tariff Act by increasing its import duties on automobiles, of which the United States was the primary supplier. Later in 1930, Italian dictator Benito Mussolini declared that Italy would only buy products from countries that bought its agricultural products. The Hawley-Smoot Tariff Act restricted imports of Italian agricultural goods into the United States. Spain reacted by withdrawing from a treaty that had been in place between Spain and the United States since 1908, ending most-favored-nation trading status between the two countries. In addition, on July 22, 1930, Spain passed the Wais Tariff, which raised duties on American goods such as automobiles, tire, rubber, and motion pictures. Although other countries were also affected by the Spanish tariff, Spain negotiated special commercial treaties with them.

Great Britain had few protectionist tariffs in place prior to 1931 and was a strong supporter of free trade. However, it passed an Import Duties Act in February 1932 and the Ottawa agreements a few months later, in July, to protect Great Britain and its colonies. These acts imposed high duties on all imports from the United States. Although U.S. imports had entered Great Britain, including its colonies, duty free 70.5 percent of the time in 1930, by 1932 this figure had dropped to 20.5 percent. The United States' biggest trading partner, Canada, was also outraged. The Canadian government passed the Canadian Emergency Tariff, which imposed high duties on U.S. imports, including textiles, agricultural products, electrical equipment, meats, gasoline, shoes, jewelry, and fertilizers.

The Hawley-Smoot Tariff Act did not have the positive effects that Congress had hoped it would have on the U.S. economy. Although it cannot be blamed for causing the Great Depression, it did contribute to the Depression, and it prolonged the economic misery that the nation suffered. It also made it even less likely that the United States would ever recover the money it had lent the world during World War I. It caused prices to increase, compounding the difficulties people faced from the Great Depression. President Franklin D. Roosevelt altered the Hawley-Smoot Tariff Act as part of the New Deal legislation he created. American politicians identified the need for a more liberal trade policy to create an economy that could thrive in a more international environment. The New Deal prevented the economy from continuing its downward recessionary spiral, and as the economy recovered there was a need to encourage a more open and free trading environment between nations.

General Agreement on Tariffs and Trade (GATT)

In 1948, following the failure of the United States to ratify the treaty for a proposed International Trade Organization, President Harry S. Truman led the United States into a new trade arrangement, the General Agreement on Tariffs and Trade (GATT), that became the basis of U.S. trade until the creation of the World Trade Organization (WTO) in 1995.

Part of the GATT's success was due to the absence of a defined institutional structure. This allowed states to introduce changes gradually and to preserve their national sovereignty. The only physical manifestation of the GATT was its Geneva-based Secretariat, which was operated well, earning the respect of the member states. The GATT was one of the very few dynamic international organizations of the era that was able to grow through consensus among its members, though its lack of enforcement capability meant that decisionmaking was sometimes considered slow and frustrating, and critics complained that there was no assurance against violations.

The GATT's primary concern was with the elimination of nontariff barriers to trade and the gradual reduction of tariffs through mutual agreement. One rule that made every GATT tariff reduction more sound was that once two or more members agreed to a new lowering of tariffs, the figure could not be raised again. Members had to be more certain of their decisions, and raising and lowering of tariffs for political reasons were not as likely to occur in this situation.

Two significant GATT provisions guided the process. First, each member state was entitled to the same benefits and concessions that any other member state received. Second, every member held the equivalent of most-favored-nation status with every other member, entitling it to the best possible benefits offered by a state. Bilateral agreements, in essence, were multilateral agreements with every other member state. Nevertheless, in order to ensure that each member had a fair chance, the GATT allowed for members, under extreme circumstances, to suspend benefits when they would unjustly cause unneeded burden to a segment of a member's economy.

Although the GATT ceased to exist with the inception of the World Trade Organization in 1995, it had enduring results. There had been an unprecedented lowering of tariffs among dozens of states, including the United States. The levels of tariffs were so low as to be almost insignificant to commercial enterprise.

One of the GATT's only real failures was in part the result of the U.S. Congress's decision not to approve the otherwise accepted GATT agreement against "dumping." "Dumping" in international trade refers to when a country exports goods to another country at a higher price than the cost of production, when the goods are being sold at prices below production in the home country. In other words, a business is able to provide low-priced goods domestically and still make a profit from its international sales. This allows it to undercut domestic producers who only sell goods in that market. The GATT and the United States have worked to develop antidumping laws that try to punish such actions by imposing tariffs or taxes on imported goods that meet these standards. As a result, the antidumping clause was dropped. The Tokyo Round of negotiations in the 1970s, however, was hailed as a success in the development of rules against nontariff barriers to trade.

Trade Laws of the 1960s: Reciprocal Trade Agreements and the Kennedy Round

After the end of World War II, the world witnessed the growing power and influence of the European Economic Community (EEC), now the European Union (EU). President John F. Kennedy wanted a way to reduce trade barriers with the EEC so that the United States could tap into its expanding market. President Kennedy, who believed the United States should take a leading role in trade, persuaded Congress to give him the power to abolish the item-by-item negotiations established under the Reciprocal Trade Agreements (RTA) Act of 1934 and adopt the European method of across-the-board negotiations.

Early in his presidency in 1961, Kennedy's top advisers warned him about the polarization of the American and European markets. Without the support of Congress, since they still favored more protectionist trade policies, Kennedy waited until 1962 to introduce the Trade Expansion Act, after gaining the support of the Committee for National Trade Policy and various business and labor leaders. The legislation included many provisions aimed at improving the international trading position of the United States. Tariffs were reduced or eliminated on many products, such as tractors, automobiles, heavy machinery, machine tools, washing machines, aircraft, and perfumes, and the tariff reductions would be implemented over a five-year period. A position for a special trade representative who would report directly to the president was to be created by the House Ways and Means Committee and the Senate Finance Committee.

Two days after its passage, the EEC announced that it was ready to discuss tariff reduction agreements with the United States. The United States recommended to the GATT in November 1962 that a ministerial meeting be convened in 1963 to discuss tariff reductions. On May 16, 1963, GATT ministerial meetings, with 600 delegates from fifty countries, met in Geneva to determine an agenda for tariff reduction meetings. These negotiations came to be known as the Kennedy Round, since President Kennedy had pushed the legislation through Congress. The actual Kennedy Round negotiations began in May 1964.

An agreement was reached on June 30, 1967, and President Lyndon B. Johnson signed the proclamations of the Kennedy Rounds into law, which would be in effect starting January 1, 1968. The Kennedy Rounds resulted in a U.S. tariff reduction of 35 percent over five years and similar reductions to European tariffs over the same period. It also lowered the investigation time for inspected goods from ninety days under existing U.S. antidumping laws. Uniform antidumping laws were applied to all countries. The United States was also supposed to end the U.S. selling price system initiated by earlier tariffs. Congress did not agree with this provision, however, so U.S. selling price regulations remained in effect for many more years.

Trade Laws of the 1970s: The Trade Reform Act and the Tokyo Round

Farmers and labor unions were not satisfied with the provisions of the Kennedy Round, and protectionist sentiments in Congress began to grow. President Richard M. Nixon was opposed to the protectionist view of foreign policy and presented Congress with the Trade Reform Act, a bill that would grant the president more power over trade policy After much debate and compromise in Congress, the Trade Reform Act was passed in December 1974. The Trade Reform Act introduced new provisions to trade laws, but in its final form it was not exactly what President Nixon had requested, although it did give the president more power in trade matters. The president had more control over tariff levels than ever before. A president could abolish tariffs entirely that were at a rate of 5 percent or below. Tariffs that were above 5 percent could be reduced by three-fifths by the president. In addition, the president was granted more power in international trade negotiations. He could change or rescind nontariff barriers such as quotas, safety standards, and special custom valuations procedures as he saw fit in exchange for other foreign concessions.

The Trade Reform Act also created the U.S. Trade Commission, which provided a way for domestic industries to make their case before a government agency if they felt they were being injured by international trade. In such situations, the commission could make recommendations to the president to grant relief to domestic industries. A portion of the bill referred to as "Adjustment Assistance" made it easier for domestic workers to make the case that they had lost their jobs owing to imports. Cash and other benefits could be provided to companies or communities that showed that import competition had damaged their businesses.

The Trade Reform Act enabled the United States to trade with more countries because it granted Communist countries most-favored-nation trading status. Tariffs were also reduced for poorer countries that wanted to export goods to the United States. Moreover, the act changed the status of the trade representative position created by the Trade Expansion Act passed during the Kennedy administration, moving it to the executive office and giving it a cabinet rank. This change helped the executive branch achieve its trade goals in the Tokyo Round trade negotiations that began in 1973.

During the Tokyo Round, representatives from the European Union, Japan, the United States, and many other nations met in Geneva to discuss the status of international trade. The negotiations were dubbed the Tokyo Round because the Japanese prime minister chaired the opening session of the discussions. The results of the Tokyo Round, including an international agreement on codes for nontariff trade barriers, were approved by all negotiating parties in 1979. However, agricultural trade barriers were left in place, leaving an area for future trade negotiations. The Tokyo Round also included the Section 301 laws, discussed below.

Trade Laws of the 1980s: Steps toward Fair Trade

Trade and budget deficits were rapidly expanding by 1980. As protectionist sentiments grew in the country, politicians were seeking new trade laws to assist the U.S. economy. A ministerial meeting was called by the GATT Consultative Group to begin in Geneva in November 1982 to improve international trade laws. The aims of the United States for what would be known as the Uruguay Round were to open up the world's agricultural markets and to modernize the GATT to include elements such as intellectual property laws.

On October 30, 1984, President Ronald Reagan signed the Trade and Tariff Act into law. The provisions of this act included a bilateral trade agreement with Israel, protection of the U.S. steel industry, an extension of duty-free access to the U.S. market to developing countries, and import relief to U.S. grape growers and wine makers.

Congress passed the Omnibus Trade and Competitiveness Act in 1988 with the purpose of creating fair trade standards for the United States. This act defined unfair trade practices and gave the United States Trade Representative (USTR) the capability to investigate unfair trade actions and issue sanctions. Super 301 and Special 301 were added to existing trade laws (see "Section 301 Laws," below).

The Uruguay Round met in Geneva beginning in 1986 with 116 countries represented and lasted until 1994. Its name comes from the fact that Uruguay's foreign minister chaired the opening session of the conference. This was the first round of GATT negotiations to address trade in services as well as of goods in its trade discussions.

Many decisions were made during the Uruguay Round. All nations agreed to reduce their tariffs by an average of one-third. The United States and the European Union made a special agreement to reduce tariffs on each other by 50 percent to help them achieve their one-third reduction average. Quotas were eliminated on most clothing items. All nations approved the Agreement on Trade-Related Aspects of Intellectual Property Rights (TRIPS Agreement), which addressed protection of patents, copyrights, trade secrets, and trademarks. The Agreement on Trade-Related Investment Measures (TRIMS Agreement) eliminated the requirement for manufacturers, such as car makers, to purchase a large portion of their products from domestic rather than international manufacturers. Countries are now allowed to alter their tariffs and other trade barriers when their local market is flooded with too much of a particular import.

The United States signed the provisions of the Uruguay Round into law on December 8, 1994, after the provisions were ratified by Congress and signed by President Bill Clinton. The United States also became a member of the World Trade Organization at this time. The WTO was created during the Uruguay Round to replace the GATT as an international economic policymaking organization.

Intellectual Property Laws

Globalization has allowed almost every country in the world to participate in an international economy. Although this has been good for many countries, globalization is often cited for the increased amount of counterfeit products sold worldwide. Globalization has created a strong interest in intellectual property laws that are relied upon to ease the economic threat of counterfeit intellectual property goods.

In most of the developed world, and especially in the United States, intellectual property laws are a necessary inclusion in trade policy. As pirating and counterfeiting of goods increases, laws are needed to protect the ownership rights of the creators of such goods. Intellectual property crimes have grown from simply copying a pattern or a logo on an item of clothing to the duplication of electronic devices and computer software. In order to maintain world trade, these infringements must be reduced and virtually halted. Furthermore, without enforcement of intellectual property laws, investment in research and development of new technology would stagnate. Even intellectual advancement would suffer as knowledge-based jobs disappeared.

Intellectual property infringements have three primary debilitating effects. First, for every pirated good sold, one less legitimate good is sold. In other words, profitability decreases and motivation for market expansion is taken away, increasing per unit costs. Second, exports from the legitimate producer's country, as well as royalties and sales based on the legitimate goods, decrease. Finally, counterfeited goods are exported to other markets, reducing the desire for more expensive legitimate goods that would otherwise be mass marketed. The major costs of developing a new product contrast sharply with the cost of duplicating it illegally. Replication often costs less than 1 percent of the original development costs, making it a profitable activity for counterfeiters, but one that is devastating to innovators. With per-unit costs included, a software title in the United States, for example, may cost over $500, but a counterfeit copy can be sold in Eastern Europe or Asia for only $5 to $8. The primary difficulty facing proponents of intellectual property laws is that no consensus exists about what amount of protection is adequate. In fact, often the introduction of high-priced goods into a state's market is deemed counterproductive to national economic security. As a result, either regulatory laws or their enforcement practices are lacking. As an example, many states protect their pharmaceutical and technology industries, allowing for blatant copyright infringement.

When such unfair trading conditions exist for the United States, a list is compiled of countries that allow intellectual property infringements, and certain extreme cases are given priority status. Each of these countries is investigated, and a plan of action is produced to stop the abuses. Though few states are placed on the priority list, the list of violating states is usually quite long. Brazil, India, Mexico, China, South Korea, Saudi Arabia, Taiwan, and Thailand have often been cited as the primary abusers since the list was started.

Unfortunately, the only realistic bilateral tools to dissuade these violations are coercion and reciprocity. For the United States, which

has strong economic and political advantages, these are viable tools. However, for weaker nations, multilateral treaties are the only logical and useful approach. Nevertheless, until the Uruguay Round of the GATT, no useful treaties existed, since those that were in effect lacked the dispute-settlement and enforcement protocol. As more countries join the developed world, more names will be added to the list of beneficiaries of a comprehensive set of enforceable intellectual property laws.

Section 301 Laws

Section 301 was introduced during the Tokyo Round. It gave the United States retaliatory powers against nations whose trade practices hurt the United States. The president was given the power to impose special duties that the exporting governments subsidized. Super 301 laws were passed as a part of the Omnibus Trade and Competitiveness Act of 1988. Super 301 required the United States Trade Representative to review U.S. trade policy starting in 1989. The USTR was to identify trade-liberalizing priorities and practices depending upon the relationship between the United States and the country under review. The USTR also had the power to initiate investigations of the trade practices of certain countries to remove measures deemed unfair. This process often took from twelve to eighteen months to complete.

Special 301 was also a part of the Omnibus act and included many provisions to promote fair trade practices. It allowed the USTR to impose sanctions against countries that did not provide adequate intellectual property laws. It also made government-funded relief available to industries that were seriously harmed by imports. It provided $1 billion worth of federal funds to the states so they could create retraining programs for workers displaced by imports, and it stated that U.S. corporate officials could be held liable if they received certain types of information from their foreign employees. Relationships between foreign investors were forced to be more equal under

Special 301, because foreign companies could only be primary dealers of U.S. government securities if their home country granted the same privileges to U.S.-owned companies. The president was given the capability to continue negotiations in the Uruguay Round under the Special 301 provisions. Moreover, under Special 301, government purchases from the Toshiba Corporation were banned for three years because the company had violated a provision of the export rules. Finally, Special 301 required notice to be given to any employees sixty days prior to any long-term layoffs or plant closings by companies that employed more than 100 people, if one-third of the workforce would be affected, or if the layoffs affected 500 people or more.

Trade Laws of the 1990s: North American Free Trade Agreement

President Ronald Reagan proposed eliminating all trade barriers between the United States and Canada in 1985 in what would come to be known as the U.S.-Canada Free Trade Agreement. Any trade disputes would be settled by a joint committee. Negotiations began between Canada and the United States in late 1987, and the agreement was ratified by the U.S. Congress in September 1988.

Mexico asked to join the free trade agreement with Canada and the United States in 1992 and the resulting treaty was called the North American Free Trade Agreement (NAFTA). NAFTA linked the United States with its largest trading partners and produced competition with the world's largest single market, the European Union. President Bill Clinton signed NAFTA into law on December 8, 1993, and it went into effect on January 1, 1994.

NAFTA included many provisions and expanded some of the agreements of the treaty with Canada. All tariffs between Canada, Mexico, and the United States were to be phased out within ten years. To be considered as coming from one of these countries, a product had to have a certain percentage of its content or production originating in North America. Agricultural trade barriers, including tariffs and quotas, were to be phased out within ten years. Automotive goods that contained 60 to 62.5 percent North American goods were to have no trade or investment restrictions after 2004. Tariffs and quotas on fabrics and clothing items were eliminated immediately. Banking, insurance, and securities companies run by a NAFTA country company can sell their products or services to anyone in a NAFTA country. NAFTA also applied the same intellectual property rights to all member nations, and applied environmental protection standards to NAFTA members.

Trade Law Enforcement Agencies of the United States

Certain federal agencies are assigned the duty of regulating trade and making policy recommendations in the United States. The U.S. Department of Commerce (DOC) has the primary responsibility for the enforcement of most U.S. trade laws. The mission of this agency is to promote international trade, economic growth, and technological advancement. The International Trade Administration (ITA) is a branch of the DOC that aims to improve the international trade position of the United States. The Bureau of Export Administration is also under the DOC and is responsible for implementing much of the export control policy, including export licensing, research on relaxation of export controls, and enforcement of export control laws.

Other agencies also play a role in regulating U.S. trade laws, even though that is not their primary purpose. Overall U.S. foreign policy is coordinated and supervised by the Department of State. Domestic and international financial, economic, and tax policy is created by the U.S. Treasury Department. The secretary of the treasury serves as the U.S. representative to the International Monetary Fund (IMF). The Customs Service, established in 1789 and part of the Treasury Department since 1927, collects tariffs, enforces customs laws, and is known as the principal border enforcement agency.

The Office of the United States Trade Representative was created by President John F. Kennedy in 1963 and became an agency of the executive branch in 1974. The USTR directs all trade negotiations and plans all trade policy for the United States. The USTR appears on behalf of the United States before the World Trade Organization, the Organisation for Economic Cooperation and Development, and the United Nations Conference on Trade and Development.

Carol Walker

See Also Antidumping and Countervailing Duties; National Government Policies; National Tax Rules and Sovereignty; Nontariff Barriers; Protectionism; Tariffs; General Agreement on Tariffs and Trade (GATT); World Trade Organization (WTO)

References

Bayard, Thomas O., and Kimberly Ann Elliot. 1994. *Reciprocity and Retaliation in U.S. Trade Policy.* Washington, DC: Institute for International Economic Press.

Committee for Economic Development Staff. 1991. *Breaking New Ground in U.S. Trade Policy.* Boulder: Westview.

Jackson, John H., and Edwin A. Vermulst. 1989. *Antidumping Law and Practice.* Ann Arbor: University of Michigan Press.

Kaplan, Edward S. 1996. *American Trade Policy, 1923–1995.* London: Greenwood.

Keohane, Robert O. 1984. *After Hegemony.* Princeton, NJ: Princeton University Press.

Lash, William H., and Robert P. Parker. 1998. *U.S. International Trade Regulation.* Washington, DC: American Enterprise Institute Press.

Mastel, Greg. 1996. *American Trade Laws after the Uruguay Round.* New York: M. E. Sharpe.

Paradise, Paul R. 1999. *Trademark Counterfeiting, Product Piracy, and the Billion Dollar Threat to the U.S. Economy.* London: Quorum.

Reinicke, Wolfgang H. 1998. *Global Public Policy.* Washington, DC: Brookings Institution Press.

Shaffer, Gregory C. 2003. *Defending Interests.* Washington, DC: Brookings Institution Press.

Thurow, Lester. 2003. *Fortune Favors the Bold.* New York: Harper Press.

Bibliography

Books

Abdel-Maguid, Esmat. *Situations and Challenges of the Arab World.* Cairo: Dar-El-Sherouk, 2003.

Abraham, John, and Helen Lawton Smith. *Regulation of the Pharmaceutical Industry.* Basingstoke: Palgrave Macmillan, 2003.

Abu-Lughod, Janet L. *Before European Hegemony: The World System, AD 1250–1350.* New York: Oxford University Press, 1989.

Acharya, Amitav. *The Quest for Identity: International Relations of Southeast Asia.* Singapore: Oxford University Press, 2000.

———. *Constructing a Security Community in Southeast Asia: ASEAN and the Problem of Regional Order.* London: Routledge, 2001.

Acheson, A. L. K. *Bretton Woods Revisited: Evaluations of the International Monetary Fund and the International Bank for Reconstruction and Development.* Toronto: University of Toronto Press, 1972.

Aghion, Philippe, and Olivier Blanchard. *On the Speed of Adjustment in Central Europe.* Cambridge: MIT Press, 1994.

Alcock, Antony. *History of the International Labor Organization.* New York: Octagon, 1971.

Al-Ibraheemy, Al-Akhdar. *The Arab Diplomacy in a Changing World.* Beirut: Center for Arab Unity Studies, 2003.

Anderson, Bridget. *Doing the Dirty Work? The Global Politics of Domestic Labor.* London: Zed, 2000.

Anderson, P., and K. Eliassen. *Making Policy in Europe.* London: Sage, 2001.

Angell, Marcia. *Drug Money: How Pharmaceutical Companies Deceive Us and What We Can Do About It.* New York: Random House, 2004.

Archibugi, Daniele, Jeremy Howells, and Jonathan Michie. *Innovation Policy in a Global Economy.* Cambridge: Cambridge University Press, 1999.

Argy, Victor, and Paul de Grauwe. *Choosing an Exchange Regime.* Washington, DC: International Monetary Fund, 1990.

Arnold, Guy. *A Guide to African Political and Economic Development.* London: Fitzrog Dearborn, 2001.

Arora, A. *Chemicals and Long-Term Economic Growth.* New York: John Wiley and Sons, 1998.

Askari, Hossein G., et al. *Economic Sanctions: Examining Their Philosophy and Efficacy.* Westport, CT: Praeger, 2003.

Aubrey, Henry. *Atlantic Economic Cooperation: The Case of the OECD.* New York: Praeger, 1967.

Axline, Andrew. *Caribbean Integration: The Politics of Regionalism.* London: Frances Pinter, 1979.

Bagwell, Kyle. 2002. *The Economics of the World Trading System.* Cambridge: MIT Press.

Balance, Robert H., Janos Pogany, and Helmut Forstner. *The World's Pharmaceutical Industries: An International Perspective on Innovation, Competition and Policy.* Aldershot: Edward Elgar, 1992.

Baldwin, Robert. *The Political Economy of US Import Policy.* Cambridge: MIT Press, 1985.

Baldwin, Robert E., and Alan Winters.Editors. *Challenges to Globalization: Analyzing the Economics.* Chicago: University of Chicago Press, 2004.

Bales, Kevin. 2000. *Disposable People: New Slavery in the Global Economy.* Berkeley: University of California Press, 2000.

Bannock, Graham, R. E. Baxter, and Evan Davis. *The Penguin Dictionary of Economics.* London: Penguin, 1987.

Barber, Benjamin. *Jihad vs. McWorld: How Globalism and Tribalism Are Reshaping the World.* New York: Times Books, 1995.

Barnes, I., and P. M. Barnes. *The Enlarged European Union.* London: Longman, 1995.

Bartlett, Christopher A., and Sumantra Ghoshal. *Transnational Management: Text, Cases, and Readings in Cross-Border Management.* Boston: McGraw-Hill, 2000.

Baskin, Y. *The Work of Nature: How the Diversity of Life Sustains Us.* Washington, DC: Island Press, 1997.

Basu, Amrita. *The Challenge of Local Feminisms: Women's Movements in Global Perspective.* Boulder: Westview, 1995.

Basu, Kaushik. *Analytical Development Economics.* Cambridge: MIT Press, 1997.

Baum, Fran. *The New Public Health,* 2d ed. Oxford: Oxford University Press, 2002.

Bayard, Thomas O., and Kimberly Ann Elliot. *Reciprocity and Retaliation in U.S. Trade Policy.* Washington, DC: Institute for International Economics Press, 1994.

Beaglehole, Robert. *Global Public Health: A New Era.* Oxford: Oxford University Press, 2003.

Becker, Egon, and Thomas Jahn. *Sustainability and the Social Sciences.* New York: Zed, 1999.

Beckford, George. *Caribbean Economy: Dependency and Backwardness.* Mona, Jamaica: Institute of Social and Economic Research, 1984.

Beigbeder, Yves. *The World Health Organization.* The Hague: Martinus Nijhoff, 1998.

Bello, Walden, Shea Cunningham and Bill Rau. *Dark Victory: The United States and Global Poverty.* London: Pluto Press, 1999.

Benn, Denis, and Kenneth Hall. *The Caribbean Community: Beyond Survival.* Kingston, Jamaica: Ian Randle, 2001.

Berger, Harris M., and Michael T. Carroll. *Global Pop, Local Language.* Jackson: University Press of Mississippi, 2003.

Berger, Mark T. *The Battle for Asia: From Decolonization to Globalization.* London: RoutledgeCurzon, 2004.

Berkov, Robert. *The World Health Organization: A Study in Decentralized International Administration.* Geneva: Droz, 1957.

Berkovitch, Nitza. *The Emergence and Transformation of the International Women's Movement.* Oxford: Blackwell, 2000.

Bernal, Richard L. *CARICOM: Externally Vulnerable Regional Economic Integration.* Notre Dame, IN: University of Notre Dame Press, 1994.

Bhagwati, Jagdish N. *Protectionism.* Cambridge: MIT Press, 1988.

Bhagwati, Jagdish. *In Defense of Globalization.* Oxford: Oxford University Press, 2004.

Bhagwati, Jagdish, and Hugh T. Patrick. *Aggressive Unilateralism: America's 301 Trade Policy and the World Trading System.* Ann Arbor: University of Michigan Press, 1990.

Bhala, Raj. *International Trade Law: Cases and Materials.* Charlottesville, VA: Michie Law Publishers, 1996.

Bhalla, A. S., and Bhalla, P. *Regional Blocs: Building Blocks or Stumbling Blocks?* New York: St. Martin's, 1997.

Blake, Byron. *Experiences and Opportunities for Capacity Sharing through Regional Co-operation and Integration: The Case of the Caribbean Community.* London: Commonwealth Secretariat, 2001.

Blomberg, E., and A. Stubb. *The European Union: How Does It Work?* Oxford: Oxford University Press, 2003.

Boltuck, R., and R. E. Litan. *Down in the Dumps: Administration of the Unfair Trade Laws.* Washington, DC: Brookings Institution, 1991.

Bond, Eric. "Transportation Infrastructure Investments and Regional Trade Liberalization." Policy Research Working Paper 1851. Pennsylvania State University, 1997.

Borrus, Michael, Dieter Ernst, and Stephan Haggard. *International Production Networks in Asia: Rivalry or Riches?* London: Routledge, 2000.

Bouzas, Roberto, and Jaime Ros. *Money and Markets in the Americas: New Challenges for Hemispheric Integration.* Vancouver, BC: Fraser Institute, 1994.

Bowen, Harry P., Abraham Hollander, and Jean-Marie Viaene. *Applied International Trade Analysis.* Ann Arbor: University of Michigan Press, 1998.

Brander, J. A., and B. J. Spencer. *Tariffs and Extraction of Foreign Monopoly Rents under Potential Entry.* Cambridge: MIT Press, 1987.

Breslin, Shaun. *New Regionalisms in the Global Political Economy: Theories and Cases.* New York: Routledge, 2002.

Brewster, H., and C. Y. Thomas. *The Dynamics of West Indian Economic Integration.* Mona, Jamaica: Institute of Social and Economic Research, 1967.

Brewster, Havelock. *The Caribbean Single Market and Economy: Is It Realistic without Commitment to Political Unity?* Georgetown, Guyana: Caribbean Community Secretariat, 2003.

Browder, John O., and Brian J. Godfrey. *Rainforest Cities: The Urban Transformation of Amazonia.* New York: Columbia University Press, 1997.

Brower, Jennifer, and Peter Chalk. *The Global Threat of New and Reemerging Infectious Diseases: Reconciling U.S. National Security and Public Health Policy.* Santa Monica, CA: RAND Corporation, 2003.

Brown, Drusilla K. *Properties of Applied General Equilibrium Trade Models with Monopolistic Competition and Foreign Direct Investment.* Cambridge: Cambridge University Press, 1994.

Brown, Drusilla K., Alan V. Deardorff, and Robert M. Stern. *Child Labor: Theory, Evidence, and Policy.* Malden, MA: Blackwell, 2003.

Brown, Lester R. *Who Will Feed China? Wake-Up Call for a Small Planet.* New York: W. W. Norton, 1995.

———. *The Future of Growth.* New York: W. W. Norton, 1998.

Buckley, J. Peter, and Mark Casson. *Economic Theory of the Multinational Enterprise.* London: Macmillan, 1985.

Budd, S. A. *The European Community—A Guide to the Maze.* London: Kogan Page, 1992.

Bueno de Mesquita, Bruce, and Hilton L. Root. *Governing for Prosperity.* New Haven, CT: Yale University Press, 2000.

Bulatao, Ronald, and R. Lee. *Determinants of Fertility in Developing Countries, Supply and Demand for Children.* New York: Academic Press, 1983.

Burfisher, Mary E., Sherman Robinson, and Karen Theirfelder. *Wage Changes in a U.S.-Mexico Free Trade Area: Migration versus Stolper-Samuelson Effects.* Cambridge: Cambridge University Press, 1994.

Burkholz, Herbert. *The FDA Follies.* New York: Basic, 1994.

Cairncross, Frances. *The Death of Distance.* London: Orion, 1997.

Caldwell, John. *Theory of Fertility Decline.* New York: Academic Press, 1982.

Callinicos, Alex. *Equality.* Cambridge: Polity Press, 2000.

Camilleri, Joseph A. *States, Markets and Civil Society in Asia Pacific: The Political Economy of the Asia-Pacific Region.* Cheltenham, UK: Edward Elgar, 2000.

Cameron, Maxwell A., and Brian W. Tomlin. *The Making of NAFTA.* Ithaca, NY: Cornell University Press, 2000.

Campbell-Kelly, Martin. *From Airline Reservations to Sonic the Hedgehog: A*

History of the Software Industry. Cambridge: MIT Press, 2003.

Camps, Miriam, and William Diebold, Jr. *The New Multilateralism.* New York: Council on Foreign Relations, 1986.

Capron, H. L. *Computers: Tools for an Information Age.* New York: Addison-Longan Wesley, 1998.

Carew-Reid, J., R. Prescott-Allen, S. Bass, and B. Dalal-Clayton. *Strategies for National Sustainable Development: A Handbook for Planning and Implementation.* London: Earthscan, 1994.

Caribbean Community Secretariat. *Caribbean Development to the Year 2000: Challenges, Prospects and Policies.* Georgetown, Guyana: CARICOM, 1988.

Casadio, Gian Paolo. *The Economic Challenge of the Arabs.* Westmead, UK: Saxon House, 1976.

Casler, Stephen D. *HarperCollins College Outline Introduction to Economics.* New York: HarperResource, 1992.

Cassen, Robert, and Associates. *Does Aid Work? Report to an Intergovernmental Task Force.* Oxford: Clarendon, 1994.

Castells, Manuel, and Peter Hall. *Technopoles of the World: The Making of 21st Century Industrial Complexes.* New York: Routledge, 1994.

Caswell, Julie A. *Food Safety Standards and Regulation.* Washington, DC: International Food Policy Research Institute, 2003.

Catley, Bob. *NZ-Australia Relations: Moving Together or Drifting Apart?* Wellington: Dark Horse, 2002.

Caufield, Catherine. *Masters of Illusion: The World Bank and the Poverty of Nations.* New York: Henry Holt, 1996.

Caves, Richard E., Jeffrey A. Frankel, and Ronald W. Jones. *World Trade and Payments: An Introduction.* Boston: Addison-Wesley, 2002.

Childers, Erskine, and Brian Urquhart. *Renewing the United Nations System.* Uppasala, Sweden: Dag Hammerskjold Foundation, 1994.

Chopra, H. S, Gert W. Kueck, and L. L. Mehrotra. *SAARC 2000 and Beyond.* New Delhi: Omega Scientific, 1995.

Chorafas, Dimitris N. *An Introduction to Global Financial Markets.* Berkshire, UK: McGraw-Hill, 1992.

Chossudovsky, Michel. *The Globalization of Poverty: Impacts of the IMF and World Bank Reforms.* New York: St. Martin's, 1997.

Choucri, Nazli. *Corporate Strategies toward Sustainability.* Boston: Graham and Trotman/Martinus Nijhoff, 1994.

———. *The Political Logic of Sustainability.* New York: Zed, 1999.

Christianson, Gale E. *Greenhouse: The 200 Year Story of Global Warming.* New York: Walker, 1999.

Cipolla, Carlo. *Fighting the Plague in 17th Century Italy.* Madison: University of Wisconsin Press, 1981.

Clark, Gordon L. *Pension Fund Capitalism.* Oxford: Oxford University Press, 2000.

Claude, Richard P., and Weston H. Burns. *Human Rights in the World Community: Issues and Action.* Philadelphia: University of Pennsylvania Press, 1992.

Coelli, T., D. S. Prasada Rao, and G. E. Battese. *An Introduction to Efficiency and Productivity Analysis.* Boston: Kluwer Academic, 1998.

Coffey, Peter. *Latin America—MERCOSUR.* Boston: Kluwer Academic, 1988.

Cohen, Joel. *How Many People Can the Earth Support?* New York: W. W. Norton, 1995.

Comunidad Andina. *How to Do Business in the Andean Community: Trade and Investment Guide.* Peru: Andean Community General Secretariat, 1999.

Cooper, Richard. *The International Monetary System: Essays in World Economics.* Cambridge: MIT Press, 1987.

Cortright, David, and George A. Lopez. *Smart Sanctions: Targeting Economic Statecraft.* Lanham, MD: Rowman and Littlefield, 2002.

Cox, David J. *Some Applied General Equilibrium Estimates of the Impact of a North American Free Trade Agreement on*

Canada. Cambridge: Cambridge University Press, 1994.

Crane, D. B., R. C. Kimball, and W. C. Gregor. *The Effects of Banking Deregulation.* Chicago: Association of Reserve City Bankers, 1983.

Cullen, John B. *Multinational Management: A Strategic Approach.* Southwestern, 2002.

Culpan, Refik. *Global Business Alliances: Theory and Practice.* Westport, CT: Quorum, 2002.

Curtin, Dennis P. *Information Technology: The Breaking Wave.* Chicago: Irwin McGraw-Hill, 2003.

Curzon, Gerard. *Multilateral Trade Diplomacy.* London: Michael Joseph, 1965.

Das, Lal B. *The World Trade Organization: A Guide to the Framework for International Trade.* London: Zed, 1999.

Deardorff, Alan V., and Robert M. Stern. *Measurement of Nontariff Barriers.* Ann Arbor: University of Michigan Press, 1998.

Dehousse, R. *The European Court of Justice.* London: Macmillan, 1998.

Demas, William G. *The Economics of Small Countries with Special Reference to the Caribbean.* Montreal: McGill University Press, 1965.

Demir, Sooman. *Arab Development Funds in the Middle East.* New York: Pergamon, 1979.

Deng, Francis Mading, and I. William Zartman. *Conflict Resolution in Africa.* Washington, DC: Brookings Institution, 1991.

Devarajan, Shantayanan. *Aid and Reform in Africa: Lessons from Ten Case Studies.* Washington, DC: World Bank, 2001.

Diamond, Larry, and Juan J. Linz. *Politics in Developing Countries: Comparing Experiences with Democracy.* Boulder: Lynne Rienner, 1995.

Díaz-Briquets, Sergio, and Sidney Weintraub. *Determinants of Emigration from Mexico, Central America, and the Caribbean.* Boulder: Westview, 1991.

Dicken, Peter. *Global Shift: Reshaping the Global Economic Map in the 21st Century.* London: Sage, 2003.

Djajiae, Slobodan. *International Migration: Trends, Policies and Economic Impact.* New York: Routledge, 2001.

Donnelly, Jack. *International Human Rights.* Boulder: Westview, 1998.

Dornbusch, Rudiger, and Stanley Fischer. *Inflation Stabilization.* Cambridge: MIT Press, 1988.

Doz, Yves L., and Gary Hamel. *Alliance Advantage: The Art of Creating Value through Partnering.* Boston: Harvard Business School Press, 1998.

Doz, Yves, Jose Santos, and Peter Williamson. *From Global to Metanational: How Companies Win in the Knowledge Economy.* Boston: Harvard Business School Press, 2001.

Dunning H. John. *Multinational Enterprises and the Global Economy.* Boston: Addison-Wesley, 1993.

Dworkin, Ronald. *Does Equality Matter?* Cambridge: Polity Press, 2001.

Easterlin, Richard A. *The Economics and Sociology of Fertility, a Synthesis.* Princeton, NJ: Princeton University Press, 1978.

Edwards, Stephen, and Sir Frank Holmes. *CER: Economic Trends and Linkages.* Wellington: National Bank of New Zealand and Institute of Policy Studies, 1994.

Ehrlich, Paul R., and Anne H. Ehrlich. *The Population Explosion.* New York: Simon and Schuster, 1990.

Eichengreen, Barry. *International Monetary Arrangements for the 21st Century.* Washington, DC: Brookings Institution, 1995.

———. *Globalizing Capital: A History of the International Monetary System.* Princeton, NJ: Princeton University Press, 1996.

El-Agraa, Ali M. *Economic Integration Worldwide.* London: Macmillan, 1997.

Elliott, Kimberly Ann, and Richard B. Freeman. *Can Labor Standards Improve under Globalization?* Vienna: Institute for International Economics, International Labour Organization, 2003.

Elson, Diane. *Progress of the World's Women 2000: UNIFEM.* New York: United Nations Development Fund for Women, 2000.

Engerman, Stanley L. *History and Political Economy of International Labor Standards.* Malden, MA: Blackwell, 2003.

Erisman, H. Michael. *Pursuing Postdependency Politics: South-South Relations in the Caribbean.* Boulder: Lynne Rienner, 1992.

Esman, Milton, and Daniel Cheever. *The Common Aid Effort.* Columbus: Ohio State University Press, 1967.

Esping-Andersen, Gosta. *The Three Worlds of Welfare Capitalism.* Princeton, NJ: Princeton University Press, 1990.

European Bank for Reconstruction and Development. *Transition Report.* London: EBRD, 1998.

European Bank for Reconstruction and Development. *Transition Report Update 2002.* London: EBRD, 2002.

Fainstein, Susan S., and Scott Campbell. *Readings in Urban Theory.* Oxford: Blackwell, 2002.

Feenstra, Robert. *Integration of Trade and Disintegration of Production in the Global Economy.* Davis: University of California at Davis, 1998.

Ferguson, Iain, Michael Lavalette, and Gerry Mooney. *Rethinking Welfare: A Critical Perspective.* London: Sage, 2002.

Finger, J. M. *Antidumping: How It Works and Who Gets Hurt.* Ann Arbor: University of Michigan Press, 1993.

Finger, J. Michael, Merlinda D. Ingco, and Ulrich Reincke. *The Uruguay Round: Statistics on Tariff Concessions Given and Received.* Washington, DC: World Bank, 1996.

Finler, Joel. *The Hollywood Story.* New York: Crown, 1988.

Flowers, E. C., Jr. *The Arab League in Perspective.* Citadel Monograph Series. Charleston, SC: Citadel, 1961.

Foreman-Peck, James. *Historical Foundations of Globalization.* Northampton, MA: Edward Elgar, 1998.

Forsythe, David P. *Human Rights and World Politics.* Omaha: University of Nebraska Press, 1989.

Foster, Janet. *Docklands: Urban Change and Conflict in a Community in Transition.* Philadelphia: Taylor and Francis, 1999.

Fowler, Edward. *San'ya Blues: Laboring Life in Contemporary Tokyo.* Ithaca, NY: Cornell University Press, 1996.

Francis, David. *Uniting Africa: Building Regional Security Systems.* Boulder: Lynne Rienner, 2003.

Francois, Joseph F., and Kenneth A. Reinert. *Applied Methods for Trade Policy Analysis: A Handbook.* Cambridge: Cambridge University Press, 1997.

Frankel, Jeffrey. *Regional Trading Blocs in the World Economic System.* Washington, DC: Institute for International Economics, 1997.

Frieden, Jeffrey A. *The Politics of Exchange Rates.* Washington, DC: Brookings Institution, 1997.

Friedman, Jonathan. *Cultural Identity and Global Process.* London: Thousand Oaks, 1994.

Friedman, Milton. *Essays in Positive Economics.* Chicago: University of Chicago Press, 1953.

Funabashi, Yoichi. *Asia Pacific Fusion: Japan's Role in APEC.* Washington, DC: Institute for International Economics, 1995.

Galenson, Walter. *The International Labor Organization: An American View.* Madison: University of Wisconsin Press, 1981.

Garber, Peter M., and Lars E. O. Svensson. *The Operation and Collapse of Fixed Exchange Rate Regimes.* Cambridge, MA: National Bureau of Economic Research, 1995.

Gardner, Richard. *Sterling-Dollar Diplomacy in Current Perspective: The Origins and the Prospects of Our International Economic Order.* New York: Columbia University Press, 1980.

Garreau, Joel. *Edge City: Life on the New Frontier.* New York: Doubleday, 1991.

Garrett, Geoffrey. *Partisan Politics in the Global Economy.* Cambridge: Cambridge University Press, 1998.

Gassmann, Oliver, Gerrit Reepmeyer, and Maximilian von Zedtwitz. *Leading*

Pharmaceutical Innovation: Trends and Drives for Growth in the Pharmaceutical Industry. Berlin: Springer, 2004.

Gebbie, Kristine, Linda Rosenstock, and Lyla M. Hernandez. *Who Will Keep the Public Healthy? Educating Public Health Professionals for the 21st Century.* Washington, DC: National Academies Press, 2003.

Gelb, Alan, and Cheryl Gray. *The Transformation of Economies in Central and Eastern Europe.* Policy and Research Series 17. Washington, DC: World Bank, 1991.

Gentle, Christopher J. S. *The Financial Service Industry: The Impact of Corporate Reorganization on Regional Economic Development.* Avebury: Aldershot, 1993.

George, V., and P. Taylor-Gooby. *European Welfare Policy—Squaring the Welfare Circle.* London: Macmillan, 1996.

Geyer, H. S. *International Handbook of Urban Systems: Studies of Urbanization and Migration in Advanced and Developing Countries.* Cheltenham, UK: Edward Elgar, 2002.

Ghali, Boutros. *The League of Arab States and Arab Conflicts Management.* Cairo: Arab Researches and Studies Institute, 1977.

Gibilisco, Stan. *The Illustrated Dictionary of Electronics.* Chicago: Irwin McGraw-Hill, 1997.

Gilbert, Christopher L., and David Vines. *The World Bank: Structure and Policies.* New York: Cambridge University Press, 2000.

Gilpin, Robert. *The Political Economy of International Relations.* Princeton, NJ: Princeton University Press, 1987.

Ginsburg, Faye D., Lila Abu-Lughod, and Brian Larkin. *Media Worlds: Anthropology on New Terrain.* Berkeley: University of California Press, 2002.

Girvan, Norman, and O. Jefferson. *Readings in the Political Economy of the Caribbean.* Trinidad: New World Group, 1971.

Global Survival Network. *Crime and Servitude.* Washington, DC: GSN, 1997.

Goodman, Neville. *International Health Organizations and Their Work.* London: J&A Churchill, 1952.

Goodman, R., and I. Peng. *The East Asian Welfare States: Peripatetic Learning, Adaptive Change and Nation Building.* London: Sage, 1996.

Goozner, Merrill. *The $800 Million Pill: The Truth behind the Cost of New Drugs.* Berkeley: University of California Press, 2004.

Gordon, Robert J. *Productivity Growth, Inflation, and Unemployment: The Collected Essays of Robert J. Gordon.* Cambridge: Cambridge University Press, 2004.

Gowan, Peter. *The Global Gamble: Washington's Faustian Bid for World Dominance.* London: Verso, 1999.

Grabbe, J. Orlin. *International Financial Markets.* New York: Elsevier Science, 1986.

Grossman, Gene M., and Kenneth Rogoff. *Handbook of International Economics.* Vol. 3. Amsterdam: North-Holland, 1995.

Guinness World Records. London: Guinness World Records, 2000.

Haass, Richard N. *Economic Sanctions and American Diplomacy.* Washington, DC: Council on Foreign Relations, 1998.

Hackett, S. *Environmental and Natural Resources Economics: Theory, Policy, and the Sustainable Society,* 2d ed. New York: M. E. Sharpe, 2001.

Hall, Kenneth O. *Re-inventing CARICOM: The Road to a New Integration.* Kingston, Jamaica: Ian Randle, 2003.

Hammelink, Cees. *Trends in World Communication.* London: Zed, 1995.

Hannerz, Ulf. *The Cultural Role of World Cities.* Edinburgh: Edinburgh University Press, 1993.

Hannum, Hurst. *Guide to International Human Rights Practice.* Ardsley, NY: Transnational, 1999.

Harrison, Christopher Scott. *The Politics of the International Pricing of Prescription Drugs.* Westport, CT: Praeger, 2004.

Hazlitt, Henry. *Economics in One Lesson.* San Francisco: Fox and Wilkes, 1996.

Heidenheimer, Arnold, and Michael Johnston. *Political Corruption: Concepts and Contexts,*

3d ed. New Brunswick, NJ: Transaction, 2002.

Heilbroner, Robert L. *The Worldly Philosophers: The Lives, Times, and Ideas of the Great Economics Thinkers.* New York: Touchstone, 1999.

Heilbroner, Robert L., and Aaron Singer. *The Economic Transformation of America: 1600 to the Present.* Fort Worth: Harcourt Brace College, 1999.

Heitzman, James. *Network City: Information Systems and Planning in India's Silicon Valley.* New Delhi: Oxford University Press, 2004.

Helal, Aley El-Din, and Nivine Mosaad. *Arab Political System Causes of Continuation and Change.* Beirut: Arab Unity Studies Center, 2000.

Held, David. *Global Transformations: Politics, Economics and Culture.* Stanford, CA: Stanford University Press, 1999.

Held, David, and Anthony McGrew. *Governing Globalization.* Malden, MA: Polity Press, 2002.

Held, David, Anthony McGrew, David Goldblatt, and Jonathan Perraton. *Global Transformations.* Malden, MA: Polity Press, 1999.

Hellman, Joel S. *Competitive Advantage: Political Competition and Economic Reform in Postcommunist Transitions.* San Francisco: American Political Science Association, 1996.

Henning, C. Randall. *Currencies and Politics in the United States, Germany and Japan.* Washington, DC: Institute for International Economics, 1994.

Hensen, Spencer, et al. *Impact of Sanitary and Phytosanitary Measures on Developing Countries.* Reading, UK: University of Reading, 2000.

Henwood, Doug. *After the New Economy.* New York: New Press, 2003.

Herman, Edward S., and Robert W. McChesney. *The Global Media: The New Missionaries of Corporate Capitalism.* London: Cassell, 1997.

Hill, Charles W. L. *International Business: Competing in the Global Marketplace.* Boston: McGraw-Hill, 2000.

Hilton, Ronald. *The Movement toward Latin American Unity.* New York: Praeger, 1969.

Hirschman, Albert. *A Bias for Hope: Essays on Development in Latin America.* New Haven, CT: Yale University Press, 1971.

Hirschman, Charles, Philip Kasinitz, and Josh DeWind. *The Handbook of International Migration: The American Experience.* New York: Russell Sage Foundation, 1999.

Hitris, Theo. *European Community Economics,* 2d ed. New York: Harvester Wheatsheaf, 1991.

Hoekman, Bernard, and Michel Kostecki. *The Political Economy of the World Trading System.* Oxford: Oxford University Press, 1995.

Holdren, J. P., G. C. Daily, and P. R. Ehrlich. *The Meaning of Sustainability: Biogeophysical Aspects.* Washington, DC: United Nations University, 1995.

Hollander, J. M. *The Real Environmental Crisis: Why Poverty, Not Affluence, Is the Environment's Number One Enemy.* Berkeley: University of California Press, 2003.

Holmes, Frank. *The Trans-Tasman Relationship.* Wellington: Institute of Policy Studies, 1996.

Hoskins, Colin, Stuart McFadyen, and Adam Finn. *Global Television and Film: An Introduction to the Economics of the Business.* Oxford: Oxford University Press, 1997.

Hossain, Moazzem, Iyanatul Islam, and Reza Kibria. *South Asian Economic Development: Transformation, Opportunities and Challenges.* New York: Routledge, 1999.

Houghton, John. *Global Warming: The Complete Briefing.* Cambridge: Cambridge University Press, 1997.

Hufbauer, Gary C. *US Economic Sanctions: Their Impact on Trade, Jobs, and Wages.* Washington, DC: Institute of International Economics, 1997.

Hufbauer, Gary C., and Kimberly Ann Elliott. *Measuring the Cost of Protection in the United States.* Washington, DC: Institute for International Economics, 1994.

Hufbauer, Gary C., and Jeffrey Schott. *An Evaluation of NAFTA.* Washington, DC: Institute for International Economics, 1993.

Hulten, C. R., E. R. Dean, and M. J. Harper. *New Developments in Productivity Analysis.* Chicago: University of Chicago Press. 2001.

Hummels, David. *Have International Transportation Costs Declined?* Chicago: University of Chicago, 1999.

Humphreys, Norman K. *Historical Dictionary of the International Monetary Fund.* Lanham, MD: Scarecrow, 1993.

Humphries, Jane. *The Parallels between the Past and the Present.* Malden, MA: Blackwell, 2003.

Huntington, Samuel P. *Political Order in Changing Societies.* New Haven, CT: Yale University Press, 1968.

———. *The Third Wave: Democratization in the Late Twentieth Century.* Norman: University of Oklahoma Press, 1991.

Hutchinson, Williams Sawyer. *Using Information Technology: A Practical Introduction to Computers and Communication.* Boston: Irwin McGraw-Hill, 1999.

Hyvarinen, Antero. *Implications of the Introduction of the Agreement of Textiles and Clothing (ATC) on the African Textiles and Clothing Sector.* Geneva: International Trade Center, United Nations Conference on Trade and Development, and World Trade Organization, 2001.

Ibrahim, Ahmed. *Introduction to Applied Fuzzy Electronics.* New York: Prentice Hall, 1996.

Inglehart, Ronald. *Modernization and Postmodernization: Cultural, Economic, and Political Change in 43 Societies.* Princeton, NJ: Princeton University Press, 1997.

Inter-American Development Bank. *Ten Years of CARICOM: Papers Presented at a Seminar on Economic Integration in the Caribbean.* Washington, DC: IDB, 1984.

International Bank for Reconstruction and Development. *The International Bank for Reconstruction and Development, 1946–1953.* Baltimore: Johns Hopkins University Press, 1954.

International Labour Organization. *A Future without Child Labor.* Geneva: ILO, 2002.

International Monetary Fund. *Balance of Payment Manual.* Washington, DC: 1993.

———. *World Economic Outlook: Growth and Institutions.* Washington, DC: IMF, 2003.

———. *World Economic Outlook.* Washington, DC: IMF, 1997.

International Organization for Migration. *World Migration 2003: Managing Migration—Challenges and Responses for People on the Move.* Geneva: IOM, 2003.

Isaiah, Frank *Breaking New Ground in U.S. Trade Policy.* Boulder: Westview, 1991.

Ivin, George, and Stuart Holland. *Central America: The Future of Integration.* Boulder: Westview, 1989.

Jackson, John H. *Restructuring the GATT System.* London: Pinter, 1990.

———. *The World Trading System: Law and Policy of International Economic Relations,* 2d ed. Cambridge: MIT Press, 1997.

Jackson, John H., and Edwin A. Vermulst. *Antidumping Law and Practice.* Ann Arbor: University of Michigan Press, 1989.

James, Harold. *The End of Globalization: Lessons from the Great Depression.* Cambridge: Harvard University Press, 2001.

Jaycox, Edward. *What Can Be Done in Africa? The World Bank Response.* Boulder: Lynne Rienner, 1988.

Joekes, Susan, and Ann Weston. *Women and the New Trade Agenda.* New York: UNIFEM, (United Nations Development Fund for Women) 1994.

Johnson, Hazel J. *Global Financial Institutions and Markets.* Malden, MA: Blackwell, 2000.

Johnston, Alastair Iain. *Socialization in International Institutions: The ASEAN Way and International Relations Theory.* New York: Columbia University Press, 2003.

Jolly, Adam. *OECD Economies and the World Today: Trends, Prospects, and OECD Statistics.* London: Kogan Page, 2003.

Jones, K. A. *Export Restraint and the New Protectionism: The Political Economy of Discriminatory Trade Restrictions.* Ann Arbor: University of Michigan Press, 1994.

Jorgenson, D. W., F. M. Gollop, and B. Fraumeni. *Productivity and US Economic Growth.* Cambridge: Harvard University Press, 1987.

Josling, Timothy E., Stefan Tangermann, and T. K. Warley. *Agriculture in the GATT.* New York: St. Martin's, 1996.

Kagan, R. *Paradise and Power—America and Europe in the New World Order.* London: Atlantic, 2003.

Kamakura, Y. *Best Practices in Work-Flexibility Schemes and Their Impact on the Equality of Working Life in the Chemical Industries.* Geneva: International Labour Office, 2003.

Kamalipour, Yahya R. *Global Communication.* Belmont, CA: Wadsworth Thomson Learning, 2002.

Kaplan, Edward S. *American Trade Policy, 1923–1995.* London: Greenwood, 1996.

Kashikar, Mohan. *SAARC: Its Genesis, Development and Prospects.* Mumbai, India: Himalaya, 2000.

Kassirer, Jerome P. *On the Take: How Medicine's Complicity with Big Business Can Endanger Your Health.* New York: Oxford University Press, 2004.

Katzenstein, Peter J. *Small States in World Markets: Industrial Policy in Europe.* Ithaca, NY: Cornell University Press, 1985.

Kehoe, Timothy J. *Toward a Dynamic General Equilibrium Model of North American Trade.* Cambridge: Cambridge University Press, 1994.

Kenen, Peter B. *Understanding Interdependence: The Macroeconomics of the Open Economy.* Princeton, NJ: Princeton University Press, 1995.

Kenney, Martin. *Understanding Silicon Valley: The Anatomy of an Entrepreneurial Region.* Stanford: Stanford University Press, 2000.

Keohane, Robert O. *After Hegemony.* Princeton, NJ: Princeton University Press, 1984.

Keohane, R. O., and Joseph Nye. *Power and Interdependence.* Glenview, IL: Scott Forseman, 1989.

Keydar, Caglar. *Istanbul: Between the Global and the Local.* Lanham, MD: Rowman and Littlefield, 1999.

Kindleberger, Charles. *The World Depression, 1929–1939.* London: Penguin, 1973.

Kleinman, M. A. *European Welfare State?* Houndmills, UK: Palgrave, 2002.

Konate, Adama. *Challenges Facing the CFA Franc.* Conjoncture, 2001.

Korhonen, Pekka. *Japan and Asia Pacific Integration: Pacific Romances, 1968–1996.* London: Routledge, 1998.

Kornai, János. *The Socialist System: The Political Economy of Communism.* Oxford: Clarendon, 1992.

Kozlow, Ralph. *International Accounts Data Needs: Plans, Progress, and Priorities.* Washington, DC: Bureau of Economic Analysis, 2000.

Krauss, M. B. *The New Protectionism: The Welfare State and International Trade.* Oxford: Basil Blackwell, 1979.

Kreinin, Mordechai. *The Canada-U.S. Free Trade Agreement: An Overview.* East Lansing: Michigan State University Press, 2000.

Krueger, Anne O. *American Trade Policy: A Tragedy in the Making.* Washington, DC: American Enterprise Press, 1995.

Krueger Anne O., Maurice Schiff, and Alberto Valdés. *The Political Economy of Agricultural Pricing Policy.* Baltimore: Johns Hopkins University Press, 1992.

Krugman, Paul. *Exchange Rate Instability.* Cambridge: MIT Press, 1989.

Krugman, Paul, and Maurice Obstfeld. *International Economics,* 6th ed. Boston: Addison-Wesley, 2003.

Kumar, A. Prasanna. *SAARC: Retrospect and Prospect.* New Delhi: Kanishka, 2002.

Lafferty Business Research. *The Allfinanz*

Revolution: Winning Strategies for the 1990s. Dublin: Lafferty, 1991.

Landes, David S. *The Wealth and Poverty of Nations: Why Some Are So Rich and Some Are So Poor.* New York: W. W. Norton, 1999.

Lang, Winifried. *Sustainable Development and International Law.* Boston: Graham and Trotman/Martinus Nijhoff, 1994.

Lash, William H. *U.S. International Trade Regulation.* Washington, DC. 1998.

Lauren, Paul Gordon. *The Evolution of International Human Rights: Visions Seen.* Philadelphia: University of Pennsylvania Press, 1998.

Lederman, Daniel, William F. Maloney, and Luis Serven. *Lessons from NAFTA for Latin America and the Caribbean Countries: A Summary of Research Findings.* Washington, DC: World Bank, 2003.

Lee, Eddy. *The Asian Financial Crisis: The Challenge for Social Policy.* Geneva: International Labour Organization, 1998.

Legrain, Philippe. *Open World: The Truth about Globalisation.* London: Abacus, 2002.

Lewis, G. K. *The Growth of the Modern West Indies.* London: Macgibbon and Kee, 1968.

Lewis, Jordan D. *Trusted Partners: How Companies Build Mutual Trust and Win Together.* New York: Free Press, 1999.

Lewis, Patsy. *Surviving Small Size: Regional Integration in Caribbean Ministates.* Jamaica: University of the West Indies Press, 2002.

Leyshon, Andrew, and Nigel Thrift. *Money/Space: Geographies of Monetary Transformation.* London: Routledge, 1997.

Libby, Ronald T. *The Politics of Economic Power in Southern Africa.* Princeton, NJ: Princeton University Press, 1987.

Lipsey, Richard G., and K. Crystal. *Alec: An Introduction to Positive Economics.* Oxford: Oxford University Press, 1995.

Lipton, Michael. *Why Poor People Stay Poor.* Cambridge: Harvard University Press, 1976.

Lissakers, Karin. *Banks, Borrowers, and the Establishment: A Revisionist Account of the International Debt Crisis.* New York: Basic, 1991.

Long, Oliver. *Law and Its Limitations in the GATT Multilateral Trade System.* London: Graham and Tortman; Boston: Nijhoff, 1987.

Lopez-de-Silanes, Florencio, James R. Markusen, and Thomas Rutherford. *The Auto Industry and the North American Free Trade Agreement.* Cambridge: Cambridge University Press, 1994.

Lorenz, Edward C. *Defining Global Justice: The History of U.S. International Labor Standards Policy.* Notre Dame, IN: University of Notre Dame Press, 2001.

Low, P. *Trading Free: The GATT and the US Trade Policy.* New York: Twentieth Century Fund, 1993.

Lowe, Boutelle Ellsworth. *International Aspects of the Labor Problem.* New York: W. D. Gray, 1918.

Macdonald, Robert. *The League of Arab States: A Study in the Dynamics of Regional Organization.* Princeton, NJ: Princeton University Press, 1965.

Maddala, G. S. *Miller, Ellen: Microeconomics. Theory and Applications.* Boston: McGraw-Hill, 1989.

Maddison, A. *The World Economy in the Twentieth Century.* Paris: Organisation for Economic Co-operation and Development, Development Centre, 1989.

Madison, Angus. *Monitoring the World Economy, 1820–1992.* Paris: Organisation for Economic Co-operation and Development, 1995.

———. *The World Economy: A Millennial Perspective.* Paris: Organisation for Economic Co-operation and Development, 2001.

Martin, Ron. *Money and the Space Economy.* West Sussex, UK: John Wiley and Sons, 1999.

Martin, Will, and L. Alan Winters. *The Uruguay Round and the Developing Countries.* Cambridge: Cambridge University Press for the World Bank, 1996.

Massey, Douglas S., et al. *Worlds in Motion: Understanding International Migration at the End of the Millennium.* International Studies in Demography series. New York: Oxford University Press, 1998.

Mastel, Greg. *American Trade Laws after the Uruguay Round.* New York: M. E. Sharpe, 1996.

Matar, Gamil. *League of Arab States: The Historic Experience and Development Projects.* Cairo: Arab Center for Development and Future Studies and Center for Political Researches and Studies, 1993.

Matar, Gamil, and Aley El-Din Helal. *The Arab Regional Regime: A Study on Arab Political Relations.* Beirut: Arab Unity Studies Center, 1988.

Mazur, Robert E. *Breaking the Links: Development Theory and Practice in Southern Africa.* Trenton, NJ: Africa World Press, 1990.

McCormick, J. *Environmental Policy in the European Union.* Houndmills, UK: Palgrave, 2001.

———. *Understanding the European Union.* Houndmills, UK: Palgrave, 2002.

McEachern, William. *Macroeconomics,* 6th ed. Mason, OH: Thomson South Western, 2003.

McGarvy, R. *Biotech Comes of Age.* Cambridge: Harvard Business School, 2004.

McKay, C. *Extraordinary Popular Delusions and the Madness of Crowds.* New York: Giroux, 1932.

McLellan, Elisabeth P. *The World Bank: Overview and Current Issues.* New York: Nova Science, 2003.

McMahon, Robert J. *The Limits of Empire: The United States and Southeast Asia since World War II.* New York: Columbia University Press, 1999.

McNeill, J. R. *Something New under the Sun: An Environmental History of the Twentieth-Century World.* New York: W. W. Norton, 2000.

Meadows, Donella H. *The Limits to Growth: A Report for the Club of Rome's Project on the Predicament of Mankind.* New York: Universe Books, 1972.

Meerschwam, D. M. *Breaking Financial Boundaries: Global Capital, National Deregulation, and Financial Service Firms.* Boston: Harvard Business School Press, 1991.

Mekky, Youssif. *Causes of Arab Nationalism Failure.* Beirut: Center for Arab Unity Studies, 2003.

Meyer, Klaus. *Direct Investment in Economies in Transition.* Aldershot: Edward Elgar, 1998.

Michaels, Patrick J., and Robert C. Balling, Jr. *The Satanic Gases: Clearing the Air about Global Warming.* Washington, DC: Cato Institute, 2000.

Miguel S. Wionczek. *Latin American Free Trade Association.* New York: Carnegie Endowment for International Peace, 1965.

Mikesell, Raymond F. *The Emergence of the World Bank as a Development Institution.* Toronto: University of Toronto Press, 1972.

Mintz, Sidney. *Sweetness and Power: The Place of Sugar in Modern History.* New York: Penguin, 1987.

Mishel, Laurence, and Paula B. Voos. *Unions and Economic Competitiveness.* Armonk, NY: M. E. Sharpe, 1992.

Mishkin, Frederic. *The Economics of Money, Banks, and Financial Markets.* Boston: Pearson Addison-Wesley, 2004.

Mishra, Ramesh. *Globalization and the Welfare State.* Cheltenham, UK: Edward Elgar, 1999.

Mockler, Robert J. *Multinational Strategic Alliances.* Chichester, UK: John Wiley, 1999.

Mohamad, Mahathir bin. *Globalization: Challenges and Impact on Asia.* Singapore: John Wiley and Sons, 2002.

Moldan, Bedrich, Suzanne Billharz, and Robyn Matravers. *Sustainability Indicators: A Report on the Project on Indicators of Sustainable Development.* New York: John Wiley and Sons, 1997.

Moody-Stuart, George. *Grand Corruption: How Business Bribes Damage Developing Countries.* Oxford, UK: WorldView, 1997.

Mooney, H. A., and R. J. Hobbs. *Invasive Species in a Changing World.* Washington, DC: Island Press, 2000.

Morawetz, David. *Economic Integration among Unequal Partners: The Case of the Andean Group.* New York: Pergamon, 1974.

Moyo, Sam, Phil O'Keefe, and Michael Sill. *The Southern African Environment: Profiles of the SADC Countries.* London: Earthscan, 1993.

Mozahem, Ghassan. The Arab Specialized Organizations at the League of Arab States. Cairo: Arab Researches and Studies Institute, 1976.

Mshomba, Richard E. *Africa in the Global Economy.* Boulder: Lynne Rienner, 2000.

Musgrave, Richard. *The Theory of Public Finance.* Boston: McGraw-Hill, 1959.

Mussa, M. *Factors Driving Global Economic Integration.* Kansas City: Federal Reserve Bank of Kansas City, 2000.

Narine, Shaun. *Explaining ASEAN: Regionalism in Southeast Asia.* Boulder: Lynne Rienner, 2002.

Nelson, Joan. "Linkage between Politics and Economics" in *Economic Reform and Democracy.* Baltimore: Johns Hopkins University Press, 1995.

Newman, M. *Democracy, Sovereignty and the European Union.* London: Hurst and Company, 1997.

Nicoll, W., and T. C. Salmon. *Understanding the New European Community.* Hemel Hempstead, UK: Harvester Wheatsheaf, 1994.

Nielsen, Henrik. *The World Health Organization: Implementing the Right to Health.* Copenhagen: Europublishers, 1999.

Nieuwenhuysen, J. *Towards Free Trade between Nations.* Oxford: Oxford University Press, 1989.

Nincic, Miroslav and Peter Wallensteen. *Dilemmas of Economic Coercion: Sanctions in World Politics.* New York: Praeger, 1983.

Nooteboom, Bart. *Inter-Firm Alliances: Analysis and Design.* London: Routledge, 1999.

Nsekela, Amon J. *Southern Africa: Toward Economic Liberation.* London: Rex Collings, 1981.

Nye, Joseph S., and John D. Donahue. *Governance in a Globalizing World.* Washington, DC: Brookings Institution Press, 2000.

O'Brien, James A. *Introduction to Information Systems.* Chicago: Irwin McGraw-Hill, 1997.

O'Hara-Devereaux, M., and R. Johansen. *Globalwork: Bridging Distance, Culture, and Time.* San Francisco: Jossey-Bass, 1994.

O'Higgins, Niall. *Youth Unemployment and Employment Policy: A Global Perspective.* Geneva: International Labour Organization, 2001.

Obstfeld, Maurice, and Alan Taylor. *Global Capital Markets: Integration, Crisis, and Growth.* Cambridge: Cambridge University Press, 1999.

Olcott, Martha Brill, Anders Aslund, and Sherman W. Garnett. *Getting It Wrong: Regional Cooperation and the Commonwealth of Independent States.* Washington, DC: Brookings Institution, 2000.

Olson, Mancur. *Power and Prosperity.* New York: Basic, 2000.

Ong, Aihwa, and Donald Nonini. *Ungrounded Empires: The Cultural Politics of Modern Chinese Transnationalism.* New York: Routledge, 1996.

Organisation for Economic Co-operation and Development. *Indicators of Tariff and Non-Tariff Trade Barriers.* Paris: OECD, 1997.

———. *Trends in International Migration.* Paris: SOPEM, 1999.

———. *Measuring Productivity.* Paris: OECD Manual, 2001.

Orme, William A. *Understanding NAFTA—Mexico, Free Trade, and the New North America.* Austin: University of Texas Press, 1996.

Osnos, Peter, and William Shawcross. *Allies: The U.S., Britain, and Europe in the Aftermath of the Iraq War.* Boulder: Perseus, 2003.

Ostrom, E. *Governing the Commons: The Evolution of Institutions for Collective Action.* Cambridge: Cambridge University Press, 1990.

Overbeek, J. *Free Trade versus Protectionism.* Aldershot: Edward Elgar, 1999.

Ozaki, Muneto. *Negotiating Flexibility: The Role of the Social Partners and the State.* Geneva: International Labour Organization, 1999.

Paehlke, Robert C. *Democracy's Dilemma: Environment, Social Equity, and the Global Economy.* Cambridge: MIT Press. 2004.

Papastergiadis, Nikos. "The Turbulence of Migration: Globalization, Deterritorialization and Hybridity." Malden, MA: Polity Press, 2000.

Paradise, Paul R. *Trademark Counterfeiting, Product Piracy, and the Billion Dollar Threat to the U.S. Economy.* London: Quorum, 1999.

Parpart, Jane, and Marianne Marchand. *Feminism/Postmodernism/Development.* London: Routledge, 1995.

Parsons, June Jamrich, and Dan Oja. *Computer Concepts.* Cambridge: Course Technology, 1998.

Pasahow, Edward. *Electronics Pocket Reference.* Chicago: Irwin McGraw-Hill, 1998.

Payer, Cheryl. *The World Bank: A Critical Analysis.* New York: Monthly Review Press, 1982.

Payne, Anthony. *The Politics of the Caribbean Community, 1961–79: Regional Integration among New States.* New York: St. Martin's, 1980.

Payne, Anthony, and Paul Sutton. *Charting Caribbean Development.* Miami: University Press of Florida, 2001.

Peet, Richard. *Manufacturing Industry and Economic Development in the SADCC Countries.* Stockholm: Beijer Institute, 1984.

Peterson, J., and M. Shackleton. *The Institutions of the European Union.* Oxford: Oxford University Press, 2002.

Philander, S. George. *Is the Temperature Rising? The Uncertain Science of Global Warming.*

Princeton, NJ: Princeton University Press, 1998.

Pierce, David W. *Macmillan Dictionary of Modern Economics.* London: Macmillan, 1986.

Population Reference Bureau. *World Population Data Sheet.* Washington, DC: PRB, 2004.

Porter, Michael E. *Competitive Advantage of Nations.* New York: Free Press, 1998.

Pratt, Edmund T., Jr. *Pfizer: Bringing Science to Life.* New York: Newcomen Society of the United States, 1985.

Preston, Samuel, and M. R. Haines. *Fatal Year: Child Mortality in Late Nineteenth Century America.* Princeton, NJ: Princeton University Press, 1991.

Price, Monroe E. *Media and Sovereignty: The Global Information Revolution and Its Challenge to State Power.* Cambridge: MIT Press, 2002.

Qureshi, Asif H. *The World Trade Organization: Implementing International Trade Norms.* Manchester: Manchester University Press, 1996.

Rama, Ruth. *Investing in Food.* Paris: Organisation for Economic Co-operation and Development, 1992.

Ravenhill, John. *APEC and the Construction of Pacific Rim Regionalism.* Cambridge: Cambridge University Press, 2001.

Raynauld, Andre, and Jean-Pierre Vidal. *Labour Standards and International Competitiveness: A Comparative Analysis of Developing and Industrialized Countries.* Northampton, MA: Edward Elgar, 1998.

Razin, Assaf and Sadka, Efraim. *The Economics of Globalisation.* Cambridge: Cambridge University Press, 1999.

Reinicke, Wolfgang H. *Global Public Policy.* Washington, DC: Brookings Institution Press, 1998.

Richards, Paul. *Fighting for the Rain Forest: War, Youth and Resources in Sierra Leone.* Wageningen, Holland: University of Wageningen, 1996.

Richards, Peter. *Towards the Goal of Full*

Employment: Trends, Obstacles and Policies. Geneva: International Labour Organization, 2001.

Richter, Frank-Jurgen. *Strategic Networks: The Art of Japanese Interfirm Cooperation.* New York: International Business Press, 2000.

Rivera-Batiz, Francisco, and Luis Rivera-Batiz. *International Finance and Open Economy Macroeconomics,* 2d ed. New York: Prentice Hall, 1994.

Robert, Maryse. *Negotiating NAFTA.* Toronto: University of Toronto Press, 2000.

Roberts, Allen F., and Mary Nooter Roberts. *A Saint in the City: Sufi Arts of Urban Senegal.* Los Angeles: University of California at Los Angeles, Fowler Museum of Cultural History, 2003.

Rodrik, Dani. *Has Globalization Gone too Far?* Washington, DC: Institute of International Economics, 1997.

———. *The New Global Economy and Developing Countries: Making Openness Work.* Washington, DC: Overseas Development Council, 1999.

Roett, Riordan. *MERCOSUR Regional Integration, World Markets.* Boulder: Lynne Rienner, 1999.

Rogers, Adam. *The Earth Summit: A Planetary Reckoning.* Los Angeles: Global View Press, 1993.

Roland-Holst, David W., Kenneth A. Reinert, and Clinton R. Sheills. *A General Equilibrium Analysis of North American Integration.* Cambridge: Cambridge University Press, 1994.

Rose, T. *Crisis and Recovery in Sub-Saharan Africa.* Paris: Organisation for Economic Co-operation and Development, 1985.

Rose-Ackerman, Susan. *Corruption and Government: Causes, Consequences and Reform.* Cambridge: Cambridge University Press, 1999.

Salda, Anne C. M. *World Bank.* New Brunswick, NJ: Transaction, 1995.

Salvatore, Dominick. *The New Protectionist Threat to World Welfare.* New York: Elsevier Science, 1987.

———. *International Economics,* 7th ed. New York: John Wiley and Sons, 2001.

Sandness, Donald H. *Computers Today.* Boston: Irwin McGraw-Hill, 1988.

Sarhan, Abdel Aziz. *The Principles of the International Organization.* Cairo: Dar El-Nahda, 1976.

Sassen, Saskia. *The Mobility of Labor and Capital: A Study in International Investment and Labor Flow.* Cambridge: Cambridge University Press, 1988.

———. *The Global City: New York, London, Tokyo.* Princeton, NJ: Princeton University Press, 1991.

———. *Cities in a World Economy,* 2d ed. Thousand Oaks, CA: Pine Forge, 2000.

Saxenian, AnnaLee. *Silicon Valley's New Immigrant Entrepreneurs.* San Francisco: Public Policy Institute of California, 1999.

Sayigh, Yusif A. *The Determinants of Arab Economic Development.* New York: St. Martin's, 1978.

———. *Elusive Development: From Dependence to Self-Reliance in the Arab Region.* London: Routledge, 1991.

Scheurer, Thierry. *Foundation of Computing System Development with Set Theory and Logic.* Workinghaw: UK: Addison Wesley, 1994.

Schiller, Dan. *Digital Capitalism: Networking the Global Market System.* Cambridge: MIT Press, 1999.

Schott, Jeffrey J. *Completing the Uruguay Round: A Results-Oriented Approach to the GATT Trade Negotiations.* Washington, DC: Institute for International Economics, 1990.

Schumpeter, Joseph. *Business Cycles.* New York: McGraw-Hill, 1939.

———. *Capitalism, Socialism, and Democracy.* New York: Harper, 1942.

Schwartz, A. J. *Real and Pseudo Financial Crises.* London: Macmillan, 1986.

Schweizer, Stuart O. *Pharmaceutical Economics and Policy.* New York: Oxford University Press, 1997.

Scott, Allen J. *Global City-Regions: Trends,*

Theory, Policy. Oxford: Oxford University Press, 2001.

Selden, Zachary. *Economic Sanctions as Instruments of American Foreign Policy.* Westport, CT: Praeger, 1999.

Selim, Mohammad. *The Development of International Politics in the Nineteenth and Twentieth Centuries.* Cairo: Dar Al-Fajir Al-Jadid, 2002.

Sen, Amartya. *Development as Freedom.* New York: Knopf, 1999.

Shaffer, Gregory C. *Defending Interests: Public-Private Partnerships in W.T.O. Litigation.* Washington, DC: Brookings Institution Press, 2003.

Shalabi, Ibrahim. *International Organization: The International Regional and Specialized Organizations.* Beirut: El-Dar El-Gamaa, 1992.

Shanks, M. *European Social Policy, Today and Tomorrow.* Oxford: Pergamon, 1977.

Shehab, Mofid. *The International Organization.* Cairo: Dar El-Nahda, 1978.

Shehab, Mofid. *League of Arab States, Charter and Accomplishments.* Cairo: Arab Researches and Studies Institute, 1978.

Shoemaker, M. Wesley. *Russia and the Commonwealth of Independent States 2001.* Washington, DC: Stryker Post, 2001.

Shore, C. *Building Europe—The Cultural Politics of European Integration.* London: Routledge, 2000.

Shue, Henry. *Basic Rights: Subsistence, Affluence, and U.S. Foreign Policy,* 2d ed. Princeton, NJ: Princeton University Press, 1996.

Sidney, Dell. *A Latin American Common Market?* New York: Oxford University Press, 1966.

Siedentop, L. *Democracy in Europe.* London: Penguin, 2000.

Silverman, Milton, and Philip R. Lee. *Pills, Profits, and Politics.* Berkeley: University of California Press, 1974.

Simons, Geoff. *Imposing Economic Sanctions: Legal Remedy or Genocidal Tool?* London: Pluto Press, 1999.

Sinclair, Timothy J. *Deficit Discourse: The Social Construction of Fiscal Rectitude.* London: Macmillan, 2000.

Singh, Kavaljit. *Taming Global Financial Flows: A Citizen's Guide.* New York: St. Martin's, 2000.

Singh, Tarlok. *Perspective after the Third Summit.* New Delhi: Vikas, 1989.

Sklair, Leslie. *Globalization: Capitalism and Its Alternatives.* Oxford: Oxford University Press, 2002.

Smith, Adam. *The Wealth of Nations.* New York: Bantam Classics, 2003.

Smolansky, Bettie M., and Oles M. Smolansky. *The Lost Equilibrium: International Relations in the Post-Soviet Era.* Bethlehem, PA: Lehigh University Press, 2001.

Soros, George. *George Soros on Globalization.* New York: PublicAffairs, 2002.

Soto, Hernando de. *The Mystery of Capital: Why Capitalism Triumphs in the West and Fails Everywhere Else.* New York: Basic, 2003.

Sowell, Thomas. *Basic Economics: A Citizen's Guide to the Economy.* New York: Basic, 2000.

Spero, Joan E., and Jeffrey A. Hart. *The Politics of International Economic Relations,* 6th ed. Toronto: Thompson Wadsworth, 2003.

Speth, J. G. *Worlds Apart: Globalization and the Environment.* Washington, DC: Island Press, 2003.

Sreberny-Mohammadi, Annabelle. *The Global and the Local in International Communications.* London: E. Arnold, 1991.

Sreberny-Mohammadi, Annabelle, Dwayne Winseck, Jim McKenna, and Oliver Boyd-Barrett. *Media in Global Context: A Reader.* London: Hodder Headline Group, 1997.

Stalker, Peter. *Workers without Frontiers: The Impact of Globalization on International Migration.* Boulder: Lynne Rienner, 2000.

Steiner, Henry J., and Philip Alston. *International Human Rights in Context: Law, Politics, Morals.* Oxford: Clarendon, 1996.

Sterky, Göran, Kim Forss, and Bo Stenson. *Tomorrow's Global Health Organization: Ideas and Options.* Stockholm: Ministry of Foreign Affairs, 1996.

Stern, Robert. *US Trade Policies in a Changing World Economy.* Cambridge: MIT Press, 1987.

Stiglitz, Joseph E. *Economics of the Public Sector.* New York: W. W.Norton, 1988.

———. *Globalization and Its Discontents.* New York: W. W. Norton, 2002.

Stroev, E. S., Leonid Solomonovich Bliakhman, and Mikhail I. Krotov. *Russia and Eurasia at the Crossroads: Experience and Problems of Economic Reforms in the Commonwealth of Independent States.* New York: Springer Verlag, 1999.

Swann, Dennis. *The Economics of Europe: From Common Market to European Union.* London: Penguin, 2000.

Szymanski, Robert A., Donald P. Szymanski, and Donna M. Pulschen. *Computers and Information Systems.* New York: Prentice-Hall, 1995.

Tajgman, David, and Karen Curtis. *Freedom of Association: A User's Guide* to *Standards, Principles and Procedures of the International Labour Organization.* Geneva: ILO, 2000.

Taylor, J. Edward. *Development Strategy, Employment, and Migration: Insights from Models.* Paris: Organisation for Economic Co-operation and Development, 1996.

Thornton, H. *An Enquiry into the Effects of the Paper Credit of Great Britain.* Fairfield, NJ: Augustus Kelly, 1802.

Thurow, Lester. *Fortune Favors the Bold.* New York: Harper Press, 2003.

Took, T. *History of Prices.* London: Longman, Brown, Green and Longman, 1858.

Torrens, R. *The Budget: On Commercial and Colonial Policy.* Smith, Elder: London: 1844.

Torres, Raymond. *Towards a Socially Sustainable World Economy: An Analysis of the Social Pillars of Globalization.* Geneva: International Labour Organization, 2001.

Trebilcock, Michael J., and Robert Howse. *The Regulation of International Trade.* London: Routledge, 1995.

Trela, Irene, and John Whalley. *Trade Liberalization in Quota-Restricted Items: The United States and Mexico in Textiles and Steel.* Cambridge: Cambridge University Press, 1994.

Tumlir, Jan. *Protectionism: Trade Policy in Democratic Societies.* Washington, DC: American Enterprise Institute, 1985.

Turow, Joseph. *Media Today: An Introduction to Mass Communication,* 2d ed. Boston: Houghton Mifflin, 2003.

UNAIDS/WHO. *AIDS Epidemic Update: December 2000.* Geneva: World Health Organization, 2004.

United Nations. *The History of UNCTAD, 1964–1984.* New York: United Nations, 1985.

———. *Trends in Population Policy.* New York: United Nations, 1989.

———. *World Population Prospects: The 2000 Revision, Highlights.* New York: United Nations, 2001.

———. *Demographic Yearbook.* New York: United Nations, 2002.

———. *Statistical Yearbook 2001.* New York and Geneva: United Nations Population Data Unit, Population and Geographic Data Section, 2002.

United Nations Conference on Trade and Development. *A Guide to UNCTAD: 30 Years and Beyond.* Geneva: UNCTAD, 1994.

———. *The DMFAS Program—A Brief Description.* Geneva: UNCTAD, 2000.

———. *United Nations Conference on Trade and Development: Trade, Investment and Development.* Geneva and London: UNCTAD and International Systems and Communications, 2001.

———. *Trade and Development Report.* New York and Geneva: United Nations, 1990.

———. *Evaluation of UNCTAD EMPRETEC Program.* No. 129. New York and Geneva: United Nations, 2000.

———. *DMFAS 2001 Annual Report.* New York and Geneva: United Nations, 2001.

———. *Trade and Development Report.* New York and Geneva: United Nations, 1999.

———. *United Nations Conference on Trade and Development, I: Final Act and Report.* New York and Geneva: United Nations, 1964.

United Nations Development Program. *Human Development Report.* New York: Oxford University Press, 2001.

———. *Human Development Report 1999.* New York and Geneva: United Nations, 1999.

———. *Human Development Report 2003.* New York and Geneva: United Nations, 2003.

United Nations Research Institute for Development. *Social Policy in a Development Context.* Report of the UNRID Conference, Tammsvik, Sweden, 2000.

Urquidi, Victor. *Free Trade and Economic Integration in Latin America.* Berkeley: University of California Press, 1962.

U.S. Bureau of the Census. *Historical Statistics of the United States.* Washington, DC: Government Printing Office, 1975.

U.S. Bureau of the Census. *Statistical Abstract of the United States, 1996.* 200th ed. Washington, DC: U.S. Government Printing Office, 1998.

———. *World Population Profile, 1998.* Washington, DC: Government Printing Office, 1998.

U.S. Committee for Refugees. *World Refugee Survey.* New York: U.S. Committee for Refugees, 2003.

U.S. Government Printing Office. *The Balance of Payments of the United States: Concepts, Data Sources, and Estimating Procedures.* Washington, DC: U.S. Government Printing Office, 1990.

Valdez, Stephen. *An Introduction to Global Financial Markets.* New York: Palgrave, 2000.

Varian, Hal R. *Intermediate Microeconomics: A Modern Approach,* 6th ed. New York: W. W. Norton, 2002.

Vautier, K. M., and P. J. Lloyd. *A Case Study of Anti-Dumping and Countervailing Duties in Australia.* Wellington: Institute of Public Policy, 1997.

Venn, Oladipo H. B. *Essentials of Government for Ordinary Level Examinations.* London: Evans Brothers, 1986.

Viner, J. *Dumping: A Problem in International Trade.* Geneva: League of Nations, 1926.

Visaria, Pravin, and Vijaylaxmi Chari. *India's Population Policy and Family Planning Program: Yesterday, Today and Tomorrow.* New York: Population Council, 1998.

Vousden, Neil. *The Economics of Trade Protection.* Cambridge: Cambridge University Press, 1990.

Wallerstein, Immanuel. *The Modern World System: Capitalist Agriculture and the Origins of the European World Economy in the Sixteenth Century.* New York: Academic Press, 1974.

Walley, John, John Wright, and John Hubley. *Public Health: An Action Guide to Improving Health in Developing Countries.* Oxford: Oxford University Press, 2001.

Watson, James. *Golden Arches East: McDonald's in East Asia.* Stanford, CA: Stanford University Press, 1997.

Weaver, Frederick Stirton. *Class, State, and Industrial Structure.* Westport, CT: Greenwood, 1980.

Webb, Michael C. *The Political Economy of Policy Coordination: International Adjustment Since 1945.* Ithaca, NY: Cornell University Press, 1995.

Weeks, John. *Population: An Introduction to Concepts and Issues.* Belmont, CA: Wadsworth Group, 2001.

Weiss, Thomas G. *Political Gain and Civilian Pain: Humanitarian Impacts of Economic Sanctions.* Lanham, MD: Rowan and Littlefield, 1997.

West Indian Commission. *Time for Action: The Report of the West Indian Commission.* Largo, MD: International Development Options, 1994.

Wichterich, Christa. *The Globalized Women: Reports from a Future of Inequality.* London: Zed, 2000.

Williamson, John. *What Washington Means by Policy Reform*. Washington, DC: Institute for International Economics, 1990.

Wilkin, Peter. *The Political Economy of Global Communication: An Introduction*. London: Pluto Press, 2001.

Wilson, Charles. *Mercantilism*. London: Historical Association, 1971.

Wood, Patricia. *World Health Organization: A Brief Summary of Its Work*. Canberra: Australian Government Publishing Service, 1988.

World Bank. *One Hundred Questions and Answers*. Washington, DC: World Bank, 1970.

———. *World Bank and IDA: Questions and Answers*. Washington, DC: World Bank, 1971.

———. *World Development 1991: The Challenge of Development*. Oxford: Oxford University Press, 1991.

———. *The World Development Report, 1997: The State in a Changing World*. Oxford: Oxford University Press, 1997.

———. *Assessing Aid: What Works, What Doesn't and Why*. New York: Oxford University Press, 1998.

———. *The World Development Report, 2000: Entering the 21st Century*. Oxford: Oxford University Press, 2000.

———. *Global Economic Prospects and the Developing Countries, 2001*. Washington, DC: World Bank, 2001.

———. *World Development Report*. New York: Oxford University Press, 2001.

———. *The World Development Report, 2002: Building Institutions for Markets*. Oxford: Oxford University Press, 2002.

———. *Transition—The First Ten Years: Analysis and Lessons for Eastern Europe and the Former Soviet Union*. Washington, DC: World Bank, 2002.

———. *Global Development Finance*. Washington, DC: World Bank, 2003.

———. *The World Development Report*. New York: Oxford University Press, 2003.

———. *The World Development Report, 2003:*

Sustainable Development in a Dynamic World: Transforming Institutions, Growth, and Quality of Life. Oxford: Oxford University Press, 2003.

———. *World Development Indicators*. Washington, DC: World Bank, 2004.

World Commission on Environment and Development. *Our Common Future*. Oxford: Oxford University Press, 1987.

World Health Organization. *The First Ten Years of the World Health Organization*. Geneva: WHO, 1952.

———. *The Second Ten Years of the World Health Organization—1958–1967*. Geneva: WHO, 1968.

———. *Four Decades of Achievement: Highlights of the Work of WHO*. Geneva: WHO, 1988.

World Trade Organization. *Uruguay Round Agreement Establishing the World Trade Organization*. Geneva: WTO, 1995.

———. *Understanding the WTO*, 3d ed. Geneva: WTO, 2003.

Yang, Xiaokai, and Yew-Kwang Ng. *Specialization and Economic Organization: A New Classical Microeconomic Framework*. Amsterdam: North-Holland, 1993.

Yarbrough, Beth, and Robert Yarbrough. *The World Economy: Trade and Finance*, 5th ed. Orlando, FL: Harcourt College, 2000.

———. *The World Economy: Trade and Finance*, 6th ed. Cincinnati: South-Western, 2003.

Yeates, Nicola. *Globalisation and Social Policy*. London: Sage, 2001.

Yoichi Funabashi. *Managing the Dollar: From the Plaza to the Louvre*. Washington, DC: Institute for International Economics, 1988.

Young, Leslie, and Jose Romero. *A Dynamic Dual Model of the North American Free Trade Agreement*. Cambridge: Cambridge University Press, 1994.

Yudelman, Montague. *The World Bank and Agricultural Development: An Insider's View*. New York: World Resources Institute, 1985.

Zacher, Mark. *International Conflicts and Collective Security, 1946–1977.* New York: Praeger, 1979.

Journal Articles, Journals, and Book Chapters

"Conflicting Pressures Plague Biotech Policy." *Oxford Analytica* 10 (September 2004).

"Facts and Figures for the Chemical Industry." *Chemical & Engineering News* (July 5, 2004): 24–63.

"ICEM World Conference on the Chemical Industries, Background Paper, 26–28 November, Bangkok, Thailand." Brussels: International Federation of Chemical, Energy, Mine and General Workers' Unions, 2001.

"New IOM Figures on the Global Scale of Trafficking." *Trafficking in Migrants, Quarterly Bulletin* (International Organisation for Migration), no. 23 (April 2001).

"Special Report. What's Going On at the World Health Organization." *Lancet* 360 (October 12, 2002): 1108–1109.

"The Unmagnificent Seven." *Economist* (January 24, 2002).

"Trafficking in Migrants." *Quarterly Bulletin,* IOM International Organization for Migration, no. 23 (2001).

"Transition: Experience and Policy Issues." *World Economic Outlook* (International Monetary Fund) (October 2002): 84–137.

"TRIP Regime Set to Bolster R&D Potential." *Oxford Analytica* (October 21, 2004).

"World Chemical Industry White Paper (Sekai Kagaku Kogyo Hakusho)." *Kagaku Keizai* (March 2004): 7–37.

"WTO Panel Hears GMO Trade Case." *Oxford Analytica* (June 9, 2004).

Abdel-Rahman, Hamdy. "Africa and US Policy: From Isolation to Partnership." *International Politics Journal* 144 (2001): 192–204.

Adam, Barbara. "The Gendered Time Politics of Globalization: Of Shadowlands and Elusive Justice." *Feminist Review* 70 (2002): 3–29.

Ades, Alberto, and Rafael Di Tella. "Rents, Competition, and Corruption." *American Economic Review* 89 (1999): 1023–1042.

Aggrewal, Mita. "International Trade, Labor Standards, and Labor Market Conditions: An Evaluation of the Linkages." USITC (US International Trade Commission) Office of Economics Working Paper, No. 95–06-C, 1995.

Al Sa'doun, Abdul Wahab. "GCC Petrochemical Industry Must Unite to Compete." *Oil and Gas Journal* 98, no. 46 (2000): 52–58.

Ali, Khaled. "New Regionalism in Africa." *International Politics Journal* 144 (2001): 185–191.

Allsopp, Christopher, and Henryk Kierzkowski. "The Assessment: Economics of Transition in Eastern and Central Europe." *Oxford Review of Economic Policy* 13, no. 2 (1997): 1–22.

Alnajjar, Ghanim. "The GCC and Iraq." *Middle East Policy* 7, no. 4 (2000): 92–99.

Arjona, R., M. Laidaique, and M. Pearson. "Growth, Inequality and Social Protection." Paris: Directorate for Education, Employment, Labour and Social Affairs, 2001.

Ark, B. van. "The Measurement of Productivity: What do the Numbers Mean?" In *Fostering Productivity: Patterns, Determinants and Policy Implications* (2004): 28–61. Edited by G. Gelauff, L. Klomp, S. Raes, T. Roelandt, Ministry of Economic Affairs, The Hague, The Netherlands, Elsevier.

Ark, Bart van, Robert Inklaar, and Robert H. McGuckin. "Changing Gear: Productivity, ICT and Service Industries in Europe and the United States." In *The Industrial Dynamics of the New Digital Economy* (2003): 56–99. Edited by Jens Freslev Christensen and Peter Maskell, Edward Elgar Publishing Cheltenham, UK.

Arrighi, Giovanni. "The African Crisis: World Systemic and Regional Aspects." *New Left Review,* no. 15 (2002).

Aslanbeigui, Nahid, and Gale Summerfield. "The Asian Crisis, Gender, and the International Financial Architecture." *Feminist Economics* 6, no. 3 (2000): 81–103.

Aslund, Anders. "Lessons of the First Four Years of Systematic Change in Eastern Europe." *Journal of Comparative Economics* 19 (1994): 22–39.

Auda, Abdel-Malek. "The Issues of Arab-African Relations." *International Politics Journal* 148 (2002): 30–34.

Avisse, Richard, and Michel Fouquin. "Textiles and Clothing: The End of Discriminatory Protection." *La Lettre du CEPII,* no 198 (2001).

Axline, Andrew. "Integration and Development in the Commonwealth Caribbean: The Politics of Regional Negotiations." *International Organization* 32, no. 4 (1978): 953–973.

Bagwell, Kyle, and Robert Staiger. "An Economic Theory of GATT." *American Economic Review* 89 (1999): 215–248.

———. "Multilateral Trade Negotiations, Bilateral Opportunism and the Rules of GATT/WTO." *Journal of International Economics* 63, no. 1 (2004): 1–29.

Baier, Scott L., and Jeffrey H. Bergstrand. "The Growth of World Trade: Tariffs, Transport Costs and Income Similarity." *Journal of International Economics* 53 (2001): 1–27.

Baker, J. "Innovate for Growth." *European Chemical News* 15–2, no. 1 (2004): 16–18.

Balassa, Bela. "Regional Integration and Trade Liberalization in Latin America." *Journal of Common Market Studies* 10 (1971).

Baldwin, Richard E., and Phillipe Martin. "Two Waves of Globalization: Superficial Similarities, Fundamental Differences." National Bureau of Economic Research Working Paper, No. 6904, 1999.

Bardhan, Pranab. "Corruption and Development: A Review of Issues." *Journal of Economic Literature* 35 (1997): 1320–1346.

Barrell, Ray, and Nigel Pain. "The Growth of Foreign Direct Investment in Europe." *National Institute Economic Review* (1997): 63–75.

Barrientos, Stephanie Ware. "Gender and Employment Relations in Global Horticulture: The Anomaly of Change in Chile and South Africa." Mimeo, 1999.

Bartelsman, E. J., and M. Doms. "Understanding Productivity: Lessons from Longitudinal Microdata." *Journal of Economic Literature* 83, no. 3 (2000): 569–594.

———. "Child Labor: Cause, Consequence, and Cure, with Remarks on International Labor Standards." *Journal of Economic Literature* 37 (1999): 1083–1119.

Bawa, K., and S. Dayanandan. "Socioeconomic Factors and Tropical Deforestation." *Nature* 386 (1997): 562–563.

Becker, G.S. 1960. An Economic Analysis of Fertility." In *Demographic and Economic Change in Developed Countries,* Universities-National Bureau Conference Series, No. 11. Princeton, NJ: Princeton University Press.

Benería, Lourdes, Maria Floro, Caren Grown, and Martha MacDonald. "Introduction: Globalization and Gender." *Feminist Economics* 6, no. 3(2000): 1–26.

Berger, Mark T. 1999. "APEC and Its Enemies: The Failure of the New Regionalism in the Asia-Pacific." *Third World Quarterly: Journal of Emerging Areas* 20, no. 5 (1999).

Bergsten, C. Fred. "APEC and the World Economy: A Force for Worldwide Liberalisation." *Foreign Affairs* 73, no. 3 (1994).

Berik, Günseli. 2000. "Mature Export-Led Growth and Gender Wage Inequality in Taiwan." *Feminist Economics* 6, no. 3 (2000): 1–26.

Bhagwati, Jagdish N. "On the Equivalence of Tariffs and Quotas." In *Trade, Growth, and the Balance of Payments: Essays in Honor of*

Gottfried Haberler. Edited by R.E. Caves, H.G. Johnson, and P. Kenen. Chicago: Rand-McNally, 1965: 52–67.

———. "Protectionism: Old Wine in New Bottles." In *The New Protectionist Threat to World Welfare.* Edited by Dominick Salvatore. New York: Elsevier Science, 1987: 45–68.

Bibers, Samia. "Sert's Summit and the Declaration of the African Union." *International Politics Journal* 144 (2001): 205–209.

Biemann, Ursula. "Remotely Sensed: A Topography of the Global Sex Trade." *Feminist Review,* no. 70 (2002): 75–88.

Bitzenis, Aristidis. "Universal Model of Theories Determining FDI: Is There Any Dominant Theory? Are the FDI Inflows in CEE Countries and Especially in Bulgaria a Myth?" *European Business Review* 15, no. 2 (2003): 94–104.

———. "Is Globalization Consistent with the Accumulation of FDI Inflows in the Balkan Countries? Regionalisation for the Case of FDI Inflows in Bulgaria." *European Business Review,* no. 4 (2004).

———. "Why Foreign Banks Are Entering Transition Economies: The Case of Bulgaria." *Global Business and Economics Review Journal* 6, no. 1 (2004): 107–133.

———. "Decisive Barriers that Affect Multinationals' Business in a Transition Country." *Global Business and Economics Review Journal,* Special Issue: The Political Economy of Transition (2005).

Blomström, Magnus, and Ari Kokko. "Policies to Encourage Inflows of Technology through Foreign Multinationals." *World Development* 23 (1995): 459–468.

Blomström, Magnus, Ari Kokko, and Mario Zejan. "Host Country Competition and Technology Transfer by Multinationals." *Weltwirtschaftliches Archiv* 130 (1994): 521–533.

Bolling, Christine, and Agapi Samwaru. "U.S. Food Companies Access to Foreign Markets through Direct Investment." *Food Review* 24, no. 3 (2001): 23–28.

Bongaarts, John. "A Framework for Analyzing the Proximate Determinants of Fertility." *Population and Development Review* 4 (1978): 105–132.

Boone, Peter. "The Impact of Foreign Aid on Savings and Growth." Mimeo. London: London School of Economics, 1994.

Bora, B., L. Cernat, and A. Turrini. "Duty and Quota-Free Access for LDCs: Further Evidence from CGE Modelling." UNCTAD Policy Issues in International Trade and Commodities Study Series, no. 14 (2002).

Borjas, George J. "The Economics of Immigration." *Journal of Economic Literature* 32, no. 4 (1994).

Bossuat, Gerard. "European Economic Areas since 1914: Old Realities and European Unity." *European Review* 5, no. 3 (1997): 323–329.

Brenton, Paul, and Daniel Gros. "Trade Reorientation and Recovery in Transition Economies." *Oxford Review of Economic Policy* 13, no. 2 (1997): 65–76.

Brewer, L. Thomas. "Indicators of Foreign Direct Investment in the Countries of Central and Eastern Europe: A Comparison of Data Source." *Transnational Corporations* 3, no. 2 (1994): 115–126.

Brown, Drusilla K. 2000. "International Trade and Core Labour Standards: A Survey of the Recent Literature." Labor Market and Social Policy, Occasional Papers, No. 43, 1994.

Brown, Drusilla K., Alan V. Deardorff, and Robert M. Stern. "The North American Free Trade Agreement: Analytical Issues and a Computational Assessment." *World Economy* 15, no. 1 (1992): 15–29.

Browning, Martin, and Annamaria Lusardi. "Household Saving: Micro Theories and Micro Facts." *Journal of Economic Literature* 34 (1996): 1797–1855.

Bywater, Marion. "Agricultural Trade Policies in the Andean Group: Issues and Options." *World Bank Technical,* no. 364 (1990).

Cain, Michael. "Risk and Fertility in India and Bangladesh." *Population and Development Review* 7 (1981): 435–474.

Caldwell, John. "Routes to Low Mortality in Poor Countries." *Population and Development Review* 12 (1986): 171–220.

Calomiris, C. W., and G. Gorton. "The Origin of Banking Panics: Models, Facts, and Bank Regulations." In R.G. Hubbard, ed., *Financial Markets and Financial Crises.* Chicago: University of Chicago Press, 1991.

Calvin, Linda, et al. "Response to a Food Safety Problem in Produce: A Case Study of a Cyclosporiasis Outbreak." In *Global Trade and Consumer Demand for Quality.* (2002): 101–127. Edited by Krissoff, Barry; Bohman, Mary; Caswell, Julie. Springer, New York.

Carroll, Eero. "Globalization and Social Policy: Social Insurance Quality, Institutions, Trade Exposure and Deregulation in 18 OECD Nations, 1965–1995." Paper presented at the Year 2000 International Research Conference on Social Security, Helsinki, 2000.

Caswell, Julie A. 2003. "Trends in Food Safety Standards and Regulation: Implications for Developing Countries" in Laurian Unnevehr, ed., *Policy Briefs: Food Safety in Food Security and Food Trade.* Washington, DC: International Food Policy Research Institute (IFPRI).

Chen, Muhua. "Birth Planning in China." *International Family Planning Perspectives* 5 (1979): 92–101.

Cheng, Wenli, Meng-chun Liu, and Xiaokai Yang. "A Ricardian Model with Endogenous Comparative Advantage and Endogenous Trade Policy Regimes." *Economic Record* 76 (2000): 172–182.

Cheng, Wenli, Jeffrey Sachs, and Xiaokai Yang. "A General-Equilibrium Re-Appraisal of the Stolper-Samnelson Theorem." *Journal of Economics* 72 (2000): 1–18.

———. "An Inframarginal Analysis of the Ricardian Model." *Review of International Economics* 8 (2000): 208–220.

Chichilnisky, G. "North-South Trade and the Global Environment." *American Economic Review* 84 (1994): 851–874.

Clark, Gregory, Michael Huberman, and Peter H. Lindert. "A British Food Puzzle, 1770–1850." *Economic History Review* 48, no. 2 (1995): 215–237.

Coale, Ansley, and Judith Banister. "Five Decades of Missing Females in China." *Demography* 31 (1994): 459–480.

Cockburn, Iain. "The Changing Structure of the Pharmaceutical Industry." *Health Affairs* 23, no. 1 (2004): 10–22.

Cohen, Ronald. "Ethnicity: Problems and Focus in Anthropology." *Annual Review of Anthropology* 7 (1978): 379–403.

Collier, Paul, and David Dollar. "Aid Allocation and Poverty Reduction." *European Economic Review* 46 (2002): 1475–1500.

Connor, John. "North America as a Precursor of Changes in Western European Food-Purchasing Patterns." *European Review of Agricultural Economics* 21 (1994): 155–173.

Cooper, Richard. "Prolegomena to the Choice of an International Monetary System." *International Organization* 29, no. 1 (1975): 63–97.

Corden, Max W., and J. Peter Neary. "Booming Sector and De-Industrialization in a Small Open Economic." *Economic Journal* 92 (1982): 825–848.

Cordovez, D. "The Making of UNCTAD: Institutional Background and Legislative History." *Journal of World Trade Law* (1967): 243–328.

Coyle, W., et al. "Understanding the Determinants of Structural Change in the World Food Markets." *American Journal of Agricultural Economics* 80, no. 5 (1998): 1051–1061.

Cranfield, John A. L., et al. "Changes in the Structure of Global Food Demand." *American Journal of Agricultural Economics* 80 (1998): 1042–1050.

Croghan, Thomas W., and Patricia M. Pittman. "The Medicine Cabinet: What's in It, Why, and Can We Change the Contents?" *Health Affairs* 23 (2004): 23–33.

Davis, Kingsley. "The Theory of Change and Response in Modern Demographic

History." *Population Index* 29 (1963): 345–366.

Davis, N. "A Year of Transition." *European Chemical News* (2004): 18–23.

D'Costa, Anthony. "Uneven and Combined Development: Understanding India's Software Exports." *World Development* 31, no. 1 (2003): 211–226.

Deininger, K., and L. Squire. "A New Data Set Measuring Income Inequality." *World Bank Economic Review* 10 (1996): 565–591.

Desai, Mihir A., C. Fritz Foley, and James R. Hines, Jr. "International Joint Ventures and the Boundaries of the Firm." National Bureau of Economic Research Working Paper, 2002.

Development Alternatives with Women for a New Era. "Securing Our Gains and Moving Forward to the 21st Century." Position paper by DAWN for the Fourth World Conference on Women, 1995.

Diao, Xinshen, and Agapi Somwaru. "Impact of the MFA Phase-Out on the World Economy: An Intertemporal Global General Equilibrium Analysis." TMD Discussion Paper, No. 79. Trade and Macroeconomics Division, International Food Policy Research Institute, October 2001.

DiCastri, F. "Ecology in a Context of Economic Globalization." *BioScience* 50 (2000): 321–332.

Diouf, Mamadou. "The Senegalese Murid Trade Diaspora and the Making of a Vernacular Cosmopolitanism." *Public Culture* 12, no. 3 (2000): 679–702.

Dixit, A. K. "International Trade Policy for Oligopolistic Industries." In *International Trade: Selected Readings*. Edited by Jagdish Bhagwait. Cambridge: MIT Press, 1987.

Dixit, A. K., and A. S. Kyle. "The Use of Protection and Subsidies for Entry Promotion and Deterrence." *American Economic Review* 75 (1985): 139–153.

Doezema, Jo. "Loose Women or Lost Women? The Re-emergence of the Myth of 'White Slavery' in Contemporary Discourses of 'Trafficking in Women.'" *Gender Issues* 18, no. 1 (2000): 23–50.

Dollar, David, and Jacob Svensson. "What Explains the Success or Failure of Structural Adjustment Programs." World Bank Working Paper, No. 1938, 1998.

Dosi, Giovanni. "The Nature of the Innovative Process" in Dosi, G., C. Freeman, R. R. Nelson, G. Silverberg, and L. Soete, eds., *Technical Change and Economic Theory*. London: Pinter, 1988.

Dowlah, C. A. F. "The Future of the Readymade Clothing Industry of Bangladesh in the Post-Uruguay Round World." *World Economy* 22, no. 7 (1999).

Dvorak, John C. "The New Digital Camera." *PC Magazine* 22, no. 20 (2003): 63.

Edgren, Gus. "Aid Is an Unreliable Joystick." *Development and Change* 33, no. 2 (2002): 261–267.

Elson, Diane. "Gender Awareness in Modeling Structural Adjustment." *World Development* 23, no. 11 (1995): 1851–1868.

Emmerson, Donald. "Southeast Asia—What's in a Name?" *Journal of Southeast Asian Studies* 15, no. 1 (1984).

Fasano, Ugo, and Zubair Iqbal. "Common Currency." *Finance and Development* 39, no. 4 (2002): 42–50.

Featherstone, Mike. "Localism, Globalism, and Cultural Identity." In *Global/Local: Cultural Production and the Transnational Imaginary*. Edited by Graham E. Johnson. Durham, NC: Duke University Press, 1996.

Fidler, D. P. "Globalization, International Law, and Emerging Infectious Diseases." *Emerging Infectious Diseases* 2 (1996): 77–84.

Fidler, David. "The Globalization of Public Health: The First 100 Years of International Health Diplomacy." *Bulletin of the World Health Organization* 79 (2001): 842–849.

Fields, Gary S. "The Role of Labor Standards in U.S. Trade Policies." Pp. 167–188 in Alan V. Deardorff and Robert M. Stern, eds., *Social Dimensions of U.S. Trade Polices*. Ann Arbor: University of Michigan Press, 2000.

Finger, J. Michael, and Ludger Schuknecht. "Market Access Advances and Retreats: The Uruguay Round and Beyond." World Bank Working Paper, No. 2232, 1999.

Frieden, Jeffrey A. "Invested Interests: The Politics of National Economic Policies in a World of Global Finance." *International Organization*, no. 45 (1991): 425–451.

Friedmann, John. "The World City Hypothesis." *Development and Change* 17 (1986): 69–83.

Fussel, Elizabeth. "Making Labor Flexible: The Recomposition of Tijuana's Maquiladora Female Labor Force in Taiwan." *Feminist Economics* 6, no. 3 (2000): 1–26.

Gehlhar, Mark, and William Coyle. "Global Food Consumption and Impacts on Trade Patterns." Pp. 4–13 in Anita Regmi, ed., *Changing Structure of Global Food Consumption and Trade*. Washington, DC: U.S. Department of Agriculture, Economics Research Service, 2001.

Gereffi, Gary. "The International Competitiveness of Asian Economies in the Apparel Commodity Chain." Asian Development Bank, ERD. Working Paper, Series No. 5, February 2002.

Gestöhl, Sieglinde. "EFTA and the European Economic Area, or the Politics of Frustration." *Cooperation and Conflict* 29, no. 4 (1994): 333–336.

Gezairy, Hussein. "Fifty Years of the World Health Organization." *Eastern Mediterranean Health Journal* 4, Supplement (1998): 6–30.

Gilbert, Christopher L. "International Commodity Agreements: Design and Performance." *World Development* 15, no. 5 (1987): 591–616.

Gould, David M. "Has NAFTA Changed North American Trade?" *Federal Reserve Bank of Dallas Economic Review* (1998): 12–23.

Greenfield, Jim, and Panos Konandreas. "Implications of the Uruguay Round for Developing Countries. Introduction: An Overview of the Issues." *Food Policy* 21, no. 4–5 (1996): 345–350.

Greenspan, Alan. "The Globalization of Finance." *Cato Journal* 17, no. 3 (1998): 243–250.

Griever, William, Gary Lee, and Francis Warnock. "The U.S. System for Measuring Cross-Border Investment in Securities: A Primer with a Discussion of Recent Developments." *Federal Reserve Bulletin* (2001).

Grossman, Gene, and Elhanan Helpman. "Protection for Sale." *American Economic Review* (1994): 833–850.

Grown, Caren, Diane Elson, and Nilufer Cagatay. "Introduction." *World Development* 28, no. 7 (2000): 1145–1156.

Haass, Richard N. "Sanctioning Madness." *Foreign Affairs* 76, no. 6. 1997: 74–95.

Habermas Jürgen. "The European Nation-State and the Pressures of Globalization." *New Left Review* 235 (1999): 46–59.

Hamilton, Alexander. "Federalist No. 1: The Utility of the Union in Respect to Commercial Relations and a Navy." *Independent Journal* (1787).

Hansen, Henrik, and Finn Tarp. "Aid Effectiveness Disputed." *Journal of International Development* 12, no. 3 (2000): 375–398.

Hardin, G. "The Tragedy of the Commons." *Science* 162 (1968): 1243–1248.

Haveman, Robert, and Edward Wolff. "Who Are the Asset Poor? Levels, Trends and Composition." Institute for Research on Poverty, Discussion Paper, No. 1227–01, 2001.

Henderson, Rebecca, Luigi Oresenigo, and Gary P. Pisano. "The Pharmaceutical Industry and the Revolution in Molecular Biology: Interactions among Scientific, Institutional, and Organizational Change." In *Sources of Industrial Leadership: Studies of Seven Industries.* by Richard R. Nelson and David C. Mowery. Cambridge University Press, 1999.

Henkin, Louis, et al. *Human Rights.* New York: Foundation Press, 1999.

Henson, Spencer, Ann-Marie Brouder, and Winnie Mitullah. "Food Safety

Requirements and Food Exports from Developing Countries: The Case of Fish Exports from Kenya to the European Union." *American Journal of Agricultural Economics* 82, no. 5 (2000): 1159–1169.

Henson, Spencer J., and Julie A. Caswell. "Food Safety Regulation: An Overview of Contemporary Issues." *Food Policy* 24, no. 6 (1999): 589–603.

Herbsleb, James D., and Deependra Moitra. "Global Software Development." *IEEE Software* (2001): 16–20.

Herrmann, Roland, and Claudia Röder. "Does Food Consumption Converge Internationally? Measurement, Empirical Tests and Determinants." *European Agricultural Economics* 22 (1995): 400–414.

Higgott, Richard. "Regionalism in the Asia-Pacific: Two Steps Forward, One Step Back?" in Richard Stubbs and Geoffrey R.D. Underhill, eds., *Political Economy and the Changing Global Order* Oxford University Press, Oxford (2000).

Hillmert, Steffen. "Welfare State Regimes and Life-Course Patterns: An Introduction." Unpublished paper, Max-Planck-Institut für Bildungsforschung, Berlin, 2000.

Hollifield, James F., and Thomas Osang. "Trade and Migration in North America: The Role of NAFTA." Unpublished manuscript, 2004.

Horton, Richard. "WHO: The Casualties and Compromises of Renewal." *Lancet* 359: 1605–1611.

Howard, Bill. "On Technology, the New Digital Camcorder." *PC Magazine* 22, no. 19 (2003): 65.

Houghton, R. A. "The Worldwide Extent of Land-Use Change." *BioScience* 44 (1994): 305–313.

Hummels, David. "Time as a Trade Barrier." Mimeo. West Lafayette, IN: Purdue University, 2001.

Humphrey, D. B. "Why Do Estimates of Bank Scale Economies Differ?" *Economic Review of the Federal Reserve Bank of Richmond* (1990): 38–50.

Hussain, Akmal. "The Imperative of a Political

Agenda for SAARC." *SAARC: Dynamics of Regional Cooperation in South Asia* 1 (2000).

Jacobson, Harold K. "International Institutions and System Transformations." *Annual Review of Political Science* 3 (2000): 149–166.

Jorgenson, Dale W., and Frank M. Gollop. "Productivity Growth in U.S. Agriculture: A Postwar Perspective." *American Journal of Agricultural Economics* 74, no. 3 (1992): 745–750.

Kanji, Nazneen, and Kalyani Menon-Sen. "What Does the Feminisation of Labor Mean for Sustainable Livelihoods?" *IIED Opinion: World Summit on Sustainable Development,* Cairo Egypt. 2001.

Kathuria, Sanjay, and Anjali Bhardwaj. "Export Quotas and Policy Constraints in the Indian Textile and Garment Industries." Mimeo. Washington, DC: World Bank, 1998.

Kathuria, Sanjay, Will Martin, and Anjali Bhardwaj. "Implications for South Asian Countries of Abolishing the Multifibre Arrangement." World Bank Policy Research Working Paper, No. 2721, 2001.

Kauffman, S. A., and S. Levin. "Towards a General Theory of Adaptive Walks on Rugged Landscapes." *Journal of Theoretical Biology* 128 (1987): 11–45.

Kinkes, Jean D. "The New Food Economy: Consumers, Farms, Pharms, and Science." *American Journal of Agricultural Economics* 83, no. 5 (2001).

Kogut, Bruce. "The Stability of Joint Ventures: Reciprocity and Competitive Rivalry." *Journal of Industrial Economics* 38, no. 2 (1989): 183–198.

Kokko, Ari. "Technology, Market Characteristics, and Spillovers." *Journal of Development Economics* 43, no. 2 (1994): 279–293.

Kolodko, Gregorz. "Ten Years of Post-Socialist Transition Lessons for Policy Reforms." World Bank Policy Research Working Paper, No. 2095, April 1999.

Kosack, Stephen. "Effective Aid: How Democracy Allows Development Aid to

Improve the Quality of Life." *World Development* 31, no. 1 (2003): 1–22.

Krueger, Anne O. "The Political Economy of the Rent-Seeking Society." *American Economic Review* 64 (1974): 291–303.

———. "Are Preferential Trading Arrangements Trade-Liberalising or Protectionist?" *Journal of Economic Perspectives* 13, no. 4 (1999): 105–124.

———. "Trade Creation and Trade Diversion under NAFTA." National Bureau of Economic Research Working Paper, No. 7429, 1999.

———. "NAFTA's Effects: A Preliminary Assessment." *World Economy* 23, no. 6 (2000): 761–775.

Krugman, P. R. "A Model of Balance of Payments Crises." *Journal of Money, Credit, and Banking* 11 (1979).

———. "Is Free Trade Passé?" *Journal of Economic Perspectives* 1 (1987): 131–144.

Kucera, David, and William Milberg. "Gender Segregation and Gender Bias in Manufacturing Trade Expansion: Revisiting the 'Wood Asymmetry.'" *World Development* 28, no. 7 (2000): 1191–1210.

Lambin, E. F., and H. J. Geist. "Regional Differences in Tropical Deforestation." *Environment* 45 (2003): 22–36.

Lambsdorff, Johann Graf. "Corruption and Rent-Seeking." *Public Choice* 113, no. 1/2 (2002).

———. "Making Corrupt Deals— Contracting in the Shadow of the Law." *Journal of Economic Behavior and Organization* 48, no. 3 (2002): 221–241.

Laursen, Finn. "EFTA Countries as Actors in European Integration: The Emergence of the European Economic Area (EEA)." *International Review of Administrative Science* 57 (1991): 543–555.

Legum, Colin. "Balance of Power in Southern Africa." Pp. 12–23 in York Bradshaw and Stephen N. Ndegwa, eds., *The Uncertain Promise of Southern Africa.* Bloomington and Indianapolis: Indiana University Press, 2000.

Lewis, W. Arthur. "Economic Development with Unlimited Supplies of Labor." *Manchester School of Economic and Social Studies* 22 (1954): 139–191.

Liebowitz, Stan. "Copying and Indirect Appropriability." *Journal of Political Economy* 93 (1985): 945–957.

Lim, Linda. "Women's Work in Export Factories: The Politics of a Cause" in Irene Tinker, ed., *Persistent Inequalities: Women and World Development.* New York: State University of New York Press, 1990.

Lipsey, R. G., and K. Lancaster. "The General Theory of the Second Best." *Review of Economic Studies* 24 (1956): 11–32.

Lloyd, Peter J. "Australia–New Zealand Trade Relations: NAFTA to CER" in Keith Sinclair, ed., *Tasman Relations: New Zealand and Australia, 1788–1988.* Auckland: Auckland University Press, 1987.

Lutz, F. A. "The Case for Flexible Exchange Rates." *Banca Nazionale del Lavaro Review* 7 (1954).

Mansfield, Edward, Helen Milner, and Peter Rosendorff. "Why Democracies Cooperate More: Electoral Control and International Trade Agreements." *International Organization* 56, no. 3 (2002): 477–513.

Marcotullio, P. J. "Globalization, Urban Form and Environmental Conditions in Asia-Pacific Cities." *Urban Studies* 40 (2003): 219–247.

Marcus, George. "Ethnography in/of the World System: The Emergence of Multi-Sited Ethnography." *Annual Review of Anthropology* 24 (1995): 95–117.

Marvel, H. P., and E. J. Ray. "Countervailing Duties." *Economic Journal* 105 (1995): 1576–1593.

Mauro, Paolo. "Corruption and Growth." *Quarterly Journal of Economics* 110, no. 3 (1995): 681–712.

McCalla, Alex F. "Protectionism in International Agricultural Trade, 1850–1968." *Agricultural History* 43 (1969): 329–343.

McCalla, Robert J. "Global Change, Local Pain: Intermodal Seaport Terminals and Their

Service." *Journal of Transport Geography* 7 (1999): 247–254.

McMichael, A. J. "Globalization and the Sustainability of Human Health." *BioScience* 49 (1999): 205–210.

Messerlin, P. A., and G. Reed. "The US and EC Antidumping Policies." *Economic Journal* 105 (1995): 1565–1575.

Meyer, Lisa B. *International Trade Liberalization and Gender Relations in Labor Markets: A Cross-National Analysis, 1970–1998.* Doctoral Dissertation submitted to the Department of Sociology at Emory University (2001).

Meyerson, L. A., and J. K. Reaser. "Biosecurity: Moving toward a Comprehensive Approach." *BioScience* 52 (2002): 593–600.

Miko, Francis T. "Trafficking in Women and Children: The U.S. and International Response." Congressional Research Service Report 98-649 (2000).

Miller, Robert R., et al.. "International Joint Ventures in Developing Countries: Happy Marriages?" International Finance Corporation Discussion Paper, No. 29, 1996.

Miranda, J. R., A. Torres, and M. Ruiz. "The International Use of Anti-Dumping." *Journal of World Trade Law* 32, no. 5 (1998): 5–71.

Moghadam, Valentine M. "Feminist Networks North and South: DAWN, WIDE and WLUML." *Journal of International Communication* 3 (1996): 111–112.

Mundell, Robert A. "A Theory of Optimal Currency Areas." *American Economic Review* 51 (1961): 657–665.

Murdock, Jonathan, and Mara Miele. "Back to Nature: Changing 'Worlds of Production' in the Food Sector." *Sociologia Ruralis* 39, no. 9 (1999): 465–483.

Naito, Takumi. "A Rationale for Infant-Industry Protection and Gradual Trade Liberalization." *Review of Development Economics* 4 (2000): 164–174.

Negroponte, John D. "Continuity and Change in U.S.-Mexico Relations." *Columbia Journal of World Business* 26, no. 2 (1991): 5–11.

Obstfeld, Maurice. "Floating Exchange Rates: Experience and Prospects." Brookings Papers on Economic Activity, No. 2, 1985.

———. "The Global Capital Market: Benefactor or Menace." *Journal of Economic Perspectives* 12, no. 4 (1998): 9–30.

Organisation for Economic Cooperation and Development. "Foreign Direct Investment Continues Downward Slide." Press release, 2003.

Otsuki, Tsunehiro, John S. Wilson, and Mirvat Sewadeh. "Saving Two in a Billion: Quantifying the Trade Effect of European Food Safety Standards on African Exports." *Food Policy* 26, no. 5 (2001): 495–514.

Oxley, Howard, et al. "Income Distribution and Poverty in 13 OECD Countries." *OECD Economic Studies* 11, no. 29 (1997).

Pape, Robert A. "Why Economic Sanctions Do Not Work." *International Security* 22 (1997): 90–136.

Parrenas, Rhacel Salazar . *Servants of Globalization: Women, Migration and Domestic Work.* Stanford, CA: Stanford University Press, 2001.

Pavitt, Keith. "Patterns of Technical Change: Towards a Taxonomy and a Theory." *Research Policy* 13, no. 6 (1984): 343–373.

Pimentel, D., et al. "Environmental and Economic Costs Associated with Non-Indigenous Species in the United States." *BioScience* 50 (2000): 53–65.

Pinstrup-Andersen, Per. "Food and Agricultural Policy for a Globalizing World: Preparing for the Future." *American Journal of Agricultural Economics* 84, no. 5 (2002): 1201–1214.

Pollock, Mark A., and Emilie Hafner-Burton. "Mainstreaming Gender in the European Union." *Journal of European Public Policy* 7, no. 3 (2000): 432–456.

Population Reference Bureau. "Population Data Sheet." Washington, DC: PRB, 2001.

Portes, Alejandro, and Manuel Castels. "World Underneath: The Origins, Dynamics, and Effects of the Informal Economy" in *The Informal Economy: Studies in Advanced and*

Less Developed Countries. Baltimore: Johns Hopkins University Press, 1991.

Price, Charlene. "Food Service." *U.S. Food Marketing System* AER-811 (2002): 34–46.

Pronk, Jan P. "Aid as a Catalyst." *Development and Change* 32, no. 4 (2001): 611–629.

Puyana, Alicia. "Andean Integration: A New Lease on Life?" *The Economist Intelligence Unit,* no. 2018 (1982).

Raeburn, John, and Sarah Macfarlane. "Putting the Public into Public Health: Towards a More People-Centred Approach" in R. Beaglehole, ed., *Global Public Health: A New Era.* Oxford: Oxford University Press, 2003.

Ragazzi, Giorgio. "Theories of the Determinants of Direct Foreign Investment." *International Monetary Fund Staff Papers* 20, no. 2 (1973): 471–498.

Ram, Rati. "Roles of Bilateral and Multilateral Aid in Economic Growth of Developing Countries." *Kyklos* 56, no. 1 (2003): 95–110.

Ranis, Gustav, and John C. H. Fei. "A Theory of Economic Development." *American Economic Review* 51 (1961): 533–565.

Rastoin, Jean-Louis, and Gérard Ghersi. "Agroalimentaire: La mondialisation en marche." *Problèmes Economiques,* no. 2719 (2001): 29–32.

Raymond, Janice G. "Prostitution as Violence against Women: NGO Stonewalling in Beijing and Elsewhere." *Women's Studies International Forum* 21, no. 1 (1998): 1–9.

Razin, Assaf, and Efraim Sadka. "International Tax Competition and Gains from Tax Harmonization." *Economics Letters* 37 (1991): 69–76.

Robbins, Anthony. "Brundtland's World Health Organization: A Test Case for United Nations Reform." *Public Health Reports* 114 (1999): 30–39.

Roberts, Donna. "Analyzing Technical Trade Barriers in Agricultural Markets: Challenges and Priorities." *Agribusiness* 15, no. 3 (1999): 335–354.

Rocha, Geisa Maria. "Neo-Dependency in Brazil." *New Left Review,* no. 16 (2002).

Rodrigue, Jean-Paul. "Globalization and the Synchronization of Transport Terminals." *Journal of Transport Geography* 7 (1999): 255–261.

Rodrik Dani. "Why Do More Open Economies Have Bigger Governments?" *Journal of Political Economy* 106 (1998): 997–1033.

———. "Feasible Globalization." Working Paper, Harvard University, 2002.

Rogoff, K "The Mirage of Fixed Exchange Rates." *Journal of Economic Perspectives* 9 (1995).

Romalis, John. "NAFTA's Impact on North American Trade." University of Chicago Graduate School of Business Working Paper, 2001.

Rosenstein-Rodan, P. N. "Criteria for Evaluation of National Development Effort." *UN Journal for Development Planning* 1, no. 1 (1969): 19–21.

Ruggie, John Gerard. "International Regimes, Transactions, and Change: Embedded Liberalism in the Postwar Economic Order." *International Organization* 36, no. 2 (1982): 379–415.

Sachs, Jeffrey D., and Andrew Warner. "Economic Reform and the Process of Global Integration." *Brookings Papers on Economic Activity.* Washington, DC: Brookings Institution Press, 1995.

Sachs, J., and X. Yang. "Market-Led Industrialization and Globalization." *Journal of Globalization* (2002).

Sachs, Jeffrey, Xiaokai Yang, and Dingsheng Zhang. "Globalization, Dual Economy and Economic Development." *China Economic Review* 11 (2000):189–209.

Sassen, Saskia. "Whose City Is It? Globalization and the Formation of New Claims." *Public Culture* 8 (1996): 205–223.

Sauvy, Alfred. "Trois Mondes, Une Planète." *L'Observateur,* no. 118 (1952).

Scheld, Suzanne. "The City in a Shoe: Redefining Urban Africa through Sebago Footwear Consumption." *City and Society* 15, no. 1 (2003): 109–130.

Seguino, Stephanie. "Accounting for Gender in

Asian Economic Growth in Taiwan." *Feminist Economics* 6, no. 3 (2000): 1–26.

Sen, P. "Terms of Trade and Welfare for a Developing Economy with an Imperfectly Competitive Sector." *Review of Development Economics* 2 (1998): 87–93.

Shleifer, Andrei, and Robert W. Vishny. "Corruption." *Quarterly Journal of Economics* 108 (1993): 599–617.

Singh, Ajit. "Aid, Conditionality and Development." *Development and Change* 33, no. 2 (2002): 295–305.

Singh, Nirvikar , "The Impact of International Labor Standards: A Survey of Economic Theory" (October 2001). UCSC Economics Working Paper No. 483. http://ssrn.com/abstract=288351.

Slaughter, Anne-Marie. "The Real New World Order." *Foreign Affairs* 76, no. 5 (1997): 183–197.

Smith, Alasdair, and Helen Wallace. "The European Union: Towards a Policy for Europe." *International Affairs* 70, no. 3 (1993): 429–444.

Smith, Dexter Jerome. "Non-Oil Industry in the GCC." *Middle East* 278 (1998): 41–43.

Smithin, John. "Money and National Sovereignty in the Global Economy." *Eastern Economic Journal* 25, no. 1 (1999): 49–61.

Sobarzo, Horacio E. "The Gains for Mexico from a North American Free Trade Agreement—An Applied General Equilibrium Assessment" in Joseph F. Francois and Clinton R. Shiells, eds., *Modeling Trade Policy: Applied General Equilibrium Assessments of North American Free Trade*. Cambridge: Cambridge University Press, 1994.

Sohmen, E. "Demand Elasticities and Foreign Exchange Market." *Journal of Political Economy* 65 (1957).

Srinivasan, T. N. "Trade and Human Rights." Pp. 225–253 in Alan Deardoff and Robert Stern, eds., *Constituent Interests and U.S. Trade Policies*. Ann Arbor: University of Michigan Press, 1998.

Standing, Guy. "Global Feminization through Flexible Labor: A Theme Revisited." *World Development* 27, no. 3 (1999): 583–602.

Stark, Oded, and J. Edward Taylor. "Relative Deprivation and International Migration." *Demography* 26, no. 1 (1989): 1–14.

Stern, Nicholas. "The Future of the Economic Transition." EBRD. Working Paper, No. 30, 1998.

Stiglitz, Joseph. "Whither Reform? Ten Years of Transition." Pp. 27–56 in *Annual World Bank Conference on Economic Development*. Washington, DC: World Bank, 1999.

Stopler, W. F, and P. Samuelson. "Protection and Real Wages." *Review of Economic Studies* 9 (1941): 58–73.

Storper, Michael. "Lived Effects of the Contemporary Economy: Globalization, Inequality, and Consumer Society." *Public Culture* 12, no. 2 (2000).

Stotsky, Janet, Esther Suss, and Stephen Tokarick "Trade Liberalization in the Caribbean." *Finance and Development,* vol 37 no. 2 (2000): 22–25.

Strover, Sharon. "Remapping the Digital Divide." *Information Society* 1, no. 19 (2003): 275–277.

Stubbs, Richard. "ASEAN Plus Three: Emerging East Asian Regionalism?" *Asian Survey* 42, no. 3 (2002).

Swinbank, Alan. "The Role of the WTO and the International Agencies in SPS Standard Setting." *Agribusiness* 15, no. 3 (1999): 323–333.

Takashi, Terada. "The Origins of Japan's APEC Policy: Foreign Minister Takeo Miki's Asia-Pacific Policy and Current Implications." *Pacific Review* 11, no. 3 (1998).

Takeyama, Lisa. "The Intertemporal Consequences of Unauthorised Reproduction of Intellectual Property." *Journal of Law and Economics* 40 (1997): 511–522.

Takeyama, Lisa. 1999. "The Welfare Implications of Unauthorised Reproduction of Intellectual Property in the Presence of Demand Network Externalities." *Journal of Industrial Economics* 17: 155–166.

Talyor, Allyn. "Making the World Health Organization Work: A Legal Framework for Universal Access to the Conditions for Health." *American Journal of Law and Medicine* 18 (1992): 301–346.

Talyor, Allyn, and Douglas Bettcher. "WHO Framework Convention on Tobacco Control: A Global Good for Public Health." *Bulletin of the World Health Organization* 78 (2000): 920–929.

Tanzi, Vito. "Globalization and the Work of Fiscal Termites." *Finance and Development* 38, no. 1 (2001): 34–37.

Tavares, J., C. Macario, and K. Steinfatt. "Antidumping in the Americas." *Journal of World Trade* 35, no. 4 (2001): 555–574.

Taylor, M. 1995. "The Economics of Exchange Rates." *Journal of Economic Literature* 33, no. 1: 19–21.

Todaro, Michael P. "A Model of Labor Migration and Urban Unemployment in Less Developed Countries." *American Economic Review* 59 (1969): 138–148.

Traill, Bruce. "Globalization in the Food Industries?" *European Review of Agricultural Economics* 24 (1997): 390–410.

Trouillier, P. "Drug Development for Neglected Diseases: A Deficient Market and a Public-Health Policy Failure." *Lancet* 359, no. 9324 (2002): 2188–2194.

Unnevehr, Laurian, and Nancy Hirschhorn. "Food Safety Issues in the Developing World." World Bank Technical Paper, No. 469, 1999.

Upadhyay, Ushma D. "India's New Economic Policy of 1991 and Its Impact on Women's Poverty and AIDS." *Feminist Economics* 6, no. 3 (2000): 105–122.

Upadhyay, U. D., and B. Robey. "Why Family Planning Matters." Population Reports of the Johns Hopkins University, Series J, 1999.

U.S. Department of Agriculture, Economic Research Service. "Embargoes, Surplus Disposal, and U.S. Agriculture." USDA/ERS, No. 564, 1986.

Verloo, Mieke. "Another Velvet Revolution? Gender Mainstreaming and the Politics of

Implementation." IWM. Working Paper, No. 5, 2001.

Vermulst, E., and F. Graafsma. "WTO Dispute Settlement with Respect to Trade Contingency Measures." *Journal of World Trade* 35, no. 2 (2001): 209–228.

Volcker, Paul. "Globalization and the World of Finance." *Eastern Economic Journal* 28, no. 1 (2002): 13–20.

Walt, Stephen M. "Fads, Fevers, and Firestorms." *Foreign Policy* 121 (2000): 34–42.

Wapenhans, W. "Report of the Portfolio Management Task Force." World Bank document, 1992.

Watkins, Kevin. "Debt Relief for Africa." *Review of African Political Economy,* no. 62 (1994).

Wei, Shang–Jin. "How Taxing Is Corruption on International Investors." *Review of Economics and Statistics* 82, no. 1 (2000): 1–11.

Wesselius, Erik. "Behind the GATS 2000: Corporate Energy at Work." Transnational Institutes, TNI Briefing Series, No. 6, 2002.

Williams, Gavin. "Why Structural Adjustment Is Necessary and Why It Doesn't Work." *Review of African Political Economy,* no. 60 (1994).

Wilson, Rodney. "The Changing Composition and Direction of GCC Trade." The Emirates Occasional Papers, 1998.

Winham, Gilbert. "GATT and the International Trade Regime." *International Journal* 15 (1990): 786–822.

Winters, Jeffrey. "Criminal Debt" in *Reinventing the World Bank.* Ithaca, NY: Cornell University Press, 2002.

Wood, Adrian. "North-South Trade and Female Labor in Manufacturing: An Asymmetry." *Journal of Development Studies* 27, no. 2 (1991): 168–18.

Yamey, Gavin. "WHO's Management: Struggling to Transform a 'Fossilised Bureaucracy.'" *British Medical Journal* 325 (2001): 1170–1173.

Yang, Xiaokai. "Endogenous vs. Exogenous Comparative Advantage and Economies of

Specialization vs. Economies of Scale." *Journal of Economics* 60 (1994): 29–54.

Yang, Xiaokai, and Dingsheng Zhang. "International Trade and Income Distribution." Harvard Center for International Development Working Paper, No. 18, 1999.

———. "Endogenous Structure of the Division of Labor, Endogenous Trade Policy Regime, and a Dual Structure in Economic Development." *Annals of Economics and Finance* 1 (2000): 211–230.

Yeager, L. B. "The Misconceived Problem of International Liquidity." *Journal of Finance* 14 (1959).

Yeats, Alexander. "Just How Big Is Global Production Sharing." Development Research Group/World Bank Working Paper, No. 1871, 1998.

Youssif, Ahmed. "Amman Summit and the Arab League Development: A Competitive Criticizing Vision." *Arab Affairs,* no. 106 (2001): 15–22.

Zia, Khaleda. "Declaration of the South Asian Association for Regional Cooperation." *Presidents and Prime Ministers* 10, no. 6 (2000).

Zwart, Anthony C, and David Blandford. "Market Intervention and International Price Instability." *American Journal of Agricultural Economics* 71, no. 2 (1989): 379–388.

Electronic Sources

Adbrands.net, "Restaurants & Bars," http://www.adbrands.net

Al-Kanaani, Khalil Ibrahim, "The Integration Attempts in the Fourth World: The Case of the Arab World," http://www.druid.dk/conferences/winter2002/gallery/al-kanaani.pdf

Andvig, Jens C., and Odd-Helge Fjeldstadt, "Research on Corruption: A Policy Oriented Survey," Chr. Michelsen Institute and Norwegian Institute for International Affairs, http://www.gwdg.de/~uwvw/research.htm

Asoomi, Mohammed, "GCC, Iraq Can Play a Significant Role," Gulf News, http://www.gulfnews.com/Articles/Opinion.asp?ArticleID=86965

Birnbaum, David, "The Coming Garment Massacre," http://www.just-style.com

———. "Life after Quota," http://www.just-style.com

———. "Marginal Countries and Marginal Factories," http://wwwjust-style.com

Bucknell University, "Russian History," http://www.departments.bucknell.edu/russian/history.html

Central Intelligence Agency, "The World Factbook," http://www.cia.gov/cia/publications/factbook/index.html

———. "The World Factbook 2001," http://www.odci.gov/cia/publications/factbook

Eisenhower Institute, "Russia and the Commonwealth of Independent States," http://www.eisenhowerinstitute.org

Embassy of Uruguay, Washington, DC: MERCOSUR," http://www.embassy.org/uruguay/econ/mercosur

European Commission, "Community External Trade Policy in the Field of Standards and Conformity Assessment," http://europa.eu.int/comm/trade/pdf/mral.pdf

Evian 2003 Summit G8 Summit, "Summit Documents," http://www.g8.fr/evian/english/home.html

Flanagan, Mike, "Apparel Sourcing in the 21st Century, the 10 Lessons So Far," http://www.just-style.com

Food and Agricultural Organization of the United Nations, "World Agriculture towards 2015/2030," http://www.fao.org

Gonsalves, Eric, "South Asian Cooperation: An Agenda and a Vision for the Future," Global Corruption Report 2003, www.globalcorruptionreport.org

Health Promotion Agency of Northern Ireland, "1974 Lalonde Report," http://www.healthpromotionagency.org.uk/Healthpromotion/ Health/section6a.htm

Heller, Peter S., and Muthukumara Mani, "Adapting to Climate Change," Finance and Development, http://www.imf.org/external/pubs/ft/fandd/2002/03/heller.htm

Hendrickson, Mary, "An Overview of Concentration in the Food System," University of Missouri, http://www.foodcircles.missouri.edu

Higgins, Kevin T., "The World's Top 100 Food & Beverage Companies," http://www.foodengineeringmag.com

Humphrey, John, and Olga Memedovic, "The Global Automotive Industry Value Chain: What Prospects for Upgrading by Developing Countries?" United Nations Industrial Development Organization, http://www.unido.org/en/doc/12769

International Institute for Sustainable Development, "Environmental Aspects of Regional Trade Agreements," http://www.iisd.org/trade/handbook/7_1_2.htm

International Labour Office, "Automotive Industry Trends Affecting Components Suppliers," Report for discussion at the Tripartite Meeting on Employment, Social Dialogue, Rights at Work and Industrial Relations in Transport Equipment Manufacturing, Geneva, 2005. http://www.ilo.org/public/english/dialogue/sector/techmeet/tmtem05/tmtem-r.pdf

Lawson, Alastair, "South Asia's Crippled Regional Body," http://news.bbc.co.uk/2/hi/south_asia/1741449.stm

Manchester Metropolitan University, Department of Computing and Mathematics, "Global Climate," http://www.doc.mmu.ac.uk/aric/eae/Ozone_Depletion/Older/Global_Climate.html

Mason, Betsy, "Man Has Been Changing Climate for 8,000 years," http://www.nature.com/nsu/031208/031208-7.html

Mbaye, Sanou, "France Killing French Africa," Taipei Times, http://www.taipeitimes.com/News/edit/archives/2004/01/29/2003096656

McCrum, Robert, "Judgement Day," The Observer, http://observer.guardian.co.uk/magazine/story/0,11913,1050825,00.html

Multinational Electronic Services Corp., "Commonwealth of Independent States Economic and Market Trends," http://www.mes-corp.com/W4_7f.htm

National Center for Policy Analysis, "Cost of Protectionism," http://www.ncpa.org/oped/bartlett/jun799.html

New Zealand Ministry of Foreign Affairs and Trade, "CER Background" and "Positive Points," http://www.mft.govt.nz/foreign/regions/australia/ausdefault.html

North American Free Trade Agreement, "Text of the Agreement," http://www.dfait-maeci.gc.ca/trade/nafta-alena/agree-en.asp

Palast, Gregory, "A High Price to Pay for the Power and the Glory," The Observer, http://observer.guardian.co.uk/business/story/0,433094,00.html

Polish Information and Foreign Investment Agency, http://www.paiz.gov.pl

Pope, Jeremy, "The Transparency International Source Book 2000—Confronting Corruption: The Elements of a National Integrity System," Transparency International, Berlin, http://www.transparency.org/sourcebook

Sellers, L. J., "Special Report: Pharm Exec 50," http://www.pharmexec.com/pharmexec/article/articleDetail.jsp?id=95192

Severino, Rodolfo C., "The ASEAN Way and the Rule of Law," International Law Conference on ASEAN Legal Systems and Regional Integration, http://www.asean.or.id/newdata/asean_way.htm

Southern African Development Community, http://www.sadc.int/index.php?lang=english&path=&page=index

Southern African Development Community, "Treaty," http://www.sadc.int/index.php?lang=english&path=about/background&page=objectives

Staverne, Irene van, "Global Finance and Gender," http://www.eurosur.org/wide/Globalisation/Global%20Finance.htm

Stein, Herbert, "Balance of Payments," Concise

Encyclopedia of Economics, http://www. econlib.org

United Nations, "United Nations Framework Convention on Climate Change," http://unfccc.int/

Wesselius, Erik, "Driving the GATS Juggernaut," www.globalpolicy.org

World Bank, "What Is the World Bank?" http://www.worldbank.org

World Health Organization, "Essential Drugs and Medicines Policy," http://www.who.int/medicines/rationale.shtml

———. "WHO Global Strategy for Food Safety: Safer Food for Better Health," http://www.who.int/fsf/Documents/fos_strategy_en.pdf

World Trade Organization, "International Statistics," http://www.wto.org

———. "Non-Tariff Barriers: Technicalities, Red Tape, etc.," http://www.wto.org/english/thewto_e/whatis_e/tif_e/agrm8_e.htm

———. "Technical Barriers to the Market Access of Developing Countries," WT/CTE/W/101G/TBT/W/103, http://docsonline.wto.org Search Results G/TBT/W/103WT/CTE/W/101

———. "Workshop on Technical Assistance and Special and Differential Treatment in the Context of the TBT Agreement-Session Reports," http://www.wto.org/english/news_e/news00_e/modrep_e.htm

———. "The WTO Agreement on Technical Barriers to Trade," http://www.wto.org/english/tratop_e/tbt_e/tbtagr_e.htm

———. "The WTO Agreement on the Application of Sanitary and Phytosanitary Measures (SPS Agreement)," http://www.wto.org/english/tratop_e/sps_e/spsagr_e.htm

Contributors

Advisory Board

Kathryn Dominguez
Gerald R. Ford School of Public Policy
University of Michigan
Ann Arbor, MI

Robert Feenstra
Department of Economics
University of California, Davis
Davis, CA

Arvind Panagariya
Jagdish Bhagwati Professor of Indian Political
    Economy
School of International & Public Affairs
Columbia University
New York, NY

Dani Rodrik
John F. Kennedy School of Government
Harvard University
Cambridge, MA

Matthew Slaughter
Tuck School of Business
Dartmouth College
Hanover, NH

Contributors

Dr. Mohammed Badrul Alam
Professor, History and Political Science
Miyazaki International College
Miyazaki
Japan

Jalal Alamgir
University of Massachusetts, Boston
Boston, MA

Dr. Maria Rosaria Alfano
Research Fellow and Professor
Università degli Studi di Salerno /
    Seconda Università degli Studi di Napoli
Fisciano (SA)/ Capua(CE)
Italy

Monica Arruda de Almeida
Faculty Fellow
University of California, Los Angeles
Los Angeles, CA

Paul Bailey
Senior Technical Specialist
International Labour Office (ILO)
Geneva
Switzerland

Claustre Bajona
University of Miami
Coral Gables, FL

Maciej J. Bartkowski
Central European University
Budapest
Hungary

Bethany Barratt
Roosevelt University
Chicago, IL

Lindsay J. Benstead
University of Michigan
Ann Arbor, MI

Dr. Mark T. Berger
Visiting Professor of International History
University of British Columbia
Vancouver, British Columbia
Canada

Aristidis Bitzenis
University of Macedonia
Thessaloniki
Greece

Steven Brakman
Professor, Faculty of Economics
University of Groningen
Groningen
Netherlands

David Brennan
Independent Scholar
Sydney
Australia

Michelle Calhoun
University of Maryland
Upper Marlboro, MD

Silvio John Camilleri
Banking and Finance Department–FEMA
University of Malta
Msida
Malta

Colin A. Carter
Department of Agricultural Economics
University of California, Davis
Davis, CA

Lucio Castro
Sr. Economist
Maxwell Stamp PLC
London
United Kingdom

Julie A. Caswell
Professor of Resource Economics
University of Massachusetts, Amherst
Amherst, MA

Nathalie Cavasin
Visiting Scientist
Waseda University
Tokyo
Japan

Lucian Cernat
UNCTAD
Geneva
Switzerland

Nazli Choucri
Professor of Political Science
MIT
Cambridge, MA

Roger Clarke
Professor of Microeconomics
Cardiff Business School
Cardiff
United Kingdom

Alfredo Manuel Coelho
Research Assistant
UMR MOISA Agro Montpellier
Montpellier
France

Meredith Crowley
Federal Reserve Bank of Chicago
Chicago, IL

Daniel Carl Ehlke
Brown University
Providence, RI

Manuel de la Rocha
Consultant
World Bank
Nairobi
Kenya

Thorgerdur Einarsdóttir
Associate Professor of Gender Studies
University of Iceland
Reykjavik
Iceland

Nilly Kamal El-Amir
Cairo Univeristy
Cairo
Egypt

S. Kirk Elwood
Department of Economics
James Madison University
Harrisonburg, VA

Jacqueline H. Fewkes
Florida Atlantic University
Harriet Wilkes Honors College
Jupiter, FL

Harry Garretsen
Utrecht University
The Netherlands

Christiana Gauger
York University
Toronto, Ontario
Canada

Steven C. Hackett
Professor of Economics
Humboldt State University
Arcata, CA

James Heitzman
University of California, Davis
Davis, CA

Stephen Hoadley
Associate Professor of Political Studies
University of Auckland
Auckland
New Zealand

Arthur Holst
MPA Program Faculty
Widener University
Chester, PA

Daniel Jacoby
Harry Bridges Chair in Labor Studies
University of Washington, Bothell
Bothell, WA

Yasuhiko Kamakura
Industrial Specialist on Chemicals Industry
International Labour Office (ILO)
Geneva
Switzerland

Nicola Simpson Khullar
University of Pennsylvania
Annenberg School for Communication
Philadelphia, PA

Bruce Kochis
Assistant Professor
University of Washington, Bothell
Bothell, WA

Dr. Kwadwo Konadu-Agyemang
Associate Professor
The University of Akron
Akron, OH

Christiane Kraus
Senior Economist
World Bank
Washington, DC

Johann Lambsdorff
University of Göttingen
Göttingen
Germany

Kocsis Laszlo
Babes-Bolyai University
Cluj / Kolozsvar
Romania

Marie Lavoie
Professeur
Université Laval
Québec
Canada

Peter Lloyd
Professor
University of Melbourne
Melbourne, Victoria
Australia

Hans Lofgren
Deakin University
Melbourne, Victoria
Australia

Charles E. McLure, Jr.
Senior Fellow
Hoover Institution
Stanford University
Stanford, CA

Lilja Mosesdottir
Bifröst School of Business
Reykjavik
Iceland

Mojmir Mrak
Faculty of Economics
University of Ljubljana
Ljubljana
Slovenia

Shoma Munshi
Consultant
UNDP & CII
New Delhi
India

R. Badri Narayan
Director (Planning)
Railway Board
New Delhi
India

Immanuel Ness
Professor of Political Science
Brooklyn College, City University of New York
Brooklyn, NY

Thomas Osang
Department of Economics
Southern Methodist University
Dallas, TX

Rose-Marie Payan
California State University Channel Islands
Camarillo, CA

Leanne C. Powner
University of Michigan
Ann Arbor, MI

Dr. Elizabeth R. Purdy
Independent Scholar
LaGrange, GA

Sean Purdy
Professor
Universidade de Brasília
Brasília
Brazil

Dipankar Purkayastha
Professor of Economics
California State University, Fullerton
Fullerton, CA

Priya Ranjan
Department of Economics
University of California, Irvine
Irvine, CA

Paul A. Rivera
Business and Economics
California State University Channel Islands
Camarillo, CA

Saffa-woya Rogers
Independent Scholar
Beijing
China

Jeff Shantz
Instructor
York University
Toronto, Ontario
Canada

Jitendra Uttam
Research Associate
Jawaharlal Nehru University
New Delhi
India

Nivedita Vaidya
Department of Sociology
California State University, Los Angeles
Los Angeles, CA

Bart van Ark
Professor, Faculty of Economics
University of Groningen
Groningen
Netherlands

Charles van Marrewijk
Professor of Economics
Erasmus University
Rotterdam
Netherlands

Jennifer Vaughn
University of California, Riverside
Riverside, CA

Carol Walker
Georgia State University
Atlanta, GA

John Walsh
Shinawatra University
Bangkok
Thailand

Richard Watt
Universidad Autónoma de Madrid
Madrid
Spain

Robert Whaples
Professor of Economics
Wake Forest University
Winston-Salem, NC

Laura L. Whitcomb
Department of Management
California State University, Los Angeles
Los Angeles, CA

Charles E. Williams
Professor of Biology
Clarion University of Pennsylvania
Clarion, PA

Geoffrey Wood
Professor of Economics
Cass Business School
London
United Kingdom

Anastasia Xenias
Columbia University
New York, NY

Xiaokai Yang
Department of Economics
Monash University
Clayton, Victoria
Australia

Beth V. Yarbrough
Willard Long Thorp Professor of Economics
Amherst College
Amherst, MA

Robert M. Yarbrough
Department of Economics
Amherst College
Amherst, MA

Derek Young
University of Dundee
Scotland, UK

Tracey Zuliani
University of Sydney
Sydney, Australia

Benjamin Zyla
Royal Military College of Canada
Kingston, Ontario
Canada

Index